THE YORKSHIRE
HISTORICAL DICTIONARY

The officers of the Yorkshire Archaeological and Historical Society would like to thank the Trustees of the Elisabeth Exwood Memorial Trust for a grant towards this publication and their continuing support for the Record Series

THE YORKSHIRE
ARCHAEOLOGIAL AND HISTORICAL SOCIETY
FOUNDED 1863 INCORPORATED 1893

RECORD SERIES
VOLUME CLXVI
FOR THE YEARS 2018 AND 2019

THE YORKSHIRE HISTORICAL DICTIONARY

A GLOSSARY OF YORKSHIRE WORDS, 1120–c.1900

L–Y

COMPILED BY

GEORGE REDMONDS

EDITED BY

ALEXANDRA MEDCALF

YORKSHIRE ARCHAEOLOGICAL AND HISTORICAL SOCIETY

THE BOYDELL PRESS

2021

First Published 2021

A publication of the Yorkshire Archaeological and Historical Society
in association with The Boydell Press
an imprint of Boydell & Brewer Ltd
PO Box 9, Woodbridge, Suffolk IP12 3DF, UK
and of Boydell & Brewer Inc.
668 Mt. Hope Avenue, Rochester, NY 14620-2731, USA
website: www.boydellandbrewer.com

ISBN 978-1-916506-67-1

The publisher has no responsibility for the continued existence
or accuracy of URLs for external or third-party internet websites
referred to in this book, and does not guarantee that any content on
such websites is, or will remain, accurate or appropriate

A CIP catalogue record for this book is available
from the British Library

This publication is printed on acid-free paper

Printed and bound in Great Britain by
TJ Books Limited, Padstow, Cornwall

Contents

L

labourer One who does physical labour, as a service or for a livelihood. The meaning may have changed little over the centuries but it cannot be presumed that labourers formerly had lowly status. In 1550, William Windle of Thorner, *laborer*, left money towards church repairs and road maintenance, made several bequests of ewes, lambs and wethers, gave *too yerdes of clothe and a half* to Elizabeth Windle for a petticoat, and left his farmhold to his wife (Th19/249). In 1558, the gift that Lionel Nailler of Wakefield, *laborer*, made to his wife was *all my landes and hows's* (Th27/259). As a group in York, the labourers were ready to defend their rights: in 1505:

> *they presented a bill of diverse wrongs don unto theym by the wryghtez, emong which
> … that the wryghts wold not suffer theym to set in a stancon with a lappe, mayk a
> bede, a shelffe, a forme, a stole, naile a burde, a dore, a yate, a wyndowe.*

The mayor and council upheld their claim (YRS106/15).

lad (1) In the early references, from *c.*1300, this was a word for a serving-man, of low birth and position, and it is found frequently in by-names: 1301 *De Johanne Hardladd*, Hauxwell (YRS21/95); 1334–5 *William Fatlad*, Pickering (NRR4/25). By the mid-fifteenth century though it was being used more generally of boys and young men: 1525 *made showtes and exclamacions, seyng Come knavez and laddes of Wortley, as many as wyll, and drynke* (YRS41/180); 1602 *He then a younge ladd thought … they would geve little enough*, Brandsby (NYRO44/25); 1684 *upon the White Moore they mett a ladd driving two horses loaden with apples*, Bolton by Bowland (QS1/23/8); 1725 *had bought it of a ladd that had found it in Knaresborough and had given five grotes for it*, Ilkley (QS1/64/1).

lad (2) A standing stone or a pile of stones. It can in some respects be compared with 'law', which was also used of boundary markers, occasionally as a direct alternative: 1594 *the heap of stones which hath in ancient times called* [sic] *Lad or Law'*, Wadsworth (WYAS276). The distinction may be that 'lad' referred initially to a single upright stone but came to be used less specifically when used as a boundary marker: 1592 *a great stone called Langshaw Ladde*, Ilkley (YNQ); 1805 *to a certain Stone called the Lad or Scarr on the Hill*, Stanbury (BAS7/72). This meaning of 'lad' has not yet been noted before the sixteenth century but numerous minor place-names testify to its use from that date. The more obvious examples include: The Lad; Ladstone (Norland); Lad Stones (Todmorden); Ladstones (Mytholmroyd); Ladhill (Saddleworth); Lad Lowe Hill (Salterforth). Ladcastle (Saddleworth) and Two Lads (Mytholmroyd) may also belong here (PNWR8/106).

ladder room The prospective owner of a new house would be granted the right to place a ladder on ground adjoining the building so that he might maintain the property: 1665 'freedom to put one or more ladders on the said land for the repair of the house', Alverthorpe (WCR5/72); 1790 *liberty for … occupiers of the intended buildings … to place ladders in the close to repair the buildings*, Holmfirth (WCR10/15). This liberty was written into title deeds where it was usually referred to as ladder room: 1629 *one ladder roume in the garden for the … needful repairing of the firehouse,*

Conistone (MD247); 1832 *subject nevertheless to a right … of Ladder room for the Owner or Occupier of the House adjoining*, Kirkburton (GRD). The term has a much longer history as 'stee-room', where stee is the dialect word for ladder.

lade Of Old English origin, meaning to bale, that is to remove water by taking it up with some suitable container: 1579 *the lading of water*, Elland (HAS35/139); 1682 *pd for ladeing in the water … 6 days*, Rotherham (QS1); 1704 *Paid for watter lading*, Farnley (MS11); 1760 *Pd for a bowl to lade water 1s 0d, Candles to Lade water by 1s 6d*, Tong (Tong/4c/5). In coal-mining it was a primitive method of draining and can be linked with 'teem'. See also sump.

lade-net A type of fishing net used by the Crowle tenants in the fourteenth century, subject to certain time restrictions: 1372 *Item piscari debent cum ladenettes inter festa Paschae et Sci Petri ad Vincula incipiendo post medium diei, scil. post prandium, et continuando ad solis occasum [Item, the fishers must fish with lade-nets between the feasts of Easter and St Peter ad Vincula, beginning after noon, namely after lunch, and continuing until sunset]*, Selby (YRS13/289). This seems to have been a type of net adapted for fishing in the 'lodes' or channels of the river Don and its feeders: *ripas alvei de Done et des les Lades ubi piscariæ arentatæ construuntur [banks of the Don channels and of the Lades where fisheries are constructed]*. See also alger, bow-net, lading (2), lode, pitch (1), pole-net.

lading (1) A regional spelling of 'loading': 1556 *ledde a lode of the wheate and rye to Bulmer tieth lathe … the Parson of Bulmer was presente … at the ladynge* (YRS114/83).

lading (2) In 1439, tenants of Shelley were accused of illegal fishing by means of *ladeyng* (MD225/1/165/1): it was one of several similar presentments in which 'machines' were used, and the poachers' method in these cases is not immediately clear. Later by-laws suggest that water channels or 'lodes' were dug, leading away from the river, which might then be dammed allowing the fish to be easily trapped: 1661–3 *we lay in payne that no person … doe ladde and cut up any mans land to dame for fishing within this liberty*, Golcar (DD/SR/1/5/9); 1739 *John Earnshaw is to … inform against such persons as destroy the fish with … daming and lading*, Meltham (G-A). See also lade-net, lode, pitch (1).

lag A curved stave for a barrel or cask: 1676 *For mendyng the church yatis and barrel laggs and nayles 4s 4d*, Sheffield (OED); 1727 *perceived the vessel (wine cask) had been opened … several of the laggs being broken off*, Pontefract (QS1/64/4); 1737 *To Mr Watts for Polls to rive into lags for Vessels 10s*, Whitley (DD/WBE/1/10).

lagan Goods or wreckage lying on the bed of the sea: *c.*1685 *goods wares … and other materialls as has been lade on board … any Shipp or vessel which perished or was lost or shipwrackt … commonly called by the names of Flotsan, Jetsan and lagan alias ligan*, York (SAH22/27).

lain To conceal: in 1513, the tenants of the grange of Haddokstones were obliged to make an annual account without any *color, withdrawynge or lainynge* (YRS140/226). In 1615, one of the conditions in the apprenticeship indenture of Richard Paicocke was that he *deligentlie doe the lawfull commaundementes of his master, his secret counsel lawfull and honneste … keep and laine*, York (YAJ17/118).

laine A thong, a strap or a chain, part of the plough-team's harness, apparently a regional form of 'lainer': 1534 *Item a pare wayne laynes and iij yrne temes*, Long Liversedge (Th24/311); 1551 *a copple of yokes with the laynes, a ploughe foote, shakill, a tug-withe and a plewbyeme*, Altofts (Th19/266); 1581 *ij pare of laynes of my master owne iron*, Stockeld (YRS161/34); 1636 *a foot laine* [ploughfoot?], Allerton, Bradford

(LRS1/87); 1754 *2 swingletrees, lains and teams*, Ox Lee, Hepworth (IH). Note: 1648 *Item 6 laned yokes 4 teames*, Sharlston (YRS134/99).

lair (1) A place for an animal to lie down, sometimes a fold or enclosure: 1672 *did see* [him] *cary a shepe into a laire*, West Riding (QS1/11/3). In upland townships the 'lair' could be simply a place on the fellside where animals customarily grazed and settled down for the night. See AW111 & 121.

lair (2), lairstall, lairstead The resting place of a corpse, a grave or tomb: 1541 *I will that my executors provide for a layer stone to cover my corps after my decesse*, Pontefract (Th19/50); 1541–2 *pro denariis debitis pro le layrestall infra ecclesiam [in moneys owed for the lairstall in the church]*, Ripon (SS81/195); 1559 *I gyve for my lare stede in the churche iijs iiijd*, Wycliffe (SS26/130). See also lay-bed.

lairpit A clay pit, from *leirr* an Old Norse word. In one very early undated reference it had already given rise to a place-name in the open field: n.d. *tres acras et dimidiam in Lairpiteflait [three and a half acres in Lairpiteflait]*, Stapleton (Th8/155). It was not uncommon through the fourteenth century: 1316 *et terciam partem cuiusdam arzilli, qui vocatur le Layrpittes [and a third of a clay pit, which is called Layrpittes]*, Moor Monkton (YRS50/120); 1341 *abutting … North on Layrepittes*, Thorpe Salvin (YRS102/137). Clay had a variety of uses in that period, as a translated court roll entry shows: 1338–9 'he took clay in a certain pit to repair his walls', Aldborough (YRS74/42). The word survived in several dialects but not it seems in Yorkshire (EDD) and from the sixteenth century at least it had been replaced by 'clay'.

lairstall, lairstead See lair (2).

lait To look for, to search: 1558 *I geue and bequeathe to the said Rowlande for laytinge of my brother Nycholas xxs*, Church Fenton (Th27/301); 1686 *For his Cow Laiting in the old pasture*, Conistone (RW27).

lake (1) The colour of certain cloths, possibly scarlet, very early examples of 'lac' or 'lake': 1391 *et ij par linthiaminum de panno de lake [and 2 pairs of lake cloth sheets]*, Lockton (SS4/166); 1397 *De 5s pro v ulnis panni de lake pro corporalibus [For 5s for 5 ells of lake cloth for the altar cloths]*, York (SS35/132); 1413–14 '8 ells of cloth *de lake* purchased for one tablecloth', Selby (SAR123); 1451 *unum par linthiaminum de panno de layke [one lake cloth sheet]*, York (SS30/144).

lake (2) A gift or offering, comparable with 'boon' according to Canon Atkinson: 1394–5 *Redditus Assis. Soca de Hakeness … redditus gallinis vocatis lakis vijs … cxl ovis ibidem [Fixed Rents. The soke of Hackness … rents in hens called lakes 7s … in 140 eggs there]*, Whitby (SS72/556n). In this series of accounts, hens and eggs feature repeatedly but with some differences in the way the items are entered, e.g. *xx gallinis de lake … De ovis lakes.*

lake (3) A play, a game, sport: 1554 *What is yon? A Christinmas play in faythe. Yonder is a gay Yole layke!* Rothwell (AGD232). See also cocklake.

lake (4) In this solitary example, 'lake' seems to be used of a stream or an area under water which was close to a spring and served to fill the moat of a newly built house: 1450–5 *byggyd hym a manor besyd the well and the lak of the bake of the well, making the lake of the well to ryn about hys uter moot on both syddys the maner*, Anlaby (YAJ39/69).

lamber An alternative of amber, via the French *l'ambre*. Chiefly a northern word (OED), found no later than the sixteenth century: 1317 'for stealing … a set of amber beads (*de Laumbre*) worth 6d', Alverthorpe (YRS78/187); 1389 *j payr bedys of lawmbyr*, York (SS4/129); 1401 *lego j par de lawmberbedes*, York (SS4/280); 1429 *his best girdell harnest, with a pare of lambre bedes*, Tickhill (SS4/417); 1498 *iij paire of laumbre bedez, price xijd*, Wakefield (YAJ15/93); 1539 *to Jennet my daughter a pare of lawmer bedes*, Leeds (Th19/8). See also amber.

lamb gate A right for a lamb to 'go' or graze on a stinted pasture: 1690 *18 lambgates on Westmoor*, Arncliffe (EG65). See also beast gate, gate (2).

lamb-hog An unshorn lamb in its first year: 1556 *to Anne Andrewe one hogg lambe*, Biggin (Th27/44); 1698 *107 old sheep and 31 lamb-hoggs*, Marsden (IMF). See also hog (1).

lampas A kind of glossy crape: 1390 *Johannæ de Carlton ... half a pes of lawmpas Johannæ Qwelpdale a volet of lawmpas neu*, York (SS4/130); 1401 *j peciam de lampas cum dimidio pecio de cypers [1 piece of lampas and half a piece of cypers]*, York (SS4/282). It is the first element in a rare compound term: 1398 *dimidiam peciam velorum lampasduke*, Beverley (SS4/240). The OED has: *a.*1548 *rolles wrethed on Lampas douck hollow so that the Golde shewed thorow.*

lamprey spit The river lamprey was apparently roasted on a special spit: 1565 *Fyve long spets, j lampron spete*, Knaresborough (SS26/179); 1582 *iiij spyttes a lampro spytt*, South Cave (Kaner119).

lancet-maker The manufacture of lancets in Sheffield was mentioned by Defoe (1724–6) and by the Rev. Goodwin (1764). Gales and Martin's Sheffield Directory listed eleven manufacturers of *Lancets and Fleams* in 1787.

land A selion or strip in the common arable field: 1315 '*two landys lying on Cafurlang*', Batley (YRS39/27); 1537 *that everyman make hys fence abowte the whete feyld of Normanton afore Thursday next apon pane of every lande end or gape 4d* (WCR9/66); 1554 *are the three lands ... now or heretofore enclosed or do they lie in the common Felde unclosed and unfenced*, Wetwang (YRS114/52). It was an element in numerous minor place-names: 1589 *novem seliones terre arrabilis (Anglice vocat' nienlandes)*, Kirkheaton (DD/WBD3/63).

landing A landing place, one where a boat might be drawn up. It is comparatively rare as a vocabulary item: 1519 *Item that no man or woman dry no hempe in the dame, nor in the lendynges goynge to the dame*, Selby (SS85/32). In fact, the use of 'landing' as a place-name element is key to the history of the word, which features regularly along the Ouse in undated twelfth-century documents, for example *Sanct Martini Lending*, York (PNER292) and *Gatelending*, Selby (YRS10/102). Perhaps the earliest and most significant reference is in a Selby charter where *Cuarlendding* is probably a misreading of *Cnarlendyng* (YRS10/103); it occurs in 1320 as '*Knarlending near Seleby*' (YRS94/63) and the prefix is interpreted by Smith as a word for a small warship. 'Lending' is ultimately of Scandinavian origin, and was formerly common along the Ouse and its tributaries. Notable examples are later associated with river ports: 1389 *Mildebylendyng*, Boroughbridge (SS120/38); 1392–3 *Draxlendyng* (HAH161); 1357 *Paradislendyng* (YAJ44/160n). The last of these was in Hambleton, held by the abbot of Selby, and from there timber and underwood were conveyed by boat to the Ouse, along Selby dam.

It was also a common element in York: 1300 *Sywinlending* (YRS83/196); 1375 'a lane called the *Lymelending*, from North Strete to the river Ouse' (SS186/9); 1398 'the lane called *Seintmartynlendyng* in *Conyngstrete*' (YRS76/178); 1401 'the lane called

Fishelendyng' (SS186/32). The latter is mentioned into the sixteenth century when it is clearly defined: 1572–3 *a pece of waist grounde ligheng … at the east end of the north syde of Ouse brig commonly called the fysshe landyng; and he to make a sufficyent landing place and way for the fysshemongars there* (YRS115/62). A foot-note identifies this site as a little quay on the east end of Ouse Bridge. On the little river Foss, in 1427, was a lane called *Sayntdinisselendyng* (SS186/91), and Lendal Bridge marks the site of St Leonard's Landing, where timber and stone for the fabric of the Minster were off-loaded. It occurs as a by-name in the poll tax returns: 1377 *de Thoma del Lendyng*, York (PTY).

A few place-names for which no early examples have come to light have the spelling 'landing', and further downstream, near to Selby, are the historic sites of Riccall Landing and Old Landing, traditionally seen as the place where the Scandinavian fleet was moored prior to the battle at Stamford Bridge. Wilfholme Landing is on the navigable river Hull and Free Landing is near Aldwark.

In recorded history the 'lendings' were simply places where a boat might unload or take on cargo, not quays or staithes where the river bank would be reinforced by some sort of stone or wooden wall. In most cases the 'landing' was linked to the village further inland by a lane, as at Hemingbrough. The evidence implies that the first 'lendings' were disembarkation sites and they are associated with Scandinavians: it was comparatively late before 'landing' emerged as the modern spelling and shook off its links with river navigation. As a word for the 'platform' at the head of the stairs it is not on record before 1789 (OED) but in coal-mining a landing was a level place where coals might be loaded, sometimes a boarded area: 1715 *from the Landing Board to the Seat under the coals*, Farnley (MS14); 1840 *landing boards at Springfield Lane pit*, Tong (Tong/4c/17). The verb 'to land' was also part of the miner's vocabulary: 1754 *landing coals*, Beeston (WYL160/129/4).

landiron (1) An andiron or fire-dog. In this spelling the definite article became attached to the noun 'andiron': 1552 *my lande iron, and gallow trees with crokes*, Pontefract (Th19/318); 1559 *the land yrons cobyrons the gallows of yron*, Ripon (YRS134/6); 1599 *two laund yrons a paire of tonges a fier shovel*, Rawmarsh (TWH16/162); 1638 *one landiron … one spet*, Selby (YRS47/82). It derived from Old French *andier* or *l'andier* but it was an iron implement and the termination was confused with English *yre* meaning iron.

landiron (2) Distinct from landiron (1). It was a kind of iron regularly imported into Hull in the fifteenth century from the Low Countries, possibly inferior in quality to osmunds: 1453 *landeiren … ½ last' osmondes* (YRS144/5); 1461 *4C lib' land eyrn* (YRS144/30). An earlier reference occurred in a case that had to do with adulterated metal: 1428 *John Lyllyng sent hym with hys awen carriage iij^c & di. of landyren, and iiij^c and mo peces of fals drosseyren … to make in osmundes*, York (SS85/2).

land-staithe The location of a bridge abutment, that is the structure which supported the bridge arch and linked it to the land: 1418 'the *landstathe* at the foot of the steps', York (SS186/57). The contract for Catterick Bridge is in English throughout and more explicit, specifying that the proposed new bridge should be *of stane … in mason craft acordand in substance to Barnacastelle brigge, aftir the ground and the watyr acordes, of twa pilers, twa land stathes, and thre arches*. The land-staithe was later listed as part of the *tymbir werke* for which the builders were responsible, and this suggests that it was a kind of wooden platform for the masonry of the abutment (NRQS3/34). If that is correct it lay over the brandreth and piles. I have not found the word later than 1595, when £20 was charged *for amending of Catterick Bridge land stare* (NRQS3/33). The editor's comment on this word was that the spelling reflected the local pronunciation of 'staithe', and this spelling can be compared with 'land-stay' below.

land-stall The OED has a single example of the word, noted in the North Riding Quarter Sessions for 1739, and the meaning given is 'staithe or landing place'. However, the passage from which the example was taken implies that it had to do with with repairs carried out on two local bridges, almost certainly work on the abutments. 'Land-stall' can therefore be compared directly with 'land-staithe' above. An earlier and more explicit reference occurs in the contract for Apperley Bridge when it was replaced in 1602. The task of reconstruction was given to a mason called Thomas Wallimsley and he was required to provide *one good and sufficient stone bridge … containing … two Landstalles or heads … one piller and two archies* (BAS6/141). Thereafter, the word is found frequently in bridge accounts. In 1678, Lune Bridge, which carried traffic from Cumberland through to Durham via Yorkshire, was badly damaged in a flood which had undermined *the groundwork of the landstalls* (NRQS7/14): in 1706, changes were made to Cattall Bridge and *it was thought convenient by the County that both the Land Stalls at eather End should be raised for conveniency of making an easier assent and that it should not in any flood be unpassable* (QS1/45/4). These were evidently masonry abutments, since the workmen were *to Raise both with stone worke and Earth at both Ends and Pave it all Annew.* Similarly, in 1702, *the Landstalls* of a bridge over the River Laver near Ripon had *to be built of good and well wrought hewen stone, well bedded and sett in lime and sand* (QS1/40/4).

land-stay There are several examples of 'stay' as a form of 'staithe' in minor place-names. The *comon stay* in Bawtry (1567–76) was said by Smith to derive from an Old English word for 'pool' but it abutted on the River Idle and seems certain to have been the common staithe (PNWR1/48). Staithgate in North Bierley is known as Staygate locally and was formerly the way to the coal staithes. The word 'land-stay' appears frequently in connection with bridges about the time that 'land-staithe' occurred as 'land stare' (see above) and it seems to have replaced it. In the 1579 contract for the building of Elland Bridge this spelling occurred several times, most relevantly in a reference to *the foundations of the said jewels and landstayes* (HAS35). More explicitly, a report on the bridge at Conistone in Wharfedale in 1684 mentioned *the excessive charge of new Oake Timber of which they made Fraimes for Lying under the Pillers and Landstays* (QS1/23/8). The flood that destroyed Cam Gill Bridge in Kettlewell in 1686 left *part of the landstayes … standinge but in danger to be carried away by the violence of the streame* (QS1/26/1). Timber remained an important bridge-building material: 1708 *Charge of wood for the Landstays wearing*, Bolton Bridge (QS1/47/9) but no doubt parts of the abutments were already of stone.

lang A regional spelling of 'long' which in turn was often an abbreviation of 'belong'. See also long.

lang settle A long bench, usually with arms at each end and a high back: 1444 *j kerven lange satill … stante in magna camera [1 carved lang satill standing in the great chamber] … j longe satill throwne*, Beverley (SS30/100–1); 1549 *a narke, a counter, a lange settill and a kiste*, Elland (Crossley43); 1729 *laid upon a longsettle asleep*, Stainland (QS1/68/4). Note the following spelling which is not unique: 1731 *a long saddle*, Austerfield (QS1/70/7).

lanner A large falcon (*falco biarmicus*), with a distribution over Mediterranean Europe, and central, eastern and southern Africa: 1311 *Adinet' le Fauconer vnum falconem Laner vel xx solidos*, Hazlewood (SS2/15); 1358 *Item Johanni falconerio meo unum laner' et xxˢ*, York (SS4/69); 1531 *to my nepevewe … my lanner and a cople of spanyelles*, Kirby Underdale (HKU144).

lant In perhaps the most explicit references, the word used by West Riding clothiers for urine was 'lant'. In 1724, the inventory of Joseph Holroyd of Upperthong included a *lant copper*, the vessel in which the urine was stored (IH) and John Brearley wrote the following in his memorandum book: 1758 *shalloons to bee scowred with hogs dung and lant hot in a tub; so sadden itt with old lant called piss*, Wakefield (YRS155/1,76). There were further details in 1761:

> The cloathiers about Wakefild the mix swine turd and piss called lant together so squeses itt out with theire hand then drains itt through a wire seiff that no moats gets in. So lecks itt over on the cloath att first when it comes out in loom and itt makes itt scowr better. But itt is apt to get some moats into the cloath (YRS155/121).

See also chamber-lee, lee, mange, mote, wash (1), and for a detailed history OWR1/2 and 2/1.

lap To wrap or enfold: 1530 *discreit women that wyndes and lappis my body in one sheit when that I am departed*, Acklam (SS79/292); 1612 *1 pese of lynsay wousay & a great sort of cruels lapt in it*, Brafferton (NYRO44/35); 1642 *Betwixt the two graininges of the rake shafte they tye a stringe which they can lappe aboute and make as longe and as shorte as they list*, Elmswell (DW53); 1647 *I came in to lap a finger which I had cutt*, Thurlstone (SS65/70); 1662 *which child she lapt in a cloth that night and going to milke the next morning shee cast it into a dike*, Rotherham (QS1). See also cloak-bag, stomacher.

lapping board A board on which things might be lapped or wrapped: 1550 *too sidebordes, one lapinge borde, one chaire*, Normanton (Th19/247).

lark net Larks were formerly netted and eaten in large numbers: 1582 *a paire of larke netts*, Colburn (SS26/71n); 1592 *3 little bordes halff a tubb a peir of bedstockes & larknates 6s 8d*, South Cave (Kaner183); 1617 *for 22 dozen larks he gott here at ijd each dozen beinge meated & lodged iijs viijd*, Brandsby (NYRO44/146). See also netmaker, plover net.

lass A word in everyday use in Yorkshire, principally for a girl but colloquially for a woman of any age: 1544 *one little lasse in the house*, Thirsk (YAJ22/224); 1586 *the Blynde Lasse was buried*, Leeds (PR).

last (1) In earlier centuries this was a wooden model of the foot on which shoemakers shaped boots and shoes, and the craftsman is likely to have had a large number at his disposal: 1541 *ten dossan lasts xs; ij pair of boytte treys xd*, Knaresborough (SS104/35); 1662 *showes & letther in the shopp, boote trees, lasts*, Selby (YRS47/77). It became a 'pub' name, evidently a house frequented by shoemakers: 1620 [met?] *my shoemaker in Blackfryers the signe of the last I payd him for blacke bootes viijs*, Brandsby (NYRO44/210).

last (2) A measure for fish, grain, cloth and other commodities, and it varied for different kinds of goods and from one region to another: 1290 *dicunt quod lesta allecis non valet nisi viginti solidos [they say that a last of herring is only worth 20 shillings]*, Ravenser (YRS23/175); 1302 *In ij laystes di et d. allec(ibus) salsatis [In 2 and half lasts and 500 salted herrings]*, Bolton Priory (YRS154/128); 1395–6 *De iij last allec. bonis i^m (pretium last) [For 3 last of good herrings 1000 (price per last)]*, Whitby (SS72/565); 1453 *2 last' 14 bund' lini … 3 last bituminis [2 lasts 14 bund of linen … 3 lasts of pitch]*, Hull (YRS144/4); 1516–17 *iij last shotyn heryng* (YRS45/40); 1566 *for every Last of Flax 3d*, Bridlington (BCP180).

lastmaker A maker of wooden lasts for shoemakers: 1717 *Richard Norman, Last Maker*, All Saints Pavement, York (PR); 1774 *John Hogg, lastmaker*, St Olave, York (PR).

latch In the *Leeds Mercury Supplement* of 20 October 1894, 'latch' was said to be used in the West Riding with the meaning of 'to survey underground workings'. In Shropshire 'to latch' a coal-pit was to measure how much of the mine had been used and determine what direction the work was taking (EDD). This was probably its meaning in earlier Yorkshire references although it is impossible to be certain without more information: 1765 *Pd Adam Harrison for latching*, Tong (Tong/4c/9); 1787 *for latching the Coal got ... by Messrs Brandling*, Beeston: the *Pillars of Coal* in this *Old Coal Works* had just been purchased by Charles Brandling from Robert Denison (WYL160/129/1).

lath-brod An alternative to lath-nail: 1534–5 *Item ij M^li· latt broydes, xxij^d*, York (CCW166). 'Prod' was an occasional variant: *c.*1660 *It^m paid for ... lat prods for nailling the steath worke*, Wolviston (HH9).

lathcleaver, lathriver Occupational, for the workman who split wood into laths: 1466 *Nicholaus Smyth, carpenter et latclever*, York (SS96/186); 1754 *Richard Dyson lathriver of Bradley*, Huddersfield (ELT23). See also rive, latt.

lathe The regional word for barn, of Scandinavian origin: 1454 *graynes herberd in the lathes of the said manor*, Cavil (YRS120/44); 1474 *sall uppe hald a fyre house ... and a lathe of viij posts*, Rawmarsh (TWH16/61); 1529 *a mease, a lathe with a close*, Lepton (DD/WBD4/77); 1588 *I made new a lathe, having ix wayne lodes of tymber towards the same*, Woodsome (KayeCP). This is one of several words which were regional in their use and which clerks began to 'translate' in property deeds from the Tudor period: 1558 *one grett arke being in the lathe or barne ther*, Hunshelf (Morehouse20); 1665 *one barne or lath joyning to a close ... called Lathyng*, Netherton (G-A). A plural form 'lathing' can be compared with folding and housing: 1753 *3 bays of laithing and one cow house*, Royston (QS1/92/4). See also lear.

lath-nail OED 1388–9. A nail for fixing laths on battens: 1351 *Et pro m^l m^l lathnail emptis ad idem, ijs, ijd [And for 2000 lathnail bought for the same, 2s 2d]*, Dewsbury (YAJ21/381); 1429–30 '4,000 *lathnails* bought for the same, 6s', Bedale (HH5); 1520–1 *Item for latt nalys, vj^d ob*, York (CCW80); 1548 *ij.m latt nayles*, York (SS35/112); 1686 *Paid for Latnailes & Spikings ... 8s 11d*, Conistone (RW33). See also latt, stone-brod.

lathriver See lathcleaver.

latt The usual Yorkshire spelling of 'lath', the thin strip of wood on which roof slates or tiles were secured, or a base for plaster on walls and ceilings: 1299–1300 *In clavis ad lates pro diversis domibus [For nails and laths for various houses]*, Bolton Priory (YRS154/105); 1357 *Item, C C centz lattes, ijs ixd [Item 200 latts, 2s 9d]*, York (SS129/5); *c.*1534 *Item for 4 bunshes lez Lattys*, Bridlington (YRS80/2); 1642 *Ashen barres ... riven very thinne, allmost like unto Lattewoode*, Elmswell (DW18). Specialist items were laths for roofs which were of stone or straw: 1396–7 *Et in C lattis pro petr'. emp. 9d [And for buying 100 latts for stone roofing slates 9d]*, Ripon (SS81/125); 1408–9 *de cc stanlat ... pro emendacione stabuli [for 200 stone latts ... for repairing the stables]*, Ripon (SS81/136); 1446 *ccc sindulis vocatis strawelat, c dimidia sindulis vocatis stanelatts [for 300 shingles called straw latts, 150 shingles called stone latts]*, Beverley (ERAS6/78). Note the use of the verb: *c.*1640 *latted and limed the chambers in the old howse*, Denby Grange (KayeCP). See also heart lath, sap lath.

latt axe One of the tools used by the lathriver: 1610 *two iron wedges, one latt ax, two iron mells*, Kirkstall (SpSt).

latten An archaic word for a mixed metal which was very similar to brass. It was used for many household items, such as basins, ladles, skimmers, but was commonly the metal from which candle-sticks were made: 1400 *j candelabrum de laton*, York (SS4/270); 1434 *duo candelabra de laton*, Campsall (SS30/39); 1535 *Item one myllen basyn iij latyn basynes with euers to them belonging*, Stillingfleet (YRS45/129); 1567 *Item tenne latten candlesticks*, Fixby (YRS134/15); 1661 *Item a latten Chaffer*, Langfield (YRS134/119). The occupational term is a guide to the early popularity of this metal: 1309 *Nicholaus Musket, latoner*, York (SS96/12). See also coin (2).

laughton A regional form of 'leighton', which meant herb garden originally and then vegetable garden. It was quite common in minor place-names but apparently remained in use colloquially into the eighteenth century at least: 1308 *moildelaghton*, Sowerby (YRS36/177); 1330 'a garden called *le littilaghton*', Shepley (WYAS824); 1583 *Mudlaghtonsteede*, Almondbury (DD/R/2/13); 1617 *one little close of meadow in Dwarriden called Laughton Croft otherwise garden Croft*, Sheffield (TWH28/176); 1775 *Laighton, a Garden*, Halifax (OED).

laund An obsolete word for an open space in a wood, akin to the modern 'lawn'. It gave rise to by-names and numerous minor place-names: 1301 *de Galfrido de la Laund*, Ugglebarnby (YRS21/111); 1384 *la Launde*, Moor Monkton (YRS50/122); 1636 *all that messuage called the greate Lawne*, Sutton on the Forest (MD87); 1651 *all that parcel of pasture ground knowne by the name of the Lawnes*, Blansby Park (NRR1/69). It remained an active word in wood leases and the like: c.1450 *in reparacione muri circa lawnd iijd [for repair of the wall around the laund 3d]*, Fountains Abbey (SS130/106); 1570 *greate covertes of underwood and tymber and large laundes*, Leconfield (YAJ17/143). See also cockglade, cockshoot, plain, quickset.

laver A basin or bowl in which to wash one's hands: 1518–19 *rasavid* [received] *of Thomas Medyllam … a bassyng, a laver and candylstyke*, York (CCW67); 1535 *Item ij laten lauers xs*, Stillingfleet (YRS45/129); 1551 *a basing and a lauer, and ij pewder dubleres*, Barkston (Th19/319); 1563 *Item, a laver 6s 8d*, Elmswell (DW230).

law As a place-name suffix this derives from Old English *hlāw* and it referred in literary texts of that period to an artificial mound, one which marked the site of a burial or a place where treasure might be hidden (EPNE1/248). More generally it is said to have meant a mound or hill, possibly one that resembled a tumulus. It survived as a vocabulary item in the West Riding, certainly into the early seventeenth century, and it is employed there in boundary descriptions, where it referred to a pile of stones, a cairn that is. Such 'laws' were probably erected as boundary markers: 1532 *and so from that Meer to another Law of stones in Smolden*, Kildwick (MD335/2/3/9/3). In 1594, a marker on the boundary between Midgley and Wadsworth was described as *one heap of stones now called Sabile's Law* (WYAS276) and the Ecclesall name Ringing Low was described in 1574 as *a great heape of stones called Ringinglawe* (PNWR1/200).

Not all the examples noted are so explicit. A Meltham indenture of 1571 mentions *one rode of land … lyinge on the west side the lawe* (G-A) and a Barkisland deed of 1611 has a parcel of land *under the Lawe att the Hystondelffe* (OWR2/1/36). Nevertheless, these almost certainly referred to heaps of stones that had been erected to serve as markers. As a small plan was drawn on the reverse of the Barkisland document we can clearly see what a 'law' looked like to our ancestors: it was a cairn. See also hoar-stone, mere (2), pike (1).

lawmber See amber, lamber.

lawn A kind of fine linen, said to derive from the French town of Laon: 1415 *j plice* [sic for plite?] *de lawnd*, Raby (SS4/382); 1429 'two garments of *lawne*', York (SS186/99); 1476 *iij plyte de lawn*, York (SS192/149); 1642 *One may buy course Lawne for iiijs vjd a yard, and the finest for vjs and vjs viijd a yard. It is much used for fine necke-kerchers … Cambricke-Lawne … the finest of them all*, Elmswell (DW111); 1755 *silk and lawn handkerchiefs*, Sheffield (QS1/94/3). See also levant.

lay (1) To re-steel a cutting instrument, a word first recorded in 1475–6 (OED): 1580 *for laynge one axe vijd*; 1581 *Item for layinge ij axes, xiiijd*, Stockeld (YRS161/17,35).

lay (2) A noun with the meaning tax or rate. The first example quoted was a payment for a ferry crossing: 1530 *for the ferelay at Lytilburgh*, York (SS35/135) although lays were more usually township or parish charges: 1579 *for on laye to the churche of Spofforthe vjs*, Stockeld (YRS161/9); 1608 *controversie touching certaine laies and sessmentes latelie imposed*, Ampleforth (NRQS1/132); 1621 *Netherthwonge is a Hamlett within the Towneshipp of Meltame and … itt bearethe a third of all layes* (G-A); 1642 *wee must pay Noutheard-wages, and Sesses and layes*, Elmswell (DW125).

lay-bed The resting place for a corpse, an alternative to lair, lairstall: 1541 *Item I gyf to the churche warks and for my labed vjs viijd*, Richmond (SS26/24); 1558 *my body to be buryed in the churche … in my chauncell and for my lay bed ther I gyve to the churche xiijs iiijd*, Richmond (YAJ38/189). See also assess.

lea (1) A measure of yarn, of varying quantity: 1399–1400 *Et in xl lee luminon' emp. pro praed. torchez 2s 6d [And for 40 lea of wick bought for the said torches 2s 6d]*, Ripon (SS81/132); 1469 *et x les de coverlet yarn*, Ripon (SS64/139); 1521 *v leye of garne that I borrowed of the wyff of Wylliam Rastryk*, Harrogate (SS104/12); 1544 *a pare of newe harden shettes and xx leas of yerne*, South Kirkby (SS106/214); 1602 *Item 18 ley of hemp yearne 1s 1d*, Knaresborough (YRS134/64); 1640 *Item, one lea of yarne 16d*, Bingley (LRS1/118); 1731 *49 lea of yarn 10s*, Spofforth (QS1/70/4).

lea (2) A regional word for scythe, noted as early as 1483 (OED) and said to differ from the southern scythe (EDD): 1559 *j turfspade iiijd, ij old leys viij* [sic], Westerdale (YRS74/57); 1559 *iij axes, ij lees*, Hipswell (SS26/134); 1573 *vij lease, iijs*, Scawthwaite, Cumbria (SS26/242); 1619 *2 leayes or sythes vs*, Brandsby (NYRO44/175). Attributive uses: 1611 *j spadeshafte … j lea craddle*; 1617 *leashaftes, pichforke shaftes, rake shaftes*, Brandsby (NYRO44/38,139). See also craddle.

leace See leash.

lead (1) A verb, to carry or transport by cart: 1690 *for fenceing of gapps to be left for leadeing or carrying away of any wood, barke or charcoale*, Tong (Tong/3/386). It was a condition in a lease of 1579 that the tenant William Lylye *leade or cause to be led Seaven wayne lodes of wodd from heaton hall to … William Beaumont his milne*, Kirkheaton (DD/WBD/3/52). See also lead stoop, pile (2).

lead (2) In 1701, the inventory of a file-cutter named John Turner listed *Two stones to grinde and two trowes, 4s 0d, Three Stockes, lead and chisels with sume steele* (IH). The 'lead' was a small block of lead on which the file was placed after one side had been finished: in that way the reverse could be worked without damage to the cuts (FBH121). See also trow.

lead (3) A vessel made of lead, used for brewing or dyeing: 1524 *a greate leede and a greate arke*, Paul (SS106/6); 1559 *Item one leyde and masfatt*, North Stainley (YRS134/6); 1617 *one lowme, a pare of geeres … one leade*, Bingley (LRS1/37). See also lead-house.

lead-house There are two distinct meanings, and the earliest references are to those buildings in which lead was kept during major construction projects, such as the minsters in Ripon and York: 1354–5 *et sculpantis thakbordes pro coopertura domus plumbariæ [and for fashioning thackboards for roofing the lead-house]*, Ripon (SS81/92); 1371 *In j ladell empto pro [bought for] le led hous, 3s 4d*, York (SS35/12); 1424–5 *Item Ricardo Horner circa ledhows … per xv dies et di. capienti per diem 6d, 7s 9d [Item to Richard Horner about the lead-house … for 15 days and a half taking per day 6d, 7s 9d]*, Ripon (SS81/152).

From the sixteenth century 'lead' more usually referred to a large vessel made of lead, which could be used in various operations such as dyeing and brewing: 1557 *In the lead house*, Thornton Bridge (SS26/100). Most of the evidence suggests that lead-houses in that period belonged to clothiers and were where dyeing took place, as in the inventory of a Leeds clothier called John Pawson: 1576 *In the Leadhowse … one Leade* (Th4/164); 1584 *Thomas Lockwood … hath encroached of the waste … and thereupon set a dyeing lead*, Almondbury (MS205); 1591 *To my son William my lome & my lead & my tenters*, Bramley (Th1/388); 1608 *John Armitage, clothier … granted all that lower and southern end of a house at Undrebanckes … half a lead house, half a fold*, Honley (G-A); 1710 *the Bayliff went to the Leade howse dore, went in and found a Leade sett there*, Oakenshaw (QS1/49/6). See also lit, lit-house.

lead-man A dealer in lead: 1519 *your orator bargayned and bought … 6 foder, 101 quarter of lede … of one Henry Yong of Appultrewyk in Craven, ledeman*. When Henry Young made his will, in 1535, he was in possession of several lead works, including mines and groves in *Appletrewicke Mores* (YRS51/175–6).

lead-nail A nail used to fasten a sheet of lead on a roof: 1354–5 *In ccc lednayle emp. [bought] 12d*, Ripon (SS81/92); 1354–5 *In C. lednayle factis de ferro ecclesiae, 2d [For 100 lead-nails made of iron, 2d]*, Ripon (SS81/93); 1399 *Et in viii.c lednayle emptis. 2s [And for buying 800 lead-nails 2s]*, York (SS35/16); 1415 *In m. ledenaile empto. prec. 2s 2d [For 1000 lead-nails bought at a price of 2s 2d]*, York (SS35/35); 1458 *Pro … vj.m ledenaills*, York (SS35/70); 1532 *Et ij.m leid nailles, 3s 8d*, York (SS35/107).

lead-pan Either a pan in which lead was prepared for use: 1391–2 *Et de j futher xiiij petr. plumbi [And of 1 fother 14 stones of lead] … Et de j Ledepan*, Ripon (SS81/103) or a pan made of lead: 1611 *j close stoole … with a lead pann nayled in it*, Brandsby (NYRO44/38).

lead stoop A locality in Scarborough, probably not a metal stoop, but one used in some way as goods were transported to and from the quay: 1522 *I will that the Grey Freres have that howse at the Leide stowpe that Alison Gilson wonys in* (SS79/153); 1633 'a moiety of a house … near the *Lead Stoope* and abutting on … *Rasinge Lane*' (NYRO47/375). See also lead (1).

leaf The layer of fat round the kidneys of a pig: 1563 *Leaves of ij swine iiij^d*, Knayton (SS2/207).

leak Probably the obsolete adjective 'leak', that is having a leak or leaks: 1611 'Johnson alleged that the Moyses was so *lecke* that he dare not sail in her', Hull (YRS116/27). The evidence for leak and its derivatives is unusually late (OED).

leap A basket made of rushes or wands which had a variety of uses but has been most commonly noted in connection with fishing: 1314 'Robert Walker 6d for putting a *fish lepp* in the mill-pond', Wakefield (YRS57/40); 1467 *machinas voc' lepes pro kepirz frye [equipment called leaps for kipper (salmon) fry]*, Quarmby (MD225/1/176); 1609 *to lay* *leapes in any brooke to tak trouts in spawning tyme*, Hipperholme (WCR11/172). Other leaps were used for carrying grain or holding bread: 1423 *j lepe facta de virgis, pro grano portando [1 leap made of wicker, for carrying grain]*, York (SS45/80); 1588 *one bread leape*, Dalton (DD/WBW/19); 1696 *one breadlip*, Holmfirth (IH). In inventories they feature alongside maunds, scuttles, skeps and the like: 1457–8 *In leps et skeps Joh'i Schau, iiijs ijd*, Fountains Abbey (SS130/51); 1580 *payd to stotele* [sic] *maker for on leape, two wyndo treles & ij stotels iijs*, Stockeld (YRS161/17); 1615 *one leape, 8 scuttles, 2 maund' cost ijs viijd at my doer*, Brandsby (NYRO44/107).

lear The context in which this word occurs suggests that it was a spelling of 'lathe': 1642 *6 barres … for the lime leare-ende fenced in one side, the hedge another*, Elmswell (DW100). Previously the writer had mentioned putting hay *in the lime-leath* (DW79) and this development can be compared with forms of staithe. Lairgate in Beverley was formerly Lathegate. See also land-staithe.

lease (1), leyes Used of pasture land, but difficult to separate from the plural of 'lea' and 'ley ground': 1398–9 'the farm of the pasture called *les leeghes*', Acaster Selby (SAR91); 1576 *all such … landes leyes meddowes … in Slawghthwayte* (YDK12); 1618 *turned the gelding lowse in my Cow leaze where he ought not to goe*, Brandsby (NYRO44/156); 1668 *they present Valentine Cletherow for putting his Sheepe into the leyes before they were common*, Bridlington (BCP243). It may be the element in minor names such as Woodsome Lees: 1566 *Edmundus Brodeheade off Lees ultra [beyond] Wodsom sepult [buried]*, Almondbury (PR). See also leasow, ley ground, and EPNE11,18.

lease (2) A verb said to mean to glean, pick or gather (OED). In the examples quoted here the grain was being sorted, a meaning that corresponds to the OED reference of 1703, attributed to the Yorkshire diarist Thoresby: 1580 *Item payd at Stockeld the same daye for bering & leasing sede wheat iiijs xd* (YRS161/23); 1619 *New wheat leazed and threshed 42 stowks*, Brandsby (NYRO44/180); 1642 *the charges he shalbe att for and aboute the leasinge, thrashing, wyneinge … the same corne*, Shipton (NRQS4/214); 1665–6 *in the latter end of harvest last* [they] *were leesing Rye togeather*, Hatfield Woodhouse (QS1).

leash In sporting language this was a set of three, used of game animals, hawks and hounds: 1614 *A lease of hawkes, xvil*, Skipton (Whit2/321); 1620 *They had at least a leashe of grewhownds*, Crayke (NYRO44/199); 1669 *did see Edward Doughty and William Richinson traycing haires in the said snow with one greyhound and … kild a Leace of haires*, Thorne (QS1/9/2).

leasow Pasture or pasturage: 1525 *orchards, gardens, meadows, leasues, pastures*, Tang Hall (SS186/276); 1566 *all heyrable grownds, medowes, leasues, closes and pastures*, Huddersfield (DD/R/4/3); 1588 *all lands, leasures*, Winterburn (MD74–5/2). The only examples found are in title deeds and I suspect that this was a lawyer's word, not part of the regional vocabulary. See also lease (1).

leather workers Leather was worked and used by a wide variety of craftsmen and it was a concern in the guild system in York that each group of workers preserve its integrity. So the curriers, *c.*1424, were warned against doing deals with the *corduaner, girdeler, cardemaker vel sadeler* (SS125/169). In 1490, the Council ordered that *all tanned ledder … putt to sail … in the Common Hall … [must] be seirched by the seirchours of the tannerez … the gyrdelers … the coverez* [curriers] *and two able men of the cordweners*, York (YRS103/59). Leather was used for a wide range of articles, including items of clothing: 1395 *pro factura unius togae et unius ledircot*, Whitby (SS72/611); 1722 *wearing … leather breeches*, Rothwell (Th22/188) and even household utensils: 1576 *a lether bottell*, Scriven (SS26/260); 1610 *one lether flackett*, Kirkstall (SpSt).

leave Willingly: 1642 *Millers will say that they had as leave have corne stricken as soe hand waved and left hollowe in the midst*, Elmswell (DW110). See also stroke (1).

leck To moisten or sprinkle with water, a form of the verb to leak according to the OED. It has several dialect usages, especially in cloth-making, but the evidence is late: 1762 *leck itt over with blak earth and mill itt well in*, Wakefield (YRS155/14). In his description of the 'home manufacture of cloth', Easther wrote: 1883 *A large kitful of urine and swine's dung was taken and strained through straw; it was then sprinkled on the cloth ... As they lecked one piece it was laid down, and so layer on layer*, Almondbury (EAHxvii). See also leak.

lee Human urine: 1650 *they searched the body of the saide Mary Sikes and founde ... a redd lumpe about the biggnes of a nutt ... when they wrung it with theire fingers moisture came out of it like lee*, Bowling (SS40/30); 1738 *her stomach sweld that her lese broak*, Sheffield (QS1/77/4). See also chamber-lee, wash (1).

leech A physician or doctor, in use in Old English and recorded as a by-name from the thirteenth century: 1379 *Thomas Leche, medic'*, Howden (PTER); 1445 *John Stevynson, leche*, York (YRS6/159); 1552 *To John Clerkeson xs which* [he] *laid downe for me to the leech*, Garforth (Th19/300). It could be used also of women: 1524 *a howsse that a lyche woman was in*, York (CCW100). See also beast leech, horse leech.

leech craft The skill of healing: 1525 *by reason of which unlawfull wounding your orator did lye att leche craft for the helyng therof*, Ouseburn (YRS41/176). Note: 1416–17 'And for one knife called a *lechyngknyf* purchased from [Robert Smith] 3d', Selby (SAR166). The editor said this was a knife for slicing meat but it was more probably one to be used by a leech.

Leeds measure One of several localised systems for measuring produce: 1606 *two loades of beans of Leedes measure*, Barwick (PR). See also Ripon measure, Thirsk measure, Winchester measure.

leighton See laughton.

leister A pronged spear, used chiefly for catching salmon. It is first noted in the Act of 1533–4, as 'lister' (OED). Yorkshire examples include: 1567 *a leade mell, and two lesters*, Mortham (SS26/201); 1611 *for taking four Salmon in the Yore ... with a lyster*, Thirn (NRQS1/209); 1638 *did kill and destroie with a certaine engine called a leister much salmon, beinge in the time of kipper*, Eppleby (NRQS4/101); 1693 *took his lyester and ... soe went downe the river to another person who stood in the stream with another lyester*, Timble (QS1/33/1).

leming A popular name for an ox, probably the Middle English word for 'lightning', an ironic nickname: 1545 *one yocke of oxen the one called Lemynge and the other Burnett*, Conisbrough (SS106/231); 1553 *and to my dowghter Alice Wattes one oxe called lemynge*, Wakefield (Th19/332); 1567 *one yoke of oxen called ... Lyghtbowne and Lemynge*, Crofton (YAJ36/440). Although the surname Leeming can derive from a place name, the nickname is likely to be the source in Ribblesdale: 1379 *sutor [the cobbler] Willelmus Lemyng*, Paythorne; *Johannes Lemyng*, Stainforth (GRDict).

lending See landing.

lesk Possibly for 'lisk', that is the flank or loin of an animal: 1471 *j vaccam [cow] with a whyte leske*, Harome (SS45/188).

let To hinder, obstruct, prevent or stand in the way of: 1419 *rutes, wedys and erthe that hafes ben casten thar out of thaire gardyns or thayre houses ... the whilk lettys the water to hafe the ryght issue*, York (YAJ22/277); 1482 *the said viage had beyn lettid for that seson*, York (YRS98/60); 1569 *Richard Hyrste ... was throughe a greate snowe letted and stopped*, Almondbury (PR). It was used also as a noun and adjective: 1587 *John Kaye ... shall have one convenyente waye ... for dryvinge and fetching of cattell ... without let of John Baylie*, Thurstonland (YDK78); 1642 *findinge of imployment for our moore folks when there is any lette weather in harvest time*, Elmswell (DW114).

letch A marshy stream, ditch or gutter: 1633 *bis presentati pro hoc et pro letches in le Forest* [twice presented for this and for letches in the forest], Galtres (NRQS3/349n). It was an element in minor place-names from a very early date and A.H. Smith quotes more than twenty examples, several with 'black' as the first element (PNWR7/216–17). Among the early references is *rivul' [stream] de Lecsha* in a thirteenth-century document, now Leeshaw in Oxenhope (PNWR3/265).

letten Formerly the past participle of to let, that is to grant possession of for a payment: 1597 *John Hutchinson for one close letten for one yeare ... 40s*, Reeth (YRS152/335); 1642 *wee have allwayes letten our lande and inclosure thereto belonging for 40s an oxegange*, Elmswell (DW130); 1686–7 *To Thomas Frankland 8 sheep gates letten in the new cloase at 8 pence apiece*, Conistone (RW31).

lettice A kind of whitish-grey fur, from the skins of the snow-weasel. It was more valuable than minever but less expensive than ermine, for which it was used as a substitute (EMV220): 1582 *Item for a timmer of lettise tewing, xxd*, York (YRS119/63). See also timber (2).

levant A type of linen imported from the Low Countries. It may have taken its name from Leuven the capital of the Flemish province of Brabant, in modern Belgium: 1465 *3 C virgis lewan* [300 yards of levant], Hull (YRS144/89); 1470 *that noo saddiller ... set no seyte but of newe cannes* [sic] *or lewent*, York (SS120/92); 1485 *de panno lineo vocato lewan lxvj ulnæ* [66 ells of linen cloth called levant], Ripon (SS64/366); 1489–90 *60 vergis lewantt* [60 yards of levant], Hull (YRS144/218). See also lawn.

level In coal-mining this was a nearly horizontal drift or gallery which might give access to the coal or help to drain a mine: 1633 *shall drive every sough which he shall take in hand till the level first begun shall withal be spent*, Northowram (HAS31/78); 1697 *Jo. Smith for takeing up Levell in the Long Endhead*, Farnley (MS11); 1761 *5 days taking up level from the throw up*, Tong (Tong/4c/6). It was employed in some compound terms: 1718 *Levell Board 35 yds from the pitt eye; Gotten in the Thirle by the Levell gate*, Farnley (MS11).

lewan A type of linen imported from the Low Countries. It may have taken its name from Leuven the capital of the Flemish province of Brabant, in modern Belgium: 1465 *3 C virgis lewan*, Hull (YRS144/89); 1470 *that noo saddiller ... set no seyte but of newe cannes* [sic] *or lewent*, York (SS120/92); 1485 *de panno lineo vocato lewan lxvj ulnæ*, Ripon (SS64/366); 1489–90 *60 vergis lewantt*, Hull (YRS144/218). See also lawn.

leyes See lease (1), ley ground.

ley ground, ley land Arable land, often in the town fields, which was left fallow or unploughed: 1545 *two leie landes in the nerre Kirkemore*, Huddersfield (DD/WBD/1/71); 1590 'the third part of a selion called a *leye*', Dewsbury (YAJ21/458); 1666 *cause to be sett ... upon everie ordinary day ploweing which they ... breake up ... out of the Ley grounde hereby demised twenty sufficient horse loades of lime*, Tong (Tong/3/292);

1720 *agreed that they neyther Let nor plow up ley three of the last years without sufishent husbrenttrey of muck and lime*, Netherthong (G-A); 1750 *will not the three last years plow, grave or rive up any ley ground*, Yateholme (G-A). See also lease (1), swarth.

liard See lyard.

lib To geld or castrate: 1395 *Item pro libbyng porcorum xd [Item for libbing pigs 10d]*, Whitby (SS72/605); 1549 *a libbed galte*, South Milford (Th19/221); *c*.1570 *small sheares to lybb lambe or foole*, Woodsome (KayeCP); 1616 *unam suellam, Angl. a libbed gilt*, Thirsk (NRQS2/123). It gave rise to early occupational by-names: 1338–9 *Robert Grislibber* or *Swynlibber*, Sandal (WCR12/31,40); 1379 *Thomas Libber*, Barnby Dun (PTWR). See also grice, unlibbed.

libard An obsolete spelling of leopard, the animal which was once considered to be a hybrid between a lion and a 'pard' or panther (OED). It was popular as a decorative motif: 1430 *unum ciphum argenti signatum cum uno liberd in capite coopertorii [one silver cup marked with a libard on top of the lid]*, Woolley (SS30/7); 1433 *unum lectum de blod cum libardhedes [a bed cover of blue with libard heads]*, Swine (SS30/25); 1454 *ij liberdhedis in le knop*, Whitkirk (SS30/177); 1522 *ij lybards of goold*, York (YRS106/85); 1568 *a Standing Cuppe with a Cover and within the cover the lione and libarde face*, Healaugh (YRS134/28).

lick Fodder for cows; chopped hay with bran, meal or anything tasty: 1816 *2 sacks of lick from Millsbridge*, South Crosland (GRD).

lick-dish This occurs as a by-name in Yorkshire from the early thirteenth century, recorded in an undated charter: *toftum quod fuit Roberti Lyckedisc*, Guisborough (SS86/64). Reaney has a twelfth-century example and it is found as a vocabulary item *c*.1440 (OED). It is said to mean 'parasite' and can be compared with other apparently pejorative nicknames from that period, several of which were listed by Reaney. Additional Yorkshire references include: 1332 John *Lekeblade*, Wakefield (WCR3/63); 1337 *Thomas Likbofet*, Pickering (NRR4/63). The frequency and variety of these names points to the importance of 'lick' in this sense in everyday vocabulary.

lidgate, lidyate A swing-gate which was formerly put in place as a barrier to animals, set up between land under cultivation and the common or waste, or between two properties: 1297–8 '10½ acres in *le Roberdriding* ... by *le Lideyhat*' Stockeld (YRS65/146); 1374 'had made *2 lideyates* at the ends of the lane between *Cliffehouses* and *Horlawegrenehouses*, to the hurt of the people', Scammonden (MD225/1/100); 1397–8 *viijd solutis ad reparacionem unius Lidyhate pro ij domibus domini in Snayth 8d [paid for repairing a lidgate for two of the lord's house in Snaith 8d]* (YAJ15/418); 1459 'that he cause the common way ... to be repaired by making a *Lidyaite*', Methley (Th35/180); 1545 'that he shall make a ladder called a *steile* between the *Lidyaite* & the wall', Methley (Th35/209). It became the generic in some minor place-names: 1514 *Kirkelidyate*, Holme (MD225); 1584 *the towne Lidyate on the east*, Holme (WCR4/140).

References from the seventeenth century suggest that by then the meaning of the place-name was no longer transparent: 1623 *that John Wood ... sufficiently make the Lidgyate yate before Maydaye next*, Lepton (DD/WBM); 1630 *That those persons to whom one yate called Lidgetyate doth belong shall keep the same up and in good repair ... upon paine of 3s 4d*, Clayton (HM/E/94). The usual pronunciation approximates to 'lidjett' and an extract from a late fifteenth-century boundary description highlights the problems this can give the modern reader: *so foloyn the raw to stawpe loyn lydche and so leffyn the same legchhett on the leffyd hand*, Bolton by Bowland (YRS56/259). The by-name occurs regularly from the thirteenth century: 1297 *Robertus Atthelidegate*, South Elmsall (YRS16/70); 1332 *William atte Lyddyate*, Holme (WCR3/102). See also yate.

lie To set in the oven, to bake: 1721 *refare* [refer] *the baking lying until another day* …
asked her again to lie her a bakeing of bread, Fewston (QS1/61/1).

lier Probably a bed cover: 1423 *Et de xxd receptis pro j lyer pro lecto, de rubeo worsted [And
for 20d received for 1 red worsted lier for the bed]*, York (SS45/72). See also ligger.

liflode For livelihood: 1483 *my liflode in Marcheland that I have purchest during the tyme
of the nonage of my son*, York (SS45/287). See also livelihood, nonage.

lig To lie: 1432 *j matres that I lige on*, Scarborough (SS30/22); 1479 *a gutter that liggez
in length from … Petergate … to the Kyngs dyke*, York (YRS98/7); 1523 *delyng of all suche
landdes as lygges dewydele* [sic] *in the biredole feldes*, Stainland (YRS50/176). Examples of
the present participle include: *c.*1450 *to haf a close lygynge in the sowth parte of Rastryke
more* (YRS65/124); 1483 *John Qwitley sall haue a sertan of land lygand in the South syde
of the Byrkfeild*, Ovenden (YRS83/151); 1500 *iij houses in Kartegaytt lyggyng under the
Blake Frere waulle*, Scarborough (SS53/184). Noted in an amusing by-name: 1301 *De
Galfrido Liggebiyefyre*, Helperby (YRS21/80).

ligan See lagan.

ligger A board or beam: 1610 *tow little presser burdes with other old liggers vjd*, South Cave
(Kaner234). See also overlier.

light (1) To settle or alight: 1642 *neare to the place wheare they* [the bees] *lighted*,
Elmswell (DW65). With the preposition 'into' it meant to come across by chance:
1669 *goeing unto the mores to worke, light into the company of Mr Thomas Canby*, Thorne
(QS1/9/2). In conjunction with 'of' it signified to find or discover: 1729 *took purpose
to travil into the west of England to get imployment … could not light of any work*, Craven
(QS1/68/4).

light (2), lights 'Tree' place-names which have 'light' as the first element include
Lighthazles in Soyland, and Lightollers in Rochdale which is close to the county
boundary. They are of a type and can be contrasted with Thickhollins, almost certainly
descriptive of woods or sections of woods where the tree cover was light, not dense.
Oliver Rackham described 'lights' as wooded and grassy compartments in a forest
(OR1/147) and this plural form occurs as an element in two neighbouring Calder
Valley place-names: 1386 *Horbury lightes* (MD225); 1525 *the Comon called the Lightes*,
Ossett (PNWR2/188). See also thick.

lighter A flat-bottomed boat, used to transport goods in harbours or along the
estuaries and rivers: 1747 *keels, lighters and other vessels bringing coal up the River Hull to
the Beck*, Beverley (YRS122/29).

lighterman One who owned or worked on a lighter: 1553 *Edmunde Johnson, Kingston
on Hull, lighterman* (YRS11/99); 1558 *Thomas Yates, Hull, lyghterman* (YRS14/188).

lights See light (2).

like on To have a liking for, to favour: 1614 *she will not sell anie of her ale forth of doors
except it be to those whom she likes on*, Easingwold (NRQS2/52).

limbeck An apparatus formerly used in distilling, a short form of 'alembic': 1520 *a
dowbyll styll to make with aqua vite that ys to say a lymbeke with a serpentyn*, Mount Grace
(YAJ18/296); 1529 *a lymbeke for stilling of waters*, Ingmanthorpe (SS79/277); 1567 *ij
olde lymbecks xxd … A stylletorye*, Richmond (SS26/197); 1614 *Stoorhouse … j lymbick*,
Stockeld (YAJ34/174). See also stillatory.

lime To put lime into a stream or river, poisoning the fish so that they could be easily taken by poachers: 1698 *Jonas Grimeshaw … brought before me for takeinge ten trouts by limeing the water*, Heptonstall (QS1); 1794 *John Ramsden and I got some Lime at Whinknowls and Limed the Beck with it … went back to the Beck to seek for fish but the Lime had kill'd none*, Keighley (ASh5/19,20).

limebearer See limeburner.

limeburner One who burns limestone to make lime: 1299 *John Lymbrinner*, Scarborough (YRS31/111); 1409 *computant cum Willelmo Lymbirner pro calce empto de eodem ad opus barræ [they settle account with William Lymbirner for lime bought from him for work on the bars]*, Beverley (ERAS4/30). The term remained in use, probably as an occupational by-name rather than a hereditary surname: 1432 *Richard Lymebirner de Tadcastre pro xxvj carectatis calcis vivi £4 2 4 [Richard Lymebirner of Tadcaster for 26 cart loads of lime £4 2s 4d]*, York (SS35/50). Sand and lime were needed to make mortar, and there was a constant demand for both in the Middle Ages when so much building was taking place. The names of the labourers who transported the lime in York were entered into the freemen's rolls: 1389 *Thomas Hughesson, lymportour*; 1394 *Thomas de Tadcaster, lymeberer*, York (SS96). See also limestone.

limehouse In York this was a building where lime was stored for the masons who were working on major projects: in 1421, 60 quarters were purchased at Sherburn and four men were paid *pro cariagio … usque lymehouse Beatri Petri infra clausum [for transport … to the limehouse of St Peter within the close]*, York (SS35/44). A Bridlington Priory place-name may have the same origin: 1541–2 *a cottage called the lime hows* (YRS80/48).

limeman An occupational term noted in York: 1384 *Hugh de Naburn, lymman* (SS96/82), and in Bingley where lime-burning was established in the seventeenth century: 1655 *Michael Maud … Lime-man de Bingley* (HP). See also limeburner.

lime pit A solution of lime and water in a pit was used by tanners to facilitate the removal of hair from the hides, also causing them to swell in readiness for tanning: 1422 'took two pits called *lez lympittes*, late in the tenure of William Barker', Bradford (CR); 1542 *Also so muche ledes in the lymme pytts as draweth xix marks, vjs viijd*, Beetham (SS26/29). In 1660, a Selby tanner had *13 hors skinnes in the lymes* (YRS47/170). Tanners who had no pits were quite often indicted for illegally using local wells. William Farrand of Kirkheaton was a persistent offender: in 1595, he was ordered to clean Ladywell and remove his quick lime *viva. calc.* and hides: in 1605 a by-law ordered him to *dresse the well called the Ladywell and take away his lyme and not occupie the same any more* (DD/WBR/2/28). At Leeds manor court in 1670, Isaac Blackburne was fined 13s 4d 'for fouling the waters at the common *stath* by washing his *lymed skins* where the people take water for preparing their victuals' (Th26/144). See also dacre.

limeporter See limeburner.

limestone The mortar used by bridge masons had two basic components, lime and sand. Its preparation involved converting the lime into quicklime which was done in a kiln, often a very primitive pit kiln. At that stage it was very volatile and dangerous to transport so the operation was usually carried out close to the place of work. Much of that is explicit in the masons' contract for Catterick Bridge:

> 1422 [they] *schalle gett lymstane and birne itte … and make thair lymkilns … and fynde and make carriage of sand als mekylle as thaim nedes … and schalle fynd apone*

thair owne cost als mykylle wode and coles broghte one the grounde as wille suffys ...
to the birnynge of alle the lymkilnes (NRQS3/34).

lince-pin nail See lin-nail.

lind The lime tree or the wood of the lime tree, also called the linden. It is found in early place-names, e.g. 1190–1202 *Lyndholme*, Hatfield (PNWR1/8) and also in the description of a boundary between Silkstone and Barnsley: *c.*1090 *per arborem quandam que vocatur Anglice Lind [per tree, the one which is called in English Lind]* (YRS25/19). In 1337, offences in Sowerby wood near Halifax included the illegal taking of *lynde* for making *sadeltres* (WYAS689). Small amounts appear to have been imported from the Baltic: 1465 *2 M waynskottes ... 3 C claphoult ... 12 lyndbordes*, Hull (YRS144/80).

line The fibre of flax or the plant itself: 1535 *lynne seude and hemp sede, iij bussheles, vjs; lyne and hempe redie to be spone and in yarne, xls,* Stillingfleet (YRS45/127); 1539 *lay no hempe nor lyne within the beke,* Normanton (WCR9/154); 1704 *having a good quantity of line lying in two barnes adjoining to his house,* Moss (QS1/43/4); 1747 *forty stones of rated line, forty unrated,* Fishlake (QS1/86/3). The thread was spun on a special line wheel: 1610 *one old lyne wheele,* Kirkstall (SpSt); 1635 *one lyne wheele, one woolle wheele,* Emley (FACccxxi); 1667 *three Lyne wheeles,* North Bierley (YRS134/127); 1796 *a line wheel and a quilting frame,* Cartworth (G-A). The finished cloth was also called line: 1327 *Ricardus le blak, lyndraper,* York (SS96/24); 1493 *the lyn wevers of this Citie,* York (YRS103/97); 1567 *neyn payre of lynne shetes,* Fixby (YRS134/16); 1756 *a piece of printed linn,* North Bierley (QS1/95/4). See also line-tow.

line-beater The rare word 'beat' was used of a bundle of flax or hemp made up ready for steeping (OED). It was the source of an early occupational by-name: 1258 *Malle Linbetere,* Rothwell (YRS12/59).

linen-draper A retail trader who deals in linen: 1576 *George Aglande, Wrenthorpe, par. Wakefelde, lynninge draper* (YRS19/2).

line-tow Tow was the fibre of flax, hemp or jute, prepared for spinning, and it gave its name to a type of linen material: 1587 *fyve yerdes of clothe made of lynetowe,* Methley (Th35/102); 1596 *Item lyne towe & yerne, 6s 8d,* Knaresborough (YRS134/60); 1658 *1 dusan of linan napkins, 1 dusan lintow napkins,* Selby (YRS47/5); *c.*1686 *napkings ... three being of lin & three of Linetow,* Conistone (RW25).

ling (1) A long slender fish found in the seas of northern Europe: 1416–17 'And for 2 salted fish called ling (*leng'*) purchased from William Benyngholm this year 3s', Selby (SAR161); 1580 *for a dry lynge ixd, for freshe fyshe xijd,* Stockeld (YRS161/17); 1613 *Saltfishe bought at Malton ... lynges a quarter cost xxviijs,* Brandsby (NYRO44/71).

ling (2) This common moorland plant had varied uses, notably as material for thatching: 1394–5 *Item ij mulieribus pro lyng mowing iiijd,* Whitby (SS72/605); 1689 *for getting ling leading & Thatching for Hilcastile house,* Conistone (RW41). See also heath, quartern.

lin-nail The linch-pin or nail which secured the wheel to the axle-tree, noted from 1496 in the OED: 1485 *ij lyn' nayles,* Ripon (SS64/373); 1558 *a wayne, to* [sic] *lyne nayles, two apiltone* [suspect axiltre] *nayles of iron,* Castleford (Th27/287); 1637 *a gang of old wayne strokes ... 2 lynnailes,* Thorpe Willoughby (YRS47/137). Note: 1580 *a lynce pynne nayle,* Beverley (YRS84/33); 1653 *bolts, shackles, runners, three lynn-pinns,* Northallerton (NRQS5/143).

lin-pin See lin-nail.

linsey-woolsey Originally a material woven from a mixture of flax [line] and wool: 1611 *1 pese of lynsay wousay & a great sort of cruels lapt in it*, Brandsby (NYRO44/35); 1631 *eleaven long & short linsne woolsne boulsters jli*, Bingley (LRS1/80); 1637 *one gowne & one linsewolsee cote*, Selby (YRS47/82).

lintycock The word 'lintie' was once commonly used in the northern counties for the linnet, a bird that ate the seeds of 'lin' or flax: 'lintycock' is not recorded independently but it was probably the male linnet and the source of the place-name Lintycock Stones in north Yorkshire.

lip See mare.

liquorice The root or rhizome of the plant *Glycyrrhiza glabra*, literally the sweet root, used medicinally and as a sweetmeat. The word is on record in England by *c.*1200 (OED) and quantities were imported into Hull probably from Spain via the Low Countries: 1463 *1 bale lycores*; 1467 *1 balle licorice* (YRS144/47,100). It was available in the monasteries: 1457–8 *In lycares d'no Abbati, jd [In liquorice for the lord Abbot]*, Fountains Abbey (SS130/67). Indeed, it is thought that the root was being used medicinally by Cluniac monks in Pontefract from a much earlier date, and its development as a confectionery item took place later in the town. Richard Cholmeley of Brandsby recorded the following purchase of the plant there: 1617 *Lycorise 100 setts cost 2s 5d from Robert Layton of Pontefract* (NYRO44/147).

list (1) The hem or selvage of material: 1433 *unam tuellam de twill, cum nigris lystez [a twill table cloth with black lists]*, York (SS30/49); 1506 *And the wever to have for … every such cloth of xxv yerds long and vij quarters and an half brod betwix the lists ijs viijd in redy money*, York (YRS106/21); 1824 *paid for some lists and thrums*, Meltham (G-A). In 1758–62, a Wakefield cloth frizzer wrote in his memorandum book: *pieces called stop lists made mostly about Dewsbury and Birstall are used in foreighn countryes for womens petticoats and the list is and [sic] ornament for border of the bottom of the coatt* (YRS155/65). Used also of a type of cloth: 1562 *One coverlet of lyste lined with fure viijd*, Richmond (SS26/162); 1598 *one white broad liste Carsey*, Hipperholme (YRS3/69). See also listing.

list (2) Short for 'enlist': 1675 *Samuel Constantine of Kettlewell listed by Captaine Cuthbert Wade … in his troope of dragoones* (QS1); 1697 *put a shilling into my hand and … towld me that I was listed*, Sheffield (QS1/36/3).

list (3) A verb, to choose, desire or please. See also lap.

listing The material of which the list or selvage of cloth is made: 1444 *cum alio coopertorio rubeo habente in lystyng volucres et albas ollas [with another cover having honey-suckle and white pots in the listing]*, Beverley (SS30/99); 1506 *in garne beside the listyng*, York (YRS106/18); 1615 *ix stone of garne, coverlait, garne and listing vijli vijs 8d*, Bingley (LRS1/24).

lit As a verb it means to colour or dye: 1617 *two dozans of woole with stuffe to litte them with all, vli*, Bingley (LRS1/40); 1621 *Item 22 pound of litted wollen yarne, xxijs*, South Cave (Kaner305); 1708 *going to buy oyle and lytting stuff*, Holmfirth (QS1/47/10).

lithe To thicken broth or milk with flour: *c.*1711 *lithe it with bean meal, as hot as can be bidden*, Scalm Park (YAJ7/58). Used also as an adjective: a recipe for oat-cakes in 1683 included *a Peck of the finest wheat-flower … strong Ale-yeast … salt … five pints of water, for itt must bee very lithe*, Methley (GWK65).

lit-house A regional word for dye-house, pronounced 'littus' locally: 1540 *lands and tenements called A lytehous now in the tenure of John Sunderland*, Sowerby (WCR9/179); 1553 *all my hool lithowse, as wadde, hardasche, with all suche thinges thereto belonging*, Birstall (Th19/340); 1635 *un domu voc a Lithouse [a building called a lit-house]*, Rishworth (MD225/1/361); 1675 *litthouses or dyeing houses erected upon the common*, Honley (YDK96). See also lead-house.

litster A dyer: 1393–4 'Stephen de Girlyngton of York, *littester*' (YRS120/6); 1427 *Thomas Bemeslay, York, litster* (YRS6/15); 1462 *John Adamson, litster,* York (YRS6/2). It was a frequent by-name and the source of the surname Lister: 1379 *Adam Litster,* Elland (PTWR). See also lit, lit-house, and GRDict.

litting lead, litting pan A vat or a pan used in the dyeing process: 1573 *one lyttinge panne*, Dalton (BIA19/677); 1588 *my great lyttinge lead, pair of tenters, and my wollhedge*, Leeds (Th1/382).

little mester A spelling of 'little master' which reflects the dialect pronunciation. The term was used almost exclusively in the Sheffield district for the independent craft workers in the cutlery trades. The little mesters worked alone or employed a small number of workers and apprentices: many had their own workshop but others rented space in a bigger establishment. The term does not appear in early records and may date only from the late eighteenth century. It has largely fallen out of use since this practice peaked in Victorian times, but continues to be used in Yorkshire, if only nostalgically. See also maister, mystery.

livelihood Means of living, maintenance: 1479 *if so be my gyft may stand, except the lyvelod that is in Garton*, Flinton (SS45/252); 1489 *that Anne my wyffe have the reule and governaunce of my yonger sonnes and of there lyvelod*, Fenwick (SS45/277). See also liflode.

liver Short for 'deliver', meaning to hand over: 1676 *offered a 5 shilling peece … layinge it on the table … Gregg snatched it upp and denyed either to liver the money or the horse*, Rotherham (QS1/13/7).

livery A distinctive suit of clothes given by a gentleman to his servants, in order that they might be recognised as his retainers: 1484–5 'The indenture to be void if Thomas [*Kame*] … take *anymans leuerey* or clothing during the said term', Thorpe Salvin (YRS102/147); 1531 *To Umfrey my brother my levera jakett*, Kirkham (SS79/306); 1555 *that euery one that shall not haue one my gownes … shall haue one cote or leueraye*, Stanley (Th27/38); 1621 *8 cloakes with gould parchment lace 2 rownd about and 5 about the coller for liveryes*, Brandsby (NYRO44/217). In a related usage the word could be applied to provisions given to servants and by extension to the items in which these were served or the place where they were kept: 1530–1 *his wages weekly viij whiett lowes of the leweray bread … iiij gallons of the leweray ayll*, Rievaulx (SS83/349); 1612 *John Graye came to serve me. I promised 4ᵒʳ markes wayges and a livery when I gave livereyes*, Brandsby (NYRO44/54); 1614 *j livery coborde*, Stockeld (YAJ34/172); 1617 *in the pantry … two livery pottes whitte*, Ripley (YAJ34/184). See also cast (2), seisin.

loaden To load, with 'loadened' as the past form: 1555–6 *and in the tyme they lodyned the wayne Ayton bated the other draught opon the balke*, Kirkham (YRS114/93); 1627 *free passage with horse or meare lodened through one foulde*, Heptonstall (LRS2/97); 1690 *after he had taken up the said money John Hardy presented a pistol at him and said it was loadened*, Silsden (QS1/29/5). See also lad (1).

load-saddle A northern term for pack-saddle: 1435 '2 *garthwebbes* for a *lodesadell*', Scarborough (SZ1/351); 1563 *a lade sadle, ij girths, a halter, and a wantow bodome xxd,*

Brantfell, Westmorland (SS26/169); 1585 *two lodesadles with garthes & wantoes 6s 8d,*
Rastrick (YRS134/56); 1636 *Item, 2 lodesadles, 2 overlayes, 2 wantowes and a tayle band,*
xs, Allerton near Bradford (LRS1/87); 1640 *Item one lode sadle tree, 16d,* Bingley
(LRS1/119). Recorded in an occupational term: 1658 *Richard Ingle, load-sadle maker,*
Bradfield (YRS1/169).

loan The usual word in much of south Yorkshire for lane: 1361 *in un lono,* Golcar
(KM69); 1379 *Richard Bithelone,* Huddersfield; 1537 *I bequeath to the mending of the*
Towne Lone iijs iiijd, Huddersfield (HPN85). See also loin.

loaning The north Yorkshire word for lane: 1313 'the way called *Spitel lonnyg* [sic]',
Bagby (YRS50/18); 1473 *le Milnloning,* Hampsthwaite (YRS55/94); 1556 *fower closes*
lyinge of the east side of the lonynge betwext Richmond and Hypswell (SS26/95); 1610 *for*
not repayring the loning between Earbie and West Ronckton (NRR1/199); 1660 *a common*
weinde or loaning, Yarm (MD302/4).

lob The pollack, a sea-fish allied to the cod. The word is first recorded in an Act of
1357 (OED): 1416–17 'for 30 salt fish called *lobbes* bought at Scarborough … at 1s
4½d each', Selby (YAJ48/124). Other purchases were *keling* and *ling.*

lock An enclosure or fold. The word is found in place-names such as Lockwood but
otherwise occurs only rarely: *c.*1562 *Hath sene the tenants build lockes and shepe fooldes*
apon the said two groundes, Marske (YAJ6/282). Angus Winchester has 'ewelocks' as a
Lake District field-name.

locket, locket-nail The locket was the iron cross-bar of a window to which the glass
was attached by small nails: 1355 *In mercede fabri facientis pragges et lokats de ferro suo pro*
fenestris ligendis 8d [In the smith's pay for making prags and lockets from his iron for window
fastenings 8d], Ripon (SS81/92); 1379–80 *Et in C loketnayles 3½ d [And in 100 locket-*
nails 3½d], Ripon (SS81/101); 1396–7 *In palis et lokytnaylis et aliis necessariis ferri, 4d*
[For stakes and locket-nails and other iron necessities, 4d], Ripon (SS81/125). In 1379, the
by-name *Johannes Loket* was recorded in Thornhill which was a nail-making centre
(PTWR).

locksmith This was a widely distributed craft, represented in all the major towns in
medieval Yorkshire and in some of the villages. In 1379, *Johannes Loksmyth* of Sheffield
paid 6d poll tax and since no occupation was listed we can be sure from his by-name
that he was a smith who specialised in making locks (PTWR321). The by-name
continued to be recorded into the sixteenth century: 1421 *in seruris, clavibus, hespes,*
stapels, jonetors … factis per Henricum Loksmyth [for locks, keys, hasps, staples, jointers …
made by Henry Locksmyth], York (SS35/44); 1454 *Et Thome Loksmyth pro reparacione et*
emendacione diversarum cathenarum portarum cerarum et clavium [And to Thomas Loksmyth
for repair and renewal of various chains gates and locks], York (SS192/78); 1513 *John*
Loksmyth, loksmyth, York (SS96/236). Nicholas Awbraye of Wyke near Bradford was an
illiterate locksmith who used a key as his mark in 1583 (YRS50/201).

lode A drain or water channel: 1410 *all others who are bound to cleanse a water lode leading*
from Hesilplace to the Kelder, Methley (Th35/168). In 1524, the mayor and council of
York wanted the name of a certain place mentioned in their charters to be corrected:
to calle yt Marslande where as yt is Marselode (YRS106/101). See also lade-net, lading (2).

lodge When lodge came into English from French it meant a hut, arbour or small
house, a temporary building. It then came to be used of a keeper's house in a deer park
and this meaning survived into the seventeenth century at least. A survey of Pickering
Forest in 1619–21 noted that there were *no keepers lodges within any part of the foreste,*

whereas in Blandsby Park there were two, *the upper and lower lodge* (NRR1/33). From the late 1400s, such lodges were being put to a variety of uses. In 1483, for example, Edward Gower was granted permission to *have low masses said in the house called le Loge in Beverley Park*: in 1489 there was *a mansion called le Loge* in Sheffield Park (CYS198,229). In *c*.1540, a dispute at the Court of Star Chamber had to do with such a lodge in the Forest of Galtres:

> Sir Thomas Curwen seyeth thatt the seid howse, wheryn the seid defendauntes have allegged a wever to dwelle, was buylded and made only for a lodge for the keper of the seid south parte of the seid foreste, for the sauegarde and mayntenaunce of the kynges dere or game there, and nott for eny wever to dwelle in. And also the seid cotage was buylded and made to kepe in the lyeme houndes of the seid keper ... (YRS41/87).

The word could also be used from that early period for the workplaces of masons, herdsmen and the like. In the fabric accounts for York Minster are: 1371 *Roberto de Ottelay operanti ibidem in logio per 41 sept*; 1399 *In le loge apud Ebor. in cimiterio lxix stanaxes*; 1409 *Item logium pro cementariis construendum [1371 to Robert de Ottelay working there in the lodge for 41 weeks; 1399 In the lodge in the graveyard at York 69 stone axes; 1409 Item constructing a lodge for the masons]* (SS35/6,17,200). Similarly, the fabric rolls of Ripon mention the *Mayson loge* in 1541–2 (SS81/194). Quite different types of lodge are found on the estates of the great abbeys: in 1366–7 Kirkstall Abbey had *in Crosdale ... vnum loghe pro pastoribus [in Crosdale ... a lodge for the shepherds]*, and the keeper or *custos* was *Willelmus del Loghe* (Th8/361). Fountains Abbey used the same word to describe specialist cattle-rearing establishments, referred to as *logias* as early as 1190–9 (SS67/9). A property they owned at Nutwith Cote in Masham is described in a lease of 1495 as a *graunge or loge* (SS42/324n) one of more than a dozen such places. More explicitly an abbey lease of 1537 described one of these at Bouthwaite as a *dare-house, loige and feahowse*, a farm therefore where dairy cattle were raised (SS42/279).

In a coal-mining context the lodge could be a temporary building at the pit mouth which might serve as a store and rest-place. A lease of 1597 granted Leonard Atkinson of Beeston *libertye to erecte and builde any Lodges over the said Coalepittes for ... any the servants or workemen ... and for takeinge downe of the said Lodges and carryeing away of the same in as large and ample Manner as is convenient and necessary* (WYL160/129/4). It can be compared with 'cabin', 'pit house', and 'shed', used in other districts.

Some keepers' lodges had been converted into farms by the sixteenth century. In 1584, a survey of the manor of Idle contained a reference to a parcel of ground *within which there standeth a pretty Lodge, wherein sometime the keeper dwelt when deer was kept there* (BAS1/192). Others were rebuilt as country houses: 1651 *a fayre howse lately built knowne by the Name of the Lodg ... which house conteyneth three severall Roomes below staires and as many above with a Court before the doore*. There were also two barns and a stable, *diverse litle yards* and a garden, all in good repair (NRR1/69). General Bernard who was related to the Beaumonts of Whitley used the word in 1793 as the name of a grand new mansion that he had built at Colne Bridge, calling it Heaton Lodge. In the basement, the domestic staff had a kitchen, pantry, shoe-room and larder; there was also a servants' hall and special accommodation for the butler and house-keeper. On the ground floor were a dining-room, vestibule and central staircase, with private family bedrooms in both wings, each with its own dressing room: upstairs were seven guest bedrooms. A comprehensive range of outbuildings, included a hot-house, and shops or workplaces for a butcher and blacksmith. The name *Heaton Lodge* was clearly intended to highlight this magnificence: the irony is that a farm called Lodge just across the river had once been the keeper's cottage in Mr Pilkington's deer park.

'Lodge' would become a popular name for villa residences from that period. See also grange, grove (2).

lodger The keeper of a lodge on the Fountains Abbey estate. In 1512, the abbot appointed Margaret and Christopher Brown as his *servauntes, loigers and feamen* at Bouthwaite, a lodge in Nidderdale (YRS140/196).

loggerhead A thick-headed or stupid person; a blockhead, used in insults: 1686 *that loggerhead, kisse my arse* (QS1).

loggin A dialect word for a bundle of straw, hay or the like: 1727 *several loggins or bundles of straw*, Wetherby (QS1/66/4).

logwood It has two quite distinct meanings. In springwood contexts it was possibly 'wood suitable for logs or sawn into logs': 1704 *And also all stovens and logwood trees in the said Spring Woods*, Bradley (SpSt). In the Colne Bridge charcoal account for 1710 were entries for *Logwood* from several local woods, e.g. *Logwood from Ethercliffe*: this was measured at *17¼ Coards, 9 Doz*[en] *and 10 S* – an abbreviation which is probably for 'seam' (SpSt). In connection with dyeing it was the heartwood of a tree found in the Americas which was imported in blocks or logs: 1600 *in dying wooll & Wollen clothe Logwood als Blockwoodd callide*, Holbeck (YRS3/174); 1668 *4 Qtrs of bluegalles; 3 Qtrs 19 lb & 1 oz Log wood; 1 Qtr of Fustick*, Slaithwaite (YRS134/137); 1758 *To dye black best way. Boyl in logwood and shumak att night*, Wakefield (YRS155/2).

loin In parts of west Yorkshire this was a spelling of 'loan', the local word for lane: 1437 *quod Willelmus Sutton, vicar de birton fecit un fossat' in le vykarloyne [that William Sutton the vicar of Birton made a ditch in the vykarloyne]*, Kirkburton (MD225/1/163); 1463 *Aspeyoleloyn*, Huddersfield (MD225/1/189); 1482 *le commonloyn*, Lepton (MD335); 1522 *Skynnerflatt and the loynes therunto adjonyng*, Nidderdale (YRS41/106); 1648 *Wainwright came and fenced the croft from the loyne*, Thurlstone (SS65/106).

London metal Thought to be an alloy of copper. In 1690, George Harrison, a Sheffield craftsman, had in his garret *36 pounds of London Mettell* and in 1692 George Bullas had *28 pounde London mettell* (IH).

long A regular abbreviation of 'belong', on record from the fifteenth century: 1443 *my chefe maner place and iiij oxgange of land langing therto*, Sheriff Hutton (SS30/89); 1486 *a halling that langith to the grete hall*, Hull (SS53/17); 1519 *a fedder bedde and that that longes to ytt*, Roundhay (Th9/89); 1540–2 *a gresse howsse … havynge no arrable land langyng to itt*, Heworth (YRS114/16).

long hundred From the thirteenth century at least, grain, livestock, timber, etc. could be calculated at the long or great hundred which amounted to six score: 1236 *et communem pasturam … ad quadringentas oues per magnum Centum cum tot agnis [and common of pasture … for 4 hundred sheep by the long hundred with all the lambs]*, Kirklees (YAJ16/465). Where that system was employed it applied to multiples such as 500 and 1,000 which in reality were 600 and 1,200. Our modern 100 might therefore be referred to as the small hundred. The distinction is explicit in references to imported clapholt or clapboard: 1483 *3 gret hundredth clapholt; two smalle hundredth clapholte*, Hull (YRS144/192,195). Other examples of small hundred include: 1562 *Clabbord the small hundrythe xd*, York (SS129/168). Both terms were used in wood management: 1574 *Okes of the secound sorte, v^c okes at vj^xx to th'undreth, at vjs 8d the pice, if li*, Aldborough (SS42/412); 1600 *in the Bushell alias Bilsdale Hagg accompting fiue score only to the 100 there hath been cut downe … Tymber trees 1581*, Settrington (YRS126/88). See also perch.

loning See loaning.

look sharp To lose no time, to bestir oneself, a colloquial usage: 1785 *If you do not look sharp about it and get Mr Fearnley to draw up the award and sign'd soon everything will be void*, Meltham (G-A).

look to To take care of; to look after, especially of sick people and animals: 1598 *Willm. Blande and one Billington were herdemen in somer tymes for the Abbott ... and kepte and loked to theyr horses and cattell ther*, Malham Moor (YRS114/168); 1638 *to Dorithe Shawe for lowkin to me in my siknes, xs*, Thorpe Willoughby (YRS47/143); 1675 *hee bought those lambs of one which was looking to a flocke of sheepe*, Bradley, Huddersfield (QS1).

loom This was the weaver's apparatus for weaving cloth, commonly referred to in the past as a pair of looms: 1588 *Item one paire of lowmbes one paire of heldes and one slaye vijs*, Dalton (DD/WBW/19); 1624 *reserved to the said Richard Swallow the roome or liberty for the standing ... of one paire of narowe loomes within the same worke chamber*, Honley (G-A).

In the Old English period it had been more generally an implement or tool of any kind (OED) and it retained that meaning: 1620 *this Courte doth request Sir Coniers Darcie ... to provide ... loomes and yrons for imployinge and ruling ... those who shalbe admitted*, Helmsley (NRQS2/235n); 1642 *An outligger carryeth but onely one loome to the fielde and that is a rake*, Elmswell (DW51). It had this sense in 'heirloom'. See also heald, web (2).

loom chamber The upper storey of a clothier's cottage: 1579 *'unam cameram voc' a lome chamber [a chamber called a loom chamber] above the said stable'*, Kirkburton (YDK116). See also work chamber.

loom house The building in which a clothier had his loom or looms, a work-place: 1576 *In the Shopp and Lomehowse ... one Lome, Damyselles, Bartrees ... and all other thynges thereunto belonging*, Leeds (Th4/164); 1724 *1 workhouse or loomhouse*, Batley (YAS/DD4).

loop-hole An unglazed opening in a wall, originally in a defensive wall, designed to allow missiles to be directed at an attacker. From the seventeenth century it was a similar opening in a barn, through which hay or straw could be forked: 1674 *did putt them through a loupe hole into his neighbour's layth*, Bolton by Bowland (QS1/13/5); 1686 *Paid to Daniell Tailforth for 6 windowes and 4 lowpeholes*, Conistone (RW45); 1722 *in a barne ... saw a riding coat ... and hid the same in a loop hole*, Heptonstall (QS1/61/4); 1756 *went to the far end of the barn and looked through a loup hole*, Birstall (QS1/95/9).

loose To 'loose' a coal-pit was to carry out all the work that was necessary for coal to be 'won' there, with proper access and freedom from water: 1633 *to loose or enable anyone else to get coals by means of the pits and soughs so made*, Northowram (HAS31/77); 1733 *convenient for the loosing and draining a coal myne*, Whitley (DD/WBW/61); 1754 *Toftshay coalmine ... cannot be loosed without buying some coals which belong to the two Cordingleys* [that is in the adjoining grounds] (Tong/4c/5); 1766 *no sough was to be cut ... so far to the extreme part of the grounds as to loose the works or coal of Mr Lister*, Halifax (HAS31/88). In his history of mining in Halifax, W.B. Trigg used the word 'water-loose' as an alternative to 'watergate' or 'sough' but the noun was absent from the documents that he quoted and may have come into use in the nineteenth century, cf. 1760–1 *Jos Cowburn and Jas Barker for feying and loosing the Water*, Tong (Tong/4c/5).

loose suit An apprentice was said to be 'loose' once he had completed his term: 1539 *I dyd lowsse John my sonne furthe his apprentyschippe which was no lytill coste*, Pannal (SS104/41); 1552 *To Barnard Spinke … when he ys loyse of his prentishipe xxs*, Featherstone (Th19/322); 1690 *Peeter Dawson hired June the 16ᵗʰ for 25ˢ & to be lowse at whitsun*, Conistone (RW27). This probably explains what a loose suit was – not a loose-fitting garment. In 1778, John Haste [Hayhurst] of Tong was bound apprentice to Samuel Pitchforth of Elland *with consent of his mother*: in the final part of the agreement was a requirement that *in due Season the said Master would finde all Aparil or Cloaths which is Nesesary … that is one sute for work days and one for Holydays and one Loose sute at the end of the time* (Tong/12a/119). See also close coat.

lop In woodmanship 'lops' were the branches cut from a growing tree, and the word occurred several times in the accounts of William Ramsden when he was Woodward General of Yorkshire: 1544–5 *Item foure tymber trees taken by the said accomptant forth of the said wodd toward the reparacion of his house at longlay the loppes expendid toward the hedgeynge of the said Coppies*, Nostell (DD/RA/f/4a). The verb to lop also occurred commonly: 1568 *to loppe alle ockes and saplynges … and for the loppyng thereof shalle have a ½d*, Esholt (BAS10/246); 1683 *as for the wood which will be convenient to be lopt or feld … & the bark coming therof, I give to my son*, Selby (YRS47/104); 1688 *that Edward Langley cutt hys hedge and lopp the trees*, Holmfirth (WCR14/122). See also offal, top.

lording A name which marked a stage in the growth of a timber tree, perhaps meaning 'less than a lord', or used more literally for the greatest trees in a wood: 1672 *leave all the lordins and blackbarkes now standing and growing*, Tong (Tong/3/321); 1687 *all the lordings and great timber trees now marked*, Beauchief (EDD); 1727 *Bought of Mr Will. Hanson his 2 springwoods at Fauthwaite, at 10£ per acre; the lordings in the wood and the hedgerows, price 150£*, Dodworth (SS65/264); 1768 *Woodsome Park lordings all sold to Mr Jonathan Roberts, tanner, of Farnley at 6,000 guineas and to take them in five years* (ELT37). See also blackbark.

lorimer A maker of small ironware, such as chains, bits, spurs and the like: 1273 *Thomas de Blida, lorimer*, York (SS96/2); 1367 *Johannes de Beverley, lorymer*, York (SS96/64); 1453–5 *Et de 6d sol. loyrymer pro faccione unius ceræ et emendale de les barres fenestrarum [And for 6d to the lorimer for making a bolt and repair of the window bars]*, Ripon (SS81/161). Examples of the by-name occur into the fifteenth century: 1421 *Radulpho Lorymar de Conyngstrete pro factura et emendacione xl cathenarum pro eisdem libris annexis in librario predicto, 23s 1d [To Ralph Loryimar for making and repairing 40 chains for those books fixed in the said library]*, York (SS35/46). The by-name gave rise to the surnames Lorimer and Loriman (GRDict) and a similar development affected the occupational term: 1577 *Symond Doddinge, Ripon, loryman* (YRS19/48).

loss'd One example noted: 1782 *heavey Showers of rain … and for that reason our warps was sorely loss'd*, Ovenden (CA106). To 'loss' as a form of to 'lose' could mean to be unprofitable, and here the inference is that the warps got wet and were spoilt as a result.

louke To pull up weeds: 1446–58 *pro messione de xij acris et di. terræ … et pro lowkyng eiusdem vjd [for reaping 12½ acres of land … and for lowking it 6d]*, Fountains Abbey (SS130/113); 1580 *to Stead wyf for lowkyng iij dais in the gardyn, iijd*, Stockeld (YRS161/45); 1624 *paid him for his mowing and his wife's lowking and hay making 12s*, Elmswell (DW175); 1786 *I was looking with the women all day*, Sessay (WM5). Note: 1642 *Lookers have (for the most parte) iijd a day, the men that whette their hookes iiijd*, Elmswell (DW148). See also louke crook.

louke crook A hook-shaped implement for weeding: 1581 *a maldbrod clowt & iij lock* [sic] *croukes*, Stockeld (YRS161/51); 1597 *Item peis houkes, loukcrouks*, South Cave (Kaner197); 1634 *3 pease hackes, 3 looke crookes*, Elmswell (DW234).

louvre A wooden, turret-like erection on the roof of a major building, with lateral openings for ventilation and the passage of smoke: 1358 *Item in loveres, vs*, York (SS129/16); 1404 *In cordis emptis pro louers, 10d [For ropes bought for the louvres, 10d]*, York (SS35/27); 1504–5 *all dorez, wyndowez, glase … lovers and almaner thing long to every house*, York (YRS106/13); 1538 *there is a kychyn of the olde fasshyon with ane upright roofe after the fasshyon of a louer*, Esholt (YAJ9/324). The slats of such louvres were operated by cords or strings: 1368 *et loverstrenges emptis vjd*, York (SS129/23); 1522–3 *for a cord to a loffer jd*, York (CCW89).

In York, the ordinances of the tilers and wrights referred in 1428 to the making of *draghtlouers* (SS125/174): this may have meant louvres which could be opened and shut or louvres which simply provided ventilation.

low–decker See collier housing.

lowke See louke.

lozengewise Here, the meaning was engraved or embossed in a lozenge pattern: 1450 *unum ciphum argenti stantem coopertum deauratum et chaceatum losengewise [a silver gilt, upright goblet, covered and chased lozengewise]*, Beverley (SS30/141).

lugged With lugs, that is 'ears' or handles: 1745 *to the said Roger Wright my two lugged silver cup*, Ripon (GRD). In a colliery account of 1711 *Lugs of Ash* were parts of corves made of alder and they were probably handles (BM82/66). Of course to 'lug' was to tug or haul and such examples appear to link the two words. See also gallow-balk, tram, tug.

lumber A word used for roughly prepared timber, or for articles of furniture and the like which take up room inconveniently (OED): 1660 *household stuff and lumber in Whitby house* (YRS9/164); 1681 *a boat with certane oke wood £2 10; the working tooles for the calling with certaine lumber in the yard and backside*, Selby (YRS47/51). See also oak.

lump stone Probably large pieces of stone which were not hewn by the masons but were suitable for rough walling: 1412 *Concessum est per Capitulum quod dominus thes. habeat lompstanes ad murum lapideum suum construendum infra clausuram [It was granted by the Chapter that the lord treasurer might have lump stone for building his stone wall within the close]*, York (SS35/200).

luthern A dormer-window, possibly a corruption of 'lucarne' (OED). The word occurs several times in a *particuler of the carpenter worke belonging to Pickering parsonage house*: 1698 *Three squaire & a halfe in 8 luteroms … Eight lutheram windows 2s a peece … eight Lutheran heads* (YAJ35/220).

lyard Gray, silvery-gray or white, used particularly of horses: 1345 *unum equum album qui vocatur lyard [a white horse that is called lyard]*, Brompton (SS4/11); 1429 *a white horse called Lyard*, York (SS30/186); 1452 *unum palefridum vocatum Lyard Gig [a palfrey called Lyard Gig]*, Masham (SS30/160); 1476 *myne graye ambuling horse callid lierd Dale*, Old Malton (SS45/224). These were effectively names, and the colour was characteristically linked with a family or place which identified where the horse came from: 1257 *et j pullum nigrum liard [and one black lyard colt]*, Harpham (ERAS21/71); 1495 *Johanni Aske lyard Otteley*, York (SS53/113); 1503 *Adæ Copley arm. j equum voc lyard Baraclogh [To Adam Copley armiger 1 horse called lyard Baraclogh]*, Clotherholme (SS53/215); 1508 *xxxiijs iiijd pro j equo succuss' vocat. Lyerd Banys [33s 4d for 1 trotting horse called Lyerd Banys],* York (SS53/289). See NH139–44.

lyke-wake The watch kept at night over a dead body: 1558 *Also I will that ther shall be no yong folks at my lyke waike but onlie xiij wydowes,* Richmond (SS26/127). See also night-wake, wake.

M

macer See mazer.

madder A herbaceous plant cultivated for medicinal purposes and the dye obtained from its root. Its use predates the Norman Conquest (OED) and it was being imported from the Low Countries in the Middle Ages: 1453 *1 poke mader*, Hull (YRS144/2); 1487 'tithes of *wald*, *mader* and *rapis*, by whatever name they are expressed', Fountains Abbey (YRS140/2); 1576 *Certeyne mather price iijs*, Leeds (Th4/164). A dye made from alum was called madder: 1510 *Item of ylke a seke or poket mader of alome jd*, York (YRS106/32).

made (1) In the inventory of John Wiseman of Selby, a shipwright who died in 1680, were: *102½ tunns of timber, at 16s, £82, in made plancke, £18* (YRS47/195). The inference may be that the timber was unwrought but that the planks were ready for use.

made (2) Mature or fully grown: used of animals. The term has been noted only in the western dales, and almost always in connection with 'beasts': 1619 *made beastes, twinter beastes*, Malham (DDKE/100/3); 1644 *2 of the said heffers were made beasts; and the other was younger*, Allerton (BAS6/275): 1674 *pasteridge for 13 made beasts*, Hanlith (MD217/187). From the eighteenth century it occurred as 'full made': 1730 *2 beast-gates or feeding and depasturing for two severall full made beasts in Cracoe Green* (MD194); 1786 *1 beastgate for one full made beast … and 21 sheepgates for 21 full made sheep*, Buckden (MD338/16).

maiden, maiden tub The OED suggests that 'maiden' was a washerwoman's 'dolly', a northern dialect word, and quotes *The Gentleman's Magazine* where it was said *c*.1752 that the term *A Yorkshire Maiden* referred to a machine for washing linen. West Riding glossaries later call the 'machine' a 'dolly' or 'peggy'; that is a wooden instrument which resembled a small stool on the end of a spade-like handle. This agitated the linen or other washing in a tub, an implement which is listed in late inventories: 1799 *tubs, churn, maiden tub*, Cartworth ; 1800 *maidening tub*, Cartworth (G-A).

maidenhair The name of some ferns, and used also of a variety of plants. In the example quoted here it was clearly a textile fabric: 1359 *et unam tunicam de maydenhare [a maidenhair jacket]*, Selby (SS4/71).

maiden tub See maiden.

mail pillion, mail saddle A saddle on which a 'mail' or pack might be placed: 1400 *pro j male-sadell*, Richmond (SS45/15); 1403 *et j malesadill*, Swine (SS4/326); 1567 *a maille and a maille pyllyone*, Richmond (SS26/197); 1658 *j bushel & maile pillion £1 4s 0d*, Barley (YRS47/16). See also pillion, trussing-coffer.

main, mainland Demesne land; the land attached to a mansion (OED): 1420 'licence … to enclose his ground from the land called the *maynland* behind the messuage', York (SS186/89); 1538 *ther manour or graunge of Greatt Broughton and all arable laund, mayn, medowe, common of moore*, Rievaulx Abbey (SS83/354). Also used as an adjective: 1601 'one acre of *mayne myddowe*', Moor Monkton (YRS150/135). It survives in a number of minor place-names: 1588 *Christopher Lowson of Munckton Maines*, Ripon (PR); 1606 *John Dodsworth of Massam Maynes* (NRQS1/48).

maine bread The finest white bread, a York delicacy. From pain–demaine, that is bread of our Lord, said to be so named because the figure of our Saviour was imprinted on it (SS120/261). The earliest references are in Latin and French, from the fourteenth century (OED) and the evidence is explicit later in the assize of bread in York: 1400 *Et in paynemayne empto vd [And for maine bread bought 5d]*, Richmond (SS45/19); 1411–12 *videlicet, panis oboulati dominici, vulgariter vocati Anglice [that is, of a halfpennyworth of pain-demaine (bread fit for the lord) commonly called in English] a halpenny symnell of mayn brede.* A memorandum in the same document then has: *touchant [concerning] payne demayn wastelles and symnelles*, York (SS120/167). Other York references include: 1452 *Pro alio pane vocato payne de mayne iiijs* (SS45/143); 1494 *he put to saile maynbred and levagn bred whiche was chaffed and myldewed and unholsome* (YRS103/106); 1533 *paid for a pottell of mavesey and mayne brede when we lokyd over the evydences, vijd* (CCW155). The word is on record over a wider area in the sixteenth century: 1528 *Item in mayne bread 1s*, Skipton (Whit2/308); 1545 *3 dussen of men bread to the said bune* [boon] *3s*, Bridlington (YRS80/70). See also scallop.

mainland See main.

maisondieu Literally 'god's house', a hospital or refuge for the old and infirm: 1374 *in domo Dei super Pontem Use [in the maisondieu on the Ouse bridge]* (SS4/93); 1398 *the Masyndew on Ouse Bridge* (SS186/90); 1432 *to the Goddes house in Paradise a rough felt*, Scarborough (SS30/22); 1434 *et pauperibus in domo dei super pontem Use*, York (SS192/14). There were several such houses in York and others in Beverley, Hull, Ripon and Tickhill, and the French word passed into general use, e.g. 1365 *in Hospitali meo juxta Kyngeston predictam vocato la Maison Dieu [in my hospital near Kingston aforesaid called the Maison Dieu]*, Hull (SS4/77); 1480 *octo pauperum in quadam Masyndew [eight poor people in a maisondieu]*, Ripon (SS78/162). In some early references where it has the appearance of a surname it may simply be a way of identifying an old or sick resident: 1553 *Alice de Maysyndw*, Ripon (SS81/299). See also measondue.

maister The usual dialect spelling of master: 1487 *I depute and make my super-visor Maister Baxter*, Hull (SS53/25); 1510 *I desir my broder … to be … good maister to my servants*, Harewood (Th24/48); 1533 *Rent servyces sute … Appertaynyng to the Sheype Maysters office*, Flotmanby (YRS80/9); 1685 *being makeinge of her maisters bed*, Almondbury (QS1). See also kirk maister, little mester, master.

make-blithe Make glad, friendly, happy. The OED has 'make-strife' and 'make-mirth' from the seventeenth century but by-names suggest that it was a frequent type of formation from much earlier: 1301 *De Ricardo Makejoye*, Whitby; *De Richedon Makedance*, Allerston (YRS21/58,108); 1324 *Robertus de [sic] Makeblith*, York (SS96/23); 1379 *Ralph Makblyth*, Dringhouses (PTWR). Earlier examples of this type are Machefare in 1176 and Makejoie in 1221 (R&W294)

makeshift In 1639, James Mauleverer of Ingleby Arncliffe had horses named *Catchpowle … Buckbraines, Silkewoorme … Twitchbell, Pepperboxe, Sugerlippes, Honni combe and Canonball* (YAJ16/177). Compared with names in the Tudor period these were eccentric and they read like individual nicknames. It is likely therefore that his horse called *Make-shifte* was something of a rogue, for this was the contemporary meaning of the word.

malacatone A peach grafted on a quince. One of several spellings of 'melocoton', found in the accounts of Richard Cholmeley of Brandsby. He experimented with it in the 1620s, planting the 'stones' and sending to London for young trees: 1620 *Yonge trees bought on William Oliver cosin 2 malacotones cost vs*; *An other bedd next it agane sowen with malacatowne stones* (NYRO44/187,189).

malison A curse or malediction: 1533 *Also I wyll and charge of payne of my malyson that all suche farmoldes as I have to equally devydyd* [sic] *betwixt my two sones John and Christopher that nother of thayme doy other wrong*, Marske (YRS152/51).

mall A spelling of 'maul', which is usually defined as 'a massive hammer' of any kind (OED). Yorkshire examples indicate that malls could be large or small, and were commonly made of iron as well as of wood: 1371 *Et in 2 novis mall' emptis pro quarera frangenda … 21s* [*And for 2 new malls bought for the opening up the quarry … 21s*], York (SS35/7); 1423 *pro iij malleis magnis de ferro … ij malleis parvis* [*for 3 large iron malls … 2 small malls*], York (SS45/81); 1569 *my greatest iron malle, foure yron wedges*, Shelf (BAS1/24); 1612 *all the wodde in the fold together with all the axes, malls, hatchetts*, Eccleshill (YRS134/69). In 1713, the cutler John Shirtcliffe had *1 Vice 1 Mall 1 workboard and other tools* recorded in his inventory (IH). See also mell (1).

mallienstane Of uncertain meaning: 1396–7 *In x carectatis de Mallienstane pro parietibus supra dicti mesuagii* [*For 10 cartloads of mallienstane for plastering about the said house*], Ripon (SS81/120). Not applicable here perhaps but worth noting is Rieuwert's reference to 'mallion' as 'an imprecise term … referring to soft gangue minerals' (JHR103).

malt This word occurs in the 1639 apprenticeship indenture of Anthony Armitage of Thickhollins, a document in which his master granted him the dressing *or malting of two oxe hides per annum* for two of the last years of his term (G-A). The verb 'to malt' usually referred to the process in which barley or other grain was initially steeped in vats, but tanners may have compared this with the tanning process in which hides were placed in pits or vats. However, the example quoted remains an isolated use of the word in such a context.

maltgrinder In late references this was a machine for cutting and crushing malted barley. The by-name is an indication that those processes were formerly done by hand: 1416 *Will. Herbotill, maltgrynder*, York (SS96/125).

malthouse A building in which malt is prepared. It occurs most commonly as a by-name or minor place-name: 1324–5 *pro ponte ultra le Malthousbek faciendo xxs* [*for building the bridge over the Malthousbek 20s*], Bolton Priory (YRS154/547); 1379 *Thomas de Malthous*, Kirkby Malzeard (PTWR); 1426–7 *William del Malthous*, 'keeper of the malt-house … and rabbit warren of Thorpe Willoughby' (SAR183n). See GRDict.

malt quern A hand-mill for grinding malt: 1551 *a pare of malt whernes*, Halifax (Crossley63); 1658 *j paire of mault whearnes*, Barley (YRS47/16). See also maltgrinder, mustard quern, whern.

maltster A person who makes malt: 1377–8 *Ade Maltester pro calciatura et stipendio per annum xs* [*To Adam Malteser for footwear and wages for the year 10s*], Bolton Priory (YRS154/561). See also –ster.

mammal An early reference to this word, used by Francis Ianson in his will in 1748. He died childless but made cash bequests to the seven children of his brother William saying that *if any die* he wanted the money to be distributed among the survivors *be* *they Males or Mamels*, Addingham (GRD). 'Mamels' clearly referred to William's four daughters.

Manchester, Manchester ware Goods made originally in Manchester: 1596 *No stranger or forrener shall … sell any lynnen cloth, seckecloth, Manchester wayres, knitt stockings,* Beverley (YRS84/57); 1663 *2 peces lon. inkell & 4 manchester, 1s 8d,* Selby (YRS47/85). An Act in 1552 *for the true making of woollen cloth* referred to *cottons called Manchester,* and to *Manchester rugs otherwise named Manchester frizes,* with regulations relating to their measurements (SAL5/359).

manchet The finest bread. According to Peter Brears pure wheat flour was sifted through a thin cloth and made into short rounded rolls: 1528 *Item, 6 doz. manchetts, 6s,* Chevet (Whit2/308); 1629 *30 cast of manchett of 2 pecks of flowre,* Thornhill (BN2/14); 1683 *For a Manshit 9d, a Browne Loafe 6d & a white Loafe 2d,* York (GWK59). See also sop.

mandril Meanings suggested in the OED include: a miner's pick, part of the lathe on which objects were turned, a cylindrical rod or axis round which metal was forged, cast, moulded, or shaped. However, the evidence dates only from 1516 and earlier Yorkshire examples from the wills of founders point clearly to a connection with the lathe: 1493 *To William Richardson the lathe that he tornys in, and all my hukes and my mawndrellis,* York (SS53/88). The reference in the OED which is given in support of the meaning 'miner's pick' is also from a founder's inventory: 1516 *Item xlvj manderelles ijs viijd. A grindstone & cruks xd,* York (SS79/80).

mange A cutaneous disease which occurs in animals with hairy or woolly coats. An account book which belonged to the Ramsden family of Almondbury contains the following:

> *c.*1575 *For curinge the Maungye: Take a groatesworth of brimston beaten, a pinte of trayne oyle, a handful of dogges grasse chopped small, some swynes greace or a penyworthe of butter and boyle them all together, let the dogge eat therof a good deale and then tye up his mouthe hard and his legges also and rubbe him hard therwith with a woollen clothe as hotte as he maye endure it. And then V or VI dayes after boyle lant and browme together and washe him sore therwith* (DD/RA/f/4b).

mangle A machine for rolling and pressing sheets, or other items of clothing after they have been washed: 1727 *Notice is hereby given … that the Mercery Goods … and a Mangle are to be sold,* Leeds (Th22/219). It was customary in working-class communities for a widow, or a woman in difficult circumstances, to have a mangle and make a living by its use: Mangle House was a frequent place-name in the 1851 census returns. *Nanny Mangle* of Sheffield may have been such a person: she was accused in 1789 of stealing, and the report in the quarter sessions records made it clear that she was actually called Ann Parkin (QS1/128/7). See NH161–3.

manor house, manor place To describe a place as a manor was immediately to give it a certain status, and people might hesitate before doing that: 1560 *John Cotes doth depose that he knowithe one hall neare unto Ledes … but whether it be a mannor or not he knowyth not* (Th9/9). The manor house was a 'capital messuage', that is the large and important house where the lord of the manor lived and where much of the business of the manor was carried on. It was a term that took a long time to stabilise: 1443 *that Jonett my wife have my chefe maner place,* Sheriff Hutton (SS30/89); 1448 *Grant by John Gomersall to … his son … of his cheyf plase or Hedplase,* Gomersal (YRS83/99); 1532 *my* *maner plase or hedhouse*, Car Colston (SS106/26); 1533 *the maner place of Calton called Calton Hall* (YAS/DD203). The continuing use of such aliases through Elizabeth's reign is a reflection of how unsure people were about the 'correct usage': 1564 *lyenge on the east syde of the hall and chappell of the scyte of the manor, or manor-place, or manor house of Manstone* (YRS50/113); 1566 *all that their manor or haule place called Baihalle*, Huddersfield (DD/R/4/3); 1587 *one capital mesuage or mansyon place callid Castelhall*, Mirfield (YDK13). See also lake (4).

mantel-tree A beam across the opening of a fireplace which supported the masonry above: 1485 *Willelmo Jonkyn carianti … mantil trees a Cawood usque Ebor, 13s 4d [To William Jonkyn for transporting … mantel-trees from Cawood to York, 13s 4d]*, York (SS35/88); 1522–3 *Item for a manthyltree, xxd*, York (CCW89); 1760 *old wood, an old mantletree, loom wood*, Thongsgreave (IH). The stone header which became usual later was called a *Mantle Stone* in a South Crosland document in 1836: it measured 5 feet 3 inches (GRD).

mantle A kind of cloth, and garments or articles such as blankets made of the cloth (OED): 1346 *Willielmo de Driffeld mantellum meum [To William de Driffeld my mantle]*, Easingwold (SS4/23); 1392 '103 dozen of *mantal clothes* 100s; 6 *mantell* 20s', Hull (YRS64/10,22); 1435 *j mantellum de albo fryssed [1 mantle of white friezed]*, Castleford (Th22/249); 1465 *7 mantell; 18 virgis panni linei; 13 virgis de Kendall [7 mantles; 18 yards of linen cloth; 13 yards of kendal]*, Hull (YRS144/81). It occurs in by-names, probably with reference to a garment: 1324 *John Blakmantel*, Brighouse (YRS109/54).

mantua A gown, cloak or other item of clothing, some times a type of cloth: 1726 *threw her mantua skirt over the child's feet*, Huddersfield (QS1/65/4); 1729 *they had in their Sacks … a Childs Coat, a Mans Coat a Woman's mantua*, Stainland (QS1/68/4); 1739 *a mantua maker*, Southowram (QS1/78/2). In one much earlier reference the meaning is not transparent: 1508 *De ijd pro j piece del bankcover. De xd pro j mantua. De xijd pro j magna laterna [For 2d for 1 piece of cloth for the benchcover. For 10d for 1 mantua. For 12d for 1 large lantern]*, York (SS53/283).

manure (1) A verb meaning to work on by hand, used in connection with wood or stone, a form of 'manoeuvre' [hand labour]: 1513 'the right to take, fell, sell or give at their pleasure from the woods growing on the farmhold and to freely *maner*, carry away … without interruption', Brimham (YRS140/186–7); 1521 'large timber which will be delivered as necessary … any further being felled, carried and *manered* at John's cost', Malham (YRS140/35). To manure land was to have the use of it, and then to work it through cultivation and enrichment: *c*.1580 *grownde whiche … is becomen very unfrewtfull and barrayne for corne and cannot be maynered witheout helppe of pasturing*, Carlton in Craven (Whit2/172); 1598 *did allwaies keipe the close in their owne occupacion and manneringe by ther owne cattell*, Kirkby Malham (YRS114/158). In turn this seems to have helped 'manure' in the sense of compost to develop its present meaning. See also husband, moldbrest, sith, teind.

manure (2) Dung or compost, spread on the land to improve the soil. Examples are quite late and the noun seems likely to have derived from the verb which had a wide range of meanings: 1555 *all mucke and maner that is at the house*, Knottingley (Th27/54); 1588 *Item in mayner xs*, Dalton (DD/WBW/19); 1599 *certayne meanor with a lytle stacke of strawe*, Rawmarsh (TWH16/162); 1675 *We present Raiph White for shovelling up great heaps of Manner Anenst his dower & Leting of it ly severall Months being in the wains way*, Bridlington (BCP278). See also manure (1), muck.

maple The field maple. In a comment on place-names Oliver Rackham said 'maple is confined to its present southerly distribution' (OR1/209) and yet the tree occurs quite commonly in Yorkshire now and it evidently has a long history there: 1617 *took a hand byll from [John] Sampson … cuttinge a thicke saughe and a thick mapple in Spellow hill*, Brandsby (NYRO44/140); 1619–21 *James Silvester for taking an Alder and a maple in Newtondale* (NRR1/30). As for place-names there are the ancient settlements of Mappleton and Mapplewell and a number of minor localities: n.d. 'next to *Mapellessic*', Farnley (YRS120/74); 1208 *cultura de Mapelwelle [the tillage of Mapelwelle]*, Lead (SS94/149); 1329 'the place called *Mapel*', Hemsworth (YRS120/99); 1383 'wood *del Mapelhirstes*', West Bretton (YRS76/14). It was also responsible for by-names: 1379 *Ricardus de Mapelbeck*; *Johannes de Mapples*, Rotherham (PTWR). The wood was used for some table items: 1618 *Rounde maple trenshers 3 dozen cost me 6s 6d*, Brandsby (NYRO44/152). It is now principally a hedgerow tree.

mar To spoil or impair: *c.*1560 *spare at the first, not at the laste for feare of marryng all*, Woodsome (KayeCP); 1571 'We pain Richard Migleye for laying litter or dung in the water course … *marring* the water that goeth to Edward Thomas house', Halifax (HAS37/73).

marble A cloth of variegated colours, resembling some kinds of marble: 1521 *pro xiij virg. panni lanei coloris marble empt. pro vestura choristarum [for 13 yards of marble coloured linen cloth bought for the choristers' vestments]*, Ripon (SS81/274); 1555 *Item vij yards of marble, xjs viijd*, Kendal (SS26/86). The adjective was used for clothes made of such material: 1527 *to my brother John a marble Jacket*, Menston (Th9/249); 1544 *to Elizabeth Gyll my marbell kyrtell*, Timble (SS104/42); 1557 *To Harry Fentyman my sonne my marble coott*, Swillington (Th27/131).

mare This is one of several words used by Yorkshire coal-miners for an obstruction in the vein of coal that was being worked, or for a 'fault', either of which could cause serious delays. Alternative terms were dike, gall and horse, all dealt with separately. A 'mare' could be a major disruption: in Shibden near Halifax, in 1660, colliers *met with a mare or gall … which hindered them from getting the coal* (HAS30/136): in 1702 a pit at Thornton was said to be *not Irrecoverably Lost by reason of Horses or Mares Lyeing and being therein* (DBB1/2/30). A later lease links 'mare' with other words which evidently had much the same meaning: 1775 *for want of driving through any galls, mares, ridges or lips*, Northowram (HAS31/83). See also dike (2), gall (1), horse (1).

marigold A name given to cows, probably a reference to colour: 1584 *one redd garded cowe called Marrigold*, Scriven (SS104/145); 1601 *one cowe called Young Marygold … one kowe called Ole Marygold*, Hampsthwaite (SS104/240). See also garded, golding.

marish A variant of marsh, used as a noun or adjective: 1619–21 *Richard Lacie of the Marish of Folketon* (NRR1/15); 1708 *pasture, meadow or marrish ground*, Skerne (MD74–5/388). Marishes is a place-name in the North Riding, near Pickering, and much of that area was marsh until it was drained in historic times: 1611 *fermer of the marrish called Keckmarris* (NRQS1/???); 1619 *the highway lying in le Marishe within the Constablery of Pickering* (NRQS2/198). Many of these marshes were recorded in 1086 (PNNR84).

mark (1) The practice of marking trees, as a sign that they were to be felled or not felled, was traced back to the fourteenth century by Stephen Moorhouse (WYAS683). In the woods of west Yorkshire they were marked with an axe and the process was supervised: an owner would have his own mark and felling might only take place where the marks were in evidence: 1316 'Adam Sprigonel with a certain false mark (*signum*) newly made on the pattern (*forma*) of the mark of the lord the Earl has marked 4 oaks in Thurstanhagh', Wakefield (YRS78/95); 1377 *set nichil succidit in quodam loco illius bosci ubi nichil est signatum [but he felled nothing in any place in that wood where nothing was marked]*, Calverley (Th6/191); 1395 'except certain trees which had been marked by Richard … in the presence of John's workmen', Creskeld (YRS63/71); 1503 *fellyd and not marked with the kings axe*, Roundhay (Th2/233).

mark (2) Individual cutlers used marks to identify their wares, and the practice had its origins in the Middle Ages. In York in the 1400s, each bladesmith had to *coupe et use son propre merkes sur ses cotels [cut and use their own marks on their knives]* (SS120/136). In 1552, a scythesmith named John Parker made provision in his will for his son to have his trademark (MW49). In Sheffield the earliest surviving examples of marks being granted by the manorial court are those of William Elles, cutler, and John White, shearsmith, in 1554. The manorial court roll of 1564–5 has hand-drawn images of the marks and a list of those who *came to the Court and took of the Lord these Marks for their knives* (HCC91). See also strike a mark.

market keeper This rare occupational term occurred in York: 1435 *John Bell, market-keper* (YRS6/14). Markets such as the city's Thursday Market had their own customs and tolls and the keeper was probably responsible for overseeing such matters.

marketstead In Yorkshire, this was formerly the usual word for market-place. In 1324, William de la Lee sued Thomas de Totehill 'for assaulting him in the town of Wakefield, in a certain place called *le Markethstede*' (YRS109/52) and references in other towns include: 1386 *un burgagio [burgage plot] in Ripon in le Marketstede* (SS74/134); 1421–2 *the Marketstyde*, Knaresborough (OWR3/1/32) and 1507 *my howse in the Markett stede*, Pickering (SS53/260). From the early 1500s it overlapped with 'market-place': property in Knaresborough that was held by the Henlake family was described in 1611 as *lying in the market stede*, whereas in 1637 it was *in the market place* (YRS55/225). When Huddersfield was granted market rights in 1671 it had a market-place not a marketstead (HPN93). However, the word survived in the vernacular into the eighteenth century at least: 1724 *a house … in the markett stead*, Skipton (QS1/63/6).

marking money See byword.

mark rent The marks used by cutlers had to be paid for. In 1662, a Cutlers Company by-law required *every person having an assigned mark to pay yearly 2d, at Pentecost* (HCC11). In 1736, an Attercliffe scissorsmith was fined 1s *for refusing to pay his mark rent* (HCC19). See also mark (2), strike a mark.

marl In regions where the soil was acid, our ancestors spread 'marl' or calcareous clay on new clearances: *c*.1323 'sufficient marl for marling the land from the marlpit formerly belonging to William son of Roold', Burton Constable (YRS83/62). In 1510, William Amyas of Horbury granted land in Hartshead to the *Dean & Chanons of Seint Stephyn's* in Westminster which he claimed to have *mended by reason of marling, to the valew of xiijs iiijd* (SS79/18): in 1582, John Kaye of Woodsome wrote: *I set xxx loades of m[ar]le in the Spring Inge banke*. He also *marlyd and stubbyd Ryshworth Yng and the Mylner Hill … and made yt plowghable and sett in ytt of marle and Lyme xxxiij loods* (KayeCP). The proportion there was usually ten loads of marl to one of lime, but marling may not have been carried out on a regular basis, unlike liming.

John Kaye also recorded setting many *loods of Pomfrett marle … in the Ladie Roods and thre Litle Clossis adioyning*. Pontefract is twenty miles from Woodsome and it draws attention to those places where marl could be extracted. In 1341, Roundhay Park had its *Merlepytte* (Th2/227) and in 1495 John Bradford possessed 3½ acres *in the feldes of Pomfrett nere the marl pyttes* (SS53/108). The practice was evidently much older: 1236 *Marleflatte*, Fyling (SS72/520); 1296 *Marleriding*, Acaster Malbis (YRS50/2). In 1570, there was *a field called marlepit felde* in Barwick in Elmet (Th17/98) and other minor place-names include: 1572 *Merled field*, Hipperholme (YRS39/54); 1621 *Marlepighell*, Whitley (DD/WBD/9/34). Typically, 'marled' soon became 'marl[e]' and the field name Marl Close is often the only reminder of a vanished practice.

marler This occurs as an occupational by-name in Rimington where marl was being excavated from an early date: 1331 'meadows, roads, paths, moors, marlpits and marshes', Rimington (YRS56/209); 1379 *Johannes Merler*, Rimington (PTWR). An implement described as *on marling wembell* in a Mowbrick inventory of 1556 suggests that borings were made to determine where marl might be obtained (SS26/93).

marrow A fellow worker or partner. The first example of its use is in a translated Latin text: 1365 'John de Roch ... says that on a certain day and year he made a pact with the said Richard [de Eltoft] that they should be partners for ploughing ... with equal animals going in the plough, which partnership is called *marows*', Thorner (Th15/168); 1530–1 *Item to Christopher Falle and ys merro ... for makyn the pentyse, xviijd*, York (CCW141). The word was also used in connection with teams of lead-miners: 1563 *I do awe nootheyng ... for I dedd pay trowelye for it when I dede take delyverans off ytt as ye headdeys man and is marrowys yt whrotthe ye grove dedd say ytt was*, Grinton (YRS152/123). It was used in an unpublished will of a pair of animals: 1662 *to my daughter one quy which was marrow to the bull*, Idle (BIA) and, in estate correspondence, to draw a comparison between two deer: 1731 *one spaved doe the marrow to this*, Woodsome (D(W)1778).

marshal A farrier or smith, especially a shoeing-smith who also tended the horses: 1379 *Roger Marsshall, faber* (PTWR); 1396–7 *In sal. Rob. Marischall fac. vj barres ferri de ferro suo*, Ripon (SS81/120); 1409 *the hale crafte of the marshals in the cite and the subbarbes of Yorke* (SS125/176); 1488 *it is registred in the Maire bukes that the marshalls, smythes and bladesmythes hath been all way a hole crafte*, York (YRS103/36).

mart, marten One of the species of martens, but used loosely in more recent times for any animal of the genus *Mustela*, including ferrets and stoats (OED): 1731 *I called at Burnley* [Burn Lee] *... to look at a wild dog which ... they took for a Martin and hunted it often before they could take it*, New Mill (YRS117/12). The fur of martens was prized in the Middle Ages and huge amounts were imported: 1424 *unam togam nigram furruratam cum marterenz [a black robe lined with martens]*, Bawtry (SS4/408); 1446 *et meam optimam togam furruratam cum martes [and my best robe lined with marts]*, Roche (SS30/121); 1453 *1 tymbre marterns*; 1463 *3 martskynnes*; 1471 *10 martfelles*, Hull (YRS144/4,61,145); 1508 *j toga scarleta penulata cum lez martrons [1 scarlet robe trimmed with martens]*, York (SS53/285). See also crop (2), foumart.

maser See mazer.

mash-fat, mask-fat A large tub or vat in which malt was mashed, that is mixed with boiling water to form wort: 1341 *unum cunam* [sic] *quæ vocatur maskefat [a vat which is called a mask-fat]*, York (SS4/2); 1395 *j vasc(ulo) pro maskilvat vijd [a small can for the mash-fat 7d]*, Whitby (SS72/606); 1485 *Item j massh fatte, ijs ijd; j wort trogh de lapide [of stone], xxd*, Clotherholme (SS64/371); 1559 *to Thomas Baytson one maskefat, one gylefate, a lead*, Pontefract (Th27/292); 1612 *1 little tubb under the maskefatt*, Brandsby (NYRO44/37). See also mash-rudder, say (1).

mashonger An unusual form of maslin (1). The source in which this occurs confirms the meaning and indicates how varied the spellings could be: 1758–62 *There is a sort of coarse flower att Wakefeild to be bought that is called measlin (or mashonger) wich makes good loaf bread and is healthful bread. Mashonger is wheat and rye ground together* (YRS155/30).

mash-rudder The instrument used to stir the malt in the mash-fat: 1508 *De xijd pro j lez toobe pro brasio, lez maskroder, et scromes,* York (SS53/289). The word 'masker' is found in some inventories, a regional form of masher: it may have been used in brewing but that is not always evident in the contexts in which it occurs: 1620 *2 maskers, 2 little tubs,* Bingley (LRS1/56); 1636 *Item, one masker and a stoole xvd,* Allerton near Bradford (LRS1/87). See also ring sieve for 'rother'.

mask A regional spelling of mesh: 1669 *for fishing with a net of which every maske was not two inches broad and one inch long,* Helmsley (NRQS6/134n). See also pole-net.

masker See mash-rudder.

mask-fat See mash-fat.

masleion An alternative spelling of maslin (1): 1698 *a sheaf of masleion ... covered with gleanes,* West Riding (QS1/37/7).

maslin (1) Mixed grain, especially rye mixed with wheat. It could refer to the mixed flour or the crop in the fields: 1612 *2 bushells of maslen whereof 5 peckes was rye and 3 peckes wheat blended,* Brandsby (NYRO44/60); 1637 *one bushel of Maslin,* Knaresborough (YRS134/82); 1798 *Shearing wheat and maslin in Lodge Field,* Sessay Park (WM75). In the first reference quoted it was contrasted with *cleane wheat.* It developed a number of different spellings, some of them erratic: see mashonger, masleion, massledine, masslejen, mastlyonis, mislin (1), misslegen, musselgeom.

maslin (2), meslin A type of brass, or a vessel made of this metal: 1434 *unum brassepott, majorem patellam de meslyn [a brass pot, the bigger meslin pan],* Campsall (SS30/39); 1481 'one basin *de Masselyn*', Thornhill (Clay21); 1506 *a basyne and oon ewere of myslyne,* York (SS53/244); 1511 *j pelvim, j lavacrum le maslyn' [1 dish, 1 maslin washing-basin],* Beckwithshaw (SS104/2); 1555 *ij messilling bassens,* Kendal (SS26/86); 1560 *one masleyne panne,* Almondbury (YRS63/3). See also messing, mislin (2), mistiltyn.

mason A craftsman who dresses and lays stone: 1322 *Testamentum magistri Simonis le masoun ... Volo eciam quod Willelmus de Dalby vendat lapides marmoreos pro tumbis [Testament of master Simon the mason ... I wish that William de Dalby should sell the marble tomb stones]* (SS4/2); 1399–1400 *in s[alario] Joh. Mason facientis et emendantis diversos parietes quæ vocantur Grundwalles et j grece de pariete ... 9s 8d [in John Mason's pay for building and repairing various walls called ground walls and 1 stairway for the wall],* Ripon (SS81/132). In 1461, Thomas Niksone of Wilberfoss made provision in his will towards *unum campanile de masoncrafte [a stone-built bell tower]* for his parish church (SS30/239).

massledine An alternative spelling of maslin (1): 1642 *lands wheare wee intende to sowe either Rye or Massledine,* Elmswell (DW19).

masslejen An alternative spelling of maslin (1): 1710 *bought a stroak of masslejen* (QS1/49/9).

master In the trade guilds of the Middle Ages the 'master' was a workman qualified in his craft and entitled to teach apprentices: 1445 *lerned his craft better to occupie as maister,* York (SS186/160). In 1479–80, the York cutlers' ordinances were approved *by thassent* and consent of all the maisters of the craftes of Cutlers and Bladesmythez (SS120/134): similarly in Beverley it was stated in 1567 that *no person ... shall sett upp and occupie the said science of a Tanner of new as a maister ... until such tyme as he be made Burges and Brother of the said occupacion of Tanners*, Beverley (BTD122). See also little mester, maister, mystery.

master cutler Before the Act of 1624 which authorised the incorporation of the Cutlers' Company, the Hallamshire cutlers were governed by the manorial court of the lord of Sheffield, where their affairs were overseen by a twelve-man jury. Standards were monitored by 'searchers' and that office was retained after 1624, although the Act also established the additional offices of assistant and warden. In a major innovation, the office of Master of the company was created, at the head of the new governing body. The title was one that had a long history in the medieval guilds and its choice is likely to have been influenced by the traditions of the London cutlers or possibly by those of York. See also master.

master mariner A mariner skilled in navigation who had control of the ship and its crew: 1582 *Peter Backehowse, Hull, marriner, and servant to James Marshall, mr and marriner* (YRS19/7); 1592 *Richard Walker, Hull, master and mariner* (YRS22/131); 1594 *Allan Pattison, Hull, maister and marryner* (YRS24/78); 1665 *Myzaell Tomyson of Selby, maister marriner* (YRS47/172).

master mason William Hyll *Maister Mason* was employed in 1486 on Lady's Bridge, Sheffield (HS1/59). The inference is that he had the skills necessary for designing and building a stone bridge, possibly with other skilled masons working to his orders.

mastiff, mastiff-dog A large powerful animal, kept as a watch dog. It was subject to certain restrictions: 1573 *if any man do keep any mastiffs unmuzzled of the day or going abroad in the street of the night he shall forfeit iijs ivd*, Doncaster (YAJ35/300); 1648 *Mitchell continues as froward as ever, but I threatening to kill his mastive hee sent her home*, Thurlstone (SS65/89); 1672 *did give out threatning words against her children ... would pull them in peeces with his mastie-dog*, Lightcliffe (QS1). In *c.*1615 a pain was laid in the Knaresborough court that *Jane Woodward ... put away a mongrell mastie ... beinge an unruly dogg and her children dogginge of men's goodes* [cattle] *with him ... upon the King's common* (SS104/xii).

mastlyonis Probably a form of maslin (1): 1461 *28 qu' mastlyonis*, Hull (YRS144/41). This is one of three unusual spellings in the Hull accounts, listed under items imported.

match The several related meanings of this word date back to 1377 at least, referring to devices which were employed to light candles, lamps, and even cannon; usually a piece of slow-burning cord or other material: 1646 *they left a lighted match in the fould*, Ecclesfield (SS40/6).

math A rare and obsolete word for the amount of a crop mowed: 1544 *ij quarters barlie math, xiijs iiijd; eighte quarters haver math, xxxiijs iiijd*, Clint (SS104/46). It survives in the word 'aftermath'.

matter Often a purulent discharge, pus, but here used more vaguely of a bodily fluid such as mucus: 1676 *upp with his cudgel, knocked him downe and soe brewsed his heade that ... he bled matter and blood at his nose*, Rotherham (QS1).

mattock An agricultural tool something like a pick-axe, used for breaking up hard or stony ground. It is not a frequent word in Yorkshire sources but Salzman noted that in 1425 *gavelockes, mattokes and wegges* were supplied for work in a Scarborough quarry and *for taking downe of the Constable Toure* there (SZ1/332). It may also have been used by pickmen at the coal-face: 1616 *Peter Pigg of Cowsterdale, collier, for stealing three mattocks, value 8d, belonging to Chr. Danby, Esq.* (NRQS2/115).

maugh A near male connection by marriage, as a brother-in-law or son-in-law. The word occurs commonly in by-names, occasionally as a simplex: 1381 William *Magh*, East Riding (PTER), but more commonly as a suffix linked to a personal name: 1316 William *Julianemough*, Hipperholme (YRS78/142); 1377–8 *allocatur [it is allowed to] ... Willelmo Adymagh*, Bolton Priory (YRS154/569); 1397 *Thomas Raumogh*, Letwell (TWH16/45). One possible earlier example is: 1297 John *Maufe*, Hipperholme (YRS29/303).

maul See mall, mell (1).

maumet A spelling of Mahomet, a false god or an image of one; an idol. The term was associated by Protestants with Catholicism, specifically with images of saints brought into the church:

> 1596 *folowed theire vanitie althe night in sekynge there Mawmet commonly called the Floure of thwell would nedes bringe the same on a barrow into the churche in prayer time ... with suche a noyse of pyping ... that the minister was constreyned to leave of reading of prayer,* Aldborough (PTD169).

Similarly, two Hunsingore men were accused in 1597 of bringing *a Toie called the flower of the Well* into the church (YRS3/57–8).

maund A wicker or other woven basket with handles, a word on record from the Old English period: 1410 *et maundes pro lina [and maunds for linen]*, York (SS45/48); 1485 *1 mande de viminibus, jd [1 maund made of withes]*, Ripon (SS64/370); 1611 *one cheist ... a bucket & a mawnd*, Cottingley (LRS1/13). Occasionally we have information about the contents: 1490 *j lez ald maund for coylles*, York (SS53/57); *c.*1534 *4 new mawndys for hoppes*, Bridlington (YRS80/2); 1638 *one maund with a few coals*, Brayton (YRS47/72). They were also being imported: 1461 *5 duss' moundes*, Hull (YRS144/30). Note: 1596 *one Maunded skepp*, Knaresborough (YRS134/60).

maze A state of bewilderment or confusion: 1673 *some good ministers about Manchester haue given over their work, most being in a mase what to doe*, Northowram (OH3/154–5). Probably 'maze' in the sense of labyrinth although a contracted form of 'amazement' also seems possible. See also amazed.

mazer This was usually a bowl or goblet, made of 'mazer' wood and often ornamented with silver: 1257 *de ij macer*, Harpham (ERAS21/71); 1348 *et unum mazerium cum pede argenti [a mazer with a silver foot]*, Emley (SS4/50); 1394 *unum ciphum de Masar [a mazer goblet]*, Birstall (Th22/241); 1433 *et unum maser flat cum singula liga argenti deauratum [a flat mazer with a single silver gilt band]*, York (SS30/48); 1558 *to Gilbert Brokebanke a maser dight with siluer*, Elland (Crossley195). Examples of 'mazer' as a type of wood are less common: 1314 'as far as a tree called *le Mazertre* growing in the said garden', Kirkburton (YRS63/65). Items imported into Hull in the late fifteenth century included: 1490 *2 massar holtes* (YRS144/206), which were possibly pieces of mazer wood. Both meanings may occur in the following: 1595 *one cupp, bowle or maser of silver and maser gilded*, Bingley (LRS2/110). It has been suggested that mazer wood was maple.

meace See mess (1).

meal A dry measure, used especially of lime: 1357 *Item pro portagio de x mele de lim, xxd [Item for transport of 10 meals of lime, 20d]*, York (SS129/6); 1371 *Et in 144 mel' calcis cariandis, dando pro la mel' 2d, et 6d ad potum [And for carrying 144 meals of lime, giving per meal 2d, and for drink 6d]*, York (SS35/7); 1404 *Et in lxvij miell calcis emptis cum portagio, 4l 16s 9d [And for 67 meals of lime bought together with carriage £4 16s 9d]*, York (SS35/26).

mean As an adjective it described possessions that were held jointly or in common, as in the case of household items or animals: 1573 *one lyttinge panne ... meane between my sonne John and me*, Dalton (YRS19/156); 1579 *three sheep at Mattershall and half a meane sheep at Hindell*, Slaidburn (CS3/12); 1617 *the thirde parte of certeyne goodes meane between the said Jennet and Thomas Lockewood*, Thurstonland (HM/C/182); 1692 *the mettall from Barnby furnace beinge a meane stock*, Colne Bridge (SpSt). It was particularly common in reference to land held in common: 1483 *to and fro the Denfeld wich is all ther meyn field*, Ovenden (YRS83/152); 1608 *a meane dicke at flaymore syde*, Hanlith (DDMa); 1664 *one daye worke in the meane close called broomefeild*, Lepton (DD/WBD/4/212). It occurs in numerous minor place-names: 1633 *a parcel of land or meadow, one rood being upon the meangateloyn and adjoining to certain lands called Meangateendes*, Holmfirth (G-A). Surviving examples are Mean Bridge in Meltham, and Meanwood in Leeds, the latter recorded as early as the thirteenth century (Th8/62).

mease (1) Originally a box or basket but first noted in Yorkshire as a container for herrings, possibly a barrel of a specific size: 1313 *Pro iij lastis di. ij mayses allec(is) emptis xiijli xiiijs [For buying 3½ lasts 2 mease of herrings £13 13s]*, Bolton Priory (YRS154/339); 1535 *tres barrel' allec' albis xlvs, x mayses allic. rub. distribut' dictis pauperibus annuatim lxs [three barrels of salted herrings 45s, 10 mease fresh herrings distributed to the said poor annually 40s]*, Fountains Abbey (SS42/259).

mease (2) See mese.

measled Infected with 'measles', a disease in swine produced by the scolex of the tapeworm (OED); 1519 *Item Hew Yeuan de Ricall for selling messell porke xxd*, Selby (SS85/33). In 1659, the butchers in Beverley were threatened with heavy fines should they attempt to sell *swynes fleshe mezled or flesh dead of the murren* (YRS84/85). The Corporation was simply responding to the laws of the realm.

measlin See mashonger, maslin (1).

measondue A typical late spelling of maisondieu which is dealt with separately. It referred to a hospital or poor house: 1590 *agreed that Anne Talor, a poore old woman, shalbe placed in the measondewe upon Owsbrigge in the place which is now voyde by the deathe of Elizabeth Trewe*, York (YRS138/129). There were probably such institutions in all the major towns and cities from the fourteenth century. See also maisondieu.

meat Food, usually solid, provided for men or animals: 1518 *of his curtisye gave the said catall meate at his proper costs and charges*, Darfield (YRS51/16); 1642 *to bee att meate and wage ... to have 3d or iiijd a day and theire meate*, Elmswell (DW31); 1689 *the constable ordered her to make James some warme meate, and shee did so, and gave it him, and he did eate parte of it and the residue being the thinne of it was kept warme for him to drinke on*, Dewsbury (SS40/287). It was also used as a verb: 1642 *Haymakers have iiijd a day and are to meate themselves*, Elmswell (DW34). See also illion, town bull.

meatboard In this early usage 'meat' was food, and the meat-board was a dining table, that is boards supported on trestles: *c*.1413 *et en un metborde de longure dun wayescotte*, York (SS120/149); 1432 *Item to Alice Page j met bord with j pare trysts*, Scarborough

(SS30/22); 1485 *j mete-burde with ij par of trystylls*, York (SS45/300); 1533 *three meate burdys, and a dische burd*, Pannal (SS104/30); 1570 *One table one little meat bourd*, Hutton Conyers (SS26/229).

medley A cloth woven with wools of different colours or shades of colour: 1346 *lego … capellano meo meliorem robam meam de medle cum omnibus apparatis [I bequeath … to my chaplain my best medley garment with all its trappings]*, Guisborough (SS4/33); 1407 *Item j garnac' de vetch medle*, York (SS4/323); 1417 *unam togam de medely lined cum rubio bukeram [a medley robe lined with red buckram]*, Durham (SS116/18); 1420 *jupam meam longam de blewmedle cum foratura in eadem [my long blue medley frock with the lining in it]*, Patrington (SS116/29); 1531 *on medly gowne furryd with blake lame*, Kirby Underdale (HKU144). Some forms suggest a link between 'medley' and 'melled': 1420 *et meum optimum capicium de moreymedled [and my best murray medled hood]*, Patrington (SS116/30). See also melle.

meet Fitting, proper, sufficiently good: 1562 *dygging up the heythe and burning the same … without whiche the inclosed growend cold never have bene made fartyll [fertile] nor mete eyther to beare good corne or good gresse*, Rawdon (YRS114/99); 1669 *some allowance made … for the repayre … as in your wisdomes you shall thinke meete*, Marsden (QS1/8/3).

meet with To encounter by chance, to light upon: 1671 *she mett with one William Sykes, a neighboure, sleeping in a waine as she came from Mr Fretwells*, Micklebring (QS1).

melancholy Suffering from the disease now called melancholia: 1673 *took away* [the] *oxen forcibly in the open market under pretence of your petitioner being melancholy*, Golcar (QS1).

melder A word of Scandinavian origin for a quantity of meal ground at one time (OED). It has been noted in different parts of Yorkshire: 1611 *a melder at Airton milne* (DDMa); 1653–5 *Item given to An the daryemaid to make the melder with 1s*, Stockeld (YRS161/84); 1719–20 *that they make their Melders of oate Shilling at their said Mills*, Beeston (WYL160/129/9).

mell (1) A regional variant of mall. As a wood-working tool it was probably a heavy wooden or iron hammer, often used in conjunction with chisels and wedges: *c.*1570 *with mell and wedge*, Woodsome (KayeCP); 1611 *a great mell and certeine rules*, Barwick in Elmet (PR). See also latt axe, sinking.

mell (2) The last sheaf of corn cut by the harvesters, also called the widow: 1786 *8 Sept We got Mell … I made the workpeople a supper* (WM9). This traditional celebration in the farming year is dealt with in detail by Wright (EDD) and by Peter Brears (TFY169).

mell (3) A verb meaning to meddle or interfere, especially where legacies were concerned: 1521 *Agnes Hemsworth … haue … a whye stirke of iij yeres olde and to clame ne melle no farther*, Bardsey (Th9/169); 1533 *thye husbondes goodes I will nott mell with*, Wintringham (YAJ15/91); 1547 *vnto Richarde my sone … all my wayne gere and ploughe gere and he to mell no forther with none of my other goodes*, Morley (Th19/200); 1573 *my wyf … when she dothe marrye … to have my house at Wilberfosse … and not to mell any further with any parte of my fermhold*, Catton (YAJ10/89). Occasionally it meant to intervene on somebody's behalf: 1428 *the parties that melled for John Lyllyng*, York (SS85/8), and 'to associate with or deal with' in trade: 1433 *als merchantz … we mell wyth Pruys, Flanders and other place*, York (SS186/157).

mell (4) To intermingle or mix: 1484 *and not to mell nor chaunge oon stuff of yerne with an othere*, York (YRS98/95).

melle, melled A mixture of colours or shades of colour, commonly used of wool, yarn and pieces of cloth: 1341 *lego Marotæ servienti meæ unum warniamente de melle [I bequeath to Marota my servant a melle garment]*, York (SS4/4); 1394 '½ a *redemelle* cloth 2d', Hull (YRS64/67). From the same century 'melled' occurred more commonly: 1388 *pur j gowne de melledi ovesque une chaperon de bloy*, Calverley (Th6/204); 1394 'for ½ a cloth of *meld* 2d', Hull (YRS64/48); 1439–40 *that noon of the said craft make no capez nother of meld woll nor meld garn*, York (SS120/78); 1446 *et dimidia panni de rede melde, xxvjs viijd [and half a red melle cloth]*, York (SS192/33); 1473 *unam togam de melled russett [a melled russet robe]*, Hampsthwaite (YRS55/94); 1504 *Item v yerdes and a half of broyd blew meld iijs iiijd*, York (SS53/191); 1546 *my melled collored jacket*, Leeds (Th19/160). See also medley.

melly A fabric of mixed colours or shades, akin to melle, melled above: 1348 *unum mantellum de brounemelly [a brown melly coat]*, Emley (SS4/51); 1359 *unam tunicam fururatam cum capucio de melly [a lined tunic with a melly hood]*, Selby (SS4/71).

melocoton See malacatone.

melting house A building or part of a building where the process of melting took place. The term is found in the wills of founders and moneyers: 1431 *omnia instrumenta et necessaria shopæ meæ ad le meltynghouse [all the tools and equipment of my workshop at the melting house]*, York (SS30/16). A York 'potter' who was evidently a metal worker had: 1402 *j meltyngpan de optimis [1 best melting pot]*, York (SS4/250).

mend (1) An aphetic spelling of 'amend', with meanings such as recompense, improve, make amends for, set to rights: 1536 *to Sir John Watson xijd and what as my wife wyll mend hym with all*, Burton (SS26/13); 1541 *to John my sone my best fool. To Richarde my sone my secunde foyll and to Robert my sone the thirde fool and his moither to mende him because his foil is warste*, Monk Fryston (Th19/48); 1556 *bated his horse upon the brode balke whilste he mendid his wooll packes*, Welburn (YRS114/87); 1558 *I wyll that the pore folks of the churche rawe be mended with bygge ... that Jenet Atkynson be mendyd with some of my clothes*, Sedbergh (SS26/122). See also amend, mensk, midden.

mend (2) To make the fire up, adding fuel and controlling the draught: 1652 *had beene at her howse, and she mending the fire with the firepoite*, Huddersfield (SS40/51); 1689 *and mended the fyer and layde more coales on*, Dewsbury (SS40/288).

menged Mixed: 1428 *stuthes of xxxiij gyrdels of menged metaill ... tin and lede was menged togedyr*, York (SS85/1).

mensk Dignity, humanity, honour, credit. John Alayn of Ossett wrote his will in 1509 clearly expressing his hope that family members would behave decently to one another: *And father, if my wif be with an other childe ye must mende her sumwhate ... and for Gode's sake rule all wisely as I have done & ye shall have moch menske thereof* (SS79/3). It survived as 'mense' in the West Riding.

mercyant An abbreviation of amerciament. See also amercement.

mere (1) A word of Old English origin which means 'boundary' and is an element in numerous Yorkshire place-names, typically as a specific. A charter of 1202–3 for Langbar near Ilkley has references to places named *westmerethorn*, *merebec* and *merestan* (EYCh7/135): Bolton Priory's expenses in 1316–17 included 10s *pro fossura circa* *le Meredyk [for ditching around the Meredyk]* (YRS154/426). It remained in use as a vocabulary item: 1457 *inter devisas et metas (anglice mers) [between divisions and bound-aries (in English meres)]*, Newland CR (JG); *c.*1490 *the whyche syke was wonte … to be drawyn with a plough for a mere on that syde*, Sand Hutton (YAJ2/91); 1632 *the meares, stones and bounders between Horton and Wibsay* (HM/A/245). As a verb it is noted in the OED *a.*950, with other references from 1507, and numerous Yorkshire examples date from the latter period: 1501 *a parcell … of a medowe … lymitted, meyred and bounded*, Barkisland (YRS39/14); 1562 *marked, staked and meared furthe*, Southowram (YRS69/143). Surviving place-name examples are: Mearbeck, Mear Clough and Mear Gill (PNWR7/222). See also mere (2), merestone.

mere (2) In the West Riding 'mere' in the sense of boundary developed a related but quite distinct meaning, serving to identify a territory rather than a boundary. Saddleworth and Holmfirth offer the most comprehensive evidence: Saddleworth was divided into four territories called Friar Mere, Lord's Mere, Quick Mere and Shaw Mere but the only early reference noted is *Frear Meere* in 1468 (PNWR2/311). This may identify the 'mere' as the land in Saddleworth which belonged to Roche Abbey. In Holmfirth, another 'forest' territory, the subdivisions of the 'graveship' were also called 'meres', and in this case the examples are earlier, e.g. 1327 *Cartworthmere, Scholemere*; 1331 *Hepworthmere* (YRS109/181). Later these places would be described as 'hamlets' and later still as townships (HFPN30–1).

The element occurs also in Slaidburn where the earliest examples noted are *Knollesmere* in 1500 (PNWR6/207) and *Riston Meere* in 1551 (YRS2/158). At the Quarter Sessions in 1720 a causeway which passed over Bowland Knotts was said to belong to *three meers equally amongst them being all within one township*: they were named as *Rishton Grange Meer, Essington Meer* and *Hamerton Grange Meer* (QS1/59/1). Although Hammerton was actually a distinct place-name in the parish, recorded independently in 1086, it is possible that three of the territories identified connec-tions with the local families named Hamerton, Knowles and Rishton alias Rushton. Rushton Hill in Easington may commemorate Rishton Grange Mere.

Similar references are found over a relatively wide area: 1317 *Carltonmere* in Royston (YRS78/184); 1539 *Soureby mere*, Halifax (WCR9/158); 1586 *Remyngton Meare* (YRS22/17) and 1590 *Thurlestone Meare* (YRS7/131). This use of 'mere' has not been explained satisfactorily. For example, the circumstances in which Thurlstone mere is recorded make it clear that it was actually a discrete area within Thurlstone township: David Hey described it as a subdivision of the township, possibly the name given to 'the rough common pastures on the edge of the moors', but he was unable to define its limits or exact meaning (Hey11). Stephen Moorhouse commented on the Holmfirth names, saying that this use of 'mere' represented an extension of the word's meaning but he remained uncertain how to interpret it (WYAS266).

The earliest example in which this 'extended' meaning has been noted is in an undated thirteenth-century charter: this records a grant to Kirkstall Abbey by *Ernaldus filius Petri de Neuhale* [Newall in Bolling], of land which extended from an oak tree *juxta Sumerwell … ad diuisas de Birle et de Birlemere [by Summerwell … to the boundaries of Birle and of Birlemere]* (Th8/244). Domesday listed only *Birle* and it is possible that 'mere' in this case testifies to a subsequent parochial division of its territory. East Bierley and North Bierley are neighbours but the former became part of Birstall and the latter part of Bradford. The prefixes East and North have not been found before this reference to Birlemere and it means we cannot be certain which of the two Bierleys was the original settlement.

Similarly, Shelf was in the parish of Halifax but a part of it lay within the manor of Bradford and the term *Schelfemere* found in another early but undated document is probably an acknowledgement of that distinction (HM/D/135). In fact, the term was characteristic of Wakefield manor, for example: 1439 *Schypedene in Northowromemer* (YRS63/120). The distinction in this case was probably made because the lower part of Shibden was in Southowram.

mere (3) A linear measurement of land which contained lead ore: the length varied from one region to another but was generally about 30 yards (R&J57). It dates from the thirteenth century in Derbyshire (JHR104) but Yorkshire examples are much later: 1504 *To William my son a more mere at Coupperthwaite whith* [sic] *I bought of Thomas Metcalfe* (YAJ6/228); 1554 *unto John Taillor my servaunt in recompence of his service two meares of grounde … next adyoineng to William Collinge grove and his fellowes*, Langthwaite (YRS152/89); 1642 *the ferst finder of any new vaine to have 2 mairs of length set forth by the barmaister*, Grassington (R&J111).

merestone A stone marking a point on a boundary, either found in situ or moved there following an agreement: 1630 *William Wharton … by consent of both parties did fixe twoo greate stone for bounders*, York (YRS50/214). In 1517, two messuages with gardens in Threshfield were *closed with olde walles and mered with two grett mere stones* (YRS140/62). An enclosure in Hepworth was said to be *devided and meared forth* in 1659 (G-A). The 'mere stones' referred to in these early documents will have been common features of the landscape and their locations are shown on some early maps. Although they marked important boundaries they could be removed and the Slaithwaite court roll of 1551 records an indictment against Thomas Hoyle for displacing the *merestones* which marked the boundary with his neighbours (M/SL). Mere Stones survives as a Wadsworth place-name. See also mere (1).

merridew A name given to cows: 1530 *to my cosyng ij oxen … and ij kye named Meridew and Strange*, Felixkirk (YAJ22/204). The meaning poses a problem but it invites comparison with Merridew as a by-name and surname: 1379 *Johannes Meridewe* (PTWR). This has usually been linked with Welsh Meredith (R&W) but that seems an unlikely explanation for a Yorkshire surname in 1379 and it raises the possibility that merry-dew should be taken at face value. In fact, it could quite easily be a development like that of merry-weather which was formerly an idiomatic phrase for pleasure or delight (Halliwell). Similarly, Chaucer's contemporary Gower described the sun as 'merry' in 1390 so it is not impossible that the dew glistening on the grass at sun-up was also seen as a happy augury. The strong associations around 1300 between 'merry' and favourable aspects of the weather, the climate, and even atmospheric conditions seem to support that interpretation.

merryman A name given to an ox: 1546 *to Robert Nelson my sone one oxe called meryman and one white cowe*, Monk Fryston (Th19/142); 1570 *two oxen called Meriman and Burnitt*, Sproatley (YAJ36/440). It was probably a nickname, to be taken literally like the surname: 1379 *Adam Myryman* (PTWR).

mese, mese stead The Old French word *mes* derives from the Latin verb 'manere', that is to dwell or remain, and it was used for a dwelling place or the site of a dwelling: *c.*1321 '*un mees*, a croft and a rood of land', Adlingfleet (YRS111/4); 1491 *the tytill of a meyss, a coteghe and vj oxgang of land*, Glusburn (YRS69/70); 1557 *one mease in Wadesworthe wythe one house buylded upon yt*, Heptonstall (Crossley158); 1590 'a messuage called a *meestead* … lately built by John Walker', Dewsbury (YAJ21/454); 1609 *a mess or house at Bothes*, Hipperholme (WCR11/170). See also messuage.

meslin See maslin (2), messing.

mess (1) A serving of food, as here at a funeral feast: 1586 'a dinner to be made on the day of my burial for ten *meaces* of my neighbours at *2s a meace*', Leeds (Th1/136n).

mess (2) The quantity of milk given by a cow at one milking (OED): 1738 *she had milked about a mess of milk in a jugg*, Halifax (QS1/77/6).

messell See measled.

messing An uncommon word, possibly a form of maslin, a metal akin to brass. The few examples noted are from Yorkshire sources: 1371 *Et in xxj lb de messyng emptis de Ricardo Kyng, 3s 6d [And for 21lb of messing bought from Richard Kyng, 3s 6d]*, York (SS35/10); 1379 *In ij petr. ij lb de messyng emp. 4s 2d [For purchase of 2st 2lb of messing 4s 2d]*, Ripon (SS81/99); 1400 *unam pelvim cum uno lavacro de messyng [a basin with a brass bowl]*, Cottingham (SS4/268); 1433 *medietatem omnium vasorum meorum de pewter et messyng [half of all my pewter and brass vessels]*, Swine (SS30/24).

messuage, messuage stead, mesuage Originally, the 'messuage' was a piece of land occupied, or intended to be occupied, as a site for a dwelling-house. Over the centuries the word then acquired new layers of meaning which reflected the individual histories of such properties. Chaucer used it, and it is recorded as early as 1290 in an official document, after which it was employed regularly in title deeds. It may appear to be simply a synonym for dwelling house, but the messuage included outbuildings such as barns and cow-houses, and also any neighbouring lands that were traditionally associated with the dwelling. These were probably distinct from the 'appurtenances' of the messuage. In 1587, John Kaye's share of a divided property was described as *the dwellinge howse, beynge the est end of the messuage* (YDK78).

Occasionally, such a property is described in detail, and the breadth of the meaning then becomes clear. For example, there is a document of 1564 entitled *A territorie or bondarie of one mesuage callid Moysey Hill*, a dwelling in the hamlet of Rowley near Huddersfield, and the survey consists of no fewer than twenty-six short paragraphs, in which the names of the enclosures and land that were deemed to be part of the messuage are given. They include *Knolgreave Close … Brodeynge … Swynes Croft … Tomrode … Armyteige … Ellys Acre* and *Gaverholme*, and *airable land at the north ende of the lane goynge to the Cowmes* (YDK57–8). The place-name Moysey Hill has not survived, but many of the fields can be identified on later maps and they allow us to locate its former site with some accuracy.

'Messuage stead' marked the site of a messuage, and can be compared with mese stead above: 1517 *two messuagez steddes and a tofte*, Threshfield (YRS140/62); 1546 *Lyonell Rolston, ij messuage steids with one kilnehouse, ijs iiijd*, Pontefract (SS92/277): in the same survey is a reminder of the word's earliest meaning: 1546 *one mesuage stede not buylded upon*, Water Fryston (SS92/334).

met A noun with various meanings, all associated with 'measure'. It was often a unit of measurement, equivalent in some cases to one bushel, or to more than one depending on the commodity: 1410 *ij scotells, iiij buschels et j met*, York (SS45/49); 1642 *when wee sende a bushel of corne to the mill, wee putte it in a mette-poake; when we sende a mette to the mill, wee putte it into a 3 bushell-secke*, Elmswell (DW108). It occurs frequently in connection with farm or garden produce: 1522 *a mette of whete*, Ledsham (Th9/168); 1549 *a met of barlie*, South Milford (Th19/221); 1581 *9 meates of pease*, Anston (G-A). Coal that was shipped into east Yorkshire was often measured by the met: 1490 *de j lez mett of collys iiijd*, York (SS53/58); 1542 *three mettes coals*, Bridlington (YRS80/48);

1706 *a water met of coal*; that is coal brought by water, Beverley (YRS84/194). The met could also be a legally binding standard measure: 1573 *the mills, the hoppers and the troughs and all other things concerning the safe guard of mens corn and meal, with a lawful mette*, Doncaster (YAJ35/297). See also mete (1), meter.

metage A duty to be paid on goods measured by a 'meter': 1699 *Every vessel of coals which comes from Hull to Beverley either to be sold or delivered shall be measured by the common Metter of the town. Penalty 10s by every owner who shall refuse such mettage to be made* (YRS84/187). See also mete (1), meter.

metal A general term for coal, ironstone, ore: 1580 *that yf any person de get cooles or stones or any kind of mettell to undermine one hiewaye called the high Skowte ... to forfeite for every such offence xs*, Dewsbury (YAJ21/412).

metal-man A dealer in metal: 1534 *Johannes Norton, mettelman*, York (SS96/254); 1585 *John Ilye, York, metleman* (YRS22/68); 1592 *Robert Cawarde of Hull, mettalman* (YRS22/99); 1657 *Farninando Garnett, mettleman*, Snaith (Th11/92). A possible earlier term is 'metler': 1490 *Henry Mettiler de Stokton*, York (YHB669).

mete (1) To measure, as by a workman or official: 1465–6 'To a labourer for *metyng* of the said plaster', Hull (YAJ62/158); 1494 *wher he had bought twenty quarter of whete of an estraunger he wold not mete the said whete with the Kyngs standard*, York (YRS103/106).

mete (2) A boundary stone, frequent in the phrase 'metes and bounds': 1574–5 *one other parcel of the same medowe as it is nowe devided, lymyted and sett furth by metes*, Thurstonland (G-A); 1587 *one medowe under the howse as it is nowe sett out and devided by metes and boundes*, Thurstonland (YDK78); 1649 *the halfe parte as it is now devided by meetes*, Wooldale (G-A).

meter One who measures, an official with that responsibility: 1675 *Jonathan Browne is appointed the common metter of coals which come to be sold in the town*, Beverley (YRS84/160). See also metage, mete (1).

meterod A measuring rod: 1473 *et pakthred pro carpentariis ac metroddes*, York (SS35/82). The term can be compared with metewand and meteyard, both in the OED.

met-poke A narrow corn-bag. See also met, poke.

mich A spelling of 'much', the dialect pronunciation: 1497 *if it will please hym to do so mich for me as to be supervisor of this my last will*, Hull (SS53/128); 1524 *for asmich as he was tenant to this deponantes Master he was moved to se him so hurt*, Malton (YRS45/74–5); 1547 *how myche money was payd for the tythes yerly*, Bradley (YRS114/21). See also sich.

mickle Great, much: 1389 *ij bras pottys & mykyl pane & ij Couerledys*, York (SS4/129); 1438 *In als mykell as hit is holden medefull to ... knowelege the treuth*, Cavil (YRS120/43); *c.*1476 *in shewing of mikle unthriftiness*, Idle (PL39); *c.*1570 *who lityll doth geat and mekill doth spend*, Woodsome (KayeCP).

midden A dunghill. 1538 *une myddyn parted att the wall hed the qwyche decays the banks off owr well*, Halifax (WCR9/88); *c.*1570 *without the dore shulve thow all up that may the mydding mend*, Woodsome (KayeCP); 1615 *straw of my stable myddyng to bed calves*, Brandsby (NYRO44/92). It gave rise to minor place-names: 1570 *one croft called Myddynge Croft*, Honley (YDK81); 1777 *the Middinghole in Ladygate*, Beverley (YRS122/57). Note its pejorative use: 1511 *fals traytour and myddyng knight*, York (YRS106/36). See also muck-midden.

midden stead The place where a midden or dunghill is sited: 1572 *Richard Brooke for one midden stead ijd*, Doncaster (YAJ35/302); 1652 *one peice of land used for a Midding stead*, Leeds (Th9/67); 1790 *a barn ... the mistall thereunder and the middenstead*, Cartworth (G-A).

middest The most central point, the middle: 1538 *apon the sowthe sid of the middist alley within the ... chirch*, Halifax (Clay116); 1541 *a great stone erected and set up in the myddest of a peat mosse*, Wibsey (LRS2/6); 1560 *to my cosyn ... a gold ring rased in the medeste and up again on boith syds*, Romaldkirk (SS26/148); 1612 *and carry all away before the myddest of June next*, Brandsby (NYRO44/31).

middle brod A nail, a medium-sized brod: 1424–5 *It. pro j m^l. myddylbrod empt. 12d [Item for 1000 middles brods brought 12d]*, Ripon (SS81/151).

middle spiking A medium-sized spiking: 1371 *Et in iij.m midelspikynges emptis pro campanis ... 15s [And for 1000 middle spikings bought for the bells ... 15s]*, York (SS35/7); 1399–1400 *Et in j mille de midelspykyng, 2s 2d*, Ripon (SS81/133); 1429–30 '400 iron medilspykyngs, 1s 8d', Bedale (HH5); 1441–2 'And for 100 *Middelspykyng ... 3d*', Selby (SAR104); 1504 *Item ij^m of mydyll spykyng ijs iiijd*, York (SS53/191).

middling A popular word in Yorkshire where it is typically used now of the weather and health. It means 'average' or 'medium'; that is nothing to get excited about. The OED has examples from 1456, and references in Yorkshire date from the early sixteenth century: 1532 *a mydlyng bordclothe and ij herden*, Hawton (SS106/28); 1551 *John Swyndell doith owe me fyve punde of mydlyn wyar*, Garforth (Th19/301); 1599 *xv payre of lynen, mydlen and harden sheetes*, Rawmarsh (TWH16/161). Later quotes reflect a broadening of its usage: 1750 *7 acres ... as good a crop of oats ... as ever he knew ... the other four Acre but Midling*, Beeston (WYL160/129/4); 1786 *Aug. 21 At Thirsk. Middling day, showers*, Sessay (WM8). The 1750 reference seems to anticipate the use of 'nobbut middlin' an almost grudging indication that things are going reasonably well.

midward The middle of, the middle point: 1420 *and that at the middeward of that lyne be set a stake*, York (SS85/17).

midwife A woman who assists other women in childbirth, noted in an early by-name: 1392 *Item lego Aliciæ Mydwyf doyxtour iijs iiijd*, East Retford (SS4/177). See also grace-woman.

milan From Milan in Italy, in many cases a reference to steelware: 1399 *lego ... filio meo unam loricam de Milayne [I bequeath to my son a milan hauberk]*, Guisborough (SS4/254); 1430 *unam loricam de Milan apud Rypon* (SS30/13); 1508 *De xd pro j pelvi del melan. De xd pro j pelvi del peuder [For 10d for 1 milan basin. For 3d for 1 pewter basin]* (SS53/290); c.1535 *Item one myllen basyn, iij latyn basynes*, Stillingfleet (YRS45/129); 1557 *to my doughter Lawson on mellan basyn*, Castleford (Th27/104). Also used of textile fabrics: 1530 *a pair of myllen sleves*, Chevet (Whit2/305); 1617 *Herbert Davis byll 3 yerds of myllan 9s*, Brandsby (NYRO44/131). See also jeans.

milk and water Milk which is diluted with water has a bluish white colour, and this word was used for a fabric of that colour: 1558 *one mylke and watter jerkyne*, Church Fenton (Th27/301); 1562 *one clock [cloak] of colour called milk and water*, Kendal (SS26/152).

milking stead A place where cows were milked, in the fields rather than in one of the farm buildings: 1695 *the newly devided Fences between the milking stead in the Nooke* *and so all along to the Bamefald nooke*, Conistone (RW6); 1711 *to Potter Lane with the milking stead and … the Black Pasture*, Kirkby Malzeard (MD16).

millstone, milnestone One of a pair of circular stones used for grinding corn in a mill: 1538 *one mylne stone for the hors mylne*, Knaresborough (YAJ30/221); 1599 *Leade, Millstones or other wares or stuffe*, Bawtry (HPP79); 1610 *Item one paire of Milne stones*, Kirkstall (SpSt); 1612 *a mylneston rope*, Gristhorpe (YRS134/72; 1636 *one wayne, wayne wheeles, and a milne stone waggon, 5 0 0*, Cottingley (LRS1/106). See also milne.

milne The regional word for 'mill', an element in numerous compound terms: 1349–50 *le watermilne*, Netherthong (G-A); 1458–9 *pro imposicione de mylnaxiltre [for fitting the mill axletree]*, Fountains Abbey (SS130/86); 1502 *volo quod Oliverus Tonge habeat meum molendinum novum cum Clauso eidem molendino pertinenti vocato le Mylneclos [I wish Oliver Tonge to have my new mill with the close belonging to it called the Mylneclos]*, Liversedge (Th24/309); 1684 *Materialls belonging to the milne … two roapes for drawing up the milnestone, one milne arke, one multer arke, one barrel to put multer in, one trough to put dust in … one dustin sieve … 20 milne pickes, one milne chisel … in the horsmilne 2 arkes*, Whitley (DD/WBD/4/314). Used also as a verb: 1539 *Cristofer Talier my sone shall haue my leis of my walke mylne … [and] shall gyve to Thomas Talier my sone … euere yere vjˢ or ells xij stokefull of clothe mylnynge*, Dewsbury (Th19/4). See also walk milne.

milnebrigg The bridge that gave access to the manorial mill, via the milnegate: 1317 'up a path where the *Milnebrigg* used to lie', Wakefield (YRS78/185); 1360 *le mylnebrigg*, Cartworth (MD225/1/86); 1472 *the Melne brige his defectyffe & be longes to the Lord to reperall*, Selby (SS85/27). It gave rise to several place-names, including Mill Bridge with five examples and Milnsbridge (PNWR8). See also milnegate.

milnegate The way to the mill. There will have been such a way formerly within each manor: 1315 'half an acre on *the Milngate*, between the land of John Wyt and *the dolys* of Kerlinghow', Batley (YRS39/26); 1589 *Milngait*, Leeds (PNWR4/127). The right to use the way was written into leases: 1630 *shall permit John Kay … to have a sufficient way … as hath bene accustomed for leading and caryinge of any tymber, woodd or stones to the fullinge milne and also for carrying … of cloth to the said milne*, Crosland (YDK90). See also milnebrigg.

milner A corn miller, the usual Yorkshire spelling. As a by-name it was in widespread use from the late thirteenth century: 1297 '*William le Milnere* is elected Grave of Soureby' (YRS29/284). It remained part of the regional vocabulary: 1657 *William Barrett … for feloniously entering into Spen Mill and takeinge … goods and moneys out of the millnere chest there*, Birstall (Th11/85).

milnestone See millstone.

milnestone-maker The millstones were quarried and shaped high above the valleys, along the grit-stone edges, and roads were made so that they might be more easily transported (HPP100–5). The occupational term occurs only occasionally: 1593 *John Harrison, Rawden, par. Guysley, milnestone maker* (YRS22/57).

milnewright The OED has references to 'mill wright' from 1481–90, but this north-country equivalent has a longer history: 1386 *Will. de Colburn, milnewright*, York (SS96/85); 1554 *Joh. Flowere of Wheldrike … husbandman and mylnewright* (YRS114/62); 1585 *William Hynchcliff of Holme, milnewright* (WCR4/122); 1678 *Godfrey Hawkyard of Barkisland, milnewright* (QS4/13). The milnewright was both a carpenter and an engineer, responsible for all the intricate wooden parts that were required in mills and mill machinery: 1596 *Millnwrightes and those that Cogg or Spindle any Wynd Myllne or Horse Myllne*, Beverley (YRS84/67).

min To remember or bear in mind. In 1444, Agnes Shirburn of Mitton had in her will: *And to the vicar of Mitton a pare of get beds for to myn my saule and mynde me in his prayers and William of Bradley prest a nother pare of get beds* (SS30/106). See also minning.

mincing-knife A kitchen knife, used for chopping up meat: 1568 *Item two mynshinge knyves … twoe Choping knyves … one Dressing knyve 2 0*, Healaugh (YRS134/32).

mind To take note, pay attention to, remember: 1642 *putte* [the lambs] *under and make them seeke for it, otherwise they will looke for suckling and bee allwayes coming to your feete, minding yow more than the Ewe*, Elmswell (DW84); 1669 *not minding the two peeces put them up in his purse*, Gargrave (QS).

minery This is an uncommon word, similar in form to 'coalery' and 'stonery': 1561 *all manner of mynerye of lead and coal within the parish*, Grinton (NYRO31/33); 1609 *James Richards a skilfull man in Mynerie who … gave my Lord his Advise therein*, Carleton in Craven (YAJ64/159). However, in these two contexts the reference may not be to mining locations but rather to mining as a skill or activity. See also coal-mine, colliery.

miniver A kind of fur which was cheaper than ermine, and used as a lining or trimming, particularly in ceremonial dress (EMV220): 1346 *unum courteby furruratam de menvayre [a short coat trimmed with miniver]*, Guisborough (SS4/33); 1388 *et le chaperoun oue* [with] *menevere*, Calverley (Th6/204); 1457 *unam togam coloris blodii penulatam cum menever [a blue coloured robe lined with miniver]*, Howden (SS30/212).

minning To 'min' was to remind, and the 'minning' was a reminder, a peal of bells rung to commemorate a departed soul. In 1524, William Greve of Penistone made a request in his will that William Benson, a priest, *for the terme of his lif … shall every yere cause a mynnyng to be rongyn* (SS79/188). See also min.

mire pits These were pits in areas of marshy ground and the term is first noted in an undated thirteenth-century charter: *novem acras terræ … quam tenui de Willelmo Tosti … viz. totam terram quam habui ad Mirepittes et apud Norlangythemore [nine acres of land … that I held of William Tosti … that is, all the land that I had at Mirepittes and at Norlangythemore]*, Marton in Cleveland (SS89/23). The same word occurs much later: 1619–21 *And thence even suth till the mire pit in the slade … And sithne fra the mire pit even suth till the greene how*, Ruston (NRR1/24); 1657 *to make her fence sufficient att the upper end of John Beaumont Mierpittes*, South Crosland (DD/WBR/2/17–20). On a map of Southowram and Rastrick, dated 1625, the place-name *Blackmyrepitts* was written in a steaner or oxbow of the Calder (DD/SR/10/218) and since 'Carr Pit' in Dalton and Nook Pitts in Linthwaite occur in similar locations, one possible inference is that these were places where alluvium or black earth was being extracted, in order to enrich land elsewhere in those townships; the practice can be compared with that of warping in lowland parishes.

It seems to be implicit in a number of documents which make no mention of the place-name. In Methley, for instance, which also adjoins the river Calder, tenants had a customary right of way to the *town Mires*, and two men were fined in 1516 because they failed to clean a ditch between the *Myers* and *Stener*, which again places the mires in an oxbow (Th35/195). In 1578, the ditch was described as lying between *Stenderfurth* and the *Towne myres* (Th35/220).

In 1755, the Rev. Joseph Ismay of Mirfield wrote in his diary about agriculture in the parish, and included 'black earth' up to twelve feet in depth among the useful commodities found there. He was clearly aware of how deep the reserves were so there may have been pits where it was being extracted. In 1851, a Meltham carrier was paid for *8 loads of black earth from Meltham Moor* (DD/WB1/1/146). The common minor place-names Black Mires and Black Pits may therefore be additional evidence of upland 'warping': 1570–1 'in the same field in a place called *black pitts*', Kilnhurst (TWH16/128). See also town mires.

mirk The use of this as an adjective has been associated with Scotland more than with England, and in the sense of dark in colour it is said to be rare (OED). In fact, it was used quite frequently in Yorkshire. The churchwardens of St Michael, Spurriergate, recorded payments in 1544–5 for candles *to cast light of myrk mornynges*, York (CCW277n) and in 1619–21 a boundary between Easingwold and Huby followed *the same hedge unto mirke nooke* (NRR1/55). Several examples have been noted where it was used in conjunction with 'grey', to describe horses: 1445 'a mare of *myrkgray* colour, *trottant*', Bolton near Pocklington (YRS63/8); 1542 *my bay horse and my yowne merke gray stage*, Cleasby (SS26/34); 1558 *my yong dyrke* [sic] *gray gelding*, Topcliffe (SS26/105). It probably had the same meaning in the river called Murk Esk, an affluent of the Esk, a name which is on record since 1230 (PNNR4); 1619–21 *Et per aquam mirke eske usque ad Wheeledale Beck [And along the river Murk Esk as far as Wheeledale Beck]* (NRR1/23). Other place-names which contain 'mirk' as a specific element are Mirk Fell and Mirk Slack both listed by Smith (PNWR8) and there was *j ten. voc. Myrke Head [1 tenement called Myrke Head]* in Harwood-dale, in the Ministers' Accounts for 1540–7 (SS72/750).

mislin (1) An alternative spelling of maslin (1): 1721 *six stroakes of misling meal in a kimlin*, Fewston (QS1/61/1).

mislin (2) A type of brass, an alternative spelling of maslin (2): 1573 'a *myslyne basyn* worth 5s', Acomb (YRS131/48).

misslegen An alternative spelling of maslin (1): 1729 *a peck of misslegen*, Saxton (QS1/68/4).

mistall A shed for cattle, a cow-house, still a well-established word in Yorkshire: 1555 *from ... the yate dearne to the east syde of the mystall dore*, Thurstonland (G-A); 1624 *one other roome called a Mistall and the chamber lying above and over the same*, Honley (G-A); 1657 *all the overend of the fould to the south corner of the mistall doore*, Hepworth (FACcclxiii); 1709 *a cow boose in the mistall*, West Riding (QS1/49/6); 1731 *three Mistalls or Cow Houses*, Austerfield (QS1/70/7). Note: 1725 *the peathouse, barn, upper Milkstall, Western foldstead*, Meltham (G-A). See also shippen.

mistiltyn Probably a spelling of maslin (2): 1452 *j par precum de mistylltyn*, York (SS30/160); 1509 *a fore basyn of mystiltyne*, York (SS79/4).

mithridate A composition of various ingredients in the form of an electuary, regarded as an antidote against poison and diseases: 1617 *a mithridate box*, Ripley (YAJ34/183); 1663 *8^{oz} methredate, 3s 6d*, Selby (YRS47/85); 1693 *London treacle, 3s; Veanas treacle 1s 6d; diascordium, 1s; middredate, 1s 6d*, Selby (YRS47/22).

mixture A type of cloth, usually made with two or more colours of wool, scribbled or mixed together before being spun: 1758 *Mr George Charnock byes a deal of mixt broods about 2s 2d or 2s per yard in bauk wich are chiefly frised and the are made of a deal of floks and coarse wooll and are dark blak mixtures otherwise called shepards att Wakefild* (YRS155/21); 1816 *March 19th Sold Luke Townend one Mixture £9 0 0*, South Crosland (GRD).

mizzling Raining in very fine drops, drizzling: 1642 *if the morning bee wette and mislinge … stay att hoame*, Elmswell (DW47); 1787 *Sept. 6 Came a mizzling rainy night; much afraid of rain*, Sessay (WM24).

mo An archaic form of 'more': 1485 *Thise beyng witnesse … Sir John Vicars, John Wederhyrde … and other moo*, Clotherholme (SS64/278); 1541–2 *what noumbre of persons did entre into the same howse … and who they wer mo that did entre with them*, Hedon (YRS69/91); 1550 *he had as he belevith … xiiij younge gese and x yonge duklings and noo moo*, Thixendale (YAJ36/446); 1617 *4 coache horses one other and 3 moe*, Brandsby (NYRO44/142).

mob (1) A mob-cap, worn by women indoors in the eighteenth and early nineteenth centuries: 1755 *j laced mobb*, Yeadon (QS1/94/4). Wright has the plural in west Yorkshire for the blinkers worn by horses (EDD): 1716 *two pair of mobbs in his stable*, Shitlington (QS1/55).

mockado A material used for clothing, hangings, etc., said to have first been made in Flanders: 1543 *to my brother Thomas Redman one night gowne of mockeado with one paire of house of the same*, Thornton in Lonsdale (SS26/51); 1568 *Item Curtans of Mockadowe for one bed*, Healaugh Park (YRS134/26); 1579 *vj yeardes of mockado for a gowne to Margrett Meddelton, ixs*, Stockeld (YRS161/6).

moise One reference only: 1506 *to crop and moise every suche cloth and it to be as good and fyn in the mydds as at the ends*, York (YRS106/21). This may be the dialect word 'moise' which means to improve, although evidence for its use in Yorkshire is otherwise lacking. Alternatively perhaps it was for 'moite'; that is 'burl' or pick out the foreign matter. See also mote.

moit See mote.

mold See mule.

moldbrest I have found no explanation of this word in the OED or in specialist glossaries but it occurs in one or two fourteenth-century court rolls for the manor of Wakefield: 1327 'land lying unoccupied at Horbury called *Molebrist*' (YRS109/125); 1338 '*6d.* for leave to take an acre lying *molbrist* on the lord', Hipperholme (WCR12/14); 1340 'eight acres in Holne … lies *moldbrest* for lack of tenants', Holme (WCR12/212). These occur in translated passages but in each case the clerk used the regional term in the Latin text. The word 'brest' could mean 'damaged' so perhaps this was a reference to 'mould', that is good land, which was deemed to be 'spoilt' because it lay uncultivated. In the notes of the Yorkshire antiquary Roger Dodsworth is a passage from the same court rolls which relates to land in Ossett. The extract is dated 1346 but will have been translated by him in the first half of the seventeenth century:

> The jurors say … that the custome is here that although any land lye fresh and unmanured whilest distresse can be found in herbage or meadow belonging to the same that the sayd land shall not be accompted for Moldebrest yet they say that there was there neither Herbage nor meadow where a distresse for the Lord's farme might be made. And so the sayd Land lay moldbrest three yeares (YAJ8/9).

See also mould (1).

molding-board See mould-board, moulding-board.

monday pot No documentary reference to this term has been noted but Trigg commented on its use in the Halifax coalfield: 'The Monday-pots amounted to 3d a man and seem to be paid pretty regularly to celebrate … *Collier Monday* when they threw up the cap to ascertain if they were to start work. It usually came down' (HAS30/147). See also pot.

mone To remember, to bear in mind, to admonish: 1438 *the menes of untreuth on to whilk men oft tymes are monet and stired thurgh couetis and other vices*, Cavil (YRS120/43). In 1640, the deputy bailiff of the wapentake of Gilling East was presented at the quarter sessions *for moyninge and warneinge a man* … to make service as a freeholder, and taking moneys and other bribes, Richmond (NRQS4/184n).

monish See admonish.

moody The modern meaning, that is 'subject to moods of ill-humour', is on record only from the late sixteenth century, and cannot be the meaning of the common by-name 'moody'. In the period when such names were in regular use it was possibly flattering (bold, brave, high-spirited) or more pejorative (proud, haughty, arrogant). 'Moody' was also the first element in a number of nickname compounds: 1253 *Ralf Modi*, Aughton (YAJ12/102); 1260 *Geoffrey Modipas*, Hilderthorpe (YRS44/102); 1274 *Richard Modisaule*, Horbury (YRS29/87). 'Modipas' can be compared with 'proudfoot' which survived as a surname and with: 1295–6 *Roger Smalpas*, Bolton Priory (YRS154/62); 1409–10 *Henricum Jolypas*, London (SS115/173). See also mothersoul.

moonlighting Carrying out illicit actions in the night-time, whether it be distilling liquor or taking a second job (OED). The examples quoted in dictionaries are no earlier than the nineteenth century but the term may owe its meaning to the medieval guild practice of restricting work to the hours of daylight. In 1307, a grant was made to the girdlers in York on condition that *nane of tham by na manere of harneys falland to gyrdels that es wroght by the mone light … that na man of girdelercrafte … wyrke … bot by clere daylight* (SS120/180–1). See also mystery.

moor barn A barn on the moor, away from the farm: 1689 *in the moore Barne all the hey £1 in the Barne; at home 10 Load of oates*, Barnoldswick (YRS118/73).

moorburn Setting fire to sections of moorland has long been a practice in the north, burning off the ling early in the year in order to promote new growth which would be suitable for pasturage. It was an offence though between 11 April and 1 November: 1610 *17–18 April, The Inhabitants of Thimbleby and those of Osmotherley for the illegal burning of linge, otherwise called Moorburne* (NRQS1/184); 1620 *11 May a Whitaside man for burning Moor-burne on the moore there*, Swaledale (NRQS2/243).

moor-cock The male red or black grouse: 1463 *iiij more cokks xd, ij fesauntes iijs iiijd*, York (SS192/110). The moor-hen in this case was the female grouse, not the water-loving relative of the coot. See also moor game, poot.

moordike In *The Harvest of the Hills* (2000) Angus Winchester wrote of ways in which the upland landscape of the north reflects centuries of land management. He described the physical division between the cultivated lower areas and the unenclosed moorland, sometimes still to be seen as a bank and ditch running across the hillside. This had a variety of names, including 'acredyke' in some regions and 'head-dyke' in others. In fact, townships at different altitudes had unenclosed areas of waste called moors and another word for such a boundary, in different parts of Yorkshire, was 'moor dyke'. The term has been noted in Durham in 1579 (OED) but the Yorkshire evidence takes its history back to the thirteenth century, in an undated deed: n.d. 'extended in length from *Moredik* on the north to *Catdikes* towards the south', Kilnwick (YRS76/105). Similarly, in 1315–16, a selion in Church Fenton lay 'next *le Muredike*' (YRS69/51) and in 1399–1400, two strips of arable land in Swaledale were said to lie between *le Muredyke* and the river (YRS102/94). The bursars' books of Fountains Abbey record a payment of 6s 8d in 1457–8 *in factura sepium circa Mordyke apud Chapelhous [for making fences around Mordyke at Chapelhous]* (SS130/55) and at a very low altitude Everthorpe in the East Riding had *le Muredyke* in 1521 (YRS39/68). See also acredike.

moor game A collective term for grouse: 1637 *moore game in abundance both black and red, as moorcocks, moorehenns and young pootes upon the moores* (HSMS4). See also moor-cock, poot.

moor gate The term 'moor gate' can have three quite different meanings. It was quite commonly a 'gate' which could be opened and shut, controlling access between land under cultivation and the moor beyond, and in this sense the word occurs frequently in manorial records. In 1734, for example, the inhabitants of Lund in the East Riding were ordered at the local court to *make their moor fences good* and not *leave the moor gate open* (YRS69/99). Similar references are found throughout the 1600s, including *the more yeate* in Malham in 1604 (DDMa) and *the moore yate* in Ardsley in 1666: in this latter case payment was made for *a crooke and loope* which would fasten the gate (WDP16/5/1). The initial 'y' in such examples is further confirmation that 'gate' was the sense intended.

On the other hand it seems likely that in some very early documents 'gate' had its origin in the Scandinavian word *gata* meaning 'road', and the 'moor gate' was the way to the moor or 'waste' from the village. That was probably true of *Le Moregate* in Wadworth near Tickhill, mentioned in 1323 (YRS83/174), and of *le Moregate* in Owsthorpe noted in 1341 (YAJ17/107). In both cases land was said to abut on *le Moregate*. It certainly had that meaning in some compound minor place-names: *c*.1300 *prope venellum qui vocatur Mynstermorgate [near the alley which is called Mynstermorgate]*, Beverley (SS89/446).

However, in some 'moor gates' the gate was neither a road nor a gate but a right of pasturage: 1724 *70 acres of arable land … 30 mooregates or depasturing for 30 beasts to goe and depasture on the freehold moore*, Norton le Clay (MD87). See also gate (2).

moor grave A manorial office for which the first example is a by-name, possibly for one whose task it was to oversee grazing and rights of way on the town moor: 1345 *Robert Moregraue of Qweldrik*, Escrick (YRS111/66). Angus Winchester has a reference to *moregreaves* in 1393 who supervised pasture rights in Bowland (AW45). See also dike grave, multure grave.

moor grime On 26 August 1786 the Rev. John Murgatroyd wrote in his diary: *A fine day – some little moorgrime*, Slaithwaite (KC242/1). The most likely meaning is that there were clouds on the peaks and sides of the moors, an explanation given in the *Sheffield Independent* in 1864. It was only in west Yorkshire that Wright found the term (EDD).

mooter An occasional spelling of 'multure': 1783 *I made at the Mill in 30 Strikes of Oat 9 strokes of Shelling besides mooter*, Ovenden (CA112). See also moulter.

mop, mope The name of one of four horses owned by the provost of Beverley: 1419 *j griseus cecus vocatus Mope [1 blind grey horse called Mope]* (SS116/25). The meaning is far from clear: it may be 'fool', on record from the thirteenth century (OED) or a term of endearment, comparable with the later 'mopsy' and 'moppet'. However, since the horse was blind perhaps 'mope-eyed' which meant short-sighted is relevant.

mopsy As a term of endearment for a child 'mopsy' is on record from 1582 (OED), almost fifty years later than it occurs as a name for an animal: 1536 *to my suster …* *one cowe named Mopcye*, Felixkirk (YAJ22/205). A link with moppet seems likely here.

morel Of a horse, dark-coloured, and then a name: 1347 *et unum equum vocatum [and a horse called] Morrellum de Tyrweyn*, Reedness (SS4/39); 1358 *Willielmo de Melton … equum vocatum Morell de Welwik*, York (SS4/69); 1495 *Edwardo Hewetson equum vocatum Blak Morell*, York (SS53/114).

more sum This term was used in bargains where a sum of money was advanced ahead of the full total due. It was particularly common in the sixteenth century: 1553 *xs parsell of a morsomm aweng to the chorche*, Sheriff Hutton (YAJ36/187); 1562 *in parte of payment of a more some for the clere bargane and sale of certen lands*, Thurstonland (G-A); 1595 *in part payment of a more sum*, Bradley (YRS63/26).

morion A kind of helmet worn by soldiers in the sixteenth and seventeenth centuries: 1568 *a morrione covered with velvet 6s 8d … a Steylle Cappe covered with velvet 5s 0d*, Healaugh Park (YRS134/34).

morling Wool taken from the skin of a dead sheep: 1524 *where as our graunt … is but wolle and wolle fells that ther be haddyd thereunto in the seid newe charter sherlyng and morlyng skynnes*, York (YRS106/101). The wording of this request repeats that of an Act of 1448 (SAL3/289), except that there the word 'shorling' was used. This is defined in the OED as the skin of a recently shorn sheep, not a shearling.

morn It means 'morning' in some attributive uses, probably the early mass in the following examples: 1510 *his dewtie to the kirk that is to say ryngyng of the morne bell and the evyn bell*, Weighton (SS35/265); 1529 *and profittes as shall happen to com of the said cottage … to the use of the morn prest and of his successors morne prestes herafter*, Halifax (Clay79); 1568–9 *To Nicholas Richardson for a rope to the morne bell, 3s*, York (SS35/115).

mort The skin of a sheep or lamb that has died a natural death (OED): 1457–8 *In Alloc. pro le Mortis pell pro ij^{bus} annis*, Fountains Abbey (SS130/65). They were used by sadlers: 1532 *and for every dacre of mortes of two yere olde and above 10s … and for all mortes under the age of two yeres, one halffe dacre of whit ledder to th'owse* [use] *of the said monastery withowt eny odre payment*, Fountains Abbey (YRS140/242).

mortuary A customary gift to the minister of a parish from the estate of a deceased person, usually the testator's best animal: 1347 *et son melior best pour son mortuer [and his best beast for his mortuary]*, Healaugh Park (SS4/47); 1393 *Item lego pro mortuario meo meliorem* [sic] *animal meum Rectori de Thornor [Item I bequeath for my mortuary my best beast to the rector of Thorner]* (Th2/98); 1448 *Et optimum meum animal nomine mortuarii mei [And my best beast by way of my mortuary]*, Leeds (Th2/100). The English word is on record from this period: 1444 *for my beriall xls … for my mortuary my best gown ford*, Hull (SS30/105). See also corse-present.

mosker To decay, rot, crumble away, now used only by dialect speakers: 1642 *The first decay of wilfes is allwayes att the hearte, for they will rotte, mosker, and bee hollowe within soe that a man may stande within them when the sides are sounde and the tree alive*, Elmswell (DW128); 1711 *the old lead was very much maskard*, Sheffield (HS4).

moss (1) The plant or plants which we refer to collectively as 'moss' are found clustered together in damp places, often on walls or trees, and this 'material' was used over a long period for bedding in slates and stopping crevices in dams and walls, from the thirteenth century at least (SZ1/266). In Durham there is a record of women collecting '*mosse pro eodem [stagno] [moss for that pond]*' in 1324–5 (OED). Evidence in Yorkshire dates from the mid-fourteenth century: 1351 *pro vadiis unius femine colligentis mosse pro reparacione cooperture [for a woman's wages collecting moss for repairing the roof]*, Hartshead (YAJ21/381); 1453–5 *Et de 5d sol. pro quinque pond. de mosse empt. ad eundem opus [And for 5d paid for 5lb of moss bought for the same work]*, Ripon (SS81/161); 1511–12 *Sclaytston, 4d, ad idem opus, ac del mose, 1d*, Ripon (SS81/267); 1570–1 *with thack, mose and morter*, Brockholes (YDK75); 1652 *to maintaine and upholde the premises with thatch, mosse, glasse and morter*, Whitley (DD/WBD/4/202). The practice is recorded regularly into the nineteenth century and gave rise to a verb: 1809 *Paid for Mossing William Charnock's House*, Ovenden (CA239).

moss (2) A swamp or morass, a peat-bog. These were common landscape features, and 'moss' is a frequent element in northern place-names from the twelfth century. Typical compounds are Moss Carr, listed seven times by Smith (PNWR8) and first recorded in Methley: 1380 'Hugh de Caille did not scour his ditches … from *Mossekerr* to the *Coitgrene*', an offence which resulted in flooding (Th35/156). Of equal interest are Moss Hagg, Mossy Sikes, Mosley Mires and two 'Moss Crops', the last of these from a word applied to various species of cotton-grass. It was a popular generic also, and *Blakmosse* was recorded in 1205–11 (PNWR7/226). Typical moorland names in this category include Fleet Moss, Holme Moss and the more evocative Featherbed Moss which occurs in Bradfield, Grassington, Meltham and Saddleworth.

The mosses were a source of peat, and responsible for a number of distinctive vocabulary items, especially 'moss room', not listed in the OED. This was a division in a 'common' moss, and it gave a tenant the right to extract peat and turf: 1556 *Item towrves oppon the mosse xiijs iiijd*, Kirkham, Lancashire (SS26/92). In 1684, William Pennington's property in Whittington included *one Mosse room* (EG42) and the term is implicit in a Rathmell lease of 1664. This granted land to Henry Walmsley on Rathmell Moor *reserving to Henry Clarke a parcel of Mosse being in the East end thereof as the same is marked and meared and staked forth for diging, getting, graveing and drying of peates, turves and fuell in the said Mosse* (MD217/300). An alternative was 'turf room': 1722 *The turbary or Turfe-Mosse in Hamerton Dalehead, One Turfe-room in Small Gill Moss, One Turfe room in the White Moss*, Wigglesworth (GRD). In a dispute about peat-getting rights in Lingards, in 1627, one witness complained that trespassers *with their Cart wheles upon the soft Mosse* had *so worne the soyle* that a boundary stream had altered its course (DT/211). See also middest, turf-pit.

mossing An obscure term, used twice in the ordinances of the York curriers *c.*1425, on both occasions linked with 'dressing': *Item for mossyng and for drissyng it clen up als it awe to be, for j dakyr of hose leddyr viijd* (SS120/65). The editor was told by a currier that the word was still in occasional use in the early 1900s and referred to the practice of 'treating the leather with a decoction of Irish and Iceland moss' in order to glaze it. It had given way to sizing the leather with glue (SS120/260).

mote As a verb this was to find fault with: 1495 *it is ordand that no man of the company sall mote another man*, York (SS129/90). Later, in the textile trade, to pick motes out of wool, was to remove minute particles of dirt or other 'offensive' matter: 1789 *my neighbour … moited and sorted into four parcels of goode and bad wool one packe his uncle sent*

him, Slaithwaite (KC242/1); 1819 *½ a pack of wool moating,* South Crosland (GRD).
See also lant for an earlier textile reference.

mothersoul In the will of John Robinson, *parson of the church of Fawkham in Kent,*
made in 1516, we read: *I will that a prest shall synge for my fader soule, my moder soule
and for all Cristen soules … within the churche of Elvington in Yorkshire* (SS116/275).
The omission of the genitive 's' is possibly an indication of his Yorkshire origins, and
his words are a link with two early northern by-names: n.d. *land once held by Ralph
Fadersaule,* Howdenshire (YRS120/41); 1313 *Ralph Modersoule* (R&W). See also
moody.

motley A type of cloth of variegated colours or shades: 1388 *Pur j gowne de bloy
mottelay,* Calverley (Th6/204); 1394 'Thomas of Gare 5 *blewe moteley* cloths and 2 *grene
moteley* and 1 *russet moteley',* York (YRS64/58): John de Thornton was a York clothier
who featured regularly in these accounts, possibly the John Thornton *motlemaker* who
was made a freeman in 1407 (SS96/111). It remained a popular fabric: 1455 *ac totum
apparatum sive ornamentum altaris de motley [and all the decking or adornment of an altar
made from motley],* York (SS30/202); 1517 *a lome to wyrk motley in,* York (YRS106/62);
1527 *to Thomas my son my motteley jackett,* Sherburn in Elmet (Th9/251); 1545 *my best
shert my motley jacket,* Marrick (YRS152/60).

mough See mow (2).

mould (1) This common place-name element meant 'earth', and from the thirteenth
century it occurred as a specific in a range of minor place-names: n.d. *following
Moldecloyh as far as Wetecroftyerd,* Hipperholme (YRS83/124); 1317 'a curtilage called
Moldyerd', Thornes (YRS78/195). A.H. Smith has 'molde' linked with 'croft, hill, royd
and thwayt' (PNWR7/225) and I have found it with *crymbyll* in 1528 (C274/1). It has
been noted several times with *lēac-tūn* (herb-garden) as the generic, e.g. 1308 *three acres
in moildelaghton,* Sowerby (YRS36/177) and this may explain an unusual Almondbury
name: 1583 *mudlaghtonsteede* (DD/R/2/13). In everyday vocabulary it was used in the
plural and meant 'lumps of earth': 1642 *When they are to make a newe barne floore they
grave it all over and then rake it … till the mowles bee indifferent small,* Elmswell (DW112).
See also mould-hill, mouldwarp, swartmold.

mould (2) A place of burial; a grave: 1371 *Et in vj serzis emptis pro le mold 18d [And
for 6 serges bought for the 'mold' 18d],* York (SS4/185).

mould-board The board or plate in a plough which turns over the earth to make
the furrow: 1395 *It. pro ix molebrodclowtys,* Whitby (SS72/618); *c.*1535 *twelue plowght
hedes … vj molberdes,* Stillingfleet (YRS45/129); 1581 *for mouldbord clout and the shares,*
Stockeld (YRS161/33); 1656 *In the Stable Chamber: Item two ploughes … and five mold
boards,* Eshton (YRS134/113); 1681 *20 mold bords, 3 harow sweards, 6 pare of plough
stilts,* Burn (YRS47/142). In cases where confusion with moulding-board might be
possible the context is important: 1612 *speakes, 2 mowlbreads 3 axle trees,* Eccleshill
(YRS134/69); 1638 *a malding bord, 2 saddels & 3 pannels,* Gateford (YRS47/66).

mould-hill The earth cast up by a mole. It was common practice to break up and
spread the earth: 1446–58 *et pro Moldhyls iijd,* Fountains Abbey. This makes sense of
the earlier entry: *et petit pro prostracione monticulorum xxd [and he asked 20d for leveling of
the mould-hills]* (SS130/209,232). It later became mole-hill by association: 1785 *Had
G. Town & C. Crowther Spreading Mole hills & dung,* Ovenden (CA161).

moulding-board A board on which dough can be kneaded and shaped. Several of
the examples noted were in brew-houses, perhaps because of the yeast used: 1450 *item*

in brasina unum plumbum unum caldarium, unum moldyng bord [item in the brew-house a leaden vessel, a cauldron, a moulding-board], York (SS30/144); 1452–3 *ij bultyng-clothes iiijd et j moledyngburde xvjd*, Beverley (SS45/137); 1485 *j plumbum magnum … j massh fatte … ij tobbes … j moldyngborde cum tristilles [with trestles], vjd*, Ripon (SS64/371); 1508 *De viijs pro iiij plumbis pro lez wort. De xvjd pro j moldingbord*, York (SS53/292).

mould-rake, mould-staff Husbandry implements used to break up clods of earth: 1574 *axes, moldraiks, pitcheforkes, sythes*, Wensley (SS26/254); 1687 *a moldstaffe … 2 drags, 3 moldrakes*, Kettlewell (GRYD159). See also mould (1).

mouldwarp The mole or 'earth thrower': 1478 'land called *Molewerphill*', Ackton (YRS61/118); 1617 *The mouldwarpe catcher I payd after jd each mowle (now before they breede)*, Brandsby (NYRO44/134); 1638 *that the said water be not also lost … by mold warpe holes or choked by sedges*, Barwick in Elmet (Th17/11). The *moldwarp stafe* noted in Wawne in the East Riding in 1584 (OED) may have been an implement to break up 'mould-hills' rather than a stick used by the mole-catcher (OED). It is also recorded in the sense of moleskin: 1570 *one mold warppe hatt*, Hutton Conyers (SS26/229). Note the ironic minor place-name: 1771 *Mouldwarp Hall*, Huddersfield (HPN96). See also mould-rake.

moulter, mouter, mowter Common alternative spellings of 'multure': 1527 *shall have ther corne grownd mouter free when the mylne of Edyngham goith*, Yedingham (YRS80/92); 1614 *for the clark of the market my mowter dishe, iiijd*, Brandsby (NYRO44/77); 1642 *very near sixe peckes of meale if the corne bee dry, or els the fault is in the Miller that taketh more mowter then is his due*, Elmswell (DW108). See also mooter, mulcture, multure.

mouse-coloured, mouse-dun Having a colour like that of the common mouse, dark grey, regularly used to describe horses: 1558 *a mowse donne gelding* (SS116/246); 1631 *a mouse coloured maire*, Adwalton (BAS7/61); 1652 *my mouse coloured gelding*, Nether Shitlington (YRS9/53). See also dunn.

mouter See moulter.

mouthed Used of hunting dogs, having a mouth of a certain kind: 1691 *she bred of a beagle and a mouthed hound*, Woodsome (C86). The OED has: 1741 'mouthed from the Beagle'.

mow (1) To grimace or pull faces: 1581 *with his face againste her, mockinge and mowinge at her and deriding of hir so that she cold not in quiet manner serve God*, Hutton Cranswick (YAJ37/177).

mow (2) A stack or pile of hay, corn or other farm produce, in a barn rather than outside: 1539 *I wull that she have the value of a mowghe of haye that my sone John dyd occupie*, Hampsthwaite (SS104/58); 1567 *In the stubbing close one stake of hay, xs. In the hudd howse one mew of hay xiijs iiijd*, Well (SS26/211); 1648 *In the barne: Item a barley mough £15 0 0. Item a wheat mough & a Ryemough £15 0 0*, Sharlston (YRS134/99); 1671 *founde the sack upon a corne mough in the barne*, Haworth (QS1/11/1).

As a verb it meant to pile up, make into a mow: 1648 *Hee opened the waynehouse dore which I had mowed with turfes to keepe the wind from my horse*, Thurlstone (SS65/89); 1783 *housed corn and mooed it*, Ovenden (CA142).

mowburnt Hay or corn spoilt by overheating in the mow: 1615 *Oats Mewburned sould at Malton*, Brandsby (NYRO44/91); 1629 'Penalty for … selling oatmeal … made of *mowburnt oats*', Beverley (YRS84/83); 1642 *It is noe pointe of good husbandry to lye such barley aside for seede as is … moweburnt*, Elmswell (DW57).

mowstead The site of a mow of corn or hay: 1578 *a jettie and a mowsteade in my overbarne*, Newton in Bowland (CS3/7); 1629 *a piece of a mewstead of wheate and maslin unthresht*, Elmswell (OED).

mowter See moulter.

moyle See mule.

muck Usually the dung of farm animals, mixed with straw and other bedding matter. It was a valuable asset, employed by farmers to fertilise the land: 1483 *to haue a lafull gait … with ther muke & ther corne to and fro*, Ovenden (YRS83/152); 1532–3 *the seyd Nycholas … to leyf the seyd howses as he finds them … & to leff hys muk at the ende of hys terme*, Bradfield (TWH20/35); 1555 *to … my sonnes all mucke and maner* [manure] *that is at the house*, Knottingley (Th27/54). It may have been refuse or offal in other circumstances, as in York: 1538 *Item rassavyd … for the moyke at the Fyshe Lendyng, if viij^d*, St Michael, Spurriergate (CCW193). This is likely to have been fish offal which would also serve as a fertiliser.

The verb meant to remove muck from stables, now more usually 'to muck out': 1642 *when they come backe they fall to mucking of the stables*, Elmswell (DW107). It had numerous attributive uses, especially in the names of the tools used to handle it and the vehicles which transported it into the fields. These are dealt with individually below.

muck-coup, muck-sled, muck-tumbrell, muck-wain The coup was the cart most commonly used to move dung: 1654 *15 dayes fillinge the muck coupe at 6d a day*, Stockeld (YRS161/97) but other vehicles are noted: 1592 *an old bound waine a mucke tumbrell*, South Cave (Kaner176); 1748 *one muck sled, one muck shool* [shovel], Sowerby (QS1/87/6); 1534 *Item a corne wayne and ij mokwanes*, Long Liversedge (Th24/311); 1636 *one old muckwayne*, Allerton near Bradford (LRS1/86). See also sled, tumbrel, wain (2).

muck-drag Wright offers two meanings (EDD), but the one which best fits the examples noted here is that it was a kind of fork, one with the tines set at an angle which made it easier to drag muck out of the midden: 1535 *three mukforkes ijs … foure pitche forkes xvjd … iij mukdragges xijd*, Stillingfleet (YRS45/130); 1578 *One mucke dragg, two iron forkes*, Ripley (SS104/135); 1581 *2 pyckforkes, 3 muckforkes and one muckdrack* [sic], Anston (G-A); 1610 *Item two Muck Forkes, one Muckdragge*, Kirkstall (SpSt); 1748 *one muck drag*, Sowerby (QS1/87/6). A rare York by-name may have been occupational, for the labourer whose job it was to move muck with such an implement: 1340 *Alanus de Wifestow, mukdragher* (SS96/35). See also drag.

mucker An occupational term and by-name found in the records of Bolton Priory; probably a servant who was responsible for attending to the muck or manure produced on site: 1298–9 *Petro le Moker* (YRS154/93); 1304–5 *xvj bovariorum, unius moker, tribus apud grang(iis), iiij apud Angrum* [of 16 ox hands, one mucker, for three at the granges and 4 at Angrum] (YRS154/189).

muck-fork A fork for handling muck, loading it or moving it from the midden: 1485 *iij mukeforkes et j mukhake, iijd*, Ripon (SS64/373); 1599 *two hackes three pitche forkes two spades a turfe spade … a mucke fork*, Rawmarsh (TWH16/160); 1671 *3 muck forks 6 pitch forks*, Thorpe Willoughby (YRS47/62). See also muck-drag, muck-hack.

muck-hack A hack for use in the stables and farmyard: 1554 *et de j mukehakk ij mukforks et j secure precii viijd* [1 axe costing 8d], Fulford (YAJ36/453); 1559 *one* *muckhacke, ij shede forks, ij shed spaids* [sic for shod?], Hipswell (SS26/134). See also hack (2), muck-fork.

muck-hott See hot.

muck-midden A dung-hill or heap of manure: 1689 *knockt him in the head and buried him in the muck-midding*, Batley (SS40/291); 1782 *I was … laying the muck miding … till 10 O clock*, Ovenden (CA106); 1786 *dressing stones by muck midding*, Slaithwaite (KC242/1). See also midden.

muck-rake A strong implement for raking muck; 1403 *Item j mukrake de ferro ijd [Item 1 muckrake made of iron 2d]*, Weighton (SS45/25). See also muck-drag, muck-fork, muck-hack.

muck-sled See muck-coup.

muck-tumbrell, muck-wain See muck-coup.

muck-wall A wall built of clay: 1539 *five acres of land … lying by the moke wall sydd*, Clint (SS104/32).

mudfish Any fish that would be found in the mud, perhaps a word for certain flat fish. They were being imported from the Low Countries: 1471–2 *14 last' allecis albi … 6 C modffysshe [14 lasts of salted herrings … 600 mudfish]*, Hull (YRS144/163). It occurs earlier as a by-name: 1409 *Et Johanni Mudfysch pro … tegularum [for … tiles]*, Beverley (ERAS4/31). The OED notes the word in Essex and Newcastle in the sixteenth century.

muffler A sort of kerchief or scarf, worn by women to cover part of the face: 1566 *j bongrace and a muflar of blacke velvet*, Hipswell (SS26/183); 1566 *iij kirchiffs, iij rayles and certen mufflers iijs iiijd*, Richmond (SS26/193).

mugg A breed of sheep with a wool-covered face. See also tup.

mulcture This spelling of 'multure' arose through confusion with the verb 'to mulct' that is to exact a fine: 1674 *in mulcts imposed on Mr Diggle and Dr Lloyd for their absences*, Ripon (YRS118/139). It occurs also in the Calder Valley place-name Mulcture Hall. See also multure.

mule A kind of shoe or slipper: 1576 *an old freese jerkyn, a paire of moldes of white rugge*, Ripon (SS64/378); 1579 *a browne jackette … a paire of moyles, and a felte hatte*, Thongsbridge (YRS39/178n).

mullion A vertical bar which divides the lights in a window: 1538 'the chapel wants … a mullion of stone', Knaresborough (YAJ30/224); 1663 *Hen: Lawson pro stones for the mullions, 8s*, Ripon (YRS118/111). The earlier history of this word is complicated but it is considered to have developed by metathesis from 'muniall' which had the same meaning: 1379–80 *Et in diversis monyeles lapid. esand et figand. cum plumbo in le Westgavell [And for setting and fixing various stone munialls with lead in the Westgavell]*, Ripon (SS81/102).

mullock Rubbish or refuse: the word remains in use in the West Riding with the sense of 'mess'. It may have given rise to a by-name: 1379 *De Agnete Mullok seruant*, Skelton in Howdenshire (YAJ9/157).

multure, multure ark, multure dish In the early history of the manor, tenants were obliged to have their corn ground at the lord's mill, and multure was a toll in kind, paid to the miller. The rate varied from one lordship to another: in 1368 for example, it was paid in Habton near Malton 'at the twentieth vessel' (YRS69/83). In New Malton the procedure was complicated:

> c.1450 *when j qwharter wheytt is sald for iiijs than schall your corne be multyrd at the xvj vessel, and qwhen j qwharter qwheytt is sold for iiijs vjd and mor to it come to vjs than the corn schall be multeryd at the xx vessel, and qwhen j qwharter qwheytt is sold for vjs then … at the xxiiij vessel* (SS85/61).

Other Yorkshire references include: 1525 *takeyng bot after the rate of xviij stroke oon stroke for thair multer*, Linthwaite (YDK106); 1546 *Item to Thomas my brother a bushel of multer corne*, Otley (Th19/141). It was occasionally used as a verb: 1590–2 *they shall … grinde all their Corne … at the said Mill called Brighouse Mill, and be multured after the Thirtieth vessel* (YRS69/18). The miller kept this corn in the mill, at least temporarily, in a wooden ark or barrel: 1684 *one barrel to put multer in*, Whitley (DD/WBD/4/314); 1714 *a moulter ark*, Whitley (GRD); 1739 *two mulcture arks*, East Riddlesden (MD194). The multure dish was a vessel in which the toll-corn was collected: 1572–3 *Item Mr Fulwood for a molter dish in his mill not sealed vjd*, Doncaster (YAJ35/302). It served as a measure locally and was frequently mentioned in by-laws. The miller at Boroughbridge Great Mill 'showed his *Moulter Dish* to the homage' in 1639 and they confirmed that 'he had used no other dish' (YAJ35/214). In 1650, the farmers of Tong mills were ordered to *show theire moulter dishes to be examined whether they be agreeable to the custome of this mannour* (Tong/8a/11). See also mooter, moulter, mulcture, multure grave, multure-ward.

multure grave The title given to an officer whose task it was to see that customary practices regarding the taking of multure were observed. The term has been noted in County Durham (OED) and north Yorkshire, in the first place as a by-name: 1301 *De Galfrido le Mult'grayve*, Sowerby by Thirsk (YRS21/86). It was a manorial office: 1572 *Radulphus Loftus et Willielmus Scrodder* [sic for Strodder?] *electi sunt in offic' le multergraves de hoc anno et jurati [Ralph Loftus and William Scrodder were chosen for the office of multure graves this year and sworn]*, West Witton (YAJ10/420). See also dike grave, moor grave, multure-ward.

multure-ward This alternative to 'multure-greave' occurs as a by-name in an undated deed for Eavestone, a village south west of Ripon, probably c.1300: *Richard le Multurward* (YRS39/65).

mumming To go mumming was to dress up in fanciful attire and move from house to house at Christmas, acting in a short play with St George as the hero: 1755 *Wife gave children mumming 2d*, Huddersfield (MS757).

muniall See mullion.

murage The toll or tax formerly levied for the building or maintenance of the walls of a town. It is recorded first in the statute of 1275, and features then in municipal accounts: 1439 *to suffer … free men and others to be quit of toll, stallage, chiminage, pontage, pavage, picage, murage and passage throughout the realm*, York (SS186/167). When Peter Symson of Leeds, a draper, enrolled as a freeman in 1447 it was on condition that he pay tolls and murage [*in solucione theolonii et muragii*] (SS96/167). In 1510, *The Murage of the Citie of Yorke* was itemised in the civic records and the fifty-two entries covered *ylka ferdell of mercerye wayre and of all other thyngs … that comys unto this Citie fro any contree* (YRS106/32–3). See also murmaster.

murk See mirk.

murmaster This was an office connected with the collection of the tax known as murage and the upkeep of the city walls of York. In 1526–7 three corn chapmen were nominated

> to be more maisters for to occupy that office truly … that is to say, to se the kyngs walls of this Citie, otherwais called the Toune walls, to be kepte clene and honest without ramell, breese and scrubs growing in and of the same, and to reparell … as much of the said walls now fallen (YRS106/107).

In 1536, it was agreed that there should be *no mo … moor maisters elect nor chossyn*, York (YRS106/174) but the office continued to be referred to for some time. In Chester and some other English towns and cities the name given to this office was 'murager' or 'murenger' (OED) and this partly explains why the dictionary had 'mure-master' in York linked to 'moor' in the sense of moorland.

murrain A disease of cattle: 1301–2 *De cor[eo] unius vacce mortue de morin[is] xijd [For the hide of a cow dead of murrain 12d]*, Bolton Priory (YRS154/126); 1446–58 *In morina in Craven ij*, Fountains Abbey (SS130/134).

murrey Purple-red, the colour of the mulberry. It gave its name to a kind of cloth, and the distinction in meaning is not always apparent: 1358 *domino J de Broddesworth cotam de murre cum cloco [to Sir J de Broddesworth a murrey coat and a cloak]*, York (SS4/70); 1394 'Joan Hukster for 3 ells of *morrey*, ½d', Hull (YRS64/50); 1401 *et unum cloke de rubeo et murray [and a red and murrey cloak]*, York (SS4/280); 1451 *Item j lectus de murray cum tapeta ejusdem coloris [Item 1 murrey bed furnishing with a counterpane the same colour]*, York (SS30/151); 1489–90 *the Common Counsaill shal in murrey or violet meit the right noble … lord Therl of Surrey*, York (YRS103/55); 1528 *To Eliz. Bolt my murray kirtle*, Sherburn in Elmet (Th9/258); 1568 *a testure of Murray Clothe fringed with Murray Silke, and 3 Curtans of murray Clothe*, Healaugh (YRS134/26).

musrol The nose-band of a bridle: 1590 *Item 2 Musrall buts north and south*, Kirby Underdale (HKU64). These were small pieces of land [butts] where a horse might be tethered according to the editor.

musselgeom A variant of maslin (1): 1578 *Item musselgeom one bushell*, Stockeld (YRS134/54).

mustard ball A leaden ball used in making sauces which had bruised mustard seeds as the main item: 1640 *one mustard ball 10d*, Bingley (LRS1/118); 1700 *two leads and a mustard ball*, Holmfirth (IH).

mustard-maker A maker of mustard: the seeds had to be ground to a powder, at which time other substances might be added, including 'must' or new wine, water or vinegar to form a paste. It was used medicinally and as a condiment, and the by-name provides early evidence of the occupation: 1379 *Alan Mustardmaker*, Ripon (PTWR); 1473 *John Musterdmaker*, Skipton (YRS6/119). Occupational references are: 1440 *John Whitgift of York, mustardmaker* (YRS6/183); 1490 *Thomas Judson, York, mustermaker* (YRS6/95). John Whitgift may have taken up his freedom as a *mercer* but he was described as a *saucemaker* in 1441 (YRS6/183). Note: 1622 *musterd money 6d*, Brandsby (NYRO44/233). See also mustard quern.

mustard quern A hand-mill for grinding mustard seeds: 1575 *j pare of mustard whernes iijs*, South Cave (Kaner90); 1581 *j payre of musterd quearnes*, Anston (G-A); 1596 *One* *paire of Musterd wheres* [sic for whernes] *6s 0d*, Knaresborough (YRS134/60)); 1611 *musterd whearnes upon a blocke*, Stearsby (NYRO44/39). 'Whern' is a variant spelling of quern. Note: 1612 *a mustard stonn*, Gristhorpe (YRS134/71). See also malt quern, qu-, quern, whern.

musterdevillers A kind of cloth which is said to take its name from the town in Normandy now called Montivilliers: 1407–8 *et unam togam de Mustrevilers furratam cum bys [and a musterdevillers robe lined with bis]*, Selby (SS116/2); 1445 'with a cloak *musterddevelance* colour', Bolton near Pocklington (YRS63/8); 1481–2 *my maisters of the chaumbre in mosterdeviles*, York (YRS98/50); 1523 *my musterdevilys gowne furride with shankkes*, Hull (SS79/171).

mynshinge See mincing-knife.

mystery The York cutlers described their craft as a 'mystery', and an order in 1477 allowed *eny maister apprentez or servant to wirke in the said misterie by candel light* under certain conditions (SS120/133). In 1565, the ordinances of Sheffield's cutlers spoke of *the cutler occupacion* and *cuttelers craft* (HCC1) whereas that had changed in 1590 to *the mystery or crafte of a Cutler* and *the said science or crafte* (HCC2). This was 'mystery' as the word was used in the medieval trade guilds, derived from Latin *ministerium*, and meaning 'craft' or 'trade': the noun 'mister' was in use from the thirteenth century, comparable with French 'métier'. There was almost certainly some confusion with 'master' and 'mastery', and also with 'mystery' in the sense of secret ceremonies which had an identical spelling but different origin. That may be implicit in article 4 of the Sheffield Orders which employs the plural of the word, referring to *personnes usinge ... the said mysteryes or scyence* (HCC2). If the term 'little mesters' has a long enough history it may have been influenced by that confusion. See also master.

N

nadge Items to be sold at auction in Holmfirth, in 1814, included a *colerake, nadge and rasp* (G-A). Wright (EDD) has nadge as a west Yorkshire word for adze, via 'a nadze', and the development is first evident in the sixteenth century, in Tusser's *an ax and a nads*, listed in his husbandry tools. See also adge, thixel.

naffe See nave (1).

nag A small riding horse or pony: 1505 *the grey Nage that awmylles* [ambles], Leeds (Th4/16); 1535 *on amling blake nage*, Stillingfleet (YRS45/126); 1557 *to Margerye my wyffe a nagge and a meyr*, Sherburn in Elmet (Th27/162); 1630 *to my father in lawe Fyve poundes to buy him a paceinge Nagg or mare*, Linthwaite Hall (YRS35/85). A minor place-name provide's an early reference: 1395 'a toft in *Goldale* called *Naggetoft*', Snaith (YRS120/82). See also ambler.

nail A measure of length, possibly because nails originally marked off sections of a yard-stick. First noted in a translated Latin passage: 1418 'from the said outer corner … towards the *fyshelendyng* 5 ells and a *nayle large*', York (SS186/57). Subsequently it was used frequently as a measure of cloth: 1434 *Et pro uno quarterio et nale rus velvet pro gladio maioris [And for one quarter and a nail of red velvet for the mayoral sword]*, York (SS192/17); 1454 *In j nayle panni empto et dato pro exemplo vesture estivalis iiijd [For 1 nail of cloth bought and given for an example of summer clothing 3d]*, York (SS192/83); 1642 *Some linen cloath … there is againe which is yard broad or yard and nayle*, Elmswell (DW111).

nail chapman The man responsible for the marketing of the nailers' wares: 1720 *Thomas Wilkinson, nail chapman*, Sheffield (PR6/132). In David Hey's history of Sheffield's rural metalworkers is a section on the nail trade in which he refers to nail chapmen such as George Guest of Thorpe Hesley in 1698 and Samuel Booth of White Lane Head in 1737 (RMH31–41). These men lived in or on the borders of Ecclesfield parish which was at the heart of the local nail trade. See also chapman.

nailer Nail-making has a long history in the south Pennines and the nailer's product had symbolic importance: in an undated thirteenth-century deed, the Farnley Tyas smith took possession of land 'at an annual rent of an iron nail' (YRS39/171). The by-name or surname is on record from the thirteenth century: 1274 '*Richard le Neyler* gives 6d for license to dig sea-coals … for his smithy', Hipperholme (YRS29/96); 1416 *Thomas Nayler, revetour*, York (SS96/125). The occupational by-name and the product are linked in the accounts of Bolton Priory: 1377–8 *Pro cc double spikyngs et di. emptis de Thoma Nayler* (YRS154/563). Nail-making flourished in and around Thornhill from the 1300s into the seventeenth century: 1368 *John Milner, nayler*, Flockton (YRS102/65); 1503 *Richard Cuke of Emley, nayler* (YRS69/40); 1601 *Ricardus Ditche de Horbury, Nailor* (YRS3/203). In south Yorkshire a nail-making family called Tinker is on record from the fifteenth century: 1437–8 *Robert Tynker of Bradfeld, le nayler* (TWH20/23); 1540 *Robert Tynker … Over Bradfeld, nayler* (TWH20/42). See also nail seller.

nail mould A mould for nail-making: 1673 *a vice 5s; a waine naile mold, 1s; other instruments, 3s 4d*, Barley (YRS47/89).

nail seller A person who sells nails, although the word was used interchangeably with nailer in Beverley: 1577 *of the naylers for a contribution 3s 4d;* 1578 *the naylesellers for a contribucon 3s 4d* (YRS84/14,19). These men may have been smiths who had a shop, or a stall in the market.

nail tool Evidently a specialist tool used by smiths and nail-makers although its precise function remains uncertain. The word is first recorded in county Durham in 1338 (OED) and frequently in Yorkshire from the sixteenth century: 1543 *Item v. nalle towlys, vjd*, Ripley (SS26/43); 1584 *all my naile tooles and all my hammers, tonges, bellowes*, Knaresborough (SS104/145); 1592 *Item 2 neale toules a pair of tongues a cuttinge iron*, South Cave (Kaner184); 1597 *3 neile towles, 4 punches and a round neile towle*, South Cave (Kaner194); 1639 *one paire of great bellow in my shop, one stiddie, one great naile toole*, Knaresborough (SS110/160). See also crooked stithy, slack-trough.

naked bed Used when referring to a person unclothed and in bed: 1504 *Thomas Slewethman lay sore seke in his naked bede*, York (YRS106/2). In later examples the term was used in depositions at the Quarter Sessions when women were on trial suspected of prostitution: 1697 *did see William the souldier in naked bed with Mary Barton*, Dewsbury (GRLD10); 1701 *went into the parlor and found Mary in bed and John Smith ... in naked bedd with her*, Keighley (QS1/40/5). In the Dewsbury case, witnesses testified to the *Lewd and Carnall* behaviour of Mary Barton, and the inn where she worked was described as *a very Lewd Bawdie House* (GRLD9–10).

nale In *The Freres Tale* Chaucer wrote, *c*.1386, 'they were gladde for to fille his purs And make him grete festes atte nale', that is 'at an ale' or drinking festival. The term survived: 1533 *We present ... for a nale keppenge Wylliam fell*, Wakefield (YRS74/17). See also ale, nat, and KHPN40.

nallbladesmith For an awlbladesmith. It was not uncommon from the sixteenth century for 'an awl' to be mistakenly written as 'a nall' which suggests that some clerks were not familiar with the term, n.b. 1655 *Thomas Ryles of Sheffeld, nallbladesmith* (PR3/197). See also awlblade.

nambry, namery For 'an ambry', a food cupboard: 1549 *4 hayll pottes a namery and a discalle*, Marrick (YRS152/76); 1551 *I geve to Agnes, my doughter, a nambrey, an arke*, Halifax (Crossley63). See also ambry, spence.

nangnail A regional form for 'an agnail', an Old English word for a corn or painful swelling. Wright has references from 1790 and offers several different definitions, mostly to soreness associated with finger-nails (EDD): *c*.1688 *how to cure nangnailes – paire your nangnailes well and then take turpen*[tine], Conistone (RW11). Highlands Lane in Halifax was known as Nang Nail Lane until residents appealed for it to be changed in the 1960s.

nans An abbreviated spelling of 'anenst': 1526 *a nans the sadler*, York (CCW117). See also anent, nens.

napery Household linen: 1378 *Deux pieces de napris [Two pieces of napery]*, York (YAJ15/480); 1521 'half of *lez* Napry, namely cloths, linen, hand-towels', Beverley (YRS111/44); 1558 *to Agnes Hudson my doughter all myne apparel and napry ware*, Knottingley (Th27/235).

naphe See nave (1).

Naples fustian See fustian of Naples.

napron An article of protective clothing, originally made of linen but then of stouter materials. The loss of initial 'n' gave us the modern spelling 'apron'; 1307 *Pro linea tela ad naperonns [For linen cloth for naprons]*, Skipton (SS35/348); 1395 *Item pro naprunis empt. ijs [Item for purchase of naprons 2s]*, Whitby (SS72/621); 1404 *In remuneracione data cementariis … cum naprons et cirotecis [In payment given the masons … together with naprons and gloves]*, York (SS35/25); 1445 *iij ulnis dimidia panni linij pro naprons [3½ ells of linen cloth for naprons]*, York (SS192/42). See also apron.

nar, narr Obsolete for nearer or 'nigher': 1546 *his marke, that is undercavelde the narre eare and sleyt the furre eare, to his owne propre use*, Halifax (Crossley20); 1580 *at the further water gate and narre water yate*, Dewsbury (YAJ21/414). The near and far sides of an animal were determined by its position in front of the farmer with the head to the right. See also underbit.

nare A nostril of a hawk: 1619 *Marlin washed … houlding up her head so as none of that water get into her eares, naires, eyes*, Brandsby (NYRO44/171).

nares For heirs, via 'mine heirs': 1488 *I wyll that it remane to my son Robert and to my nares folowyng*, Bardsey (YAJ16/222); 1502 *and if my nayres pay nott the ijs aforesaid I will that the prest strayne* [distrain] *on the sayd grownd in Echwra for the said ijs*, Sherburn in Elmet (Th33/36).

narke Ark, for 'an ark': 1549 *I bequeathe to John Ramesden … to be heirlomes ij scleddes, a plughe, a narke, a counter, a lange settill and a kiste*, Elland (Crossley43).

narr See nar.

nat, natt A mat for use in the house, either as a bed cover or against a window: 1399 *Et in nattes emptis de [bought from] Johanne de Francia, 8d*, York (SS35/17); 1443 *In nattes emptis pro fenestris vitriis in Ecclesia, 7d [For natts bought for the glass windows in the church, 7d]*, York (SS35/58); 1574 *Item j old natte & a coverlet ijs*, South Cave (Kaner84); 1698 *a straw natt reared upp in the windowe*, Haworth (QS1); 1748 *one bednat*, Sowerby (QS1/87/6). Hence: 1669 *For covering the seates with natting in the Dean's closet*, York (SS35/348). See also gnat, knat.

nathe See nave (1).

natt See nat.

naught, naughty, naughtiness See nought (1), noughty.

naunt, nont For aunt, via 'mine aunt', pronounced like 'haunt': 1505 *To myn Awnte Alison*, Guisborough (SS116/270); 1545 *I give to my nawnte Warrayn the graie horse*, Seaton (SS106/225); 1570 *to Thomas Eyon … and every one of his children which he had with my nante xijd*, South Cave (Kaner73). The moorland inn *Nont Sarah's* near Scammonden commemorates a nineteenth-century licensee.

nave (1) The hub of a wheel, that part into which the end of the axle-tree is inserted: 1581 *7 elme naves*, Anston (G-A); 1664 *9 pair of waine naves*, Elmswell (DW239). A variety of alternative spellings has been noted: 1588 *certen wayne nathes and carte nathes*, Dalton (DD/WBW/19); 1643 *a gauge* [sic] *of felkes and naphes in the barne*, Pudsey (LRS1/128); 1648 *6 axletrees two paire of naffes a gange of felkes two gange of speaks*, Sharlston (YRS134/99).

nave (2) An alternative spelling of 'knave', a carpenter's tool, although it remains uncertain which is the correct form: 1471 *j wodax, ij brode axis, j brysse, j naffe, a wombyll*, Harome (SS45/188). See also knave.

navigator One who navigates a boat, a sailor or seaman. It was regularly used for sailors on inland waterways: 1596 *Robert Mydleton, Navigator*, All Saints Pavement, York (PR); 1673 *Leonard Wilkinson junior of Selby, navigator* (YRS47/192); 1681 *John Hurst, navigator … of Selby* (YRS47/9).

nawb For 'an alb', a white tunic worn by priests: 1558 *to the churche of Stavelay a westyment an a nawbe* (SS26/120).

nawgur For 'an auger', a boring tool: *c.*1530 *Item ij sthelegys a ship nawgur & ij gymbles*, Hull (YAJ2/250). The *sthelegys* may be 'stee legs' – for support. The item quoted is followed by *iij Cumpas with iij rennyng glasses*.

nawmbling For 'an ambling', referring to the gait of a gentle horse: 1552 *to my cosyn Dorothie Skergell … a nawmbling meare and hir foole*, Womersley (Th27/33). See also amble.

nawn, nown For 'mine own': 1538 *To be buried in the churche … at my nawne stalle ende*, Thirsk (YAJ22/223); 1578 *one petticoat … maid upon my nowne wolle*, Barwick (PR).

nawt, nout, nowt Alternative spellings of a regional term for cattle, derived from a Scandinavian word. It was a dialect alternative to 'neat': 1442 *Willelmo Rilleston fratri meo septem animalia vocata twynternawt … Ranaldo Gibson servienti meo quatuor catalla nominata stirknawte [To William Rilletson my brother seven cattle called twinter nawts … To my servant Ronald Gibson four cattle called stirk nawts]*, Rylstone (SS30/87); 1502 *all maner nowte as fatte nowte, drapez or yong stote to be brought into Fyschergate and ther to be put to sale*, York (YRS103/174); 1518 *catall, sheippe, and nowte*, Flamborough (SS79/91); 1521 *I will that … my son haue his porcion xx markes with xx nawte and xx sheipe*, Bardsey (Th9/161). It was the first element in several compound terms: 1543 *John Blande for nawte skynnes xvs*, Kirkby Lonsdale (SS26/38); 1557 *my lease and intreast of the stonne howse wyth two naut gayth [gates?] in the lee feld*, Yeadon (Th27/128). See also geld, neat, note, noutgang, stirk, twinter.

nawt hair Hair from the hides of cattle had a variety of uses, not all of them legal. A complaint by the saddlers of Wakefield in 1539 was that *dyvers persons byeth nawtte herre [hair] of the tannerrs and sells it to Cendell [Kendal] men to blend it with woile and make cloth of it callyd pawmpillzon cloth* (WCR9/86). See also hair (1), Kendal, kendalman, pampilion.

nawtherd, noutherd Regional by-names for the cattle herd or herdsman: 1296 *Nicholas le noutehird*, York (SS96/7); 1309 *German le Nauthyrd*, Wakfield (YRS36/197). In 1280, *Robertus Noutmaysterman* was a witness in a dispute between Rievaulx Abbey and Kirkham Priory: his name suggests that he was responsible for all the cattle in one of those monastic houses (SS83/406). The word remained in use as an occupational term: 1642 *they would not take under iiijs a gate and wee must pay Noutheard-wages*, Elmswell (DW125). It had the same meaning as neatherd, a point appreciated by a clerk who chose to demonstrate his knowledge of the regional terms used in a local place-name: 1705–8 *there is a lane leading from Helaugh to Harkaside called Neatherd Lane or Noutherd Lonning … it got that name by the Helaugh mens using to drive their neat or cattle from Helaugh to Harkaside* (YRS162/262). See also neatherd, noughter.

nawt-house Apparently a rare alternative to cow-house or mistall, although the references point to an important and substantial building. The word occurs in a series of title deeds for property in Highburton, some in Latin the others in English: 1610 'one house called *a nawtehouse* in the occupation of Thomas Sonyer'; 1619–20 *one house called a nawtehouse ... and all and everye the outshuttes, elinges and buildinges to the Nawtehowse belonging*; 1629 'a house called *a nawtehowse*, a chamber above the same, one other house adjoining to it now used as a *mistall* with a chamber above it' (YDK63). See also eyling, outshot.

nawtmarket The cattle market in Pontefract was *le Nawtmerkette* in 1426 (PNWR2/78) and the *Nawtmarket* in 1546 (SS92/277). The site of the market was *the nawte market steade* in 1552 (Th19/310). The place-name was still in use in the seventeenth century.

nay The regional form of 'no': 1487 *I askid hyme if he wold to York and he said nay, I must to Hull* (YRS103/4).

nayres See nares.

naystre See aster.

nazzard Probably for 'an hasard', that is gray-haired, hoary, used of animals: 1557 *a hassart whye of the same aige*, Tynemouth (SS2/155); 1619 *Peter's little meare and a nazard coult*, Brandsby (NYRO44/180).

ne An archaic word for nor: 1528 *Residue of al my goodes not yeven* [given] *ne bequeathed, also that I dois not yeve ne bequeath in my lyve ... to Richard Hemyngwaye*, Halifax (Clay77); 1542 *he never harde* [heard] *ne knew the contrarie but that every person being in Heworth ... paith tith woll and lambe to Sainct Savior Churche* (YRS114/13).

neafe A clenched hand, a fist. See also nieve.

neald See neeld.

near hand Almost, close to: 1642 *aboute noone or when wee thinke they have nearhande halfe done*, Elmswell (DW20); 1647 *This day I ... cast up the accounts ... and I find them to be nere hand £100*, Thurlstone (SS65/81). See also in-field.

neat The word 'neat' was formerly in general use for animals 'of the ox tribe' (EDD): although it could, like sheep, be both singular and plural it was usually plural in Yorkshire and the term included heifers, oxen, bullocks and cows. In 1512, when Guy Wilstrop was accused of destroying land in Moor Monkton, by enclosure, one of the specific accusations made against him was that *he bredes nete and schep ... uppon the seid grounde* (YRS41/168). It is plural in that case, as it is in a Richmond inventory of 1541 which lists *40 heade of yonge neyte* (SS26/20). In *c*.1570, when John Kaye of Woodsome put his ideas on husbandry into verse for the benefit of his heirs, his advice was: *thy yong neat see abroad thow kepe ... unto yll wether make them meke* (KayeCP). See also nawt, note, twinter.

neatherd In the past the term 'neatherd' was almost as frequent as 'shepherd'. John Coy of Azerley near Ripon was listed as a *netehird* in the poll tax of 1379, and several individuals in the same township bore the by-name or surname *Netehird*. The surname does not seem to have survived, but the occupational term certainly did and in 1606 Christopher Pressick had *sundry misdemeanours proved against him ... being late neathird of Carlton* (NRQS1/30). See also nawtherd.

neat's foot, neat's tongue The foot and tongue of a bovine animal. We should not be surprised that neat's tongue was formerly a delicacy, but the feet are a less obvious attraction. In the seventeenth century the variety and the amount of food eaten by the Saviles at Thornhill was recorded in their kitchen accounts, and Barbara Nuttall's transcription for 19 January 1629 includes *23 neates tongues* and *7 neates feet* (BN2/14). See also noutfoot.

neat's leather Top-quality leather, made of the hides of 'neat' or cattle. In the Act of 1558 it was ordered that 'No shoe-maker shall make any shoes or boots of any neats-leather mingled, but only of itself' (SAL6/137). That regulation was incorporated into the cordwainers' ordinances: 1627 *their wares ... to be of leather well tanned and curried ... and stitched hard drawn with handleathers without mixing the overleather part of neats leather and part of calves leather*, Beverley (YRS84/79). In 1666, *shooes taken in Bridlington market were seased* and declared unlawful, *being not well tanned leather ... with calfe leather and neats horse leather mixt* (BCP227).

neb The beak or bill of a bird. It was customary in the past for swans to be marked, and the practice is commented on by Henry Best: 1642 *the kings swanner hayth all the markes, both nebbe-markes and foot-markes, sette downe in his book; Our marke is 3 holes boared with an hotte-swipple in the right side of the nebbe*, Elmswell (DW129). It is still in regular use, especially for a person's nose or the peak of a cap.

necessary, necessary house A useful or necessary house, commonly a privy or toilet, abbreviated by dialect speakers who refer to it as the 'nessy': 1717 *order that a necessary house be built in some convenient place*, York (QS1/57/8); 1743 *pulled down a necessary house next the town gate*, Gargrave (PR); 1788 *A Boy about 12 years old ... hang'd Himself in the necessary House*, Slaithwaite (KC242/1). In July 1785, an Ovenden farmer was *in the lathe Croft Cleaning the Necessaries*, and in August 1815 he was paid 2s *for Thatching Jo⁵ Blagbrough's (Coal) Necessary* (CA177,272). The OED evidence dates from 1609 but the word has a much longer history: 1413–14 'for one iron bar purchased from Robert Smyth for the door of the privy (*necessariorum*)', Selby (SAR224).

necklace A piece of lace or ribbon to go round a person's neck: 1558 *one ounce of blake silke ... iij necklaces and ij paire of gloves*, Knaresborough (SS26/126); 1636 'a woman for stealing a piece of a necklace, a childes bibb', Thirsk (NRQS4/62). As an item of jewellery 'necklace' is on record from *c.*1590 (OED).

neeld, nild Regional spellings of 'needle': 1567 *vij quyshinges of nealde worke xiiijs*, Esholt (SpSt/6/4/2); 1614 *j neeld wrought chear ... ij nild work quisshons*, Stockeld (YAJ34/172–3).

negligee A word on record from the mid-eighteenth century when it was usually a garment worn by women, a sort of loose gown. A tradesman's bill for Mrs Armitage of Thickhollins in Meltham included: 1765 *a large Negligia Cap 8s, 3 yards pampedore Ribon ... book Muslin, rufles* (G-A). See also silveret.

neighbour 'Functions that are today performed by nurses, physicians, social workers, secretaries, real estate agents and lawyers were among the countryfolk of Elizabethan and Stuart days performed by neighbours for each other' – so wrote Mildred Campbell in *The English Yeoman*, finding the right words to define the word 'neighbour' as it came to be understood in the Tudor period. The word is found in numerous contexts where it is clearly more than just a reference to a person living next door or close by: *c.*1545 *agreyd ... that all maner ways and gates shall be hade and occupyd after the old maner and custom amang all neghburs*, Thurstonland (G-A); 1578 *every tenant of this manner ...*

who kepe any cattell goinge on the Common, shall bear and pay all layes, taxes and assessments rateably … and shall be assessed by their neighbours, Dewsbury (YAJ21/404). In 1584, a papist named Richard Lumby died in Leeds: he had been excommunicated but his body was taken to the church *by hys kynsfolks and neighbours* in an attempt to have him buried there (PR). Note the by-name or surname: 1481 *William Gudeneghbour*, Doddington in Northumberland (SS85/38). See also neighbourhood.

neighbourhood The way that 'neighbour' was used in the Tudor period influenced the meaning of 'neighbourhood', placing emphasis on the values shared by the community: 1503 *she shuld have ben grievously punished and amercyd bot for pitie and neghbourhed and remitted hir punnyschment unto viijd*, York (YRS103/183); 1503 *accordyng to olde neghburode & gude custome with oute grugyng of ather party*, Selby (SS85/30); 1668 *such part and rate of cattlegates, woods, underwoods, turbaryes and other profits and commodities … as are allotted … within Hanlith according to the order of neighbourhood there used* (MD217/170). See also swine root.

nens An abbreviated spelling of anenst: 1533 *we present Myles Jenne that he fey hys donge hyll a way nens hys grownde*, Wakefield (YRS74/17). See also nans.

ness A headland, sometimes on the coast, but particularly a semi-circular piece of land around which a river flows. It is found from the twelfth century in place-names such as Cotness and Reedness and is very common along the Ouse and its feeders. Typical examples of minor localities so called are at Rawcliffe and Wistow: 1272 *infra villam et territorium de Drax in loco qui dicitur le Nesse ex opposite villæ de Routheclif [within the township and lands of Drax in a place called the Nesse opposite the township of Rawcliffe]* (YRS13/105); 1558 *I gyve the lease & yeares which shalbe to come in the Nesse at Wistowe to … my sonne in law* (Th27/240).

nest A set or series of similar objects, especially those crafted so that a smaller one can fit into one that is next in size: 1461 *1 nest cofers*, Hull (YRS144/31); 1489–90 *8 nest countours*, Hull (YRS144/207); 1524 *I will my wif enyoye to hir owne use my nest of my goblettes*, Guisborough (SS79/190); 1531 *a nest of bollis of silver with one covering*, Wilton (SS79/310); 1567 *One nest of goblets with a cover*, Richmond (SS26/197); 1617 *a nest of baskets*, Ripley (YAJ34/193); 1693 *3 nests of boxes £1 10*, Selby (YRS47/22).

nether Lower, in contrast to upper, although in Yorkshire the contrast was originally with 'over': 1377–8 *Pro quodam Louthyr fact[o] apud Nethyrmylne*, Bolton Priory (YRS154/564); 1489 *a certan ground at the neder end of the … holme*, Ovenden (YRS69/122); 1552 *a payre of bede stockes likewise in the nether parler*, Pontefract (Th19/318); 1647 *I went to Shore hall, and so through the nether part of the town*, Thurlstone (SS65/40). Its use in everyday vocabulary declined, in favour of lower, and this affected many minor place-names. Low Moor in North Bierley was, in 1579, *the nether common next adjoining Okenshaye* (LRS2/115) and Lower Houses in Almondbury developed in a similar way from Nether House: 1635 *John Kaye of Netherhous;* 1636 *John Kaye of Lowerhouse* (YDK111). The element survived in Netherton, Netherthong and other major names, but see 'over'.

nether stocks Stockings, also referred to as under stockings, and apparently worn with slops: 1577 *all my hosen as well sloppes as nether stockes*, Burton Constable (SS26/273); 1589 *a graye frisse jerkin and a peire of nether stockes*, South Cave (Kaner155); 1607–8 *my best over hoose and my best netherstockes*, Clint (SS110/2). See also overstocks, slop, undersock.

netmaker A maker of nets, especially those for trapping birds or catching fish. The by-name occurred several times in south Yorkshire in the poll tax returns: 1379 *Henricus Nettemaker 4d*, Doncaster (PTWR). See also lark net, plover net.

net prick A piece of wood similar to a skewer, used for attaching nets: 1683 *purss nets, yate nets, nett pricks*, Doncaster (QS1/23/3); 1739 *an haze net and twenty netpricks … in the warren*, Rawmarsh (QS4/29). See also pack prick.

nettle-cloth A cloth said to be made of nettle fibres: 1544 *to Gilbert Browne wif a kirchif of nettill clothe*, Wakefield (Th19/103); 1572 *viij yeards of nettell clothe, viijs*, Richmond (SS26/233). See also scotch cloth.

never heed Still a common colloquial expression which means 'pay no attention to' or 'never mind'. It is on record in the deposition of a highwayman in the West Riding: 1722 *but never heed Dick, before the weekend we'll make somebody's purse pay for it* (QS1/61/4).

newark Not a reference to a place-name but to 'new work' on a building project, recently completed or close to completion: 1508 *my bodye to be buried within the newwarke of the college church of Ripon* (SS64/330); 1510 *To be buried in the Newarke of Halifax* (Clay37).

newitie See annuity.

nib One of the two short handles which project from the shaft of a scythe: 1697 *making search for some horse shoes taken of William Pullen Horse feet found … a sith (being then out of the shaft) and likewise two handles or nibbs … covered with some cloaths*, Spofforth (QS1/36/1).

nieve A clenched hand, a fist: 1642 *there are holes of that bignesse that one may thrust in theire neafe*, Elmswell (DW132).

nifle As a plural noun it meant trifles, items of little value: 1577 *with inkhorns and other nyfles*, Birstall (Sheard343). As a verb it was to steal trifling objects (EDD): 1755 *guilty of nifling at Barnby Dunn* (QS1/94/3).

nightertale A regional word for the night time: 1499 *Sir Roger Hastynges the xiij day of October last past with Force and armz of the nyghtertall sent hys houshold servants to the Castell of Pykeryng* (NRR1/189).

nightingale The bird renowned for its song, but a name traditionally given to cows, probably ironic: 1486 *ij kye called Nightigale and Luffley*, Felixkirk (YAJ22/203); 1547 *to John Morton one cowe called Nyghtingegaile with one quie crumble headed*, Great Preston (Th19/184); 1557 *two kye the one called whytehorne and the other nyghtgaill*, Methley (Th27/112). It can be compared with 'throstle', dealt with separately, which was a popular name for a horse. The poet John Gower linked 'The Throstle with the nyhtingale' in 1390.

night-wake The vigil beside the body of a dead person: 1416 *Capellani parochiales de Masham … pro qualibet nygwake, 7d [To the parish chaplain of Masham … for each night-wake, 7d]* (SS35/249); 1521 *to the vicar of Knares[borough] for nyght wakes and hedemasse pennys viijd* (SS104/13); 1556 *paid his oblacions … to Mr Walter Pullan who he thinks hath righte thereunto And he thinks he ought to pay nothinge nor hath paid nothinge for no nyght wakes*, Farnham (YRS114/76). See also lyke-wake, wake.

nild See neeld.

nine-holes A game played in the open air, with nine holes cut in the turf: stones or other rounded objects had to be rolled into the holes, and three in a row was a winning score. Alternatively, a similar game could be played indoors using a board: 1611 *James Kendroe and Will. Nelson of Northallerton for using unlawfull games on the Sabaoth daie, viz. at Nyenholes* (NRQS1/240).

nipping irons Possibly tongs or pincers: 1636 *three shovel shaftes and a chesfatt xijd, and nipping irons, xijd*, Allerton near Bradford (LRS1/88). Later, 'nippins' referred to short ends of thread, waste yarn or useless scraps more generally (EDD). White's *West Riding Directory* has: 1837 *John Hall, dealer in nippings*, Huddersfield, and Nippins Row was the unofficial name for houses in Hopton.

nobit For 'an obit', that is a ceremony performed at the burial of a deceased person, or a gift in commemoration of the deceased: 1488 *I wylle that a nother nobylle of the same land be takyn euery yer to make a nobette with alle in Bardsay Kyrke* (YAJ16/224); 1506 '*a noppyt for Jenet Palmar's soul*', Leverton (YAJ2/250n); 1557 *I will that twentye shillings rente shalbe taken fourthe of the byrk nabbe for a nobyt … to be downe yearely for my sowle healthe*, Rothwell (Th27/109).

noble A gold coin introduced in 1344 which had a value of 80 pence; that is half a mark. It was discontinued in 1465 after being revalued and gave way to the angel which had the same value: 1487 *I witte to my eame John Gyldous … a old nobill*, Hull (SS53/25). In fact nobles continued to be passed down the generations: 1542 *to Margaret my doughter v nobles beside her parte oute of the holl goodes*, Leeds (Th19/80); 1558 *to my broder William Atkinson twentie nobles*, Pontefract (Th27/201). Mathew Witham of Brettanby left nobles to several people to be made into gold rings, for example: 1545 *to George Jakeson my son a nobyll to mak hym a ryng of* (SS26/56). See also angel, eme.

noffisour For 'an officer': 1483 *it is agreed … that then the said brygmaisters shall have a noffisour of the Maiour to distreyn the said Richard for the said debbts*, York (YRS98/67).

noggin A small drinking vessel, a mug or cup (OED): 1610 *four cannes and a noggen xijd*, Kirkstall (SpSt); 1622 *16 noggans, skales, dishes, butter coffens & 3 dossen of trenchars*, Cottingley (LRS1/61).

noil A word used in the textile industry for the short pieces of wool combed out of the staple, usually in the plural. It is on record in an Act of 1623–4 and then frequently from the eighteenth century: 1738–9 *Recd 13 Stone of Noyls and a half after … £5 9 8*, Honley (Crump94); 1747 *John Hepworth stole half a pound weight of woollen noyls, 2d*, Huddersfield (QS4/30/216). It could be applied to the short ends of other materials: 1761 *hair shagg made of mohair or sopose you was to make of silk noyles … is grett profitt*, Wakefield (YRS155/18).

nold For 'an old': 1540 *unto John Watson wif a nolde blake colte*, Scarcroft (Th19/12); 1554–5 *a nolde horse price 10s*, Aysgarth (YRS130/4).

nolmary See ambry, nambry.

nolt Probably for 'nowt', that is cattle: 1552 *sex young nolte, thre score shepp*, Lowther (SS26/74). See also nawt, neat, note.

nonage The condition of being under age, the legal period of infancy: 1462 *that myn executours have the … surplus of my livelode during the nonage of my said sone*, Mirfield (SS30/257); 1504 *the marriage and custody aswele of the body of the said Nicholas as of the* *said maner of Newsom ... during the nownage of the said Nicholas belongith ... to Sir James* [Strangwais], Farnley Tyas (YDK33); 1543 *the gouernance of the saide Elisabeth and Agnes my doughters with ther goodes unto the saide Margaret ... during ther none aiges*, Halifax (Clay171). See also liflode.

nont See naunt.

nook A corner or a recess: 1642 *The pinnes were made of wilfe ... One of them was strucken downe close to the side of the west house ... two att the turne of the nooke*, Elmswell (DW152–3). It was used especially of a field corner, and so features in boundary perambulations: 1466 *and so estward to Woddall feeld nuke*, Sand Hutton (YAJ2/92); 1556 *the Curate of Bulmer ... in Crose weke ... goeth in procession about Hardie Flate and saith a Gospell at the Sowthe nowke of the same and hath a pott with aill* (YRS114/92); 1606 *one higheway ... betweene Canswick Park-nooke towards Nosterfeild and Massam Bridge* (NRQS1/57); 1637–42 *towardes Theast, includeinge the Crookes or Nookes beelonginge to Haram Haw* (HRD432). Found also in minor place-names: 1572 *Salondynenoke*, Lindley near Huddersfield (KM352). See also crook (1), milking stead.

Norway oak Pine and oak were imported from Norway from the Middle Ages but early direct references to the country are not common in Yorkshire sources: 1661–2 *Anthony Marsingale had not paid them their wages from Norway ... [he] said that 150 deals were missing from the ship*, Hull (YRS105/153); 1694 *Paid to Mr Haworth for 10 firdeels & one Norway oake £1 5s 0d*, Conistone (RW45); 1701 *deals fetch'd from Norway and deliver'd at Scarborow*, Castle Howard (CSS60); 1751 *9 Stockholm deals, 3 Norway oak boards*, Branton Green (QS1). A catalogue of the boards purchased at Hull by Sir Walter Calverley in 1705 included *10 Norway oak boards of 2 inches thicknesse*, which cost 6s 2d each (SS77/110). See also board (2), easting board.

note In general, the meaning was profit, advantage, usefulness, but in Yorkshire the word was often applied to cattle and it could have several distinct shades of meaning. These all had to do with the animal's profitability in the period it was able to give milk after calving: 1545 *I bequeath to ... my father the proffettes of a cowe iij yeres ... to Leonarde my brother a cowe not ij yeres ... to William Dicconson of Harrogaite a cowe noyte one yere* (Th19/141); 1551 *I gyff to Elisabeth Turner one cowe ... and ijs viijd for the nawte of the saide cowe*, Fewston (SS104/61). In this period the cow was said to be 'at note': 1552 'and deliver to Henry Jesope *one cowe at noyte*', Cumberworth (YRS102/113); 1557 *Crister Leche owes me for a cow noyt iiijs*, Monk Fryston (Th27/167). In an agreement drawn up *c*.1635, William Haigh of Falhouse near Thornhill, asked that his brother Francis *buy a new noyted cowe for him* and *allowe her summer and winter keeping*: in return William was agreeable to *paying him an indifferent rate for the noyte and 30s for the ... keeping*, Thornhill (YDK71). The spelling 'noyt' is a characteristic of the dialect in the south-west of the county.

The 1557 spelling 'nawte' seems to suggest that not all clerks were aware of the distinction between 'note' and the two similar words for cattle; that is nawt and neat. Examples which seem to make this same point are frequent: 1512 *Fyrst viij oxyn ... xiiij ky ... xij yong noyt of on yere ... xvij noyt of a noder yere*, Fewston (SS104/5); 1568 *Item 9 hede of yonge noit, the pric' £4 10s*, Grinton (YRS152/159); 1596 *Item Elizabeth Clarkeson of Sattron for the neat of a coowe 4s*, Crackpot (YRS152/321), 1678 *We present Thomas Ellis for not sending to the feild coman noate*, Bridlington (BCP279).

nouch For 'an ouch', a clasp, buckle or brooch: 1430 *cum uno nowche cum lez perlez [with a nouch with the pearls]*, Woolley (SS30/7); 1443 *j nowche de auro [1 gold nouch]*, Well (SS26/1). See also ouch.

nought (1) Naught, nothing. To 'ail nowt' is still to be in good health: 1538 *to the orgone maker of London for ys fey when he comys in to this countre and seys that owr orgons haylles* [ails] *noght*, York (CCW194); *c.*1570 *the heire owght to be carefull that nowght perished be*, Woodsome (KayeCP). It was derogatory when used of individuals: 1725 *said that Jonas Horsfall is nought*, Ilkley (QS1/64/1) and could mean useless in references to tools and implements: 1642 *the naughtinesse of the Mowers cradle*, Elmswell (DW49). It occurs occasionally in by-names but these were probably nicknames and their real significance remains uncertain: 1379 *Adam Costenoght*, Conisbrough (PTWR). Smith has *Costnoght place* (1452) in his list of Sheffield field names (PNWR1/220). See also craddle, flite, noughty.

nought (2) A rare spelling of nout, that is cattle: *a.*1731 *Yorke hath 7 head fairs that is Whitson Monday, St Peeter day & lammas day, Cald the nought fares*, Scalm Park (YAJ7/53).

noughter Probably for 'nawtherd' or 'noutherd': 1669 *the said George Whittin doe hereby promise to repaire, maintaine and uphould all the cow fould till Martin next and if he sufer any beast to be pinded by reson of his nectlect the Noughter to borrow them out of his wages*, Bridlington (BCP274). See also nawt, nout.

noughty From nought, an alternative spelling of naught. When used of people it had a range of meanings which included abject, evil, wicked, worthless: *c.*1515 *dyueres other light lude and noughtie persons to the noumber of twentie*, Ilkley (YRS41/173); *c.*1536 *he was a nowghty person*, Tadcaster (YRS51/102); 1568 *did imprison Ric. Londesdaill, clerk, for his evell behaviour and noughtie lieffe*, Tickhill (YRS114/109).

nout, nowt Cattle. See also nawt, nolt.

noutfoot This rare word occurs as a by-name: 1301 *Thomas Noutfot*, Richmond (YRS21/17). It means 'cow foot' but is likely to have been a nickname and the allusion is lost. See also neat's foot.

noutgang Cattle way or lane: 1259–60 'From a place called *noutegang*', Kayingham Marsh (YRS12/80).

noutgelt Literally, cattle money. In 1676, *Noutgelt* was one of several payments listed in the will of Lady Anne Clifford, due to her from tenants on her estates (YAJ18/402). See also nawt.

noutmaysterman See nawtherd.

novel For 'an oval': 1731 *a novel table*, Austerfield (QS1/70/7).

nown See nawn.

nowt See nout.

Nowtgate A York street-name which has not survived, literally Cattle Lane. It was recorded in 1612 (PNER300) and Angelo Raine identified it as today's George Street (YRS103/174n). It has a much longer history, though, for 'gate' had replaced the earlier word 'geil' which also had a Scandinavian origin and meant 'narrow lane or passage between houses'. In 1353, land released by Walter de Kelsterne was said to stretch from 'the highstreet of Walmegate in front as far as the lane called *Noutegale* behind' (YRS102/177) and in 1365 property in Walmgate and Fishergate was said to abut on *Noutgaile* (YRS111/184). Similarly, in Beverley: 1366 'a lane (*venellam*) called *Noutdritlane*' (YAJ16/88). See also gale (2).

nox For 'an ox': 1519 *to Richard Hardestie that hayth weddyd my doughter a nox*, Clint (SS104/8); 1521 *to my broder doughter … a nox stirke of ij yeres olde*, Bardsey (Th9/170).

noyt See note.

nut A cup formed from the shell of a coconut, mounted in metal: 1378 *Item domino Johanni Carp unum nutte nigrum cum cooperculo et pede argenteis [Item to sir John Carp a black nut with a silver lid and foot]*, York (SS4/105); 1433 *unum ciphum vocatum le nutt coopertum cum pede argenti stantem [a lidded standing cup called the nut with a silver foot]*, York (SS30/47); 1534 *To Richard Derelove one nut as one harelome belonging unto this house*, Knaresborough (YAJ14/417n).

nuthack, nuthagg These are possible spellings of the bird we call the 'nuthatch' and they occur in several by-names: 1359 *Walter Nuthak*, Dale; 1387 *John Nuthagg*, Hawnby; 1389–90 *Walter Notehagg*, East Heslerton (YRS50/58,74). If that is not the meaning it should be noted that similar by-names and place-names are found in other parts of Yorkshire where they probably refer to small hazel woods: 1274 William *de Nuteschawe*, Sowerby (YRS29/93); 1379 John *Nuttehirst*, Saddleworth (PTWR); n.d. *terram suam de Noteherst [his land at Noteherst]* (SS72/682). See also hagg, pile hagg, wand hagg, wood hagg.

nutt, nutty Traditional names for a cow, possibly for 'nutbrown': 1412 *lego Ricardo fratri suo vnam vaccam que vocatur Nutte [I bequeath to my brother Richard a cow called nutt]*, Winestead (ERAS10/7); 1553 *to my dowghter Elizabeth Wattes one cowe called nutt*, Wakefield (Th19/332); 1619 *one cow called Nuttie*, Harrogate (SS110/54); 1708 *Nutty buld Aprill 16th*, Conistone (RW50). Found also as a by-name: 1379 *Johannes Nutte*, Rotherham (PTWR), as is 'nutbrown': 1260 *Geoffrey Nutebrun*, South Cave (YRS83/83). See also GRDict.

O

oak England's most popular tree over the centuries, responsible for hundreds of place-names, many of them recorded in Domesday Book. Typical examples include Ackworth, Acomb, Oakenshaw and Oakworth, all of Old English origin, whilst Aketon and Aikwood have spellings which testify to Scandinavian influence. Solitary oaks were boundary markers and meeting places, as in Shire Oaks and Skyrack. Scores of minor settlements have survived with simpler names, such as The Oak in Sowerby and Oakes in Almondbury.

The oak was our major source of timber in the past and it is referred to countless times in wood leases and wood management documents: 1316–17 *Pro j quercu et j rota molendini empt(is) apud Ryther pro domo in Holdernesse [For 1 oak tree and 1 mill wheel bought at Ryther for the house in Holderness]* (YRS154/425); 1470 *Johanni Rawdon de Wystow … pro xlv quercubus 4li [To John Rawdon of Wistow … for 45 oaks £4]*, York (SS35/73); 1599–1600 *Oke Tymber trees Super le Wham Hagg*, Settrington (YRS126/29). A Dissolution survey of the woods that had belonged to Fountains Abbey divided oaks into several categories: 1574 *Okes of the best sorte* were valued at 13s 4d *a pice; of the second sorte* at 6s 8d; *of the third sort* at 3s 4d *and speres of okes* at 12d (SS42/412).

The historian T.D. Whitaker offered an insight into how fashion changed when he said of English oak in 1816 that it had traditionally 'formed the great material of our furniture as well as of our floors and roofs', but then added that it 'was a stubborn log, dark and unsightly; and as soon as the first plank of mahogany' was imported from Jamaica, people 'began to discard the lumber of their dwellings and to adopt the new material' (Whit1/80). See also border.

oakarmy See alchemy.

oakum The coarse part of flax, separated in the hackling process: 1676 *one firme with a parsill of ockem*, Selby (YRS47/2); 1704 *for 2 Bushells of hair & Ockham, 3s*, Camblesforth (QS1).

oatmeal maker Oatmeal was made by grinding 'shilling', that is oats from which the husks had been removed, and it was formerly a major element in the diet of most Yorkshire families. John Beamonde of Birkhouse died in 1577, leaving Jennett Hopkinson *one stroke of shilling at harvest*: Frances Collins transcribed the will and quoted the explanation of 'shilling' by the Kirkburton historian Morehouse: 'this refers to oats, which, previous to being ground, are taken and dried on the kiln. They are next taken and shelled, or denuded of the husk or shell. In this state the corn is called by the miller shilling, or shelling, being then ready for grinding' (FACcciii).

There is evidence of a guild of oatmeal makers in Beverley from the late fifteenth century (VHER6) and they are referred to in a variety of documents: 1576 *no otemeall maker or otemeal seller eyther brother of that occupacon or contrybutor shall carry or send to the Toune of Hull above one quarter of otemeal on the Market Day there* (YRS84/5); 1591 *James Hartesse, otemealemaker* (PR); 1642 *the Lincolnshire men come over to hull and to these doe Beverley oatemealemakers vente and sell a greate parte of theire oatemeale* (DW106). See also shill, shilling. Note: 1317 *Cicely Melemaker*, Rastrick (YRS78/181).

oat shiller A rare word, probably an alternative of oatmeal maker: 1726 *Paul Wilson, shiller*, Richmond (NRQS9/74); 1763 *Joseph Clark, oat shiller*, Beverley (YRS122/43). See also shill, shilling.

obit A service or gift in commemoration of a deceased person: 1522 *he shall provide … yerly, for the term of his lyff, an obbett to the valow of ijs*, Knaresborough (SS104/17); 1533 *the said prest to syng … Messe of Requyem at the principall altar … for all Cristen saules whiche said obbite I wil be celebrate and kepid the first Sonday next after the Inuention of the Holie Crosse*, Halifax (Clay88–9); 1558 *I will that myn assignes that shall have the yshewes and proffettes of my fermholdes shall yearlye make one obytt at Swillington Churche* (Th27/341). See also nobit.

occupation lane, road These were lanes or roads which were constructed as a result of the Parliamentary inclosure Acts, designed to provide access for landholders to the newly created allotments. As a minor place-name it has escaped attention although it occurs several times in and around Huddersfield, perhaps most obviously in Lindley's long and very straight Occupation Road. It is uncertain just when and where the term was first used but it occurs in the Inclosure Award for Honley: 1782 *And we do set out … one other private Occupation Road … for the Use and Improvement of all such landes* (I/Ho) and Huddersfield: 1789 *One private occupation Road … branching out of Fixby Road … leading … to an allotment and certain tenements of Thomas Thornhill* (I/Hu). It was later used of roads created to give access to pits, quarries and the like: 1860 *an occupation road leading to Eastwoods Coal Pits*, Meltham (G-A).

occupier A trader or dealer, especially mariners or ship-owners: 1567 *Thomas Sherwodd, Bridlington Key, occupier* (YRS14/143): 1569 *Robert Storye, Bridlington, occupier* (YRS19/150). See also wood vessel.

occupy To employ oneself in, to exercise a craft or trade: 1417 *if any man come fra other cites or tounes and will occupy here in this cite in girdelercrafte als a maister he sall pay at his first setting up of his shoppe xs*, York (SS120/182); 1428 *charged hym that he suld noght occupy in bying nor in selling*, York (SS85/4); 1487 *haith occupied within the Citie as a fraunchest man in his craft of glasier*, York (YRS103/3). See also able (2), dairyman, freeman, maister, occupier.

ocknomy See alchemy.

offal This word has become more restricted in meaning over the centuries, and for many people now it signifies those parts of a butchered animal which remain when the carcass has been dressed, i.e. the kidneys, heart, tongue and liver. It is said to have passed into English from the Dutch *afval*, literally the 'off-fall', that which has fallen off, and its wide range of early meanings included wood or leather that was not of the first quality: 1547 *all the topes, loppes, barkkes and offall*, South Crosland (DD/WBD/2/44); 1577 *certen old planks and other offall of wood 6s 8d*, Beverley (YRS84/9); 1580 *and also the offall of all the said trees, viz so much … as wilbe no tymbre*, Thurstonland (YDK77). It was also a term in the fish trade, used of inferior or low-priced fish, not prime fish such as haddock, plaice and whiting: 1396 *v last vi^{ml} allecis bonæ et iii last vii^{ml} de offall [5 lasts of 6000 good herrings and 3 lasts of 7000 offal]*, Whitby (SS72/565).

In the tanning industry, the word was used of inferior leather: 1622 *Item, dry ouffel lether*, Cottingley (LRS1/62). A shoemaker called Stephen Embley of Slaidburn died in 1719, and the inventory of his goods included items *In the shop* such as *leather curried … sole leather and Offall leather* (CS1/91). This was defined in a Quarter Sessions document of 1736 as *pieces of leather called offolds of cows' hides … the least useful scraps*

(QS1). A tannery in Keldgate, Beverley which specialised in the early 1900s in the processing of bellies and shoulders was known locally as *the Offal Yard* (BTT15).

The meaning was not 'waste' or 'superfluous', but simply 'not of the first quality', for in every early instance the offal was being put to good use. That was still the case in Henry Best's advice on bee-keeping in 1642: he recommended that after the honey had been extracted, water should be put into a tub – *for every hive 3 gallons of water, for every hive's offell will serve to sweeten 3 gallons,* Elmswell (DW70). Presumably the 'offal' in this case referred to bits of the comb that had broken off as the honey was being extracted. The liquid would then be used to make mead.

office See house of office.

oilcloth See oiled cloth.

oil-drawer A term for a drysalter, one who dealt not only in chemical products used in the arts, drugs, dyestuffs and gums, but also in oils and sauces: 1732 *a Lamentable Fire Accidentally and Suddenly broke out in or neare the Roofe of a Shop Scituate in Westgate in Wakefield … in the possession of Mr Thomas Walker, Oyledrawer or Salter* (QS1/71/4).

oiled cloth, oilcloth A name for any fabric such as canvas, cotton or linen which was prepared with oil to make it waterproof: 1721 *there being a piece of oyled cloath a wanteing,* Wakefield (QS1).

oil-mill A mill for extracting the oil from rape, linseed and the like. Oil was being imported into Hull in barrels in the fifteenth century, certainly from 1453 when it was described simply as *oile.* More specific references soon followed: 1461 *2 parva bar' cum lynsede oyle*; 1463 *1 bar' rape oyle,* Hull (YRS144). In Bridlington in 1679, the pier toll *for every Barrelle of Oyle* was 2d (BCP180). Mills to crush the oil-giving seeds are in evidence in Hull from the early sixteenth century: 1525 *… to my son John … my oile mylne with the garthyng, with all the cisternes of leede,* Hull (SS79/212); 1527–8 *John Harryson for … his oil milne at a terme ijd,* Hull (YRS141/123); 1550 *my messuage commonly callyd the Oylemylne with cesterns and all other implementes,* Hull (SS116/206). Hull was later to be a world centre of the seed-crushing industry but by the 1700s oil-mills were more widely distributed. The clothier John Brearley drew a diagram of a windmill in his *Memorandum Books* (1762) saying: *This mill grinds logwood chips and rasps and grinds rape seed for oyle,* Wakefield (YRS155/134).

oil-miller The person who operated the oil-mill: 1785 *William Townsley, oilmiller,* Aberford (PR).

olivant This is an obsolete spelling of 'elephant', less usual than 'oliphant', but retained in the sense of ivory, especially as one of the hafting materials used by Sheffield cutlers. In 1616, an Eckington cutler called Roger Barber had a quantity of *olivant* in his smithy and when George Harrison died in 1690 the finished goods in his inventory included *6 olivante Spring knives*; that is ivory-hafted penknives (IH). See also ivory, spring knife.

oliver The 'oliver' was a tilt hammer, used by early iron-workers. The OED evidence for the word is limited to nineteenth-century quotations, the first dated 1846, although a reference to a description of the 'contrivance' indicates that it was in use in 1686. The first Yorkshire examples are in Warley near Halifax, in 1350 (WCR2/260), and Creskeld in Arthington in 1352. In that year Richard de Goldesburghe leased two 'olivers' to a man called Robert Totte; supplying him with charcoal and iron ore which is confirmation that Totte was operating a smithy. The original deed is in French and relevant extracts include: *deuz Olyveres contenaunz vynt quatre blomes [two* *olivers containing twenty-four blomes]* and *urre suffisaunt pur les ditz Olyvers [sufficient ore for the said olivers]* (Th41/302). The inference is that 'oliver' had already come to be used of the site of the hammer, of the smithies itself, a development similar to that of 'wheel'. Stephen Moorhouse notes the use of *olyvers* in Clayton West in 1418, and more specifically in the Wakefield area: 1479 *le smethys called Olyver*, Crigglestone (WYAS775). In sixteenth-century accounts for the smithies at Farnley near Leeds, the building which housed the hammer was known as the 'Oliver': 1582 *Paid to the smethe men for scouring and trimming the Olyver and mending the great dame 14s 4d: Item for theakine the olyver 10s 8d*: 'theakine' or theaking is a reference to roof repairs (Th41/304).

The etymology of 'oliver' remains uncertain but it has been plausibly suggested that the hammer in early forges may have been named in honour of the legendary hero Oliver who was renowned for the mighty blows he struck in battle. A reference in 1637 to *a meadow Called ye Oliver* in Ecclesfield, may be evidence that an 'oliver' had once been in use there (HSMS280). Smith listed Oliver Wheel in Ecclesfield (PNWR1/251). See also dint, tilt-hammer.

ollar An alternative regional spelling of alder: 1549 'has cut down and carried away one *ollar*', Slaithwaite (MMF); 1743 *peeling some ollars*, Mirfield (DD/WBE/1/18). It is found in a number of minor place-names, for example: *a*.1290 *Ollirsayhe*, Shelf (TWH30/52), that is 'alder shaw'. See also owler, pill.

oncost The churchwardens of St Michael, Spurriergate, regularly completed their accounts with a request for extra money: 1520–1 *Also we aske a lowans that we have laid down a bowt the repracion of the kyrke and the londes and of other oncostes to the sume of xvj^li xv^d: ob.*, York (CCW81). This may be 'running' costs or expenditure outside what was usual.

on life, on live Early forms of 'alive': 1486–1500 *William Otes the son had issue by the said Johanet and dyed and the said issue yit being on lyff*, Shibden (YRS63/125); 1529 *when so euer it shall happen my said feoffees to decesse, so many of them that ther be bot sex or four of them on lyve*, Halifax (Clay79). Similar terms had the same meaning: 1478 *his godfaders called Thome Smyth the whilke is yit of live and Jellyne Disforth*, York (SS85/37); 1519 *the saide feoffees, or suche of thayme as at that tyme shalbe upon lyffe*, Golcar (KM177); 1521 *To every of my god childer now being of lyve, iiijd*, Mexborough (SS106/5).

on-shoot In the one example noted it was used of trespassing animals, almost with the sense of invasion: 1609 *escape or on-shote of forrend beasts into Barden* (WHD14).

ooze, ooze pit In the earliest contexts 'ooze' meant juice, sap; the liquid obtained from a plant, fruit or the like, and a fifteenth-century reference described squeezing the 'wose' out from grapes (OED). It is distinct from 'ooze' in the sense of mud but the meanings of the two words overlapped from the sixteenth century when the tannin liquor in which the hides were steeped was called ooze, probably ground oak bark in water. Distinctive spellings had initial 'w': in 1673 a Selby tanner had *1 back in lime, 12s: 6 hides in wouse, £3 1 8* (YRS47/33). The spelling had changed by the early 1700s: 1707 *Sixteen Hydes and six Necks lately in the Lime and now in the Owse*, Frizinghall (YAS/DD187). In the inventory of Benjamin Empson of Sandal, an early eighteenth-century tanner, are nine references to Ouse Pitts, e.g. *Item In Other Ouse Pitt twelve Bend Leather Hides* (NSI/38).

open When there was water in a coal-mine it presented colliers with problems that could only be solved by draining, that is by 'opening' soughs or watergates: 1640 *did stope the soowe … so that no man can get coles … til itt be opened and the way to* *open itt is to Sinke a pitt within three yeards of it*, Sharlston (GSH2); 1653 *he would join with him in opening a sowe upon Baildon Moor* (WPB); 1774 *sow opnin 2 men 2 days*, Tong (Tong/4c/11). Alternatively a pit that had been sunk and was being worked was said to be 'open': 1597 *the myne or mynes of Coales opeind and not opnyd*, Beeston (WYL160/129/4); 1699 *all that my … coalmine … open and not open*, Goldthorpe (WN). This last item demonstrates how late a 'coal-mine' might consist of more than one coal-pit.

open cast This term became popular in the twentieth century when it was applied to mines where the ground surface was removed and the coal removed without shafts or galleries. It is actually on record though from the early 1700s when the verb 'to cast' still retained the meaning of 'to dig', as when throwing up a bank or earthwork: 1754 *to dig, sink or open any Pitt or pits … make any water gate or water gates, open cast or open casts, board gate or board gates*, Beeston (WYL160/129/9).

open tail See sough.

open time The time after harvest: in a quitclaim of land to Sawley Abbey in 1319 the grantor relinquished his right to use a footpath which passed through the property, except in 'open time': *aut aliquem transitum, fugacionem vel passagium per predictam semitam excepto tempore aperto [or any crossing, driving or passing by the said path except in the open time]* (YRS87/107). See also fence month.

orache A plant of Asiatic origin, introduced in the late Middle Ages, and recorded here in a list of spices: 1395–6 *Item pro dim. lib. de orage viijd [Item for half a pound of orache 8d]*, Whitby (SS72/622).

orange, orange-coloured There are references to the fruit from the fourteenth century and to its use as a colour from *a*.1600 (OED). Early Yorkshire examples include: *c*.1504 *Item xj yerdes reyd orryge viijs*, York (SS53/191); 1522 *I gif to William Marshall an orege colour gowne furred with whit lame*, Doncaster (SS79/154); 1539–40 *one orige tawnaye dosyn of my best making*, Leeds (Th19/10); 1559 *a jirkin of orysh colour cloth furred with fox*, Hipswell (SS26/133); 1568 *Item a quilt of orange color Satten abridges*, Healaugh (YRS134/25).

ore-blower Early spellings of the place-name Kirkby Overblow preserve what is likely to be an early term for 'smelter': *c*.1270 *in territorio de [within the district of] Kerkebi Oreblauhers* (YRS90/38); 1355 'the church of *Kirkeby-Oreblawers*' (YRS52/49). See also blow.

oregate A highway along which lead ore was transported. It gave its name to a farm in Marske in Swaledale which was owned by the Conyers family and named as *Orgate* in a charter of 1477 (YAJ6/225n). In 1531–2, William Conyers left to his son the lease of his *leid mynes … and Orgate* (YAJ6/229).

oregrave A place where iron ore has been extracted, a word which seems to have a longer history than 'orepit'. Indeed, its origin goes back to the Old English period, since the West Riding place-name Orgreave was listed in Domesday Book: minor place-names include *Orgraveker* in an undated thirteenth-century deed for Sharlston (WYAS776) and *the Orgraves* in Rawmarsh in 1574 (PNWR1/177). See also orepit.

oregraver An ironstone miner, noted in by-names: 1308 *Robert le Orgraver*, Sowerby (YRS36/155); 1327 *Adam le Orgraver*, Ossett (YRS109/120); 1416 *Johannes Uregrafer*, barker, York (SS96/125). In York, the evidence may point to a hereditary surname.

orelay A dialect spelling of overlay: 1705 *Four load saddles, wantoes & orelays 10s 0d*, Slaidburn (CS1/76).

orepit An ironstone pit, possibly a later word than 'oregrave' but in evidence from the thirteenth century at least. An undated Byland Abbey charter mentions 'land in *Orpittis* between the old forge (*vetus forgium*) and Alexander's land' (WYAS774) and an assart in Flockton in the same period had the name *Orpitterode* (YRS69/55). References to similar place-names in Sheffield are probably responsible for the place-name Pittsmoor: 1315 'the field *del Orepittes*' (TWH38/8); 1655 *Suzanna Tingle of Orepitts*, Sheffield (PR3/195). Since 'orepittes' here named one of the open fields the inference may be that ore had been mined there much earlier than 1315. Other place-names listed by Smith include: 1309 *Orepittes* in Hemsworth (PNWR1/267); 1403 *Orepitt*, Ecclesfield (PNWR1/256). See also oregrave, Toppit(t).

orestone The early regional word for ironstone: 1411 'Thomas Thorne made fine with the lord of 20d for licence to carry *le Urston* over the moor', Bradford (CR); 1450 'licence to fetch and carry ironstone (*petras ferreas*) called *Ureston* to … *lez Smythiez*, Tong (YRS120/63). In 1454, Sir John Langton leased to his son *all his … mynes of Iryn Ure* in Farnley (YRS120/64). See also ironstone, ure.

orfray Rich embroidery or an ornamental border or band, especially on an ecclesiastical garment: 1375 *Pro iiij ulnis et dimidia orfrayes 22½d [For 4½ ells of orfray 22½d]*, York (SS35/127); 1455 *lego … fratri meo usum vestimenti mei de albo fustian cum rubeis orfrayes [I bequeath to my brother the use of my white fustian vestments with red orfrays]*, York (SS30/202); 1471 *Item iij orferays to Seynt Mary kirke*, Beverley (SS45/195); *c.*1500 *Quatuor capæ de sateyn … cum le orfreys de viridi panno aureo [Four satin copes … with orfrays of green cloth of gold]*, York (SS35/229); 1531 *written on the orfray of the bak*, Doncaster (SS79/304). Used occasionally as a verb: 1455 *unam capam de blewe satyn cum operibus de velvet orfraid cum checkty velvet [one cap of blue satin with works in velvet orfrayed with checked velvet]*, Masham (SS30/188).

organ-maker A maker or builder of organs. The craft was established in York from the early fifteenth century: 1431 *Johannes Gyse, organemaker*, York (SS96/145); 1435 *John Seymour, organmaker*, York (YRS6/148). A by-name is evidence of the craft in Ripon: 1453–5 *Et de 20s solutis Will. Organmaker pro emendacione de organicis cum le belousse earundem [And for 20s paid to William Organmaker for repairing organs together with their bellows]* (SS81/161–2).

orish See orange.

orman See overman.

orphrey See orfray.

osier hope The osier was a type of willow and it had tough pliant branches which once had a variety of uses, especially in basket-work: the word came to be applied more generally to willows and to the branches themselves. 'Osier hope' is a rare term, recorded in the OED under 'hope': 1607 *I have planted an Ozier hope … in a surrounded ground, fit before for no vse, for the too much moisture and overflowing of it.* It was said to be a word found also in Essex and can be compared with osier holt and osier bed. Two Yorkshire examples are from roughly the same period: 1615 *lez Eightes, Les Osier hopes, vineyards, willow trees, Lez wares, mildames & Fludgates*, Almondbury (DD/R/2/27); 1623 *all messuages … eightes, les osiers, hopps, fishwandes, sallowes, the weares, mildames, rundells*, Butterwick (NRQS4/159). I believe the punctuation in this transcribed indenture masks the second example of 'osier hope', and since 'eightes' were aits or small islands it seems clear that willows were being coppiced in enclosed, marshy areas by the river or possibly on small islands. Halliwell described 'ait' as a little island where osiers grow. Objects made with osiers are on record from the same period: 1621 *Two little osier baskettes and one greater*, Slaidburn (YRS63/47). See also maund.

osmund It is known that Sheffield cutlers were using iron and steel imported from other countries from the sixteenth century at least, and much of it came via Danzig (FBH184). In fact iron had been imported into Yorkshire from a much earlier date, and the key to that is in the word 'osmund' which has an uncertain origin but referred initially to high quality iron from Sweden: the term later came to be used more generally for iron from a number of countries, imported via the Baltic. It was imported as small bars or rods, and the OED notes examples from 1280, with one for Hull in 1400–12. In York, a case in 1428 against John *Lyllyng* proved that he had forged *fals osmundes* by mixing tin and lead: *William Kyam saw ij barells of osmundes market* with John Lilling's mark (SS85/2). The published customs accounts for Hull contain numerous references, starting with a cargo from Danzig brought in the *Jacob*: 1453 *1 last' osmondes* (YRS144/3): an editorial note says that a 'last' was 12 barrels of osmunds. In the same period (1453–90) there are entries for iron imported into Hull from Germany, Hungary, Liege [lukys], Scotland and Spain. See also Dansk iron, German steel, landiron, Spanish iron.

ostery, ostre, ostry Characteristic spellings of hostelry or hostry: 1477 *that no man ne woman within this said citie … holde non osterie commune without that thai have a sygne ower thare dore*, York (YRS98/21); 1554 *a payn that everye man that kepethe anne ostre or In shal set uppe a Syne before hys doure*, Wakefield (YRS74/19). The meaning is not always so clear: 1583 *with other hustilment in the barnes, viijs, in the ostry cart gere and hustilment ijs*, Ripon (SS64/381).

other A spelling of 'either', although in the case quoted here it means 'both': 1548 *I geve to my sone George 2 chyldren other of thayme a lame*, Grinton (YRS152/66).

otter fur Otters were one of the wild animals trapped locally which were regularly used by the skinners: 1442 *unam togam russetam et penulatam cum otyrs [a russet gown lined with otter fur]*, York (SS30/84); 1559 *Item I gyffe to John Royston clarke a gawne furryd with otter*, Middleham (SS26/128).

ouch A clasp, brooch or buckle, used to hold together the two sides of a garment. They were often valuable objects, made of gold and set with jewels: 1347 *Une nouche dor [a golden ouch]*, Conisbrough (SS4/42); 1366 *unum par de paternosters et unum ouche de auro [a pair of rosary beads and an ouch of gold]*, York (SS4/79); 1437 *lego Margaretæ filiæ meæ unum uche de auro [I bequeath to my daughter Margaret an ouch of gold]*, York (SS30/61); 1498 *a nowche of gold, the wiche weies iij quartains of an unce*, Wakefield (YAJ15/92); 1550 *one owche of baysgold set with peyrll and one precious stone in the myd parte therof*, York (SS116/209). See also nouch.

ought (1) Anything, a variant spelling of aught, still in regular use: *c*.1570 *yf owght be gone than neds not Ile complayne to hadywiste* [had I known], Woodsome (KayeCP); 1786 *one mason dressing Stones at Stonepit … Joseph Pogson there for ought I know*, Slaithwaite (KC242/1).

ought (2) The past of the verb to owe: 1496 *for the tendir love that he hath ought to my husbond*, York (SS53/117); 1521 *iijs iiijd that his fader owght me*, Pontefract (Th26/344); 1557 *Detts that the testator ought the daye of his dethe*, Thornton Bridge (SS26/102); 1685 *his father ought him seven shillings for lamb summering*, Gargrave (QS1/24/5); 1727 *Daniel Brear ought him money*, Bradford (QS1/66/6).

out Out of or away from the village nucleus. The frequent use of the word by our ancestors emphasises their sense of 'belonging' to a tight-knit community, both territorially and in terms of the population more generally. Places and people were 'in' or 'out', of the extended family and its affinity, of the manor, township or parish, and 'out' was used in a score of compounds which articulate that sense of identity. Several of the more important usages are dealt with individually, for example, outgang, outlane, outpasture, outrake and outwood, but additional attributive uses are given here: 1725 *found him in an out barne*, Ilkley (QS1/64/1); 1564 *that every tenant … make their partes of the out-dykes*, Giggleswick (CR); 1634 *that every man make his outfences*, Meltham (G-A); 1593 *fenses called the outhedges*, Slaithwaite (MMF); 1609 *dwelling at an outhouse distant a good space from any towne*, Exelby (NRQS1/162–3); 1622 *Sent 4 of these kine to Skipsea outleyes to feed*, Elmswell (DW168); 1574 *11s 6d p. a. and all owte rentes, that is 18d to George Wodrove esquire and 15d to the castle of Pountfreit* (G-A); 1533 *We present mylner … for sarvyn folke of howt townes and will not serve folke of towne*, Wakefield (YRS74/17); 1671 *the poore of the Outtownes, not the Townsmen*, Fishlake (QS1/10/5). See also ley ground.

outbreak An alternative word locally for 'outcrop'; that is where a vein of coal appears at the surface. Yorkshire examples include: 1714 *the outbreak … in Agill and other places* [is] *most hopeful*, Colsterdale (BM82/71). The context does not always make the meaning clear: 1761 *2 days and a ½ at outbreak*, Tong (Tong/4c/6). It was called an 'out-burst' in *The Compleat Collier* (CC2). See also shiver, skirt coal.

out-door The door of a house which gives access to places outside, as on to the village street: 1685 *he broke open the out doore which was bar'd with a wooden barr*, Rigton (QS1/24/8); 1690 *found a child … laid upon a bench near his out doer*, Burley Woodhead (QS1); 1740 *standing in the porch at the out door*, Hartshead (QS1/79/2). See also in door.

outfolk All those who are not part of the community or not tenants of the same lord: 1519 *that the mylners grounde my Lord Abbott & his tennantez off Selby afore any owte folks* (SS85/32). See also outman.

outgang A word for a way or road out of a township or hamlet, often one which was used regularly by cattle on their way to pasture. The term has an Old English origin and it occurs frequently in Yorkshire documents over a wide area: 1189–99 *xv acris terre … inter Vtghang Johannis de Laxington et Vtghang de Skeltun [for 15 acres of arable land … between John de Laxington's outgang and the Skelton outgang]*, Howden (YAJ11/187); 1324 *usque ad portam de Norwragrene et sic transeundo per viam suam que dicitur le Owtegange [to the Norwragrene gate and thus crossing by his road called the Outgang]*, Healaugh (YRS92/53); 1413 'abutted on a meadow … on the north side *and le Westutgange* on the south … the said *utgang*', Bagby (YRS50/19); *c*.1450 *common pastur' to all their bestes … with fre entre and goynge owte to the mor' by a large way, the qwhyche is called the owtegang*, New Malton (SS85/58); *c*.1516 *apud le owte gange abbuttandam super Todhill gate [at the outgang abutting onto Todhill gate]*, Wombwell (YRS92/205). A few examples point to the outgang as a way to a neighbouring locality: 1442 'a Watergate in the *outegange* which leads to the forest of Galtres', York (SS186/132). Settlement sites might take their name from a location adjoining the way: 1301 *De Galfrido Atteoutgang' iiijs jd*, Wath (YRS21/6); 1608 *John Hyl of the outgange*, Malham (DDMa). See also outlane.

outlane A lane leading away from a hamlet or township: n.d. *unam venellam quæ dicitur Owtlane [a lane which is called Outlane]*, Balne (YRS13/163); 1311 'a certain *hutlane* ... in *le Holeclough*', Hepworth; 1327 'a path in *Littelwood* called *Outelone*', Cartworth (WYAS619); 1461 *le Outlane*, Hipperholme (PNWR3/83); 1556 *through one lane called the outelayne in Westgate*, Wakefield (YRS74/24).

outman A stranger, one who is not part of the community: 1483 *that melners is not deligent to serve the Lorde's tennandes be for owte men*, Selby (SS85/29); 1510 *Item in wod to the nowmer of four hundredth treis, with better, sold to owte mene*, Husthwaite (SS35/264). See also outfolk.

outmoor An area of moorland that belonged to a township but was located some distance away: 1615 *common of pasture upon the outmores*, Embsay (LRS2/91); 1642 *1 parcel of land upon the common out moore of Rauthmell* (MD217/294).

outpasture An area of pasture located at some distance from the dwelling or township which had grazing rights there: 1661 *To ... my sons in law ... two beast gates in the out pasture ... to my sons 6 beast gates in the out pasture*, Lees in Bowland (CS1/52); 1664 *all his part of the outpasture in Whessenden*, Marsden (G-A).

outrake A pasture or right to pasture away from the village, or the right of way leading to the pasture. The meanings are closely connected: 1425 'Robert Maleverer has *utrake* in the moor of Potterton this year only ... 2s', Barwick in Elmet (Th28/243). See GRYD19–22.

outset In October 1664, a group of tenants from the manor of Wakefield raised what they considered to be a case of discrimination within their own community. They were described as *the Inhabitants of the out-setts of the hamlett of Linley* (WCR5/139) which was then part of the vast township of Quarmby, so the inference is that *out-setts* is a reference to their outlying locations, away from the nucleus of houses in Lindley. That meaning may be shared by two Derbyshire places named Outseats which date from 1566 and 1683 respectively (PNDb156,189). In Harrison's survey of Sheffield manor, in 1637, a tenant called William Hincliffe was said to hold *at will a Cottage being an out sett adjoyneing to the East side of Alsoppe Farme house in Sheffeild Towne* (HSMS69), possibly a comment on its status although the meaning in this case is obscure.

outshot, outshut The first dictionary evidence for this word is a Yorkshire example of 1624, so it is likely to be a regional term. The outshot was an extension built onto the side or rear of an existing building, and the suffix describes the projection thus made. References occur commonly from the first part of the sixteenth century: 1533 *buyld ... one house to have two outshittes* [sic] *at either ende*, Halifax (Clay89); 1538 *2 outshoits joined to a new house lately of William Waddesworth*, Sowerby (WCR9/44); 1542 *le Owteshott near the cemetery*, Huddersfield (DD/R/2/6). Two of these spellings clearly point to the influence of dialect on 'shoot' as the suffix.

The frequency of the word in those years may imply that building such extensions was only then becoming popular in that part of Yorkshire, and a variety of almost explanatory examples have been noted subsequently: 1594 *one messuage, one owtshott adjoined and affixed to the said messuage*, Kirkheaton (DD/WBD/3/72); 1666 *in the Outshoote joining to the Kill*, Brayton (YRS47/75). In the seventeenth century, the spelling 'outshut' became more frequent and the term was increasingly taken as a synonym of 'eyling': 1604 *one eling or outshutt adjoining the said bay*, Hopton (YRS39/92); 1640 *a house and barn and le Outshutt or Eelinge adjoining*, Holme (WCR1/25). See also eyling, pentice, shot (2), shutt.

outwood The 'out wood' was a wood situated away from the village nucleus, and the place-name occurs frequently in Yorkshire. References not noted in PNWR include: 1543 *there is within the saide Lordshipp of Hamelton, Woode called the Owt Woode* ... (YRS13/362); 1572 *a great wast ground ... called the Owt woodes ... in the nature of a chace*, Spofforth (YAJ17/142). Wakefield's 'outwood' is well documented and it has been shown that it lay in the township of Stanley and part of Alverthorpe, rather than in Wakefield itself: it was distinct from the common wood (WYAS690–2). James said the name was sometimes used for a wood 'within the forest purlieu'; that is land which had been disafforested (Cox, *Royal Forest*, 9). See also scrud oak.

outwork This was probably work done by a miner for his employer away from the site, or at another of his pits: 1707 *out worke at pit at wood*, Farnley (MS11).

oven house A building in which an oven or furnace was located: 1569 *a crofte in Bradforde nere the Vicarage, in the occupation of* [William] *Rookes upon one half of which ... two ovens belonging to the vicarage are buyldede* (LRS2/14); *c.*1624 *an old howse caled an ovenhouse nere the said dwelling*, Honley (G-A); 1647 *one little House called an Ovenhouse standing in the North Side of the Fould there*, Bowling (MMA/28); 1697 *had an Iron Pott stole out of his furnass which stood in his oven house*, West Riding (QS1/36/6).

over Through the late Middle Ages, 'over' had the sense of 'upper' and it was used in contrast to 'nether' or 'lower': 1517 *half an acre lying in Aykden goyng downe from the over ende ... also half an acre ... at the nether ende*, Threshfield (YRS140/62); 1564 *the Intacke callyd Rawden Moore butteth upon ... the over end of Deane Moore*, Rawdon (YRS114/104). These were regional usages and they would survive only in dialect from the seventeenth century. Two entries in the court roll of Wakefield for 1609 are evidence that this was the transitional period: (1) *Longwood, Charles Kirshawe for nether end and John Haighe de Slake for over end*; (2) *the water runnynge from the upper end of Shepley unto the nether end* (WCR11/179,187). Both overend and netherend were frequent place-names, and the former survives as a common Yorkshire surname, first recorded in 1297 (GRDict). Upper Heaton near Huddersfield was Overheaton in 1578 and is 'Ower Yetton' still in dialect.

overbit A rare term which referred to a cut made on an animal's ear as an aid to identification, the opposite of the much more frequent underbit: 1730 *the wether was under bitt of the far ear and over bitt of the near ear*, Wetherby (QS1/69/1). See also nar.

overbody A woman's garment, clothing for the upper part of the body: 1572 *one kirtle of clothe of golde ... with overbodie of yalow damaske*, Skipton Castle (Whit2/330); 1615 *stealing a woman's overbody value 8d and a pare of sleeves, value 20d*, Carlton Miniott (NRQS2/98); 1629 *one white coat, one green overbody*, Lees in Bowland (CS2/52). It was frequently linked in wills with 'sleeves'. See also bodies, upperbody, welt (2).

over end The upper end: 1420 *a house at the over ende of the hedge of Mergaretes Hetche*, York (SS85/17). It gave rise to several by-names and a West Riding surname: 1297 *per ... Robertum del Overend*, Austwick (YRS16/4). See GRDict.

overlay A piece of material placed under the load-saddle of a packhorse: 1614 *2 load sadles panelled, ouerleys, wantoes*, Stockeld (YAJ34/178); 1636 *2 lodesadles, 2 overlayes, 2 wantows and a tayle band, xs*, Allerton near Bradford (LRS1/87); 1656 *five load sadles fower overlayes fower wanteyes fower colesackes*, Eshton (YRS134/113); 1712 *a horse a lode sadel ouerlay wantaw and a Colle sake, £4*, Barnoldswick (YRS118/62); 1719 *2 saddles, wantoes & overlays, 9s 0d*, Slaidburn (CS1/90). See also packing house, panel (3), orelay.

over leather The regional alternative to 'upper leather': *c*.1424 *pro aptacione duodecim parium de les over leders jd ob [for fitting twelve pairs of over leathers 1½d]*, York (SS120/193); 1458 *unum daykyr de over ledder*, Wakefield (SS30/218); 1627 *without mixing the overleather part of neats leather and part of calves leather*, Beverley (YRS84/79). The inference is that only the hide of a full-grown beast was of the right quality. See also neat's leather, sole leather, upper leather.

overlier, overligger A horizontal beam: 1579 *Item post sparres & overlyers over & under the helmes*, South Cave (Kaner103); 1620 *all the old wood as overligers in the helme*, South Cave (Kaner299); 1642 *one helme with overlyers and all the loose wood about the yeard*, Broomfleet (Kaner347). See also overwhart.

overlive To survive, outlive, live longer than: 1472 *And if God fortonne theis childer to over life their modir*, Pontefract (Th26/326); 1488 'lands and tenements ... to Elizabeth, the wife of John Kay *and she over live hym*', Woodsome (YDK11); 1549 *yf she forton to survyffe and overlyve ... hir husband*, Copley (YDK99).

overman A man having authority over others, especially over a body of workmen: 1539–40 *Item to Wm hart owerman for his quarter wages at Lammes 4s his liverey for 3 quarters 3s*, Wykeham (YRS80/95); 1578 *Thomas Robynson the overman his account sens Martynmes*, Stockeld (YRS161/43): in December that year he was *Robynson the orman* (YRS161/2).

over-measure In excess of the proper measure:

> *c*.1535 *John Bever of Umforth ... opon his othe deposith ... that he hath taken of the kynges wast by copye of court rolle within the time of Sir Richard Tempest ... too acres of lande ... he saith that he hath ouermesure iiij acres*, Holmfirth (YRS51/60).

Such grants were illegal but the testimony of other tenants shows that the practice was widespread and that the land was passed down the generations: 1546 *I bequest to Alison my wif, Edwarde Mawde, etc. ... all myne intereste ... of certan lande ... and they to fine for it ... as other men doth for ther ouermesser*, Warley (Crossley14–15); 1585 *which lands and tenement called Overmeasure ... the said John* [Mitchell] *late purchased*, Thornton near Bradford (LRS2/56). It is commemorated in a minor place-name found across the region: 1584 'Cotton Gargrave ... surrendered into the lord's hands ... a half rood of land called *Overmeasure* with the buildings thereon', Hepworth (WCR4/73).

overplus An additional amount, a surplus: 1481 *if so be the same money be not fully spendit ... that than the same ... to be delyverd ayane to the said wardens and they to delyver the overplus ayane*, York (YRS98/45); 1507 *I forgyve Walter Bubwythe the overpluse that is over & aboyff the some of viij marks*, Pontefract (Th26/343); 1558 *my parte of goodes equally amonges my wyff and my childer ... savynge that I wyll gyff to Margaret my dowghter a why stirke overplus*, Westerdale (YRS74/56); 1611 *If it be more my father is to pay the over-plus*, Brandsby (NYRO44/53); 1658 *paid him ... 7s more ... for his overplus worke at New-Hall*, Elland (OWR8/2).

over press In general the verb means to overburden, and in this case a tenant had too many beasts on a common pasture: 1603 *we present John Preston for over press in the new close called the Pryer Raike*, Malham (DDMa).

overquart A common alternative spelling of overthwart: 1500 *Item, for a tymmer of putts sewing the overquart semys, jd*, York (SS186/221); 1517 *north and sowth betwixt raynes and the waynway goynge overqwhart it*, Threshfield (YRS140/63). See also quart saw.

oversea From overseas, a term used for imported items: 1509 *To Sir Thomas Pilley …
a overse bed,* York (SS79/5); 1544 *an oversee coverynge of a bedde,* Wakefield (Th19/102);
1562 *A carpet of overse worke, xiijs iiijd,* Allerton Mauleverer (SS26/154); 1612 *j paynted
oversea chist with bands locke & key,* Brandsby (NYRO44/34); 1636 *an over-sea hanging
of wrought stuffe,* Richmond (NRR4/56).

overseer One who oversees or supervises, as in a will: 1530 *And also that … my
kynsmen be helpars and oursears with hir,* Heptonstall (Clay83). Also a title given to
the officers of a township or parish who were responsible for the poor and the
highways. More generally it was used of a person who surveyed work carried out on
an important project. Before Apperley Bridge was rebuilt in 1602 the mason Thomas
Wallimsley came to an agreement *with the overseers* who *of their own costs* were held
responsible for the provision of *all the tymber stone and lyme needful* (BAS6/141–2).
When Huddersfield Bridge was destroyed in 1647–8 Sir John Ramsden appointed
overseers to consult with two workmen and *agree with them for building the said bridge*
(QS10/2/75). See also oversight.

overshot A payment over or above what was necessary: 1619 *in part of a rente and
overshotte of five shillings,* Burnsall (MD87). See also shot (1).

over shuttle See shuttle.

oversight Supervision, work carried out by overseers: 1517 *Residewe of all my goodes
… I give … to my sonnes … that they the same goodes well and trewly dysposse … by the
ouersyght of Edward Saltonstall my broder,* Halifax (Clay50); 1552 *that the paving in the
way doune to Saynt Leonards Lendyng … shalbe sufficiently repayred of the common cost by
oversight of the Chamberlaynes,* York (YRS110/71). In 1562, money for the poor in
Thirsk was *at the disposycion of the churchwardens and oversight of the poor* (PTD146); that
is by the overseers of the poor.

overstocks Knee breeches (OED): 1565 *Item to Samuall Pullayne a pare of black
overstocks cutt in long paynes,* Farnham (SS26/177). See also nether stocks, pane.

overthwart Placed across or lying athwart something else, crosswise: 1417 *Thomas
Duffeld hafe sextene yerdys over thwart of the garthe fra the wall,* York (SS85/12); *c.*1535
*the seyd riotous persons dyd … cast the seyd dame Anne ouerthwart apon a horse bakk lyke a
sekk,* Egton (YRS45/4); 1537 *and from thence south overthwart to a close called Carr-rode,*
Calverley (DB5/C12/17a); *c.*1570 *begynyng at the overthwart aley,* Almondbury church
(KayeCP); 1603 *the way from the Oldgarth to go overthwart the Colgarthes,* Airton
(DDMa); 1611 *one stone sett overthwarte betwene one house of Nicholas Fenay … and the
groundes there of the said Robert Kay,* Almondbury (YDK109). Used occasionally as a
verb: 1573 *the accustomed way for cart and carriage which lyeth overthwarting his great new
close,* Doncaster (YAJ35/300). See also overquart, overwhart.

overthwart saw A cross-cut saw: 1544 *one over thwarte sawe and one chessell,* Harrogate
(SS104/47). See also quart saw, thwart saw.

overwhart An occasional alternative spelling of overthwart: 1590 *Item 4 ouerwhart
sykes north and south,* Kirby Underdale (HKU61); 1643 *for the helmewood and props and
the overwhart liers* [cross-beams], Elmswell (DW235); 1703 *shee falling ill and not able to
goe, the Constable took her up and laid her over whart a horse,* Hunshelf (QS1/42/7). As
a noun it could mean a lintel: 1537 *ij doore cheyks & a fresholde with a overwhart to the
same,* Bridlington (BCP24). See also overlier.

over work A word found in the accounts of a colliery in Tong: 1760 *pd one of the miners for over work 6d*, Tong (Tong/4c/5). This seems likely to have been payment for work carried out in excess of the hours contracted for.

owler A common local spelling of alder: 1572 *at the north end of the dame begynnyng at one owlar bushe*, Honley (KayeCP); 1592 *That no person pill anie owlers, crabtries or hollyns*, Dewsbury (YAJ21/466); 1690 *a close called Owlers*, Almondbury (DD/R/M/3). In the late sixteenth century, the Kayes of Woodsome *brought water in Owler troughs to the Brewhouse* (KayeCP). Smith indexes numerous minor place-names such as Owler Greave, Owler Wood, Owlers Wood, Green Owlers (PNWR8). See also cart legs, ollar.

own To claim or recognise as one's own: 1679 *upon notice given by the clarke or pindor, that they doe come and owne their fence*, Kirkheaton (DD/WBR); 1698 *found a parcel of turf in Josias Cowper's house which Elizabeth Parkin owns to be hers*, Slaithwaite (QS1). In 1681, after the theft of a brewing pan at his house, Oliver Heywood was asked by the constable *to come and own* it, Northowram (OH2/228). It could also be used meaning to admit or acknowledge: 1607 *having owned himself the father of Barbary Anderson's base child, shall pay 20s yearly*, Hinderskelfe (NRQS1/72); 1687 *does owne that he sold the foure sheepe to Thomas Lee*, Flockton (QS1); 1718 *George Myers own'd that he stole the hanks of yarn*, Knaresborough (QS1/57/8); 1789 *Edmond Littlewood owned that he … graved the turfs*, Meltham (G-A). See also drugget.

oxbow The wooden bow which forms a collar for a yoked ox: 1433 *In oxbose de lignis facto empto in domo Joh. Hovyngham 6s 8d [For wooden oxbows made and bought in John Hovyngham's house 6s 8d]*, York (SS35/54); 1580 *for a dossion oxe bows xijd*, Stockeld (YRS161/25); 1614 *garthes, ox bowes, cogges, spindles*, Stockeld (YAJ34/177); 1617 *oxe bowes, wayne stowers, leashaftes*, Brandsby (NYRO44/139); 1622 *12 clapsoles and 9 oxebowes, 4 old stroakers*, Bingley (LRS1/56).

oxgang A measure or quantity of land. The word has an Old English origin and its equivalent under the Normans was 'bovate': 1506 *one oxgang of land … otherwise called a bouett of land*, Ripon (YRS51/78). Conventionally a carucate was an area that an ox team of eight animals might plough and the oxgang was considered to be the contribution of a single ox. In reality, the quantity varied from region to region: 1628 *what Acres an oxegange doth Conteyne we Cannot Certainlie sett downe but that it hath been reputed that xxtie acres goes to ann Oxegange*, Leeds (Th57/160). Moreover, the oxgang could be made up of selions located in different parts of the town fields: 1673 *to George Fish my sonne one halfe oxgange of land lyinge dispersed in the towne feild*, Brayton (YRS47/62). It could serve as a unit on which rates might be assessed and responsibilities and privileges allocated: 1621 *a common pasture belonging to Thwongestowne and there was to everye oxgange in that towne a parte of that pasture*, Netherthong (G-A). See also tether.

ox gate The OED has examples of this word as a Scottish equivalent of oxgang but that is not the meaning in Yorkshire where the 'gate' was a right for the ox to 'go' onto certain grazing lands. It was a right to pasturage: 1539 *de firma unius clausi … vocati Welborne Oxe-close in tenura diversorum tenentium … qui quidem tenentes habent inter se pasturam pro vj^xx bobus, Anglice vj^xx oxegates ibidem [In farm of a close … called Welborne Oxe-close in the tenure of various tenants … who have between them pasture for 6 score oxen there, in English ox gates]* (SS83/321). See also gate (2).

ox hide The skins or hides of oxen, important to both butchers and tanners:

> 1579 *By the consent as well of the tanners as by the bochers of this Citie, and diverse*
> *of theyme being present, it is now agreed that no bochers shall by any indirect meanes*
> *make any bargayne or put to sale any oxskynnes or cowe skynnes before the beast*
> *wherapon the said skyns ware growing shalbe killed, to any tanner … but to buye the*
> *same as the said oxen or kyne shalbe killed* (YRS119/7).

In 1730, a south Yorkshire tanner records in his diary his bargain of 26 August with
Mr Watson of South Sheilds, a butcher, *for all the ox hides he shall kill betwixt now and*
Christmas, weighing 5½ stone a pece, for 1s 11d per stone (SS65/298).

P

pace (1) The Christian festival of Easter: 1561 *In pace money vijs xd*, Richmond (SS26/149). It was a regional word, noted in the York Mystery Plays in 1440 (OED) and preserved in the Pace-egg plays, still acted out in Yorkshire and Lancashire. See also pasch.

pace (2) In the single reference noted it was probably a step:

> 1590 *wheras Thomas Graves haith layd and sett downe his pace and paving before his dwelling howse bothe higher and further out then the same ought to be … it is nowe agreed that he shall … cause the same pace and paving to be made level and equall with … his next neighbours*, York (YRS138/117).

pack cloth A coarse material used to wrap up the packs carried by pack animals, particularly wool: 1394–5 *Item pro xxvj ulnis canaby emptis pro pacclathis xijs iijd [Item for 26 ells of canvas bought for pack cloths 12s 3d]*, Whitby (SS72/621); 1539 *I witto John Taliour my sone all the wooll in the pake clothe with the pakclothe*, Woodkirk (Th19/11); 1642 *For selling of woll … It was weighed in the hall, the packe-cloath beinge layd against the skreene; it was weighed all in single stones*, Elmswell (DW33); 1742 *wool packed up in packs of canvas commonly called packcloth … stamped or marked on the outside with the word wool in large letters 3 inches in length*, Rawcliffe (QS1/81/7). See also packsaddle, wool pack.

pack–horse A horse used for carrying packs of goods: 1517 *To Thos Warde xls & a packe horse with all thynges to hym belonging*, Leeds (Th4/144); 1522 *a pakehors with all things belonging*, Sheffield (HPP64). The phrase 'all things belonging' occurred several times and it covered items such as overlay, packsaddle and wantow, all dealt with separately. See also packsaddle.

packhorse bridge For centuries, and certainly into the early nineteenth century, goods were transported by packhorses, occasionally in 'gangs' of 18 or more but perhaps more usually in small groups. They followed customary tracks and roads, up hill and down dale, crossing numerous rivers and streams en route, and yet there is no entry in the OED for the term 'pack-horse bridge'. It has been used frequently enough by transport historians in recent years, as when W. B. Crump wrote about 'causeys' and claimed that they 'originated, along with the pack-horse bridges, in the sixteenth century' (Crump31). Now, any bridge that is old and narrow and has a single arch is likely to find itself described as a packhorse bridge. There were alternative words: bridlesty bridge was recorded in 1688 (QS1/27/1) and 'horse bridge' was quite frequent from the late sixteenth century. In 1598, the West Riding magistrates ordered the inhabitants of Trumfleet and Thorpe to *make the horse bridge sufficient between trumfleete Marshe and thorpe Marshe … upon payne of xls* (YRS3/129). The context suggests that this may have been a causeway, but the term occurs in all three Ridings after that date and some of the bridges so described seem likely to have been what we now call packhorse bridges. 'Evill-slack bridge' in Skelton near York was also a 'horse bridge' in 1606 (NRQS1/35). A later word was 'pack and prime bridge', recorded in

1798 but probably much older, since the term 'pack and prime way' is on record from 1628. See also bridlesty bridge, foot bridge, horse-bridge.

packing house A place where packs were prepared for transportation by pack-horses: 1672 *five stone of hempe stolen out of his packing house in Skipton … did not know who to suspect but Jonas Paite called on to justifie the selling of 2 overlaies for pack-sadles … confessed* (QS1/11/4).

packing shop Part of the retail premises of John Taylor, a Gomersal merchant: 1779 *stable, hay chamber, a packing-shop, a counting house and warehouse* (MD292/30).

packing ware See pack ware.

packman A man who makes a living by selling goods from a pack which he carries from place to place, a pedlar. I have found no examples of the word in Yorkshire sources but the by-name is on record from *c*.1160 (R&W) and minor place-names are also evidence of its use: 1625 *Buried … a poore traveller dying at Brampton hige* [high?] *packman gate 29 Sept*, Wath upon Dearne (PR).

pack prick A skewer, probably made of wood, an item first mentioned in 1430 (see packsaddle). It secured the pack cloth in which goods were wrapped: 1718 *can do nothing for a livelihood save onely a few packpricks*, West Riding (QS1/59/2). See also net prick, prick (1).

packsaddle A saddle adapted for supporting a pack to be carried by a pack-animal: 1398 *unum equum optimum … et j paksadyll [a best horse … and 1 pack saddle]*, York (SS4/250); 1430 *Et Adæ famulo meo sellas vocatas paksadyls, pakclathes, pakprykkes [And to my servant Adam saddles called packsaddles, pack cloths, pack pricks]*, York (SS30/9); 1549 *I bequeathe vnto John Chrashelaye … one horse and paksadle, one paire of hampers, a teylde, with all other thinges belonginge vnto a packhorse*, Wakefield (Th19/230); 1680 *I met a man riding on an horse and driving two horses before him with pack-saddles on, yet empty*, Northowram (OH4/20); 1713 *Four Little Gallowaies with four old Pack saddles sursingles Wanties and Panyers for Coal Carriage*, Sheffield (HPP64). See also packing house, teld.

pack sheet A sheet of cloth used for packing up goods that were to be transported: 1703 *coarse wooll black wooll, pack sheets, 3 packs of wooll*, Holmfirth (IH); 1731 *new wolle, a packshet*, Austerfield (QS1/70/7). The Rev. Lewthwaite wrote in the Newsome parish magazine for 1882 that he knew of *many a dish of trout caught in a pack sheet*, Almondbury. See also pack cloth.

packthread Stout thread, employed especially to secure packsheets, but with a variety of additional uses: 1371 *In pakthred empto pro celura, 5d [For packthread bought for the canopy, 5d]*, York (SS35/11); 1399–1400 *Et in pacthrede emp. pro prædictis organis 3d [And for packthread bought for the aforesaid organs, 3d]*, Ripon (SS81/132); 1473 *Pro greas, tallow et pakthred pro carpentariis [For grease, tallow and packthread for the carpenters]*, York (SS35/82); 1534–5 *Item hare and pakthreid, jd*, York (CCW164); 1617 *Ribboning 9d, Tape, 6½ yards 1s 0d … Packthridd 2d*, Elmswell (DW160–1).

pack up To cease trading, to place goods in a pack and be ready for departure:

> 1596 *All forren butchers that bring any dead victuals to the Market to sell shall not open any pack or show any victuals before 12 o'clock that the bell be ronge. And likewise to pack up at 4 o'clock when the bell shall be rung again*, Beverley (YRS84/63).

pack ware, packingware A type of coarse cloth made in York, as defined in the references given here: 1474–5 *no brother of the said fellyshipp shall bye no clothe of Yorke makynge that is called pak ware but if it hald in length xxviij yerdes and in bred two yerdes* (SS129/65); 1484 *course cloth called packyng ware shalbe perfitly made in length and breed … xxviij yerds in length … and in breed ij yerds,* York (YRS98/94).

pageant A wheeled stage or platform used in the open air performances of the mystery plays: 1394 *quod omnes pagine Corporis Christi ludent in locis antiquitus assignatis [that all the Corpus Christ pageant plays in their places designated of old],* York (SS120/47); 1467 *payd ijd pykes and gret nayles for the axeltre, and burdes and nales and warkmanship to the grete paujand xxd,* York (SS129/63); 1500 *And the cartwryghts to make iiij new wheles to the said pagiaunt,* York (YRS103/162). See also red leather, turner.

pain A threatened penalty or fine, to be paid for an offence. It is found from an early date in manorial court rolls, where the threatened 'pains' were listed, originally in Latin. It could be a noun or a verb: 1549 *Item pena posita est qd [Item a pain was laid that …] … or Item penat' est qd [Item a pain was laid that …] …* Lepton (DD/WBM). English examples of the word are less common: *c.*1488 *commaundyng them … to appere before youre highnes … at a certen day upon a certen peyn as shalbe lymyted,* Markington (YRS41/6); 1584 *under a payne to repaire their porcons of the said damme,* Wakefield (WCR4/32); 1688 *Paines layd by the Constable and sworn men,* Holme (WCR13/164).

pain-demaine See maine bread.

painful Of a person it was 'painstaking', a complimentary reference to the care and attention bestowed on a task: 1613 'free … to serve in any office … they having been long *industrous and painefull* members of the House', Hull (YRS116/57); 1642 *often-times a painfull fellowe will not refuse to stooke after 7 or 8 sythes, if the binders will but doe soe much as throwe him in the sheaves,* Elmswell (DW56).

painted cloth In the Tudor period the walls of wealthy families were hung with tapestries, partly for ornament but also no doubt to exclude draughts. We are less familiar with the term 'painted cloths', items which may have been a cheaper substitute but served a similar function: the images often had a religious theme. They feature in many inventories in the sixteenth century but the term is recorded earlier in Latin: 1392 *lego … meliorem pannum meum pictatum [I bequeath … my better painted cloth],* York (SS4/173). Such items were among goods imported from Veere in the Low Countries: 1483 *3 pannis depictis £1 [for 3 painted cloths £1];* 1490 *a dos' pantyd clothys,* Hull (YRS144/196,203). They were also used in churches: 1498 *Item ij awterclothes peynted price iijs,* Wakefield: these were recorded in the chantry chapel on the bridge (YAJ15/93).

Some references provide us with details of the paintings, as in the inventory of the goods in St William's Chapel on Ouse Bridge: 1509 *ij curtyns longyng to the hie alter of rede payntid damaske wark … ij alter clothes and ij curtyns of white damaske flowers payntid … ij olde alter clothes payntid with rede and ij curtyns for the werk day,* York (YRS106/29–30). In Sir Thomas Wentworth's house at Bretton in 1542 were numerous expensive tapestries, and *hanginges … of red say with two paynted clothes fixed on the same, on* [one] *of our lady of pitie and thother of mary mawdelen* (YRS134/2). Cushions and bankers were also painted and the custom survived into the late seventeenth century at least: 1550 *old payntid clothes 12d,* Richmond (YRS152/78); 1628 *4 old paynted cushyons, 2s 6d,* Pudsey (LRS1/76); 1684 *2 pented quishens,* Cartworth (G-A). See also stained.

painter An artist who painted images on cloth, wood, etc. The by-name continued to be active well into the sixteenth century: 1399–1400 *Et in salario Johannis Payntour* *pictantis j magnum vale ad cooperiendum crucem stantem infra corpus ecclesiæ … ij alias ymagines [And for John Payntour's pay for painting 1 great veil for covering the cross standing in the nave of the church … and 2 other images]*, Ripon (SS81/129); 1439 *to David Paynter for xxiiij baners peyntyng wyth canvas langyng thereto and peyntyng of vj castyls, xs*, York (SS129/49); 1522 *empcione stuffuræ pro le paynting cum vadimonia Thomæ Payntour pro pictura prædicti operis hoc anno [for buying painting equipment with pledges to Thomas Payntour for the painting of the said work this year]*, Ripon (SS81/182). In 1421–2, *David Payntour* of the *payntourcrafte* in York was working with the stainers for a Corpus Christi play (SS125/103).

pair Often used of single things where the perception is that two or more parts are involved: 1548 *a paire of jeate beades*, Bishop Burton (SS106/272); 1573 *ad quoddam forgam vocat' a paire of Smythies [at that forge called …]*, Honley (YDK85); 1588 *one paire of lowmbes, one paire of heldes and one slaye*, Dalton (DD/WBW/19); 1655 *desired a little parcel of land of the waste … for building a pair of staires*, Leeds (Th9/75). See also bodies.

pairater, pariter, paritor Abbreviated spellings of apparitor, an officer of an ecclesiastical or civil court: 1570 *The obligacon & to the pairater vjs viijd*, South Cave (Kaner72); 1671 *spent upon the pariter which brought the book of artickles 6d*; 1674 *paid to Aparitor*, Bradford (BAS3/482,486); 1743 *In the terrier and to the parretor 8s 0d*, Kirby Underdale (HKU152).

pale, pale-board 'Pale' would have been used initially for the vertical pieces of wood in a fence, especially of a medieval deer park, but it then came to mean the fence itself: 1505 *beilded a palle betwixte the said Parke and woode*, Healaugh (YRS92/198); 1524 *all the wode within the new payle that is newlye theyr made, as it is set and founded*, Moor Monkton (YRS50/125). Interesting details are found in documents which related to a recently created park near Leeds: it was described in 1600 as *all that parke or grounde inclosed with a Paille … commonly called Beeston parke*, and a lease of 1597 reserved to the landlord *libertie to sett stayes or Proppes and to repayre the Pale … at all times*: the land on the outside of the pale, which made such maintenance possible, was referred to in 1589 as *le paile walke* (WYL160/129/4).

The term pale-board seems likely to have developed as a result of the changed meaning of 'pale': 1489 *shall not take payle boordes upon payne of 3s 4d* (CHT126); 1528 *Item to a slede man for carryng of payll bordes, ijd*, York (CCW131); 1624 *take no Pallbordes out of the Pall of Hunesworthe Parke* (DD/SR/1/6/14). The transcription of a document in Latin is evidence that the practice has a much longer history: 1315 'Richard del Bothem, pale setter in Stanley wood, 12d for not making an adequate paling' (YRS57/99).

pale boot The right to take wood to be used as pales, noted once only, as *paleboote* in a Cawthorne lease of 1626 (OC7). See also boot (1).

paled Marked with stripes, probably vertical like 'pales': 1306 *j lectum de serico paleato cum rubeo et nigro [1 bed cover of red and black striped silk]*, Raby (SS2/39); 1414 *cum costeris paled de colore rubeo viridi et albo [with red green and white striped side curtains]*, Middleham (SS2/70); 1423 *et meliore say, viridi, palyd et brod [and the better silk, green, striped and broad]*, York (SS45/69). See also sindon.

paler A workman employed to set up a pale: 1581 *payd to pallors for palinge & dychinge ix acres on halfe acres & halfe on rode*, Stockeld (YRS161/24). See also pale.

palership, palisership These are rare terms which I have not seen listed elsewhere. In 1490, two officers of Blansby Park near Pickering, in the Duchy of Lancaster, were

at variance over *the palership of* the said park and the judgement was that the responsibility belonged to the master of the game, not the keeper (NRR1/124). Alternative
spellings occur in documents which in 1553 were concerned with the rights and titles
of *the keepership, bowberership and palastershipe of the parke of Spofforde* (YRS76/142) and
in 1607 with the fees of *the pallisershippe of Bilton parke* (YAJ35/423). See also paliser.

palfrey–man A person in charge of the palfreys or saddle horses, a well-documented
by-name which was active into the fifteenth century at least and also gave rise
to surnames: 1301 *De Willelmo Palefreyman, vjd*, Pickhill (YRS21/2); 1381 *Joseph
Palfrayman*, Scorborough (PTER228); 1404–5 'And he has delivered to John *Palfayman*
for the fodder of the horses in the lord abbot's stable', Selby (SAR147). See GRDict.

palis A fence made of pales; an alternative to 'pale': 1468 *the uphaldinge ande making
of the forsaide pales*, York (SS85/19); 1479 *concessio custodiæ palasij circa parcum nostrum
Ripon, vulgariter nuncupati Paleses [the grant of oversight of the fences around our park of
Ripon, commonly named palises]* (SS78/161). It gave rise to a number of minor place-
names, including Palace House near Hebden Bridge: a rental of 1536 has *the palys called
Palishous* and the allusion is said to be to the pale which surrounded Erringden Park
(PNWR3/189). In the early thirteenth century, Adam de Bestun granted to Kirkstall
Abbey four acres of meadow in Beeston *quod dicitur pratum del Paliz [that is called the
meadow of the Paliz]* (Th8/245): its local name was *Palis Henge* [ing] (PNWR3/220).
In 1669 Thomas Morritt of Brayton died at *Pallice Field House* (YRS47/117).

paliser The man responsible for the 'pale' or 'palis' of the medieval park, usually
said to be either the woodman who made the palings or the officer who managed
the park. It is one of several spellings and the term is first recorded as a by-name:
1315 *Roger Paleser*, Stanley (YRS78/39); 1379 *Robertus Palycer*, Brearton (PTWR).
Examples of the occupational term include: 1488–9 *Johannes Conceytt … Forestarius
dicti Leonis Percy et palicer de Blandesby [John Conceytt … forester of the said Leo Percy
and paliser of Brandesby]* (NRR1/145); 1516 *George Myllet, servaunte unto my said lords
grace, and palasoure of the parke of Beverlay* (BTD137); 1622 *Pallisor et Keeper de Blandsbie*
(NRR2/10). The wood-worker responsible for making the 'palis' had a distinctive
by-name: 1379 *Willlmus Palycemaker*, Arkendale (PTWR). See also keeper, pale,
palership, palis.

pampilion The OED gives two meanings for 'pampilion', the first as a word for fur,
of unknown origin but possibly from an unidentified animal: the second as the name
of a coarse woollen fabric, derived from one of two similar place-names in France and
Spain. As a word for fur it dates from the fifteenth century and Veale suggested that it
was 'lambskins presumably from Pampeluna, the capital of Navarre' (EMV217). As a
fabric it is on record from the sixteenth century when pampilion was characteristically
used for trimming garments. A definition offered by John Brierley, a cloth frizzer in
Wakefield in 1761, throws light on its later meaning:

> *A sort of hair cloath called pompilion in Yorkshire itt is made of that cow hair wich
> comes of salted hides. Itt is a sort of strong stapled hair and free from lime or dirt but calf
> hair has the finest staple to make cloath. Cloath on pompilion is made like wadding
> and is used for to lay shear boards with all in Yorkshire* (YRS155/101).

It was actually a traditional material in the West Riding and some of the points made
by John Brearley appear in a much earlier reference. In 1538, complaints were made
by a number of Wakefield men that *dyvers persons byeth nawtte herre of the tannerrs and
sells it to Cendell men to blende it with woile and make cloth of it called pawmpillzon cloth*

(WCR9/86). The complainants were saddlers who were objecting to hawkers selling *unlawfull ledder* so the inference may be that 'pampilion' was being used in some of the products, perhaps as wadding in saddles, although saddles were not actually mentioned. It seems possible though that 'animal hair' in these references may link the two quite distinct meanings offered in the OED.

That is not the first reference to this word in Yorkshire sources for it occurs as the specific element in a minor place-name more than two centuries earlier: *Pampellion Holme* was an enclosure held by the Earl of Surrey in 1316, located in Thornes which formed part of Wakefield parish (YRS63/156). It is explained by Smith as deriving from a nickname but I find no evidence for such a name locally. However, examples occur in other counties, notably in East Anglia: 1310 *John Pampiloun*, Suffolk (R&W); 1381 *William and John Pamphilonn*, High Easter in Essex (PT). This does not clear up the origin of the word which may have to be looked for much earlier than has been thought.

pan It has more than one meaning and in some late examples was a 'panel', a square, timber framework filled in with bricks or plaster (OED). More usually it was the horizontal timber along the top of a wall which received the ends of the rafters, although the evidence is not always explicit: 1284 'one *pannepece* of oak, 40ft long', Scarborough (SZ1/203); 1420 *in hys tenement in Coppergate … walles … fra the grunde uppe to the panne*, York (SS85/15); 1501 *the sparrez & tymbre … is shot & hyngeth over the ground … by viij ynchez and more anenst the pan of his house*, York (SS85/22); 1519 *stayd with proppes haldyng up the pannes*, Bishop Burton (SS35/271); 1576 *for a dogg of yron nayled on the joynynge of two pannes in the new house*, York (SS35/116); 1682 *well wrought roof … with pans or wall plates*, Scriven (YAJ16/112); 1739 *2 pann pieces 22 yards in length*, Lofthouse (QS1/80/1).

The term 'post and pan' has a long history: 1341 *et les pannes et les postes au tizon seront de leaese et espesse solonc le scanteloune fait entre les parties*, Brandsby (SZ1/595); 1617 *stronge poasts and pannes*, Brandsby (NYRO44/139); 1619–21 *an auntient howse buylte upon timber or postes and pan*, Pickering (NRR1/27). See also sole, wallplate.

panch, paunch As a verb it means to cut open the paunch or belly of an animal and take out the entrails, together with the heart, liver, lungs, etc. (OED). In Yorkshire the examples are found in the records of the Quarter Sessions: 1670 *founde a doe hid in a bush … and there hee pansht her*, Barnsley (QS1); 1675 *they found the belly and the guts of a sheepe greene and newly paunch't, for it did not smell at all*, Slaidburn (QS1/14). The noun referred to what was removed: 1670 *one or two sheep panches new put in the midding on the backside*, Kirkby Malzeard (QS1). A fourteenth-century by-name points to a much earlier use of the word, proably a nickname: 1312–13 *Symoni Paunche pellipario* [skinner] *viijs*, Bolton Priory (YRS154/346).

pane As a noun a 'pane' was a distinct portion of a garment or piece of cloth, set alongside other panes or strips, possibly of different colours. To 'pane' was to make up such an item: c.1537 *hanged with fyne say paned and fringed with borders*, Halifax (YRS45/188); 1565 *quyshens of silke xxxs … two panyd with tawney sattan … two panyd with yellowe velvett*, Temple Newsam (YAJ25/95). See also overstocks.

panel (1) A section or compartment of woodland set out to be felled: 1574 *division into panels or fells* [sic], Sheffield (HS13). See also fall (2).

panel (2) Used adjectivally of a chest made of thin boards, similar in meaning therefore to wainscot chest: 1640–1 *one panill chiste*, Hampsthwaite (SS110/176).

panel (3) The protective pad under the load-saddle of a pack horse: 1377–8 *In j panell[o] emp[to] per eundem viijd [Item for 1 panel bought by the same man 8d]*, Bolton Priory (YRS154/567); 1394–5 *Item pro ij panels et j howse ad sellas nostras iijs vjd [Item for 2 panels and 1 house for our saddles 3s 6d]*, Whitby (SS72/601); 1581 *one old saddell with panels*, Anston (G-A); 1587 *certayn tethers & bandes 1 pecke skepe a pannyll*, South Cave (Kaner136); 1614 *2 load sadles panelled, ouerleys, wantoes*, Stockeld (YAJ34/178); 1642 *On market-dayes our folkes … give to every 2 horses a bottle of hey and that serveth them till theire pannells bee sette on*, Elmswell (DW107); 1692 *Two hackney saddles three pannells and garthes … two wantowes*, Worsbrough (HPP67). See also crutch (1), pillion.

pannage A word of French origin which had several related shades of meaning. It could refer to swine fodder such as acorns or beech mast, in which sense Chaucer used it *c.*1374 (OED) or it could be the right to pasture swine in the forest. Finally it was often the payment made for that privilege. In 1245–6, for example, Thomas de Auno had pannage in his woods at Burneston valued at 6d (YRS12/3). In Pickering, in 1250–1, the tenants had mast for their swine without paying 'pannage': *et pessonem ad porcos suos sine pannagio reddendo [and the mast for his/her/their pigs without paying pannage]* (NRR1/1). See also estover, stower.

pannier-maker A maker of panniers: 1358 *Joh. de Cotingham, paignermaker*, York (SS96/53); 1472 *Item that oone panyermaker houses & harbers suspect persones in his hous*, Selby (SS85/25); 1614 *Fr. Harwood, pannier-maker*, Egton (NRQS2/64). See also pannierman.

pannierman In theory this word might refer to any hawker or tradesman who carried his wares in panniers, but in Yorkshire it was used principally of fishmongers who operated from the eastern half of the county. Panniers were said *c.*1300 to be made 'to beren fish inne' (OED) and the early link between fishermen and panniermen is clear-cut: in 1467, traders in Beverley were referred to as *piscarii viz. panzaremen*; that is fishermen or panniermen (BTD58): in 1468 *Ricardus Pannyerman, fisher* was granted the right to trade in York (SS96/188). The link with east-coast fishing towns was often specific: 1476 *de Thoma Webster de Sywardby* [Sewerby], *Fisher alias panyerman*, York (YHB24); 1553 *William Storie, Skardburghe, panyerman* (YRS11/169); 1558 *John Storrie, Bridlington, panyer man* (YRS14/155). In fact, 'pannierman' as a by-name survived over several centuries: 1301 *de Thoma le Paynerman*, Skelton (YRS21/37); 1486–7 *Elizabeth Ricardby, wife of Thomas Panyerman of Filey* (YRS103/3). In 1522, the will of a prosperous merchant called Robert Skyrley cancelled the debts of *Robert Panyerman*, and this is almost certainly a reference to the man's occupation and not his surname (SS79/154). Throughout much of that period the men who were selling the fish had probably caught them also.

The emergence of the pannierman as a middleman may be implicit in that relationship between Robert Skyrley and Robert Panyerman, and it is explicit in 1583 when reference was made to licences granted to panniermen *to buy and Carye fish from the sea syde contrary to the Custome* (NRR1/251). These panniermen may not have been fishermen but the two occupations had strong family links. The saying 'Mock no panyer-men your father was a fisher' dates to before 1678 (EDD), and a study of family names along the coast points to such connections much earlier. John Skirlay of Hornsea Beck *fyscherman* died in 1512 (YRS6/151) and William Skyrlay of Hornsea Beck, *fyschmonger* in 1503 (YRS6/152): these two men seem certain to have belonged to the same family as the merchant Robert Skyrley, mentioned above, who left lands *at Hornsebeke* to his son in his will. There are similar links in the Storry family.

From that time therefore, the panniermen were small merchants who met incoming fishermen at the coast and purchased their catch. They loaded the fish into panniers on the backs of horses and then made their way inland, to major markets across the region (EDD). In a Starchamber case in 1534 the plaintiff Robert Goldsborough stated 'that he was a fishmonger as well for the … town of Pontefract' as for other market towns and 'Commonly every market day he conveyed fresh fish from the sea to Pontefract and brought it into the market place to sell' (YRS41/140). The Panniermens Causeway in North Yorkshire serves to remind us of the routes used by these men.

pan piece See pan.

pant In parts of Scotland and northern England the 'pant' was a public fountain or water supply and the earliest reference is in 1661 in Northumberland. In Cumberland, Lancashire and Westmorland it was more commonly the word for a cesspit or sump, especially the pool below a midden or dung-heap and the gutter down which waste water flowed. The word was used also at Spurn and along Yorkshire's east coast for pools left by unusually high tides (EDD). Where it occurs in the place-names Pant Head (Austwick) and Pant Foot (Ingleton), it seems likely to have had the Cumbrian meaning. Smith suggested that these two names, and similar examples in Westmorland, derive from Welsh *pant* which means valley but the origin remains unknown (OED).

pantable, pantocle Spellings of 'pantofle', that is a slipper or any kind of loose, indoor shoe: it could also be used of overshoes that were worn outdoors (OED). The word became frequent in the latter part of the sixteenth century: 1573 *j paire pantocles*, Gilling (SS26/241); 1585–7 *To Randall Webbe, shoemaker, in parte payment of his bill for bootes, shoes, pinsons and pantables* (HPP58); 1596 'Every cordiner or jerkin maker who shall *shapp, cutt* or make … *buskinges, pantables* or slippers', Beverley (YRS84/74). In Beverley in 1627, the cordwainers' searchers had the job *at least once a month* of checking *all boots, shoes, pantables and other wares* (YRS84/79).

pantry Originally the place where bread was stored but then a more general provision room: 1528 *In the Pantree*, York (SS79/254). By-names provide the earliest examples: 1266 *Thomas de la Panetrie*, York (YRS17/30); 1381 *Robertus del Pantry*, Cottingham (PTER219).

papejoy, papenye, papingay Typical spellings of popinjay, an old word for a parrot. Images of the bird were popular in tapestries and decorative material: 1380 *unum vestimentum album, braudatum cum compass' et infra compass' papingays [one white vestment embroidered with circles and within the circles papingays]*, York (SS4/111); 1390 *unum lectum cum tapete de viridi et albo cum papenyes [a bed with a green and white counterpane with papenyes]*, Skeckling (ERAS10/2); 1414 *ij worsted beddes … unum rubeum et alterum embroded cum j papejoy cum celuris [2 worsted bedspreads … one red and the other embroidered with 1 papejoy together with canopies]*, Pontefract (SS4/375); 1444 *cum tapeto operato cum papynjoys [with a counterpane worked with papingays]*, Beverley (SS30/107).

paper For press papers, that is sheets of paper placed between the folds of cloth in preparation for transportation: 1618 *papers for papering clothe & two prasse boards, xxijs*, Bingley (LRS1/54); 1641 *two pair of lombes, one sheare boarde, one pair of cloth sheares with the papers and handles*, Fulstone (PR1/248n). See also press paper.

papingay, papynjoy See papejoy.

parcer See parser.

parchmenter, parchmentmaker Makers of parchment. In *c.*1395, these craftsmen were in the same guild as glovers and tanners: 1301 *Thomas le Parcheminer,* York (YRS21/119); 1349 *Rob. de Habton, parcheminer,* York (SS96/48); 1465 *William Whyte, parchementmakere,* Beverley (YRS111/25); 1488 *Thomas Holgyll, parchiemyner,* York (SS96/213); 1550 *John Burland, parchementmaker,* York (YRS11/30).

parchment lace A kind of lace, braid or cord, the core of which was parchment: 1558 *in silke parchennett laice ijs … a dussand of parchment crulis vd,* Patrick Brompton (SS26/126); 1621 *8 cloakes with gould parchment lace 2 rownd about and 5 about the coller for liveryes … bought on Mr Marshall draper,* Brandsby (NYRO44/217).

parclose A partition, screen or railing, which served to enclose or shut off a space in a building: 1422 *the perclose that standys betwixt the entre and the shop,* York (SS85/16); 1505 *dorez, wyndowez, glase and other perclosez … and almaner thing long to every house,* York (YRS106/13); 1536–7 *for making of a parclose in ys hye chawmer ijs viijd,* York (CCW182); *c.*1538 *the same hall is closed at the southe end with a parclose of bordes,* Esholt (YAJ9/323).

pare To take the top sods off the land: 1694 *for pareing the grounde where the bricks are to be made,* Tong (Tong/4d/3). When land was being prepared for cultivation, the sods were burnt so that the ashes enriched the soil: it was a practice that seems to have gathered momentum in the eighteenth century: 1755 *Some sour, marshy grounds are made arable by spading the turf from the surface and then burning it in heaps. This is called Pairing and burning,* Mirfield (WDP1/192). The practice was discouraged in some manors: 1742 *if any person grave and burn any turf or sods … in order to convert the same into tillage, 3s 4d,* Meltham (G-A); 1749 *not to pair, flee or burn any of the surface or swarth of any of the closes,* Calverley (MM82).

parget To cover a wall with plaster; to decorate a plastered surface. The occupational by-name is on record in East Anglia from 1207 (R&W) but Yorkshire references are scarce: *c.*1570 *he dyd pargett and whyte the topps of the chambers,* Woodsome (KayeCP). The alternative spelling 'pargen' has been noted in co. Durham from 1449–50 and later in York: 1541–2 *settyng up off wallys and pargenyng xv^s x^d,* York (CCW238).

parish bridge This was a bridge that served only the local community and had to be maintained at the parish's expense. Local people were sometimes successful in having the status changed so that the Wapentake or Riding shared the cost. In 1683, for example, Cottingley Bridge was described as a useful bridge, lying *in the direct … waine roade from Kighley to Bradford … formerly a parish bridge* (QS1/22/5).

parishing A regional word, apparently an alternative of 'parish': 1436 *geven to xiij pure folke in ilke parisshyn underwretyn xiijd,* York (SS30/217); 1487 *in the said parisshing of Saint Elyn,* York (YRS103/4); 1511 *To the well of my parishyng iijs,* Leeds (SS79/24); 1524 *William Hall of the paryshynge of Pannall* (SS104/19); 1549 *I George Cowtus of the parischyng of Westerdayll* (YRS74/49); 1593 *I geve unto the poore of the parishing … 13s 4d,* Felliscliffe (SS104/194).

pariter, paritor See apparitor, pairater.

park The word has a French origin and was brought here by the Normans. It is now associated with recreational facilities and industrial complexes but it was originally an enclosed tract of land reserved for beasts of the chase, and held by royal grant. It was distinct from a 'forest', not least because it was enclosed by a deer-proof pale, and Blansby Park which lies within Pickering Forest is an example of that distinction. The place-name Blansby is evidence of a Scandinavian settlement but in the Domesday survey it already had the status of a 'berewick', as a demesne farm attached to Pickering. That relationship continued after the Conquest, when the castle was built and the surrounding district converted into Royal Forest. A memorandum in the records of the Duchy of Lancaster states that *A Parke taken out of a Forrest may ly within and bee surrounded by the Forrest … and yet be no part of the forest* (NRR1/94). Blansby was probably a separate reserve from the early twelfth century, and an inquisition of 1251–2 details its links with Pickering, touching on the customs and rights that tenants had in the Forest in the time of King John: it was expressly stated that the *haya de Blaundeby*, that is the territory within the enclosure, did not belong to the manor, and the men of Pickering were not even allowed 'housbote' there. It is referred to as *le Parkes de Blandesby* in a petition in the reign of Henry III (NRR3/242) and an extent of the king's lands in Pickering in 1297–8 listed 'the park of *Blaundebi*', with agistment worth 100s p.a. and meadow 40s (YRS31/73). Income from what was essentially a deer park clearly included profits from the sale of hay and grazing rights for live-stock.

Parks remained a landscape feature for centuries and are regularly mentioned in manorial documents:

> 1584 *a few old doted trees which are good for nothing except it be for the fire, which underwood and old doted trees do grow within her Majesty's park of Almonburie* (MS205); 1599 *all that great Close of land Wood and pasture Commonlye called Roydes hall parke … parcel of the landes belongeinge to the Capitall Messuage called Rodes hall*, North Bierley (MMA/249).

See also herbage, pale, palership, palis, paliser.

parker A man in charge of a park. The by-name is recorded in Domesday Book, and Reaney quotes other very early examples (R&W). Yorkshire references include: *c.*1244 *Ego Hugo Parcarius de Pontefracto* (YRS30/329); 1258 *David percarius*, Rothwell; *Adam Parcur*, Kippax (YRS12/58,64); 1310–11 *De Roberto le Parkour xls*, Bolton Priory (YRS154/289). In 1390, when Sir Philip Darcy sold woods in Aislaby which included *le Oldepark* it was required of the purchaser that everything should be done 'at the view of the parker' (YRS102/1). In 1516, the archbishop of York granted to Miles and John Staveley 'the office of parker of his park of Rypon' (YRS102/103).

parkin Parkin is still a popular cake in Yorkshire, traditionally associated with Bonfire night: 1729 *her Mistress did persuade her to ask Sarah Priestley … to steale meal from her master to make a parkin on*, Elland (QS1/68/4). The parkin 'pigs' made for that occasion have currents for eyes, or 'curn een'. According to Peter Brears the earlier parkins were thin oatmeal cakes, baked directly on the 'bakstone', and it was the use of ovens and bicarbonate of soda from the mid-nineteenth century that led to the modern parkin. Treacle or golden syrup was an essential ingredient and references to its use date from the early 1700s. The origin remains obscure and it is tempting to link the word with 'Parkin' as a pet form of Peter, or with Parkin as a surname. However, no evidence for such an origin has been discovered. See also treacle.

parpoint The regional spelling of 'parpen', a stone with two smooth, vertical faces which passes through the thickness of a wall. A parpoint wall was a partition: 1657 *shall raise a parpointe wall of a yard high for battlements*, Barden Tower (Whit2/239); 1739 *parpoint wall … at 6s a rood*, Lofthouse (QS1/80/1); 1812 *Paid James Pickles for Parpoints 6s 6d*, Meltham (G-A); 1830 *12 yd of Parpoints from Dean*, South Crosland (GRD).

parretor See pairater.

parrock An early spelling of paddock: 1641 *all the doles and parrocks of land belonging,* Fulstone (PR1/248n); 1696 *two parrocks or little closes of land in Bradford, near …* *Sill-briggs* (LRS2/137). Paddock as a district in Huddersfield is now an established place-name but this is a relatively recent spelling: 1568 *Edmond Hyrst of Parockfote*; 1625 *Parockfoote mill*; 1768 *Parrockfoot alias Paddock Foot* (HPN109). Paddock has been described as a corruption of parrock, another form of park: 1729 *the paddock or parrock called Butt-paddock*, Dalton Travers (NRQS9/107n).

parser An obsolete spelling of 'piercer', that is a tool or instrument for piercing or boring holes. The earliest references occur in connection with coopers and masons: 1400 *duo parsures, unum spigot, wymbill, unum thixtill*, York (SS4/265); 1498 *ij les parsors pro cementariis [2 parsers for the masons]*, York (SS35/92); 1541–2 *Item for a parser, jd*, York (CCW236); 1589 *2 iron wedges a parcer*, South Cave (Kaner156). See also bowsaw, gauge, parser bitt.

parser bitt The bit of a 'parser' or boring tool: 1576 *ij percer bitts*, Aske (SS26/261); 1692 *one chezell, two fyles, one gimlet … a parsey bitt*, New Malton (NRQS9/4). In 1567, in the inventory of Sir George Conyers were *v wombles iiij percers bittes and a brace*, Harpurley (SS2/268).

parsneb A spelling of parsnip: 1628 *half the parsneb garth*, Abbotside (YRS130/49).

pasch The Christian festival of Easter: 1495 *Agreed that the buchers … for that they had not flesche on the synod day next after pasche … shal pay unto the Chamberleyns v^{li}*, York (YRS103/121); 1518–19 *Item for a seyke of sharkoll for Pash evyn iiijd*, York (CCW68); 1539 *weshyng the curche [sic] clothis at Cristenmas 4d; and the same at Pashe*, Sheriff Hutton (YAJ36/183); 1548–9 *Item paid for a torche off vj^{li} and di. aganst Pashe day, xiij^{d}*, York (CCW331). See also pace (1).

pash A crash or heavy fall: 1677 *as I was preaching there was suddenly a pash of a chamber floore down into the room*, Northowram (OH3/149). The verb was to smash or cause to break by a violent movement: 1736 *Joseph Vickars … had struck up his heels and had like to have pash't out his brains*, Bradford (QS1/75/6).

passage A narrow entry which gives access to or from a house or row of houses: 1735 *they ran down a narrow passage adjoyning the said house, into the street*, Wakefield (QS1/74/4). In 1762, a way in Almondbury that gave access to several houses and even to adjoining closes was described as *All the long entry or passage* (DD/R/M/7). See also entry.

paste board A board on which pastry was prepared: 1614 *Pastry – ij past boards*, Stockeld (YAJ34/175). In such inventories the 'pastry' was a room: 1565 *Pasterie. One bultinge table & knedinge troughe iijs iiijd*, Temple Newsam (YAJ25/98); 1617 *and in the Pastrie a kimlin & five shilves*, Ripley (YAJ34/201).

pastry See paste board.

pasture master A town official with responsibility for the common pastures: 1533 *that the common pasture of Knaismyer be oons in a moneth dryvin by the pasturemaisters*, York (YRS106/165); 1536 *agreyd that John Wedderall shalbe pasture mayster of the … common of Knaysmyer and to tayke in all geyst … to the common profet of this citie … shall have yerely in fee for excercisyng of the seyd rowme of pasture master fowre marks*, York (YRS108/1); 1644 *pasture maisters to have … as formerly hath beene … every one of them a horssegaite*, Scarborough (NYRO49/36); 1671 'The Pasture Masters of Westwood, Swinemoor and Figholme … ordered to account for their receipts & payments', Beverley

(YRS84/152); 1792 *The pasture masters of Westwood empowered to make such plantations … as they shall think proper*, Beverley (YRS122/75). See also drive (2).

pate A regional word for the badger: 1743 *Pd to John Kirby for a pate head* [sic] *and two foumarts 1s 8d*, Kirby Underdale (HKU152). See also bawson, brock, gray (3).

patlet A ruff or band worn round the neck. The word is on record from *c.*1500 and in early examples the fabric was often velvet: 1532 *to my aunnte … my velvett patlett*, Seacroft (Th11/48); 1559 *a petticote and a pattelet of velvet*, Treeton (YAJ17/365). In 1522, Robert Skyrley of Doncaster bequeathed *a patlett of velvett* to Agnes Bukton and his *velvett jacket* to Laurence Foster, *to make his childer pattelettes and cuyffes* (SS79/153–4). References in the early seventeenth century include: 1615 *iij patlets and iij course bendes*, items bequeathed by Walter Morvell of Bingley to his sister (LRS1/24). See also safeguard.

patron An early spelling of pattern: it occurred several times in founders' inventories where it clearly referred to a model or mould of the objects they produced: 1492 *To William myn apprentice … vj bell fete patrones*, York (SS53/78); 1512 *Item xxj ladill and scomer patrons*; 1516 *Item … vj floure patrons*, York (SS79/36,79). See also wood pattern.

pattener A maker of pattens, a type of footwear: 1381 *Laurence Patener* (PTER); 1412–13 *Nicholaus Jacobson, pataner*, York (SS96/119); 1427 *John Tunstall, pataner*, York (YRS6/172). See also spring (2).

pauncer A piece of armour that covered the lower part of the body, used in the fourteenth and fifteenth centuries. The pieces were imported into Hull and will have been made of either metal or leather: 1453 *8 duss' pauncers; 6 dacres pauncers* (YRS144/6).

paunch See panch.

pause To kick, a frequent dialect word in Yorkshire: 1650 *the saide Thomas … paused him soe vehemently that the saide Robert cryd 'awe'. And by reason of the saide pawseing the issue was stopt*, West Ardsley (SS40/32); 1673 *laid on her with a great staffe … paused her with his feet*, Northowram (OH3/204).

pautener A small bag, purse or wallet (OED): 1459 *j broche de auro cum uno pawtener de auro [1 gold broach with a gold pautener]*, Hull (SS30/236); 1465 *meum nigrum pawtener [my black pautener]*, York (SS30/269).

pavage A payment or toll towards the laying of pavements in a town, or their maintenance: 1228 *et de tol, pontagio, passagio, pavagio [and in toll, bridge-toll, passage-fee, pavage]*, Ripon (SS74/53).

pave, pavement To pave was to lay stones closely together in order to create a compact, smooth surface, particularly for the public highways in major towns: the word was responsible for an important York street name: 1376 *De terra Thome de Strensell, goldesmyth, super Pavimentum xxiiijs [From the land of Thomas de Strensall, goldsmith, on Pavement 24s]* (SS120/2); 1417 *super Pavimentum* (SS125/63). The maintenance of the pavements in Doncaster was an ongoing problem and numerous tenants incurred fines, e.g. 1572 *Thomas Cockson for a broken pavement unmade we merce him ijd* (YAJ35/293).

The surface of the way between the battlements of a bridge was also referred to as the pavement. In 1602, the mason Thomas Wallimsley was hired to build *one good and sufficient stone bridge at Apperley* and he agreed *to pave and battle all the said bridge throughout* (BAS6/141). When Wetherby Bridge was in need of repair in 1614, the townsmen alluded to *the decay of the pavement ... with the continuall travell of cole waines over the same* (YRS54/17). Similarly it was claimed in Birstall in 1706 that *great quantities of Lyme in wagons Excessively loaded* [had] *much impaired the paveing* (QS1) and at Cottingley, in 1683, men were instructed *to fill up all the holes in the pavement* (QS1).

The approaches to bridges, causeways across marshland, and riverside stathes also required paving and from an early date testators contributed towards their upkeep. In 1393, John Weste of Roundhay Grange made the following bequest: *Item Pavimento [for the paving of] de Ferrybryg vjs viijd* (Th2/98). An account in 1421 had *Pro cariagio de chyngell per navem a Hesill et Humbre pro pavimento ejusdem staith 16s [For transport of shingle by ship from Hessle and the Humber for paving that staith 16s]*, York (SS35/44). The accounts for Brotherton causeway in 1717 included payments *for leading earth to Pavers* (QS1/56/4). See also bound wain, paver.

paver The by-name and occupational term became important in York from the fourteenth century: 1387 *Memo. qd Ricardus de Bakewell paver admissus est ad libertatem pro pavimento per ipsum facto in ... de Munkegate [Be it remembered that Rochard de Bakewell paver was admitted to the freedom for the paving he did in ... Monkgate]* (SS96/85n); 1421 *Thomas Paver de Ebor. pro mundacione dictæ quareræ [Thomas Paver of York for cleaning the said quarry]* (SS35/43); 1455 *Robert Cambysshe, paver*, York (SS96/176). No fewer than six pavers were enrolled as freemen in the period 1474–6 (SS96).

pawn A thing left in the possession of another person as security for a debt: 1578 *certen lyninn geare of the goods of Thomas Brande, baker, layd in pawne to George Barthram draper, for the sum of 17s 2d*, Beverley (YRS84/21); 1615 *November 19 And I payd 44s for lowsing of my pawne*, Brandsby (NYRO44/88); 1688 *did borrow an axe of Matthew Ingleson ... and left a paire of knitt gloves ... as a pawne*, Hampsthwaite (QS1/27/4). See also pinner (2).

pax, paxbred The pax was a tablet of gold, silver or other precious material, which bore an image of the crucifixion or the Saviour, and it was kissed by the celebrating priest at mass before being passed to other clergy and members of the congregation. The paxbred had a similar function but was so called because it was originally a wooden board: 1377 *unum paxbrede vocatum relik [one paxbred called a relic]*, Bewick (SS4/101); 1424 *j paxbrede argenti et deaurati [1 silver gilt paxbred]*, York (SS35/277); 1497 *Item a paxe of every* [ivory] *and silver, price xs*, Wakefield (YAJ15/93); 1524 *a pax with the crucyfix Mary and John, of laton*, Sheriff Hutton (YAJ36/179); 1535–6 *for helping of the paxe and the lettron, ij^d*, York (CCW173).

peark, perk Regional forms of perch, in the sense of placing in an elevated position, with a number of distinctive usages: 1617 *plowe geare pearked in the top of the house*, Ripley (YAJ34/188). In wood management, for example, springwood leases were often taken up by several individuals or by partnerships which might include sawyers, charcoal-burners and tanners, and the tanners or their workmen will have been the first into the woods, to remove the bark. In order that the woodmen might then fell the trees without delay the tanners were allowed spaces where the bark had time to dry: 1672 *the Tanners and their servants may sett their Barke to dry in the Lands of any of the Tennantes ... neare the woode*, Tong (Tong/3/320). The use of the word 'peark' implies that it was probably done on wooden frames: 1672 *full & free libertie to sett and pearke the barke ... for the drying thereof in the pasture groundes lying neare unto the sayde wood*, Tong (Tong/3/321); 1704 *free liberty for pillinge the Bark and Pearking the same in any of the grounds near the said woods*, Bradley (SpSt). A wooden frame was also employed by clothiers in the finishing processes: 1506 *to send for suche on walker as shall walk and* *wyrk that cloth and he to cast the same cloth on a perk and see it thorowe*, York (YRS106/21). Raising the nap of the cloth may have been done on a 'perch': 1703 *Handle brake, Handles and Raizing Peark*, Skircoat (HAS25/45–6) as was the process of 'perching', that is placing the cloth over the pole or frame so that motes and burls could be removed: 1761 *att Leeds the[y] perk all theire frises att after frised to see if aney spots bee in* (YRS155/18). See also bark stack, mote, rail boot.

pearl shell Mother of pearl which is the shining iridescent inner layer of some shells. Its use for ornamentation is on record in Yorkshire from *c*.1500 (OED). Cutlers used it as a hafting material: in 1726, for instance, the inventory of Charles Stuartson listed 9½ pound of *pearl shell*, valued at £1 13s 3d (IH).

pease, peasen The original singular and plural of pea, peas: *c*.1527 *Item di Barell peson*, Hull (YAJ2/250); 1632 *Received for one load of payson, 5s 10d*, Sprotbrough (YAJ56/121); 1724 *stole the said Pease to make Pease Pottage of*, Spofforth (QS1/63/4). Pease, like corn, hay, etc. was a singular: 1642 *in this corner was allsoe a pease-stacke sette on the grownde*, Elmswell (DW78).

peck A measure of capacity for dry goods, equal to two gallons or a quarter of a bushel. Also the vessel which held that amount: 1357 *et j pec de plaster vjd*, York (SS129/13); 1581 *j bossell skepe … and one peyck skepe*, North Cave (Kaner134); 1602 *Item a bushel a peck & a half peck 1s 4d*, Knaresborough (YRS134/66); 1644 *one strocke a pecke & a half pecke 3s*, Lepton (HM/C/180).

peckled A regional form of 'speckled', noted by Wright in Lancashire and Cheshire but not Yorkshire (EDD): 1616 *a white peckelled oxe hide*, Huddersfield (DD/RA/f/4a).

pedder A regional form of pedlar: 1588 *Henry Wethereld of Bellerby … being a souldyar in Flaunders and his wife coming to Holbeck with a pedder packe is delivered of a child*, Leeds (Th1/62). A man described only as *Nelson, pedder*, was involved in an affray in Halifax in 1585 (WCR4/143).

peel (1) A shovel-like implement used principally by bakers to place loaves into the oven: 1532 *also the broken breid of the latter oven broken with the peele*, Rascall (SS83/356); 1597 *In the kitchin … a boarde a tubb a swill a peile*, South Cave (Kaner195); 1622 *Item, iron peale, 2 shoules*, Cottingley (LRS1/62); 1671 *one iron range & one iron pelle, 3s*, Thorpe Willoughby (YRS47/61–2). Compound terms could be more specific: 1674 *Two py peales*, Doncaster; 1675 *One pasty peall*, Bretton (YRS134/142,150). Mostly made of iron, but not always: 1612 *The Buttrie … j wodd peele*, Brandsby (NYRO44/36). It was also a name for a kind of fire shovel: 1664 *for braggs nayls spade bars & peel for the smelters*, Ripon (YRS118/116).

peel (2) Historians now use this word for the fortified houses and towers in the border regions of England and Scotland. Originally, the 'peel' was a stake or palisade but then a building within the palisade and by the fourteenth century a small castle (OED). Its use as a place-name element reflects that semantic history, for the site of Bolton Peel seems to link it with the enclosure now known as Hague, formerly *Le Haie de Boulton* (YRS56/7); n.d. *the hede of pele owteloyn* (YRS56/260); 1577 *Henry Peele, the Pele, Bolton nighe Bollande* (YRS19/120). Hellifield Peel is first mentioned in 1537 (YAJ55/85) and later spellings include: 1551 *Hallyfeld Pile* (YRS2/251). Peel Hill in Thorne was *le Pele* in 1483 (PNWR1/5) and was said *c*.1760 to be a corruption of Pile Hill (YAJ7/203). See also pale, pile (2).

peeler An alternative to 'piller', that is one who removes the bark from trees: 1810 *Paid the Peelers at Grimescar and Calverley 5s.* (DD/T/R/a/33). The *Peelers* in a

Cawthorne wood were given small sums in 1626 'to be careful they peeled nothing that was marked to stand' (OC8). See also pill, piller.

pelerine From the word for pilgrim, used of capes or mantles worn by women, and fashionable in the mid-eighteenth century: 1745 *it stays the making of a pillereen for Molly*, Meltham (G-A).

pell A skin or hide, a term found occasionally in connection with furriers (OED): in 1354, the Beverley skinners were ordered not to mix lambskin (*agnorum pelles*) with budge fur (BTD41) and a Scarborough inventory of 1395 had a cloak *mixto cum pelle de bevyr [combined with pell of beaver]* (SS45/4). In 1667–70, Isaac Blackborne of Leeds was fined 13s 4d for scouring hides *levand' pelles*, or 'fouling the water by washing his lymed skins where the people take water for preparing their victuals' (Th26/135,144). In the inventory of a Selby fellmonger we have: 1685 40 *calfe skins, 4s; 3 doz. of pells at 4s, 12s* (YRS47/198). See also back.

pell-mell In a great hurry, rushing, even reckless: 1733 *coming along the road from Frizinghall to Idle, in a bridle road leading through Bolton ... mett with Mrs Henry Swaine a pile mile riding* (QS1/72/6).

pelter A dealer in skins or hides. Reaney noted the by-name in Yorkshire in 1219 and it was not uncommon over the next 200 years: 1251 *Simon le Peleter*, Pontefract (YRS82/61n); 1372 *Johannes de London, pellter*, York (SS96/70); 1386 *Alexander de Ripon, pelter*, York (SS96/85); 1413 *Johannes Pane, pelter*, York (SS96/121). The register of York freemen suggests that the craft established itself in the city in that period and at least one of the earliest men to be enrolled was an immigrant from Hainaut, a province in what is now French-speaking Belgium: 1376 *Petrus Petyte de Hanawde, pelleter*, York (SS96/75). The ordinances of *les gentz del artifice des pelteres [the men of the pelters' trade]* are undated but may be *c*.1400, York (SS120/60).

pelyment See belyment.

penard See penner.

pendant A hanging on a girdle: 1467 *if any man of the sayd craft ... sett outher buccle or pendante uppon any girdilles that er made of threde or of cruyles he schall lose and pay at every tyme vjs viijd*, York (SS120/185). See also pendle.

pendle Almost certainly a hanging ornament, an alternative form of pendant (OED), although there is scope for confusion with 'penner': 1527 *on velvett girdle with penall and bukill gilte*, Whitkirk (Th9/247); 1531 *Item a lytyl buckyll and a penell and vj stoythes [studs]*, York (CCW64); 1558 *my late wife girdle with that pendall and buckle of silver*, Fairburn (Th27/266). It may have been used more generally for any hanging object: 1588 *one iron range with all the pendles therunto belonging*, Barwick (PR).

penistone A kind of coarse cloth which presumably took its name from the town of Penistone in south Yorkshire. It is referred to in an Act of Parliament: 1552 *clothes commonlye called Pennystones* (OED) and at intervals thereafter: 1617 *a greene penny stone cover*, Ripley (YAJ34/190); 1653 *Item paid for a yard of pennisston & halfe a yard of fustion 2s 8d*, Stockeld (YRS161/79); 1693 *In the shop ... 3yds penneston, 3s 9d*, Selby (YRS47/22).

penknife This was originally a small knife intended for making and repairing quill pens and it was kept in a sheath. References date from the 1400s (OED) and there is mention of *your pen knife, a right Sheffield knife* in 1590 (FBH111). Later, 'penknife' was used of almost any kind of folding knife, although one used for shaping quill pens is said to have developed in the early eighteenth century. The type of penknife that we are now familiar with has a jointed blade or blades which fit inside the handle, and among those found in the mud banks of the Thames are several which are considered to date from the late 1600s (FBH111). In 1733, Richard Oates of Barnsley was stabbed *with a penknife into the breast* (SS65/321); William Birks was a *penknife and razor maker* in Norfolk Street in Sheffield in 1766 (HCC54) and Gales and Martin's directory of 1787 lists *pen and pocket-knifemakers*. Cutlers took the skill to other areas, as this entry in a York register shows: 1812 *Joseph Fletcher of Fossgate, cutler (son of the late George Fletcher of Sheffield, pen-knife grinder)*, St Crux (PR). See also spring knife, trumpmaker.

penknife grinder A late specialisation: 1818 *John Oates, penknife grinder, Grogram Wheel*, Sheffield (WPS112). See also penknife.

penner A case or sheath for pens, formerly carried at the girdle: 1504 *vj long pennurs vd*, York (SS53/192); 1558 *my silke girdle with a siluer pennar and a siluer bockle*, Ledstone (Th27/225). Alternative spellings were common: 1557 *a gyrdyll hernysyd wyth a pynder of siluer and a buckle*, Pontefract (Th27/134); 1558 *Thomas Dursay … a garnished girdle with buckle and penard of silver*, Warter (BIA15/3/200). See also pendant, pendle.

penny dole Charity to the value of one penny handed out at a burial, often in the form of bread or ale: 1487 *To poore people be penydale iiijl iijs iiijd; for to pray for soule*, Hull (SS53/26); 1509 *I will that peny dole be dalt the day of my beriall*, Dewsbury (SS79/7); 1524 *that my executors dispose appon my beriall daye to poore people penny deale … for my saull … to every house … a penny and a pece of bef*, Paull (SS106/6); 1558 *I gyve to be distributed in the day of my buryall in penny dole as far as it wyll goo … iiij markes*, Richmond (SS26/113). See also dalt.

penny farm See penny ing.

penny grass A popular name for several different plants, influenced by the shape of the leaves or seed-pods. Henry Best was probably referring to the meadow plant yellow-rattle when he wrote: 1642 *soe soone as the pennie-grasse beginne to welke and seeme dry, then is it time to beginne to mowe*, Elmswell (DW33). This was widely held farming wisdom, articulated by Markham in *The English Husbandman* (1613).

penny ing, penny land, penny place These terms were once customary in the neighbourhood of Cawood and Sherburn in Elmet, estates of the Archbishop of York. In 1699, for example, a tenancy described as *one halfe Penny place nere piperbridge in Cawood* was surrendered to Henry Garbut of York: in 1700 Francis Brindholme surrendered *three acres of penny land called the Haggsteeles and … one penny place in Ryther gate* (MH/DC). Similarly, when Edward Barkston died in 1556, he bequeathed property described as *one penny place … in Shereburn* and *fyve rodes of pennye land in Barkestone Feildes* (Th27/69). In 1711, William Storr listed the dues payable to the archbishop: *Fines for a messuage, head of a whole oxgang, penny place, cottage, penny land, penny ings* (YAJ7/55).

Perhaps these developed from the term 'penny farm', used of lands which were free of services but subject to a money rent: 1398–9 'farm of Hillam … leased at *Penifarm*'; 1404 'all the remaining bovates there are leased at *Penyferm*', Selby (SAR47,141).

pennyman A name for the men who worked alongside urban butchers in the Tudor period but who were subject to different regulations: 1589 *ordeinid that no maister … shall by him self … dresse anie manner of fleshe … furthe of there owne howses or shoppes … but that the pennymen … shall have the dressing of all suche fleshe with the whole benefit* *thereof*, York (YRS138/58); 1610 *that no butcher dwelling within this towne commonly called a penny-man, shall take for wages of any other butcher for killing of meat above 2d for every beast*, Doncaster (OED). The inference may be that slaughtering and dressing animals was the pennyman's task and the butchers were retailers. The earlier history of these trade practices is likely to be found in York's records: 1483 *in esyng of the tolls, murage, bucher penys and skaitgyld*, York (YRS98/82).

penny nail From the fourteenth century the custom of classifying nails according to the original price per hundred became increasingly common, so a five-penny nail was a nail which cost 5d a hundred. The accounts for the rebuilding of Trinity House in Hull, in 1470, record the purchase of '2C of four-penny nail 8d', and even of '2C of three-halfpenny nail 3d' (YAJ62/164). After the prices changed, as they began to do in some places before 1500, the names persisted and were eventually used to designate the sizes of nails: 1538 *pro v.c pennye nayll 2s 6d*, York (SS35/109); 1548 *A m penny nayles, 5s*, York (SS35/112). Examples of different sizes are frequent from this time: 1539 *Item for sixpenny nalles and dubbyll spykyng, ijd*, St Michael's, York (CCW201); 1596 *one hundred of tenpennye nayles & one hundred of sixpennye nayles for naylinge downe lead and sarking bords on the roufe of the churche*, Howden (YAJ19/462); 1704 *for 7 Firrdeales and 100 12d. nayles*, Camblesforth (QS1).

Most references are from tradesmen's accounts of one kind or another so the following extract from Henry Best's Farming Book is of real interest:

> 1642 *a barre ... goeth straight downe the middle of the spelles and is nayled to each spell with a single 8 or 10 pennie nayle ... if the barres should bee cutte soe thinne till a 4 pennie nayle woulde nayle the swordes and spelles togeather, they woulde not bee halfe soe stronge*, Elmswell (DW17).

penny place See penny ing.

penny-prick A game, the nature of which is uncertain, although it is recorded in the early fifteenth century in Essex and subsequently over a wide area. Hunter said of it in his *Hallamshire Glossary* (1829) that it consisted 'of casting oblong pieces of iron at a mark'. A much earlier Sheffield reference refers to a similar practice and the circumstances in which a young man was injured: 1753 *several youths was tumbling in a ... garding and using ... a piece of iron call'd a file, us'd at a game call'd Penyprick ... [William Fox] was passing betwixt the fall of the file and the young man's inadvertanly casting of it* (QS1/92/10).

pennyroyal See pudding grass.

penny-stone A game in which a flat round stone was used as a quoit: 1519 *Usi sunt infra cimiterium ludi inhonesti prout pililudus pedalis & manualis, viz tutts & handball ac penyston [There were practised in the cemetery disgraceful games such as ball games with foot and hand, that is tuts and handball and penny-stone]*, Salton (SS35/270); 1595 *were lookinge upon strangers playinge at peniston in the churche yarde in devine service tyme*, Topcliffe (PTD95).

penny town In 1641, the inhabitants of *Hampall cum Stubbs* complained at the court of Quarter Sessions that the rating system locally was not fair, since they were being *assessed after the rate of a two penny towne*, whereas *Langthwaite cum Tiltes nere adjoyneing* was not *assessed* at all. In a Solomon-like judgement the court decided that both territories would in future be *chardged ... after the proporcon of a pennye towne*

(YRS54/282–3). This order by the court is clear up to a point but the exact interpretation of the term penny town remains uncertain.

penny ware Apparently goods to be purchased with one penny. An undated York inventory, probably of 1504, lists the contents of Richard Bishop's shop with valuations of the goods for sale, including: *Item v dosan and v knyfes of peny ware ijs viijd; Item ij dussan and a halfe of halpeny ware beddes vijd; Item iij dossane fardyng ware glassys iiijd* (SS53/191–3). Perhaps the inference is that the mark-up on the items was just over one hundred per cent.

pennyworth The amount of something bought for a penny or that which may be bought for a given sum in contrast to the money itself: 1516 *To pay … iiij markes in money or ells in such convenient pennyworth as they will take for the said money*, Wakefield (OED); 1530 *I giff and bequeath to John Sheffeld … iiijli in money or pennyworths*, Houghton near Pontefract (SS79/284).

penstock The shuttle which regulated the flow of water through the pentrough: 1732–3 *Nether finery wheel … Trough and Penstock New*, Colne Bridge (SpSt).

pentice, pentis A structure attached to a larger building, often with a sloping roof, a lean-to: 1450 *In Clx thakbord' emptis … pro j pentyce ibidem inde faciendo vijs [For 560 thackboards bought … for building 1 pentice there 7s]*, York (SS192/66); 1464–5 'making *lez pentessez in le Chirchelane*', Hull (YRS141/103); 1550 *I give … for the making of a pentice or a covering rounde aboute the crosse in the market plaice … substanciall and stronge with tymber and tyell vjli xiijs iiijd*, Newark (SS106/293–4). Popular etymology was responsible for the modern spelling 'penthouse': 1714 *an incroachment in the street before the Swan Tavern, 15 yds long and 2 foot in breadth, and a penthouse along the said front*, Leeds (Th9/286). See also outshot.

pentrough A word used in connection with water-powered mills, first noted in the OED in 1793. Presumably, the 'pen' was the dam or store of water and the trough was a channel or conduit between the head of the water and the overshot wheel, capable of being closed by a 'shuttle' or penstock. Examples are late: 1791 *to make a water wheel 20ft high and 5ft wide and … make a large pentrough*, Beeston (WYL160/129/1); 1811 *Pd Joseph Mitchel for New Shuttles, Penn Trough and other jobs about the same*, Meltham (G-A). See also falltrough, penstock, shuttle.

pepper-quern See quern.

perceive To receive or take in rents, profits or dues: 1484 *aggreed … that the said mynstrals from now forth shall have and perceive yerely … of every Alderman of the said citie xxᵈ*, York (YRS98/102); 1505 *that my sone John yerely take and perceve other xxᵗⁱ marks of the said George*, Birstall (Th24/307); 1512 *I will that … my dogthters have and persayve all the revenyeuse, ishues and profettes coming … of all the forsaid landes*, Fewston (SS104/4); 1528 *to perceive yerely hir joinctour & dowre of xxᵗⁱ marc*, Sheffield (SS79/248).

percer See parser.

perch This was a rod of a definite length used for measuring land, and in standard measure it was equivalent to 5½ yards. There were local differences, and in 1684 Black Carr Wood in Tong was estimated at *36 acres alloweing sixe yards to the pearche*. The woods could not be *exactly measured until they shalbe sprung … and cleansed* (Tong/3/377). The *Coucher Book of Furness* has an even earlier local example: 1200–26 *et campis de Hetoun mensuratas per perticam de Wyntirburne* (Furn2/392). See also long hundred.

perk See peark.

phillip To hit with the fist or open hand, a spelling of 'fillip': 1681 *he did arise from his seate and phillipped him over the noase*, Doncaster (SS40/249).

phodre A variant spelling of fother: 1545 *3 phodre of leade*, Grinton (YRS152/63); 1567 *Roger Cherye xix phodres of leade at vijl a phodre*, Richmond (SS26/198).

piannet The common magpie, a pied or black and white bird that was very familiar to our ancestors. Like other birds seen close to the village, the jackdaw for example, it was given a personal name. The 'mag' of magpie is of course for Margaret, and this alternative regional name has a suffix probably derived from 'Annot', a diminutive of Agnes: 1632 *A paine laid that noe tenant … shall suffer any glead pyannatt water Crowe or Ruckes or any such Verment to brude but destroy either their eggs or young ones*, Burton Agnes (YRS74/88). Pyenot Hall in Liversedge dated from 1785 but was demolished in the 1990s.

pick (1) A regional spelling of pitch, the black substance obtained from the boiling or distillation of tar: 1395 *It. pro j barell de pyk, iijs*, Whitby (SS72/615); 1446 *pro rosyn [rosin] et pyk*, York (SS35/61); 1510 *Item of ylk a barrell terre of pyke, q^u*, York (YRS106/33); 1789 *pick and tar for pump*, Tong (Tong/12f). Inventories for South Cave have: 1589 *a pick pann*; 1603 *a little panm & a pick pan*; 1616 *a tarpan* (Kaner156,214,260). See also blare (2).

pick (2) As a verb this could mean to rob or plunder: 1728 *was driving three Horses throo the towne of Cumberworth loaded with wheate Flower and … Mary Pease … told this informant that some persons had pick'd the loads … and was deviding it emongest them* (QS1/67/6).

pick (3) To vomit, a regional usage: 1781 *I called and smok'd 1 pipe with Mr Stansfield at night, had an overloading on my stomack and pick'd in the lane just below Mr Stansfield*, Slaithwaite (KC242/1).

pick (4) To abort or miscarry: 1723 *Mary Mangham … calling her whore … told her she was with a cubb and if she wud come to the doore she would make her pick it and wud rasle [wrestle] her to pieces*, Skipton (QS1/62/5); 1798 *A Wye had picked her calf*, Sessay (WM64).

pick (5), pickman The work-force in the first commercial coal-pits was small and it consisted of a few face-workers, a labourer or labourers who moved the coal to the bottom of the shaft, and a worker on the surface who hauled up the coal. The man hewing the coal was the élite workman and the pick which was his main tool served to identify him: 1486 *3 picks, one barrow-man, one bank-man*, Cortworth (YAJ12/236); 1601 *the said John Boys … shall not at any tyme … digge or gett coles … in Northowram with above three pickes at once* (HAS30/132); 1666 *to keepe in worke eighte pickes*, South Crosland (DD/WBD/2/81).

This gave way to the term 'pickman' which featured prominently in a legal dispute: *c*.1730 *priviledge to sink, digg … with five Workmen Commonly called pickmen and with no greater number at once … he that works the strait work being allways to be reconed one of the said pickmen*, Beeston (WYL160/129/4). When a Featherstone miner was killed by falling rock in 1323, a coroner decided that his pick had caused the accident: *pro quodam picosio per quem Simon Galpyn fodebat carbones in quodam puteo [for the pick with which Simon Galpyn was digging coal in that pit]* (YAJ15/210). See also collier (1), deodand, strait board.

pick (6) The verb is found as the first element in numerous by-names where it seems to have meant 'to eat', possibly pejoratively, although that remains speculative: 1301 *De Willelmo Pykepasteth'*, Felixkirk (YRS21/84); 1301 *De Hugone Pykewastelle*, Skelton in Cleveland (YRS21/38); 1316 *John Pykehuskes*, Stanley (YRS57/103); 1379 *Nicholaus Pykhauer*, Rimington (PTWR).

pickfork For pitchfork: 1454 *a pikeforke, a hande spade*, Nottingham (SS30/173); 1614 *12 pykeforkshaftes*, Stockeld (YAJ34/175). See also pitchaxe.

pickle A common late spelling of Middle English *pightel*, that is a small enclosure: 1551 *Henpyghell*, Cartworth (PNWR2/238); 1752 *Eneas Ramsden of Henpickle Mill*, Cartworth (PR). See also pightel, and PNWR7/231.

picklock A long schedule of the utensils which belonged to a mill in Riddlesden included: 1739 *1 large gavelock, thirteen picklocks, two great hammers, two long chissels*, etc. This is said to be an instrument for picking locks, but the number in this case seems unusually high (MD194).

piece (1) A portion or space of time, a dialect usage: 1787 *At Thirsk … Stayed a piece*; 1797 *I stopped a piece at both places*, Sessay (WM23,50).

piece (2) A length of woollen cloth: 1492 *any husband man … being unfraunchest that maketh a pece or two of woollen cloth in a yere within his awn house*, York (YRS103/91); 1588 *to John Kylner for mylninge of peces*, Dalton (DD/WBW/19); 1599 *a pece in the lowme*, Bingley (LRS1/2); 1703 *13 plaine pieces at £1 6 0 a piece; 2 couple of broad pieces £13 in all*, Holmfirth (IH).

pier A structure extending into the sea or the waters of a tidal river, designed to form a partial enclosure protective of shipping, and a place where goods might be loaded and unloaded: 1530 *Also to the peir if it go furthwardes, xls*, Whitby (SS79/300); 1537 *the pere or haven there is in great decay and like to be loste*, Bridlington (BCP4); 1566 *wheare the same peare is nowe and heretofore haith bene all the owte sides made of tymber framed like two house sides filled within with stones*, Scarborough (YAJ70/83); 1600 *The groundage of every ship landed Filowe peere … of every cole ship two bushel coles to the Bayliffe*, Filey (YAJ70/74). See also key.

pierage A toll or fee, paid for the privilege of bringing a vessel alongside a pier: 1516–17 *wulde neither suffer hym to departe with his seid shippe … from thens onto the tyme the seyd Thomas yaffe [gave] … as well the forseid xviijs ijd … as xd for his ankyrage and peerage*, Hull (YRS45/41); 1601–2 *all the proffittes & receipts which doe come for pereage*, Scarborough (NYRO47/11); 1647 *for collecting the duties of the perridge*, Bridlington (BCP180).

pig An ingot of smelted metal: 1648 *Item a pigg of lead 15s*, Sharlston (YRS134/99). See also pig-iron, sow (2).

piggin A wooden vessel with one stave extended to form a handle: 1567 *In the mylke howse. Item one kitt, thre piggins, one cherne*, Fixby (YRS134/15); 1621 *foure great piggans, 8d, two dozen of little piggans, 2s 6d*, Hammerton (YRS63/48); 1659–60 *In the Celler – 1 wooden piggon*, Knaresborough (SS110/245); 1720 *saw a child coming out of the house with a piggin … and set it downe upon the stepps* (QS1); 1731 *a kit and 4 meight-pigenes*, Austerfield (QS1/70/7). See also say (1).

pightel A small enclosure, a croft: *c*.1220 *unum essartum quod vocatur Hirst et aliud quod vocatur Pichel [an assart called Hirst and another called Pichel]*; 1254–80 *cum uno pychel prati*

in Ouerseleby [with a pightel of meadow in Ouerseleby], Selby (YRS13/15,81); 1312–13
Pro herba vendita in le Pighell' ibidem xijd [For grass sold in the Pighell' there 12d], Bolton
Priory (YRS154/335); 1346–7 'one place of land and wood which is called *un pickell*
… in the *Westewode of Gouldekerres'*, Golcar (DT/257); 1540 '16d … for the farm of
two *pightells* called *Frontes'*, Mount St John (YRS94/123); 1570 *butting of the west parte
of one little pighell called the hoyll*, Honley (WDP231/18); 1675 *the pighills adjoining upon
Honley Bridge* (YDK96). Late spellings of the place-name included pit hill and pigtail.
See also pickle, pingle, and the surname Pickles in GRDict.

pig-iron, pig-metal Pig-iron is produced in a furnace by smelting iron ore with
a high-carbon fuel: charcoal was used in earlier centuries and then later coke. The
molten iron thus produced is run off into rough moulds where it solidifies and forms
'pigs'. The first reference to pig-iron in the OED is in 1665 and the term was used
in a south Yorkshire document in 1676. The accounts of Colne Bridge Forge contain
entries in 1745 for *Barnby Piggs*; that is pig-iron brought over from Barnby Furnace
(SpSt). In that state it contains impurities and is brittle; unsuitable for making edge
tools. It can be converted into cast iron by remelting and blowing air into the molten
mass. The Cutlers' Company had strict rules about the use of pig iron and cast iron but
their records show that these were not always observed: 1779 *Resolved that all suspicious
places shall be searched for Forks made of pig metal*. Two cutlers called Parker were later
suspected of producing 'deceitful wares' and the Company's searchers found metal
forks in their warehouse *made of pig iron or cast metal* (HCC24). See also cast (7), pig,
shoat, sow (2).

pike (1), piked Said to mean 'pointed' in the place-names Pike Law and Pike Low,
both recorded by Smith three times and both having *hlāw* as the suffix. The 'law'
could refer to a hill or burial mound but in Yorkshire it was also used of boundary
cairns in the Middle English period. Since so few of the Pennine hills are pointed
it prompts me to suggest that 'piked law' meant a hill which had a pointed heap of
stones rather than a pointed hill. In a description of the bounds of Gisburn Forest in
1205–11 the line ran *usque ad [as far as] Pykcros super [on top of] Manebent* (YRS87/31).
A map of common lands in Ingleborough, dated 1619, places *The Pyke aboue Hamerton
folde* on the hill called Moughton which is undoubtedly rocky but not pointed, often
described as a limestone plateau (MPC1/235). The pointed symbol on the map almost
certainly identifies a prominent boundary cairn.

   Some of the earliest examples of the compound Pike Law are in charters relating to
the lands held by Kirkstall Abbey, notably those for the period 1329–33 which define
the boundaries between Blackburnshire and Barnoldswick, for example *de Oxgille
vsque Pikedlawe que vocatur Aleynsete [from Oxgille as far as the piked law called Aleynsete]*.
This was hilly country, even if the hills were not 'pointed', but the same cannot be said
for the low-lying land between Alwoodley and Chapel Allerton near Leeds which is
mentioned in an undated charter: *vnam acram terre in campo de Alretun, iuxta Pikedlawe
[an acre of arable land in Allerton field, next to the piked law]* (Th8/105,326). The two
names are part of a substantial corpus of similar names which includes several Pike
Hills and Pikedaws: the latter has the suffix *haugr* which is the Old Norse equivalent
of *hlāw* and it was also commonly used as a boundary marker. See also howe, pike (3).

pike (2) A pitchfork:

> 1642 *theire flayle-handstaffes they … putte them into an oven … and lette them
> lye there a whole night, and this will dry up the moisture and make them lighter …
> and keepe them from casting* [warping]. *This is the course they take with their pikes*,
> Elmswell (DW128–9).

pike (3) The pike was a stack of hay made up of several hay-cocks, with a pointed top: 1563 *one pike of haye att langmouthe*, Leake (SS2/213); 1642 *if there bee any hey to spare … wee either stacke it abroade or else make it up in a pyke … therewith intending to fother our sheepe in winter*, Elmswell (DW39). The verb is also on record: 1787 *Aug. 1 Men mowing Barley Garth … Got half into pike. Aug. 4 Our people piked rest of the Ings*, Sessay (WM23).

pilch This was an Old English word for a garment and it derived ultimately from Latin *pellis*, that is 'skin' or 'hide'. In some early examples these were made of expensive fur: 1395 *pro j pilch de scrank et bys [for 1 pilch of shank and bis]* (SS45/13); 1410 *De xviijs de una pylchia de gray. De xxiijs iiijd de una pylchia de bever [For 18s from a pilch made of gray fur. For 23s from a pilch of beaver]*, York (SS45/45): in the accounts of Fountains Abbey in 1446–58 *j pelch* was valued at 18d (SS130/230). A monk who moved to Mount Grace in 1520 brought with him *a newe pylche of the gyft of Mr Saxby* and *an olde pylche* (YAJ18/295). In 1522, Robert Skyrley of Scarborough made the following bequest: *and to v men that goys in my bote, every oon of them a pilche* (SS79/154). These were presumably coarse garments suitable for hard work at sea, and the inference may be that they were made of cowhide or sheepskin. Veale's definition was 'a garment of skins, fur side outwards' (EMV221). One possible earlier reference is a by-name: 1301 *De Thoma Pilcheprest vjd*, Skelton (YRS21/37).

pile (1) A pointed blade of grass: 1562 *some gresse pyles that grewed emongest the ling bent and brakens*, Rawdon (YRS114/103); 1642 *they will not leave soe much as a pile of grasse or a windle-strawe*, Elmswell (DW79). See also windle (2).

pile (2) A substantial length of timber, usually oak or elm, with the lower end sharpened, sometimes tipped with iron. They were used in the construction of weirs, dams, fish-garths, bridges and the like: 1322 *& in pilis pro nouo stagno molendini faciendis [and in piles for building the new mill dam]*, Leeds (Th45/86). Archaeological evidence shows that huge numbers were driven into the bed of a river to support bridge foundations, weirs or water-banks (DHB124–6): 1398–9 *quod omnes pile, pali et kidelli in aqua de Ouse positi ammoveantur citra festum Pasche [that all piles, stakes and kiddle-nets in the river Ouse are removed before Easter]*, York (SS120/45). In 1422, Thomas Rawson was indicted because he 'made *1 weyr* with *pylles* … on the north side of the water', thereby diverting it from its 'ancient course', Bradford (CR).

Piles are mentioned frequently in Yorkshire bridge documents from the seventeenth century: 1616 *For thre hundredth and fortye pyles with leading, workinge and dryveninge we estimate at 3s 4d*, Kirkstall (BAS6/146); 1705 *the Pyles … for repair of the Banks and Wears*, Bradley (SpSt). It was used also as a verb: 1682 *For wood … to be well piled downe there … and to be Fastned with Coupleing the same … to the old frame*, Cottingley (QS1/21/5). See also pile hagg, hoop (1), shoe, weir.

pile hagg These place-name references surely indicate that some woods or sections of woods were managed in order to produce piles: 1399 '30 pairs of ash trees purchased … by the lord abbot, with transport of the same *del pilehag* to Cawood 10s 6d', Selby (SAR82); c.1690 *In pile hagg, that is that part that lyes betwixt the dam & A bank which goes from Rist Park … Contains 220 Acres*, Scalm Park (YAJ7/49). See also wand hagg.

pilerow A row of piles: 1630 *to maintain and defend the howses and buildings, the walls, ditches, piles and pilerowes and other defences*, South Crosland (YDK90); 1638 *the dam was raysed by pilerows halfe a yeard higher*, Woodsome estate (DT/266).

pill To 'peel' or remove the bark from trees. It was evidently an ancient practice: 1277 'He is also accused of barking hollies (*de hussis escorchiatis*)', Wakefield (YRS29/167). Later references include: 1501 *Thomas Ternour … has pylled hollynnes … and cutt esshwod* *by divers tymes*, Selby (SS85/30); 1564 *noe inhabitant … shall pill any barke of any oake, ash, holling or elder*, Giggleswick (CR); 1658 *to pill, fell, cut downe … the wood, trees, underwood and barke in Dodger Roide Springe*, Tong (Tong/3/267); 1739 *To the Pillars when Pilled the Reign*, Whitley (DD/WBE/1/12). In a colourful deposition at the Quarter Sessions in 1682 it was claimed that the

> *servants of John Firth did in a very riotous manner enter into the groundes and woods of Sir Lyon Pilkington … and did take away his barke which was pilled and turned the ladders where severall of the workmen were pilling … and carried the same awaie*, Bradley (QS1).

In the East Riding the word was also used in the preparation of flax and hemp for spinning: 1587 *Item certain pillyd tow and unpylled towe vjs*; 1606 *Item sommer hempe pilld & unpild*, South Cave (Kaner141,220). Other inventories for South Cave have references in 1588 to *a stonn of pilling towe* and in 1592 to *certayne pylling hemp* (Kaner151,168). See also unpilled, waver (1).

pillar (1) A pillar was a solid column of coal, left unwrought in order to support the roof of a working. It is first recorded in a case of encroachment brought to the attention of the Chancellor of the Duchy of Lancaster by Henry Farrer:

> 1591 *John Drake and John Roebucke have now of late at several times in most forcible manner, felled and cut down all the heads, pillars and other work being placed and made within the grounds of your orator's mine at his great charges for bearing up the ground there*, Northowram (HAS31/75).

More usually it is found in leases, included in the list of conditions under which the coal-mine might be worked: 1659 *doth … agree … that he will at all tymes … durynge the said term keep and maintaine in all such pitt or pittes … good and sufficient pillers for the upholding and supporting of the groundfeild … as is used and accustomed*, Wibsey (MMA/255); 1777 *and leave the Pillars thereof of a sufficient size and strength*, Southowram (HM/C/10). Such pillars might at a later stage be exploited, especially if at ground level there was no important building, and that is implicit in the *Sale of pillars of coal left unwrought* in Beeston in 1787 (WYL160/129/1).

pillar (2) Although this is in regular use for the pier of a bridge, the first OED evidence is in a Nottingham document of 1579 – relatively late. The new stone bridge at Catterick in 1422 was to have *twa pilars* (NRQS3/34) and Elland Bridge had two substantial *juells or pillors* in 1579 (BAS6/138) but the word is seldom used after that. I have found no examples locally of 'pier' although its history in this sense goes back to the twelfth century in Kent.

piller This was usually occupational, for the man who pilled or peeled the bark from trees, as in 'pill' above, but it was also a 'pilling' implement: 1622 *choping knives, 4 pillers*, Cottingley (LRS1/62). Elsewhere in this man's inventory were the items *in barke and toyles* and *barke unpilled*. See also peeler.

pillever A pillow-case, a variant spelling of pillow-bere: 1572 *iij pillevers and one paire of harden sheets*, Wensley (SS26/252).

pillion, pillion seat A kind of saddle on which loads could be placed: 1673 *one pannill & one pealyon seat with other formitory* [furniture?] *5s*, Hambleton (YRS47/138); 1676 *one pillion seate*, Selby (YRS47/2); 1693 *j pillianseat & cloth*, Selby (YRS47/21). See also load-saddle, mail pillion, panel (3).

pillion–cloth A cloth to cover the pillion saddle or seat: 1616 *A pyllyon cloth orynge and black fringe and buttons*, Brandsby (NYRO44/120); 1682 *2 pilyon cloths 11s*, Selby (YRS47/88). See also pillion.

pillow–bere A pillow-case: 1542 *Item one fine pillober wroght with silke: Item ij course pillobers*, Lindley near Otley (Th19/133); 1574 *Item tene pillibers of lyne, viij pillibers of femble*, South Cave (Kaner85); 1602 *8 lynnen sheetes 4 harden sheetes ... & 6 Pillowbers*, Knaresborough (YRS134/65); 1611 *two codds, a pillow beare*, Bingley (LRS1/13); 1700 *the linnen found in his possession ... one sheet, one shirt and a pillowbeare, he tooke out of a close ... as they were laid to whiten*, West Riding (QS1). See also pillever.

pinchbeck An alloy of copper and zinc which resembles gold: 1771 *my metal or pinch back watch*, Slaidburn (CS2/87). The alloy was invented by Christopher Pinchbeck (1670–1732), a London clock and toy maker, whose surname derives from a village in Lincolnshire.

pind To shut up or enclose, to impound an animal that has trespassed: 1466 *I never knewe no pyndyng off noo catell off the tenantes ... oonly fro scapes makyng*, Sand Hutton (YAJ2/92); 1522–3 *if it happen the cattalle of the said abbot ... to come ouer the water of Swaile to put thame ouer agayn without pyndyng ... to pynd any catalle ... for damage fesaunte*, Hudswell (MC79); 1643 *and 2s 6d he laid out for pinding*, Elmswell (DW195). As a noun it had the same meaning as 'pinfold': 1674 *taking horses away violently from the common pinde*, Elmswell (DW227). See also noughter, pinfold.

pinder The manorial officer who was responsible for impounding stray animals: 1219 *Richard le pynder*, Yorkshire (R&W); 1286 Henry the *Pynder*, Hipperholme (YRS29/227); 1672 *Thomas Batson being pinder of Tinslow and in pursuance of his office ranging the towne fields*, Tinsley (QS1/11/3). Examples in the OED indicate that the occupation survived into quite recent times. See also noughter.

pinfold The fold where stray animals were kept until payment was made to secure their release. The spelling variations reflect its association with the verb to pind and with pound meaning enclosure. First noted in an undated thirteenth-century document: 'taken away on account of the *pondfald*', Drax (YRS12/124). Later examples include: 1335 'which toft lay between *le Punfald* on the east side and the road', Sewerby (YRS69/130); 1473 *unius parcellae terrae ... vocatae Pynfald [of a plot of land ... called Pynfald]*, Ripon (SS81/241); 1509–10 *pro firma unius horti 8d nuper Pynfolde [for farm of a garden 8d formerly the pinfold]*, Ripon (SS81/174); 1522–3 *shalle lowse thame oute of the pynde folde*, Hudswell (MC79); 1611 *the pindfould*, Malham (DDMa).

pingle A small enclosure of land, a paddock: 1546 *Roger Blythe for one pyngle, with libertie ... for the conveyans of the water to hys mylne*, Todwick (SS91/154); 1577 *all the pingles, pastures and fedings*, Aldbrough in Holderness (YRS65/9); 1608 *a close called Pingle*, Fixby (YRS76/120); 1680–1 *also one little pingle of meadow at the bottom of the Cliff Close*, Brampton (YAJ6/72). See also pightel.

pink Originally a type of small vessel from the Low Countries, first referred to in English sources in 1471 (OED). In Yorkshire, such boats were in use along the coast and inland waterways but there is evidence later that they were capable of sea-crossings: 1575 *John Adams for refusing to pay primage on a voyage from Hamburgh in Christopher Wormeley's pink*, Hull (YRS116/64); 1639 *complained of Henry Appleton for hiring Henry Hodgson whom [Mr] Crew had first shipped too go in his pink*, Hull (YRS105/39). The merchants who used pinks as trading vessels often had only a share of the boat: 1669 *alsoe that 16ᵗʰ part of one pink with the tackling*, Selby (YRS47/35); 1678 *the one halfe of my parte of George Bell pincke*, Selby (YRS47/192). They were being built in Selby shipyards in the 1600s. See also shipwright.

pinmaker, pinner (1) The occupation of pinmaker is recorded occasionally in Sheffield from the seventeenth century (FBH134) but the craft flourished from an earlier date in York: 1349 *Ricardus Spenser, pinner;* 1350 *Robertus de Badby, pinmaker* (SS96/44–5).

pin-nail Only one possible reference has been noted although Salzman had 'pynail' in Cockermouth in 1322, used in roof-work (SZ1/316): 1530 *For a thousand lattnells and ij penyworth pennels, 10d*, York (SS35/135). It is possible that these were slate-pins.

pinner (2) A type of coif or close-fitting cap worn by women of better rank. It had long flaps pinned on each side of the head: 1652 a case *against a woman for stealing a pynner*, Thirsk (NRQS5/103); 1676 *layd her in pawne … one handkercheife and a pinner*, Mirfield (QS1).

pipe (1) The OED has one or two early references to pipe in connection with horse-harness [1309–1418] and suggests the meaning which is explicit in this much later example: 1726 *a tanned horse hide … to be made into pipes for iron traces*, Potterton (QS1/65/8).

pipe (2) A large cask used principally to hold and transport wine but which at times served as a container for other provisions: 1395 *Emptio vini. inprimis pro iv pyps vini [Purchase of wine. First, for 4 pipes of wine]*, Whitby (SS72/616); 1445 *una pipa vini rubei iiijli vs … cariagione eiusdem pipe de taberna usque domum fratrum [for a pipe of red wine £4 5s … for carrying the pipe from the tavern to the brothers' house]*, York (SS192/41); 1502–3 *the awners … if it be a pipe to sett the mark on the pipes hede*, York (SS129/106); 1528 *paid for a old pyype and a old hoghed, xijᵈ*, York (CCW131).

pipe (3) Used of the flue or 'tunnel' which conveyed smoke upwards from the fire into the open air. See also chimney.

pismire The ant, so called because of the smell of urine associated with ant-hills: 1642 *take a spade … and goe twice a day to the Aunthills and there digge … for pismire egges and those pismires which have wings like unto flyes*, Elmswell (DW116). Pismire Hill occurs several times as a minor place-name, possibly a derogatory nickname: 1548 *a cottage called Pyssemyre Hill at the end of le Shyregrene*, Sheffield (TWH28/30).

piss To urinate. Not now in polite use but frequent formerly: 1519 *the hangynges of the where* [choir] *lyeth opynly in the presbitory, dogges pysses of thame, wax droppys of thame*, York (SS35/267); 1544 *the place of Owsbrige callyd the pyssing howes*, York (YRS108/122); 1677 *Hall tooke his hatt from him and pissed in it*, Barnsley (QS1/16/10). Its use as a name for a boundary marker may suggest that this was where the walkers traditionally relieved themselves: 1707 *and so goeth North to a place called Pissinghow*, Brompton (NRR1/112).

pitch (1) An implement used to catch fish. Canon Atkinson's comment on the term 'fishlock' in a Thirsk case of 1661 (NRQS6/43n) includes a reference to a *pyche or fyshe lepe*, which suggests that the pitch was probably a kind of basket, 'pitched' or set in the stream, or in a dam or weir: 1372 *injunctum est … quod nullus de cetero præsumat piscari cum rethibus aliquibus vel pyches ponere prope gurgites domini [it was enjoined … that nobody at all presume to fish with any kind of nets or place pitches near the lord's fish-traps]*, Selby (YRS13/290); 1657 *every person that shall take any fish … by any netts, nighthookes,* *pyches, Angleroddes, ladeing or otherwise 3s 4d*, Meltham (G-A); 1667 *that no person doe fish with pytches or spoile our water waires* [weirs] *with fishing*, South Crosland (DD/WBR/12/13). The Wakefield cloth frizzer John Brearley described its use:

1758 *Gett one of them piches such has people catch minnows in only let itt bee twise has large ... gett some live fish ... aney small fish. Putt them in the piche and sinke your piche in a mill dam and tye itt to some willow.*

The advice was that eels could go into the pitch but would be unable to get back out (YRS155/33). See also eel-ark, lade-net, lading (2).

pitch (2) In the few references noted this was a bee-hive: 1612 *one old tub three hive pitches*, Eccleshill (YRS134/68); 1729 *Isaac Mawd Senior Stole from the said Thomas Sutcliffe One Hive of Bees ... Elizabeth Mawd strain'd the honey and Isaac ... carried the pitches back*, Stainland (QS1/68/4). The hive may have been made of 'basket' material, similar in appearance therefore to pitch (1).

pitch (3) As a verb this could mean to pave with small irregular stones (EDD): 1736 *leading earth and sand to rase the ground and piching the cobles*, Hammerton (QS1/75/8).

pitchaxe A spelling of pickaxe: 1614 *j iron mall, j pitchaxe*, Stockeld (YAJ34/178). See also pickfork.

pitch the bar To throw or toss the bar, a simple game which sounds similar to tossing the caber, possibly using a heavy piece of metal: 1567 *Robt Jonson ... de Flamburghe ... is presented to have misused him selfe in his pastymes in ... that he one tyme did pitche the barre in the churche yearde* (PTD85).

pit eye Few examples of this term have been noted in reference works and the only quotation in the OED is for 1881 where it is explained as 'the bottom of the shaft'. It has a much longer history than that: 1574 *when they dryve owte of the eye*, Sheffield (SYC3); 1690 *parte of pitt eye coale getting*, Farnley (MS11). The same term was used by miners of ironstone and lead: 1630 *1 pickman or hewer will require 1 carrier from him to the neyt or eye pit, there one winds it up*, Derbyshire (R&J68). In fact, it was an alternative word for 'pit' in ironstone-mining: 1576 *one Pitt or Myne called One eye of Iron Stone*, Farnley (BM82/15). The inference is likely to be that in shallow pits the 'eye' marked the place where daylight gave way to darkness, although few of the references are detailed enough for that to be evident: 1706 *framed the fallen pitt eye*, Farnley (MS11); 1714 *from the old pitt eye*, Shibden (HAS30).

At times it is as though the 'eye' was the whole shaft. It should be quite distinct from the 'pit mouth' which was the pit head but the two are on occasion used confusingly as apparent synonyms: 1754 *to lay, dispose and place on such part of the said demised premises as shall be near to the mouth or eye of the pit*, Beeston (WYL160/129/9); 1806 *about eight yards from the eye or mouth of the pit*, Horsforth (SpSt/5/2/7). Of course in drift mines, those with a horizontal gallery, it would be more difficult to draw a distinction between the eye and the mouth. See also pit mouth.

pit greave A local word for a steward or overseer, noted only in Lepton. In the 1530s, several of the tenants there were indicted for selling coal to persons outside the township, and fines of 12d were exacted for each cart load. The rolls continued to list numerous offenders and in 1540 four men were elected as *Pyttegreyffes*. They could be called on to serve more than one term but there is no obvious pattern to the appointments. In 1547, *Adam Hochonson, Robert Bayldon, Robert Crawshay and John Coken* were named as *pittgreves* and supervisors (DD/WBM).

pit–hill In the more recent history of coal-mining the pit-hill was the mound of waste close to the pit-head, of little value perhaps but scratched over for small pieces of coal in hard times. Sixty and seventy years ago such pit-hills were a common sight and they provided exciting play-grounds for youngsters. The Rev. Lewthwaite wrote an account of Newsome (near Almondbury) in the church magazine in the 1880s and said of the hamlet of *Coalpit Hill* that

> *a stranger might very reasonably ask why should this place be called by such an incon-*
> *gruous name … neither coals, coal-mines, neither banksmen nor tips may be seen now*
> *… still if we skip backwards 100 years or more these were all to be found on Coal*
> *Pit Hill. Then indeed there were no houses and coal getting was the principal thing.*

There was an attempt in many pits, certainly from the eighteenth century to get rid of the waste and restore the land to its former condition: 1767 *2 men one horse and Cart one day removing the Hill*, Tong (Tong/4c/10); 1777 *at the end of the said term remove and carry away … all the Pitt Hills, scale, stones, wood, gravel, earth and rubbish … and make the soil and surface … as level arable and good in every respect*, Southowram (HM/C/10).

In an alternative, earlier use the pit-hill was a hill or mound of coal close to the pit-head, where it would be stacked ready for sale, a valuable resource. In 1647, Adam Eyre wrote in his diary: *we parted at the Coyle-pitt hills*, Thurlstone (SS65/54): in 1672 a man was indicted at the West Riding Quarter Sessions for carrying *away certain Coales from the Coale pitt hill*, and in Bradford in 1702 *a collier at Mr Rawson's pitt came to the pitt hill of Mr Edward Stanhope and gave the colliers their notice* (QS1). The word could retain this meaning long after it had also started to be used for the spoil-heaps: 1819 *every square yard of this bed will yield five loads of coal, which on the Pitt Hill are worth 2s 6d*, Birstall (DD/CA/5). See also Beeston Pithill, slack (2), spoil.

pit house This was one of several names given to buildings erected at the pit head, and a *Colepithowse* is shown on Robert Saxton's map of Baildon for 1610 (BM101/50). In 1622, the death was recorded of *Symond Moore of Coalle Pitts House*, in Masham (PR). The accounts for a new pit in Shibden in 1750 have entries which point to a relatively permanent structure: *Pd H. Mallinson for making the pithouse 5 days at 1s 4d; Pd for nails 1s 6d; Pd for pithouse theaking 4s; Pd for 200 of slates for pithouse 12s; Pd for laths and nails 3s 1d* (HAS30/151). Buildings at Pit House in Shepley, south east of Huddersfield, are on a site where early OS maps show a drift mine and the words *Coal got*. See also cabin, lodge, shade.

pit mouth Formerly this could be used for the pit head. In the years before coal was delivered to home-owners, the pit mouth was where it was purchased: 1755 *great plenty of coal which is usually sold for 2d the Horse Load at the Pits mouth*, Mirfield (WDP1/192); 1761 *1 day helping to repair the pitt mouth*, Tong (Tong/4c/6). See also pit eye.

pit-prop The OED has references to this word only from 1883 but it was in use much earlier: 1815 *Joseph Rhoades for pit props £3 18s 6d*, Soil Hill (HAS32/282) and it may be implicit in an even earlier Northowram lease: 1633 *all the charges of tools, props and stoops* (HAS31/79). See also pillar (1), post (2), punch (2), puncheon.

pitstead The site of a coal-pit, particularly a place where it was intended to open up a new pit: 1713 *The Workemen was at the setting out of the new pittstead*, Shibden (HAS30/142); 1780 *sold a pitstead in my lands*, Birstall (TW150). It could also refer to a site in the woods where charcoal was burnt; a charcoal pit: 1795 *and make pit steads for Coaling the same*, Calverley (DD/T/V/3).

pix See pyx.

place Included here because it could mean 'residence' and was a significant place-name element: 1344 'a certain place called *le Priour Place de Drax*', Hook (YRS17/41); 1419 'Grant … of two messuages which are called *William Symplace and Clerkplase*', Farnley near Otley (YRS111/81); 1486 'a messuage called *Jenett Swaldale place*', Thornton on the Hill (YRS63/139). It could refer to more than one property: 1410 'two messuages and four acres of land and meadow in *Melmorby* called *Rosseplace*' (YRS69/101) and even to a capital messuage: 1448 'the *Cheyf plase or Hedplase*, Gomersal (YRS83/99).

It was a very important element in some parishes, especially in Methley where it featured more than forty times in a list of the manorial greaves for the period 1592–1642. The names there survived the departure of the families after whom they were named: 1594 *Tho: Beckellanes … pro Porter place [for Porter's house] in Thorpe quondam [formerly belonging to] Richardi Bunnye et Roberti Brigges* (Th35/79). Many examples survive and they can be important clues to the antiquity of settlements: 1387 *Henry Wade*, Cartworth (MD225); 1578 *John Crosland de Wadeplace*, Cartworth (G-A); 1663 *Abraham Kaye of Wardplace*, Cartworth (PR).

plack A small copper coin worth four pennies, current in Scotland in the fifteenth and sixteenth centuries: 1504 *enacted … that all grotts plakks and pens of two pens being silver not clipped nor rongged shalbe curaunt*, York (YRS106/5).

pladd A spelling of 'plaid', a twilled woollen cloth: 1617 *one bedstead with a canopie of pladd*, Ripley (YAJ34/195); 1764 *A Bedstead with Plad Hangings*, Ecclesfield (EDH24).

plain An open space, usually within a wood or forest: 1549 *any playnes or cokglades within the seyd woodes*, Bradley (DD/WBD/8/60); 1571 *Thomas Smythe shall have a right of waye … to the towne … over the West Wood plaine*, Ilkley (CHT129); 1636 *as the same dothe lie in a plain called Coit Green*, Fixby (DD/T/S/a/13); 1742 *a spring wood and the plain ground in the same*, Holmfirth (G-A). There is evidence that such open spaces might be deliberately created: 1752 *William Tingle for paring and Stubbing a Plain in Tibnetherend Wood 10s 6d*, Kirkheaton (DD/WBE/1/25). The word was probably in use from the twelfth century at least, since charters contain references in Latin to 'wood and plain': *c.*1148 *in bosco et in plano [in the wood and in the open]*, Sawley (YRS87/2). Used at times also for a space in the midst of houses that was open, free from obstructions: 1534–5 *he used to sell in an open shop opening towards the market place or plain street*, Pontefract (YRS41/141); 1642 *as they come out of the Calf-house … all ditches and dales are (with them) plaine way*, Elmswell (DW124). See also cockglade, laund.

plancher A wooden plank or board, suitable for dam repairs, internal floors, etc.: 1309–10 *Pro sarracione plaunchure … ijs vjd [For sawing planchers … 2s 6d]*, Bolton Priory (YRS154/271); 1322 *& plaunchur inde pro fundo eiusdem brecce sarrandis [and for sawing planchers from it for the base of that breach/break]*, Leeds (Th45/88); 1408 *Item et in j roda planchoure cmp. pro stauro*, Ripon (SS81/137); 1416 *meremium [timber] et plaunchors*, Masham (SS35/249); 1535 *Item in bordes for planchers xiijs iiijd*, Stillingfleet (YRS45/128); 1588 *with the shelfes … stone flagges, glasse, boyses, plawnchardes, heckes*, Leeds (Th1/382).

planish The verb meant to make level or smooth and it occurs in the inventories of goldsmiths, in contexts which suggest that metal was flattened on a small anvil by blows from a special hammer: 1374 *unum planyssch stythy*, York (SS4/92); 1458 *j planysshing stithy et j planysshing hamer*, York (SS30/214); 1490 *De v lez planeshyng* *hamers xijd*, York (SS53/58). The term remained in use and can be found in cutlery records: 1766 *all that newly erected mill now used for planishing*, Sheffield (WPS178). See also stithy.

plank Planks were frequently used to bridge narrow water courses: 1610 *the planks between Brampton & Acley*, Auckley (PR); 1623 *the bridge ... on the highway within ... Kirkby Wiske and Ottrington commonly called Newby Planckes* (NRQS3/172); 1679 *noe man shall make their waye over a planke in the middle of a close called the long Holme*, Slaithwaite (DT/287). North Riding bridge accounts suggest that in some places a wooden foot-bridge was erected which linked the causey with the main bridge. In 1624, a Kirby Wiske yeoman was indicted *for not repairing his parte of the cawsey att the bridge-end over the Wiske, besides his planckes, as others his neighbours usuallie doe* (NRQS3/191). See also causey, cobble, foot bridge, hebble, rail (2), tree-bridge.

plantation In early uses of this word the references are to placing plants in the ground or to establishing settlements of people overseas, as in Ireland and New England. As a word for a new wood of planted trees it is recorded from 1669 (OED). Estate accounts in Yorkshire contain references from the late eighteenth century: 1781–2 *Ambrose Lockwood and D Sykes weeding and cleaning the plantation on the Hill side and at top of Quarry near Whitley Hall* (DD/WBE/1/82); 1810 *3 days setting out Firs in Fixby Plantations 16s 6d* (DD/T/R/a/33). The Huddersfield *Nurseryman and Ornamental Gardener* William Pontey emphasised *the Use, Ornament, or Shelter* of plantations in *The Forest Pruner* (1805). See also top.

plash To lay a hedge, cutting into the stems so that they can be bent over and the branches interwoven or 'plaited: *c*.1560 *fell, plashe and twyste hedges*, Woodsome (KayeCP); 1642 *that Janet Richardson doe cut and plashe the hedge and scoure the ditch between Alverey Whitley Shawes and her crofte*, Lepton (DD/WBM); 1651 *That Owners and occupiers ... hereafter plash theire hedges and scower theire ditches*, Wakefield (WCR8/143); 1725 *it would be ... of great use if a clause could be obtained in any publick Act of Parliament to oblige the owners of lands adjoining upon the Highways to cutt and plash their hedges notwithstanding the Highways be 20 foot broad* (QS10/15). See also stoving.

plasterer The skilled workman who applied plaster to walls, especially the outside walls of buildings. The plaster was evidently white: 1333 *Willelmus Whitebrow, plasterer*, York (SS96/28). The by-name 'plasterer' remained in use well into the fifteenth century: 1396–7 *Et in solucione facta Ricardo Plasterer et fratri suo ... pro parietibus prædicti tenementi plastrandis, 6s 8d [And in payment to Richard Plasterer and his brother ... for plastering the walls of the said tenement, 6s 8d]*, Ripon (SS81/120); 1453–5 *Et de 22d sol. Johanni Plastr' pro platsteryng muri aulæ ibidem [And for 22d paid to John Plastr' for palstering the wall of the hall there]*, Ripon (SS81/160); 1466–8 'Paid to William *Playsterer* ... plasterer ... for plastering £1 10s 0d', Hull (YAJ62/160).

plat A patch of flat land, usually quite small, a word akin to 'plot': 1562 *no green grass in the land ... onles it were in some places emongest the ling bent or brakens thereof that some little plattes of grene grasse grewed*, Rawdon (YRS114/103). A frequent minor place-name and by-name: *c*.1300 *Roger del Plat*, Saddleworth (GRDict). It is easily confused with 'plat' meaning footbridge, and I suspect that Smith's explanation of White Gate in Cartworth may illustrate that point. For much of its history the name was White Plate and the modern form dates only from the seventeenth century: 1657 *Whitegate or Whiteplate*, Holmfirth (YRS1/169). With that as his only evidence Smith gave the meaning as 'a footbridge; it is a road over the moors' (PNWR2/238). However, references from the court rolls point to this as a patch of land in Cartworth where wheat was once grown: 1435 *Qwateplatefelde*; 1515 *Whateplates*; 1616 *Whiteplattes*; 1651 *Whytegate or Whiteplattes* (MD225).

plate (1) A piece of iron, fastened to corves and other moveable wooden items as a form of protection in the shafts and galleries: 1754 *two plates for a corf 2d*, Beeston (WYL160/129/4). See also coal-mining tools and implements, scoop shoes.

plate (2) Precious metal, especially silver, from Spanish *plata*: 1528 *ex summa omnium vasorum argenteorum de le plate [from all the silver vessels and from the plate]*, York (SS79/251). See also silver-plate.

plate-coat A corselet of leather on which small plates of metal were sewn: 1567 *one plate cote one styched Tacke two Salletts one gorgett*, Fixby (YRS134/16). Sometimes 'coat of plate': 1563 *2 coats of plate and a Jacke*, Elmswell (DW229); 1568 *a steylle Cappe … An Armyng Sword … twelve Cootes of playt*, Healaugh (YRS134/34).

plate-lock A rare word, for which the OED offers two possible meanings, either a lock in which the works are pivoted on an iron plate or one for an outside door, encased in wood. The sole example noted was for locks on doors which gave access to local woods: 1446–7 *Et in iij seris vocatis platelakes cum ij clavibus emptis pro ij portis in bosco vocato Ryg et j porta in bosco vocato Berkyng [And for 3 locks calls plate-locks with 2 keys bought for two gates in the wood called Ryg and 1 gate in the wood called Berkyng]*, Beverley (ERAS6/82).

plate-shears Strong hand shears for cutting sheets or plates of metal. The term is first recorded in 1599 (OED) and occurs in the inventory of Francis Brownell, a Sheffield boxsmith: 1689 *1 Vice, 16s 0d, 1 paire of plate sheares 4 little hammers* (IH). See also plating-hammer.

platesmith A maker of plate-metal. In the West Riding poll tax returns the word occurs as an occupational surname or by-name: 1379 *Johannes Platesmyth serviens [servant]*, Barnsley; *Johanna Platesmyth*, Cawthorne (PTWR). See also plate-shears.

plating-board The meaning is uncertain but it evidently had something to do with the shearing of cloth. See also shearman.

plating-hammer A hammer used by a blacksmith. The only example found occurs in the will of a Ripley shoeing-smith in 1543: it is in a list of tools that includes several different types of hammer. See also fore-hammer.

play-day For a dialect speaker 'to play' is not to work, so this was a day free of work:

> 1754 *William Buxton charged with casting a roap and a horse rack into the pitt of William Spencer … being in liquor … at the instigation of Jonathan Bramall, a coal getter at the said works, with an intention to stop the works in order to obtain a play-day*, Attercliffe (QS1/93/10).

playing-table A board on which a game such as chess might be played: 1568 *Item 3 pare of plaing tables with men for the same 4s 0d*, Healaugh (YRS134/34). See also tables.

plight (1) Condition: 1393 *I will that thay reparell it and kepe it in the plyte … it es in now, as wele als thay may*, York (SS4/186); 1642 *remoove them to some fresh pasture … And by this meanes may yow have them in very good plight against Easter*, Elmswell (DW11–12); 1674 *she shall deliver the same [goods] againe unto John Armitage … in as good plight*, Meltham (G-A).

plight (2) Possibly a layer: 1377 *de nouo cooperient de unica plita de Thakborde [newly rooved with a plight of thackboard]*, York (SZ1/453–4) but more usually a fold in drapery: 1433 *unam albam pelliciam et duas plytes de wolas [a white cloak and two woollen plights]*, York (SS30/23). It may have referred also to a pleated material, as in the following: 1398 *et vestimenta mea … et unum velum vocatum plytts et unum de cypres [and my clothing … and a cloth called plights and one made of sipres]*, Beverley (SS4/240). See also lawn.

plodding pole Evidently an implement used by men fishing in rivers but the exact meaning is uncertain: 1617 *Saunder Peckett with a poad nett and his man with a plodding powle was fyshinge in the downewodd becke*, Brandsby (NYRO44/139). See also pod-net.

plough Although 'plough' itself needs no explanation it could have unusual spellings: 1552 *such instrumenttes as belongithe unto the pleght*, Beckwithshaw (SS104/64) and it was the specific in some more difficult compounds: *c.*1535 *twelue plowght hedes, xij beames, xij plowght shethes*, Stillingfleet (YRS45/129); 1551 *a ploughe foote, shakill, a tugwithe and a plewbyeme*, Altofts (Th19/266); 1580 *Item 2 plowe soles taken of John Cawthroppe*, Beverley (YRS84/33); 1667 *plew beames … plewstillts, moulboards & plewheads … 1 plewfootboult*, Brayton (YRS47/31). The plough-beam was the central longitudinal beam or bar to which other parts were attached; the head was a wood frame to which the share was fixed and the foot was an attachment to the beam which regulated the depth of ploughing; the stilts were handles. Less straightforward are plough-sole, possibly an alternative of 'beam' and plough-sheath, described by Fitzherbert as a thin piece of wood, set fast in the plough-beam and also into the share-beam, which was 'the keye … of all the plough' (FH10).

plough-beam See plough.

plough-boot, ploughbote The liberty to have wood for making a plough or its wooden parts: 1457 *to have housbote, heybote, ploughbote and waynbote*, West Bretton (YRS102/24); 1524 *housbote, axbot, ploughbot, cartbote and fyrebot*, Thorpe Underwood (YRS140/107); 1579 *competent hedgboote and plowboote in and upon the premises*, Whitley (DD/WBD/3/52). See also boot (1), ploughwright.

plough-foot, plough-head, plough-sheath, plough-sole, plough-stilt See plough.

plough-tilt, plough-tilth The OED has a reference to this term in 1494 in which it was used as a measure of tilled land, equivalent in the example quoted to 160 acres. In Yorkshire it occurs very rarely but was recorded in 1598 when the highway between Leeds and Wike near Harewood was *in great decay* (YRS3/104). The matter was taken up at the Wakefield Quarter Sessions and the justices of peace laid a pain *that euerie person occupieng a ploughe tilth of land* in certain villages around Leeds should *send their draughts and sufficient labourers … and repaire the same waie*. The injunction can be traced to an Act of 1555 which dealt specifically with highway maintenance and required those persons who were in possession of 'plow-land in tillage' to provide carts and labourers when repairs were in hand (SAL6/71–3). The Statute was revived in 1562 and 1587 and the Leeds case confirms that it was being enforced. An East Riding reference shows that the possession of plough-land continued to be a measure of a person's communal responsibilities: 1734 *That every Husbandman for one Plow-Tilt of Land do send a sufficient Person to gather Stones at the Common Day work*, Lund (YRS69/100).

ploughwright A carpenter who specialised in making ploughs: 1269 Robert *Plochewrychte*, Saxton (YRS12/110); 1285 Robert *le Plogwryth*, Ossett (YRS29/195);

1381 *Willelmus Ploughwryght*, Etton (PTER226). He would need to be able to fashion the plough-beam, the plough-foot, the plough-head, the plough-sheaths and the plough-stilts: 1540 *Item to a ploghe wright for makynge ploghes harowes axillyse waynes and hewynge felewes and other tymbre*, Hampole (YRS80/125). See also felf.

plover net A net for trapping plovers, to be eaten: 1550 *To Thomas Parwyne on plower nett with all geyr pertenyng to it*, Morton upon Swale (SS26/71). See also lark net.

plumber Originally a man who worked and dealt with lead, especially on the roofs of great buildings. The by-name probably persisted into the sixteenth century: 1354–5 *In mercede Johannis Plumbarii cooperientis et soudantis diversos defectus super ecclesiam … 2s 6d [For wages of John the plumber for covering and soldering various defects above the church]*, Ripon (SS81/92); 1421 *Custus plumbi. Roberto Plumber operanti ibidem tam in arte sua quam in aliis laboribus [Costs of lead work. To Robert Plumber who worked there both in his trade and on other jobs]*, York (SS35/43); 1476 *Et solutum Willelmo Plomer pro x libris plumbi pro solduracione Stathe vd [And paid to William Plomer for 10lbs of lead for soldering on the staith 5d]*, York (SS192/153); 1538 *pd to Thomas Plummer … for solder to the Church leads iiijd*, Sheriff Hutton: subsequent payments in the accounts were for *solder to the plummer* (YAJ36/181–2).

plump Used originally of a compact body of persons or things, and of a clump of trees from 1470–85 (OED). In 1525, *Herry Savyll* was accused of breaking into Wortley Park where he set his men *in dyuerse plumps and busshementes* (YRS41/180). Much later it was the word for clumps of trees planted in parks and gardens: 1818 *walling plumps in Ridge*, Meltham (G-A); 1847 *a Hill where … a plump of firs had been planted*, Tong (DD/S/I/25).

plunket A woollen fabric of varying texture, blue or grey in colour (OED): 1394 'Of Alice Hukester for ½ a *plunket* cloth', York (YRS64/48); 1407 *Item j garnac' cum capucio de plunkett liberaturæ lineatæ cum tartarico blanco [One robe with a hood of plunket livery, lined with white tartaric]*, Durham (SS4/323).

pocket A small bag or pouch: 1316 'Geppe son of Richard stole 1 *pokett* full of oatmeal', Halifax (YRS78/85); 1471–2 *5 saccis 18 petris lane in 2 serp[lers] et 1 pokette [for 5 sacks 18 stones of wool in 2 sarplers and 1 pocket]*, Hull (YRS144/174); 1692 *one leather pockett worth 2d*, Bowland (QS1/31/2); 1735 *made her a pockett to bring her goose-berrys in*, Bingley (QS1/74/9). See also madder, poke, purse-net.

pocket-knife A folding knife to fit in the pocket. Originally the blades opened at one end only. The few OED references are late and the term has not been noted in local records until the 1700s. In 1721, the inventory of John Woolin of Sheffield listed *1 doz. horne hafted pocket knives* worth 1s 6d and *3 doz. bone penknives* with the same value (IH). Today the terms 'pocket knife' and 'penknife' are used interchangeably. See also penknife, spring knife, trumpmaker.

podiger, podinger See pottinger.

pod-net A net with a narrow neck for catching eels: 1619 *John Pattricke alias Fowler, excellent fisher and fowler of Scruton, sent me a poad nett without cords, lead, shafte or bowe … ijs viijd*, Brandsby (NYRO44/169). See also plodding pole, purse-net.

pogmire A regional word for a miry pit or hole: 1681 *fill up the pogmire neare unto Wiskithill*, Tong (Tong/8a/22). It gave rise to a number of minor place-names, for example Pogg Myers in Liversedge: 1748 *Poggmiers* (SpSt); 1799 *John Sheard of*

Pogmires, Hartshead (PR). It can be compared with Pog Moor in Barnsley which gave rise to a surname (GRDict).

point (1) To fill the spaces in lines of masonry or brickwork with mortar or cement, applying the point of the trowel: 1391–2 *In salar. Willelmi Sklater punctantis super dictam domum per iiij dies, 20d [For William Sklater's pay for pointing on the said house for 4 days, 20d]*, Ripon (SS81/107). In 1682, the masons who contracted to repair Cottingley Bridge had *to point the bridge with good Lime and haire and fill up all the holes in the pavement* (QS1).

point (2), point-maker Points were the tagged laces or cords which served to fasten garments where buttons are now used: *c.*1504 *Item vij groys qwyth poyntes ijs iiijd [Item 7 gross white points 2s 4d]*, York (SS53/192). The making of points became a craft in its own right: 1453 *Willelmus Lutton, poyntemaker*, York (SS96/174); 1500 *Robertus Gettyns, poyntmaker*, York (SS96/225); 1597 *John Hall, pointemaker*, Skelton (YRS24/45). See also dress.

poke A bag or small sack: 1490 *De j ald sekk ijd. De ij lytill ald poyckes iijd*, York (SS53/57); 1505 *that thei open not theyr sakez and pokez and put non to saile*, York (YRS106/14); 1612 *stealing thence a poke and a pecke of barley meale*, Cropton (NRQS1/260); 1662 *he found a quarter of lambe put into a poake and laid there with a stone upon it*, Rotherham (QS1); 1725 *gave him a peck of apples and lent him a poak to put them in*, Ilkley (QS1/64/1). Some pokes were used as measures: 1731 *five mett poakes, two bushill poakes*, Spofforth (QS1/70/4). See also pocket, pudding, seck, sprout.

poked One reference noted: 1615 *An ould cow … She calved shortly after and dyed 6 wekes after being poaked*, Brandsby (NYRO44/91). The meaning is not certain but since the writer had 'poad' for pod the word may be pocked. This was used of diseased sheep and Wright has 'poked' as an alternative (EDD).

poland oats A variety of oats which became popular with Pennine farmers two centuries ago because of its high yield: 1809 *Paid 8 Bushels of Oats Called Poland Oats to Sow in Wheat field 2 8 0*, Ovenden (CA207). It was soon abbreviated to Poland: 1829 *10 stroke Poland … 10 stroke Freesland*, South Crosland (GRD). See also friezland oats.

pole (1) Used of the saplings which sprang from the stool or stoven of a tree in the coppice cycle. They could be felled at the end of the cycle or allowed to grow into more substantial trees: 1528 *Item for iiij pollys off wode, ijd*, York (CCW130); 1530 *for ij eller powylles to a stey* [ladder], York (CCW147); 1675 *thirtie such polles or dooble wavers*, Tong (Tong/3/334); 1719 *polls now allready marked, ringed and sett oute for standing for future growth*, Tong (Tong/3/505); 1755 *to John Earnshaw for felling polls in Boyfall wood 10s 6d*, Kirkheaton (DD/WBE/1/33). Specific uses are mentioned: 1737 *for Polls to rive into lags for Vessels 10s*; 1739 *for Polls to weer, and falling £7 11s 8d*, Lepton (DD/WBE/1/10,12). Note: 1756 *a piece of polewood*, Airmyn (QS1/95/4). See also eller, raff.

pole (2) A pole set up in marshland or on the moors as a way-marker: 1607 *from thence to a certain powle or stowpe set in the moors*, Crowle (ERAS13/202). In 1775, the Halifax historian Watson wrote: *the Botheroyd … family … had a privilege belonging to their lands that they might hawk and hunt between Worset Pole … and Spend Bridge*. This was the pole that gave its name to Pole Moor in Slaithwaite, located at Wortshill.

pole-net A net attached to a pole, used to catch fish. In 1372, at a manorial court in Eastoft, the tenants of Crowle claimed an ancient fishing right: *quod … antiquitus usi fuerunt et adhuc uti debent piscari in comuni aqua totis temporibus anni cum polnettes [that … they had been accustomed of old and still ought to be accustomed to fish in common waters at* *all times of the year with pole-nets]*, Selby (YRS13/288). In the debate about the tenants' rights it is made clear that fishing might take place, but only at certain times of the day and year and then with nets of a defined mesh size, that is allowing the passage of a man's two fingers up to the second joint: *licete* [sic] *piscari possunt cum retibus vocatis polnettes quæ erunt in mascis amplitudinis ut duo digiti hominis ingredi poterit* [sic] *usque secundam juncturam [permitted that they can fish with nets called pole-nets which in mesh size will be such that two fingers of a man can be put in up to the second joint]* (YRS13/289). See also alger, bow-net, lade-net, pitch (1).

polished See pullished.

polling tree Apparently a pole or tree reserved for timber, not one to be cut off near the ground:

> 1543–4 *Ther be growing aboute … the seyd tenements and in hedgis inclosinge lands parteyning to the same ix polling okes aishes and elmes of lx and lxxx yeres growthe whereof xxx resservid to the fermour and tenauntes there for tymber for housebote to repayre their forseyd tenements*, Liversedge (YAJ16/347).

See also pole (1).

ponder To ascertain the weight of, to weigh: 1509 *A chales ponderyng xx uncs, ij cruetts of silver and gylt pondyng iiij uncs*, St Annes Chapel, Foss Bridge, York (YRS106/28); 1528 *Three pannes pondering xxx li, iijs ixd*, York (SS79/255).

pondfald See pinfold.

pontage There are references to pontage from the twelfth century (OED): it was a toll levied on goods that crossed certain bridges and it was supposed to contribute to their maintenance. A writ of 1155 allowed the servants of Fountains Abbey to cross the Ure at Boroughbridge free of *passagium* and *pontagium* (EYCh1/73). There were tolls at Ferrybridge from 1228 (DHB208) and at Cottingham: 1282 'the men of Sokene for pontage of Saltenges' (YRS12/241).

poot The young of game birds, especially grouse, a dialect form of 'poult': 1609 *buying … 12 moorpowtes, 11 doves, 20 fowls*, Northolme (NRQS1/159); 1637 *moore Game in abundance both black & red … and young pootes upon the moores*, Sheffield (HSMS4); 1653 *Not a poute left on all the mores soe we are idell*, Stockeld (YRS161/121); *c*.1730 *some young poots*, Meltham (G-A). See also moor-cock.

popel Descriptive of squirrel skins taken in the early summer (EMV228): 1388 *la goune furre ovesqe popile [the gown trimmed with popel]*, Calverley (Th6/204); 1404 *alia chimera de eodem panno foderata de populo [another chimer of the same material trimmed with popel]*, Durham (SS4/322); 1415 *unam togam de violet furruratam cum popill womes [a violet robe lined with popel skins]*, Wollaton (SS4/381); 1456 *unam togam de violet penulatam cum popill [a violet robe lined with popel]*, York (SS30/201).

popinjay A parrot, see papejoy.

poplar The wood of the poplar was not prized as a building material but it features occasionally in the records: 1423 *vj bords of popill … for amending of the louer of the quyen-eschambre*, Scarborough (SZ1/250). This spelling suggests that the tree may sometimes be the first element in place-names such as Popplewell, although two alternative possibilities are usually given.

porr As a verb, to thrust or poke, as with a stick or sword: 1575 *Simon Tanfeld, a dronkarde, drue his knife and porred with it at Ambrose Jackson in Acaster church upon a Sondaie* (YAJ15/224). The noun usually referred to an iron poker: 1451 *unum porr ferri [a poker of iron]*, Brandsby (SS30/153); 1559 *a brandrethe and one iron porre*, Hipswell (SS26/134); 1612 *four iron porres and one iron cowlerayke*, Brandsby (NYRO44/61). See also pote.

porringer See pottinger.

portas A portable breviary, that is the book which in the Roman Catholic church contained the 'Divine Office' for each day, and had to be ready to hand for those in orders: 1439 'one portiforium *Anglice a portus*', Southowram (Clay8); 1454 *I witt Robert my son the old Portos*, Bossall (SS30/176); 1459 *a Graile, a Manuell, a litel Portose the which … Sir Thomas toke with hym always when he rode*, Wiverton (SS30/227); 1497 *an old portous noited, price xvjs*, Wakefield (YAJ15/93); 1520 *a printyd portews by the gyft of Mr Rawson*, Mount Grace (YAJ18/296); 1541 *I bequith to the new chapel one greate portesse*, Fewston (SS104/34); 1557 *to Wathe churche a Almere, a vestement and a portys* (SS26/97). It was meant to be carried from place to place, which may explain the following: 1454 *my Portatyve which I say opon my selfe*, Bossall (SS30/175). See also reparel (2).

porter The by-name and occupational term were common: 1242 'Walter the Porter', Wetherby (YRS67/114); 1317 *Adam le porter*, York (SS96/17); 1401 *Willelmus de Man, portour*, York (SS96/106). It usually referred to the carriers or workmen who transported goods on their backs, in what were described as burdens: 1433–4 *Et Philippo Simondson porter pro portacione eiusdem calcis, vjd [And to Philip Simondson the porter for carrying that lime, 6d]*, York (SS192/17); 1476 *that no sleddman nor other persoune carie by cart, slede nor horse, any thing that belongis to the saide porters to bere*, York (SS186/191); 1495 *That the porters of this Citie … shall bere from the water of Use unto Trenite Kirk … iiij byrdens for a peny*, York (YRS103/122). Less commonly it was the person responsible for a door or gate, as in a walled town. The origin is clear in three references to one man in the period 1322–6: *John ad Portam; John le Porter; John Atteyate*, Wadworth (YRS83/174–5).

portiforium The Latin word for a portable breviary, found occasionally in English texts: 1351 *lego unum portiforium ecclesiæ parochiali de Kyrkeby super Moram [I bequeath a portass to the church of Kirby on the Moor (Kirby Hill)]* (SS4/64). See also portas.

portmanteau A case or bag which would hold clothing and other necessaries; used by those riding on horseback: 1610 *one port mantæ*, Kirkstall (SpSt); 1632 *A Port Mantua 4s*, Sprotbrough (YAJ56/120). 'Portmantle' was a regional spelling: 1700 *One port Mantle 2s*, Elland (OWR1//2/8); 1721 *had his portmantle cut from behind his horse, with a buckskin and above twenty pair of shoes in it … port mantle or cloak bagg*, West Riding (QS1/61/1).

posnet A small metal pot in which liquids could be boiled over a fire: 1304–5 *Et in j patella, posceneto, navicula [And for 1 pan, posnet, a little boat]*, Bolton Priory (YRS154/182); 1348 *lego Beatrici Daunee unum possenet [I bequeath to Beatrice Daunee one posnet]*, Blyth (SS4/46); 1362 '2 small pots (*posenets*) for the fire', Mitton (YRS111/127); 1451 *Also j posnet to Anne*, Guisborough (SS30/149); 1567 *fowre brasse pottes, one possenett*, Fixby (YRS134/16); 1729 *a brass posnet*, Stainland (QS1/68/4).

poss To thrust or push violently, especially with the feet: 1758 *Shalloons to bee scowred with hogs dung and lant hot in a tub and att after take them to the river and pos them weel* *with your feets so there swill them clean*, Wakefield (YRS155/1). Still a dialect word in regular use, more familiar in the wash-day 'posser'.

posset A drink of thickened milk or cream enriched with spices, alcoholic liquors, eggs and sugar (GWK95). Henry Best gave possets to his sheep-washers half-way through their working day in the sheep-dyke:

> 1642 *sende for a groates-worth of ale and a White loafe … take a quart or 3 pintes of milke and boyle it and then putte to the ale … take the white loafe and either grate or crumme the same very small into the possettes … throw in some pepper and grated nutmegges*, Elmswell (DW20).

Details of the contents are occasionally given in other sources: 1662 *shee made a possitt and putt therein one penyworth of saffron*, Rotherham (QS1). Peter Brears gives recipe details for *Sack-posset* and *Ale-posset* from recipes of 1669 and 1741 (GWK97).

posset pot The containers used for possets could be bowls: 1618 *Item 9 puther dublers, 3 sawcers, a posset boule*, South Cave (Kaner271); 1669 *4 dozen trenchers, a possett bowle*, Elmswell (DW243); 1675 *one puter possit boule*, Hambleton (YRS47/108), or cups, pots, etc.: 1655 *one possitt cup*, Whitley (DD/WBM/69); 1674 *a possitt pott*, Doncaster (YRS134/141); 1700 *1 pewter posset cup*, Holmfirth (IH).

post (1) The vertical timbers in a building or other construction were referred to as posts: 1433 *In diversis peciis meremii … vj duble postis, vj thoregistes [For various pieces of timber … 6 double posts, 6 through joists]*, York (SS35/53); 1498 *with axis hewid in sonder the postez of the hous and pulled it downe*, Wilstrop (YRS41/17); 1509 *I will that the Chappelle … in Estburne be beylded … of viij postes* (SS79/9); 1521 *a kilnehouse of x postes that lieth in the laithe*, Pontefract (SS106/4); 1570 *one baye of a laythe containing fouer postes*, Falhouse (YDK68). The verb to post was usually to prepare timber for use as posts: 1312–13 *Pro meremio prosternendo, postando et sarrando ad grangiam [For timber felled, posted and sawn at the grange]*, Ryther (YRS154/341); 1418–19 *In expensis iiij carpentariorum postantium easdem quercus 3s 4d [For the expenses of the 4 carpenters who posted those oaks 3s 4d]*, York (SS35/38); c.1520 *Will'mo Howyd posting tymber for the said fertter per iij dies and sawyng 18d*, Ripon (SS81/205); 1570–80 *For posting and squarynge syplinges for the mason's scaffaldes 16d*, York (SS35/117); 1580 *maye … cutt downe, fell, post, breake and carye awaye the same trees*, Thurstonland (YDK77); 1707 *paid for timber … paid for posting it*, North Bierley (QS1/46/9). It could also refer to setting up the 'posts' in the new building: 1561 *I postyd new my lathe* [barn], Woodsome (KayeCP). See also balk (2), pan, square.

post (2) A section of coal left unworked in order to support the roof of a colliery, an alternative to pillar. The first example given here may be early evidence of the post and stall method of working: 1486 *with poste and thyrle*, Cortworth (YAJ12/237); 1704 *paid for 2 dayes in a post*, Farnley (MS11); 1714 *there must be care taken … that there be sufficient strong posts*, Shibden (HAS30/146). The term 'post and stall' is in the OED from 1839 but it has not been found in early documents. It describes the method of working coal in which 'posts' of coal were left uncut and the coal-getters worked in the spaces or 'stalls' between them. The practice in some parts of Yorkshire evidently goes back to the fifteenth century at least. See also board (1), pillar (1).

post (3) For postman, a carrier of letters: 1621 *May 9, George Andrew, the towne's foote post, buried*, Hull, St Mary's (YAJ12/467).

postle spoons See apostle spoons.

posture master An expert in assuming artificial postures, especially a contortionist or acrobat: 1741 *William Parkins hath played tricks as a paster master or tumbler … showed tricks or activity of body for reward,* West Riding (QS1/80/4).

pot This was an allowance for drinks or an actual pot of ale given to certain workmen as a bonus, and references to the custom occur in a variety of early documents linked to building: 1332 *In potu quando levaverunt meremium castelli [For drink when they constructed the castle's timber],* York (SS81/198); 1355 *In potu dato eidem et aliis auxilian- tibus circa facturam eorundem 3d [For drink given him and others helping with their making 3d],* Ripon (SS81/91); 1404 *In expensis custodis fabricae versus eandem quareram, cum potu dato operariis ibidem, 3s 6d [For the expenses of the keeper of the workshop adjoining that quarry, with drink given the workmen there, 3s 6d],* York (SS35/26). From the late seven- teenth century it is again well documented in building accounts: 1719 *Gave the mason for a thacking pott 2s,* Bradford (BAS1/54).

Expenses for 'pots' granted to colliers are on record from the latter period but it is likely that the practice was already traditional. In the accounts for a colliery in Farnley near Leeds, payment is recorded in 1718 for a *Holeing pott;* that is probably 'a pot' for driving a tunnel or ventilation hole. A *Wake pott* in 1691 and a *Wake supper* are less easy to explain since 'wake' had a variety of meanings which included festivals and funerals (MS11, MS14). A Shibden reference to the marking out of a new pit contains rather more information: 1713 'all the colliers assembled and Mr Lister allowed them a 'sod pot' of two shillings with which to celebrate the occasion; that is the cutting of the first sods as the ground was opened up' (HAS30/147). In Tong, it was linked with 'earls': 1760 *given for earls of pit and sod pot* (Tong/4c/5). Note the rare alternative: 1749 *gave sinkers to drink for a sod-cup 2s 6d,* Halifax (HAS30/150). See also set pot.

pot-crook A hook suspended from an iron bar over the fireplace, from which to hang a pot or kettle: 1557 *to John my son … pot crokes a raken and my barres of yron in the chimney,* Huddleston (Th27/105); 1612 *2 pottcrooks 1 racke of iron,* Brafferton (NYRO44/37). There were similar alternative words: 1578 *a gallow balke of yron iij crowkes twoo payre of pott howkes,* South Cave (Kaner102); 1581 *1 rekyne … 1 payre of pothockes,* Anston; 1684 *1 paire of pot grips,* Cartworth (G-A); 1558 *one rekane with pottkylpes and tanges,* South Cave (Kaner53). See also crook (1), kilp (2).

pote, poyt A pointed iron bar used to stir the fire: 1628 *one yron poate, one payre of tongs,* Pudsey (LRS1/76). See also fire-point, porr.

potekary, pothecary, poticarie, pottecary Abbreviated spellings of apothecary: 1473 *Georgius Essex, potekary,* York (SS96/194); 1492 *Lauraunce Swattok, Hull, poticarie* (YRS6/162); 1526 *To Edmund, the pothecary his man,* Hazelwood (SS79/6n); 1655 *Item paid to Pottecary Elwick,* Stockeld (YRS161/108). See also treacler.

poteller See pottle-pot.

pot-grip, pot-hook, pot-kilp See pot-crook, kilp (2).

pottage Broth, porridge or similar: 1260 'flesh one day and fish the other with pottage *(potagio)*', Pocklington (YRS12/74–5); 1443 *iij disshys of silver for potage,* Wollaton (SS30/133). In later references it was probably for porridge which dialect speakers treated as a plural: 1789 *I had boil'd milk pottage to my breakfast in plenty and took 'em with pleasure,* Slaithwaite (KC242/1). In my own experience children had to 'eat them up'. The surname Pottage provides evidence of how the spellings porridge and potage interchanged: 1573 *Robert Poddage alias Porrage,* Doncaster (GRDict).

pottecary See potekary.

potteringly In an ineffectual manner: 1708 *the bridge ... was repaired potteringly but who was at the charge of laying the said trees ... he cannott tell*, Skelmanthorpe (QS1).

pottinger A vessel to hold broth, soup, porridge and the like, or one from which these could be eaten. They were often in sets of six: 1520 *ij pewtyr dysshes ij saucers an a podynger*, Mount Grace Priory (YAJ18/296); 1557 *iij podigers*, Pontefract (Th27/152); 1559 *Item 6 pottingers at 6d a peice*, Ripon Park (YRS134/6); 1559 *to eyther of them one potynger and a saucer*, Pontefract (Th27/292); 1588 *six podyngers*, Dalton (DD/WBW/19); 1727 *a Pottinger near full of honey*, Keighley (QS1/67/1). A later spelling was porringer: 1667 *two silver porringers*, North Bierley (YRS134/128); 1691 *6 pewter porringers*, Selby (YRS47/4).

pottle A vessel for liquids, or a measure, usually half a gallon: 1446 *Et in ij lagenis, j potell, j quart' vini rubei ... xxijd [And for 2 flagons, 1 pottle, 1 quart of red wine ... 22d]*, York (SS192/33); 1528 *iij pottells of ypocrace to present my lorde of Northumberland*, York (YRS106/119); 1635 *Item one Pottell, 8 panns and one brasse pott*, Knaresborough (YRS134/80); 1652 *a wainded botle which will hold about a potle of wine*, Malton (SS40/56); 1694 *paid for pottles for the wine*, Almondbury (WDP12/181).

pottle-pot A pot, tankard or similar vessel capable of holding half a gallon: 1392 *Item lego eidem domini unum potelpot et unum quartpott [Item I bequeath to the same master one pottle-pot and one quart pot]*, York (SS4/183); 1426 *et unam ollam argenti vocatam potelpott [and a silver pot called a pottle-pot]*, Spaldington (SS30/11); 1507 *iij wyn pottes of pewder, on potell pott, on quart pott and a pynt pott*, York (YRS39/189); 1548 *To Isabell Larynders a ... pottell pot of pewder*, Bishop Burton (SS106/275); 1578 *Item one sylver pottell pott parcel gylte*, Stockeld (YRS134/50).

pottler Apparently a variant of pottle or pottle-pot: 1306 *ij ollas potellers argenteas [2 pots, silver pottlers]*, Raby (SS2/39); 1414 *et j ollam poteller argenti*, Middleham (SS2/71); 1455 *Item ij pottis of silver potellers parcel gilt*, Masham (SS30/189).

pounce A punch or stamp used to make a defining mark on work done by goldsmiths and silversmiths: *c.*1420 *toutz ceux choises qi ne purront mie porter la dite touche serront touche ovesqez le pounce de luy a quy mesme la choise appente [all those articles which cannot carry the said mark at all will be struck with the pounce of him to whom the article belongs]*, York (SS120/75); 1561 *touched with the pounce of this Citie* (YRS112/9).

pounced Of metal, embossed or chased by way of ornament: 1426 *a gilt cop pownsed with boores*, Holme upon Spalding Moor (SS4/410); 1463 *unum punced pece cum coopertorio argenteo [a pounced piece with a silver cover]*, Leeds (Th24/55); 1519 *a siluer peice pouncede*, Roundhay (Th9/90); 1542 *a nest of thre grett goblettes pounsed gilt ... ij little saltes pounsed*, Lindley near Otley (Th19/133); 1546 *with the pudre pounced basing and laver*, Richmond (SS26/63).

poundstone Probably a natural stone or pebble of a pound weight: 1668 *one paire of weigh scales & 1 pundstone, 6s*, Selby (YRS47/58). As *pundston* it is in the Whitby Glossary (1855), said to have been used by farmers whose butter was weighed by *the lang pund* of twenty-two ounces.

pourprise An enclosure, a word of French origin: 1423 'the meadow called *Powreprice*', Tickhill (YRS120/165); 1553 *on the eest syde of the said Purprise*, Wadsworth (Crossley86). See also purpresture.

powder-box Probably a box which contained perfumed powder, evidently a fashion item: 1421 *Pro j pouderbox … ijs viijd*, York (SS45/64); 1437 *unum pouderbox argenti [a powder-box of silver]*, York (SS30/62); 1444 *a poudre box of maser gilt*, Lincolnshire (SS30/111); 1454 *j powdyr box of silver*, Brandsby (SS30/174).

powdered Used of fabrics decorated with small spots or figures: 1392 *lego dicto Thomæ unum lectum integrum de viride sandal poudred cum rosis [I bequeath to the said Thomas a complete bed furnishing of green sandal powdered with roses]*, Ingmanthorpe (SS4/170); 1565 *a credle clothe of redd velvett lyned with powdred armynze xls*, Temple Newsam (YAJ25/94). See also tunicle.

poyt See pote.

prag A spike or small nail, although the exact meaning is uncertain. The two examples found both occur in Ripon, with almost forty years between the references: 1354–5 *In mercede fabri facientis pragges et lokats de ferro suo pro proprio pro fenestris figendis 8d [For the smith's wages for making prags and lockets from his own iron for fastening the windows 8d]*, Ripon (SS81/92); 1391–2 *In vj pragges ferri emp. pro dictis domibus, 2d [For 6 prags bought for the said houses, 2d]*, Ripon (SS81/108). A connection with 'brag' is unlikely, since these were 'great' nails, so perhaps it is an early form of 'prog' for which there is evidence from 1615 in the sense of 'skewer'. See also prod.

praise See appraise.

prass A frequent alternative spelling of press (1): 1528 *In the Prasse … a gowne of rede scarlet furred*, York (SS79/253); 1559 *one greate cubbord ore prasse*, Treeton (YAJ17/364); 1700 *2 cupboards, 2 prasses, £2 10s 0d*, Holmfirth (IH), and press (2): 1560 *a paire of tenters, ij payre of loymes, a paire of my best sheyres and a prasse*, Birstall (Th27/309); 1582 *A pare of prasse bordes*, Slaithwaite (IMF); 1599 *one sheareboarde, one prasse, lowmes*, Cottingley (LRS1/2); 1607 *sheares, sheareboard and prasse*, Golcar (IMF). See also presser.

prasser See prass, presser.

premises Literally 'the aforesaid', the things mentioned previously. It is now usually understood to refer to a building or buildings, and this meaning came about via title deeds and other legal documents which referred in the first place to a piece of property and then to the aforesaid property. Early usages include: 1564 *Nicollas Tirner … animated his fellowes, saying pull hym … fourth of the quere And the premisses were don*, Slaidburn (YAJ37/178). In 1754, it was argued at the Quarter Sessions that people in the Sheffield area were escaping prosecution simply because there was no place locally to hold prisoners. Their *worships* were asked *to take the premises into consideration and to order a House of Correction to be built* (QS1/93/5).

prentice Short for apprentice: 1544–5 *Item to his prentyse for xij days, vs*, York (CCW280); 1675 *Henry Scholay which was putt as a towns prentice to me*, Gateforth (YRS47/6).

prepresture Probably for purpresture, in the sense of trespass, in this case an unauthorised chimney: 1527–8 *for a chimney at Edmond sheffeld hows being a perpresture*, Hull (YRS141/129).

presently At the present time, immediately or promptly, meanings which it retained into the late seventeenth century: 1642 *take a branch of a willowe or saugh-tree and sticke it into the ground, and it will take presently*, Elmswell (DW127); 1669 *he desired … that they should hide the iron and bring no more to light at once then what they presentlie wrought*, Wickersley (QS1).

press (1) A large cupboard, usually with shelves: 1495 *a presse of waynskott*, York (SS129/87); 1556 *on presse, on almery and on gret chiste standing in the firehouse*, Scarcroft (Th27/63); 1646 *Item one Presse & a Safe xxxs*, Lepton (HM/C/180); 1693 *one presse or cupboard*, Slaidburn (CS1/65). See also prass.

press (2) Implements used by clothiers in the finishing processes, possibly two boards between which the cloth was pressed: 1541 *unto … my sone the best half of all my lomes, walker sheres, cloth presses, and sherbordes*, Halifax (Clay147); 1558 *all my sheres, sherebord, lowmes, and clothe presses*, Warley (Crossley171); 1758 *Shalloons when prest to bee made up on a board … and before you fast the end put them in press*; 1762 *a master dresser … is obliged to have tenters and preses of his own*, Wakefield (YRS155/1,129). See also paper, prass, pressing boards, pressing iron.

press–bed A bed so constructed that it will fold back into a cupboard: 1614 *Mr Woods chamber … one presse bed, j matteris, j payre of sheets*, Stockeld (YAJ34/180).

presser A large cupboard; an apparent alternative of press (1): 1444 *1 pressur pro pannis*, Beverley (SS30/100); 1454 *To the making of a presour for the capys to be kepyd in*, Hull (SS30/171); 1559 *Item one presser … one greate chist*, Ripon Park (YRS134/5); 1570 *One cupboard, a prysser and one old almerie*, Hutton Conyers (SS26/229); 1592 *one presser standing at my bedd head*, Birstwith (YRS55/106). See also pressing iron.

pressing boards 1543 *one pare of hose cloith; also one kiste, one hoode and my pressinge bordes*, Halifax (Clay167). See also prass, press (2).

pressing iron The usual meaning offered for 'pressing-iron' is that it was a sort of smoothing-iron, used by tailors or dressmakers: 1485 *Item ij pare of scherys with ij presyng yrnes xiiijd*, York (SS45/302); 1660 *one pressing iron and one paire of sheres & a bodkinge, 8d*, Selby (YRS47/82). However, that seems an unlikely explanation for the implements used by Sheffield's cutlers, which are referred to in 'pairs' and were probably vices. In 1689, Francis Brownell had *1 paire of pressingirons* and in 1696 Joshua Barnsley had in his smithy *2 pressing Vices 3 other Vices £5, 22 pair of presses 2. 4. 0.* In 1717, George Cartwright had *2 p[ai]r of pressors* in his Tiphouse and *4 vices 1 of 'em a pressing vice* in his Work Chamber (IH). They were evidently vice-like contrivances designed to hold an object and exert pressure on it, perhaps used in the hafting process. See also razor scales, scale-presser.

pressing–nail John Preston was a *bukelermaker* in York who made the following bequest in his will: 1400 *Johanni filio meo omnes formellas meas coopertas et non coopertas cum cornibus clavatis & non clavatis cum clavis artificio meo pertinentibus vocatis pressyng-nayle [To my son John all my moulds covered and uncovered with horns nailed and unnailed together with the nails belonging to my trade called pressing-nails]* (SS4/269). The nails were evidently connected with his craft, possibly as decoration, although the exact meaning remains uncertain. See also buckler-nail.

press paper In a textile context this was paper placed between the folds of cloth when it was ready for transportation: *c.*1758 *Where to light of good press papers at Sheffeild paper makers or att Halifax*, Wakefield (YRS155/1). See also paper.

prest A loan, a part payment in advance: 1481 *which sowgers wer destitute of money … for the which cause and for the Kyngs plesour they desired a prest of money*, York (YRS98/47); 1554 *ther hath been therfor toward the amendment therof and saving of old tymbre delivered in prest to dyvers honest men of the same towne, 13s 4d*, Bridlington (YRS80/71).

prick (1) A metal or wooden skewer: 1562 *One brulinge iron viijd. One paire of pryckes iiijd*, Richmond (SS26/163). As a verb it was to secure with a skewer: 1671 *Simeon Crosley ... had a parcel of wooll stollen out of his barne ... his servants saw her* [Sarah Carter] *have her apron prickt full of wooll*, Sowerby (QS1/11/1). See also broach (1), pack prick.

prick (2) To urge on or incite. In 1482, defending an action of his questioned by the mayor and council, *John Brompton ... said that he was not prickyd by no person so for to doo*: his companions claimed they were *not mewyd nor intysed*, York (YRS98/61). More literally it could mean to spur on a horse and in this sense gave rise to several by-names: 1259 *Peter Prikehest*, Tholthorpe (YRS82/111); 1286 *John Prykmare*, Hipperholme (YRS57/164); 1327 *Nicholas Prikhors*, Shipton (YRS74/157); 1377–8 *John Prichors*, Bolton Priory (YRS154/567). In one undated example the meaning seems more likely to be 'goad': n.d. *Henry Prikestirke*, Elland (Font137). In turn these were responsible for minor place-names: n.d. *Prikestirkrode* (Font136); 1435 *Prikmeyrebank* (MD225/1/161/1). See also stirk.

prick (3) To select or name, that is to choose a person, perhaps by 'pricking' his name on a list, ticking it off: 1754 *my neighbour Mr Melladew, the bearer, is pricked on for Chief Constable by the name of William Melladew but his Christian name is John*, West Riding (QS1/93/4).

prick (4) To hang up greenery as a decoration, presumably securing it with pins or something similar. Tolson noted *Pricking the Church with Green at Christmas* in the churchwardens' accounts for Kirkheaton. He gave no date but subsequently quoted: 1822 *The Church Pricking* (LTK112–13). Similarly, there was *Church pricking* or *decorating with evergreens* at Brodsworth in 1784 (HS7/34).

pricker (1) On stocktaking day, 1 November 1681, the scissorsmiths' storehouse in Sheffield contained *sheaths, namely prickers, razor cases and crooked sheaths* (IH). It seems likely therefore that prickers were the sheaths that contained knives and which were attached to men's belts around the waist.

pricker (2) Only one example noted: 1639 *Edward Horsfall, pricker, sep*, Almondbury (PR). It was evidently occupational but the meaning is uncertain. In some contexts a 'pricker' was a huntsman and in others a witch-finder (OED). A by-name which may derive from witch-finder is: 1168–94 *Helya Prickescin*, Fountains Abbey (EYCh4/145).

pricket (1) A buck in its second year. An undated document which dates from the reign of Henry VII lists the terms which denoted the age and sex of red and fallow deer. Those of the second year were: *knobber or brocket, hearse, hyrsel, pricket, teg*, Pickering (NRR1/139). A count of the deer in Woodsome Park lists: 1698 *of full bucks four brace, that are now bucks of the first head three brace, that were this year sores six brace, sorels four brace, prickets six brace*, Woodsome (C86). Probably the source of the by-name: 1259–60 *Ralph Priket*, Scarborough (YRS44/117); 1384 *John Priket*, Wharram Percy (YRS65/117).

pricket (2) A spike on which to stick a candle, or possibly the candle so placed: 1397–8 *Et in torchiis, torticiis et prikett' emptis de Symone Chaundeler pro camera domini abbatis per billam xlvs [And for torches, candles and prickets bought from Simon Chaundeler for the lord Abbot's chamber by receipt 45s]*, Selby (YAJ15/415).

prick in the belt A trickster's game, played with a stick and a belt, arranged so that the operator could always win: 1748 *an unlawful game ... prick in the belt*, West Riding (QS1). It is described by Halliwell under fast-and-loose.

prick song Originally pricked-song, that is music sung from notes 'pricked' or written down, as distinguished from that sung from memory: 1527–8 *Edwardo Huby pro xiij libris de les priksong, 40s [To Edward Huby for 13 books of prick songs]*, York (SS35/103); 1546 *to too scollers that is useall to singe prik songe of thame ij^d*, South Milford (Th19/167). Charges were made for writing such music: 1526 *Johanni Gibbons pro le pricking diversorum ymnorum et Te Deum in diversis libris in choro, 3s 4d [To John Gibbons for pricking various hymns and the Te Deum in various books in the choir, 3s 4d]*, York (SS35/101); 1675 *Mr Shaw pro pricking songbooks pro Choristers*, Ripon (YRS118/141).

prick wage A single example of this term has been noted and the context helps to define the meaning: in 1694–6 Thomas Hallas was a collier who did not serve out his time and found himself at the centre of a settlement dispute at the Quarter Sessions. The depositions illustrate the complicated way in which some miners were employed:

> 1694 *Thomas Hallas … was hyred by one John Armitage at Lepton … to get cooles as a collier … Armitage gave him 6d in hand and in a weeks time after gave him 2s more for a gods penny and was to pay him dureing the year pricke wage, viz 1s 6d a score provided that he serve his tyme* (QS1).

His wage therefore depended on how many 'score' of coals he 'got' which may suggest that the daily totals were marked or 'pricked' on a tally of some kind. See also god's penny.

priest nail An entry in the colliery accounts for Beeston, of uncertain meaning: 1754 *To priest nailes, 5d. To brag nailes, 4d*, Beeston (WYL160/129/4).

prig A small pan of brass or tin: 1567 *fowre great pannes fowre litle pannes and two little prigges*, Fixby (YRS134/16); 1588 *two pottes, three pannes … one olde fryenge panne and one prigge*, Dalton (DD/WBW/19); 1612 *one litle panne 2 prigg pannes & a dripping panne*, Eccleshill (YRS134/68); 1644 *Item foure prigges & two pannes*, Lepton (HM/C/180).

primage A duty paid to the guild known as Trinity House in Hull. The money was due for the loading and unloading of cargo in Hull and, under certain conditions, in ports such as Bridlington and Grimsby: 1505 'An order for the gathering and paying of primage', Hull (YRS116/47); 1632 'a ship of Grimsby … whose anchor has been taken for non-payment of primage' (YRS105/1); 1662 'Mr Arthur Greame … appointed deputy for the collection of primage at Bridlington … to collect primage from every ship according to her lading entered in the Custom House', Hull (YRS105/156). The word features regularly in the records through that period, but the spelling seems to have been modernised, except in one reference in 1615 where it is called *premidge* (YRS116/31).

print A pat of butter moulded to a shape: 1727 *Joseph Earnshaw had his house broken open and several prints of butter, oatcakes, part of a sixpenny rye loaf and a harding bagg … thence conveyed*, Soyland (QS1/66/9).

privity A thing kept private or hidden, used in the plural for the private parts or genitals: 1686 *was assaulted, knockt down, almost strangled with his cravat and cruelly bruised on the privities*, Wigton (QS1).

privy Short for 'privy room', that is a room where privacy is possible, a toilet or lavatory: 1419–20 *remove thayre pryves that standys upon the kynges dyke*, York (YAJ22/277); 1538 *an entry into a privy or jaques*, Knaresborough (YAJ30/224); 1654 *paid for 3 times dressing the previe*, Stockeld (YRS161/92). Used attributively: 1528 *In his owne chamber … A prevey stole*, York (SS79/254). See also jakes, necessary.

prod A type of nail, probably an alternative spelling of 'brod': 1675 *pro stone prods & stubbs; pro broad prods & nayls*, Ripon (YRS118/146–7). See also lath-brod, stack-prod.

prop Traditionally, animals such as cows and sheep have been marked by their owners so that the farm to which they belong might be identified. The practice is on record from the sixteenth century but it probably has a much earlier origin (AW105–9). In some cases, the horns were burned but more usually the marks could be distinctive cuts to the ears, or colours applied to the hide or wool. It is in these circumstances that prop has been recorded in the Dales: 1685 *one Weather which had A prope on the nar shoulder & A prope on the far hugh bone*, Conistone (RW20); 1688 *a prop of the farr hook-bone*, Litton (QS1/27/4); 1698 *sheep marked with a prop of the nar side*, Ingleton (QS1/37/1); 1729 *a prop of the far hook-bone*, Greenfield (QS1/68/8). The mark was probably made with ruddle, as in an example from west Yorkshire noted by Wright in an advertisement for a lost sheep (EDD). However, the origin of the word is obscure, although a connection with 'property' may be possible.

provin tub Possibly a tub for 'provend' that is food for a horse: 1617 *two buckettes two provin tubes, three ould colleres*, Ripley (YAJ34/187).

pruce Of Prussia or produced in Prussia. It was used particularly in consignments of timber, flax, or skins for the fur trade, all of which were imported into Hull: 1453 *5 duss' pruce skynnes*; 1463 *1 scok prusse delys*; 1471–2 *1 last pruce line* (YRS144/4,60,161). Chests and coffers were often made of wood from Prussia: 1485 *my pruce kyst*, Bridlington (SS53/6). See also spruce.

prune To cut off branches in order to promote fruitfulness and induce regular growth, to trim (OED): 1620 *a rowe in the myddest of little slipps of peartrees proyened to see if they will take*, Brandsby (NYRO44/189).

pudding As a plural noun the puddings were the entrails: 1556 *that neyther man nor woman frome hensfurthe washe anye clothes, woole, puddynges … in the waver*, Wakefield (YRS74/22); 1632 *A paine laid that noe man woman or child shall wash any puddings Fish Cloathes or any other filthy thing above the washing stone*, Burton Agnes (YRS74/90).

The washed stomach or entrail of an animal was used to hold mixtures of minced meat, oatmeal, suet and seasoning which were then boiled to produce dishes that were called puddings. Henry Best's servants were fed such preparations: 1642 *Wee sende for the folkes puddings a bushell of barley, but neaver use any Rye for puddings because it maketh them soe soft that they runne aboute the platters*, Elmswell (DW109). The research of Peter Brears has introduced us to many varieties of pudding, for example, *Herbe-Pudding* and *Kidney Puddings* in 1683; *Carrot Pudding* in 1735 and *Colliflower Pudding* in 1741 (GWK79–85). The meaning of pudding has expanded over the centuries, reflecting developments in food preparation.

From the early twelfth century, Pudding was actually a common by-name (R&W). In 1275 *Johannes Pudding* played an active role in a serious affray at Stainland (YRS29/73) and in 1301, 3s 4d tax was paid at *Lythe cum Sandesend … de Willelmo Puddinge* (YRS21/45). It was also a common first element in minor place-names, linked with –bag, –dike, –hall, –hill and –poke. Smith listed the names but in most cases offered no meaning: John Field suggested convincingly that *Puddyngholm* in Cambridgeshire (1438) was a reference to 'soft, sticky land', presumably having in mind the consistency of a soft, boiled pudding, not one of the early savoury puddings.

That interpretation might also apply to place-names with a similar generic, such as –acre, –field, –hole, –mead, –meadow and –patch, but it cannot explain 'Pudding Bag' or 'Pudding Poke'. The latter is the most popular combination in Yorkshire and it is surely a name for an enclosure which resembled a pudding bag or poke, perhaps an allusion to the shape and tiny point of entry. It is worth noting that in some dialects the wren and the long-tailed tit have 'pudding poke' as a nickname, almost certainly because of the shape of their nests. See also poke.

pudding grass The regional word for penny-royal, a plant that thrives best in moist locations according to the diarist Ismay: 1756 *Pennyroyal or Pudding grass. In most places where the water stands in winter*, Mirfield (WDP1/193). In fact *Penny-royall* was used to season puddings and was an ingredient in *Herbe-Pudding* in 1683 (GWK81).

puke This sometimes described a dark colour, but more commonly it referred to a dark and expensive woollen cloth used for items of clothing: 1485 *una toga de pewyke furrata cum shankes, xiijs*, Ripon (SS64/369); 1486 *To my cousin … a fyne blak puke bonet, nekked*, Beverley (SS53/19); *c.*1537 *a gowne of pewke, furred with blak cony*, Halifax (YRS45/189); 1561 *to the said Nicholes my cote of black puke*, Leeds (Th27/338).

pull To draw up a mine-shaft, using a windlass or gin: 1690 *halfe a day to pull watter*, Farnley (MS11); 1729–30 *a Horse and Lad pulling of Coals*, Swillington (CKY37); 1762 *Thomas Sugden 2 days helping to pull rubbish out of the pitts*, Tong (Tong/4c/6). Note the occupational term 'puller': 1715 *poolers Kilping and Child at 3½d per score 3s 11d*, Farnley (MS14) and the noun, used as a measure: 1752 *39 pooles is a pitt load*, Elsecar (HS9). See also cabin, dress.

pullan A colt, from Old French *poulain*. It was used as a by-name from the twelfth century (R&W) and is the source of the surname Pullan: 1348 *Margaretæ filiæ meæ tercium jumentum melius equicij mei cum pullano … quartum jumentum melius cum pullano [To my daughter Margaret the third best mare in my stud with colt … the fourth best mare with colt]*, Emley (SS4/51); 1349 *unam bonam equam cum pullano in parco de Spofford [a good mare with colt in Spofforth park]* (SS4/60). It was occasionally used as a 'colour', presumably a shade of gray-brown: 1400 *pro j supertunica fururata cum puleyngray [for one surcoat furred with pullan grey]*, Richmond (SS45/12); 1437 *lego nomine mortuarii mei unam togam nigram furratam de poleyngray [By way of my mortuary I leave a black robe lined with pullan grey]*, York (SS30/61). See also grizzle.

pullen Poultry, domestic fowl: 1329 *xij pullan precii xviijd*, Ripon (SS78/102); 1485 *establisshed that the common powters [poulterers] that cometh to the citie … sell there pulan in noo place but in the common market*, York (YRS98/113); 1546 *the thirde parte of all my pulleyne and geise*, Wakefield (Th19/164); 1585 *in pulleyne about the howse 4s*, Rastrick (YRS134/56); 1642 *fatt geise, tenn Capans, thertene hens, sex turkes and other pullan xls*, Cannon Hall (BAS7/192); 1710 *did attempt to steal pullen from about the house*, Clifton (QS1/49/4). They were housed at night: 1617 *December 1 Theaker 5 dayes on the pullayne house*, Brandsby (NYRO44/149).

pullished Made smooth by friction, an obsolete spelling of polished: 1538 *the walls thereof four yards thick … of fine hewn stone clene pullished within and without*, Knaresborough (YAJ30/223).

pull to To close, drawing the door towards one: 1739 *he pulled to the door*, Haworth (QS1/79/4). See also put to.

pump (1) The OED has examples of this word from *c.*1440, long after pumps are known to have been in existence. They were being used at sea, for example, to pump out bilge water, and a ship in the Humber estuary in 1528 had *a newe sofe for the pompe* listed in its gear (YAJ2/250). They were also employed in coal-mines, and Salzmann noted that a pump worked by horse power was raising water from a pit as early as 1486 (SZ/9). However, the first Yorkshire evidencefor such a pump dates only from the seventeenth century: *c.*1640 *All 96 yeards left to be recovered by drawing water only 14 or 15 y*[ard]*e: which was the length of the old Pumpe and as the Ginn was first made by my father*, Barnbow (Th17/10). Note: 1617 *a pumpe wimble that lyeth in the hall end and bitts therto belonging*, Ripley (YAJ34/202).

pump (2) A kind of light shoe: 1614 *a payre of new … stockings promised, a payre of pumpes and some ould clothes*, Brandsby (NYRO44/87); 1750 *the pumps he had upon his feet*, Wetherby (QS1/89/1); 1770 *Benjamin Pumps heelespecht*, Meltham (GRD).

punch (1) To deliver a sharp blow with the foot or knee: 1675 *threw her downe, trayled her upon the ground and punched her with his feet*, Meltham (QS1); 1754 *did punch him upon the body with his knees*, Sheffield (QS1/93/10). See also bunch (2).

punch (2) This word is discussed at some length in the OED but its origin remains uncertain. No mention is made there of Wright, who listed it as a West Riding coal-mining term for a pit-prop and compared it with 'puncheon' which had that meaning (EDD). There is earlier evidence in south Yorkshire accounts which supports that connection: 1637 *they get Punch wood for the use of the coale pits*, Sheffield (HS13); 1778 *for Felling and Boughing punch wood*, Elsecar (HS9). See also steal.

puncheon A short upright piece of timber which served to support the long horizontal beams in a house frame, something like a 'stud'. Salzman has examples from 1369, so the Yorkshire evidence is late: 1639 *Rayles for sealeing Punchones for the same*, Swinsty (YRS134/91). It may also have referred to fence-posts: 1658 *2 newe yaits … 20 yayte barrs … 200 punchions*, Beckwith (SS110/229). It occurs most frequently in coal-mining contexts, but only from the seventeenth century and it was probably 'borrowed' from the carpenters' vocabulary. Puncheon in this sense was a pit-prop:

> 1683 *the grounds, when the puncheons let in to the pitts by the Collyers to support the roof of the work are removed, will sink and fall in and be sore shaken, and in case the puncheons bee not removed yet ordinarily … the same will rott and break and the grounds fall in*, Whitkirk (YAJ36/331).

Later examples include: 1693 *paid for 20 punshons borrowing*, Farnley (MS11); 1760 *William Barker for setting puncheons and forcing vent in upper end*, Tong (Tong/4c/5). See also corf, couple (1).

punfald See pind, pinfold.

punt A flat-bottomed, shallow boat, used on inland waters as a ferry or for fishing: 1653 *paid for fower punts at Borrowbridge £1 19 6*, Stockeld (YRS161/82).

pured grey Used of fur from the back of the squirrel, trimmed so that none of the white belly fur can be seen: 1450 *toga … penulata cum bisse et capucio cum puredgrey [a robe … lined with bis and the hood with pured grey]*, Beverley (SS30/141). Pured miniver was the white belly part of these furs: 1379 *togam meam de scarlet cum furrura de pured menver [my robe of scarlet with a lining of pured miniver]*, Swillington (SS4/107). See also tavelin.

purfle To decorate the borders of a garment, as with gold or silver thread: 1388 *la goune oue* [avec] *la perfulyng du mesme et la lynure del chaperon xxijs [the gown with the same* *purfling and the lining of the hood 22s]*, Calverley (Th6/204); 1532 *To Isabell Harbatill a blacke gowne purfilled with shankes*, Seacroft (Th11/48); 1558 *to my doughter Anne … a gowne purfeld with veluett and wide sleues … to Jennett Gaston … a gowne vnpurfelde*, Pontefract (Th27/234). See also purl (2).

purl (1) A rill or small stream, flowing water: 1584 *the[y] came nere a little becke or pirle of water called Slabecke where the same faleth into the sea*, Falsgrave (NRR1/231). It occurs as a specific element in a number of place-names: 1246–55 *Pirlewelle*, Batley; 1331 *Pirlwelle*, Kirkheaton (PNWR2/180,228). Smith suggested 'bubbling spring' as the meaning here.

purl (2) A spelling of 'purfle', to edge with gold or silver thread: 1544 *unto his wif one gowne of sade tawney purflyde with tawne velvet … unto my suster Nelson one gowne purled with shankes*, Pontefract (Th19/106).

purlin Examples in the OED date from 1447 and it is said to be a horizontal beam which runs along the length of a roof and rests on the principal rafters. Salzman found the word a century earlier in a building contract written in French and suggested that it referred there to the roof timbers generally: 1341 *le scentelon de leesse et del espessour del meryn demort devers Hen. le Stedman et est merche de purlens de la sale Mons. Thomas Vghtred [the scantling of width and the thickness of the timber will be decided by Henry le Stedman and is marked on the purlins for the hall of Sir Thomas Ughtred of York]*, York (SZ1/595).

purpose In the reference quoted here, 'to purpose' meant 'as a result' or just 'considerably': 1677 *in the way I had a dangerous fall, was durtyed to purpose, not hurt, preacht there, found much assistance*, Northowram (OH2/45). The editor described it as 'A Yorkshire idiom still' (1881).

purpresture A legal term for an encroachment or trespass, recorded from *a.*1190 (OED). It often referred to illegal clearances in waste and woodland, as when Adam de Baggebi claimed in an undated charter that Byland Abbey had encroached on his land: *de purprestura quam fecerunt super me versus moram de Baggebi [for purprestures they have made against me onto Bagby Moor]* (YRS50/12). In the settlement of a dispute between Fountains and Sawley, 'assart' was used almost as a synonym: 1279 *quod nulle … ibidem … fiant purpresture vel assarta [that nobody may make purprestures or assarts there]* (YRS90/15), either of which would have been illegal in this case. Similarly, in 1498–9, the officers of Pickering Forest were informed that certain persons had *made divers assartes and purprestures within the Forest* (NRR1/130). The fact that a Methley tenant was indicted in 1377 because he 'made a pourpresture by planting a hedge on the waste' may imply that enclosure alone might constitute such an offence (Th35/152). See also prepresture, pourprise.

purse-net A net like a purse, with ends which could be drawn together by string. It was used principally to catch rabbits: 1612 *taking from him … divers other nets called pursenettes*, Brandsby (NRQS2/1); 1613 *2 foxe nets on the pursnett fashion*; 1622 *one rabbet in his pocke(t) and pursenetts and a ferritt*, Brandsby (NYRO44/61/,232). See also net prick, pod-net.

push-plough Noted as a verb: 1816 *April 2ᵈ pd for push plowing 2a 1r 8p – £3 18 0*, South Crosland (GRD). The noun push-plow occurred in Staffordshire in 1686 and was described as a sort of spade, shod in the form of an arrow: the term breast-plough dates from the same period (OED). The workman's breast applied the force and the implement was used in paring the top sods.

put forth To place an apprentice with a master, now more usually to put out: 1625 *my mynde … ys that … my sonne shall … be brought upp att Schoole in good Learninge untill he attaine to yeares of strength and discretion fytt to be putt forth to be an Apprentice*, Lepton (DD/WBW/25); 1698 *the townsmen … certifie that the … overseer hath put forth certaine children of the poore to sufficient men*, Slaithwaite (QS1).

put off To pass counterfeit or clipped money: 1701 *asked if he could put her off any bad money and told him that if he could putt off for her tenn pounds of bad and counterfeit he should onely returne her five*, Wakefield (QS1).

put to To close a door by pushing it away from one's body: 1699 *he put the forke into the laith … and put to the dore*, Conisbrough (QS1/38/3). See also pull to.

puttock A bird of prey, probably the kite, although the by-name occurs much earlier than examples quoted elsewhere: 1304–5 *Thomas Puttock*, Bolton Priory (YRS154/183). Reaney noted it as early as 1034.

putts Furs made of the paws of an animal, usually the squirrel according to Veale (EMV221): 1500 *Item for a tymmer of putts sewing the overquart semys 1d*, York (SS186/221); 1531 *to have a fur of fox putez*, Harewood (Th11/39). See also overquart, overthwart.

pyx A box or coffer but principally the vessel in which the consecrated bread of the sacrament is reserved: 1490 *I bequeath my saltcellar and a silver box for a pyx to be made thereof and for the body of Christ to be placed in the same*, Halifax (Crossley204); 1542 *to be bestowed of the pix of the hie alter of Otteley vjs viijd* (Th19/67).

Q

qu- In regional spellings this was a common alternative for initial 'wh' or just initial 'w'. Examples are given below and under 'w' but the practice affected a much wider range of place-names, surnames and vocabulary items.

quaking, quakerly Words used pejoratively when referring to Quakers, the religious society founded by George Fox in 1648–50: 1656 *quakeing and disgraceful speaches*, West Riding (QS10/3/271); 1662 *as hee came from a quakeing meeting at Thorne* (QS1); 1723 *he was a lying quakerly knave and wanted his bones breaking*, West Riding (QS1/62/5).

quare, quere Spellings of 'where': 1489 *qwere diuers contrariis & wareans* [variances] *was had … betwixt John Bairstow … and his son*, Ovenden (YRS69/122); 1542 *to be buryed … quare my frends thynks best*, Richmond (SS26/24).

quarrel (1), querrell Early alternative spellings of 'quarry', a place where stone is excavated: *c*.1290 '*torfgravyng, qwarel* with opening up *(apercione)* the land', Ilkley (YRS69/126); 1316 '3 selions under *le Aldequarel*', Richmond (YRS102/92); 1425 *pro xij carect. petrarum a le quarel [for 12 cartloads of stones from the quarry]*, Ripon (SS81/153); 1581 *payd to John Shotley for gettinge slayt at Carlton Quarrell*, Stockeld (YRS161/36). This word, along with a local variant spelling, occurs in the masons' contract for the rebuilding of Catterick Bridge in 1422: one of the clauses granted the masons *free entre and issue … to the qwerelle of Rysedale berkes*, and then, using the alternative regional form, *to the wherelle of Sedbury* (NRQS3/34). The two spelling were used in minor place-names such as Quarry Hill, Almondbury: 1634 *Wharrel alias Querrellhill* (DD/R/3/14) and Quarry Gap near Bradford: 1693 *Quarrell gapp* (DBB/5/C12). When Mr Armytage was building or repairing Kirklees Hall, in 1609, he wrote to Mr Beaumont of Whitley Hall saying that he was *destitute of much stone* and desired *such like as your quarrell affordeth* (DD/WBC/32). 'Quarrel' survived as a dialect word but it is interesting to note that in 1672 a Quarter Sessions clerk crossed out the final 'll' in the words *John Blackburn's quarrell* and substituted the letter 'y' (QS1). See also wharell.

quarrel (2) A square or diamond-shaped piece of glass, of the kind used in lattice windows: 1575–6 *two pannes in the new house, 20d … for xx quarrels, 3s 4d*, York (SS35/116); 1577 *to uphoulde and manteyne the glase windowe quarelles in theme*, Birstall (SS35/350).

quarrier The workman responsible for a quarry of stone, or a worker in a quarry: 1297 *Radulpho le Quarreur*, Bolton Priory (YRS154/81); 1323 *Henry le Quarriour*, Sandal (YRS109/17); 1379 *Henricus le Qweriowre*, Embsay (PTWR). These were occupational by-names: 1400 *Custus Quarerarum: Soluti Henrico Quareour per xx sept 26s 8d [Costs of quarries: Paid to Henry Quareour for 20 weeks, 26s 8d]*, York (SS35/20). See Warrior in GRDict.

quarry In occasional use for a coal-pit, possibly a 'day-hole': 1615 *the North Wood in Baildon … and all pits or quarries of coal there* (WPB1/542). See also delf.

quart A measure for liquids, and the container which held that amount: 1407 *duos quartpottes argenti*, Warsop (SS45/42); 1686 *she stole one ale quart out of the hall*, Ripley (QS1). See also pottle-pot for earlier examples.

quarter A measure of capacity, commonly used for grain, and usually equal to eight bushels: 1343 *et xxx quarteria avenae … xl quarteria siliginis [and 30 quarters of oats … 40 quarters of rye]*, Ryton (SS4/6); 1393 *sex quarteria frumenti, decem quarteria brasei ordei [six quarters of wheat, 10 quarters of barley malt]*, Walton (SS4/187); 1522 *I wytt … a quarter of malt, half a quarter of whete*, Knaresborough (SS104/16). It served as a standard measure, and in 1642 Henry Best wrote: *To our thrashers that bury* [beat] *by quarter-tale wee have allwayes given heretofore iiijd a quarter for oates, vd a quarter for barley, vjd a quarter for pease, and viijd a quarter for winter corn*, Elmswell (DW148). As a measure for coal it was probably the fourth part of a chalder or chaldron: 1333 *quolibet anno de predicti minera de Colsterdale viginti quarteria carbonum [every year from the aforesaid mine at Colsterdale twenty qurters of coal]* (MC133). At Stanley, in 1339, a quarter of coal was valued at two pence (WCR12/84). A later dialect spelling of the term was 'wharter', dealt with separately. See also Rale coal.

quarter cliff Wood cut into four parts: 1642 *The best wood for barres is the willowe … wee gette the biggest of them riven with iron wedges into quarter-cliffe*, Elmswell (DW17); 1686 *one Rood of good and sufficient Quartercliff boards*, Conistone (RW33); 1694 *Paid for quartering and cutting one tree 4s 6d*, Conistone (RW45). Henry Best wrote: 1642 *One may buy alsoe att Malton shorte forke shaftes made of seasoned Ash and quarter cliffe for ijs or xxijd a dozen*, Elmswell (DW36).

quarterdware One example noted, in the ordinances of York's shoemakers: *c*.1424 *Item pro xij paribus de quarteredware or crested hottes xd ob. [Item for 12 pairs of quarterdware or crested hots 10½d]* (SS120/194). The meaning is uncertain but in the same list are *xij paribus de syngleware vijd ob.* so they may have been shoes made from four pieces of leather.

quartern A quarter of anything, a measure of numerous commodities, especially wool: 1312–13 *Pro … j quarteroun de maces*, Bolton Priory (YRS154/340); 1399 *iij quartron vitri albi empti pro magnis fenestris novi chori [3 quarterns of clear glass for the great windows of the new choir]*, York (SS35/18); 1484 *a quartron of woll*, York (YRS98/95); *c*.1504 *iij qwaterons of crules viijd*, York (SS53/192); 1576 *a quartron and a halff of allum vij^{li} x^s*, Leeds (Th4/164); 1605 *for five stone and half a quarterne of wooll at 9s 6d a stone*, Abbotside (YRS130/32); 1615 *and a quartram of lynges with corde to pack them up in*, Brandsby (NYRO44/124); 1622 *3 stone of woll lacking quarteron xxiiijs*, Cottingley (LRS1/61); 1686 *For a quartron of tobacco*, Conistone (RW21). See also ling (2), tick, whartern.

quart saw A regional spelling of thwart-saw, via 'whart-saw': 1561 *one hand sawe … 1 whart saw*, Spaldington (YRS134/10); 1576 *one quarte sawe*, Leeds (Th4/164); 1637 *6 wombles, 2 wedges, 3 hatchets, 1 quart saw, 1 handsaw, 1 thistle, a broadax, a woodax, a paire of pinzers, 2 iron frets*, Barley (YRS47/87); 1671 *1 acks, 1 hack, 1 quart sawe*, Thorpe Willoughby (YRS47/62). The spelling alternative has been noted by earlier Yorkshire writers: Canon Atkinson observed that 'overthwart' was often 'overquart' in the Danby area (NRQS5/143n), and the Whitby Glossary has 'to quart' for 'to thwart'.

queat For wheat: 1568 *Strake queate iiijs viijd*, Kendal (SS26/224).

quelewright A regional spelling of 'wheelwright': 1399 *Et de 20s de Johanne Quwelewright in emendacione facta pro convenc' fracta in cariagio meremii [And for 20s from John Quwelewright for payment made for the broken agreement made for carrying timber]*, York (SS35/14). See also wheelwright.

quell, qweyll, qwhell Regional spellings of wheel, usually in the sense of spinning-wheel: 1542 *Item a spynnyng qweyll viijd*, Bedale (SS26/30); 1557 *to … my maid all suche thinges as belonge to the quell*, Wakefield (Th27/177). Used also of a bell-wheel: 1522–3 *paid for mendyng of the grett bell qwhell viij^d ob*, York (CCW88). John Daille of Attercliffe near Sheffield died in 1547 and the word 'qwell' was used several times in his will (TWH13/82–3). The editor T.W. Hall said in a footnote that *a qwell* was a spring of water; that is a 'well': he was aware that names and words which begin with 'w' were locally given an initial 'q' by clerks who were reporting what they heard, but I believe that his interpretation was mistaken and that 'qwell' in this instance was a spelling of 'wheel'. It can be compared with spellings of spinning-wheel above, and the surname Wheelwright in the following example: 1379 Richard *Qwelwryght*, Halton West (PTWR). The testator's reference to the *qwell which stands in Porter Felde Side* is confirmation that the reference was to a building which housed a grinding wheel. It should be noted therefore that 'wheel' in the Sheffield area had come by then to mean 'mill'. See also wheel.

quenshe For wench, a girl, a characteristic regional spelling: 1558 *to the littill Quenshe iiis iiijd*, Knaresborough (SS104/82).

quenter See quinter.

quere (1) A spelling of 'where', see quare.

quere (2) A regional spelling for choir or quire, that part of a church reserved for the choristers: 1487 *singing solemplye in the high qwere of the said church*, York (YRS103/24); 1491 *my body to be beried in the Lady qwer of my parissh chirch of Allerton Mauleverer* (YDK119); 1555 *sitting in the quere*, Glaisdale (YAJ37/167); 1559 *nere the altar in the qwere at Mydelham* (SS26/128). See also where.

querell An early alternative spelling of 'coral', used in necklaces: 1415 *j par parvum de bedes de querell cum gaudiis [1 pair of small rosary beads of coral with gaudies]*, Wollaton (SS4/382).

quern Used for grinding, typically for malt, mustard or pepper: 1410 *de j pari peper-quernis [for 1 pair of pepper querns]*, York (SS45/48); 1444 *j maskefatt cum j par qwernes*, Beverley (SS30/100); 1455 *j parr qwerens*, Bossall (SS30/180); 1485 *duo paria pepyr-qwernys, ijd*, York (SS45/300). A Sheffield boxmaker named William Harrison made smoothing-irons, and in his smithy in 1692 were the usual bellows, stithy, vices, hammers and tongs, plus *a paire of Quernes* (IH). If these were not for domestic purposes, that is grinding corn, mustard or pepper, it is difficult to say what their function might have been as smithy gear. See also malt quern, mustard quern, whern.

querrell See quarrel (1).

quest Short for inquest: 1594 *Elizabeth the wife off John Eastwodde … was cruelly kylled with an axe … and the crowner queste goynge on her then buryed the Tuesdaye after*, Almondbury (PR1/239).

questor A pardoner, an official appointed by the Pope or a bishop to grant indulgences. In the York Mystery plays they were linked with the scriveners and limners (OED) and enrolled in the city's register of freemen: 1419 *Rogerus Whetely, questor*; 1436 *Thomas Gosberkirk, questour* (SS96/129,151). Other references are also to York men: 1470–1 *Et de Johanne Kirkeby questour quia utlagatur xxd [And from John Kirkeby questor because he is outlawed]* (SS192/134); 1509 *William Smyth, questor* (YRS6/154).

quey See quy.

quick Short for quick-grass, a term used for weeds, especially couch grass. As 'quicks', or its dialect form 'whicks', it remained in use among farmers for whom the collection [samming up] and burning of weeds was a task that went hand in hand with ploughing: 1740 *some quicks or rubbish burning in the fields*, Morley (QS1/79/4). Its use as a verb is also on record in farmers' diaries: 1796 *Quicking in Rush Fields*, Sessay (WM38); 1809 *I was Emplyd in Breaking Clod and Whicking in the afternoon*, Ovenden (CA209).

quicken, quickenberry The mountain ash or rowan: 1729 *This month, the quicken berry, being full of berries, made a brave shew all over the country*, Dodworth (SS65/291). See also whicken, wiggen.

quickfall I have found no reference to this word in dictionaries although it occurs repeatedly in early Yorkshire documents: 1391 'making 18 acres of ditch with *whykfall* around the said wood', Wakefield (WYAS691); 1457–8 *W^mo Plumland pro colleccione de qwycfall ijd [To William Plumland for collecting quickfall 2s]*, Fountains Abbey (SS130/48); 1474 *quod nullus eor' succid' aliq' boscu vel Whicfall infra dominum [that no one of them shall cut any wood or quickfall within the demesne]*, Kirkheaton (DD/SR/213/24); 1488 *Agreed that … the fermours opyn ther yatts [gates] of thare furmolds … that no hurt be don upon the whikfall belonging to the same*, York (YRS103/38). It was said by J. T. Fowler to refer to the haws that fall from hedgerows in winter, or perhaps to the hedge itself (SS130/265). Since the Fountains Abbey accounts refer to collecting quickfall and transporting it he speculated that the haws may have been for the propagation of quicksets. In several examples though the sense of 'hedge' is clear, although there may occasionally have been confusion with 'quickset', as in a 1488 reference to a *hege of whiksall* [sic] *late set … with whitethorn* in York (SS186/198) or a *whiksatt hedge* in Kirkham in 1556 (YRS114/82). See also quickset, quickwood.

quick goods Quick or live animals, livestock: 1485 *my best quyke goode to the kyrke in the name of my mortuary*, Ripon (SS64/275); 1556 *all my goodes quicke and deade*, Yeadon (Th27/128); 1642 *earemarke lambs as they fall for feare that some exchange a dead lambe for a quicke*, Elmswell (DW6). See also good.

quickset Slips or cuttings of plants, especially whitethorn, set in the ground to form a hedge: *c*.1560 *lay qwycksett … the Spring is at hand*, Woodsome (KayeCP); 1609 *diverting the King's way … in Danby Lawndes … by digging and setting of quicksetts*, Danby (NRQS1/158). It came to mean 'hedge' early in its history via the compound 'quickset hedge': *c*.1530 *dyd hew and cut down a great part of the quyk sett or spryng growing in and aboute the … two closez*, Kirby Misperton (YRS70/48); 1580 'a certain hedge or *quicksette*', Dewsbury (YAJ21/414); 1597 *Milncroft field as inclos'd with Quicksetts*, Beeston (WYL160/129/4). See also fence, hedge-breaker.

Quickstavers A place-name in Sowerby near Halifax. It means 'live stakes' and was evidently a location where such stakes had taken root: 1515–16 *apud Whykstaver* (MD225/1/241). 'Whick' is the dialect form of 'quick' in the sense of 'living'. See also wilf.

quickwood Living wood, commonly used of whitethorn as a hedge plant: 1436 *to dyke with qwykwode*, Huddersfield (DD/WBD/8/10); 1545 *for the wages meyt and drynke of ten workmen … in dichynge and laynge qwikwodd aboute the said wood*, Spofforth (DD/RA/f/4a); 1573 *none shall … cut no quickwood*, Dewsbury (YAJ35/299); 1614 *3900 of quick wood after 4d each hundredth*, Brandsby (NYRO44/74). 'Whickwood' was an alternative spelling: 1455 'made one ditch with *Whikwod*',Yeadon (SW172); 1492 *they found no hegges brokyn, whikwod pulled up*,York (YRS103/94); 1562 *as enclosed with a whykewode hedge*, Southowram (YRS69/143). See also quickfall, quickset.

quilk An obsolete form of which. See also workman.

quillet A small plot or narrow strip of land, first on record in an Act of 1533–4 (OED): 1600 *I do deuyde the lordship into … the freholdes … husbandryes … grasse farmes … Cotages wich haue onely Crofts & common … quillets & new rents*, Settrington (YRS126/4).

quilting-frame A frame on which a counterpane is stretched during the quilting process: 1756 *a chair quilting frame & ladder, 10d*, Slaidburn (CS2/85).

quince Used here of the tree, one of several experimental plantings by the Cholmeleys in the seventeenth century: 1621 *William Oliver brought me … Also a white great quenshe tree*, Brandsby (NYRO44/216). An earlier reference to quincetree is given under 'set' (1). See also malacatone.

quinter A regional spelling of twinter, that is a 'two-winters old' animal: 1508 *one qwynter qwhye*, Breckenbrough (SS53/272); 1556 *one qwintter bulle price xxs*, West Layton (SS26/88); 1571 *thre qwenteres called sterkes 40s*, Grinton (YRS152/170). See also quy.

quishing, quissyne Typical obsolete spellings of cushion: 1304–5 *pro baunkers et quissynes xiijs iiijd*, Bolton Priory (YRS154/185); 1430 *iij banquers, xij quysshyns cowched*, York (SS30/8); 1535 *vj qwisshinges of Carpet and tapester werke*, Stillingfleet (YRS45/127); 1588 *Six quyssyns iijs*, Dalton (DD/WBW/19); 1689 *they let him lye by the fier-side in an old coverlet and a quishing under his heade*, Dewsbury (SS40/287). A long list of cushions in an inventory for Temple Newsam includes the following: 1565 *two sewed quyshens of silke xxx⁵ … one of black velvett & damaske vj⁵ viijᵈ … one of verie olde tissue garded vj⁵ viijᵈ, two of crewlez nedle worke iiij⁵ viiiᵈ* (YAJ25/95). Note the occupational by-name: 1367 *Willelmus Qwsshyynmaker*,York (SS96/65). See also banker.

quitclaim See whiteclamed.

quoif See coif, cross cloth.

quoin See corner, coyne.

quome, qwom Obsolete forms of 'whom': 1489 *to all men to qwom this wrytyng of awarde indent schall com*, Ovenden (YRS69/122); 1557 *my chyldryn quome I make my treue and lawfull executors*, Ledstone (Th27/134).

quy A heifer, or a young cow up to three years old that has not calved. The OED headword is quey, a spelling which I have not yet noted in Yorkshire: 1455 *j blake qwy*, Bossall (SS30/180); 1485 *I will that Elyne Peke have a quye*, Ripon (SS64/277); 1559 *one quye to be kepte of the cost and charges of my Executors unto … fully thre yeares olde and upward*,Wombwell (ΓAClvi), 1600 *two heffers (als quyes) prassed to £3 6s 8d*, Marrick (YRS152/358); 1616 *6 quhyes bought whereof the biggest tow branded cost £4 5s*, Brandsby (NYRO44/126); 1662 *Thomas Brockhole … bred att Thorne a redd quy with a little white under her belly which will bee att Christmas next about three yeares old … will calve … he verily believes about tenne daies hence* (QS1). See also appraise, quyherd, why.

quyherd The herdsman responsible for a herd of quys or heifers.These occupational by-names take the history of 'quy' back to a much earlier period: 1301 *De Willelmo*

Quihird xxjd o, Bainbridge (YRS21/90); 1327 *De Willelmo le Quyhird 2s 6d*, Sowerby near Thirsk (YRS74/120).

quyssheld One example noted, in the undated ordinances of the York cordwainers. It was evidently a process in their work but the meaning is uncertain: *c.1430 xij parium ocrearum in mundumque linate fuerint, quyssheld, lased vel clasped xix d [of 12 pairs of leather boots that were neatly lined, quyssheld, laced and clasped]* (SS120/194). If it were a variant of 'qwysshened' it might mean padded.

quy-stirk According to Wright this was a heifer up to two years old (EDD): 1542 *a qwy steirke, vjs viijd*, Bedale (SS26/30); 1563 *Item, 3 quye stirkes, a bull stirke*, Driffield (DW231). See also stirk, why-stirk.

quytyd For 'requited': 1575 *fyrste I causyd the common to be sowen at iiij severall tymes and every man to have his porcion … although yt was paynfull and chargeable yet yt quytyd the travell*, Woodsome (KayeCP). In other words it repaid all the hard work.

qwerfor A spelling of 'wherefore': *c.1450 qwerfor the sayd howmpers* [umpires] *gafe award*, Rastrick (YRS65/124). See also quare.

qweyll, qwhell See quell.

qwhos An obsolete spelling of 'whose': 1450–5 *thus the sayd prior has desheryd this William and us tyl this day qwhos lyn ys worn and passyd away*, Anlaby (YAJ39/84).

qwom See quome.

qwycche, qwylk Obsolete spellings of 'which': *c.1450 certan landes … within the town of Rastryke the qwylke the sayd Bryan [of Thornhyll] had in occupacion … and at qwycche tym … to suffyre the sayd Jon to occupy*, Rastrick (YRS65/124). See also house of office.

qwyett, qwyth Typical obsolete spellings of 'white': 1442 *v yerds of broude qwyett xijs*, Bedale (SS26/31); *c.1504 xij yerdes of qwyth fusgyn vs*, York (SS53/191).

qwylk See qwycche.

R

rabbet An earlier spelling of rebate, used as a verb, meaning to cut a groove along the edge of a piece of wood: 1620 *for paling the swine sty with sawn ashepayle ... he is to saw them and ... the rails and posts and set them in a grundsell and rabbit them into the rail above*, Elmswell (DW166). See also groundsel, thwart saw.

race out For 'erase', that is take out: 1609 *Ordered that James Raper of Holme, convented at the last Sessions for raceing out one name in a Warrant ... be fined 20s* (NRQS1/155).

rache (1), racke A line down a horse's face, usually said to be white: 1512 *a trotting stag, blak, with a rache in the face*, Well (SS79/27); 1556 *my bay stagge with a long Rache*, Farnley (Th27/59); 1617 *my blew Dand horse with a whyte racke*, Barmston (YRS63/54); 1689 *one bay guelding with a black list and a white rache down his face*, Middleton (NRQS7/99); 1726 *an Old Single Eyed bay Mare, a White Rach down her Face*, Whitkirk (Th22/209). See also rache (2).

rache (2), ratch A hunting dog which pursues its prey by scent: 1514 *browght a grett multitude off dogges both grewhondis and ratches*, Moor Monkton (YRS41/168); 1665 *a strange noyse in the aire ... this winter called Gabriel-Ratches by this country-people, the noyse is as if a great number of whelps were barking and howling*, Northowram (OH3/91). It was probably the source of a by-name given as a nickname, although rache (1) is also possible: 1298–9 *domus Gilberti Racche in Halton* (YRS154/92).

rack (1) A verb, descriptive of the gait of a horse when the two feet on each side are raised simultaneously: 1490 *all my riding horses ... except the raking gelding*, Batley (SS53/49); 1549 *my yonge daple gray geldyng rackyng and trottyng*, Newby near Topcliffe (SS106/191); 1562 *one trotting mare ... One old rackynge nagg xxs*, Thrintoft (SS26/166); 1631 *one sad bay maire trots ... one bay fillie with a white starre racks*, Adwalton (BAS7/58–9).

rack (2) A bar or set of bars used to support a spit or other cooking utensil: 1400 *Et respondent ... pro ij paribus [And they account ... for 2 pairs of] de rakkez, j brandereth*, Richmond (SS45/14); 1434 *unum yren spytt, duos yren rakkes*, Campsall (SS30/38); 1535 *ij pare rakes of Iron iijs*, Stillingfleet (YRS45/129); 1567 *fowre spittes two Iron Rackes, one gyrde Iron*, Fixby (YRS134/16); 1669 *a rainge, a pair of racks and 3 spits*, Elmswell (DW243).

rack (3) A frame designed to hold a cross-bow when it was not in use: 1520 *To Mr Vavasour my crosse bowe with rake*, York (SS79/120); 1548 *a crossebowe with the rakke for the same*, Norton, Wath (SS26/61); 1565 *a crosbowe & rack xxs*, Temple Newsam (YAJ25/99).

rack (4), rake Commonly used by dialect speakers in the phrase 'by the rack of the eye', that is estimating an angle or a distance without any rule or measurement. No early example has been found but 'rake' was formerly used in estimating distances: 1647 *one yeard and a quarter broad and a yeard deepe, more or lesse according to the ... rake*, West Riding (QS10/2).

rackabones 'Rack' could be the bones of a dead horse, and the OED has 'rack of bones' for an emaciated person, although the examples are late. In a much earlier reference it was clearly pejorative, evidently a lean or very thin person, a 'bag of bones', or simply a 'good-for-nothing': 1533 *that Wyllm smythe & hys wyffe be brought befor master stawerd for harbryne of rakckabones*, Wakefield (YRS74/17). Wright has 'rackapelt' and 'rackatag' which are also pejorative (EDD).

rackan, reckan An iron bar mounted in a chimney from which cooking implements could be suspended: 1400 *unum par tongis, unum flechok … et unum recawnt de catenis ferreis [a pair of tongs, a flesh-crook … and a reckan of iron chains]*, Cottingham (SS4/268); 1453 *Johannæ Grafton j rakand*, Ripon (SS30/165); 1552 *a spytte a rekan a payer of tonges*, South Cave (Kaner47); 1485 *j racand, j pare of tongys*, York (SS45/300); 1630 *a dripping panne, 2 raggins and a frying pan*, Abbotside (YRS130/52); 1648 *one Reckin balke a paire of tonges*, Sharlston (YRS134/97). See also gallow-balk, pot-crook, reckontre.

rackan crook A crook or hook suspended from the rackan in a chimney: 1544 *a raking crooke and a pare of tonges*, Brignall (SS26/53); 1571 *a rekand crooke*, Abbotside (YRS130/8); 1621 *two spittes … two reckon crookes*, Slaidburn (YRS63/48); 1685 *a reckincrewke is the pot hanger* (Meriton).

racke See rache (1).

rack–rent A very high or extortionate rent, equal or nearly equal to the full annual value of the land: 1755 *tenants at rack rents and cottagers employed in the spinning of wool*, Wetherby (QS1/94/5).

raddle, reddle, riddle Alternative spellings of ruddle, also called red ochre, found as a verb or noun. The ochre was used especially to mark sheep: 1648 *I marked my sheepe, 101 ewes of my owne with fresh redle on the narr sholder*, Thurlstone (SS65/113); 1669 *a fat Wether out of his Croft, marked with raddle on the head, one Eare slitt the other cropt*, Sheffield (QS1/9/2); 1688 *one other sheep ridled on the head*, Kilnsey (QS1); 1701 *a raddle marke along the Rigg*, Skipton (QS1). The varied spellings are found also in minor place-names: Raddlepits, Riddle Clough, Riddle Pit (PNWR8).

raddlings A collective term for poles, rods, twigs, possibly with regionally distinct meanings, referred to by historians as panels in a timber-framed wall (HH6). In the *Hallamshire Glossary* 'radlings' are described as 'hazel or other boughs, put within the studs of a wall, to be covered with lime or mortar'. In 1680, the tenants in Woolley were *allowed to take radlins for the thatch and mortaring of their houses* (YAJ27/284). The verb 'to raddle' is also on record: in 1713, for example, James Fausit was paid *for Studin and radlin the chim*[neys] of five cottages in Wibsey (MM82). In 1457–8, fourpence was paid at Snape for 'raddling', the earliest usage noted (HH5).

raff A map of Huddersfield for 1820 has the word 'raff' written in the enclosure by the corn mill, on one side of the mill goit (HPN15): it was a timber yard, and there have been 'raff-merchants' in Yorkshire from the seventeenth century at least: 1642 *the Raffe-merchant may lawfully stile them good deales*, Elmswell (DW132); 1656 *John Peckit, Rafmerchant*, Hull (YAJ14/206); 1756 *Mr Osborne, Raff merchant*, Sculcoates (PR). The *Leeds Mercury* of 28 Nov. 1738 gives notice that Martin Browne *keeps a Raff Yard … where is to be sold (dry and fit for present use) all Sorts of single and double Deals and Poles at reasonable Rates* (Th26/73). 'Raff' was foreign timber, mostly deals imported from Prussia and the Baltic: the history of these two words is closely linked. See also deal (2).

rag A coarse, hard building-stone, a term with locally distinct meanings: 1409 *Et pro cariagio sabuli et rag xijd [And for transport of sand and rag]*, Beverley (ERAS4/37); 1741

A very good Slate Quarry, the Slate Bed upwards of five Yards thick and very easy to get, the Ragg of a very good Nature, and fit for any Uses about Buildings, Leeds (Th26/95). See also Clifton-Taylor, *English Stone Building*.

raggan, raggin See rackan.

ragged staves This unusual term occurs in the will of Sir Thomas Neville of Furnival: 1407 *unum alium ciphum auri cum cooperculo ejusdem cum ragged-staves [another gold cup with its lid having ragged-staves]* (SS45/41). Under 'ragged staff' the OED says it was a knobbed staff in the badge or crest of the Earls of Warwick: Shakespeare referred later to it as 'Old Neuils Crest', that is a bear chained 'to the ragged staffe'.

raggin See rackan.

raggled Probably a form of ragged, used as a name for a rough-coated animal: 1582 *I geve unto her more one other cowe called Raggalt*, Grinton (YRS152/252). A public house called the *Raggalds*, high above Bradford, is on an ancient highway used by drovers, and 'raggled' may explain the unusual name. See also flowereld, spangled, sterneld, taggle.

ragmop wheel In the grinding and polishing process a final shine was provided by a 'rag-mop' wheel, also called a 'dolly' (CAT36). Many smithies had a work chamber where such a small wheel could be operated by a foot treadle. See also glaze.

rail (1), railway These were ways or roads laid with rails which allowed heavily laden wagons to move more freely, and in this sense the words are first on record in coal-mining districts. Such railways are said to have existed in Newcastle from the early seventeenth century (OED). They were originally of wood but rails made of cast iron came into use in the 1700s. The evidence in Yorkshire for these words dates from the early nineteenth century: 1816 *Taking down and laying iron rails £4 13s 4d*, Bradshaw (HAS32/282). See also tram, wagon-road.

rail (2) A bar of wood, varying in size but usually between six and ten feet long, four inches broad and an inch or more thick. They were used in the construction of carts, fences, staircases, balconies, etc.: 1658 *8 score yeard of reales; for Seelling of a roome ... 15 Duble reales 22 single reales*, Elland (OWR8/2/11). Many wooden bridges must have had hand-rails but there is little evidence for that in bridge documents and the OED has no record of it in connection with bridges until 1726. In fact, a bridge at Knaresborough was brought to the attention of the Justices of Peace in 1695 because it lacked such an obvious structural feature. It was described as *a bridge over A deep Houll ditch* and was actually called *Houll Becke Bridge*. A petition by local people for its repair is lengthy and full of terrifying details. The following is an extract:

> ... *it doth stand High from the water and it is made of two slender narrow plankes which is much decayed, almost Rotten and Shrunk from together ... that Chillder feet may slipp Betwixt them ... neither hath it foot rile nor Hand Rile ... In the night it is said that severall have fallen of it, now of Late two servant girles and an old man who had been drowned but that by accident George Hayge came and helped him out of the water* (QS1/34/2).

See also alder, axle-tree, puncheon, stoop, wood-house.

rail (3) A woman's garment, formerly a piece of linen or other cloth worn about the neck: 1566 *I gyve to Alison Theker on raile*, Richmond (SS26/192); 1611 *to Issabell Mitton ... my best duble raile*, Eldwick (LRS1/11); 1544 *Also the wench ther suster to haue* *a … kirchif, a rail,* Wakefield (Th19/102); 1585 *a kirchyfe and a Rayle which are for the holie days,* Slaithwaite (IMF); 1612 *3 railes, an apperne, a smocke 3 crosclothes 3 old necker-chiefs,* South Cave (Kaner241). Occasionally recorded as 'railband': 1558 *Fower crepings vjs … iiij railbanndes iijs,* Knaresborough (SS26/126). See also upperbody.

rail boot, rail bote The right to take wood suitable for making rails, noted as *rayle-boote* in a Cawthorne lease of 1626 (OC7). In this case the right was connected with the stacking of bark which may have been placed temporarily on rails outside the woods. See also boot (1), peark.

rain(e) See rein.

raise (1) In the process of cloth-finishing, the nap was formerly raised by teasels set in an implement referred to as 'handles', and this was possibly a similar implement: 1556 *two payr of walker sheres and ij payr of lomes a shere borde and a rayse,* Halifax (Crossley145). The *Raizing Peark* mentioned in 1703 under 'handles' is likely to have been the wooden perch or frame over which the cloth was draped. See also peark.

raise (2) See rear.

rake (1) It had two closely related meanings, referring firstly to a rough path in a hilly landscape and secondly to a pasture ground used by sheep and cattle. The dual meaning seems likely to have developed as access to hill-pasture along such tracks became customary: 1564 *in and about the sheppe Raikes or paithes,* Rawdon (YRS114/101); 1598 *had stint and rake of goodes* [livestock] *in Fountans Fell in the Abbey tyme and since* (YRS114/164); 1688 *a rent for a catlerake over Raskelfe Common* (NRQS7/277). From the Tudor period the use of 'rake' as a pasture was well established: 1520 *binds himself … to keep a wether flock … on such raykkes and grounds,* Darnbrook (YRS140/47); 1664 *all that flockraike or sheep pastures,* Hanlith (MD217/167).

Almost inevitably the word became a common element in minor place-names: 1495–6 'from which a payment of 26s 8d to Lord Scropp is mad ann. for *le Cowrake*', Pott (FAR4); 1536 *to pay an out-rent … of 26s 8d for a cow pasture now named the Cowe Rake,* Pott (YRS140/301). In fact, Cow Rake became quite a frequent place-name: 1641 *present … a Slingsby yeoman for an assault … at a place called le Cow Raikes* (NRQS4/212). Two additional examples are Cow Rakes Lane in Whiston and Cowrakes in Lindley near Huddersfield (PNWR8/45).

The use of 'rake' as a verb with the meaning 'to pasture', especially to pasture illegally, is recorded from the seventeenth century: 1617 'the cattle might *rake over* into the disputed ground but they were not herded there', Oakworth (BAS8/8); 1661 *and lette his sheepe rake over all theire oats sowne on this south-side of the sayd heads,* Cottam (DW221). It was used also when permission was granted for red deer to feed on moorland in Swaledale: 1653 *quietly to leap, rake, depasture and lodge on the premises,* Healaugh (NYRO31/21).

The offence of permitting animals to stray onto land sown with oats, as in Cottam above, is evidence that 'rake' was not confined to upland areas but could also be used of pasturing or pasture rights on lowland farms: *c.*1624 *a sheep rake in Cottam Field for eighteen score sheep £6,* Elmswell (DW218). Of course, this right could be exercised only after the harvest had been taken in, and there is similar evidence in a sequence of deeds for Hanlith in Malhamdale: 1662–76 *winter stint or raike … the edige and winter raike within the open fields of Hanleith … herbage and feeding for the said beasts to raike, feed and depasture* (MD217/165; MD217/175; MD217/185; MD217/191).

None of the above evidence touches on the earliest use of the word in Yorkshire, and for that the only information we have is in by-names and place-names. In the accounts of Bolton Priory, for example, are entries which make it clear that as early as the fourteenth century 'rake' was used not of a path but of a territory, probably one used as pasture: 1311 *Pro assartacione in le Rakes vjs [For clearing in le Rakes 6s]*; 1314 *Pro fossura apud le Rakes iiijs jd [For ditching in le Rakes]* (YRS154/293,365). This is likely to have been an area of waste or common in Halton East for *le Rak'* featured there in a priory rental of 1538 (YRS132/30). Even earlier is a by-name in the Calder Valley, also in the plural: 1275 *Adam del Holirakes*; 1376 *Johannes de Holinrake* (GRDict383).

rake (2) An alternative spelling of rack.

Rale coal This obscure term occurs in the north of the county from the fifteenth century: 1457–8 *In exp. carr. ad Rale pro carbon', vijs viijd [In costs of transport to Rale for coal, 7s 8d]*, Fountains Abbey (SS130/58); 1473 *Pro viij quarti et j bus. carbonum voc. ralycole [For 8 quarters and 1 bushel of coals called Rale coal]*, York (SS35/81); 1485 *in carbonibus de Rale*, Ripon (SS64/374); 1603 *Everye tenant … shall everye yere lead me a loade of of coels from Raylye pitts*, Brandsby (NYRO44/23). Similarly, in 1538, Leland stated that *Most of the Coale that be occupied about the Quartars of Richemount Toune be fetched from Rayle Pitts toward … Akeland* (YAJ10/476) and such references are confirmation that 'Rale' was a place. One editor suggested that the coal was brought south from Relly near Durham but it seems more likely that it came from Railey in the same county. Coal-mines were in operation there as early as 1385 according to Victor Watts, and in 1460 a week's production at 'Raly' amounted to 1,800 corves.

ramell It has a general meaning of 'rubbish' but in wood management the reference was to fallen branches or what was left over when the tanners and charcoal burners had used what they wanted, usually branches but sometimes whole trees. It could clearly be used in fencing: *c*.1270 *Habeant ramillum ad claudendas sepes circa terram [They may have ramell for closing fences about their land]*, Whitby (SS72/450); 1307–8 *De ramill(is) quercuum, alnetis et de alio bosco prostrato per ventum … et venditis [For ramell of oaks, alders and from other wood blown down by the wind … and sold]*, Bolton Priory (YRS154/228); 1373–4 *Et in v plaustris cariantibus ramallum de Benetbank [And for 5 cartloads of ramell carried from Benetbank]*, Leeds (Th45/111); *c*.1495 *50 plaustrata de subbosco* [underwood] *vocato ramyll [50 wagonloads of underwood called ramell]*, Pickering (NRR1/155); 1549 *bushes, thornes and other ramell … for fuel*, Stockeld (YRS50/164); 1711 *Hessell, Birch and such like ramill*, Hunsworth (DD/SR/28/6/1). See also blown wood, copy, dry wood, windfall.

rammer A metal instrument used to ram shale or dirt into a bore-hole where a charge of gunpowder had been placed: 1754 *to two drills, one ramer, two spindles*, Beeston (WYL160/129/4). See also gunpowder, tar band.

ramper, rampier, rampire These archaic forms of 'rampart' appear to have two distinct meanings in connection with bridges. In the first, the word was used of a reinforced river embankment, and there is a descriptive reference in the repairs to Kettlewell Bridge: 1686 *the rampier on the south end to extend 20 yards in length up the water and to be carried 12 yards in length below the bridge; and that on the north end to bee 12 yards in length on each side* (QS1/26/1). The rampire may originally have been the earth embankment itself but in such cases it was clearly the wing or wing wall of the bridge. A reference to *the old ramper wall* of Hampsthwaite Bridge, in 1717 (QS1/57/5) may represent a transitional stage in the word's semantic development. The second meaning occurs when 'rampire' is used as a synonym of causey, as it is several times from 1687, e.g. *with a Ramper or Cawsey … from the foot of the bridge 67 yards in length* (QS1). Here also the rampire must initially have described the raised earthwork.

ramson The broad-leaved garlic, abundant in some Pennine valleys in the spring, well known for its smell and taste: 1540 'a close called *Ramson* containing 8 acres of arable land, worth yearly 4s', Grosmont (YRS80/111). Old English *hramsa* or *hramse* is likely to have been the first element in most of the numerous places named Rams Clough and Rams Gill, although Smith opted for 'ram', the male sheep.

ran(e) See rein.

range In early references the meaning is not absolutely clear but this was evidently an iron fireplace of some kind, the fore-runner of the ranges used for cooking which were frequent from the nineteenth century: 1423 *pro j longo brandyryn pour le range [for one long brandiron for the range]*, York (SS45/79); 1559 *to the same Edward one yron raunge standing abowte the fyre*, Aberford (Th27/260); *c.*1585 *The house betwixt the buttery and the kytching … for making of a range in the same*, Fenton (YAJ36/332); 1613 *a range, tangs, reckon*, Cottingley (LRS1/7); 1632 *one iron range 20s*, Ripley (YRS55/115); 1669 *an iron range, gallowbalk and crooks*, Elmswell (DW243); 1678 *to Samuell Abbot my sonn the great range & the grat brasse pott*, Selby (YRS47/1). More explicit details are given in a deposition alleging wrongful distraint:

> 1689 *there being a range fixed in the chimney stead and a table that was nailed to the frame he the said John Hulley pulled up the range and John Loftus pulled the table in pieces and they carried the goodes away*, Wetherby (QS11/29/1).

rape See reap.

raper A rope-maker, the northern form of roper: 1347 *Willelmus le raper*, York; 1436 *Johannes Rapour, rapour*, York (SS96/40,151); 1444 *Willelmo Raper pro factura dictorum cabyll et hausers 24s [To William Raper for making the said cable and hawsers 24s]*, York (SS35/60). The craft was established in York in the 1400s, where the ropers were linked with 'hairsters' as a guild (YRS103/16).

raper staff The meaning is not absolutely clear, but it was evidently a weapon, perhaps similar to a pikestaff, with a short blade or rapier fastened into a wooden handle: 1559 *to George Parker my brother one raper sword*, Rothwell (Th27/278); 1568 *An Armyng Sword with a pare of gawntletes … a Rap* [sic] *to put in a staff … twelve Cootes of playt*, Healaugh (YRS134/34); 1677–8 *found two earthen pots full of rendred tallow, and a broken raper staffe, two poakes full of woll*, Wetherby (QS1).

rase To make a mark with a sharp instrument, to inscribe or write: 1497 *all the above* [will] *rasyd I Thomas Dalton, rasyd with my hand*, Hull (SS53/128); 1561 *To my cosyn … a gold ring rased in the medeste and up again on boith syds*, Romaldkirk (SS26/148). The verb was employed several times in the accounts of the carvers who worked on the high altar in Ripon Minster *c.*1520, for example, *Will'mo Caruer rasyng tymber per v dies et di. 2s 9d; Will'mo Caruer rasyng carvyng works per iiij dies & di. 2s 3d* (SS81/202–3). It is probably a reference to the symbols carved on the wood. Stone was also said to be 'rased' when carved: 1627 *a stone with crosses rased with a workman's toole*, Slaithwaite (DT/211).

ratch See rache (2), reach.

rate (1) The regional spelling of 'ret', that is to soak in water or expose to moisture, used especially in the preparation of hemp and flax. The plants were placed in a pit or pool and as putrefaction occurred the fibres were separated or split from the stem: 1533 *That no man shall rayte nowther hempe ne lyne*, Selby (SS85/34); 1617 *Item sommer*

& winter hempe rated 40s, South Cave (Kaner268); 1630 'They present the inhabitants of Aldburgh because they have retted hemp in an unlawful manner' (YAJ35/203); 1747 forty stones of rated line, forty unrated, Fishlake (QS1/86/3). It was used more widely for the effects of exposure to moisture, as with hay: 1642 When hey is beginninge to be rated the best helpe is to throw it out a little and then … sette it on a newe … staddle, Elmswell (DW36). More unusually, Stovin said of a body discovered in the peat on Thorne moors in 1747 that the Bones was Rated Black (ERAS12/39). See also rating dub, unrated.

rate (2) Manner, style, way, an obsolete usage: 1674 Mr Horton asked him if hee would talke to Sir John Armitage that rate with his hatt on, Stainland (QS1).

rathe A wooden frame or shelving fixed to the side of a cart so as to increase its capacity: 1449 unum antiquum plaustrum cum iij temes ferri et j par de Rathes pro j cortwayne [an old wagon with 3 iron teams and 1 pair of rathes for 1 cortwayne], Featherstone (Th22/258); 1535 iiij pare of Wayne rathes, Stillingfleet (YRS45/129); 1545 one pair of couppraithes, Knaresborough (SS104/47); 1639 two paire of Cart Raths, Swinsty (YRS134/91). Note: 1656 fower Coopes three paire of wreathes, Eshton (YRS134/112); 1716 one oxe cowp 1 pair of wraiths, Slaidburn (CS2/74); 1741 felks, Cart Wrayes & ash bords, Wakefield (QS1/80/9). See also coup, shelving.

rating dub, rating pit, rating pool A pool of water in which quantities of hemp and flax were left to putrefy in order that the fibres might be more easily separated from the stems: 1600 and one hempe pitt for to rayt hempe in, Malham (RMM24); 1611 makeinge a rating dubb in the syke, Airton (DDMa); 1636 land at the towne end of Kylnsey and 1 rating dubbe (MD247). Such pools were necessary because it was forbidden by law from the reign of Henry VIII to place the stems in any running water: in 1607 a number of North Riding men were indicted for watering or rating their hemp … in the brook or watercourse called Kyle Water, Easingwold (NRQS1/85–6). There is early evidence for this process in an undated Monk Bretton charter of the thirteenth century: 'Grant by Adam de Byri … of land in … Hepworth … following the causeway … to the great water of Rachet and thence to Retingpolsnappe' (YRS66/208). See also dub (1), hemp dub, and MHW125–35.

ratsbane Poison for rats, especially arsenic: 1616 Arsnyck to kyll rats 4 oz vjd, Brandsby (NYRO44/129); 1694 Esther Harrison beleeves Ann Bingley hade givne her poyson for it is commonly beleeved the Bingleys carried rats bane or mercury a longe with them in their pocketts, Middlestown (QS1). In 1644, the body of Thomas Sandeman of Scarborough was exhumed and examined for traces of ratsbane, ersemicke [sic] or roseager (NYRO49/40). See also ratton bread.

ratton bread 'Ratton' was the regional word for a rat: it derives from Old French ratoun and its use dates from c.1300 (OED). The animal was considered a pest which needed to be controlled: 1510 like wise vestimentes … are gretly fawtie, some worne full of holles some ettyn w[ith] rattons, York (SS35/263); 1576 a ratton fell, Scriven (SS26/260). Ratton bread was a poisonous paste used for that purpose: 1395–6 It. pro sperstane et ratonbrede empt. ijs ijd [Item for spar-stone and ratton bread bought 2s], Whitby Abbey (SS72/623); 1532 Ser Wylliam Gascoignes servaunte had lad raton brede in the house, Wombwell (YRS70/124); 1679 searching his pockets they found ratten bread and he confessed he intended to poyson himself, Northowram (OH2/266). In minor Yorkshire place-names the word was characteristically linked with water-courses, for example Ratten Clough, Ratten Gill, Ratten Gutter and Ratton Syke (PNWR8/148). See also ratsbane.

ratton row 'Ratton Row' is a minor place-name which occurs so frequently across the north of England that it is tempting to see it as a generic, applied to any row of houses or cottages which was rat infested or perhaps just run down. One possible Yorkshire example occurred in Swaledale in 1297–8 (YRS31/80) but the earliest confirmed reference in the county is in a list which had to do with property in the Mirfield area, that is: 1405–6 *Nethirholes, Brygelone, Ratunrawe, Whitleghes* (DD/WBD/12/4). Not long afterwards it was the name of buildings in York, mentioned in a lease of 1420–1 which placed a garden 'between the tenements of *Ratonrawe* and the stone wall of the city' (SS186/59).

A locality with the same name is mentioned in the will of Humphrey Waterhouse in 1545 when he bequeathed to his son Laurence *all the meases in Hallifax called Ratton Rawe* (Crossley8): there is no doubt that this was by then an established place-name and references in the court rolls include: 1574 'one house or cottage in a place called Rattonrow in Halifax' (HAS37/106). The Halifax historian John Watson said it was a very ancient name and wrote in 1775 *Rattan-row is the name of some ground adjoining to the church-yard, on the north side ... where the fair was kept.*

The inference in this case may be that the Halifax name had survived the demolition of the old buildings on the site but the truth is that some references, even from an early period, were not to bricks and mortar: in 1553 for example 'half an acre of pasture called *Ratton Rawe* in Etton' was in the tenure of John Anleby (ERAS24/60). Other East Riding examples noted are: 1667 *an hous in Rattan Row*, Bridlington (BCP273); 1772 *Ratten Row*, Kilham (YAS/DD147). From the sixteenth century, 'row' had begun to replace 'raw' as the suffix, as in Leeds: 1578 'my other cottages ... in a place called *Ratten Rowe* (Th1/109): in the parish register it was *the Rattanrawe* in 1580 (PR). Many of the latest examples are in villages rather than in towns, that is in Dodworth, Garsdale, Lepton, Long Preston, Swillington and Thruscross, already recorded by Smith (PNWR8). However, the list does not end there, for example: 1736 *A Large well built House, opens two ways, to Westgate and to Ratton Row in Wakefield* (Th24/100); 1777 *Charles Utley, hucster ... at Rattenrow in Addingham* (PR). If these were genuinely late they suggest that the term had become part of a common regional vocabulary.

The area nationally in which 'Ratton Row' can be found has not yet been clearly defined but it occurs in many northern counties and with earlier references. Three Cumberland examples have been recorded, starting with 1410 *Rattanrawe*, Arlecdon (PNCu337) whilst *Ratteonrawelane* is listed among 'lost' Kendal street-names, found between 1575 and 1620 (PNWe1/118). In 1633, Rattenrow was one of several commons in the Redesdale 'marches' of Northumberland (AW32). The county town of Nottingham had *Ratounrowe* as early as 1308 (PNNt16) and John Markham held a toft in *Rattenraw* in East Markham in 1513 (YRS55/174). No examples have yet been noted in Derbyshire.

Whilst the etymology is clear enough the interpretation remains a matter for conjecture. The editors say of the Nottingham place-name that it was 'a common nickname of contempt in medieval street-names', whilst Diana Whaley said of Ratten Row in Caldbeck that it was a 'semi-jocular name for a dismal row of dwellings'. The late examples and the use of the word for areas of common and pasture may point to a more complicated meaning and its use as a generic.

raw An early spelling of 'row', with reference to a hedgerow or a row of houses: 1460 *j shopam cum una camera in rangia vocata Boucher Rawe [1 shop with a chamber in the row called Boucher Raw]*, Beverley (SS30/239); 1531 *the third part of one Raw called Scherome Raw*, Sprotbrough (SS106/19); 1558 *the pore folks of the churche rawe*, Sedbergh

(SS26/122); 1576 5 Feb. *Wyllelmus Turnebull … was weatherbette on candlemasse daye as he came from Marsden and died on the moore under a rawe or hedge*, Almondbury (PR). See also hedgerow, house-row, ratton row.

raw hide Used of untanned or undressed skins: 1579 *Agreed that no tanner, glover, parchment maker … shall buy anie rawe hydes untanned of any forreyner in anie place within this Cyttie, but onelie in the Common Market upon payne of vjs viijd* (YRS119/23). In 1747, Stovin said of a woman's body discovered in the peat of Thorne moors that her *Skin was Like a peece of Tannd Leather* whereas one of her sandals *was made of one whole peece of a Raw Hide* (ERAS12/39).

ray A kind of striped cloth: 1438 'a gown *de ray* … a new hood *de ray*', Hedon (SS30/68n).

rayn(e) See rein.

razor grinder, razor hafter See razormaker.

razor hone A whetstone for sharpening razors. In 1720, the inventory of the Sheffield cutler James Barnes listed 7 *razor Whones* and *a Certaine number of Rasors unfinished*: in 1733, John Justiss had *A parcel of Hones* worth ten shillings (IH).

razormaker, razorsmith In 1285, *William le Rasorer* was a tenant of Wakefield manor, living at Thornes (YRS29/195), and it is possible that he made razors. Otherwise the first mention of the occupational term is in Rotherham, more than two centuries before it has been noted in Sheffield: 1459 *John Dolfyn, rasursmyth*, Rotherham (YRS111/144). Nevertheless, there can be no doubt that Sheffield cutlers were making razors long before it became recognised there as a specialist occupation. In 1681, for example, the Cutlers' Company presented Sir John Reresby and his clerk with six razors, two of them with silver caps, in recognition of their help in the fight against the hearth tax, and in the same year John Greaves was described as a *razor-maker* (FBH129). References in the Sheffield parish register increase from the early eighteenth century: 1709 *Thomas Wilson, Razorsmith* (PR7/33); 1710 *John Slack Rasor smith* (PR7/37); 1721 *Thomas Betts, razorsmith* (PR6/134). The Castleton family of Dove House followed the trade over several generations and they were at the heart of a close-knit community: 1737 *John Castleton, Razer smith*; 1770 *John Castleton, Razorsmith*; 1883 *William Castleton, Razor-hafter* (GRD). Specialist razor grinders are on record from the 1700s and not just in Sheffield: 1786 *Samuel Knot of Ackworth, Razor Grinder*, Wragby (PR); 1786 *Joseph Turnpenney of … Birstall, Razeor Grinder*, Hartshead (PR). The concentration of the trade in Sheffield gave rise to razor strap making as a subsidiary industry by the late eighteenth century (FBH130).

razor scales The scales were the coverings on the handles of razors. In 1731, Jeremiah Rollinson was fined 40s by the Cutlers' Company for selling *Presst Tip Razor Scales … to London unhaft*; that is not attached to the handles. He was said to be *an old offender* (HCC17). In 1721, Samuel Boulsover of Longley in Ecclesfield parish had eight pairs of *razor presses* in his inventory (IH) See also ivory, scales, tip

razorsmith See razormaker.

reach The stretch of water in a river, between two bends: 1693 *Certaine stumps remnants of an old fish garth in Sandall ratch … being very dangerous to ships*, Hook (SAH22/25). Fareswell Reach on the Wharfe at Cawood is on record from 1700 (MH/DC).

realm, ream For 'cream', an obsolete usage: 1559 *The mylke house ... ij reame kitts*, Hipswell (SS26/135); 1579 *In the Mylkhouse ... a realme pott*, South Cave (Kaner102).

reap As a noun it dates from the Old English period and can mean 'bundle' or 'sheaf'. In Yorkshire it is much used with reference to bundles of peas from the sixteenth century: 1592 *Mr Gayton oweth me 40 rapes of peas*, South Cave (Kaner177); 1642 *Pease pullers ... break the stalkes, cutte the stalkes, or else pull them up by the rootes, and then ... they rowle them on forwards, tumbling them over and over till they bee as many as they thinke sufficient for a reape*, Elmswell (DW60); 1671 *reaps of fitches lapt within some reaps of pease*, Tinsley (QS1/11/1); 1677 *there was many reapes of cleane pease whereas George Bollers land was throughout struck with wild oates or thistles*, Barnsley (QS1/16/10). No connection has been established with 'reap' as a minor place-name which occurs several times in the Pennines, especially near woodland or on the moor edge. The earliest evidence for this word is in Heptonstall: 1578 *Henry Bawmefurth surrendered a parcel of land taken from the waste containing forty-three acres and three roods called parcel of the Reapes* (HAS37/141). Reap Hirst in Huddersfield dates from 1658 (HPN118) and Reaps in Slaithwaite from 1710 (SLPN28). The meaning remains uncertain although it has been suggested that it referred to 'shrubs, brushwood' (PNWR7/235). One possibility is that it related to ling or other moorland plants, marking locations where they were formerly bundled up and harvested, although no evidence for that has been found. See also ling (2).

rear To set up or erect a building, originally bringing the main trusses of a timber-framed house into a vertical position. R. W. Brunskill defines different aspects of the task in *Timber Building in Britain* (1985) with diagrams on p. 45 which show successive stages of the process and the number of men involved. Early documentary references are quite rare: 1583 *John Hanson ... 36 years ago did know certain buildings in the town ... at the setting up of which* [he] *was a helper to rear or set up the same amongst other neighbours*, Huddersfield (DD/R/2/16); 1678 *for twoe Timber trees for Parsonage barne ... for bringing them from Yestrop parke ... to 4 carpenters 4 dayes worke apece ... in ale at the rearinge the timber*, Pickering (YAJ35/414). Completing the rearing was clearly a cause for celebration, and a good excuse for ale-drinking: not surprisingly the custom outlived the timber-framed house and became associated with completing work on the roof of a house, whatever materials it was made of. In 1776, workmen in Meltham had ale supplied at four different stages, ending up with *rearing – meat for workmen* (G-A). In 1796, a North Riding farmer recorded a visit to friends, saying *They had a supper about the rearing of their new house* (WM34) and in Mirfield in 1818 William Carr provided *a bottle of rum* and *a Shoulder of Mutton for the rearing supper* (DD/CA/5). In an earlier document the verb to 'raise' probably had the same meaning: 1465–6 'To William Yonge labourer ... at the *raising* of the said house', Hull (YAJ62/157).

rearbrace Part of the armour which covered the arms. See also umbras, vambrace.

reck This alternative spelling of wreck occurs frequently from the mid-1700s. In 1748, there is reference to payments made to John Storrey of Kirkham *for the trouble he has been at for eight years last past in clearing away all the reck and timber that lodged against the jewels of Kirkham Bridge* (NRQS8/275). Similarly, in 1753, Joseph Aneley of Almondbury was paid *for taking Reck from the foot of Armitage bridge* (WDP12/176A).

reckan See rackan.

reckontre An isolated and late reference: 1684 *one range, reckontre and tonges*, Marsden (IMF). Perhaps this was a gallows-like contrivance, serving the same purpose as a rackan but not mounted in the chimney. See also rackan, rackan crook.

recusant One who refuses; that is in England a person who refused to accept the religious changes of the Reformation, to acknowledge the supremacy of the Crown, to conform to the Book of Common Prayer and to attend the services of the Church of England (PDE165): 1575 *Joh. Belhouse wife beinge excommunicate for Recusancie was buried in the churche yarde by the forcible meanes of Joh. Belhouse her husbande*, Saxton (PTD79); 1605 *That Barnabas Pearson of Pickton is a Recusant and does not come to his parish church* (NRQS1/4); 1680 *there is noe popish Reccusantes within our said townes of Kirkeburton, Shelley, Shepley*, etc. (QS1).

reddle See raddle.

red leather References date from the fifteenth century: 1435 *unam tunicam rubeam de rubeo corio [a red tunic of red leather]*, York (SS30/46); 1444 *my litil Sauter coveryd with reed ledir* (SS30/113). In 1476, the ordinances of the York tanners included the following paragraph: *the sersours [searchers] of the saide craft shall yerely ... receive of every foreine barker that commyth to this citie and accustumably sellith rede ledir or byeith rouch ... that they paie unto the sustentacion of the pageaunt ... yerely, iiijd* (SS125/167). It is one of several references to 'red leather', a term that I have not seen mentioned elsewhere in accounts of the industry's history. In 1491, for example, the cordwainers paid *xiijs iiijd to have ther old ordynaunces agayn delivered with serche of blake and rede lether*, York (YRS103/74) and in 1546 it was *agreyd that the cordyners shall bring to my Lord Mayer ther graunts whiche they have for licence to serche red ledder*, York (YRS108/143). The York cobblers' ordinances of 1582 stated that they must mend only *old bootes with read leather ... and not with blacke leather* (YRS119/60).

Evidently the distinction between the two had to do with more than just the colour. Nevertheless, it seems safe to assume that tanned leather was dyed red using a colouring agent, possibly the 'rouch' referred to above in 1476. If this is a spelling of French 'rouge' it may have been a solution in which there was iron oxide, although natural red dyes from plants and insects had long been used on textile fibre: kermes or grains was a scarlet dyestuff brought into Hull: 1490 *½ dos' graynes* (YRS144/204). In the Act of 1558 it was said that *tanned leather red and unwrought* should be sold only *in open fair or market* (SAL7/137) and by the Act of 1662 persons buying *any red tanned leather within the city of London or three miles thereof* were required to give notice of their purchase *to one or more of the company of curriers* (SAL8/70). See also vamp.

red tin The only reference located is in the inventory of George Bullas: 1692 *21 pound red tin* valued at 14 shillings (IH). The significance is uncertain.

ree To sift grain, peas, etc. by giving a circular motion to the contents of a sieve (OED): *c.*1580 *March wynd, I trowe things dry doth blowe, thy warecorne sede ree cleane*, Woodsome (KayeCP). In 1642, Henry Best of Elmswell wrote: *When wee ... take up Corne for the mill ... wee ... looke out ... a sieve to rye the Corne with*. He described making brown bread from rye, pease and barley, *viz a bushel of pease and a bushel of Rye into which wee putte a Ryinge or 2 or 3 of barley* (DW171–2). The reeing sieve was one of several similar implements, each specially designed for its own task: 1611 *1 rye riddle one haver riddle 1 reeing sive*, Brandsby (NYRO44/38). See also ring sieve.

rein A narrow piece of land, although the precise meaning has varied from one district to another and even from one parish to another. Several writers commented on the word in the nineteenth century, among them Joseph Lucas in *Studies in Nidderdale* (1872): 'the country is covered with little step-like terraces called 'raines' ... each being twenty or thirty yards long and two or three yards wide', the feature that is which landscape historians call lynchets. These strips are now under grass but are said by some to have been arable formerly: 1517 *two half-acres of lande callyd Grenhowbuttes, lying est and west of either side a rane,* Threshfield (YRS140/62); 1607 *Henry Deane for getting gress in the Raines in the Field,* Kirkby Malham (DDMa); 1748 *four rains called Cross Green or Cross Green Lands in Malham East* (MD217/256). In 1894, Canon Atkinson wrote: I made oral inquiries in Wensleydale about 'reins' and got the answer 'the grass headland … all round a field' then 'terraces on a hillside, like steps on a stair'. The other day they were 'grassy banks … between the arable steps' (NRR1/61n).

In fact, different shades of meaning are implicit in early records: in some south Pennine townships the word referred to thin strips of woodland where fields dropped steeply down to a stream: 1519 *all the wodes within the birke stubyng except a reyne in the north syde,* Tong (Tong/3/3); 1611 *one little reyne of spring wood of small value,* Almondbury (DD/R/5/29); 1704 *And all Reines belonging and usually fallen with the same,* Bradley (SpSt); 1739 *To the Pillars when pilled the Reign instead of making mares* [meres, i.e boundary markers] *3s 6d,* Whitley (DD/WBE/1/12). It survives as the minor place-name Reinwood in both Lindley and Horsforth. In other contexts its meaning overlapped with 'hedge': 1608 *followinge a certaine rayne or hedge devydinge Gomersall and Liversedge* (Peel125); 1676 *set his nett at the end of a reine or hedge,* Sprotborough (QS1/15).

However, even in those regions where 'rein' was used of wooded strips of land or hillside lynchets, it could also be part of the open field vocabulary: 1517 *one acre called Gosepittes lying north and sowth emongest raynes … also one acre callyd the Brode Rayn … betwixt raynes and the wainway,* Threshfield (YRS140/62–3); 1609 *all the common or waste grounds or soyle commonly called balks and reanes situate in the Biredolefeilds of Wibsey* (LRS2/160).

The evidence of minor place-names takes the word's history back to the twelfth century, although some of the references are undated: *c.*1192 *septem acras terre … ad [seven acres of arable land at] Cumbedenerane … et ad Henganderane et ad Goditrane et ad Hermitrane,* North Stainley (YRS102/185); 1300 'three acres at *Henryran,* two acres at *Ryflatte* … one acre and one rood at *Doweranes,* Bishopton (YRS102/18); 1481 *veridi bosco crescente plantatum vulgariter vocatum le call raynes [for green wood growing at the plantation commonly called the call raynes],* Ripon (SS64/340). The diversity of the spellings in these examples, and the varied meanings, may be a reflection of the word's complex etymology, for Smith lists his examples under two distinct headwords, that is *rein* and *⋆rān,* the former Old Norse in origin and the latter Old English. The meaning given is 'boundary strip' in both cases although they are, he said, 'often indistinguishable' (PNWR7/235).

reins (1) The kidneys: 1708 *in this as in all other chronicall distempers I suppose her reynes or matrix may be out of order if not decay'd,* West Riding (QS1).

reins (2) Used of a fabric suitable for sheets, towels, etc., possibly linen from Rennes in France: 1378 *Trois touails de Reyns [Three reins towels],* York (YAJ15/484); 1380 *unum par linthiaminum de Reyns … et xxvj ulnas telæ de Reyns [a pair of reins sheets … and 26 ells of reins cloth],* Howden (SS4/112); 1400 *cum linthiaminibus, videlicet unum par de reyns cum matresse [with sheets, that is, one pair made of reins with a mattress],* Castle Bolton (SS4/275); 1404 *j par linthiaminum de panno de reyns [1 pair of reins cloth sheets],* Sigglesthorne (SS4/332); 1437 *et unum volet de lawne vel de renys [and a kerchief of linen or reins],* York (SS30/62); 1451 *unum curtum tuellum de reynes [one short table cloth of reins],* York (SS30/144); 1477 *j par linthiaminum de panno de Reynes [1 pair of reins cloth sheets],* York (SS45/235).

rembland, remland A remnant or remaining portion: 1434 *I will that the remlande of my gude be partid in thre*, Ousefleet (SS30/41); 1442 *paid in hand xls and syr Jo Fox plege for the remland*, York (SS129/53); 1482 *all the remland of the soghers* [soldiers] *in the same oppenion*, York (YRS98/60); 1508 *a prest for ever to synge ij daiez in the wek at Brakenbargh and the remland at Kirkby oppon Wisk* (SS53/272). Latterly, it was commonly used of remnants of material: 1643 *unto Anne Slater … a rembland of wollen cloath*, Cottingley (LRS1/130); 1758–62 *Tim Oxley 2 remblands frised scarlit and green*, Wakefield (YRS155/82).

remove When a horse was being shod the remove was a shoe taken off but then refitted: 1563–5 *for the shoeng of his* L[ordships] *horses and remoues*, Topcliffe (SS134/100); 1647 *In the morning to Birchworth, to remove an horse shoe*, Thurlstone (SS65/4); 1690 *for 3 new shooes & a Remove of the sorrelld gall*[oway] *10d*, Farnley near Leeds (MS11).

renew In animal husbandry it was a concern to keep herds and flocks at the desired size, so older animals that were fattened and slaughtered had to be replaced by a new generation. The verb used was 'to renew', as in a tithe cause: 1553 *the custome in the parishe is that for everie cowe which reneweth … they use to pay ijd … the first yere … he hade xvj kie that renewed and the secunde yere he hade xviij kie that renewed*, Gargrave (YRS114/49). See also crochon, drape, strip.

reparel (1) To repair, an obsolete spelling: 1393 *And I will that thay reparell it and kepe it in the plyte that it es in now*, York (SS4/186); 1457 *shall make and reparell all the hegges*, West Bretton (YRS102/25); 1499 *the fence, wall and yates … shalbe cast downe and broken and … at no tyme repareld* (YRS140/65). Also as a noun: 1550 *The churche is owte of reparell so that no man can well abyde in the bodie of the churche for rayne when it is fowle wether*, Kirkby Wharfe (SS35/274).

reparel (2) An alternative of apparel: 1521 *a jacket, a paire hoose and other of my reparell*, Pontefract (Th26/344); 1557 *I bequyth all my reparill belongyng to my body to Agnes my doughter*, South Milford (Th27/165); 1562 *to M^ris Cleasbie … wydowe, for the reperell of Umfraie Cleasbie*, Thrintoft (SS26/167). More generally it could include fittings or 'furniture': 1517 *I woll that the masse booke, portace, chales, vestementt and all other reparell to oon preiste to say masse with*, Clint (SS104/6).

resiant Resident, as a noun or adjective, a status within a community that could guarantee a person's rights and liberties: 1476 *the tenauntes of oure Duchie of Lancastre and thinhabitaunts and receants*, York (YRS98/112); 1534 *then habytances* [the inhabitants] *and receauntes within the said towne … shuld elect … gouerners*, Beverley (YRS41/34); 1570 *tymbre for necesarie buyldynges … to be takyn by the appointment of the officers … resiant within the seyd manor*, Honley (YDK81); 1596 'Any person chosen Governor shall be *Resiant, Inhabytinge and keepe house* within the town', Beverley (YRS84/39).

ret The standard English spelling of rate (1). It occurred also in a detailed description of the marks which were used to identify sheep, and may have meant 'split' in that case. However, that suggestion is speculative. See also underbit.

rial, ryal A form of 'royal', a name given to certain coins, including one of silver struck in Scotland. In England, the name dates from 1464 when Edward IV abandoned the noble and introduced the angel at the noble's old rate of 6s 8d. The ryal or 'rose-noble' also dates from that period and there were subsequent issues: 1535 *in Seuerall places and chistes ther, in Rialles, nobles and King Hen' pence*, Stillingfleet (YRS45/126); 1560 *vnto my good m^r Sr Edmond Maliuerer … one old Riall of golde and to my lady his wife one old angell*, Thorner (Th27/310); 1577 *an ould ryall for a remembrance*, Burton Constable

(SS26/273). A later issue was in 1558, for Elizabeth I: 1612 *I pawned to him 17 owld angels & one Elizabeth white ryall*, Brandsby (NYRO44/58). See also angel, ducat, noble.

rib See thirl.

rid To clear or rid an area of trees: 1578 *to burne, faughe, to Rydd, stubbe, hewe and Cut downe all maner of woodes growenge within the sayd Close*, Cartworth (G-A). See also ridding.

riddance Rescue, deliverance, as in an appeal to the court of Star Chamber:

> 1514 *the forsaid Joseph ... entred into the quere and violently ... strake your said orator upon the bare hedd ... ran to the quere dore for a stafe ... and yff good riddance of other people had nott beyn ... had slayn your said orator in hys owne quere*, Moor Monkton (YRS41/168).

riddel See ridel.

ridding An assart; a piece of land cleared of shrubs and trees, found principally as an element in minor place-names from the twelfth century. These often occur in territorial 'groups': 1320 *Edmundridding ... Lyngridding ... le Pynderriddyng ... Wylkocridding*, Hambleton (YRS94/68). See also rid, rodeland, royd.

riddle (1) See raddle.

riddle (2) A type of sieve with coarse mesh, suited to a particular task: 1446 *j whetridell, j bigridell*, Durham (SS2/94); 1563 *on haver rydle, j wheit rydle*, Knayton (SS2/208); 1713 *one weighbalk scales & riddle*, Barnoldswick (YRS118/63). They were used by colliers to separate small coal and rubbish: 1729 *coal pit riddle 1s 6d*, Horsforth (SpSt); 1761 *1 day riddling and helping to pull*, Tong (Tong/4c/6). One such implement was described as *a wire riddle* in Tong in 1763 (Tong/4c/6).

ridel, riddel A curtain, especially for a bed: 1358 *et lectum meum in quo jaceo cum tapetis et ridellis [and my bed in which I lie with covers and ridels]*, York (SS4/69); 1380 *unum coopertorium lecti ... unum dimidium celur' de card' cum uno riddell [a bed covering ... a half canopy of card with a riddel]*, York (SS4/112); 1403 *ij linthiaminibus novis, cum tribus ridels de blueto [for 2 new sheets with three bluet ridels]*, Swine (SS4/326); 1449 *Item j par ridels de rubeo tarteryno et viridi [Item 1 pair of ridels made of red and green tartarin]*, York (SS30/151).

rider See horse (1).

ridge See mare.

ridgel, riggon, riggot These are regional words for a male sheep, as defined by Henry Best: 1642 *Riggon tuppes are such as have one stone in the codde, and the other in the ridge of the backe*, Elmswell (DW3). Earlier he listed: 1620 *10 wether lambs, 5 riggons* (DW164). It is a word with a great variety of spellings: 1549 *Item ... tups & regoltes price 18s*, Marrick (YRS152/70); 1559 *xxij^tie tupes and rygetts xliiijs*, Hipswell (SS26/135); 1657 *sheepe called Riggalds or ridleinges*, Meltham (G-A); 1664 *such persons as have tups and ridges shall ... let them have liberty till the 22th of this instant October*, Holmfirth (WCR5/158). It was used occasionally of other animals: 1734 *That none keep any Riggan Horse or Nagg in any of the Fields for every Default 3s 4d*, Lund (YRS69/99).

ridge-tree, rig-tree A horizontal timber, the highest beam in the roof-frame of a building: 1642 *aboute a yard or more belowe the rigge tree*, Elmswell (DW154); 1672 *we had* *busy work in laying our rig-tree*, Northowram (OH1/289); 1733 *7 spars and one ridgetree*, Wakefield (QS1/73/4). See also roof tree.

ridging, rigging The rig or ridge on the top of a building, sometimes used less precisely of the roof itself: 1399–1400 *Et in s. j hominis temporantis lutum pro ryggyng pro prædicta domo 4d [And for 1 man's pay for mixing the clay for the rigging of the aforesaid house 4d]*, Ripon (SS81/130); 1700 *was seen upon Thomas Hodgson's house rigging, going on the slate*, Bradford (QS1). The stones used for the ridge were described in a number of ways: 1658 *for Leading of slate & rigging stones 7s 4d*, Elland (PR2/263); 1710 *for lime, latts, nailes, ridgeing stones, moss*, Colne Bridge (SpSt); 1815 *Ridgins fetching 5s*, South Crosland (GRD). It could refer to other roofing materials: 1675 *to digge, grave and carry away morter, stones and rigging sods*, Hanlith (MD217/188), and to covers or 'roofs' more generally: 1642 *cutte of one of the endes of the stacke … takinge of as much as wee thinke will serve our turnes for toppinge up or rigginge of the same*, Elmswell (DW62).

Riding Bridge In Yorkshire, each of the three Ridings was responsible for the maintenance of certain bridges and these were known as Riding Bridges. The term is likely to have come into use in 1530–1 when the Statute of Bridges placed that responsibility on county authorities (SAL4/199). In 1674, in a report to the Quarter Sessions, the local Justices referred to Sowerby Bridge as *a Rideing Bridge* – having had occasion to *refer to the Booke of Bridges* (HAS4/181).

rig The northern form of ridge, used of the back of a person or animal: 1471 *j togam … penulatam cum gray rygges [1 robe … lined with rigs of gray]*, Beverley (SS45/183); 1582 *wambes and rigges* that is backs, York (YRS119/63); 1736 *thou knows I laid a beesome start upon thy rig last night*, Baildon (QS1/76/2). Sometimes found in compound adjectives: 1554 *one whyte Rygged quye*, Swillington (Th27/32); 1588 *a white rigged whye*, Scalby (YAJ36/436). As a verb it could be to put something on the back in order to carry it: 1739 *took 5 shalloons of the tenters and rigged them and carried them into his masters shop*, Haworth (QS1/78/4). Additionally it meant 'put a roof on a building', with special reference to the ridge itself: 1399–1400 *pro ryggyng pro prædicta domo 4d*, Ripon (SS81/130); 1561 *I riggyd the hall with atchlar*, Woodsome (KayeCP); 1682 *shall slate all the aforesaide roofe … and … rigg the said building with good stone riggs*, Scriven (YAJ16/113). See also raddle.

rigald A rail or spar of wood, usually listed in the same contexts as wainscot and timber: 1357 *Item, in vj regald et vj waynscotes vjs iiijd*, York (SS129/7); 1371 *Et in ij magnis arboribus emptis pro celura … 13s 4d. Et in lxxx rigald emptis pro eadem cum cariagio, 40s [And for 2 large trees bought for the ceiling … 13s 4d. And for 80 rigalds bought for the same together with the transport 40s]*, York (SS35/8); 1399 *Et in sarracione meremii righolts et waynscots, per annum, 38s 10d [And for sawing timber rigalds and wainscots, for the year 38s 10d]*, York (SS35/16); 1409 *pro j rygalt*, Beverley (ERAS4/36); 1415 *In sarracione meremii, ryghold, waynscott … 100s 10d*, York (SS35/35). Salzman noted the spelling *rigallis* in Scarborough in 1343 and considered that the word originally referred to wood from Riga, the Baltic seaport (SZ1/246). They were imported as boards and cut to the required size locally. See also clabbord, deal (2), wainscot.

rigg, rigg and furrow Rigg was used in several ways for land, presumably meaning 'ridge' initially: 1735 *six riggs or parcells of ground lying in the middle of a close called Bell-close*, Barton St Cuthbert (NRQS9/130); 1751 *ordered to turn her out onto the rigg or common*, Hemsworth (QS1/90/3). The term rigg and furrow is more commonly associated with ploughed land: 1590 *the lands lying in Medydall and the cownne which are fur and ryg are growne out of knowledge by name by reason they were imployd to an ox* *pastur*, Kirby Underdale (HKU62–3); 1629 *It is easelie to be discovered that their is rigge and furrow wheare the hedge standeth*, Scriven (YAJ37/202). However, it was used in Colsterdale of coal seams, possibly a reference to the undulations of the strata: 1705 *the seam of coales 14, 15 or 16 inches high and goeth much Rigg and Furrow* (BM82/53). See also swelly.

rigging See ridging.

riggon, riggot See ridgel.

right Used colloquially to mean thoroughly, completely or just 'very': 1556 *he hathe tane* [taken] *paynes for me right oft*, West Layton (SS26/87); 1727 *his foot slipt and he fell upon his back, and was never right well after*, Barnsley (SS65/276). In a letter of *c*.1500 the rector of Slaidburn wrote that he was *right glade*, Whitley (BP2).

rightwise Just, rightful, etc., an early spelling of 'righteous': 1404 *the other ryghtwis heire of the Says londes*, Durham (SS45/27). See also wrangwise.

rig tile A tile used for ridging the roof of a building: 1415 *In lx rygtiell emptis de eodem Willelmo* [*Welwyk*] *20d* [*For 60 rig tiles bought from the same William 20d*], York (SS35/35); 1446–7 *c tegulis vocatis rigtiell* [*100 tiles called rig tiles*], Beverley (ERAS7/60).

rig-tree See ridge-tree.

rind An iron fitting which serves to support an upper millstone on the spindle (OED). The early Yorkshire evidence lends weight to the argument that the final 'd' is excrescent: 1322 *Et in la Ryne molendini anterioris de nouo faciend*[a] *cum j pecia ferri empta ad idem, vjd* [*And for renewal of the upper millstone's rind together with 1 piece of iron bought for it, 6d*], Leeds (Th45/86); 1399 'one *Ryne* for the said mill', Selby (SAR88); 1512 *Item ii ryne spyndilles xijd*, York (SS79/36).

ring (1) As a verb it is used in colliery accounts for Farnley near Leeds, although with a mistaken spelling: 1718 *Rob. a day to wring the pitt*; 1719 *Titus and Tho. Savage a day wringing the pitt and takeing up earth 2s 0d* (MS11). The meaning is not absolutely certain but the noun 'ring' was used in the north-east for a circular spout or crib which was placed in the shaft of a coal-pit to collect waste water. It was made of oak or metal and had a channel on its top side (EDD). There were expenses at Beeston colliery, in 1754, for *Making a Ring Dam* (WYL160/129/5).

ring (2) To put a ring in the snout of swine in order to stop the animals rooting too deeply: 1519 *Item that the swyn be rynged be Saynt Elene day excepte sewes with piges*, Selby (SS85/32). See also swine root, yoke.

ring (3), ring about To mark a ring round a tree as a sign to the workmen about to fell a wood: 1686 *the woods ... all marked by ringing*, Tong (Tong/3/377). It could be a painted ring or a cut made with a scrive iron: 1763 *reserving thereout all Those Trees and powles and wavers therein which are marked and Rung about with Red, with the Bark and Ramel thereon to be and Remain*, Esholt: in this case though the ring warned the woodmen not to fell the tree. In the same indenture 'ringing' was defined more explicitly: *cause the Wood & Trees to be so pilled and Rung about that the same be felled within or Under the Ringing of the Bark and that Low near the Earth*, Esholt (MD93/19). It raises the question of whether the colour indicated whether or not a tree was to be felled. The word occurs also in a reference to timber rights in Wistow woods, although the meaning here is obscure: 1711 *tenants may take competent wood in the Lord's woods for daubing standers and windings to the houses and for rings, ring stowers and shellrings to the ways* (YAJ7/56). See also mark (1), set out (2).

ring sieve A reeing sieve: 1410 *j schakyngsiff, j tempse, j ryyngsiff cum iiij rothers*, York (SS45/49). Noted in several South Cave inventories: 1558 *one meyll syve one ryenge syve one temse*; 1609 *2 Rying sives two riddles & a temse* (Kaner53,227). In the meaning suggested by the editor the first element was interpreted literally but I believe these were 'reeing' sieves. See also ree.

rip To slash or tear apart violently: 1725 *Ann Milnes promised she would be ripped if she ever told*, West Riding (QS1/64/2).

Ripon measure Although there were attempts to standardise measures during the Tudor period, the records contain numerous examples of local measures: 1526 *to receve two quarters of malte at the malte garner after Rypon mensure upon the liberalitye of the seid abbot and convent*, Fountains Abbey (YRS140/166). See also Leeds measure, perch, Thirsk measure, Winchester measure.

ripper A spelling of 'rippier', that is one who carries fish inland to sell: 1623 *Marmaduke Potter of York ripper Recognizance £20*, Scarborough (NYRO47/104). This man was elsewhere described as a pannierman, the usual word locally for such a trader. As 'rippier' was more usual in Sussex it is possible that the word had been brought into east Yorkshire by fishermen from the south.

ripple A regional word for a slight scratch: 1666 *knocked him downe to the ground … demanded his purse … and gave him some rippills with his knife on his brest*, Hutton (SS40/141).

ripple comb A toothed implement used in the preparation of flax and hemp: 1481 *De ij hekills et uno repplyng kame iijd*, York (SS45/261); 1499 *a hekyll, A ryppyll came iijd*, Northallerton (SS2/104); 1570 *3 heckles one ripple canne* [sic] *for lyne*, Spaldington (YRS134/40); 1585 *a ripple comb 2 heckles*, South Cave (Kaner130); 1639 *In the Chamber a ripplecame*, Selby (YRS47/43); 1667 *a ripple coame*, Barley (YRS47/44). A by-name is evidence of the word's much longer history: 1316 *Alice Ryppelcombe 1d*; 'to the house of *Alice Reppelcombe of Werloley*', Sowerby (YRS78/145–6).

rise (1) The headword 'rice' is preferred in the OED but 'rise' is a more common spelling in Yorkshire records. As a noun it meant twigs, small branches or brushwood, a valuable commodity which formerly had a variety of uses, particularly for hedging and making causeways. In 1393, woodmen in Langwith were lopping off the branches and taking them away: *amputando et cariando les ryse [for cutting and carrying the rise]* (SS35/130). By-laws were put in place which aimed at preventing illegal practices: 1601 *Henry Lynthwate succid. boscu (voc ryse) [for cutting wood (called rise)]* in *the Cliff* without licence; that is 'cut down wood called *ryse*', Farnley Tyas (DT/193). It could be used for firewood but excessive amounts may have posed a problem and were possibly burnt on site: 1649 *helped Wm Wainwright to hurdle up rise in the Rocher, and burnt some* (SS65/100). It may also have given its name to patches of woodland: 1579 *A certain Thycke or Ryse of Thornes and Underwood*, Arncliffe (Whit2/492). A Sawley Abbey charter of 1279 has *de bosco Ris nominato [for wood called rise]* (YRS90/15). See also rise bridge, stoprise.

rise (2), rise-end, rise-side The 'rise' is the upward direction of a vein or bed of coal, contrasted with the 'dip'. The advantage of this to miners is expressed in some documents: 1819 *if the coal rises in the field it is better for that and worth more*, Birstall (DD/CA/5). The 'rise-end' may have been a gallery driven on the rise parallel to the cleavage of the coal. Examples have been noted in Halifax and Leeds: 1704 *Jo. Harrison paid Adam in parte of 9 yards Rise end*; 1718 *Robert end or Rise end*, Farnley (MS11); 1765 *taking up stone in the rise end*, Tong (Tong/4c/9). The 'upper end' mentioned in some pit accounts may have the same meaning. See also dip-side.

rise bridge Formerly, a 'bridge' could be a causeway across marshy ground rather than a structure across a stream or river. This best explains the meaning of the popular minor name Rise Bridge, since 'rise' was brushwood, the material used to make the causeway. The name occurs as *Risebrige* in a Pool charter of around 1195–9, which then continues 'and so through the midst of the marsh' (YRS63/81). Similarly, there are references to *Rysbriggs* in Thornton in Craven (PNWR6/34) and *Risebriggkerr* in undated deeds for Selby Abbey: in the latter case the marsh or *kerr* took its name from the causeway (YRS13/28). See also fleak bridge, stock bridge.

rised wough A partition or internal wall, with 'rise' or small branches interwoven between the stakes: 1627 *the West end … of one lathe or barn containing two bayes … which was lately divided from the East end … with a rysed woghe*, Allerton (MD178); 1634 *one watled wanded or rised woghe*, Addingham (GRD). See also wand (2).

rise-end, rise-side See rise (2).

rish The early spelling of 'rush', the grass-like plant found in marshy locations. These were traditionally strewn on the floors of dwellings and more important buildings as late as the seventeenth century: 1525 *the expence of my lords house att London … rishes ivd* (WHD39); 1609 *for 10 burden of rishes against the judge coming 20d*, Skipton (WHD89). The spelling change to 'rush' influenced surnames such as Rushton and Rushworth but had less impact on the place-names from which they derive; that is Rishton and Rishworth (GRDict). See also rush-bearing.

rive To split or cleave wood with iron wedges and malls or mells, found commonly as a past participle: 1457 *pro c long revyn burdes*, York (SS35/69); *c*.1565 *certayne Isshies* [ashes?] *… which was reyvenn for Sparis*, Pickering (NRR1/209); 1580 *payd to William Watson for ryvinge of wodde*, Stockeld (YRS161/18); 1648 *Thomas Milnes who riv mee some staves for pitchforks*, Thurlstone (SS65/96); 1694 *Paid to Rob' Wiggon for riving Lattes*, Conistone (RW45). See also lag, lathcleaver, pole (1), quarter cliff, sagen, treenail.

riveter A workman who made or used rivets. The occupational term is found in York from the early fourteenth century: 1307 *gyrdelers and revettours*, York (SS120/180). It occurred also as a by-name: 1313 *Ricardus le riveter*. 1419 *William Revetour, clericus fil' Rogeri Morbell revetour* (SS96/15,130). Some of these craftsmen provided ornamentation for girdles but others may have been engaged in making the armour known as 'almain rivets' which owed its flexibility to the riveted and overlapping plates which were capable of sliding. No early references to the occupation have been noted elsewhere but in 1724 the inventory of Samuel Taylor, a Sheffield cutler, listed *4 revitting Stithys … 3 revitting hammers* (IH). See also boring stoop.

road, roadway The noun 'road' originally referred to the act of riding but then it became associated with the horse-riders' route or way and eventually it took the place of 'highway'. The change appears to date from the second half of the sixteenth century: 1569–72 *Tadcaster … tenn myles from Yorke in the rode wey towards London* (YAJ17/141); 1618 *and soe directly upward … towards one common roode waye leading from Roodeshalle to Bradfourth* (MMA/239); 1669 *a wooden Bridge over the River at Marsden the same beeinge a greate Roade for a greate parte of Lancashire and Cheshire* (QS1/8/3); 1755 *situate about the middle of the Road betweene the Towns of Wakefield and Halifax*, Mirfield (WDP1/192).

It came into regular use in the seventeenth century, sometimes as 'high-road', and was particularly frequent in the records of the Quarter Sessions: 1649 *ridinge on the high rode way betwixt Lincolne and Doncaster* (SS40/25); 1686–7 *to the damage of Carriers and Packmen who use the road betwixt Lancashire and Newcastle*, Kettlewell (QS1/26/1). The idea that it referred to the 'route' survived through that period: 1725 *I veued the highway in the high roade betwixt Leeds and Harewood* (QS1).

roast iron A gridiron, a device for broiling fish and meat dishes over an open fire: 1377 *2 kymnays … 1 rostyrin*, Hackness (YRS76/129); 1395 *It. pro j rost yryne xviijd*, Whitby (YRS72/617); *c*.1500 *j gratt and j royste yryn iiijd*, York (SS53/193); 1519 *the roste yerne in the same where [choir] set in the chapitour*, York Minster (SS35/267). In view of the strange location in this latter case it was suggested by the editor that it served to bake the singing-breads.

rocher A word of French origin, meaning a large rock or a steep rocky place: 1637 *very stately Timber … & they grow out of such a Rocher of stone that you would hardly thinke there were earth enough to nourish the rootes*, Sheffield (HSMS3); 1675 *Ann Wood … by reason of a fall she had from a Rotcher … hath been lame ever since*, Wortley (QS1). It continued to be a meaningful term: 1647 *stayed all day at the Rocher and got great stones out of the quarry there*, Thurlstone (SS65/52); 1651 *James Sykes of Lingarthes for cutting wood in the Rotcher 3s 4d*, Slaithwaite. It gave rise to a number of minor place-names (PNWR7/236) and one early compound was the source of the surname Gaukroger: 1403 *John de Gawkerocher*, Halifax (GRDict).

rochet, rocket An outer garment, of the nature of a smock or cloak: 1377–8 *Pro consuicione rochet(i) pannorum secr' et linthiam(inis) pro eodem ijs [For sewing a rochet out of cloths from the sacristan, and linen for the same, 2s]*, Bolton Priory (YRS154/559); 1547 *To Edward Hungaite my sone my velvet rochett*, Saxton (SS106/257). There was a regional form of this word: 1657 *the felonious stealing and carrying away a certaine White Gray Cloake or Rokitt*, Earlsheaton (Th11/99).

rodeland, roydland A regional word for land cleared of trees, first encountered in an undated thirteenth-century document: 'that parcel of land called *rodeland*', Thurstonland (YRS65/154). The term was used in the Wakefield area to distinguish between ancient town arable and land that had been assarted: it was a type of land and I have found no evidence to link it with place-names, unlike 'royd' and 'ridding' with which it shares much of its meaning: 1307 'it is called *rodeland* because it was cleared (*assartata fuit*) from growing wood', Alverthorpe (YRS36/81); 1339 'John de Bouderode gave 40d to the lord for … an inquiry as to whether the land which he holds is from the ancient bovates or *rodeland*', Ossett (WCR12/134). The dialect spelling 'roydland' is on record from the early fifteenth century: 1402 'one acre of meadow called *Roideland*', Methley (YRS83/146); 1515 'half a bovate of land, four acres of land *de Roidelande*', Hipperholme (MD225/1/241). See also assart, ridding, royd.

rod iron Used of iron in the form of a rod. In 1690, the Act which sanctioned new taxes on imported iron wire, metal and metal products defined it thus: *iron slit or hammered into rods, commonly known by the name of rod iron* (SAL9/89). In the late seventeenth century the slitting mills at Wortley and Rotherham were the sole suppliers of rod iron to the south Yorkshire nailmakers (RMH37). Further north, in August 1745, Mr Spencer of Cannon Hall wrote to Francis Watts of a contract with John Stringer which was to bring him *5 tons Rod Iron from Colne Bridge to Barnby Furnace*: he added that *there's none Slit of the sort at Rotheram* (SpSt). In that financial year the Colne

Bridge accounts have payments to customers over a wide area, including Lancashire, for the *Carr:* [carriage] *of Rod Iron* (SpSt). See also ironmaster, nail chapman, slitting mill.

roll A type of windlass which consisted of a cylindrical piece of wood or metal, evidently similar to or synonymous with 'turn': 1655 *the Roule and Turne, geares and other utensils belonging to the sayd Coal pitts*, Sharlston (GSH3); 1754 *Iron work for a new Roole 39^{pd} at 3½ per pound*, Beeston (WYL160/129/5); 1761 *fetching the Coal pitt rowl and frames from Holme*, Tong (Tong/4c/6). See also gin, turn, windas.

roller An occasional term for one who operated a rolling mill. See also slitter.

rollers The cutlers had rollers in their smithies long before there were rolling mills, although it is not clear how they were powered. In 1692, for example, Robert Nicholls had possessions which included three 'engines' with a total value of £4 10s 0d and *a pair of rollers* worth £1 2s 6d (IH). The inference is that the rollers and one or other of the contrivances described as 'engines' were used to form metal into bars or sheets. See also engine, rolling mill.

rolling mill A mill in which metal is rolled out or flattened (OED). References in Yorkshire date from the second half of the eighteenth century: 1760 *Places where cast iron work and rowls iron into plates of aney sise or thickness is has at Coln Bridg near Healland in Yorkshire and att Wotley near Penistone … and att Rotherham* (YRS155/9). In a history of Cooper Wheel on the river Sheaf, it was said that in 1766 four men took a lease of the *rolling mill lately a cutler wheel*, and by 1794 *six pairs of rollers had to be powered* (WPS178–9). Similarly, Middlewood Wheel on the river Don was the site of a rolling mill by 1794, and a sales catalogue of 1828 lists *forges for rolling and making German steel* (WPS4).

Elsewhere in the West Riding, other rolling mills came into operation from roughly the same period, and the clerk at Colne Bridge forge entered in his diary for 12 July 1776: *At the Forge all day, they began rolling hoops, the first that were ever rolled at Colne Bridge* (LTK144). See also rollers, slitting mill.

rood A cross, as an instrument of execution: 1518 *to the Roode of Dancastre at the brigge end* (SS79/95). It referred particularly to the cross upon which Christ suffered and in English churches was the word for a crucifix, often set above the rood screen: 1567 *an image with a crosse that the Roode hanged on*, Skeffling (PTD29).

rood-loft A narrow loft or gallery across the top of the rood screen: 1399–1400 *pro serracione omnium meremiorum ad prædict. rodeloft [for sawing all the timber for the aforesaid rood-loft]*, Ripon (SS81/133); 1470 *ad sustentationem le rudeloft infra ecclesiam [for mainte-nance of the rood-loft in the church]*, Kirkby Fleetham (SS26/9); 1530 *To the reparacion of a new Rode loft in Darfeld church x markes* (SS79/299).

roof In a mine this was the top of a working or gallery. In 1708, in the north-east, it was thought best to 'leave perhaps about a Foot thick of the Coal top for a Roof' (CC22) but that would not have been possible where the seams that were being worked were thin. Roof falls killed and injured many miners: 1575 *Thomas Boothe by sodeyne mischaunce was slayne in a cole pytte, the roofe falling upon hym*, Almondbury (PR); 1682 *John Green of Bradforthe, Collyer, by accident … is maymed in one of his armes by the fall of a greatt Stone in the Coale Myne* (QS1); 1755 *Thomas Pickering was working in a Colepit and the roof of Cole fell upon him … about a tun weight … and he was dead when they found him* (QS1/94/4). Roof falls also made the getting of coal more difficult so it is not surprising that roof maintenance was stressed in contracts. In 1666, Mr

Beaumont leased a pit in South Crosland to three sinkers and required them *to leave the Roofes … where they have gotten and under myned for cooles in sufficient repaire as shall be thought fittinge.* This was not simply trusted to the colliers for it was stipulated that their work should be examined by *two work men to be made choyse of* (DD/WBD/2/81). See also dead work.

roof tree A substantial section of a tree, suitable for the ridge-pole of a roof or other main timbers: 1466–8 'To John Ricard to a *roof-tree* had to the said house', Hull (YAJ62/160); 1686 *21 yards of roofetrees 4 inches square*, Conistone (RW33). See also ridge-tree.

room (1) A word of Old English origin with more shades of meaning formerly than it has now. It was commonly an office, position or function: 1514 *we have yeven* [given] *… unto hym th'office and rowme of baner berer*, Ripon (SS74/303); 1530–1 *the rowme and office of their common stable to hymsylffe*, Rievaulx (SS83/349); 1725 *in the Room of Mr Henry Adams lately deceased*, Leeds (Th22/200). In this sense it was a 'space' occupied or left vacant: 1700 *recommending your son … as theire representative in Parliament in the room of Mr Fleming*, Castle Howard (CSS13). In fact, it was used in many contexts where 'space' or 'place' was the meaning: 1538 *one rowme in the xxvj stall apon the sowthe sid of the middist alley within the said chirch of Halifax* (Clay116); 1564–5 *to sett and plant vj yonge trees … and if any dye to sett … so many other of the like … kynde in their roome*, Hemsworth (YRS63/51). More particularly it was used of the 'compartments' in structures such as piers and fish garths, recorded as *rowmes* as early as 1394 (YRS64/xvii).

As a compartment within a house, the most frequent meaning now, it is found in a Durham document in the mid-fifteenth century (OED). Examples which illustrate that development include: 1586–7 *to haue a bed Roome in my house*, Huddersfield (BIA23/434); 1618 *all and euery the roumes and parcels of that messuage … vizt all the dwelling roumes*, Handsworth Woodhouse (YAJ20/16–17); 1642 *Mary Goodale and Richard Miller have a Cottage betwixt them. Mary Goodale hath two rooms and the orchard*, Elmswell (DW131); 1705 *20s to his daughter Alice Tatham and a room in which to live while unmarried*, Eshton (EG73). In numerous compound terms it was linked with specific elements such as fire, house, moss, stee and tenter. See also pasture master, roomstead, roomth, seal, standing.

room (2) An undated thirteenth-century charter for Worsbrough has a reference to 'two assarts (*essarta*) called *Rokelay stubbing* and *Rockelay Roum*' (YRS39/183) and in the latter the use of 'room' as a place-name element is sufficiently rare to deserve comment. The context suggests that the meaning is 'cleared space', roughly equivalent to 'stubbing', and it is additional evidence that the word was an active vocabulary item. This name has apparently not survived but it may share the same origin as the Morley place-name 'Rooms' which also dates from the thirteenth century. In 1202, Adam *de Beston* purchased lands in the township which included an assart lying *inter le Ruhm et domum Adæ filij Hugonis [between the Ruhm and the house of Adam son of Hugh]* (SS94/32): Smith gave the meaning as 'an open space, a clearing' (PNWR2/183). Later in the deed there is mention of forty acres of land *in le Ruhm*, so the name can be seen to emphasise how spacious or expansive the initial clearance had been. Almost incidentally it suggests an alternative meaning for the local surname Room(e) which flourished for several centuries in the Beeston and Morley area. It had previously been considered to derive from Rome in Italy, as a name given to pilgrims (GRDict).

roomstead A particular section or compartment of a building: 1642 *the greate roomestede in the North ende of the rye-barne*, Elmswell (DW49); 1754 *2 roomsteads or bayes* *of building*, Hutton le Hole (MD437/519). An earlier reference occurs in a survey of Settrington, where it is one of the particulars in the preamble: 1600 *What roomesteedes be in euery house that waste hereafter may be preuented* (YRS126/4).

roomth An early alternative spelling of 'room': 1556 *from the middle dore inward all the roomthes called thopper parte of the house*, Beeston (Th27/57); 1644 *all that one stall or forme containeing four seates or roomethes*, Heptonstall (PR45).

rope See coal-pit rope.

roseager An alternative spelling of rosalger, resalgar or realgar, a disulphide of arsenic (OED). See also ratsbane.

rosell A rare alternative spelling of rosin: 1588 *Canvasse threde wax and rosell 4s* Ingleby Arncliffe (YAJ16/114); 1596 *Item for wax & rosell 3ᵈ*, Howden (YAJ19/463). In 1612, an inventory taken at Brafferton had *Glewe, brimston, resell waxe lether* (NYRO44/35) and this seems to be another alternative, if not an error for 'rosell'.

rose nail A wrought nail having a round head, made with or cut into triangular facets 1640 (OED): 1471 *j bigam ligatam with rosse nallys*, Harome (SS45/188); 1572 *iiij thousand of rose nayles, xxs*, Richmond (SS26/233).

rosin Etymologically a word akin to resin, a substance which is obtained as a residue after the distillation of oil of turpentine from crude turpentine (OED): 1392–3 *In xxvj lb de Rosyne pro eisdem torch' emp., 2s 2d [For 26lbs of rosin bought for those torches, 2s 2d]*, Ripon (SS81/110); 1444 *lego Quinquaginta libras cere et rosyn ad quatuor torcheas comburendas [I leave fifty pounds of wax and rosin for burning four torches]*, Harpham (ERAS21/75). It was listed in the inventory of a Knaresborough shoemaker: 1541 *one stoyne of sett likoure and oille and sex dossan of rossen xs* (SS104/35). As a verb its use is illustrated in early building accounts: 1409 *Et Johanni Lytster pro roseynyng portarum viid [To John Lytster for rosining the gates 7d]*, Beverley (ERAS4/36), and in the ordinances of the Beverley cordwaners: 1627 'sewed with good thread well twisted and sufficiently waxed with wax well *rosond*' (YRS84/79). In Sheffield, the cutlers used it for varnishing their products and in 1709 Joseph Webster had *A pair of bags Emory and Rozin* in his inventory. In 1723, Elizabeth Thwaites had *Rozen* in her shop and in 1735 Joseph Morton also had some *Rossin* (IH).

roswek For ruswerk, that is the skins of squirrels from Russia (EMV225). See also timber (2).

rotten Used of soft barren ground although perhaps originally ground covered with decaying vegetation: 1562 *in the same Intake there nether* [sic] *was … any moorishe, weet sobbed or rotten ground but … always hayth bene a good and fair ground meet for gyrs [grass] and corne*, Rawdon (YRS114/101). In 1682, Thoresby wrote *thence over the rotten Moors for many miles without anything observable*.

rotten wood A not uncommon term in the seventeenth and eighteenth centuries, possibly for wood that was partly decayed but useful at least for firewood: 1677 *a sacke fill'd with rotten wood and straw*, Quarmby; 1686 *there was laid on her house side to dry betwixt two or three strokes of rottnewood*, Golcar (QS1). However, it had a valuation in some inventories and was brought to clothiers in Wakefield as cargo: 1696 *in Rotten Wood £1 11s*, Holmfirth (IH); 1759 *things … that comes up bye watter are … plaister, iron, rotten wood*, Wakefield (YRS155/27). It was evidently used in the domestic cloth industry, so it should be noted that Wright lists it as an ingredient in dyeing, albeit without examples (EDD).

rouch See red leather.

rough arch See arch.

rough mason The OED defines a rough mason as one who built only with unhewn stone, and examples of the word are given from 1444. Yorkshire references show that some men so described were dry-stone wallers: 1579 *Anthony Whiteheade of Emmotte and John Reade, roughemasons*, Elland (BAS6/138); 1612 *Oswold Collyson, waller or rough maison*, Birdforth (NRQS1/252); 1629 *Richard Walker of Birstall, rough mason* (YAS/DD4). However, the term is much older than that, and several rough masons are named in the York freemen's rolls, for example: 1379 *Rad. de Holdernesse, rughmason* (SS96/78). See also arch.

rout (1) A variant spelling of root, used of swine which turned up the soil with their snouts in the search for food. They were capable of laying waste to the landscape if not ringed and their movement also had to be controlled, as the following indictment makes clear: 1687 *John Tailler, Oliver Wallker ... presented for their swine goeing into the Chourch yearde and routing up the grawfes*, Wakefield (WCR13/86). See also ring (2), swine root.

rout (2) An isolated and obscure example: 1353 'drove away beasts with instruments called *Rowtis*', Bradford (CR). Possibly connected with 'rout' in the sense of making a loud noise (OED).

row A row of trees, houses, etc., an early street name. Smith has examples from the thirteenth century (PNWR7/235). See also house-row, ratton row, raw.

rowell A wheel-shaped chandelier, a fitting in many churches: 1522 *I witto the rowell in my parishe chirche iiijd*, York (SS79/147); 1531 *I witt ijd to the mindyng of the rowell in the sayd churche of Saynt Feles*, Thirsk (YAJ22/204); 1539 *I will that the xs which I delivered to the churche grevis shall remane to be a stoke to find one Rowell befor the blissed sacrament*, Methley (Th35/101); 1557 *I bequeath towards the making of the Rowell iiijd*, Woodkirk (Th27/95). An occupation noted in York may refer to a maker of such rowells rather than to a specialist spurrier: 1390 *Johannes Fauconer, roueller* (SS96/90).

royal aid A royalty; the payment due to a landowner by the lessee of a mine in return for the privilege of working it (OED): 1690 *second payment of Royall Aide*, Farnley (MS11). See also coal-mine, king's rent.

royd A dialect spelling of *rod*, a word for an enclosed clearing or assart, often the work of an individual rather than the community as a whole. It was particularly frequent from *c*.1150 into the 1300s and gave rise to numerous place-names in parts of west Yorkshire, many in undated early charters: 'three acres of land within the close of *Hetonerodes* which is called *Walthefrode* which acres the same *Walthef* held', Kirkheaton (Font361); *c*.1260 *de uno essarto quod vocatur Hervardrode [for an assart which is called Hervardrode]*, Calverley (Th6/20). The dialect spelling dates from the early fifteenth century: 1437 '4 acres were *Roideland* lying in an assart called *Maymoundroide*', Stanley (WCR17/55). See also rodeland.

roydland See rodeland, royd.

ruck A heap or pile, as of stones, turf or hay, a word found in several glossaries: Canon Atkinson defined 'rook, ruck', as 'a carefully made heap, of no great size; of turves, stone, etc.' Isolated examples illustrate its use in the everyday vocabulary: 1577 *vj rookes of peise strawe vs*, South Cave (Kaner97); 1590 *2 lytle ruckes of hay*, Marske

(YRS152/289) but it occurs more commonly in traditional boundary descriptions: 1637 *unto one howe called Cooke Howe and from thence to one rooke of stoanes in Arnesgill heade and soe to one rooke of stones above Hew Hill Brow*, Bilsdale Kirkham (NYRO23/1); 1642 *to a great Ruck of Stones aboue Stainedale Farm*, Helmsley (HRD433). In fact, it has a much longer history in such contexts: 1294 *et abinde usque locum vocatum rukke super Cockhowe et deinde sicut aqua cæli dividit [and from there as far as the place called rukke on top of Cockhowe and from there just as the water from heaven divides (i.e. along the watershed)]*, Marske in Swaledale (YAJ6/218). It is likely therefore to be the first element in place-names such as Rookstones in Rishworth, listed by Smith but with no explanation (PNWR3/48) and there are others where it may be preferable to 'rook' meaning the bird. It seems as though 'ruck of stones' was the original expression but that 'ruck' could be used on its own when the sense was clear.

Its use for stacks of turf or peat, both used as fuel, may have something to do with its early history in Nottinghamshire, where it was used of a particular measure of coals, possibly a pile of a certain size originally. The movement of miners from one coalfield to another may explain its later use in south Yorkshire. It is found there as a measure in colliery records from the early eighteenth century: 1729–31 *three Rooks or Stacks being two Dozen Of Coals*; *Colliers shall get the Coals at 18d per ruck*; *thirty Corfs to each Ruck*, Swillington (CKY37–8). See also ruckle.

ruckle The *Craven Glossary* has: 'ruck, ruckle, a great quantity; a heap of stones' which may point to ruckle as a diminutive of 'ruck'. Only a few examples have been noted but the word occurs in an Elizabethan transcript of a medieval charter: *neare the great stone Ruckle*, Arthington (Th2/125) and again in a deposition from the Quarter Sessions: 1721 *hidd them in a ruckle of stones* (QS1/61/1). In *Local Studies in Nidderdale* (1882) is a reference to stacks of peat called 'ruckles'. It has not yet been found as a place-name element.

rud An occasional alternative to ruddle, as both noun and verb: 1688 *one stroake down the neer Ribs one other down the tayle head, all with Rud*, West Riding (QS1); 1700 *Rudded in the neck*, Nidderdale (QS1/39/5).

rudder A kind of paddle, used by brewers to stir the malt in the mash-tub: *c*.1534 *In the beyrhowsse ... on greitt maskfatt ... 4 rudders*, Bridlington (YRS80/2). A Lancashire by-name takes the word's history back to a much earlier period: 1379 *John Masshrother*, Lonsdale (PTLa). See Masheder (GRDict).

ruddle A red variety of ochre found in several localities in Yorkshire: in 1755 the vicar of Mirfield wrote of the *ruddle or red chalk found in a quarry near New Hall in Hopton* (WDP1/192). It was used principally for marking sheep: 1669 *the Lambes marked with Ruddle on the near Buttock like a crosse*, Shelley (QS1) but occurs occasionally as a verb in wood accounts: 1810 *7 days ruddling wafers*, Fixby (DD/T/R/a/33). It gave rise to the minor place-names Ruddle Clough, Ruddle Dike, Ruddle Pits. See also canker, raddle, rud, and NH157–9.

rugg A rough woollen material, first referred to as *Manchester rugs otherwise named Manchester frizes* in an Act of 1551–2 (SAL5/359). References are mostly from that century: 1576 *a pair of moldes [slippers] of white rugge*, Ripon (SS64/378); 1585 *one blacke broadcloth gowne lyned with black conny skines and white rugge*, Marrick (YRS152/264). It could also be used of a kind of coverlet: 1611 *1 payre of blankets, 1 seagrene rugge*, Brafferton (NYRO44/34). Possibly an element in the by-name: 1285 *Robert Ruggebagge*, Wakefield (YRS29/198).

rugged In general it meant rough or hairy, so when it was used of items of clothing there may have been a direct connection with 'rugg' as a material: 1558 *ij ruggid hats*, Knaresborough (SS26/126): in the same inventory are *one Welvet capp, one sattan cappe* and *seven worsett hatts*.

rulley A word of obscure origin, found mostly in Yorkshire sources, but only from 1806 (OED). It was a flat four-wheeled wagon used to transport goods: 1759 *July 14 Mary d James Firth who was killed by a Rulley running over her*, York, St Mary Castlegate (PR84).

runagate Literally a 'runaway', but used in the Tudor period of an apostate or renegade: 1571 *sayd ... he wold put the vicar ... and the Curat and such as they were oute of the towne by the eares and that he wold get dogs to byte such ronnagates*, Masham (PTD151).

run behind To get into arrears: 1689 *Joseph Holiday ... had a portion with his wife, took £120 upon his land and is run behind £100, skulks for fear of being apprehended*, Northowram (OH2/193).

rundle A runnel, a local alternative spelling: 1591 *the said gill, becke or rundell*, Ilkley (YNQ); 1601 *make a goite, sough or rundell to draw away the water from under the said bridge to a lower water*, Apperley (BAS6/142). The place-name Rundleside in Stonebeck Up was *Runnalside* on the Jefferys map of 1771 (PNWR5/219).

runlet A cooper-made cask of varying capacity: 1463 *1 roundlette cum haberdaysh' et glasses*, Hull (YRS144/63); 1616 *And he promised to send me good Canarye sack a rundlett of 8 gallons at the least*, Brandsby (NYRO44/121); 1621 *Tenn barrells, two rundlettes and two standes*, Slaidburn (YRS63/48); 1655 *in the seller five hogsheades and 6 runletts*, Whitley (DD/WBM/69); 1688 *two runletts with some ale in them* (SS40/286); 1695 *severall barrells and rundletts*, Holmfirth (IH).

runt An ox or cow of a small breed or size: 1658 *4 runttes £10 13 4; 4 smale runtte steares £9*, Selby (YRS47/17).

runted oak A runt was said by Halliwell to be the stump of a tree, but it may simply have been a reference to size and age. In any case the value was not high: 1543 *Esthagge ... conteyneth by estimacion xxx acres sett wth manye olde runted okes*, Hambleton (YRS13/361); 1642 *Best okes ... Worser okes ... Runt okes*, Bilsdale (NYRO23/62).

rush-bearing A ceremony in parts of the north, formerly widespread but surviving now in one or two localities only, notably in Sowerby Bridge. Typically, rushes and other greenery were borne to the church and spread over the floor, and the evidence suggests that it was an opportunity for singing, dancing and general merry-making. It was evidently a custom with a long tradition: 1510 *of old custome it hath beyne used that evere yere at the festes of Whitsonday and Sanct Petir day the kirk was wount to be strewed with ryshes ... and now it is not so*, St Michael le Belfrey, York (SS35/262). In 1583, the churchwardens of Bolton Percy *were commanded ... to certify ... of there ... strawing the church with rushes*, and in 1595 Hugh Gryme of Fewston was accused of offensive behaviour *aboute caryinge in of rishes into the Chapell* (PTD60,95). Local diaries and accounts provide evidence of the custom into the early nineteenth century: 1690 *On Hebden Reshbearing day 8s 0d* (RW7); 1781 *5 Aug. Luddenden Rush-bearing was last Wednesday* (KC242/1); 1815 *4 Aug. Being what is Called Illingworth Rush bearing we had 5 of Joshua Stancliff Children on a visit*, Ovenden (CA275). See also rish, summer games.

ruskin A squirrel skin imported from or via the Baltic, particularly the fur of an animal trapped in the summer (EMV228). Examples taken from goods imported into Hull from Danzig include: 1453 *2 tymbres roskyn*; 1490 *½ dakar russkyns* (YRS144/4,207). The OED has an example from 1287 without an explanation of the etymology so Veale's reference to squirrel skins called 'ruswerk' which were Russian skins is worth noting (EMV225).

russel A woollen fabric, noted in 1488 and 1493 (OED), but more frequent in the sixteenth century, with reference to items of clothing such as doublets, jackets, jerkins and kirtles: 1551 *as much Russell as will make her a kirtill*, Pontefract (Th19/289); 1560 *my best jerkynge of russell*, Church Fenton (Th27/301). It was occasionally used attributively: 1543 *one dublett of russell worstede*, Otley (Th19/79) and was quite frequently in the plural: 1549 *a jakett of russelles*, Knottingley (Th19/223); 1552 *two kirtelles, the one of russels*, Womersley (Th27/33); 1558 *xxxix yeards of russhels … fower hole peaces of russhells*, Knaresborough (SS26/126). It cannot mean 'red' since early examples were specifically black, green, or grey but may take its name from a Flemish town (OED).

russet A reddish-brown, homespun woollen cloth, traditionally associated with country-folk: 1257 *Swaynthur supertunicam suam de Russeto [Swaynthur's russet surcoat]*, Harpham (ERAS21/72); 1346 *Roberto filio meo j remenant de panno russeto [To my son Robert a remnant of russet cloth]*, Easingwold (SS4/23); 1347 *cum supertunica' de russeto*, Catfoss (SS4/40); 1394 *et unam togam coloris russet' pelulatam cum grisio [and a russet coloured robe trimmed with grey fur]*, Roos (SS4/201); 1437 *unam novam togam de russet [a new russet gown]*, York (SS30/62); 1470 *meam tunicam de russett [my russet tunic]*, Kirkby Fleetham (SS26/9); 1558 *to my brother … one russet jackett*, Poole (Th27/214).

rust One example noted, but possibly having the sense of 'rust-coloured': 1558 *ij fynne red capes, vj round capes, j doble rust cappe*, Knaresborough (SS26/126). Alternatively it may be for 'russet' which was both a material and a reddish-brown colour.

rustic The earliest examples of this word date from the fifteenth century when they referred to countrymen, or men who followed country pursuits (OED). In the records of Healaugh Park are much earlier Latin uses which seem to point to workers of villein status working in the park. The charters are undated but probably of the thirteenth century: *servicium rusticitatis Waltero Tornario [the rustics' service to Walter Tornarius]* (YRS92/37); *cum duobus rusticis et eorum catallis … scilicet Johanne filio Matill et Roberto fratre ejus [with two rustics and their cattle … that is, John son of Maud and his brother Robert]* (YRS92/42). They are also directly compared with free men: n.d. *liberis hominibus meis cum eorum tenementis et rusticis meis cum eorum catallis [for my free men with their tenements and my rustics with their cattle]*, Healaugh Park (YRS92/92). See also turner.

ryal See rial.

S

saa See say (1).

sack and seam A rare expression, used to mean pack-horse traffic: 1631 *stopping up the kings highway for sacke and seame betwixt Rounckton North moor and the Milneholme wath* (NRQS3/312).

sackcloth A coarse textile fabric, so named because it was intended originally to make sacks or wrap up bales, but used subsequently for items of clothing: 1394–5 *Item xij ulnis de secclath iijs [Item for 12 ells of sackcloth 3s]*, Whitby (SS72/603); 1562 *one dublet of sackclothe iijs*, Thrintoft (SS26/166); 1576 *Item vii yerds of sackcloth*, South Cave (Kaner94). Apparently also called sackweb: 1444 *j web de sac xxd*, Northallerton (SS2/90); 1580 *for xij yeardes of secke webe iijs iiijd*, Stockeld (YRS161/18); 1616 *Sackwebbe bought at Malton … of 22 yeards*; 1616 *a new sacke of sack webb*, Brandsby (NYRO44/124,129). See also barehide, Manchester, seck.

sacking yarn Yarn to be used in the making of sackcloth: 1638 *fower hankes of sekan yairne*, Thorpe Willoughby (YRS47/143). Sacking was a coarse cloth: 1631 *three sekkin boulsters iijs 4d*, Bingley (LRS1/80). Note: 1658 *20 hespes of seck waft [weft] 15s*, Barley (YRS47/91).

sackless Innocent of wrong intent, secure from accusation: 1664 *The men that sufferd at Appleby were proper and able men and dyed sacklesse* (SS40/124n); 1670 *as for the bewitching of any of his children shee is sacklesse*, Alne (SS40/177). It was already being used pejoratively, of a person weak in mind or body and gave rise to a nickname: 1662 *Sackles Sam: a poore fellow of New chappell*, Leeds (Th7/429).

sackweb See sackcloth.

sad Dark or deep when used of colour, in contrast to 'light': 1415 *j lectum de worsted de light blewe et sadde blewe [1 worsted bed cover of light blue and sad blue]*, Wollaton (SS4/382); 1451 *Item iiij peciæ de light blew and sade blew operatæ [Item 4 pieces of light blue and sad blew, worked]*, York (SS30/151); 1454 *unam togam de sadgrene*, Whitkirk (SS30/177); c.1504 *Item vij yerdes of sad tawne iiijs*, York (SS53/191); 1682 *one sad colerd peticote*, Brayton (YRS47/103); 1722 *a sad brown Bay Gelding*, Leeds (Th22/191). It could mean compact or dense: 1691 *I … found the snow deep where drifted but sad and bearing*, Slaithwaite (GRD). The meaning is likely to be pejorative in the following by-name: 1305–6 *Nicholao Saddebely pro uno termino ijs [To Nicholas Saddebely for one term 2s]*, Bolton Priory (YRS154/199). Employed at the same time was *Symon Paunch*.

saddle-back A live horse might be described as saddle backed if it had a depression where the saddle would come: 1618 *one saddleback black oxe hide 18s 6d*, Huddersfield (DD/RA/f/4b).

saddle-tree See lind.

sadness Seriousness, gravity of mind: 1496 *we be content that they [go unto the said diette] in the companye of our said ambassadours soo that they be men of good sadnesse and honour*, York (YRS103/124).

safe, safe-keeper A ventilated chest or cupboard for protecting provisions from insects, etc. It was not a cheap item: 1621 *A safe keeper for meate and a keeper for glasse, 33s 4d*, Slaidburn (YRS63/48); 1644 *one Presse & a Safe xxxs*, Lepton (HM/C/180); 1667 *In the Buttry: one safe £1 6 8*, North Bierley (YRS134/126); 1701 *One great safe or Cupboard 10s*, Elland (OWR1/2/8).

safeguard An item of clothing, worn as a protection over other garments. It appears to have come into use in the Elizabethan period and was mainly for women: 1578 *an old safegarde forfayted by Jane Clark*, Beverley (YRS84/19); 1587 *unto Ann Hodgeson a workedaye savegarde*, South Cave (Kaner143); 1619 *To Jane Walmesley a safegard, one canvas sheet, one canvas smock, one petticoat, 2 cross cloths and 2 patletts*, Gisburn (CS3/36); *c.*1686 *two Savegards in Linning Left in the Cubbert*, Conistone (RW25). Items of clothing given to the poor in Bridlington in 1636 included nine *safegardes*, one to Matthew Man and eight to women (BCP160).

safe-keeper See safe.

sage This is the dialect word for the carpenter's 'saw': 1639 *Item one whipp Sage, two cutting Sages and one hand sage*, Swinsty (YRS134/91); 1689 *one hammer, one sage, one gourge*, Slaidburn (CS3/62); 1721 *a Cutting saige*, Salterforth (YRS118/73). See also whip-saw.

sagen From the verb 'to sage', the dialect equivalent of 'sawn': 1658 *sagon timber aboute the house*, Beckwith (SS110/229); 1689 *new Sagen bords and 2 ash baukes, £3*, Barnoldswick (YRS118/72); 1693 *all the sagen wood and riven speakes*, Holmfirth (G-A). In the Colne Bridge forge accounts for 1729 are entries for lordings and polls *felling and saiging* (SpSt).

sager, sagher The dialect equivalent of 'sawyer': *c.*1360 *pro duobus saghers 12d [for two saghers 12d]*, York (SS35/2). It was responsible for many by-names, and the surnames Sagar and Sager, common in the Bradford/Colne area: 1317–25 *Philip Sarrator*, Stanley (YRS78/202); *Philip le Sagher*, Stanley (YRS109/61); 1379 *Willelmus Sagher, sagher*, Beamsley (PTWR); 1590 *the searchers of cowpers and the saigers shalbe called into this court*, York (YRS138/94). See also saw-pit.

sailyard One of the radiating beams of a windmill, bearing the sail: 1364 'The said Thomas shall make at his own charge *axiltres* and *sayleyerds*', Thorner (Th15/163).

sall A regional form of 'shall': 1483 *John Qwitley sall haue … land lygand in the South syde of the Byrkfeild*, Ovenden (YRS83/151); 1501 *Thomas Hawme sall have … and occupie such two clauses [closes] called Tuche Rod and Hertley Rod hole*, Barkisland (YRS39/13).

sallet In medieval armour this was a light helmet or head-piece, with an outward curve at the back: 1438 *unum salett*, York (SS30/63); 1476 *De ijs iiijd de precio j salett cum visura capto pro libertate Firthbank [For 2s 4d the cost of 1 sallet with vizor taken for the liberty of Firthbank]*, York (SS192/148); 1504 *every inhabitant within his ward to have a staffe and a salet*, York (YRS106/7); 1526 *To Thomas Milner my salett and a pare of white hoise*, Halifax (Clay72). See also splents.

sallow, sally A willow or the wood from it, said by James to be the goat willow: 1546 *Ther is a wood callyd Welskough conteynyng by estimacion xx acres of okes, asshes, salyes and other woodes there, valued at xxli*, Well (SS91/113). In *c.*1570 John Kaye of Woodsome recommended to his son that he *sett whithorn on good ground sallow on clay* (KayeCP). Some variant spellings are dealt with under 'saugh'.

salmon hecks A contrivance which consisted of wooden bars, designed to catch salmon in a river: 1462 *le Samonde hekkes*, Wakefield (PNWR2/173); 1540 'for the farm of *le salmon heckes* in Wetherby' (YRS94/138); 1624 *Matthew Harland of Egton, capper, for suffering his salmon heckes to stand in the Esk in unseasonable times, thereby killing many salmons in the time of kipper* (NRQS3/199). See also heck, kipper.

salt Short for salt-cellar: *c.*1537 *Item ij saltes of Syluer with a couer halfe gylt*, Halifax (YRS45/186); 1541 *to … my sone a siluer pece, a siluer salte*, Leathley (Th19/49); 1588 *one Candle sticke thre saltes one pewder canne*, Dalton (DD/WBW/19); 1675 *a silver salt with a coote of armes*, Richmond (SS40/218).

salt-ding A building where salt was stored. See also ding (2).

salter, saltery, sawtry A kind of deer-leap which involved a modification of the pale around a park. It allowed deer to enter the park but made it difficult for them to leap out again. Mary Higham discussed the word in connection with Leagram Park within the Forest of Bowland: 1603 *with a pale of wood and divers salters left therein for the deer to come out of the forest* (MHW17). It is said to derive from Latin *saltatorium* and is clearly a vernacular form. What is probably an unusual Latin spelling is found in the Ministers' Accounts for Pickering Forest where expenses 'for stopping up an old deer-leap' are detailed: 1314 *pro uno insultorio antiquo obstupando* (NRR2/21). An alternative English spelling is 'sawtry': 1526 *Herry Savyll … and his adherentes … came to the seid park pale and satt upon the sawtryez of the seid pale*, Wortley Park (YRS41/180); 1621 *and so back agane on the common to the Sawtrye into Sir Henry Bellasis parke*, Brandsby (NYRO44/227). The word may survive in some of the many minor place-names with 'salter' as an element.

salt-fish chamber An upper room where salted fish might be stored: 1528 *In the salte fyshe chamber*, York (SS79/255). See also salt-house.

salt hay, salt meadow The ings or meadows along the tidal rivers produced this special crop: 1577 *to Isabell my wiefe five acres of salt medowe*, South Cave (Kaner94); 1589 *15 loades of salt haye & 10 loades of freshe haye*, South Cave (Kaner157); 1618 *Item salt hay being inned vli*, South Cave (Kaner275).

salt hide If untanned hides had to be transported over a long distance they were soaked in brine to save them from decay: 1465 *3 salthydes* – from Dysart in Fife to Hull (YRS144/73); 1476 *saylinge oute of Scotland with his merchaundise ther bought … salt hides to the nombre of iiij^c lxx*, York (YRS98/13). In the Act of 1535, by which the king sought to ensure that customs dues were paid on all exported leather, certificates had to be obtained for the movement of *salt or untanned hides … or any leather called backs or sole leather* (SAL4/375).

salt-house Either a place where salt was made or refined (OED) or, more usually, a building where it was stored: 1503 *To my wif a meise with one salt howse in Whitby*, York (SS53/213); 1528 *M John Langton for a salthows wiche paid at a terme vs now iijs iiijd*, Hull (YRS141/122); 1542 *To John Maister … my salte house with the newe tymbre that I bought for it*, Whitby (YRS51/199). Salthouse Lane in Hull takes its name from such a building: 1465 'the decay of a tenement called *Salthous*'; 1465 *the Comon seuer in Salthouslane by yere ijs* (YRS141/119,122). See also salt-fish chamber.

salting-fat A tub in which meat and fish were cured: 1533 *to Agnes Northend a saltyngfat and on arke*, Skircote (Clay99); 1588 *one Saltingefatt one dishcratch & one breadleape iijs*, Dalton (DD/WBW/19); 1610 *one saltin fat, kneding trough*, Cottingley (LRS1/7); 1644 *three Saltingfattes & a kneading trough*, Lepton (HM/C/180); 1693 *j* *salting fat*, Holmfirth (G–A). It was sometimes called a salting-tub: 1556 *iij sowttyng tobbes*, Mowbrick (SS26/92).

salt meadow See salt hay.

saltpetre man A man appointed to obtain saltpetre for the manufacture of gunpowder: 1590 *This is the clause in the salt petermans patent … wherby he demaundeth to have cariages in the Ainstye to fetch him coles from Mr Gasconge pittes*, York (YRS138/124).

salt-pie A container for salt: 1597 *a Cradle & a salte pie*, Wakefield (SpSt); 1622 *pecks, mandes … salt pye*, Bingley (LRS1/62); 1676 *a saltpye, 1 pigin*, Selby (YRS47/2); 1700 *a salt pye, two leades and a mustard ball*, Holmfirth (IH); 1731 *a salt py and salt in it*, Austerfield (QS1/70/7). It gave its name to a type of lean-to building and this in turn explains a number of late minor place-names.

sam (1) To collect together, to pick up, a regional word which has survived: *c*.1570 *all ewes with lam together sam, in one spare close them kepe*, Woodsome (KayeCP).

sam (2) A spelling of seam, that is lard or grease: 1742 *goose grease, sam dish, dripeing pan*, Holmfirth (G–A). Wright has 'saim' as the headword (EDD).

sameron A word noted only in Yorkshire sources. It was a cloth, defined by Meriton as 'between Linnen and Hempen, not altogether so coarse as the one nor fine as the other': 1525 *a paire of sheittes of sameron, a codwer*, Saxton (Th9/184); 1535 *Item lx pare shetes lynnyn Samaron and harden … tenne Tabilclothes, lynnyn and Sameron*, Stillingfleet (YRS45/127); 1567 *Item 11 payre of sameron shetes*, Fixby (YRS134/16); 1598 *Item samoran yearne £6 0 0*, Knaresborough (YRS134/61). The spelling varied in the sixteenth century: 1544 *one pare of shettes samerell … and a samerell towel*, Pontefract (Th19/106); 1559 *a payre of sameroll shettes*, Pontefract (Th27/291); 1581 *for workyn xxxiij yerdes of samarant iijs*, Stockeld (YRS161/45).

sampler A young tree: in a survey of Bilsdale in north Yorkshire the word was used frequently for ashes and oaks which were almost always valued at 1s, the same as a sapling: 1642 *30s Best okes; 6s 8d Of the second sort; 3s 4d The worser sort; 1s 0d Samplers* (NYRO23/60).

sandal A thin rich silken material: 1378 *Un matras de sendal rouge [A red sandal mattress]*, York (YAJ15/480); 1382 *westimentum meum de taune sendyl cum duabus tuniculis [my tawny sandal vestment with two tunicles]*, Richmond (SS4/96); 1392 *lego dicto Thomæ unum lectum integrum de viride sandal poudred cum rosis [I leave to the said Thomas one complete green sandal bed furnishing powdered with roses]*, Ingmanthorpe (SS4/170). See also sindon.

sanders A flavouring derived from sandal wood: 1394–6 *pro sandre et ficubus empt. pro eod. festo [for sanders and figs bought for that feast day]*, Whitby (SS72/621); 1417 'And for 2 pounds of *Saundrez … 2s 5d'*, Selby (YAJ48/125); 1616 *Cloves j lb … sanders ½ lb … Nutmeggs 4 oz*, Brandsby (NYRO44/129).

sand-leader A labourer who made a living by transporting sand: 1384 *Edm. de Paterdale, sandleder*, York (SS96/83); 1469 *Et solutum Andree Blythe pro cariagio xv summagiorum sabuli ad eundem opus xjd [And paid to Andrew Blythe for transporting 15 horse loads of sand for that work 11d]*, York (SS192/129); 1503 *apon the payment of pagiaunt money of the … sandeleders within the said Citie*, York (YRS103/183). In 1476, the above Andrew Blythe was described as *sandsleder* (SS192/144).

sand–walker Of uncertain meaning, although evidently a trade within the juris-diction of the Court of Admiralty: 1695 *Fishermen, Ship-wrights, Sand-walkers, Cadgers and all others Exercising any mistery or Trade*, Mappleton (SAH22/24).

sanguine Blood-red in colour: 1359 *lego robam meam integram sanguinei coloris nomine mortuarii mei [I leave my complete sanguine coloured gown by way of my mortuary]*, York (SS4/70); 1394 '2 *blewe* cloths and 1 *sangwyn* cloth', Hull (YRS64/48); 1435 *lego … capellano j capucium de Sangwyn [I leave … to the chaplain 1 sanguine hood]*, Castleford (Th22/249); 1442 *my scarlet gowne and my best sangweyne cloke*, Hemingbrough (HAH176); 1545 *unto … my doughters my sangwen gowne*, Woodkirk (Th19/153).

sap lath A lath made from sap-wood, that is the softer, more recently formed outer wood of a tree. In most examples 'lath' has the dialect spelling 'latt': 1415 *In m. ccc saplattes emptis de Johanne Bateman [For 1300 sap laths bought from John Bateman]*, York (SS35/35); 1446–7 *m^l sindulis vocatis saplatt'[1000 thin pieces of wood called sap laths]*, Beverley (ERAS7/60); 1525 *Item for ij bonchis of sape lattes, vd*, York (CCW111); 1694 *Paid to Will: Stackhouse for 300 Sap lattes 6s 6d*, Conistone (RW45).

sapling A young tree: 1415 *In ij sappelynges emptis … pro gauntrees, 3s [For 2 saplings bought … for gantries, 3s]*, York (SS35/35); 1617 *Fower trees, a sapling for ladders*, Ripley (YAJ34/199). For the alternative spelling 'sypling', see post (1). See also sampler, severy, spile sapling, wood collier.

sap wood The outer wood on a tree through which sap was still circulating. Woodworkers in guilds were forbidden to use sap wood: the craft ordinances stated that their work had to be honestly done *sauz* [sic] *ascun sappe*, York (SS120/149); 1629 *If any joiner, carpenter or wright … find stuff himself he must not put in any sappie or unseasonable wood*, Beverley (YRS84/81). Moreover, felling trees had to be done at the right time of the year: 1580 *to fell … in the wyntre season or out of sapp tyme*, Thurstonland (YDK77). Note: 1795 *ten bluecoat boys with branches of plane or sap tree*, Ripon (SS64/337n). See also sap lath.

sark (1) A garment such as a coat, or one worn next to the skin, a shirt or chemise: 1472 *for ij sarkkes mendeng ijd*, York (SS129/71); 1534 *a white cotte and an new sarke*, Liversedge (Th24/311); 1552 *two pare of hoose and one sark*, Huddersfield (BIA13/930). Occasionally it was a coat of mail: 1515 *my sark of mayll and a battell axe*, Hunmanby (SS79/62). It is found as an element in early by-names: 1301 *Henry Whitserk*, Carleton juxta Snaith (YRS31/173); 1332 *William Whiteserk*, Thornes near Wakefield (WCR3/86). See also spannall.

sark (2), sarking boards The verb meant to cover (a roof) with wooden boards (OED): 1458 *pro sarracione [for sawing] … de les sarkyng bordes*, York (SS35/71); 1538 *the sarking underneath if it might be seen is sore chauffyd and will have much new timber*, Knaresborough (YAJ30/224); 1582 *In laying the gutters and in sarkinge about the chime*, York (SS35/118); 1596 *one hundred of sixpennye nayles for naylinge down lead & sarking bords on the roufe of the churche*, Howden (YAJ19/462). Note: 1464–5 *Pro M^l sarkyngnale, 5s*, Durham (OED), presumably the nails used to secure sarking boards on a roof. See also penny nail (1596).

sarken In the single example noted the reference was to a type of fabric, possibly one such as 'sarks' were made of, or a misreading of 'sacken', for sack cloth: 1581 *iij payer of sarken sheates*, North Cave (Kaner114).

sarking boards See sark (2).

sarsenet Literally 'Saracen cloth', a very fine and soft silk material, both plain and twilled: 1463 *j mantellum linatam cum sercenet [1 cloak lined with sarsenet]*, Leeds (SS30/258); *c*.1504 *A yerd and a half sayrsnyt iiijs*, York (SS53/191); *c*.1537 *tawny and blak sarcenett lyning for a gowne*, Halifax (YRS45/188); 1542 *curtens of chaungeable sarcenet*, Bretton (YRS134/2); 1618 *Gownes makeinge and trymbinge up with … changeable sarcenett to lyne the hynginge sleeves*, Brandsby (NYRO44/152); 1675 *seaventy yeards of Indian sersnit for 25li*. Richmond (SS40/218).

sart A short form of 'assart', found frequently in early charters: *c*.1148 *et duas bovetas in Hilleclaia cum sartis eidem terre pertinentibus [and two bovates in Ilkley with sarts belonging to that land]*, Sawley (YRS87/3).

sashed Possessing sash windows, a fashion which dates from the late seventeenth century: 1722 *a large sash'd House late Lawyer Gill's*, Ripon (Th22/191); 1737 *A Handsome Sash'd House fit for a Gentleman or Merchant*, Leeds (Th26/64).

sass A sluice, a word of Dutch origin, evidently introduced in the seventeenth century during the drainage schemes carried out by Vermuyden and others. Stovin's manuscript contains information about the damage done to the *Sasse at Turn Brigg* in 1645 (ERAS13/230) and the decree made at Thorne the following year *for reedifieing the Sluces and sasses pulled up by malicious People* (ERAS12/27).

satin bridges Satin from the city of Bruges: 1531 *for iij yerdes of Burges satan vijs*, York (SS79/324); 1537 *a crosse of greyne sattin brigges imbroided with floures of golde*, Wighill (YAJ8/403); 1564 *yowlowe sattane in brygges*, West Applegarth (SS26/171); 1575 *xij yeards of saten bredges, xvijs*, Richmond (SS26/233).

saucemaker, saucer (1) Makers of sauce, that is condiments or spicy, appetising preparations to accompany food: 1296 *Johannes de Weteley, sauser*; 1395 *Johannes Heselden, sawser*; 1416 *Willelmus Rukeby, salsemaker*; 1440 *Johannes Kylburn, sausmaker*, York (SS96).

saucer (2) A deep dish or plate for holding condiments and sauces, often of metal: 1546 *my pewther vessell as well chardgers, dublers, sawcers, salte sellers and Counterfottes*, Wakefield (Th19/164); 1557 *to Jenet Lawson ij brasse pottes, v pece of pewther, ij sawcers*, Castleford (Th27/104).

saugh A willow, a common alternative spelling of sallow: *a*.1568 *Hagges Mete to be solde att this Present and are besett with hasell, Sawyhe and Thornes*, Pickering (NRR1/210); 1577 *for cutting of saughes in Westwood unlycenced, 12d*, Beverley (YRS84/9); 1615 *one saughe and two ashe tree for xiijs viijd*, Brandsby (NYRO44/95). See also maple, seal, season, strum, within.

saw–cutter, saw–maker References to saw-making are late at the national level and the occupational term is first recorded in 1662 (OED). The business letters of George Sitwell of Renishaw in Derbyshire, an ironmaster, refer to the manufacture of saws at Pleasley and it is known that saws were being produced in Yorkshire in the sixteenth century. In 1787, ten manufacturers were listed in Sheffield in Gales and Martin's Directory and the term saw–cutter occurs occasionally from the same period: 1794 *William Johnson late of Tanner Row, sawcutter*, York (St Crux PR2/37).

sawn boards, sawn timber Boards that were sawn as opposed to riven: 1485 *ij flekes pro plaustro [for the cart] xd. sawane bordes, viijs*, Ripon (SS64/373); 1510 *all necessary wood to his husbandry geare … except sawne timber for the body of their waines*, Shitlington

(FACcclxxxiv); 1558 *all my tymbre lying … within my croft … and all my sawen bords*, Hunshelf (Morehouse20). See also sagen, sark (2).

saw-pit A location where trees could be sawn, usually in woodland: 1663 *W Lynus & 2 sons pro sawing in Allerton parke £1 5 0; to other workemen pro helping them & making sawpitts £0 4 4*, Ripon (YRS118/102); 1717 *to Digg upp any part of the said Linecroft or West Park for making of Saw Pitts … for working of the said Trees*, Bradley (SpSt). See also sager.

sawther A regional spelling of solder: 1568 *amendynge the leades with sawther*, Sheffield (HS4). Used also as a verb: 1685 *the clippings … doe belonge to his trade, that is for sawtheringe of brasse withall, and that all whitesmiths have them*, Almondbury (QS1). See also souder.

sawtry See salter.

say (1) A large tub which had two 'ears' through which a pole might be passed: 1468–9 'For 5 *girths* bought for the Trinity *saa*', Hull (YAJ62/162); 1497 *j maskfatt, j gylefatt, et j saa*, Adel (Th22/94); 1530 *for two gyrthys to a say, 1d*, York (CCW142); 1554 *ij kymmeles, a sea, an arke*, South Cave (Kaner47); 1566 *a masken fatt, 3 cowlinge tubes, a saye, a swine tubbe and thre gallons*, Grinton (YRS152/142); 1663 *J Briggs pro watersea & piggen*, Ripon (YRS118/105). See also soe.

say (2) A cloth of fine texture, like serge, formerly made partly of silk but later entirely of wool: 1310 '*Sayes of Worstede* price £4', Hull (YRS64/5); 1394 *et sur mon corps un drape de blew saye [and over my body a cover of blue say]*, Wighill (SS4/198); 1432 *unum lectum de rede say enbrowded [an embroidered red say bed cover]*, Lead Grange (SS30/36); 1490 *a vestiment of blake seye*, York (YRS103/63); c.1537 *the halle … hanged with fine say … Normandy sey with moche other Englysshe saye*, Halifax (YRS45/188); 1636 *scotch cloth and say garters*, Thirsk (NRQS4/50); 1697 *one green say appron*, East Ardsley (QS1/36/6).

scabbed Having the scab, a skin disease. Animals which might infect others were commonly the subject of orders to tenants: 1573 *no man shall keep no scabbed horses nor no other infected cattle within the common field or other common pasture … but keep them within his own ground*, Doncaster (YAJ35/299).

scabell, scaytbell A word found only in York where it was the bell rung on Foss Bridge to declare the fish-market open: 1519 *Also that the bell of Fossebregg called the Scaytbell shalbe rong at viij of the clok in the morning on the market dayes* (YRS106/68). Previously, it had been mentioned when restrictions were placed on 'foreign' traders: 1481 *Et eciam quod nullus piscenarius forensicus qui portat pisces marinos ad istam civitatem vendendos non vendit pisces suas nisi ad scabell' omniam etc. [And moreover that no foreign fisherman who brings sea fish to this city for sale sell any of his fish except at the scabell]*, York (YHB230). The reference is probably to skate meaning fish, especially since 'skategeld' was apparently a toll on fish coming into the city: 1483 *our said sovereyn lord … grauntid … releve of the said Cite in esyng of the tolls, murage, bucher penys and skaitgyld* (YRS98/82). See also skategeld.

scaffold, scaffolding In early contexts, the scaffold was probably a temporary platform, supported on poles or trestles which gave workmen access to the higher sections of the building that they were working on: 1354–5 *Laur. Wrigth sublevante le skaffald in choro [To Lawrence Wright for supporting the scaffold in the choir]*, Ripon (SS81/94); 1360 *Pro flekes emptis pro skaffald [For fleaks bought for the scaffold]*; 1371 *Et in cc de firspars pro le scaffold [And for 200 fir spars for the scaffold]*, York (SS35/2,8);

1409 *Et aliis necessariis pro scafald* [*And for other requirements for the scaffold*], Beverley
(ERAS4/30); 1485–6 *tymber to mak the centres of the scaffyldes*, Sheffield (HS1/59);
*c.*1520 *Johanni Henryson making scaffaldes*, Ripon (SS81/202). A more complicated
framework of platforms and poles required substantial amounts of timber: 1399 *Item
xviij magnæ arbores pro scaffaldyng, precii 60s* [*Item 18 large trees for scaffolding at a cost
of 60s*], York (SS35/19). Bridge building records have references from the fifteenth
century: 1422 *schaffoldynges*, Catterick Bridge (NRQS3/33); 1485–6 *the centres of the
scaffyldes*, Lady's Bridge in Sheffield (HS1/59). See also centre, post (1), scatch, severy,
tree.

scald Having the scall, a scabby disease which often affected the scalp: 1638 *Ordered
that Robert Clough shall take the saide poore childe Apprentice if he have not a scald head*,
Keighley (YAJ5/378).

scale (1) A regional form of shale. The search for coal obliged miners to sink shafts
and drive passages through earth, rock and a variety of minerals which they considered
to be of little or no value, and all this waste matter had to be taken out of the pit and
stacked or distributed on ground close to the pit-head. It is in such contexts that we
find the word 'scale'. In 1665, two Bradford men were ordered at the manor court
to *remove all the gravel of earth and scale digged forth of the … Cole Pitts, which by their
procurement was throwne into the high wayes and ditches belonging to Heaton* (BAS7/42). In
1777, the lessees of a pit in Southowram were granted room where they might store
the coal and also *all such gravel, Stone, Scale and Rubbish as shall arise in Sinking of the
same pitts*; spoil heaps that is (HM/C/10). See also black scale.

scale (2) A drinking bowl or cup: 1616 *Who present … Geo. Smales … for keeping
an alehouse and selling ale in scales and pottes not sealed*, Hutton Bushell (NRQS2/118).

scale-presser A specialisation in the cutlers' hafting process which involved the use of
vices. For example, horn scales were first heated gently, roughly shaped with a knife,
then 'placed in a *die* of of heated steel' and 'subjected to heavy pressure in a hand
screw vice' (CAT36). In 1690, George Harrison of Sheffield had 3 *dossen plain knifes
to presse* (IH) and in 1818 John Bellamy was described as a *scale presser* (WPS112). See
also presser.

scales The scales are the coverings used on spring knife handles, that is materials such
as horn, pearl, wood and even silver. We know little about the word's earliest history
since 'hafting' developed as an independent craft only in the eighteenth century, but
the first references in Sheffield inventories include those of George Harrison in 1690
who had *17 dozen of horne scale* and John Shirtcliffe in 1713 with unwrought silver
for embossed handles and *silver scales and weights* (IH). It was used also of sword hafts:
1463 *6C swerdscales*, Hull (YRS144/61). See also bone.

scallop In this case used of bread which will have had the shape of a scallop shell:
1509 *I will have my Derege in my house and therto be had comfettes, sugar plates and suckittes
… and at tharbe skallapis of mayne breid*, York (SS79/5).

scantling The scantling was a carpenter's or builder's measuring rod, but used in
the plural the word meant 'dimensions': 1682 *the timber … to be of such scantlings or
dimencions as may be strong and substantiall for such a roofe*, Scriven (YAJ16/113). It seems
occasionally to have referred to the timber itself: 1793 *32ft of scantling for a shoring*,
Thurstonland (M55). See also pan, purlin.

scapple A word used by both masons and carpenters to describe work done on newly
cut stone or timber so as to reduce the faces of the material to a plane surface: 1322

Et in xx blettron' prosternend' & scapland in bosco de Secroft [And for felling and scappling 20 saplings in Seacroft wood], Leeds (Th45/86); 1399 *Pro scorpillyng lapidum [For scappling stones]*, York (SS35/15); 1422 *the wherreours brekes the saides stanes and schapels thaim in the saides qwerrels*, Catterick (NRQS3/35); 1433 *in iij quercubus scapulatis et ij quercubus squararatis pro balkes [for 3 scappled oaks and 2 squared oaks for balks]*, York (SS35/52). The small pieces of stone removed by masons in that process were referred to as 'scapplings': 1745 *24 load of small stone and two load of scaplings*, Bradfield (HPP50). See also broach (2), dress, rough mason, scrapplings, stone-breaker.

scar A cliff or a precipitous, rocky slope: 1673 *had trailed a horse of the said Geo. downe a great scarr*, Ridley (SS40/196); 1706 *the inhabitants of Ealand are great sufferers by their cattell falling down the hills and scarrs … they have petitioned that a convenient wall or defence be made to prevent the same* (QS1/45/9). It is a common place-name element, with examples quoted by Smith from the thirteenth century (PNWR7/244).

scarth A regional form of 'shard, sherd', used here for fragments of tile or brick: 1421 *Soluti pro viij sarcinis de telescarthes a Telehouse de Clifton usque eundem locum 8d [Paid for 8 loads of tile scarths from the tile house at Clifton to that same place 8d]*, York (SS35/45). In the same accounts is a reference *Pro cariagio [For transport of] … mason chippes*, possibly used as hard-core (SS35/95).

scatch The two contexts in which this word has been noted suggest that it may have referred to scaffold poles, and that the 'bridges' were the platform for the workmen: 1420 *William of Alne … sall fynde the brygges, the scaches, nayles and all the tymbre that sall ga un to the gutter* (SS85/15); 1533 *for v bordes to the guttors, iiijd. Item for wood to make scatchys and bryges iijd*, York (CCW157).

scathe fire A destructive fire, a conflagration: 1666 'Two dozen leather buckets and two fire *houkes* or clamps to be provided for the public use in case any *scath* fire happen', Beverley (YRS84/141).

scaytbell See scabell.

scissor grinder 1812 *Thomas Dyson, scissor grinder, Lescar Wheel* (WPS133). See also grinder, scissorsmith.

scissorsmith The making of scissors and shears were ancient crafts in Yorkshire, especially in Sheffield. The scissorsmiths saw themselves as distinct from shearsmiths and claimed the right to manufacture any item which operated on the pin principle, even some that were named 'shears'. When the Cutlers' Company was incorporated in 1624 marks were immediately granted to 28 working scissorsmiths, and references to the occupation are frequent from that period: 1638 William Newbold, *scissor-smith*, Handsworth (YRS54/112); 1653–4 *William Grimeshawe of Sheffeld scissorsmith* (PR3/189).

sconce A candle-holder: *c*.1392 *Pro reparacione de iiij skonses fractis in vestiario, 12d [For repairing 4 broken sconces in the vestry, 12d]*, York (SS35/129); 1506 *on of my sconsis and a writyng candlestik*, York (SS35/353); 1567 *a sconsse to set before the fyre*, Mortham (SS26/201); 1610 *In the Lobby … two skonzes iiijd*, Kirkstall (SpSt); 1641 *two voyders, a hand sconce*, Thornton near Bradford (LRS1/122).

scoop A word applied to various implements used for ladling liquids, or shovelling sand, grit and the like. Often the context does not make the exact meaning clear: 1395 *pro j skowp Willelmo Plomar vjd [to William Plomar for 1 scoop 6d]* (SS72/605); *c*.1450 *brosches et scopis emptis pro purgacione les reredose in choro, stallorum et murorum Ecclesiæ [for*

brushes and scoops bought to clean the reredos in the choir, the stalls and the church walls], York
(SS35/65); 1454 *Et in iiij scoupes emptis pro jactacione aque ad huiusmodi opus xijd [And
for 4 scoops bought for casting water for that kind of work 12d]*, York (SS192/82); 1642 *to
stande ready with a scoupe … and water it sowndly all over*, Elmswell (DW145).

In some West Riding coal-mines the scoop was a container in which coal was
drawn to the surface: 1666 *keepe in worke eighte pickes five Skuppes foure Spades two
Shoufles*, South Crosland (DD/WBD/2/81); 1702 *hurt by the end of a scoop in pulling up
coals*, Shelley (QS1). Oliver Heywood likened it to a basket in 1673, in which colliers
were raised and lowered at the scene of an accident, and that is the meaning given
in the OED. However, few examples are quoted there and the evidence is far from
conclusive, especially the east Yorkshire reference 'scopp' which may be a mistaken
reading of 'scepp' (DW109). Colliery accounts make it clear that by *c.*1700 the scoop
was a box-like construction, made of wood with iron fittings: 1713 *two boarded scoops*,
Shibden (HAS30/147); 1732 *two scoops mending with staples and nailes*, Whitley (DD/
WBE/1). Scoop and corf are listed together in the accounts for a pit in Tong, so they
were distinct items. See also coal-mining tools and implements, corf, scoop shoes.

scoop shoes The under-side of the scoop used in coal-mines may have been
fitted with iron plates which allowed it to be dragged across rough ground: 1707 *2
spades 4s and 6 scoopshoes 5s*, Huddersfield (QS4/20); 1732 *two pair new scoop shoes*,
Whitley (DD/WBE/1); 1750 *Pd smith for … 3 pair of scoop shoes and nailes*, Shibden
(HAS30/151). See also scoop.

score In the fifteenth century, pigs and other farmyard animals were weighed by the
'score' which was equivalent to twenty or twenty-one pounds. It was used for a wider
range of materials in the sixteenth century: 1539 *a score off sand viijd*, York (CCW215);
1593 *a score of harden cloth*, South Cave (Kaner188). It also occurred regularly in
colliery accounts from the seventeenth century: 1694 *was to pay him 1s 6d a score*,
Lepton (QS1); 1710 *Coales on the Hill 35 Sc. at 2s 6d a score*, Farnley (MS11); 1760
Pd for 9 score of wood borrowing 1s 1½d, Tong (Tong/4c/5). See also chalder, quarter.

scotale Literally a payment or 'tax' on ale. This was a forced contribution, paid for
ale at a celebration organised by some official (OED): 1395 *Item pro j scotall ibid iijd*,
Stakesby (SS72/619).

scotch cap When Thomas Greenwood died he had unfinished business, and in his
will he sought to set matters straight:

> 1551 *unto Edwarde Sundderland as it apperethe in my booke of parcels for a
> remnantte of calve skynes so that the said Edward do allowe to me xxs whiche I paid
> for hym to William Parkyns, besides a Scotche cappe that he had of me, and I owe unto
> hym for whitte carsaye*, Wakefield (Th19/261).

The OED has examples of this word from 1591 and it is described there as 'a man's
head-dress made of thick firm woollen cloth, without a brim, and decorated with two
tails or streamers'.

scotch cloth A textile fabric which resembled 'lawn' but was cheaper: 1636 *stealing
cambric and Scotch cloth*, Thirsk (NRQS4/50). It is sometimes said to have been made
from the fibre of nettles. See also nettle-cloth, scotchman, whisk.

scotchman This was formerly the English word for a man of Scottish nationality,
now usually 'Scotsman': 1681 *John Marshall, Scotch man*, Skipton (PR). It was applied
in particular to travelling drapers, hawkers, and pedlars of scotch cloth who called

regularly at out-of-the-way places: they are said to have been successful partly because they used a credit system.

The term occurs regularly in Yorkshire records from the early eighteenth century but will have been in use much earlier: 1705 *Alexander Miller ... and another Scotchman taken up with a pack on his back*, Gisburn (QS1/44/4); 1721 *Mary Hanson had bought the musling of one Robert Maxfield a Scotchman* (QS1/60/1); 1731 *William Rowan, scotchman pedlar*, Sheffield (PR); 1738 *one piece of red and white printed linen which she saith she exchanged with a Scotch Man for her son's hair in 1736*, West Riding (QS1/77/6). In 1755, a coroner's inquest called David Anderson *a travelling Scotchman* (QS1/96/4). Some early depositions contain good biographic information, as when John Smith was arrested in Kirkheaton:

> 1682 *saith that he was borne in Scotland and Dumfrees and he came into England the fooreende of May last and sells hollan and scotchcloath, cambrick, muslins, callecoe and blew linne and that he came from Almondbury to Kirkheaton and there was taken up by the watch and hath used this pedding traide for five yeares last paste in England and that he byes the comodityes, except the scotchcloath, of Mr Hardwick and Mr Hey both of Leeds* (QS10/8).

In the 1881 census the occupation of Joe Whiteley of Holmfirth was given as *scotch traveller:* his local surname suggests that the term had by then acquired a more generic sense.

scotsemnail Noted as *scotsem* in Nottingham in 1273 (SZ1/314). It was frequent in Yorkshire from the early fourteenth century: 1313–14 *Pro ij. M^L scotnayl hoc anno iij s [For 2000 scotsemnails this year 3s]*, Bolton Priory (YRS154/364); 1318–19 *Pro dcccc. di. de spikings et scottesem [For 950 spikings and scotsemnails]*, Bolton Priory (YRS154/464); 1371 *Et in 10.m de Scotsomnail emptis pro celura, dando pro c. 5d, 41s 8d [And for 10,000 scotsemnails bought for the timberwork, giving 5d per 100, 41s 8d]*, York (SS35/7). The inference may be that 'sem' derives from the word for 'nail' or 'rivet', on record in the most northerly counties and especially in Scotland. It was used there of a nail that fixed together the planks of a clinker-built boat (CSD) and may therefore have meant simply 'scottish nail', one that could be clenched. In that case the suffix 'nail' will have been added by clerks who were unfamiliar with the regional word. Later examples include: 1379–80 *in scotsumnayle, 3d*, Ripon (SS81/101); 1434 *In v. m Scotesemnailes, 5s 5d*, York (SS35/53); 1518 *Item paid for ij M skotsym, ijs*, York (CCW/70); 1535 *It'm twoo thowsand skott Semes*, Stillingfleet (YRS45/130); 1537 *scotsem nayles otherwise called lathe nayles*, Sheriff Hutton (SZ1/314).

scraggy On record from 1611 with the meaning lean or bony, chiefly depreciatory (OED). Possibly a nickname several centuries earlier: 1270 *Simon Scraggy*, Hunmanby (YRS12/113); 1360 *Adam Scraggy*, York (SS96/55).

scrapplings An alternative of 'scapplings': 1818 *clearing away masons scraplings*, Mirfield (DD/CA/5). See also scapple.

scrath An obscure term with a variety of spellings, found only in documents to do with cloth-dressing, always in similar contexts: 1618 *half a warping wouthe, half a brack of handls and scraths iijs vjd*, Bingley (LRS1/54); 1703 *Handle brake, Handles and Raizing Peark ... Three Shear Boards ... and Scraths*, Skircoat (BAS7/229n). Spellings with final 'th' omitted, as in dialect more generally, occur from the sixteenth century: 1576 *one shearborde, iiij paire of walker sheares, viij course of handles, one scraye*, Leeds (Th4/164); 1701 *handle brake, shearebord, skreas*, Holmfirth (IH). W.B. Crump thought it possible that these were pairs of wire cards, although he was uncertain whether 'scray' and 'scrath' were the same word (BAS7/229). However, I believe Wright had the meaning under 'scray' which he noted in Yorkshire and defined as 'A low wooden frame with cross-pieces used for laying cloth upon' (EDD).

scree A type of sieve used to separate corn from dust and other unwanted matter (EDD): 1657 *1 credle, 1 skree*, Gateforth (YRS47/32). Occasionally also as a verb: 1700 *it was of his best mault and he screed it with his own hands*, West Riding (QS1). The spellings invite comparison with screen and scry (OED) and with screel below.

screel A 'screen' for dressing corn, noted under 'skreel' as a North Lincolnshire term (EDD): 1658 *one screl & one bushel 15s*, Selby (YRS47/124); 1669 *the milne kilne hare, screele, shovels and scuttles belonging to the said kilne*, Brayton (YRS47/118).

scribble A term for one of the processes by which wool is converted into yarn, originally using hand cards but later a machine which had rollers covered with card wires: 1727 *2 pairs scribblers and stocks*, Holmfirth (IH); 1741 *he was to have £4 15s wages and was to scribble nine pounds of wool each day and then to be at liberty to go where he pleased*, Churwell (QS1/80/9); 1758 *The quantity of wooll … for a man to scribble of one d(ay) is 36 pound if itt is for mixt(er)*, Wakefield (YRS155/4); 1788 *engines for scribbling or carding of wool*, Hunsworth (MD292/59); 1794 *Occupier of Scribling Engeons*, South Crosland (GRD).

scrimple Apparently a form of 'crumple': 1758–62 *so put in streight with cuttles so lett itt go about 10 minutes and that will take outt all the scrimples*, Wakefield (YRS155/29).

scrive iron An iron, marking tool, recorded in the OED from the nineteenth century. The Yorkshire evidence is not clear-cut but there is a link with marking trees: a Tong wood lease of 1806 has *numbered with scrive irons* (Tong/4f/15).

scrogg See shrogg.

scrow Short for escrow, a scrap or strip of parchment, a land deed: 1561 *with all my landes, howses … and with all deeds, charters, escriptes, scrowes … concerning the said land*, Ebberston (NRQS4/131); 1637 *this to be my last will revooking all others as scrowes and unperfecte papers*, Barwick in Elmet (PR). See also craw.

scrub oak In an undated survey of Pickering Forest, earlier than 1568, a clear distinction was drawn between an oak classed as 'a timber tree', with a usual value of xijd, and 'a scrubb' worth ijd. A typical entry reads: *Item att Hunt House, Skethewyck and Swyne Gill 1000 scrubb okes and Sepeinges* [sic] *and 360 Timber trees*. In other entries the order of the words is reversed: *Item in Bryghton bank xl okes scrubbes* (NRR1/211). See also scrud oak, shrub oak.

scrud oak The Dissolution rental for Selby Abbey contains the following entry: 1540 *ther ys a wod upon the common pastur called Selby out woddes wherin ys conteyned by est[imacion] mccc scrudde okes worth vijd le oke* (YRS13/354). Halliwell and EDD both have 'scruddy' as a northern word for dwarfish or stunted, but no examples are given and the OED makes no mention of it. Similarly: 1579 *certain olde Skruddle Hessels*, Arncliffe (Whit2/492).

scrutore A writing desk or cabinet, from French escritoire. The OED has similar spellings from 1665: 1728 *a scrutore and chair*, Wooldale (IH); 1755 *'unto my son John Frankland £40 and a scrutoe* [sic] *standing in the parlour'*, Lees in Bowland (CS3/83).

scry A shout or cry: 1487 *And that noo maner of persones … make noo skryes, showtings nor blowing of hornes … after the wache be sett*, York (YRS103/27). In a much later reference the meaning seems to be 'don't betray our presence' so it may be an apheptic form of descry: 1755 *James said they were there to be sure but don't scry us and accordingly on the search they found a goose and three other fowles secreted in a treacle barrell*, Rawcliffe (QS1/94/3).

scummer A 'skimmer', a shallow ladle or sieved spoon used for removing scum or other unwanted matter from the surface of liquids: 1399 *j scomor cum j podyngiren*, York (SS35/18); 1445 *et j ladill cum ij scomeres de auricalco [and 1 ladle with 2 scummers made of brass]*, Beverley (SS30/100); 1515 *pro … j skomer*, York (SS35/97); 1567 *a latyne Ladill a Latyne scomer*, Fixby (YRS134/19); 1619 *one scomber, one latine ladle*, Bingley (LRS1/30); 1700 *one Brass scumber 4d*, Elland (OWR1/2/8). In some inventories it was a kind of fire shovel or riddle: 1490 *De j fyre scomer cum j pare de taynges vjd*, York (SS53/57); 1507 *a rost yren with a fyer scomer*, York (YRS39/189); 1528 *A scomer for the fire and a great pare tonges xvjd*, York (SS79/255); 1669 *3 broyling irons, 2 pr racks, j fire scumer*, Selby (YRS47/36). In 1735, William Hawkesworth of Longley in the parish of Ecclesfield had *tongs Scimmer and Hammers* (IH).

scuncheon A kind of chamfered brick used for jambs and arches (SZ1/141): 1409 *Et Johanni Elward pro mille squynchon et vj walltill vjs [To John Elward for 1000 scuncheons and 600 wall tiles 6s]*, Beverley (ERAS4/31); 1446–7 *Dc [600] tegularum vocatarum qwynshontylle 2s 8½d [600 tiles called scuncheon tiles 2s 8½d]*, Beverley (ERAS7/54).

scurf A fish, also known as the salmon-scurf or sea-trout (OED): 1678 'for catching ten unseasonable fish called *scurfes*', Startforth (NRQS7/6).

scutt A rare word with just one OED reference, in Nottinghamshire in 1561. It means embankment or possibly water channel: 1704 'unless care be yearly taken for cutting destroying and clearing weeds … and removing the sand bed from the Mill Scutt, the Beck or River will in a short time be grown up again', Beverley (YRS84/114).

scuttle Typically a large basket made of wickerwork, used for carrying corn, vegetables, sand, etc.: 1357 *Item j scutil ijd ob [2½d]*, York (SS129/5); 1399 *in scutells et schovells*, York (SS35/17); 1446–7 *ij scutellis 2d*, Beverley (ERAS7/60); 1457–8 *In Scafis et scutellis de Joh'e Schau iijs xd*, Fountains Abbey (SS130/50); 1535 *Item baweles, seues and skutteles xs*, Stillingfleet (YRS45/128); 1642 *two olde scuttles to carry up morter in*, Elmswell (DW151); 1663 *pro scuttles & traces, 6s 8d*, Ripon (YRS118/103); 1679 *with hoppers, troughs, sckepts, scuttles*, Selby (YRS47/48). Early Latin examples point to more ornate domestic items: 1356 *do et lego … uxori suæ scutellam deauratam melioremquam voluerit eligere pro speciebus dandis [I give and bequeath to his wife the better gilt scuttle which she wished to choose for the reasons given]*, Lincoln (SS4/25).

scuttle maker A maker of scuttles or baskets: 1580 *Imprimis payd to stotele [scotele?] maker for on leape, two wyndo treles, & ij stotels [scotels?] iijs*, Stockeld (YRS161/17); 1586 *Edward Crawe, skutlemaker*, Wighill (YRS22/32). In Beverley, the *scuttellmakers* were linked in 1596 with the carpenters and joiners (YRS84/67). When George Murrey of Nosterfield was described as a *scuttle maker* in 1611, the editor, Canon Atkinson, said that in his day, that is 1884, the scuttle was a shallow open basket with a wide mouth, used for gathering potatoes and the like (NRQS1/208). The occupation was sufficiently distinctive to serve as a by-name as late as the seventeenth century: 1625 *James Scuttlemaker alias Tayler, younger*, Spofforth (YRS32/81). See also carpenter.

scythe boon See boon, sickle boon.

scythegrinder Until well into the eighteenth century most Hallamshire metal workers who needed to grind their own wares rented space at grinding wheels, and only scythe-grinding was a specialist occupation (FBH103). In Derbyshire, a scythe-mill was established at Holbrook in 1489 but the first references to the occupation are much later: 1603 *Robert Barnes, scythe grinder*, Norton (WPS171). However, it was an established craft in Sheffield later that century: 1674 *Rob. Hawksworth, Heeley, scythgrinder* (QS1/13/10); 1704 *ux Georgii Marriott Sythgrinder de Eccles*[all] (PR7/5); 1728 *James Oates, sythgrinder*, Sheffield (PR.6/64). In 1729, the Cutlers Company paid Joseph Lord *for getting information ag*[ain]*st Scyth Grinders* (HCC23). See also scythesmith.

scythesmith Sheffield historians have made the point that scythesmiths were operating in the Norton area of Derbyshire before the craft had independent status in Sheffield (FBH95), and references to the occupation bear that out: 1599 *Edward Gill, scythesmith*, Norton (WPS166); 1653 *Lawrence Savage of Woodsetts in the p'ish of Norton, sythsmith* (PR3/189). That is not to say that scythes were not being made in Sheffield at that time, for there is proof in wills that they were: 1545 *bellowes, sithes, hamors and tonges*, Attercliffe (TWH13/73); 1551–2 *smythe geyre and two dossen sythes readye to the chapman*, Sheffield (TWH13/100). There were also scythesmiths elsewhere in south Yorkshire: 1556 *Thomas Blithe of Hymmysworthe, scithesmythe* (YAJ20/13); 1575 *blades-mythes, blacksmythes and sythesmythes* (YRS115/108); 1580 *Nicholas Beckett, Hoghtone hall in Worsbroughe, siethsmythe*, York (YRS19/12).

The Sheffield scythesmiths were admitted into the Cutlers Company in 1682 but references to the occupeation occur much earlier: 1654 *Thomas Wright of Hawslinbanck in the p'ish of Sheffeld sythsmith* (PR3/191). In 1639–40, Thomas Maude of Sheffield, *sithersmith* [sic – so possibly a scissorsmith] was indicted for stealing *a teame, two paire of plowe shackles and two pair of waine shackles*, all iron objects which he had no doubt intended to sell or convert to his own use (YRS54/178). See also bloomer.

scythe-striker The striker assisted the smith by hammering the scythe when instructed: Norton examples include: 1559–60 *Thomas Rose*; 1579–80 *William Barten of Grennell* (PR); 1670 *George Anderton, Woodseats … sythestriker* (IH). Across the border in Heeley, George Denton and Richard Broadbent were both described as *sythstriker* in 1674 (QS1/13/10).

sea See say (1).

sea-coal This early word for 'coal' has been explained in a variety of ways but one important theory is that it first described coal which had been cast ashore from seams exposed on the sea bed. The diarist Abraham de la Pryme knew that coal was obtained in this way on the Yorkshire coast, and he wrote in 1697 of great quantities washed up in Holderness. It was, he said, little more than dust, *so exceeding small that it commonly smothers all their fires out, unless they keep perpetualy blowing the same*. In towns along the coast the people therefore had special chimneys, and set their houses in positions which ensured a constant draught (SS54/166).

The main alternative theory is that sea-coal was so named because for many people it was literally brought to them by sea, especially from Newcastle upon Tyne. Oliver Heywood wrote in 1665 of an *exceeding scarcity of sea-coal in great towns that have been supplied from New-castle, especially London, Hul and York by reason that the Hollanders lye upon the sea-coast and hinder passage* (OH3/92).

Neither explanation seems entirely satisfactory, especially if we consider that sea-coal was the name given to coal dug out of the ground in the Pennines as early as the thirteenth century. In Old English, sea-coal or *sæcol* was actually jet, also cast up on the east coast, and this may have been an influence when it became necessary to distinguish between charcoal and mineral coal. Most early references are in Latin: 1306 'and he is digging sea coal (*carbones maris*) therein, damages 6s 8d', Sandal (YRS36/59); 1446–58 *Et petit pro labore suo ad carbon. marin. per iij dies, vjd [And he asks for his labour with sea-coal for 3 days, 6d]*, Fountains Abbey (SS130/174). An earlier English reference is listed under 'coal'. See also chalder.

seal To fasten a cow in its stall. The origin appears to be an Old English word for a rope, although in Sheffield in the nineteenth century it was 'a piece of wood put round a cow's neck' which was then fastened to a chain in the cow house (EDD). The verb is recorded from the sixteenth century and was confined to Scotland and the northern counties. In *c*.1570 Mr Kaye of Woodsome Hall advised his son that at certain times cattle and sheep should not be allowed into the pasture grounds: he was to *sele them upp to brede … mucke* (KayeCP). In 1682, part of a property in Monk Bretton was described as a *house for sealinge their cowes in and roome over them for lying of hay for the said cowes* (YAS/DD116b). A very similar description in the Huddersfield will of Richard Williamson, in 1686, referred to part of the barn and *mistell … sufficient to seale one cow and lay hay* for it (BIA/VR/478). Later, the word may have been used more generally, for Joseph Exley of Rawdon had geese *to sele* in 1740 (QS1). The buildings at Esholt Priory were surveyed in 1538 and they included *a cowe-house of iiij rowmys seyled abowte*, but this was perhaps for 'ceiled' (YAJ9/322). See also breed.

seale spars See ceiling board, seal.

sealing See ceil, ceiling board.

sealing board A board which could be used for panelling and for doors, as in 1472 when repairs were being carried out to the Pageant House in York: items in the accounts for the doors (*pro hostiis*) included *selynges et barres … burdes … bandes et crokes* (SS129/69). See also ceiling board, syling.

sealsmolt Almost certainly seal blubber. There are numerous references in early customs accounts for Hull although the spelling varied considerably: 1453 *6 bar' selsmelt*; 1463 *2 bar' sellsmought*; *5 bar' scelsmought*; 1465 *6 bar' selsmouthe*, Hull (YRS144). See also train (1).

seeled, seild, seled, selyd, seylid Spellings of ceiled. See also ceil, seal.

seeling A spellings of ceiling. See also ceil, seal.

seam (1) This is a word already in use in the Old English period when it referred to the seam formed when the edges of two pieces of cloth were joined by sewing. A much later example indicates how it came to be used of rock strata: 1687 'that which at first seemed to be seams or joynings of the Stones are only veins in the rock' (OED). Coal-mining examples date from that period. See also coal-bed, vein, win.

seam (2) A measurement, used for a variety of commodities: 1419 *Custus vitri: Et in iij sem' et in iij pais' albi vitri emptis de Johanne Glasman … prec. le seme, 20s [Costs of glass: And for 3 seams and 3 weys of clear glass bought from John Glasman … priced at 20s the seam]*, York (SS35/37); 1456–7 *pro ij seym salmon de Joh'e Neusom xvs [for 2 seams of salmon from John Newson 15s]*, Fountains Abbey (SS130/11). It is found in charcoal accounts as equivalent to a horse-load, one of three alternative terms for the same quantity: 1567–8 *the quarter ys a seame and the seme ys 8 busshell; the quarter ys a horsselode; the dusson ys 12 seme or 12 quarter alle one mesuer*, Esholt (BAS10/246–7). See also dozen (1).

searcher The office of 'searcher' was already established in the medieval guilds. In York in 1477 the cutlers' guild ordered *that whatsomever he be of the said craft that will not obbey his serchiours … shall forfett xijd to the chambre* (SS120/133). It became a traditional custom too among the Sheffield cutlers whose ordinances in 1565 included an obligation to be *yerelie … searched by xii men of the said crafte* (HCC1).

season To keep timber after it has been cut so that it might dry out and harden. Examples of the word date only from the 1600s but the practice is much older: 1529 *also tymbre lying drye for the use of husbandrie*, Ingmanthorpe (SS79/277); 1617 *2 oake boards well seasoned beinge 8 foet longe and 11 inche broad to make up my new barne doers with*, Brandsby (NYRO44/139); 1642 *A Sweathrake hath usually xxxiiij teeth … of yron, the heade of seasoned Ash and the shafte usually of saugh*, Elmswell (DW53); 1671 *found 2 boards neare fower yards long, foot broad and about 12 years seasoning in a chamber of an out-house*, Kimberworth (QS1/9).

seave A regional word for a rush or rushlight: 1579 *candel seaves vjd*, Stockeld (YRS161/11). Angus Winchester has commented on the plant's domestic uses and noted a reference in 1579 to mowing *lez seavethacke* in Littondale, and another in 1659 to *thatche seaves* in Lartington (AW138). It is a frequent element in minor place-names: 1443 *seueker*, Tadcaster (YRS38/164); 1564 *the Sevye closes*, Ingleby Arncliffe (YRS50/114); 1631 *Rushie close or Seavy close*, Spofforth (YRS69/118). 'Half a rood at *Seneker*' in an undated thirteenth-century Tockwith deed should probably be *Seueker* (YRS80/183).

seck A regional spelling of sack: 1522 *for a sek of coylles iijd*, York (CCW88); 1579 *of Mr Robert Wytham for a secke of haver 3s 4d*, Stockeld (YRS161/9); 1693 *six sex and three pockes*, Holmfirth (G-A). Early examples of the spelling are found in Yorkshire in by-names for a maker of sacks or sack-cloth: 1277 *Eva la Seckere*, Ossett (GRDict). See also sackcloth, sacking yarn.

seeing-glass A mirror or looking-glass: 1619 *a baskett a seing glasse certaine old ireon*, South Cave (Kaner279); 1658 *1 seeinge glasse & 1 paire of curling irons 5s 4d*, Barley (YRS47/16); 1731 *one larg seeing glas*, Spofforth (QS1/70/4).

seentree, signtree, sinetree In Wright the 'sign-tree' or 'sine-tree' is explained firstly as 'one of the principal timbers of a roof', and secondly as the 'centerings of an arch' (EDD). The word was in use in both Lancashire and Yorkshire. As no examples are quoted, either there or in the OED, the following references to its use as a roof timber are of interest. In 1817, a Slaithwaite diarist called Hirst wrote of damage to the 'thack' or roof of his house: he had been awakened in the middle of the night by a very loud noise and discovered that *the sine tree [had] slipped out of the mortis in the balk end* (KX390). In 1686, the accounts for the building of an extension to a house in Conistone mention *Fower paire of sinetrees bought of … John Piccard* (RW33). In this case the dimensions of the timbers are given as *10 inches deep and 5 inches in thicknesse*. In 1739, *1 pair of signtrees* at Lofthouse measured *10 fot* and cost one shilling (QS1/80/1).

The following references support the idea that 'sine-tree' and 'sign-tree' share the same origin as 'centre'. For example, *signetrees* were required for the arches of Elland Bridge in 1579 (BAS6/139) and in 1698 *one paire of senters* referred to timbers for Pickering tithe barn (YAJ35/221). In 1747, *sintrees* for Clapham church bridge were listed in the same context as the frame and the arch (QS1/86/5). The semantic change can perhaps be explained by the fact that both meanings carry the idea of 'load-bearing timbers', and the orthographic connection may be via the word 'tree', commonly used in the past instead of 'wood' or 'timber'. As 'sine' is an early and alternative spelling of 'sinew', Wright plausibly suggested that it was the first element in 'sine-tree' (EDD) but the Yorkshire evidence points to an alternative explanation. See also fork.

seethe To cook food by boiling or stewing: 1444 *a chafir to seethe fish ynne*, Lincolnshire (SS30/112).

sege See siege.

segg A bull, castrated after it has grown to maturity: 1581 *Item on bull segge pryse 28s*, Stockeld (YRS161/33); 1605 *one segge hide*, Almondbury (DD/RA/f/4a); 1655 *one bull and one segg*, Whitley (DD/WBM/69); 1667 *two fatt segges £7 0 0*, North Bierley (YRS134/130). However, fully grown animals such as pigs or sheep could also be called segs (EDD).

seiling, seillyng See ceil.

seine draught McDonnel noted that seine nets were used by fishermen on Yorkshire rivers from the twelfth century at least, and in salt-water estuaries soon afterwards (YRS62/122). The net was designed to hang in the water, and the ends were drawn together to prevent the fish from escaping: the practice meant the fisherman had to stand on the bank above the water in order to draw the net tight and the term 'seine draught' seems to have become associated with the right to do that: 1435 *Lease of le seynedraght*, Wakefield (WCR15/140); 1540 *ther be certen fyshynges late in thandes of the house, that ys to say the fyshyng and signe draughtes in the water of Ouse, lately demised*, Selby (YRS13/351); 1572 *Ther is in the gallery netts, viz a great sene and less sene as draught netts*, Skipton (Whit2/335).

seised of In possession of a property: 1530 *I will that my feoffees shall stand and be seaissid of and in all my landes and tenements in Waddisworth* (Clay83); 1546 *I wul that they stonde and be seased of v acres of the same*, Kettlesing (SS104/48). See also seisin.

seisin Literally 'possession', a word found in connection with the conveyance of property: 1251 'their attorneys put themselves in seisin of the manor', Stokesley (YRS12/26). It occurs especially in the phrase 'livery of seisin'; that is the formal handing over of a house, land or the like, e.g. 1488 *sall not delyv(er) seasyn unto aftir such a day in the next weyk after lowgh Sonnday*, Golcar (KM146). The particular interest in the word is in the money or items that were handed over by vendors as symbols of the change in ownership.

The earliest example that I have noted is in an undated twelfth-century charter which transferred land in Skelbrooke to St John's Priory, Pontefract: *Quam terram Oliverus frater eius prius donaverat, et super altare obtulerat per cultellum plicatum [Which land his brother Oliver had given earlier, and on the altar offered through a clasp knife]*; that is 'at the altar of the church by a clasped knife' (YRS30/433). In 1567, the manor of Skewkirk changed hands and the symbol was a pair of knives (*unius paris cultellorum*): Skewkirk was a former cell of Nostell Priory (YRS2/340). Later deeds provide details of a wide variety of objects: 1610 *lease of Roger Weddell's farme sealed upon the grownde in the myll close and a sod cut up by me … and delivered … as possession of all therein conteaned*, Brandsby (NYRO44/48); 1611 *one peece of silver of the value of sixepence in the name of possession and seison thereof*, Kilnsey (MD247); 1666 *one pewter doubler in stead and name of all the premises*, South Crosland (G-A); 1693 *by presentation of a clod of earth and a warming pan*, Arncliffe (EG26); 1766 *one pewter spoon at the time of the selling and delivering'*, Heptonstall (MD43/J17). In 1777, Anthony Green of Austonley had debts that he was unable to pay because of *losses in trade … and other unhappy misfortunes* and he was obliged to sign over his real and personal estates to his creditors. When the deed was executed in November he agreed to put Christopher in full possession *by delivering to him one Silver cup in the name of the whole* (G–A). See also sneck (1), surrender with straw.

selion An individual strip of arable land in the common field of a township, found as an English word from *c.*1450 (OED) but much earlier in Latin documents, some undated: *a.*1272 *de dimidia acra terre in Boultona et j selleione [for half an acre of arable land in Bolton and 1 selion]*, Bolton by Bowland (YRS87/85).

selyng See ceil.

sennight A period of seven days and nights, a week: 1482 *of fryday was a senyt*, York (YRS98/67); 1496 *deliver the said bill unto theyr wardeyns afore Friday come a seven nyght*, York (YRS103/126); 1579 *that wyddowe Rawson make her fence betwixte her ynge and little common tofte betwixte this and Sonday cum a sennet*, Dewsbury (YAJ21/411); 1615 *put 2 kyne … into Steresby clyffe on Monday was a sennet*, Brandsby (NYRO44/98); 1642 *If pease bee dry they may bee ledde the same day senight after they are pulled*, Elmswell (DW98); 1729 *Tuesday was sevennight before*, Stainland (QS1/68/4).

serge (1) A typical English spelling of French 'cierge'. It was a large wax candle, especially one used in religious ceremonies: 1371 *Et in vj serzis emptis pro le mold 18d [And for 6 serges bought for the mold 18d]*, York (SS35/9); 1393 *I wyte xx^lb of wax in v sereges to birn a boute my body*, York (SS4/185); 1492 *also 1lb of wax to be made in a serge*, York (SS35/352); 1533 *I will that x or xij serdges and tapers shalbe kepid and upholden in the said parishe churche*, Halifax (Clay88); 1548 *I will haue a serge of waxe sett opon the herse ouer me the spaice of one yere*, Saxton (Th19/200). See also mould (2).

serge (2) A woollen fabric, latterly durable, twilled worsted: 1710 *In the shop … browne searge, stript searge*, Holmfirth (IH).

serve their turn To answer a purpose or requirement: 1634 *that the people of Thwongsgreave shall turne [into its right course] one springe of water which they have taken out of the Lordshipp of Meltham to serve their owns turnes* (G–A). Used ironically by a man in possession of an offensive weapon: 1677 *a very desperate person and often drunke … he had something in his pockett that would serve their turns*, Halifax (QS1).

serving-man A male servant, attending on a gentleman: 1552 *John Perte, sarvinge man*, Everingham (YRS11/135); 1565 *Lewis Thomas, serving man*, Seamer (YRS14/162).

sess, sessment See assess.

sestern, sestrin Common alternative spellings of 'cistern', for example: 1481 *De j sestryn xvjs viijd*, York (SS45/261). See also cistern.

set (1) The verb 'to set' could be to plant seeds or cuttings, and in some leases the tenants moving into a new property were held responsible for setting and planting a number of trees: 1737 *To Mr Watts for 6 Trees to set in the Garden … For six baskets to set 'em in*, Whitley (DD/WBE/1/10). The instructions were occasionally detailed and explicit:

> 1564–5 *to grafte or have upon the grounds specified … in some convenyennt place within foure of the first yeares of the terme of the said lease six appletrees, two peare-trees, one wardentree, one quyncetree, one walenuttree, four cherytrees, a plumbtree; and in the hedge or other convenyentt place … to sett and plant vj yonge trees of the*

oke, ashe or elme, and preserve all the same trees during the said terme; and if any dye, to sett and preserve so many other of the like and same kynde in their roome, Hemsworth (YRS63/51)

See also spire (2), wilf.

set (2) To encourage or incite a dog to attack another animal or a person: 1616 *the spanyell … which he had taught to sett for her,* Brandsby (NYRO44/128); 1767 *The Reverend John Gray Curate of Swillington died suddenly … as he was setting Partridges with a Dog in … Black-well Close* (PR). See also setting-dog, sleat.

set (3) To accompany a departing guest on the first stage of their journey home: 1726 *John Holt said he would sett him part of the way,* Erringden (QS1/65/2); 1798 *I set them to the Brick pinfold,* Sessay (WM75). See also agateward.

set (4) Probably a shortened form of set work: 1601 *eight sett quishions,* Slaithwaite (IMF); 1622 *6 sett quishings,* Cottingley (LRS1/61); 1684 *2 set whishens,* Cartworth (G-A); 1699 *five seeld chears … ten set chears,* Meltham (G-A). See also set work.

set (5) To lay or set stones, in bridges, highways, walls, etc.: 1579 *able men … to help in the setting of the jewells, casements, springers,* Elland Bridge (BAS6/139); 1602 *to help the said Thomas Wallimsley to sett the ground worke,* Apperley Bridge (BAS6/142); 1665 *Wee present Thomas Hartley for settinge stones to stop the high street in Hallefax* (WCR5/184); 1719–20 *Cowcroft and his servant seting the edge of the Causway,* Brotherton (QS1/60/4); 1735 *ordered that the town streets of Rotherham be repaired, new set and paved with bolders and levelled* (QS10/17). We have some information about the equipment used: 1399 *stane hamers … magnæ [large] setting chisiles,* York (SS35/18); 1508 *approns and glovys for settyng to the masons,* York (SS35/94). The verb could also be used when single stones were being placed, as at intervals against the side walls of narrow bridges: 1697 *setting severall stones upon the said Bridge to keepe Waines and Cartes from Comeing to neare the Batlements,* Horbury (QS1). See also set stones, setter (1&2).

set ale A term found only in York, meaning old or stale ale: 1579 *doo sell within there howses a wyne quart of sett or stale ale for a penye* (YRS119/4); 1590 *that every tipler within the … cittye shall sell their aile being olde and sett aile for vjd the aile gallon aswell within their howses as without* (YRS138/120).

set forth To mark out a piece of land with boundaries: 1555 *the mydle parte … boundid and set furth betwix the other too partes,* Almondbury (G-A); 1575 *one other parcell of the same medowe as it is nowe devided, lymyted and sett furth by metes,* Thurstonland (G-A); 1590 *in sutche part of the said ground as ys nowe appointed lymyted and set fourthe bye us … with meares and bounders,* Shelf (HM/A/96); 1597 *lands lieing in their Townefields … as the same is now allotted mered and set forth,* Hepworth (FACcccxciii). Note: 1538 *landes shalbe devyded, marked and lymyted furth by indyffrent persons,* Barkisland (HM/B/10).

set on work To employ, give work to. This phrase was used in the earliest surviving Orders of the Hallamshire cutlers: 1590 *no person … shall … sett on worke in the said science or occupacon anye jurnyman … under the age of twentye yeres* (HCC3). It was part of the traditional language of the guilds, repeated at regular intervals: 1690 *No maker of knives, shears … or other cutlery wares … to employ or set on work any foreigner* (HCC11).

set out (1) As a verb 'to set' was used in a general sense when the location of a new pit had been decided on: 1704 *setting a Coale Mine a foot,* Farnley (MS11); 1718 *drinke at pitt setting,* Farnley (MS14); 1754 *setting the pitt 2s,* Beeston (WYL160/129/4). Once the exact site had been confirmed the pit was 'set out', which is likely to mean that stakes or other markers were placed in the ground where sinking was to take place. It was another occasion for colliers to receive free ale: 1713 *the setting out of the new pittstead*, Shibden (HAS30/142). See also set out (2).

set out (2) To mark trees in a way that made it clear to workmen which should be felled and which should be left standing: 1704 *as many straight poles fit for standing as will make the same Lordings and Blackbarks … to be chosen and set out by his servants*, Bradley (SpSt); 1719 *Timber Trees now Allready marked and sett out to be felled*, North Bierley (Tong/3/505); 1746–7 *Mr Goodall for Valueing and setting out Lepton Wood* (DD/WBE/1/20); 1766 *All such Trees & Polls as are set out to be felled in three Spring Woods in Quarmby* (DD/T/33/1). See also plantation.

set pot The OED has a reference dated 1839 which shows that the word 'set-pot' sometimes referred to a container used in the making of varnish or for heating items such as oil or size. It may have no direct connection with the word 'set-pot' as it used locally: Wright listed it in several counties in the north and north midlands (EDD), and in that region the set-pot was a fixture in the kitchen; a cauldron or boiler, usually made of iron or copper. It stood above a fire-grate and was used principally for the washing of clothes in boiling water.

It actually had a variety of functions: Easther noted that it was 'for brewing purposes' and in the *Leeds Mercury Supplement* of 1897 it was stated that it also had a culinary role, 'being found useful on occasions when an extra quantity of things' had to be cooked, 'on the occasions of tides, feasts and at Christmas time'. In 1976, Miss Annie Walker of Slaithwaite reminisced about the traditional rent dinners provided for tenants on the Dartmouth estate and spoke nostalgically of *mutton, tongues, beef, veal and bacon all cooked together in the set-pot … then plum pudding and rice pudding.* In November, *they had boiled turnips in a big set-pot.* The dinners were held in local public houses, and in the evening whatever was left over was put in the set-pot with dumplings and *the company* had it.

The word appears to have come into use quite late, for the earliest references I have found are in undated documents of the eighteenth century. In *c*.1740 a *set pot* was listed among numerous items at Green House in Austonley and an inventory for the same property in 1799 has *oven, great range and sett pot in House* (G-A). The term occurs regularly in that sort of context in the nineteenth century: in one Gomersal document of 1829 the fixtures included *ranges, ovens, set pots … sinks, cisterns* (MD292/75): similarly in Halifax in 1834 we find *ranges, ovens, set pots, bakestones* (YAS/DD118). It had probably been in popular use from the time when it became customary to 'set' the boiler or pot in a stone or brick surround, a practice implicit in the following reference: 1743 *1 Pott set and stone furniture*, East Marton (GRD).

There is evidence that similar utensils such as brewing leads, kettles and pans were 'set' or fixed from a much earlier date, e.g. 1481 'Also two brass pots, one standing in *le fournes*, the other *sine fournes*, Thornhill (Clay21); *c*.1537 *a grett pann sett in a fournes*, Halifax (YRS45/187); 1565 *a panne sett in a furnace xiijs iiijd*, Temple Newsam (YAJ25/98); 1596 *settinge of leades with stone or claye* Beverley (YRS84/71); 1699 *one keetell which is sett in a furness*, Brayton (YRS47/71). The setting of bakestones seems to be contemporary with that of set pots: 1734 *a sett baking stone*, Holmfirth (IH); 1785 *setting a Range, setting a Pan, setting a Bakeing Stone*, Ovenden (CA185).

Previously such implements were almost certainly moveable objects: 1485 *the grete brasse pot that stands in the fornese*, Ripon (SS64/277), but by Elizabeth's reign wooden frameworks probably provided the first 'settings'. The clue to that seems to be in the rare word 'crubb' an alternative form of 'curb': 1565 *1 brode pan and a crubbe to the same*, Knaresborough (SS26/178); 1636 *a great brewing copper … set in a wooden crubb*, Hull

(OED). In this sense the 'curb' may have been a ring of timber which held the pan securely in place, possibly a cylindrical construction. See also crubb.

set stones Shaped stones set in the ground as a type of paving, especially in a highway: 1580 *to the sett stones on the east*, Rastrick (HAS44); 1664 *Wee lay a paine … that the sett stones about the middingstead before his stable … be removed*, Halifax (WCR5/132). These were later called 'sets' or 'setts' and the word features regularly from the 1800s, as in the council minutes for Huddersfield in 1881: *that the whole granite setting be taken up … that the slippery blue sets be done away with altogether and that … gray granite sets only be used*. See also set (5), setter (1&2).

setter (1) A mason whose task it was to set or lay the shaped stones in a building or wall: 1401–3 *In remuneracione data cementariis vocatis setters ad parietes cum cirothecis [For pay together with gloves given the masons called setters on the walls]*, York (SS35/21); 1432 *In regardo facto Johanni Taillor et Johanni Bultflow cementariis vocatis settars, 26s 8d [For payment made to John Taillor and John Bultflow the masons called setters]*, York (SS35/50).

setter (2) A precisely cut stone: its meaning is best illustrated in the conditions that applied to the tenant who leased Wakefield bridge-house:

> 1683 *That he … after any Flood of Water do observe and take notice … when any of the Stones commonly called Setters within any of the frames or Jewells under the bridg, chance to shrinke or fall by reason of the Washing of the gravell from under them* (QS1).

In 1717, payment was made for *setters hewed at Fairburne* for Brotherton Causey (QS1/56/4).

setting-dog A dog taught to 'set' hunted birds or animals, used by huntsmen and poachers: 1551 *my setting spanyell doge with all netts and geyr pertenyng*, Morton on Swale (SS26/71); 1594 '*a setting spaniell* for the Earl', Batley (Sheard154); 1635 *to kill any more game … with setting dogges*, Meltham (G-A); 1671 *the constable … hath made search for gunns, bowes, greyhounds, setting doggs, haies, netts or other engins used for the destruction of game*, Skelbrooke (QS1/11). See also set (2).

setting stick Possibly an implement for setting plants although it has also been suggested that it was used when making the pleats or sets of ruffs (RMG): 1618 *a steele settingestick*, Brandsby (NYRO44/158); 1628 *one old settinge sticke*, Pudsey (LRS1/76).

set up This is a traditional part of the vocabulary of the medieval guilds. A man was entitled to set up in business only after completing his time as an apprentice and journeyman: in 1475 the brethren in York would not permit *any estraunge man to sett up as maister* unless it could be shown that he was *able and connyng* in the craft (SS186/182). In Sheffield, a pre-incorporation Ordinance of 1565 said that *no maner of person shall sett up the said occupacion … oneles he have beyne apprentice vij yeares* (HCC1). It gave rise to the noun 'upset': in Beverley in 1577 William Blenkarne, a coverlet weaver, paid 20d *for an upsett* (YRS84/13). See also upset.

set work A kind of embroidery, used especially for carpetwork, chairs and cushions: 1621 *Three cushions, two of needleworke, one set worke 3s*, Slaidburn (YRS63/47); 1675 *Three settwork Carpitts … One Duzon of settwork Chaires*, West Bretton (YRS134/148); 1695 *8 settworke chaires*, Selby (YRS47/45). See also set (4).

several Separate, it was used of land held by an individual, not in common ownership: 1491 *vij acres of land and medowe … lying severalle in iiij felds of Pudsey* (Th6/284);

1564 *Rawdenfild ... for this xxx or xl yeres continually haith bene and yet is a severall inclosid ground* (YRS114/105); 1566 *all those landes ... liyinge severally in the Townefeldes of Thurstonland* (G-A). It had legal implications, as in this use of the noun: 1535 *towchyng his title whereby he clamys to have severaltie in certeyn closys,* York (YRS106/170). Examples where the meaning is 'separate, distinct' illustrate how the modern usage developed: 1529 *the seruandes and tenantes of the seid Erle at twoo seuerall tymes toke certen wheate,* Scorborough (YRS45/137); 1622 'Robert Wrangham for breaking the pinfold 3 several times', Acomb (YRS131/136). It was responsible for minor place-names as open-field enclosure took place: 1558–9 *had the Agiestment of a Large parcel of Ground called the Severals which the Tennants ... fenced for him,* Hatfield (ERAS12/60); 1719 *Great Severals,* Beeston (WYL160/129/3). See also shelving.

severy A compartment of a vaulted roof or a section of scaffolding: 1399–1400 *j porcione meremii empta ... pro sewerwus pro præd. tenemento [1 piece of timber bought ... for the severy for the said tenement],* Ripon (SS81/131); 1422 *pro vj magnis saplyngs emptis pro scaffaldyng in le severy Archiepiscopi, 14s [for 6 large saplyngs bought for scaffolding in the Archbishop's severy, 14s],* York (SS35/47). Also used as a verb: 1530–1 *Item to iiij wrightes for on day severlyng the hye chawmer syde,* York (CCW141).

sewer An artificial water-course designed to carry water to a dam or drain marshy land of excess surface water, taking it off into a river or the sea: 1352 *Cum walliæ, fossata, gutteræ, seweræ, pontes, calceta et gurgites aquarum de Trent et Done [the walls, ditch, gutters, sewers, bridges, causeway and drains of the rivers Trent and Don],* Selby Abbey (YRS13/392); 1527 *als well the watter dame belonynge [sic] the milne as the watter sewer for the redy passaige of the watter to and frome the seid milne,* Bewerley (YRS140/212); 1540 *one close called the Vevers ... overflowed the moste parte all winter with water, charged with a sewer & lyenge in common pasture from Michalmas to Martynmas,* Selby Abbey (YRS13/349). As a channel for waste matter in a town it is on record from the mid-fifteenth century. See also salt-house.

seylyng See ceil.

shackle An iron ring or U-shaped piece of iron used as a coupling device: 1485 *ij shakels de ferro viijd [2 iron shackles 8d],* Ripon (SS64/373); 1548 *a wayne schakell and a bolt a plowe schakell and a bolt,* Todwick (YAJ36/439); 1628 *two teames, 3 tugwythies, 4 shackles, bolts,* Pudsey (LRS1/76). See also shackle bolt, striving irons.

shackle bolt The bolt which passes through the eyes of a shackle, with which it is often listed in inventories: 1530 *a wayne and yoke with bolte and shakyll,* Clint (SS104/26). It occurs less commonly as a compound term: 1549 *a yocke, a wane heade shakill bolte,* South Milford (Th19/221); 1581 *one coulter & a socke & one shackell boulte,* South Cave (Kaner116). See also shackle.

shackle net A regional word for a type of fishing net, compared with a flue or dragnet in glossaries. Examples generally are late and infrequent but it occurs quite regularly in the Pennines: 1624 *no man shall fishe neyther with rod nett nor sha[k]ell nett,* Golcar (DD/SR/1); 1705–8 *presented for fishing with a shakle net in the river of Swale* (YRS162/280); 1726 *there were other two persons with a shackle nett fishing in the river,* West Riding (QS1/65/5).

shade A former spelling of shed, a small building: 1763 *Richard Hopwood, ship carpenter, to have leave to erect a shade in Grovel for building boats,* Beverley (YRS122/43).

shaft Usually a vertical or near vertical excavation which gives men access to the minerals underground. The earliest OED examples noted are connected with mining, either in Durham (1434) or in Cornwall (1602). In Yorkshire the references are from the latter period: 1600 *libertie for digging and gettinge … and making waies and shafts*, Northowram (HAS30/132); 1668 *a shaft put downe cost £18*, Tan Hill (NYRO36/79). The meaning of this word may be self-evident but it is of interest because of the way it came to symbolise the ability of a lessee to gain access to the riches underground and the landowners' need to control that access. In 1739, for example, a lease to John Kaye of Lepton finished with the words *and shall not get Coals with above one shaft at a time* (DD/WBD/4/320). It was occasionally used of a horizontal gallery. See also thirl, vent.

shag A material having a velvet nap on one side, usually of worsted but sometimes of silk: 1607 *two blacke cloakes thone lind with velvet thother with shagge*, Whitley (DD/WBW/20); 1622 *one white shage boulster*, Cottingley (LRS1/61); 1693 *6yds shag £1 13s*, Selby (YRS47/22). The meaning had expanded by the eighteenth century: 1761 *long cut shagg made of goats hair or hair shagg made of mohair*, Wakefield (YRS155/18).

shake (1) The noun is used of a fissure or cleft in timber which developed during a tree's growth: 1686 *boards without either shake or sappe or any other thing which may be thought to be hurtfull*, Conistone (RW33). The condition is considered to be a defect and was so described by the Lepton horticulturist William Pontey in *The Forest Pruner* (1805). Under the heading *Shaken Timber (or what we call Wind Shakes)* he gave some credence to the view that such cracks might be wind damage but cautioned against thinking that might be the only cause. A North Riding document also gives it as a defect: *a.1660 many old doterelles … decayed and shaken trees*, Wheeldale (NRR1/81). It could also refer to the harm caused by coal-getting, both underground and on the surface: 1683 *the grounds are so shaken and spoyled by the undermining thereof and by the coal slack and rubbish that lye upon the same that little or no profit can ever be made*, Whitkirk (YAJ36/331). See also spoil.

shake (2) As a verb it could refer to the customary right of turning animals or poultry into the stubble after harvest (EDD): *c.1547 the inhabytantes of … Saxton … have usyd tyme owte of mynd yerely after harvest done to shake wyth theyre beastes and cattelles in the sayd too closes* (YRS51/123). Perhaps this was originally to feed on the shaken corn, the grain that had fallen to the ground: 1642 *Oates are a graine that may bee cutte greener then any other white corne … the hinder ende of them will shake afore yow can gette to mowe them*, Elmswell (DW52).

shakeragg In a case at the Quarter Sessions in December 1639 a Bramley yeoman was accused of addressing 'contemptuous words' to Henry Sikes of Hunslet, viz: *thou shakeragg blewe beard* (YRS54/173). According to Halliwell a shake-rag or shagrag was a mean, beggarly fellow, and the OED has both spellings from the sixteenth century.

shalloon A closely woven material, used particularly for linings and bed coverings: 1346 *Item in unam robam et unum chalonem et unum linthiamen [Item for a gown and a shalloon and a sheet]*, York (SS35/166); 1455 *2 duss' chalons … 32 pannis sine grano [2 dozen shalloons … 32 undyed cloths]*, Hull (YRS144/15). Clearly some were being imported but more than a dozen examples of the occupation of chaloner were recorded in the West Riding poll tax, where it occurred also as a by-name: 1379 *Willelmus Shalunhare*, Elland (PTWR). The subsequent lack of evidence may point to a decline in its production and popularity but references are again numerous from the eighteenth century: 1739 *John Windle … one afternoon at Keighley took five shalloons of the tenters* (QS1/78/4); 1751 *a coat lining of shalloon*, Pontefract (QS1/90/4); 1762 *orders for 15 or 16 hundred shalloons wich are low prised ones*, Wakefield (YRS155/131).

shamble A table, counter or stall where goods for sale could be displayed, recorded as *shamells* in 1357 in Bradford (CR). More particularly it was used of stalls where meat and fish were sold: 1429–30 'William *de Hotone … fissher … a parcel of waste …* in a corner by *Fisschamyll*', Richmond (YRS39/142); 1517 *declared by my lorde Maire that where he went to se the Flesshe Shamells … Richard Coke sold unholsom flesshe*, York (YRS106/63); 1556 *a payne is sett that the baylye do see the fyshe shamells furneshed with fyshe*, Wakefield (YRS74/22). The street in York now called the Shambles is recorded as *Marketskire alias Flesshamelles* in 1316 (PNER297). See also swale.

shammy A spelling of chamois, the antelope which inhabits certain mountain ranges in Asia and Europe. From the skin was prepared a soft pliable leather: 1720 *a doe skinn, two shamey skins, one shamey leather skinn*, West Riding (QS1/59/2).

shank(s) The lower leg, but in the plural it was used for fur taken from the legs of animals, especially black lambs, used for trimming outer garments: 1463 *j togam pennulatam cum buggishanks [1 robe lined with budge shanks]*, Leeds (SS30/260); 1497 *my cremesyn gowne furred with blake shankes*, York (SS53/121); 1531 *for iij blak-lamskynnes viijd, and for a pursell of shankes & v caulinge of shankes ijs vjd*, York (SS79/324); 1544 *one gowne purled with shankes*, Pontefract (Th19/106). See also budge, musterdevillers.

shapen, shaping Used of clothes, shaped, fashioned or tailored: 1434 *Lego Johanni Webster … vestes meas usui meo aptatas Anglice shaping apparel [I bequeath to John Webster … my apparel fashioned for my use in English shaping apparel]*, York (SS30/25); 1444 *to my doghter Elizabeth … xxx yerdds of lyn cloth shappyn in shetes*, Mitton (SS30/106); 1506 *to Thomas and Nicholas Tempest all my shaping close* [clothes] *at Bealrapar*, Bracewell (SS53/251); 1533 *all my shappyn clothes*, Marske (YRS152/130); 1576 *all my shappen clothes*, Slaidburn (CS1/20); 1618 *shapen clothes 20s*, Abbotside (YRS130/41). See also buskin.

shape to To act in such a way as to achieve an intention: 1738 *he flung stones at [the greyhound] and shaped to send him home*, Pannal (QS1/78/1).

shaping board Noted in a tailor's workplace, probably a board or table on which garments were cut out: 1485 *in the schoppe j schapyng borde with ij schelfys viijd. Item j nodyr schapyng borde with the trystylls xvjd*, York (SS45/302). See also shapen.

shard See tile house.

share The past tense of the verb to shear: 1648 *This morne came shearers and share the Coytfeild head*, Thurlstone (SS65/110).

sharking The several meanings are all pejorative, that is cheating, swindling, sponging and the like: 1668 *Mr Savil of Marley having sold his land and living a sharking wandering life*, Northowram (OH3/100).

sharp (1) To sharpen: 1424–5 *Item Thomæ Qwernside pro scharpyng et wellyng of wegges de ferro*, Ripon (SS81/152); c.1540 *for shoyng oxen and sharpinge the mylne pikks 20d*, Esholt (YRS80/84); 1642 *Clippers bringe … 2 paire of sheares and one or other of them … a whetstone to sharpe them withall*, Elmswell (DW23); 1708 *for sharping masons tooles*, Wetherby (QS1/47/9). In collieries, a blacksmith had to be 'at Hand' to sharpen the colliers' tools, especially their picks and wedges (CC12): 1616 *picks sharpin 4d*, Brandsby (NYRO44/119); 1717 *Sam. Bywater for worke sharping 1s 6d*, Farnley (MS11).

sharp (2) The common admonition 'look sharp' requires immediate action from the listener, with no delay allowed: 1785 *if you do not look sharp about it ... everything will be void*, Meltham (G-A).

sharpling A type of nail, although the exact meaning is uncertain. It was probably a regional term since the few references recorded were mostly in the north (SZ1/316): 1415 *In cc sharpelynges emptis, prec. 16d*, York (SS35/35); 1475 *Et pro sharplynges, xjd*, York (SS129/74); 1548 *ij.c sharplynges, 18d*, York (SS35/112); 1577 *For sharplinges for naylinge the clowtes on the table feete in the chapter house, 3d*, York (SS35/116).

shaving, shaving knife The craftsmen who worked leather used knives when they removed flesh and hair from a hide: *c.*1425 *what man as wyrkys a dakyr of backes, for the fyrst drissyng, colouring and shafyng ... he shall hafe iijd*, York (SS120/65). Robert Gale, a Methley tanner, made his will in 1570, and this word features in an interesting bequest to his brother in law – in his words: *to Arthur Peise ... after my wyf gevithe up my occupacion of Tannynge, my barke and tubbes with my shaving knyfes* (Th35/102). It occurred also in the leather Act of 1662: *divers tanners do shave, cut and rake their upper-leather hides all over, and the necks of their backs and butts to the great impairing thereof* (SAL8/69). At the West Riding Quarter Sessions in 1713 reference was made to tanners *dressing and setting out their bends for sale ... which the officers call shaving* (QS10/13/30). See also thixel.

shaw A word used from the Old English period, usually said to mean a thicket or copse. However, it is actually more complicated than that, and the places so named should always be interpreted in their local context. It probably remained in occasional use as part of the regional vocabulary during earlier centuries, e.g. 1329 'land ... above *le Schaghe* near the dike', Hemsworth (YRS120/99). In Tong, it became the name of an early settlement and *c.*1323 Margery *del Schagh* was in possession of a house and 'land in *le Schagh* in the vill of Tong': in a deed of the same period it was called *le Schaye*, an example of a common alternative spelling (YRS69/172).

sheaf Familiar still as a word for a bundle of corn but formerly a more general measure, used for a variety of commodities: 1453 *24 shife tasilles [teazles]*, Hull (YRS144/3); 1503 *ij sheff of blew glasse, one sheff of red*, York (SS53/217); 1508 *x shaffe Renysh glase*, York (SS35/3); 1515–16 *Pro j c ferri, iiij sheiffes de calabe [For 100 pieces of iron, 3 sheaves of steel]*, York (SS35/96).

shear When applied to sheep this was an indication that an animal was past its first shearing: 1549 *Item in shere shepe, wedders and yowes*, Westerdale (YRS74/49); 1554 *20 shere wedders 33s 4d*, Aysgarth (YRS130/4); 1588 *viij wedders and ten sheare sheepe*, Westerdale (YAJ36/436). See also shearing, shearling.

shearboard The board on which the cropping or finishing of cloth was done: 1535 *to William my sone my greatest arke, his own paire of sheites and shereborde*, Halifax (Clay101); 1599 *one shearboarde, one prasse, lowmes & all other thinges ... to clothinge apperteyninge*, Cottingley (LRS1/2). See also handles.

sheargrinder The earliest sheargrinders of whom we have any record worked in towns, and they were probably providing shears for the finishing process in cloth-making: 1345 *Will. de Lincoln, cheregrinder* [sic], York; 1440 *Thomas Elez, York, sheregrynder* (SS96/39,159); 1598 *Hugh Fayrbancke ... sheareginder*, Halifax (YRS24/37); 1598 *Lancelotus Norden de Wakefeild sheregrynder* (YRS3/62). The occupation was established in the textile area: 1664 *Thomas Fairbanke lately of Warley, shear grinder, deceased* (WCR5/124); 1674–5 *Joseph Turner of Leedes, sheere grinder* (SS40/214).

shearing A regional equivalent of shearling, that is a sheep that has been once shorn: 1545 *x yowes and sherynges*, Westerdale (YRS74/55); 1570 *sex score wethers … lxxvj sheringes*, South Cave (Kaner69); 1582 *lxxx wedders and wedder shearinges*, South Cave (Kaner118); 1617 *two sheering shepe viz one gimber and one tuppehogge*, Aughton (YRS55/228–9); 1642 *Ewes are such as have beene twice shorne … after that they are once shorne they are called gimmer shearings … yett is it a custome with many … sheep-men to clowte their shearings to hinder them from tuppinge*, Elmswell (DW4); 1686 *24 shearings bought of R^{ic} Wharton 7^s 6^d apiece*, Conistone (RW19). See also clout, shear.

shearling A yearling sheep, once shorn. The spelling is first noted in the ordinances of the skinners which are undated but probably of the fifteenth century: *si ascun homme vende … sherlynges en fururs dagneaux … qil paie di. marc [if any man sell shearlings … in lambskins he pays half a mark]*, York (SS120/60); 1500 *furrs of boge or scherlyngs*, York (SS186/219); 1515 *v yowes and shirlings*, South Ottrington (YAJ36/438); 1582 *fell or furre of broge or sherlings lambe furre*, York (YRS119/61). See also shear, shearing.

shearmaker A maker of shears for the cloth trade: 1665 *Mark Fawbert of Wakefeld shearemaker* (WCR5/72).

shearman A cloth-finisher: 1400 *Thomas de Thorneton de Ebor. scherman … duo par forpicarum & duas mensas pro cessura' panni & unum platyngborde [Thomas de Thorneton of York shearman … two pairs of shears & two tables for cutting cloth & a plating-board]*, York (SS4/260); 1534 *Richard Grenwod of the towneshype of Northowrome in the parishing of Halyfax, shereman* (Clay107).

shearsmith 'Shears' are tools which operate by the simultaneous cutting action of two blades, larger than scissors but sharing many of the same characteristics. They were used particularly by shearmen in the final processes of cloth-making and for sheep shearing, and examples of the word are on record in the Old English period. These shears would have been made by smiths and yet the earliest example of 'shearsmith' in the OED as an occupational term is in the Act for Hallamshire in 1623–4. That takes no account of early surnames though, and Reaney has an example in 1325.

In Yorkshire, the first evidence dates from later that century: 1391 *Galf. [Geoffrey] Sheresmyth*, York (SS96/91); 1481 *John Childe, York, sheresmyth* (YRS6/37). The making of shears must have become a more specialised occupation in the Sheffield region by the sixteenth century: 1552 *John Staynfurthe, sheresmythe*, Tinsley, Rotherham (YRS11/167); 1592 *Arthur Byrley, Sheaffeild, shearsmyth* (YRS22/22); 1620 *Nicholas Staniforth, shersmith*, Sheffield (TWH16/179); 1655 *W'm Bamforth of Darnoll in the p'ish of Sheffeld shersmith* (PR3/194). The status of these workers is emphasised by their position alongside the cutlers and scissorsmiths when the Cutlers' Company was founded in 1624, but they were a comparatively small and localised brotherhood, confined mostly to urban centres. The Sheffield marriage register of 1653–60 recorded four shearsmiths in Sheffield town and three in Attercliffe-cum-Darnall township, but numbers remained small. The tools listed in the inventories of Hallamshire shearsmiths were similar to those found in the smithies of other local craftsmen (FBH117–18). However, the occupation was not confined to York and Sheffield: 1571 *William Awemunde, shiersmythe*, North Cave (YRS19/6).

sheather, sheathmaker A maker of sheaths for knives, usually of leather. In York the sheathers had traditional links with the cutlers: in 1445, for example, *the cutlers, bladsmythes et shethers* supported the Pageant of Corpus Christi (SS120/136). The term has been noted there from the early fourteenth century: 1302 *Henricus le Schether*, York (SS96/9), and sheathmaker occurs as an occasional alternative: 1523 *Christopher*

Beilby, shethmaker, York (YRS11/15). The occupation is on record in Sheffield from the mid-sixteenth century: 1554 *William Spownare, sheather and yeoman,* Sheffield (TWH16/89); 1591 *Robert Hill, Sheffeild, sheather* (YRS22/61); 1610 *Godfrey Harwood of Sheffeld, sheather* (TWH20/132); 1654 *Joshua White of Sheffeld sheather* (PR3/190). Like the cutlers in York they were subject to the rules of the Company: 1693 *Charges expended att severall meetings this year about deceiptfull Sheathes* (HCC22). There was less demand for sheaths once forks began to be used along with knives as household items, so the workers had to find different outlets for their skills.

sheath knife A sharp, dagger-like knife kept in a sheath. The sheather had an important role in the cutlery trade, and sheath knives would have been a common sight in the centuries before knives were linked with forks as tableware. It is surprising therefore that the term has not been noted in the OED earlier than 1837. In Sheffield *sheath knives* were listed in Thomas Scargell's inventory in 1714 (IH).

sheathmaker See sheather.

sheath mould The *sheath molds* recorded in the inventory of Anthony Hall of Sheffield (1698) and the *sheath moulds* of Robert Couldwell of Attercliffe (1736) were possibly pieces of leather cut out for stitching or gluing. The inventory of Joshua White of Sheffield (1694) included *Glew Stuff, £1* (IH).

sheep brand An iron for burning or branding sheep: 1581 *1 shepbrand,* North Anston (G-A).

sheep coloured Used of fleece-coloured clothing: 1558 *I bequeath to Henry Hillam a cote of shepe colour,* Whitkirk (Th27/195); 1573 *two jackets, one of shepe colour the other of blacke,* Timble (SS104/113); 1578 *a shepe culered gown xxxs,* Kendal (SS26/281).

sheep gate A grazing right for a sheep in a stinted pasture. See also gate (2).

Sheer Thursday The Thursday before Easter: 1505 *William Wrangwysche, contrary to the act maid the xvj day of Marche, on shyre thuresday, went into the common crane and wold have occupied,* York (YRS106/14); 1520 *no man … shall suffer ther children to go with clapers upon Shere Thursday and Good Friday,* York (YRS106/70); 1550 *For breade spente at the maundye upon sherethursdaie 2s,* York (SS35/136). An editorial footnote to the 1520 reference says that 'clappers' were rattles, used to summon people to church on the last three days in Holy Week.

shelf A horizontal piece of wood, or other material, attached to a wall or set in a frame, designed to hold books, crockery, food, etc., a cupboard or cabinet: 1594 *two partes of my goodes, the shelfe with all things thereupon which I reserve to my selfe,* Lingards (IMF); 1621 *One chest, frames and shelues in the larderhouse 10s,* Slaidburn (YRS63/48); 1638 *my part of the shelfe in William Sonniare house,* Slaithwaite (IMF).

shelling See shilling.

shelved wain A wain with side shelving attached: 1648 *two shilved wanes & 2 Coopwanes,* Sharlston (YRS134/99); 1655 *2 shilved waynes,* Whitley (DD/WBM/69). See also shelving.

shelving, shilving A board attached to a cart or wain so as to increase its load capacity, usually in the plural: 1642 *lay them in 4 severall rowes crosse over the shelvings of the waine and none in the body,* Elmswell (DW18); 1642 *for stealing two shillvins 2d,* Great Ayton (NRQS4/224); 1686 *shilving for 2 cartes,* Kettlewell (GRYD159). See also rathe, shelved wain.

shide A piece of wood split off from timber: 1469–70 'For wood *shydes* had for the *shoring*', Hull (YAJ62/166); 1519 *paid for iij shydys, iiijd*, York (CCW75); 1551 *To my brother … my shidewode*, Great Ouseburn (YAJ14/418); 1638 *certain shyees* [sic] *of wood*, Barley (YRS47/72).

shift A body garment of linen, cotton or the like, worn by men, women or children. The word came into regular use in the seventeenth century, replacing smock: 1692 *had taken or stollen out of his laith … a pair of breeches, two pair of mens stockings and two little shiftes*, Hellifield (QS1/30/1); 1710 *a shifte or smock*, Tong (QS1/49/4).

shill An alternative spelling of 'shell', that is to remove the husks from grain, usually with reference to oats: 1631 *buying of oates in the Kinges markett to shill and convert in oatmeal*, Ayton (NRQS3/310); 1754 *three pair of stones for grinding and shelling of corn and grain*, Beeston (WYL160/129/9).

shiller Occupational, a short form of 'oat shiller' and dealt with under that heading.

shilling This was the usual word in many parts of Yorkshire for oats from which the husks had been removed, ready for grinding, often at the local mill: 1685 *she did entice Joseph Cliff to goe into Kings Mill and take some shillinge out of a Chist which was unlocked*, Huddersfield (QS1). The shilling had to be ground to produce oatmeal: 1760 *the* [they] *grind shilling for to make oat meal*, Wakefield (YRS155/11). In the earlier references noted, 'shelling' was an alternative spelling: 1510 'John Ley my tenant *oon quarter sheling*', Copley (Clay38); 1783 *9 strikes of shelling*, Ovenden (CA112). The word was in frequent use: 1545 *to … my sone xijs and a bushell of shilling*, Otley (Th19/121); 1647 *3 loods of shilling*, Thurlstone (SS65/22). See also oatmeal maker.

shilved wain, shilving See shelved wain, shelving.

shingle (1) Light boards used for roofing houses: 1376 *Pro iiij centenis de chyngyl, 9s 4d* [For 4 hundredweight of shingles, 9s 4d], Weston (SS35/128); 1379 *Pro tectura chori de Brodsworth cum chyngyll, 3s 8d* [For roofing the choir at Brodsworth with shingle, 3s 8d] (SS35/128–31). Attached by shingle nails: 1541–2 *pro clavis sindul*, Ripon (SS81/195).

ship carpenter A carpenter employed in the construction or fitting out of ships, an occupational term first noted in an Act of 1495 (OED). It was well established later in Hull, and a dozen examples have been noted there in the second half of the sixteenth century: 1570 *Thomas Adamson, shipcarpenter*, Hull (YRS19/1); 1601 *Henry Browne, shipcarpenter*, Hull (YRS24/16). See also shipwright.

shipful As much as a ship will hold: 1403 *caryyng unius shipfull petrarum per aquam* [carrying one shipful of stones by water], Tadcaster (SS4/327).

shipman A sailor, although most of the evidence relates to men who operated boats on the Ouse, the Trent and their tributaries. Several villages and towns in that region were ports: 1379 *William de Seyton, schypmane*, Rawcliffe (PTWR); 1398 *William Bird, schipman*, Beverley (SS4/240); 1421 *In cariagio xlvj tuntight lapidum a Cawod usque Ebor. per aquam in valde magna siccitate per botes, per iiij vices per Johannem Blacburn, 27s 2d* [For transport of 15 tuntights of stone from Cawood to York by water in very great dryness by boats, 4 times by John Blacburn, 27s 2d] (SS35/43). By-names provide many early references: c.1280 *Benedictus le Scipman*, York (YAJ50/85); 1301 *De Roberto Schipman, Catton juxta Swale* (YRS21/82); 1320 *Adam Schipman*, Hambleton (YRS94/64); 1379 *Robertus Shypman*, Rawcliffe (PTWR). See also shipwright.

shippen, shippon A cattle shed or cow house, a word of Old English origin. It gave rise to the place-name Shippen House in Barwick in Elmet, recorded as *Scipene* in Domesday Book, but is a rare vocabulary item in Yorkshire until the early eighteenth century: 1705 *loose wood in the turf house, shippen and baulkes in the barn*, Slaidburn (CS1/76) 1707 *the Milneholme, one house, a shippon therein*, Horton in Ribblesdale (YAS/DD117); 1717 *into the shippen where the cows lye*, Bracewell (QS1/56/8). See also mistall.

shipping timber Probably timber that was suitable for building ships. George Bushell of Whitby was a merchant and shipowner, and in his will he made the following bequests: 1541 *my wif to haue … ij partes of all my shipes and taykell, and the said Robert the thirde parte with all my tymbre called shipping tymbre*, Whitby (YRS51/199).

shippon See shippen.

shipwright A carpenter with the special skills required for building ships. It is found initially as a by-name: c.1280 *Willelmus Skipwryth*, York (YAJ50/89); 1308 *Johannes le schipwrith*, York (SS96/121); 1377 *Johannes Schipwryght*, Hull (PTER189); 1379 *Henricus Schypwryght*, Rawcliffe (PTWR). Not surprisingly, many examples of the occupation are found in coastal towns and the Humber estuary: 1446 *Gilbert Kyllyngholme, shipwright*, Hull (YRS6/99); 1527 *William Watson, shipwright*, Scarborough (YRS11/191); 1539 *John Person, burgess and shipwright*, Scarborough (YRS11/135). However, the Ouse and its feeders were navigable and there were several inland ports where shipbuilding flourished: 1379 *Johannes Botteler, shippewryght*, Doncaster (PTWR); 1417 *William Bouwer, schippewrighte*, Snaith (YRS120/156); 1586 *Robert Jenkinson, shipwrighte*, Beverley (YRS22/71). Other centres were Selby and York, so the craft was established on the Ouse, Aire, Don, Wharfe and Beverley Beck. An item in the Records of the Admiralty Court of York contains a fascinating deposition made on behalf of a shipwright called William Peirson. He had entered into an agreement with Robert Pallister for the building of a ship but the vessel had been *built beyond and above the Covenants* and William Peirson was accused also of not using the materials stipulated. In his defence the following statement was made:

> … *the deck by the original Covenants was to have beene made of Oake, but is made of Firr wood, which is more used and by experience found to be better for that purpose then Oake, for that Oake splitts with the heate of the Sun, and warps up at the edges, and wears slape* [slippery], *whereas Firr keeps thighter and streighter and is better for walking on* (SAH22/17).

shive A slice: c.1690 *take A shife of wheate bread & Toaste it well*, Conistone (RW7). An undated recipe, probably from the early eighteenth century, gave the following advice: *Take two young rabbets … boil them in milk … until tender … pull the meat in shives* (GWK39). It could be used of detached pieces of wood or metal: 1669 *received two shillings for the said iron … bid this informant … throw the greater peeces into a shive tubbe that stoode by*, Rotherham (QS1/9/2).

shiver Slaty debris, shale or flakes. Shivers of hard stone had a market value: 1432 *De 2s de Thoma Mix pro quadam porcione de shyvers*, York (SS35/49). In coal-mining contexts the word is referred to in 1708, in *The Compleat Collier* (CC14), and also in a letter written to Thomas Metcalfe: 1746 *whether it is all clean coal or mixed with shiver as the outbreak was I cannot tell*, Askrigg (NYRO62/41).

shoat A young, weaned pig: 1563 *40 swine and 6 shotts £10 0 0*, Elmswell (DW231); 1566 *ij sowes v shottes & iij peiges*, South Cave (Kaner65); 1585 *two hoggs, a brawne and two litle shotes*, Knaresborough (SS104/151); 1618 *unto my sonne Thomas a shoat in the garth over and besyd the shoat that is marked for him*, South Cave (Kaner269). See also pig-iron, skote, sow (2).

shod Probably for 'iron-shod', used of a wooden implement furnished with a shoe or sheath of iron: 1485 *j shod shole* [shovel] *ijd ob*, Ripon (SS64/373); 1576 *two shodd forkes, two Iron forkes*, Leeds (Th4/163); 1632 *one Iron forke one shodd Shovell and one shodd spaid 2s 0d*, Scriven (YRS134/79). A shod cart or wain was one with iron-bound wheels: 1515 *unum le shodd wayne, ij oxen*, North Frodingham (YAJ36/436); 1557 *ij unshod cowpes*, Thornton Bridge (SS26/101); 1577 *for shodcartts ... 33s 6d*, Beverley (YRS84/14). See also iron-bound wain.

shoe The wooden piles used in dams, river defences and bridge foundations were often provided with an iron shoe at the pointed end: 1675 *shoeing the Piles with Iron*, Ilkley Bridge (QS1); 1682 *three Smithes for hoopes and shoos for piles*, Bolton Bridge (QS1). The practice had a much longer history: 1322 *Et in iiij peciis ferri pro pilis inde ferrandis [And for 4 pieces of iron for piles shoed therefrom]*, Leeds (Th45/88). See also hoop (1), pile (2).

shoe-broad A common field-name, said by John Field to be 'found all over England' (EFN132). In south Yorkshire and neighbouring counties it is on record from the twelfth century at least, and examples were noted by Smith (PNWR7/282). There has been some speculation about the precise meaning but it is considered to derive from 'shovel broad' and to have referred originally to a narrow strip of land. Among early references are: *c.*1312 *et una particata jacet super Schouelbrode [and 1 perch situated above Schouelbrodes]*; 1346 *una perticata jacet in le Shovelbrodes*, Pudsey (Th6/80,163). An undated thirteenth-century document has: *Scouelbrayd ... Schouelbrad*, Spofforth (YRS76/139). It is included here partly because the development of the spelling shovel-board for the game of shove-board has been described as 'an unexplained alteration' (OED).

shoemaker board Presumably a shoemaker's working bench. These were imported into Hull from the Baltic: 1483 *1 duss' shomakere bordes*; 1490 *60 shomakar burdes*, Hull (YRS144/191,207).

sholve See shovel.

shoon The old plural of 'shoe', still used by dialect speakers, with 'shooin' as the form in much of the West Riding: 1460 *1 C horsshone*, Hull (YRS144/19); 1509 *to lytyll Byly Malson a cote & a peire of showne*, York (SS79/7); 1519 *that the shounemaker sewe well thayre shown*, Selby (SS85/32); 1543 *Item l horsse showne iijs iiijd ... Item, oxe shone with nalls xijd*, Ripley (SS26/44); 1570 *to Hewgh Howden my best shone*, South Cave (Kaner74).

shooting glove A glove worn to protect the hand when drawing a bow: 1525 *Item a shotynge glove ivd*, Skipton (Whit2/258); 1537 *Item for a harrow cayse and a shottyng glove viij^d*, York (CCW181); 1542 *A pair of perfumed gloves and a shoting glove*, West Bretton (YRS134/2); 1558 *to my brother ... my bow, my quyver, my shaftes, my braser and shoting glove*, York (YAJ15/196).

shop A building where goods were made and prepared for sale, also used frequently of work-places: 1374 *non omnia instrumenta ejusdem schopæ [not all the equipment of that shop]*, York (SS4/92); 1399 *quatuor shoppys sicut jacent in Ripon in le Kyrkgate [four shops* *are thus situated in Ripon in le Kyrkgate]* (SS74/147). In 1584, a Scriven blacksmith wrote: *I give to Edward my sonne two stiddes in my shopp att Knaresburghe* (SS104/145): in 1619–21 a Pickering survey listed *fowre shopps nere the Churche yarde ... wherof one is a smythes forge* (NRR1/19). It was used particularly of cutlers' workplaces and in Harrison's *Survey of Sheffield* featured repeatedly in lists of tenants and their holdings although sometimes a distinction was drawn between a shop and a smithy: 1637 *William Skargill for a Shop; Robert Clerke for a Smithy and 2 gardens* (HSMS18). In 1730, Thomas Taylor was 'a small employer with three smithies and a cutting-shop', Sheffield (FBH122). The Ordinances in York prohibited the 'hawking' of goods and obliged each cutler *to sell all such stuff within his shop* (SS120/135). See also ware (1).

shore (1) A regional spelling of 'sewer': 1664 *A man about Ealand went to the Colepit on Monday last, fel to drinking and as he came home ... fel down a shore and brake his neck* (OH3/89); 1766 *There hath been and still is a common Shore in the Township of Wakefield called Skiterick, in the King's Common Highway ... leading from Sandal to Stanley* (QS4/35/118).

shore (2) Land by a river (OED), or a precipitous slope (PNWR7/242). Research by David Shore suggests that it was more accurately 'an arc of rising land above a river or stream'. In several cases a highway passed down the 'shore' to a river crossing, as at Shore in Huddersfield (HPN125). It occurs several times as an element in minor place-names, and occasionally as a vocabulary item: 1456 *quandam parcel terr. juxta ripam aque prope Thwongesbrigg sub le shore [a parcel of arable land next to the river bank close to Thwongesbrigg beneath the shore]*, Netherthong (G-A).

shored In this isolated example the meaning is obscure. It may have meant 'shared', or possibly 'brought ashore': 1797 *John Pallister and I went to Helperby in the afternoon to look at some lime which Mr Roulstone had shored us. I have got 17 dozen and John Pallister 16. The keel containing 33 dozen*, Sessay (WM49).

short end Of uncertain meaning, but evidently a short section of a felled tree. An Almondbury rental of 1629 records the expense of cutting and felling *x skore weavers at 3d a peece ... ix skore shorte endes at 2d a peece* and *7 loades of bindinge*. An additional sum was paid *for bearing all out of the wodde* (DD/RA/f/4b).

shot (1) The reckoning or bill, especially one in an ale-house, an obligation discharged: 1640 *who having drunck ther wyne and paid ther shott were coming forth*, York (SS40/3); 1647 *I sent to Jo. Wordsworth for my shott to an ale hee had me to for Christopher Batty 1s 6d*, Thurlstone (SS65/42); 1676 *did tender a pewter shilling to Susan Ogden for his shott*, Oxenhope (QS1); 1736 *James paid the shott*, Meltham (G-A). See also ale.

shot (2) Thrust out or projecting: 1501 *his said tenement ther ... which is shot & hyngeth over the ground of the same Ric' [Thornton] ther by viijth ynchez*, York (SS85/22). See also outshot.

shot (3) Of uncertain meaning but descriptive of a process in tanning: 1660 *18 hors skinnes shott in the bark*, Selby (YRS47/170); 1720 *bought six shott calve skins ... intending to dress the same*, Knaresborough (QS1/59/1). See also ooze.

shote, shott See shoat.

shotten herring A reference to fish that have spawned. The term occurs in a list of items on which duty had to be paid in York: in 1510 one halfpenny was received for *ylke barrell of shoton heringe* (YRS106/33). In Hull soon afterwards 'shotten herring' are contrasted with full herring; that is fish charged with roe: 1517 *vj last full heryng and iij last shotyn heryng* (YRS45/40).

shoul, shoule These are the usual dialect forms of 'shovel': 1395 *j spad yryn et schole yryn*, Whitby (SS72/606); 1557 *an olde fyere showle*, Thornton Bridge (SS26/99); 1655 *Paid for 2 new shoole Irons 2s 2d*, Elland (PR2/259); 1704 *a new shoule*; 1707 *for a shoule shaft 10d*, Farnley (MS11). The verb had the same spelling: 1789 *Leting water of in Street and shouling Roade and breaking stones*, Tong (Tong/12f/1). See also bank shovel, bottom pick, shod, shovel.

shout A flat-bottomed boat. The word has a Low Countries' origin: 1457 *Lego Thomae Dauson apprenticio meo j naviculam vocatam le Showte [I bequeath to my apprentice Thomas Dauson 1 little boat called the Showte]*, York (SS30/209).

shove–board An alternative of shovel-board: 1648 *shall not permit any playing at tables, dyce, cards, shove-board, bowles, nor any other unlawful game*, West Riding (QS10/2). See also shove-groat.

shove–groat An alternative of shove- or shovel-board: 1594 *suffred dyvers persons to play at unlawfull games in his house in service time, viz at showgrote or sloppthriste* [sic for slip-thrift?], Marston (YAJ15/233).

shovel Many shovels were wooden implements, 'shod' with iron: 1616 *2 shovel irons xvjd*, Brandsby (NYRO44/119). The shovel, like the pick, could also stand for the person who would employ it: 1666 *promise ... to keepe in worke eighte pickes ... two shoufles*, South Crosland (DD/WBD/2/81). Note: c.1570 *Both forke and spade must use his trade To Shulve from Oxe and kowe*, Woodsome (KayeCP); 1614 *j pare of tongs j fyre sholve*, Stockeld (YAJ34/172). See also iron.

shovel–board A game in which a coin is driven by a blow with the palm of the hand along a board marked with transverse lines: 1607 *unlawfull games viz Shovell a board*, Middleham (NRQS1/90); 1619 *Paid to his lo[rdship] losses at shovelboard xs*, Skipton (Whit2/321). It had numerous alternative forms and spellings: 1575 *plaienge at Showlay bourde ... in service tyme*, Thirsk (PTD77); 1608 *playing ... at shoule-bord in the Evening prayer-time*, Bagby (NRQS1/100). See also board-end, shoe-broad, shoul, shove-board, shove-groat.

showing For shoeing, as when shoeing animals: 1543 *iiij showyng hamers iiijd*, Ripley (SS26/43–4), or when working on bridge foundations: 1675 *Layinge the foundation of one Piller and Landstall and showing the piles with iron*, Ilkley Bridge (QS1). See also pile (2).

shred See stove, stoving.

shrogg A regional word for scrubby woodland, first recorded in the Towneley Mysteries: c.1460 *I haue soght with my dogys All horbery shrogys* (OED). In 1697–8, James Jackson of Nether Shitlington was ambushed by two thieves on *the common high roade* near Brighouse and he told the magistrates that afterwards *other two men came out of a little shroge or wood* and joined his attackers (QS1/37/1). Easther thought that it might usually have referred to woodland 'on a bank side' and certainly in the Huddersfield area that fits well with the place-name. A particularly good example is *Dogkennel Shrogg* recorded in 1871 (DD/WBD/3/264). The wood in this case is very narrow but it covers the slopes on either side of a beck which divides Kirkheaton and Whitley. The same meaning may be implicit in 1763 in *the Brow or Shrogg Close* in Esholt (MD93/19).

It was actually a common element, but found only in minor place-names, so it has received little attention. Smith listed more than a dozen examples in the West Riding and although much of the evidence was late several names are on record from the seventeenth century, e.g. *Shroggywood* (1662) in Hoyland Swaine and *Shrog* (1688) in Thornhill (PNWR7). Most of the names noted are in the southern half of the West Riding and the adjoining counties of Lancashire and Nottinghamshire, which may mean that it was simply a regional variant of 'scrog'. This has a longer history and it is found over a wider area, including Cumberland, north Yorkshire and Scotland: Catterlen Wood in Cumberland was *boscus de Caterlenscrok* in 1292 (PNCu490) and *scrogscugh* was a Sedbergh name in 1479 (PNWR7/242).

In view of that it is curious to find that Long Tongue Scrog Lane in Kirkheaton is only a few hundred yards from Dogkennel Shrog. Since no early references to this name have been found it is possible that clerks or map-makers will have been responsible for the 'educated' spelling. This particular 'shrog' is again on a bank side, named after the adjoining field 'Long Tongue' (KHPN38).

shrub oak An alternative form of scrub oak: 1543–4 *ther be growing in the seyd copp' woodes lx short shrubbyd and polling okes of xl and lx yeres growth valuid at iiijd the tree*, Kexbrough (YAJ16/347); 1574 *ij shrubed ashes, at xviijd a pice; in the close called Woodd close, ij shurbd okes* [sic] *at ijs a pice*, Aldborough (SS42/413,416). See also scrub oak.

shruff brass A term first recorded in an Act passed in 1541–2 which prohibited the export of *Shroffe Metal into any parte … beyond the Sea*, that is old or broken metal that might be converted into weapons (SAL5/78). In later contexts, the inference is that it was usually old brass or copper. In 1709, a Sheffield cutler called Joseph Webster had *some Shruff brass* in his inventory, valued at ten shillings (IH).

shulve See shovel.

shutt The word 'shot' has numerous meanings and in one definition it is said to be a division of land. 'Shutt', which occurs in Yorkshire, is a variant spelling and the evidence we have at present suggests that it may have come into use towards the end of the sixteenth century, as a synonym of 'furlong': in some cases it identified part of the unenclosed town field: 1601 *septem seliones terre arrabilis iacen in le overfield super shuttam sive furlangam voc. le Overshutt [seven selions of arable land lying in the overfield above the shutt or furlong called the Overshutt]*, Kirkheaton (DD/WBD/3/77a). In other cases it was an enclosure in what had formerly been a town field: 1604 *that … Thomas Wood by exchange of lands might take in and inclose one close called the Neither Shuttes*, Lepton (DD/WBD4/156); 1687 *the footway leading downe their groundes unto the shutt*, Northowram (WCR13/110). It remained in use after land had been in the *now in a close taken in under Bincliffe House*, Brampton (YAJ6/71): in this deed of exchange four divisions in the Cliff Field of Brampton had 'shutt' as a place-name element.

Lepton field maps of the 1700s show the Nether Shutts as large enclosures to the north of a town field that was still in common ownership: it is clear that this land had been cleared of trees at some early date and brought under the plough as an extension of the older Northfield. Downshutts is a relatively common field name in the south Pennines and more research may show some comparisons with Nether Shutts. Certain aspects of the history of 'outshut', which was similarly an extension, are worth noting.

shuttle In contexts which relate to water mills, reservoirs or drainage systems, a 'shuttle' was a flood-gate; that is a hatch or 'door' which controlled the flow of water and needed to be raised to allow it to flow freely. In 1880–1, the Minutes of Council for Huddersfield recorded that the Waterworks Committee *proceeded to Wessenden Head*

Reservoir ... and the keys of the inlet shuttle at Shing [sic for Shining] *Brook* were delivered to the Commissioners. Much earlier references have been noted: 1549 *to make a over shotyll a honest goyt to brynge watter to the sayd whell*, Ecclesfield (Miller85–6) and some of them suggest that it could be a substantial structure: 1612–16 *all the tymber ... needfull for the shuttlestocke ... all boards for an over shuttle*, Golcar (DD/RA/f/4a): the 'over shuttle' may have been part of the 'pentrough'. Later references include: 1659 *we lay in paine that one shutle att Armitage, standing in the ground of Matthew Blackburne, in the water course ... be taken up for the space betwixt Michaellmas day and Martinmas day every yeare*, South Crosland (DD/WBM); 1789 *for a fulling mill ... weirs, dams, goits, shuttles*, Kirkburton (G-A). The word gave rise to a number of minor place-names, e.g. 1638 *noe man shall make a foote waye from Upper Shuttle upp Myres unto Ridingswell*, Lepton (DD/WBM). Other examples include 1720 *Shuttle Ing* (DD/WBE/32); 1798 *Shuttle Close* (DD/WBE/60). Such field-names may serve to identify mill sites when the building itself has disappeared. See also goit stock, pentrough.

shuttle–maker A maker of the shuttles used by weavers: 1377 *Willelmus Schitelmaker*, Hull (PTER).

shuttle–stock See shuttle.

Shyre Thursday See Sheer Thursday.

sich A dialect spelling of 'such': *c*.1537 *he was olde and feble and nothing mete for siche busyness*, Jervaulx Abbey (SS42/276); 1542 *shetys, coverlets and sych other*, Stanwick (SS26/27). See also mich.

sickle An obsolete word that meant sickly, used here in a by-name with wether, a male sheep,: 1332 *Michael Sekilwether*, Hipperholme (WCR3/67). Possibly also: 1326 *Richard Sicel*, Holme (YRS109/88).

sickle boon A manorial service which obliged the tenant to work with his 'sickle' for a number of days on the lord's land: 1463 *lettyn to ferme ... gyvyng therfore yerely xiiijd ... and oon sykylboyn*, Rowley (YDK4). See also boon.

sicklesmith The making of sickles was a trade particularly associated with the Moss Valley in the north Derbyshire parish of Eckington, just beyond the Yorkshire border. It had been established there in the late Elizabethan period, apparently by a group of families which included the Staniforths, originally from Attercliffe. The mark assigned to John Stanyford at the Lord's court in 1564–5 stood for *falcir ferreis*; that is iron sickles (HCC91). When John Staniforth of Eckington died in 1597, his inventory recorded *Syckles ready made xxix dozen* (IH). However, the term 'sicklesmith' is unrecorded there until 1690 when John Turner of Ford, *sicklesmith* made his will (IH).

Early Yorkshire references to the occupation are: 1699 *Robertus fil' Joh'is [Robert son of John] Taylor sickelsmith, Parke*, Sheffield (PR4/173); 1706 *John Waller of Woodthorpe Moore Side in ... Handsworth, sicklesmith* (TWH14/88). In 1729, *Adam Waller, sicclesmith, laid down his fine for selling sickles without a mark* but 5 shillings was returned to him since this breach of the ordinances was considered to have been done in ignorance, not maliciously (HCC17). The OED has references to 'sickle-maker' in 1483 and 1619, but there is no entry for sicklesmith. The word was certainly in use, for Bardsley quoted 'John *Sykelsmith*' as an early undated surname, though he considered it to be the origin of Sixsmith, wrongly I suspect.

sideboard Originally a dining table placed against the side of a room: 1530 *A brew lede & ij side bords in the hall*, Worsall (SS2/109); 1536 *The side borde in the haull with the* *tristillis sett in the ground*, Car Colston (SS106/26); 1574 *yokes, harwyes, tenter, sideborde*, Hipperholme (HTu224).

side-waver, side-wiver A regional word for 'purlin': 1446–8 '10 sawn spars for *side wyfers*', Hull (YAJ62/160); 1524–5 *Item payd a wryghte for a syde whiner* [sic] *setting*, York (CCW104); 1544 *for a syd wyvere for his hye chamer*, York (CCW282); 1617 *strong poasts and pannes and good side wavers*, Brandsby (NYRO44/139); 1694 *hewing 10 spars 1s 3d; hewing a sidewaver 3d*, Tong (Tong/4d/3); 1739 *4 dormonds, joists … side wavers*, High Lofthouse (QS1/80/1). In his Almondbury glossary (1883), Easther had 'sidewires' which he defined as roof beams, used for laying the spars on. This was a local form of side-wiver and in telling us how it was pronounced it explains a much earlier reference: 1672 *laying our rig-tree and siduire*, Northowram (OH1/289). See also fork, waver (1), wiver.

siege A privy: 1448–9 'For making, dyking and walling of a *sege* in the Trinity House', Hull (YAJ62/161).

sievewright An early occupational term not found in the OED which has sieve-maker. Nevertheless, in 1301 *Laurence Syffewrythe* of Farndale was one of four scattered North Riding taxpayers with the same by-name (YRS21/48), so the craft may then have been regionally important. In 1590, John Beley of Beverley was a *syve maker* (YRS22/11). There was a craft of sievewrights in Edinburgh, certainly from the early 1500s, and the surname survives in Scotland (Black). See also riddle (2).

signtree, sinetree See seentree.

sile A strainer or sieve, especially for milk: *c.*1504 *ij tubes j syill and j skeyll iiijd*, York (SS53/193); 1579 *xij mylkbowles with a syle*, South Cave (Kaner102); 1612 *Milkehowse … 1 syle, 3 chesfatts, 2 synkears*, Brafferton (NYRO44/37); 1683 *4 skeles 6s, 3 chesfatts & 3 siles 10s*, Gateforth (YRS47/27); 1731 *4 large bowls, one milking pail, 3 siles*, Spofforth (QS1/70/4); 1799 *small milk can and sile*, Cartworth (G-A). The occupation is on record as a by-name: 1381 *Johannes Sylemaker*, South Cave (YAJ20/343).

silk An obsolete spelling of 'such': 1457 *a corse present to be takyn of my gudis silke as the custom of the kirk … requires*, York (SS30/207). See also sich.

sill The pole or shaft of a cart or wain, a regional word listed by Wright. In a list of attributive uses he wrote of 'the arrangement on the collar of a shaft-horse to which the shafts are attached by chains; hames having chains on each side' (EDD). That seems to be the meaning in the following example: 1739 *a pair of sill hames*, Emley (QS1/78/4). Perhaps also here: 1667 *Three coupe waines & two silld waines*, North Bierley (YRS134/130). However, 'sills' could also be the timber sections which formed the body of a wain (EDD).

silly The former varied meanings included 'simple' and 'trifling', either of which might be applicable here: 1630 'He recalled that … there had been kept at Bradford … *a little sillie* market for corn, butter, cheese … but not for cattle, horses or sheep', Adwalton (BAS10/287). It could also be 'blessed' in earlier centuries, as in a variety of by-names: 1268 *William Selisaule [soul]*, York (YRS12/265).

silveret A type of fabric for which one example has been noted: 1755 *a piece of stuff to sell called a silveret … to make into a negligee*, Huddersfield (QS1/94/9).

silver-plate In 1764, the Rev. Edward Goodwin commented on *the principal manufactures* in Sheffield, and included in the list *various kinds of goods … plated with silver*. In fact, the trade dated only from 1743 when Thomas Boulsover discovered how to plate copper with silver, partly by chance it is said. He successfully sold silver-plated buttons which were hardly distinguishable from those made of solid silver: his wares were convincing alternatives and much cheaper (FBH125). He did not patent his find, and other metal workers were quick to exploit the discovery, especially Joseph Hancock, and they established a reputation for 'Old Sheffield Plate' that still survives. The occupational term was in use soon afterwards, for example: 1796 *Godfrey Machon, silverplater*, Broad Lane, Sheffield (GRD). See also plate (2).

silversmith Sheffield had craftsmen who made silverware from the seventeenth century at least: 1641 *Edward Fisher of Sheffeld, silversmith* (TWH16/188). They were independent of the Cutlers' Company and the craft did not really prosper until the 1700s when the success of the silver-plating industry gave it a new impetus. The trade grew in importance and in 1773 an Assay Office was set up in Sheffield that eventually expanded its influence well beyond the city's boundaries.

sind To rinse or wash out, a regional word: 1664 *we present Mary wife of Isaac Longbottom for defileing the town spring by sinding and washing yarn in the same, 10s*, Halifax (WCR5/132).

sindon A fine, thin fabric of linen; a kind of cambric or muslin: 1257 *et zonam suam de Rubea Syndone [and her red sindon girdle]*, Harpham (ERAS21/71); 1300 *quodam panno de sindone [a piece of sindon cloth]*, Harpham (ERAS21/74); 1380 *lectum meum de sindone palatum de rubio et glauco integrum … unum matras de sindone [my complete sindon red and silvery-grey striped bed furnishing … a sindon mattress]*, York (SS4/112); 1393 *et capucium dupplicatum cum taphata vel syndone [and the hood lined with taffeta or sindon]*, York (SS4/170).

singing bread The wafer used in the celebration of the mass: 1453 *j box of silver covered for syngyngbrede*, Castle Bolton (SS30/190); 1490 *a thrawen boxe of tre for syngyngbreid*, York (YRS103/62); 1524 'the seal is round about the quantity of one *lez synging bread not of the lest*', Kirkby Malzeard (YRS114/1); 1567 *trueth it is that I had in a box certayne syngyng breads remanyng*, Beverley (PTD67).

single See cingle, kingle.

single spiking A spiked nail, probably the smallest of the three types on record: 1504 *iiij.m singlespikyng, 6s*, York (SS35/93); 1543–4 *Pro v.m single spykynges, 7s. 6d*, York (SS35/111). See also spiking.

sink (1) To excavate a vertical shaft. The term is found in Durham as early as 1358 (OED) and it is explained with some care in *The Compleat Collier* (1708); that is 'when we sink a pit, at first we break or cut the ground four square, and the diameter of the square is generally … about 9 quarters' (CC12). As the pit was deepened, timber was used 'in the same four square form', until the underlying rock was reached. A Bradford lease of 1599 granted the colliers *libertye for sinkeinge and diggeinge of pittes* (MMA/249). It could be a very dangerous operation: in 1672, for instance, *Robert Flowar of Sandal was sincking a coolepitt and … a great stone … fell about six yerds height upon his back* (QS1/11/8). The sinker's wages in the north-east were 'about 12d or 14d per day' in 1708 (CC6), and the expense of sinking a pit in Birstall was *fivepence per yard* in 1819 (DD/CA/5).

sink (2) A pit into which water or waste matter might flow, serving as a drain, sewer, or sump: 1524 *payd the plummer … for a synke mendyng xiiij^d*, York (CCW104); 1527 *for a graytt to the seynk hede v^d*, York (CCW117); 1641 *Present … Robt Harrison Cowper for*

*making a sinke to convey his corrupted washyngs & other offensive matter into … the Fryaridge
to his neighbours annoyance*, Scarborough (NYRO49/9); 1648 *he doth covenant to make
one sinke through the ould parlor underlinde and covered on the top with paveing and waled on
the side with stone*, Sowerby (YAJ16/110). See also sink-stone.

sinker (1) This was the occupational term for the men who dug the early pit shafts,
and the colliery accounts for Tong have the following entry: 1760 *paid sinkers 10s
6d* (Tong/4c/5). A story in the note-book of J.S. Nowell of Almondbury, writing in
1861, recounts how a collier known as 'Sinker' Kaye acquired his nickname: he was so
called because he would *delve for the new houses* after completing his shift as a collier;
making extra money by excavating or sinking draw wells.

sinker (2) The circular board which compresses the curds in the cheese vat: 1579
iij chese fattes, a sinker & a wood doubler, South Cave (Kaner102); 1593 *chesfaittes a
cheise presse & a synker 2s*, Hudswell (YRS152/311); 1676 *26 chesfats & sinkers*, Selby
(YRS47/2).

sinking This element occurred in a variety of compound terms which described
the implements used by sinkers. There is a reference to *one sinking pick* in Shibden in
1713 (HAS30/147), and to *one sinking hammer* and *6 sinking picks* in Beeston in 1754
(WYL160/129/5). Two *sinking corfs* were valued at five shillings in 1727 (SpSt) and
sinking wimbles at 8s 4d in 1815 (HAS32/282). In Colsterdale, a blacksmith was paid
in 1736 for making *sinking hacks* and *a sinking mell* (BM82/86). Sinkers had a very
important role in the development of mining and they were doubtless conscious of
their status: an illiterate sinker called Thomas Hallas used a pick as his mark in 1666
when he signed an agreement with the landowner Sir Thomas Beaumont (DD/
WBD/2/81).

Sinking Wood The diarist Oliver Heywood wrote in 1684 of a visit he made on
horseback to New Mill, a former coal-mining area near Holmfirth. He lost his way
in the snow and *got intangled in a wood, among bogs, and very dangerous precipices*: it was
moonlight when he reached his destination, where his host told him that the wood
was so *full of pits … that its called Sinking Hills* (OH3/343). It is still known as Sinking
Wood and if the local story has any truth in it there must have been coal-pits there
many centuries, since it was called *synkynge wodd* in a title deed of 1545 (KC315/3/3).
In the Thurstonland township book is a payment in 1778 to *Mr Banks's Colliers for
searching Pit in Sinking Wood for Mary Firth* (KC271/1).

sink-stone The stone basin of a font, from which water could be drained: 1432
*Willelmo fratri meo unum lavacrum cum le synkestane [To my brother William a laver with the
sink-stone]*, York (SS53/23); 1445 *unum lavacrum pendens cum le synkstone [a laver hanging
with the sink-stone]*, York (SS30/195).

sipe To drain or leak, a dialect word that is still in use: 1503 *shall wall up … the utter
west syde of his swynstye … so that no filth … or dunge come nor discend … into the grounde
of the said John Goldall excepte that it be by sipinge or casualtie*, Selby (SS85/30); 1519
*Porticus ecclesiae est defectivus in tegulis. Lez holywater stane sipis [There are broken tiles in
the church porch. The holy water stone leaks]*, Strensall (SS35/272).

sipling See post (1), scrub oak.

sippet Apparently a diminutive of 'sop', a small piece of bread, often toasted or fried,
used to garnish or accompany soups and stews. In a recipe of 1683, entitled *To stew
Pigeons*, is the following item: *so thicken the liquour then putt in the herbes again and serve
them upp in sippetts of bread* (GWK40). See also sop.

sipres An alternative spelling of cypress which has two distinct origins and meanings. It was the name of rich textile fabrics which were apparently imported from or via Cyprus: 1398 *dimidiam peciam velorum de sipirs … Unum [velum] de cypres [half a piece of sipres cloth … a [veil] of sipres]*, Beverley (SS4/240); 1402 *ij flameola de cipres [2 sipres headscarves]*, York (SS4/289); 1419 *j flameolum de Sipres*, Pontefract (Th26/341). Many references are to the tree of that name or the wood of the tree, and references are given under 'cypress'.

sith, sithen, sithence Obsolete forms of 'since': 1487 *with … repentance of all my synnes that ever I did sith the first houre I was born*, Hull (SS53/23); 1515 *if eny suche lees were made, where it was made and what tyme and how long sithen*, Gleadless (YRS41/84); 1525 *dymysed the premysses to the said defendaunt* [who] *peasibly manured and occupied the same euersythen until this day*, Leeds (YRS41/182); 1583 *sythence the same purchase have barganed and sould … one messuage*, Meltham (G-A); 1607 *about xxiiij yeares sithence*, Salton (NRQS1/79). See also manure (1).

sixpenny nail From the fourteenth century, nails began to be classified according to the original price per hundred, but when prices changed such terms were more an indication of size: 1524 *Item payd for two hunderethe sex peny naylles <dubyll spykynges> x^d*, York (CCW102); 1538 *iiij.c sex penny nayll, 2s*, York (SS35/109); 1544 *pro j.m v.c sex penne nail 5s*, York (SS35/111). See also penny nail, sark (2).

size An abbreviated form of assize.

skategeld A toll paid on bringing fish called skates into the market: *c.*1450 *the qwhyche schall gyffe for selling of m^l heryng jd, or ellys for selling of the same thay schall gyffe to the skattegyld iiijd*, Malton (SS85/60). See also scabell.

skeel A pail for milk or water: 1558 *j skyle with j barrel*, South Cave (Kaner59); 1577 *iiij skeiles*, North Frodingham (YAJ36/450); 1598 *One greate skeile, One little gallon*, Knaresborough (YRS134/62); 1615 *brought them [fish] in a skeele of water on her head*, Brandsby (NYRO44/98); 1642 *a little two gallon skeele to fetch water in*, Elmswell (DW151); 1743 *1 wooden scheele*, East Marton (GRD).

skeg A species of bearded oats: 1637 *3 pecks of skegg 1s*, Hambleton (YRS47/98); 1658 *Skeege sowne upon the ground is valued at £1 5s*, Thorpe Willoughby (YRS47/125); 1674 *Courn … rye … barlie … oates and scog* [sic] *one acar & a hauff*, Thorpe Willoughby (YRS47/9).

skein A rare usage of this word, with an obscure meaning. In 1555, Sir Edmund Mauleverer sold 'three parcels of wood *as by the skeyne apperithe … within a portion of ground called the Park in Ingleby Arncliffe (YRS63/58). It may be a reference to how the woods had been measured since a skein was a certain quantity of thread on a reel (OED).

skell-boose Although this term finds no place in most dictionaries its meaning has been discussed by several writers who agree that it referred to the stalls in a cow-house. For Stanley Ellis, the *skell-bewse* was the boarded wall at the head of the stall, through which there was access to the *mewsteead* (YDS9/46) and that was also the opinion expressed by Marie Hartley and Joan Ingilby (DM). In both these accounts a drawing showed the position the skell-boose occupied. That appears to differ from the definition offered by Canon Atkinson who defined it in his *Cleveland Glossary*, under the heading *skel-beast*, as 'a boarded partition between stall and stall'. The distinction may be one of chronology or geography but as recently as 1985, Miss Annie Walker of Slaithwaite in the West Riding said that her family used the word for 'the divisions between the beasts in the mistal'.

Early references confirm that it was made of wood but they do nothing to further clarify the meaning: 1362 'Megota broke burnt and destroyed one *Skelbose*', Yeadon (SW9); 1456–7 *In repar. de Skelbuse per Wm Horner xxd*, Fountains Abbey (SS130/55). On other occasions it was used in contexts that link it with other wooden objects and place it in a barn or cow-house: 1570 *horse hecke and skelbuses* (Kaner69); 1571 *skelboises with the horse crib and the manger* (DW233). See also skell-booth.

skell-booth A form of skell-boose. The suffix was confused in dialect with the plural of 'booth': 1577 *ij skell booths*, North Frodingham (YAJ36/450); 1634 *j horseheck and a manger with skelbouthes*, Elmswell (DW235); 1642 *stealing two skell-booth boards*, Exelby (NRQS4/224n). See also wright.

skene A type of knife or dagger, traditionally associated with Ireland and Scotland: 1578 *A stele coite … a shert of male … A sword and a skeane*, Kendal (SS26/281).

skep This is a word of Old Norse origin which had passed into English by the eleventh century and was subsequently used over a wide area. A skep was a kind of basket or container, typically used for grain and charcoal, and these came to be associated with specific measures. In an undated charter, Peter de Brus was to pay to Nostell Priory *decem sceppas bladi* for the sustenance of one of the canons, that is three of wheat, three of oats and four of barley or rye (YRS80/199). In 1225, in Whitby, an annual tithe payment of oatmeal was said to be *sex sceppas pacabilis farinæ de avena [six skeps of saleable oatmeal]* (SS69/220); in 1274 Peter de Brus had the right to one skep of salt (*unam skeppam salis*) from salt-pans in Coatham (YRS12/140), and in 1371, York Minster fabric accounts listed *vj skeppes carbonum [6 skeps of charcoal]* (SS35/9). Similar references to 'coal' in Ripon were to charcoal: 1470–1 *Et in ij skeppis carbonum vocatorum charcole [And for 2 skeps of coal called charcoal]* (SS81/216). Barley is specifi-cally referred to: 1208 *j skeppam ordei [1 skep of barley]*, Fimber (SS94/129) and wheat in four *skeppes* was paid as a kind of rent for land in Selby in 1404–5 (SAR141). A smaller basket was *the holy brede skepe* for which the churchwardens of Sheriff Hutton paid 1d in 1539 (YAJ36/182).

The full skep came to be thought of as a bushel, although I cannot say precisely when. Examples noted include *a bushel skepe* in South Cave in 1570 (Kaner69), *1 bushell sckep* in Selby in 1679 (YRS47/48) and *four bushel skepps* that were used for measuring coal in Beverley in 1755 (YRS122/36). Also in Beverley, following complaints of short measure, new regulations were drawn up in 1766 to make the skep *conformable to the Winchester bushel* (YRS122/46). The 'bushel-skip' was still 'a familiar term' in Cleveland in 1868.

The likelihood is that the skep was usually made of wicker, that is osiers or other small, pliant twigs, and there is evidence for that in the OED. In nineteenth-century Yorkshire glossaries it was variously described as a 'round-bottomed willow basket without a bow' (Whitby), 'a basket made of willow' (Almondbury) and 'a basket of willow or flag-fabric' (Cleveland). That seems to be explicit in the reference to *one wanded skepe* in the inventory of William Myddilton of Stockeld in 1578 (YRS134/52) and implicit in the entry *leps et skeps* in the Fountains Abbey accounts of 1457–9 (SS130/51). Bee-hives made of straw were called skeps from 1494 at least although the earliest relevant Yorkshire reference I have seen is to *foure bees skeps* in Faxfleet in 1578 (Kaner99): an Elmswell farmer had *15 skepps of bees* in 1664 (DW239).

Wright has examples of the word used both domestically and in collieries and mills (EDD). A coal scuttle, for example, has invariably been referred to in parts of Yorkshire as a skep whatever material it is made of, a point made by Easther in 1883. On the other hand the *coal skep* listed in a Farnley Tyas inventory of 1814 (G-A) may have been the much bigger container used by colliers to haul material up the mine shaft. Watson (1775) defined a 'skip' as *a Box to carry coals in* but I do not know if he meant the domestic implement or the industrial skep.

skepful This was a rare term, possibly because for much of its history the skep had a precise meaning. The OED has one example in Durham as early as *c.*1570 where the materials in the skep were sand and clay, but no others until the nineteenth century. In York, in 1579, it was agreed that anybody who deposited dung or filth at Skeldergate postern should be fined 12d for every *skepfull or burden* (YRS119/8). Elsewhere, of course, a 'burden' was deemed to be the amount that a man might carry, as opposed to the 'horse load' or 'cart load'.

skewbald Irregularly marked with white and brown or red, or some similar colour, used especially of horses. The diarist Adam Eyre had a horse so called: *1647 Oct. 8 This morne I putt Scue to grasse … Oct. 12 This morne I rid on Scueball to Carlecoates*, Thurlstone (SS65/67–8).

skift This is a dialect form of 'shift', that is to move. It was used in an undated document, possibly from the late eighteenth century: *An Account of Money disburst on Skifting the Old Coal pitts out of James Holden and Broadbent Close by the Farmers booning July 12*, Tong (Tong/4c/20). That was not the meaning in early wills: *1479 it is my will that my silver spones be skift betwixt my doughters*, Flinton (SS45/253); *1523 I will that my cosynge Matilde childer have to be skifted amongst them xl wedders, xl yowes, xl hogges*, Linton (SS53/84). The inference here is that 'skifted' meant 'shared'. See also pit-hill.

skillet A cooking utensil, typically made of brass or copper, which had three or four feet and a long handle, used for boiling and stewing: *1520 a lytell brasyn skelett with a stele*, Mount Grace (YAJ18/296); *1669 3 kettles, 5 brasse pots, 2 skellitts, a brass mortar*, Elmswell (DW243); *1676 one skellitt with pot kilps*, Selby (YRS47/2).

skin wool Wool taken from the skin of a dead sheep. In a Quarter Sessions case, Robert Webster of Carlton said in 1669 that sheep had been stolen from him, and named two suspects *for that upon a search made by the Constable … in their houses hee … found … severall parcells of skin wooll for which they* [could] *give no good accompts*, Monk Bretton (QS1/9/2).

skirmisher From an Old French word for a fencing-master which survived as the surname Scrimgeour (R&W): *1202 Inter Reginaldum Eskermissur … et Radulfum le Waut*', Teesdale (SS94/75); *1298 'the wife of le Scirmissour for a house 12d'*, Scarborough (YRS31/91).

skirt (1) In 1272, a butcher named as *Robertus Witheskirtes* was enrolled as a freeman of York (SS96/1) and the interpretation of 'skirt' in this by-name poses a problem. The more obvious possibilities are a garment worn by men, recorded *c.*1330, or the flaps of a saddle, usually in the plural as here, a term known from the thirteenth century (OED). If the man's occupation is considered perhaps 'midriff of an animal … especially as used for food' (OED) should be considered. See also taffeta.

skirt (2) An outlying piece of land, away from the main holding: *1697 beinge upon a skirt of land of his within Ossett, called Barefoote Crofte* (QS1).

skirt coal A rare term, defined by William Hooson in 1747 as coal which 'bounds and limits' the seam. It was used later in a survey of lands near Huddersfield: 1845

There is in the hilly parts of the Almondbury estate skirt coal that lays in long ranges between the old workings and the outbreak of the coal to the surface (DD/RE/C8).

skitterick A 'skitterick' was a stream which served as an open sewer, and it derives from two Old English words meaning 'excrement' and 'ditch'. The present spelling is evidence of Scandinavian influence and the word has survived as a minor place-name across the county. The best documented of these names was in Kirkgate in Wakefield, although the exact site cannot now be identified. It is mentioned regularly from the early fourteenth century: 1313 'in *Kergate* between *Hesperode* and *Schiterike*' (YRS57/5); 1533 *We present Rowland tode and smallpage wyffe that tha skore skyttyryge … betwyx thys & sent tellynge [St Helen] day* (YRS74/17); 1688 *his ditch wherein runs the water called Skitterick* (WCR13/130). See also shore (2), stone bridge.

skote A dialect spelling of 'shoat', a young weaned pig: 1621 *two boares, two sowes, three hogges and two skotes*, Slaidburn (YRS63/49).

skrike To shout or cry out, a regional form of shriek: 1597 *Samuel Wade skryked and said 'he kills me, he kills me' upon whose skrytchinge this deponent … ran in*, Sowerby (HAS14); 1666 *was a gun discharged and … William Knaggs … gave a skrike and turned round and fell downe dead*, Birdsall (SS40/142); 1686 *Elizabeth Taylor beinge in the parlor he took a candle and went to her and instantly after she scriked out*, Elland (QS1).

slab A verb meaning to dress timber, that is by removing the bark and possibly some of the sap wood: 1719–20 *Spent when the balks were slabbed*, Bradford (BAS1/54). See also slob.

slack (1) A hollow, depression, or shallow area between two stretches of rising ground: 1205–11 *et inde per la slake super Brokthornes usque ad Blakmore [and from there by the slack on Brokthornes as far as Blakmore]*, Gisburn (YRS87/31); 1331 *at Ryehill in le Slak … ½ an acre*, Marske in Cleveland (YRS102/85); 1541 *a great stone erected and set up in the myddest of a peat mosse or slacke*, Wibsey (LRS2/6); 1562 *ther was some grene gresse that growed in some slackes*, Rawdon (YRS114/103); 1697 *one half day-work in the slack of the field*, Holmfirth (Morehouse214). The turnpike records for the Keighley to Bradford road contain: 1755 *An account of the slacks filling and hills lowering, from the Two Laws to Toller Lane* (WRT13). See also water slack.

slack (2), sleck A term for small or refuse coal, recorded from *c*.1440. A witness in a case that had to do with the 'dilapidation' of the parsonage in Whitkirk, in 1683, blamed the vicar Mr Dade who had allowed coal to be extracted from ground under-lying the church, and *Coal, slack and rubbish* to accumulate above ground (YAJ36/331). Slack was sometimes taken as fuel to nearby works: 1773 *13 load of sleck for furnish*, Elsecar (HS9); 1775 *18 Load of Sleck for Brick Makers 9s* (Tong/4c/11) or used to back-fill quarries, along with other colliery waste: 1792 *carry away into the quarry or stone pit … all the sleck, earth and rubbish from the pit hills* (DD/WBD/3/222). The dialect spelling 'sleck' was very common.

slack trough A northern word for the water trough in which a smith cooled or 'slaked' heated metal. It can be compared with 'coltrough' which served the same purpose in the Sheffield area: 1445 *unum stethy de ferro … unum slek trough [an iron stithy … a slack-trough]*, York (SS30/116); 1613 *two vices the great steedye and the croked steedy … sleck troughes and other*, South Cave (Kaner248); 1638 *a stythie and a slecktrough and a nayle toole*, Elmswell (DW237). Slacking trough is an occasional late alternative.

slade In general a shallow valley, or an open space between wooded slopes, although the exact meaning often depends on the regional context. It is used several times in the description of a boundary between Easingwold and Huby: 1617 *westwarde downe a sladd unto an oke marked with a crosse … to another oke … nere unto long bridge, from thence as a slade leadeth unto another crosse in an oke* (NRR1/55). In the same sequence is a more puzzling reference: 1617 *another plough furrow or slade leading to a crosse*, Alne (NRR1/56), although this may express a doubt whether the slade or the furrow marked the boundary. See also slode.

slag Refuse matter separated from the metal in the smelting process: 1721 *all the waste of Lead ore or slagge*, Buckden (QS1/60/1). The slag from former bole hills was evidently worth re-smelting and is referred to as slagwork or blackwork: 1427 *antiquum slagwerk remanentem ex antiquo [old slagwork left over from long ago]*, Stanhope Park, co. Durham (R&J54). A 'slag hearth' used for that purpose is mentioned in Derbyshire in 1572 (JHR137). See also black work.

slam Impurities which resulted from the preparation of alum. In 1651, several North Riding men were presented *for throwing the slam of allome into the water-course at Slape-wath* (NRQS5/65). The processes which created the refuse are commented on in a foot-note by Canon Atkinson who mentioned also that a drain at Saltburn was called a 'slam-hole'.

slang A thin strip of land. A privately published account of the Woodsome estate quotes the instructions given to Jonathan Senior, a woodman: 1806 *The Range, Farnley Tyas – a slang of land at top of Roberts Mill Farm, about 2 acres, should be thickened with oak and ash* (DMB34).

slant gate This survives as a place-name in the Huddersfield area, in Fixby, Kirkburton and Linthwaite, descriptive in all three cases of a linking lane or road which ascends a hill directly and obliquely. It seems likely to have been a generic term locally, with a long history, especially since it occurred in other townships. In 1516, for example two acres of land in Austonley were said to lie *inter hoywodde bothomehede ex parte orient Slantgaite ex parte occident [between hoywodde bothomhede on the eastern side Slantgaite on the western side]*, Austonley (MD225).

slatemonger Probably a dealer in slate-stone: 1332 *De Roberto Sklatemanger xviij^d*, Brompton cum Sawdon (NRR4/158).

slate pin The peg which passed through a hole at the top end of a stone slate, thereby securing it behind the laths on a roof. Formerly the pins were made of wood or bone: 1410–11 *Item pro xx^{ml} sclat pynnes vjs viijd [Item for 20000 slate pins 6s 8d]*, Sibthorpe (MC285); 1648 *he is to make slate pins for them and he is to theack, rige and pave the whole … having mosse found*, Sowerby (YAJ16/110); 1705 *slate pins of wood or bone*, Methley (Th11/279); 1733 *slate pin wood*, Wakefield (QS1/73/4); 1740 *600 of Slate Pins for the barn*, Whitley Beaumont (DD/WBE/1/14).

slate-stone The thin 'flags' of sandstone which were used as a roofing material in many parts of Yorkshire: 1298–9 *Pro sparstan, sclatstan et aliis ad camaram [sic] de Rither [For spar-stone, slate-stone and other such for the chamber at Rither]*, Bolton Priory (YRS154/91); 1395 *Item pro boring 1^m sclatstane 20d [Item for boring 1000 slate-stones]*, Whitby (SS72/617). The most explicit information, and the link with Slater as a surname, is found in the fabric rolls and chamberlains' rolls for Ripon: 1392–3 *Et in sal. Simonis Sklater cooperantis et ponentis lapides de sklate et pro coopertura cujusdem domus … cum sklatestane [And for the pay of Simon Sklater for roofing and laying slate-stones and for roofing that building … with slate-stone]* (SS81/116); 1475–6 *uno plaustr. tegularum vocatarum Sclatestane 2s 6d … et vad. Ricardi Sclater tegentis super magnas cameras [a cartload* *of tiles called slate-stones 2s 6d … and wages of Richard Sclater for tiling on the great chambers]* (SS81/246); 1511–12 *Rogero Sclayter 6d tegenti super cameram … per unum diem, Sclaytston 4d ad idem opus ac del mose 1d [To Roger Sclayter 6d for tiling on the chamber … for one day, slate-stone for that work 4d and for moss 1d]*, Ripon (SS81/267). Only certain quarries had the right kind of stone: 1399 'three acres at *Stondelfs*'; 1400 'three acres at *Sclaftonedelffe* [sic]', Rastrick (YRS65/121) and the slates required preparation before they could be attached to a roof: 1608 *Robert Davyson for slating, dressing, holeinge, latting & pynnynge each roode vijs iiijd*, Brandsby (NYRO44/45). See also slate pin, stone-delf.

slaughter hide A word which is used in the lease of Fountains Abbey tannery, granted to Richard Paver: 1532 *grauntteth … all ther slawghter hydes as shalbe slayn to th'owse* [use] *of the said monastery: he was to pay 20s for every dacre, able and not able* (YRS140/242). See also mort.

slay A word of Old English origin, on record from before the Norman Conquest. A local glossary has the following definition: 'an instrument used in weaving to keep the threads straight. It also acts as a support to the shuttle as it runs, and, on being pulled to the piece, it drives the threads of the woof closer together'. In most references it is linked with 'heald': 1498 *unum bastard-lome cum iiij heyldes et slayes pro panno lato [one bastard-loom with 4 healds and slays for broadcloth]*, Beverley (SS53/137); 1559 *I give to Thomas Dawtre one wolane slea and one pair of heldes*, Wombwell (FAClvi); 1602 *to William Simpson my new lynnen loame with all the slayes saving thre or fower of the smallest*, Winsley (SS104/241). See also slaymaker.

slaymaker A maker of slays, that is the wooden instrument used in weaving to beat up the weft: 1602 *my new lynnen loame with all the slayes*, Winsley (SS104/241). The occupation and the occupational by-name are on record from the fourteenth century: 1379 *Johannes Slaymaker*, Doncaster (PTWR); 1389 *Johannes Whyt, slaymaker*, York (SS96/89); 1451 *fil. Johannis White, slaymaker*, York (SS96/172). In 1754–8, *John Kilner, slaymaker*, is listed in a trade directory for the Huddersfield area (EJL2) and in 1822, the entry for Huddersfield in Baines's directory has a separate section devoted to *Slay and Heald Makers*. Slaymaker Lane is in Oakworth, near Keighley.

slaywright An alternative for slaymaker, a rare term, noted in the North Riding: 1633 *two men, one a coverlet weaver, the other a sleawright*, Yearsley (NRQS3/348).

sleat, sleit Alternative spellings of 'slate', that is to set a dog at an animal, especially at sheep and cattle: 1555 *No man shall chase or sleit their neighbours shepe or cattell with dogges*, Lepton (DD/WBR/4); 1665 *wee lay in paine that noe … person … shall sleat any shepe belounging to the common*, Cartworth (WCR5/212); 1680 *tyed his horse to a gorse bush and slett his dogg at the sheep*, Dinnington (QS1/19/9); 1785 *the sheep was slet off by Meltham people*, Lingards (G-A).

sleck (1) A regional alternative of slake, that is to reduce lime to a soft white powder by the action of water: 1519 *payd for a loyd of lyme ij^s ix^d … paid for beryng and slekyng of the same iij^d*, York (CCW75); 1581 *For sleckinge, beating, and sifting of lime 9d*, York (SS35/118); 1697 *for 6 load of lime 6s … for slecking and blending and getting of sand 3s*, Long Preston (QS1/37/1).

sleck (2) See slack (2).

sled A sledge, used to transport a variety of heavy goods, not just in winter but at all times of the year, especially in places where wheeled vehicles with loads were impractical: 1454 'making a *Sled* for carrying stones 2d', Kirkby Malham (Morkill239); 1506 *yf ony man will have his turffs by sled it shalbe lefull*, York (YRS106/25); 1555 *all maner* *of thynges that belongith to a draughte, that is to saie wayne, plewghe, couppe, sledde, temys and other gere*, Beckwithshaw (SS104/66); 1616 *led home with a sledd the great wood*, Brandsby (NYRO44/109); 1748 *one muck sled*, Sowerby (QS1/87/6).

Also used as a verb, meaning to transport by sled: 1400 *in sledding lapidum … usque aquam [in sledding stone … to the river]*, York (SS35/21); 1409 *Et Johanni Holme … pro plumbo et sleddyng [And to John Holme … for the lead and the sledding]*, Beverley (ERAS4/37); 1434 *Et pro sleddyng batelli communitatis de aqua Fosse usque in aqua Use [And for sledding the common boat from the river Fosse to the river Ouse]*, York (SS192/18). Sleds were farm vehicles in the Pennines into relatively modern times and could still be seen in the Calder Valley fifty years ago: *c.*1570 *when comys great froost … sled home loggs for fier*, Woodsome (KayeCP); 1713 *Besids his hors to sled morter and fetch Slate, hay, wood*, Bradford (MM82).

It may be that 'sledful' emerged as a term similar to burden or horse-load, a standardised measure that is: 1450 *pro quolibet sledful ijd*, York (SS192/65); *c.*1540 *4 Sledfull wood yerely 16d*, Grosmont (YRS80/112); 1657 *Thomas Greene did unjustly carry away two sled full of manure*, Ecclesfield (QS4/5). Underground, sleds were used to convey corves of coal along the galleries: 1814 *Old axle trees for corve sleds 6s 0d*, Bradshaw (HAS32/280). It is difficult to interpret this reference but it may mean that the runners for the sleds were to be fashioned out of old axle-trees, which by this date were quite often made of iron. 'Sledge' was a less-common spelling: 1715 *for 4 sledge sides 1s 0d*, Farnley (MS14). See also car, corf, sledman.

sledman An occupational term in York for labourers who transported goods by sled, distinct from porters: 1402 *Johannes Hardy, sledman* (SS96/107); 1469 *Et solutum [And paid to] Christoforo Batell' sledman* (SS192/128); 1476 *Item that no sleddman … carie by cart slede nor horse any thing that belongis to the saide porters to bere* (YRS106/185); 1519 *for iiij peyse of temer iij^s v^d … payd to a sledman for ledyng of thame ij^d* (CCW69). The occupation was not confined to York: 1528 *William Clark, Sledman*, Hull (YRS141/123).

sleeper A strong beam used in the construction of bridges, houses, mills, etc. References in the OED date from 1607 but in Yorkshire the term has been noted only from the eighteenth century. Accounts relating to Batley Bridge include: 1733 *the long pieces … to be three in number … all of heart of oak and the sleepers, or cross pieces at the ends … of yew or good oak* (Sheard199). In unpublished documents for Cawood there were requests by tenants in 1756 for *new Slepers* for the mill and *Slepers … which shou'd be 10 Inches deep for a barn floor* (MH/DC). In 1786, William Metcalfe of Sessay, near Thirsk, wrote in his diary: *Leading sleepers from the wood* (WM6). In areas where there were collieries, a sleeper was a piece of timber used as a transverse support for the rails of a tramway or railway: 1817 *Moses Barker for sleepers*, Halifax (HAS32/282). The word can be compared with 'dorman, dormand'.

sleeve An item of attire to cover the arm. Formerly, it was not attached to a gown or coat and could be worn with a variety of garments: 1544 *to Margarett my servante … my beste paire of scleves*, Timble (SS104/42); 1559 *I geue to Isabell Walter my sister my bed gowne & my best sleves*, Otley (Th27/299); 1565 *a parre of wide sleves of clothe of golde*, Temple Newsam (YAJ25/94). Note the by-name: 1335 *Petrum Sleveles*, Pickering (NRR1/68). See also alb, tissue.

sleit See sleat.

slice A kitchen utensil although the word has a wide range of meanings. In the following context it was possibly a kind of fire shovel, or an implement for turning roast meat: 1644 *one gawbeiron and one slice*, Lepton (HM/C/180). See also gobirons, gawbiron.

slidder Noted in a hill-farm inventory, possibly a type of sledge, the runners of a sledge, or 'sliders', that is planks used for moving heavy objects (EDD): 1743 *a sledge and snout, 3 slidders*, Holmfirth (IH).

sliding rule A mathematical measuring instrument: 1698 *John Scott … had one Slideinge rule, an instrument used in his office or place of gauging* which [he] *did cause to bee cryed in Bradford* when it was stolen: *it was full of figures or Letters* (QS1).

sling yoke An obscure term. It is found in contexts which fail to clarify the meaning but was possibly a yoke slung across a person's shoulders which made it possible to carry heavy loads: 1596 *a bill, a spade, a slinge yoake, a muckforke*, South Cave (Kaner192); 1681 *8 felkes, a brake, a sleing yoke, 4 payre of hames*, Lund (YRS47/66). See also yoke.

slip (1) A narrow piece of land: 1775 *a small slip of land between this and the bounds of Sowerby township*, Halifax (Watson); 1834 *pieces or slips of woody ground and land*, Northowram (MD43/C10/6). It gave rise to a small number of minor place-names, for example 'Slip' in Northowram (PNWR3/103) and probably the 'Slip Inn' in Longwood: 1812 *A Slip of land beginning at a place called Haughs lane top and extending … about 300 yards in a line towards the Guide Stone at Raw Nook*, Longwood (DD/T/E/10).

slip (2) To take a slip or cutting from a tree for the purpose of propagation: 1778 *shall not Commit … any Manner of Waste … Fell Crop top prune Slip or Destroy any Timber*, Addingham (GRD).

slipping A skein or hank of yarn: 1725 *she took five slipping of yarn*, Pontefract (QS1/64/4).

slit deals Used of deals 'a full half inch thick', in contrast to whole deals which were 'one inch and a quarter thick' (OED). The examples listed here predate that definition by two centuries: 1673 *for slittdeals to J Brown 4s 3d*, Ripon (YRS118/137); 1689 *40 slitt deales att 8d, £3 6 8*, Selby (YRS47/186).

slitter An occasional late term for one who operated a slitting mill: 1849 *tilter, roller, forger and slitter*, Wadsley (WPS12).

slitting mill The first slitting mills were introduced into England from the Continent at the end of the sixteenth century and they were established in Yorkshire during the 1600s which led to a considerable expansion of the nail trade. In these mills, flat bars of iron were formed into plates between rollers and then passed between grooved rolls or 'slitters' to produce rod iron for nail-making. The first slitting mill in the Sheffield district was probably the one built for George Sitwell at Renishaw (Derbyshire) in the 1650s. The one at Masborough (Rotherham) was recorded in 1678 and another at Wortley, next to the forge, was first mentioned in a lease in 1684 (FBH174). Further north a lease of 1665 granted Thomas Dickin of Colne Bridge *liberty to erect, build and make use of a slitting mill … near the place where a corn mill … formerly stood* (MD335/3). A slitting mill at Kirkstall near Leeds is said to have been built in 1676, and Thoresby said in 1714 that it had been *erected for slitting iron into small Bars or Rods, by which Means there is a considerable Manufacture of Nails* (RTD167). When the lease of Wortley slitting-mill expired in 1738 the 'utensils' to be left there were listed as:

> *The Engine (viz. slitting machine) with 1 pair of cutters and 1 pair of Rolls, 2 Spanners, 1 Hammer, 2 pairs Furnace Tongs, 2 pairs Draw Tongs, 2 pairs Middle Tongs, 2 small Furgins, 1 Ringer, 1 Hook, 1 Chizel, 1 Weigh Beam and Scales with ½cwt., 1 Binding Bench, 2 pairs Binding Tongs, 1 Pestle, Hams [sic] and Grease*

Dishes, 2 Furnace Hooks, 1 Coal Rake, 1 Box to Break iron on, 1 Box to put Cutters in, 3 Furnaces, 2 with Bars, one without (AND82).

Rolling and slitting would often take place in the same mill and it was not unusual for the terms to interchange. See also draw out, rolling mill, rod iron.

slive (1) A verb meaning to cleave or cut: 1617 *thornes … had bene ether stubbed or sleven*, Brandsby (NYRO44/144). The noun is also recorded: 1617 *some slyvings of yonge oaks from ould stovens*, Brandsby (NYRO44/135). The OED has a reference from 1688 to 'A Sliven, Shivered, or Cloven tree'.

slive (2) The verb meant to slip on a garment such as a hood. Here it is linked more unusually with clothing for the legs: 1518 *I give to Robert … a par of Whit Slyvyng hose*, Barkston (Th9/87); 1558 *I bequeath to Robert Reame a paire of old slyve hose*, Whitkirk (Th27/195).

slob A rare word, recorded just once in the OED. It may have been a riven oak or ash pole: 1793 *ash boards, heart laths, saps, slobbs*, Thurstonland (M55). See also slab.

slobbery Slushy, miry, muddy: 1683 *Nov. 29 was very dirty, slobbery, but the day after it was a very hard frost*, Northowram (OH2/235).

slode The meaning is uncertain. Smith raised several possibilities in his comments on the place-name Slode which is in Warley near Halifax and provided references from 1624 (PNWR3/125). One earlier example has been noted: 1593 *escurare et purgare debent cursu' aque inter le Slode et le turffgates [they must scour and clean the river between Slode and the turf-gates]*, Slaithwaite (M/SL). See also slade.

sloe-thorn The blackthorn, a word on record from the Old English period. Found in Yorkshire as a minor place-name element: 1377 'a hedge at *Slothorncarr*', Methley (Th35/152).

slop A type of loose-fitting garment, breeches, mantle, or more usually over hose: 1520 *a wyde sloppe furryd to put over all my gere*, Mount Grace (YAJ18/295); 1542 *to Anne Heire my next best sloppe and best cloke*, Beverley (SS106/168); 1566 *one payre of sloppes of crayncoloryde fustyane and the undersokes belongynge the sayme*, Catterick (SS26/190); 1574 *a felte hatte with one paire of redde sloppes*, Thongsbridge (YRS39/178n); 1582 *my best paire of sloppes*, Slaithwaite (IMF); 1593 *my best overhose or sloppes … my best under stockinges*, Killinghall (SS104/195). See also nether stocks.

slot A bar or bolt for securing a door, often of iron: 1368 *in quadam serura empta, ij slottes de ferro emptis xxd ob [for purchase of that lock, for 2 iron slots bought 20½d]*, York (SS129/24); 1485 *et pro operacione les crestes pro dictis altaribus, seris, clavibus, les tyers et slotes [and for making the crests for the said altars, bars, keys, the tiers and slots]*, York (SS35/87); 1537 *for making of banddes, slottes, barres and staples to the new church and the offices*, York (SS35/109); 1619 *jembers for … doer(s) and 3 iron slotts and staples iiijs*, Brandsby (NYRO44/175); 1681 *a slot iron*, Lund (YRS47/66).

sludge In coal-mining vocabulary this was used as a verb, meaning to scour a water channel or clear the sludge from it: 1693 *paid for gate sludgeing 6d*, Farnley (MS11); 1765 *2 days sludging the water gate*, Tong (Tong/4c/9). In 1702, colliers in Colsterdale had to *clear the level of sludge at their expense* (BM82/48).

sluice This was in effect a small bridge, built into the raised embankment of a causey so that flood waters might flow through and not accumulate around the bridge approaches. None of the meanings of sluice listed in the OED adequately describe this feature and they are referred to as 'flood arches' by Harrison (DHB112). See also causey for an example of its use; and spring (3) for additional information.

smalegarne 'Small' or narrow yarn: 1453 *2 petris smalegarne [2 stone of smalegarne]*, Hull (YRS144/6). Apparently in contrast to 'grosgarn', but see grogram.

small hundred See long hundred.

smelt To melt ore in order to extract the metal: 1543 *for smelting one pece leade that was of the leade ashes whan the howse at Brymbem was thekydde, vs*, Fountains Abbey (SS42/403). The term 'smelt-lead' was used: 1446–58 *et de vij pese de smeltled liberatis Joh'i glassyn [and for 7 weys of smelt-lead delivered to John glassyn]*, Fountains Abbey (SS130/241).

smelter A workman who smelts ore: 1377 *Henricus Smelter*, Appletreewick (PTWR); 1455 *Nicholas Bucke, smeltar … pro labore suo ad le smeltes [… for his labour at the smelt-house]*, Heyshaw (SS42/364); 1580 *John Haykin the smelter of Marricke oweth one foother of lead* (YRS152/246); 1688 *Humphrey Chaddocke a smelter at the smelt mills*, Hampsthwaite (QS1/27/4); 1721 *Cuthbert Watson of Buckden, smelter* (QS1/60/1).

smelt-house, smelt-mill, smelting-mill Places where ore was smelted: 1446–58 *Rob'to Merbek pro carr. plumbi de smeltmyln ad Ripon [to Robert Merbek for transporting lead from the smelt-mill to Ripon]* (SS130/150); 1669 *the Smeltyng Mylne near Kettlewell with the wheel* (OYD48); 1688 *at the smelt house*, Hampsthwaite (QS1/27/4); 1721 *the smelt mills in Buckden* (QS1/60/1). Bale-hills were sites where smelting took place but possibly without any buildings: 1446–58 *apud [at] lez Smeltes*, Fountains Abbey (SS130/155). See also smelter.

smit (1) Probably an outbreak of black shale (EDD): 1714 *a Black Smitt which … may lead to coal or worse*, Colsterdale (BM82/71).

smit (2) A mark on the fleece of a sheep which identified the owner, a necessary practice where livestock from different farms or different townships used the same pasture grounds: 1593 *to Stephen Harisonn the smitte of my sheep and to Richard Harisonn the ear mark of my sheep*, Tosside (CS3/22); 1632 *two hogges that hath a smitt of Tar on the shoulder*, Kirby Underdale (HKU187). It could be used as a verb: 1579 *that every inhabitor shall smytt ther shepe which they fest with a buy smytt to be knowne from them which they kepe at home*, Halton Gill (AW173).

smith This common occupational term has had a range of related meanings over the centuries which includes farriers, marshals and ore-smelters. In Sheffield in particular it is clear that the numerous 'smiths' listed in the poll tax of 1379 were not shoeing smiths but craftsmen who were producing a variety of iron wares. The *Ordinances for the occupation of Smithes in Beverley* offer an insight into those workers who were considered to be 'smiths': 1596 'Every master of the said *arte of smithes, armourers, cutlers, swordslipers and hardewayremen*', and an earlier paragraph has the following interesting definition: 'any smith *working upon any stithie of iron (except could smithes)* shall be obedient to the Wardens and Stewards' (YRS84/69). See also cold smith, smithy.

smithies, smithy place The word 'smithy' was used for the forge or workshop of a blacksmith but iron works on a larger scale were being called 'smithies', from the early 1400s at least. A Derbyshire reference suggests that such smithies had a number of ancillary buildings, however modest: 1387 'houses, buildings and *Smythyhouses*', Barlborough (TWH16/43). In some early Yorkshire examples, 'Smithies' is a surname, possibly already hereditary: 1425 *Thomas del Smythies*, Sawley (WF1/11); 1432 *de Roberto oftheSmethies*,York (SS192/10).Among early West Riding ironworks so named are: 1450 *lez Smythiez in Tonge* (YRS120/63); 1538 *unius Molendini vocati le Yron Smithes [of a mill called the Iron Smithies]*, Rievaulx (SS83/312); 1598 *Ecclesoule Smithies*, Sheffield (WPS159). There is evidence in a Honley deed of how the plural usage may have originated: 1573 *quoddam forgam vocat' [that forge called] a paire of Smythies* (YDK85).

The alternative 'smithy place' has a similar history and the two terms may have been interchangeable: 1482 *usum et occupacionem tenure de Hundesworth et fabrice ibidem vocate Smythplace [the use and occupation of the holding of Hundesworth and the workshop there called Smythplace]* (Th22/244); 1507 *a Syte of a Smethe place to bylde an Irnesmethe both blome herth and strynge herth* and also the *Course of the Water … to turne the said Smethes*, Hazlebarrow, Norton (TWH14/124). In *Spen Valley Past and Present* (1893), Peel (*Spen Valley*) refers on page 131 to *one tenement made into two dwellings called the Smythies Place where some time stood Iron Smythies long since decayed* (1608). Such 'smithies' are distinct from the plural of 'smithy' as a blacksmith's forge: in 1557 property leased to Francis Swift of Sheffield included *tooe cotages and tooe smethes* on *the northweste syde of … Pinchen Crofte* (TWH16/105): a lease of Sir Francis Wortley's ironworks in 1621 covered *All those Iron Smythees … with all houses, buildings, stringe hearths, bloom hearths, dames, streames, goats [leats] and water-courses thereunto belonging … with all the bellowes, tools and implements now at the said smythees* (AND22). Smithies and Smithy Place are still relatively common place-names in the West Riding. See also iron mill, smithy, smithystead.

smithy In general, the 'smithy' is thought of as the workplace of a blacksmith, a village forge, but in Sheffield the word had associations from an early date which require comment. Those associations are already evident in the poll tax returns of 1379 when one Sheffield resident had the by-name *John de Smethe* and paid 6d tax as a working *smyth*: no fewer than eight neighbours were also classed as smiths and there were twelve more near by in Handsworth. These were communities of smiths producing iron goods for a wider market, and the townspeople would have been familiar throughout their lives with the sound of hammers on iron. As a by-name 'smithy' survived in that part of Yorkshire well into the fifteenth century but perhaps not later: 1384–5 John *del Smythy*, Bradfield (TWH26/4); 1440 *Thomas de Smythy*, Ecclesfield (TWH26/9).

Even in later centuries, many Sheffield cutlers had what might be called a domestic smithy, and they literally worked from home: 1498 *a house called a Smethy and iii gardens lying to the same* (TWH13/109); 1615 *one bay of housing … used for a smithy* (TWH20/145). The premises were humble buildings, often lean-tos or in backyards: Richard Kirk was taxed on two hearths in 1677, but protested that the former kitchen hearth had been converted into a smith's forge three years earlier (FBH102). When the burgesses of Sheffield leased a house in *the Castlegreene* in 1610, to a cutler called Laurence Braywell, with *all smithyes fouldes*, they used 'fold' in an urban context that foreshadows its development in the nineteenth century (TWH20/133). See also smithies.

smithy gear A frequent word in the wills and inventories of cutlers, which covers the range of implements and tools that one would expect to find in a smithy, such as bellows, hammers, stithies, tongs and vices. In 1542, Richard Boyer of Sheffield 'willed that Richard his son and John Hobson have all his *smythe gere and the coltroughe*' (TWH13/71). Similarly, Edward Hawke bequeathed all his *smethie gere* to his two sons (TWH13/76). In 1557, Robert Skergell made a distinction in his will between his *smythe gaire* and his *whelle gaire*, Sheffield (TWH16/109). See also stone-getter, working tools.

smithyman Not a farrier or shoeing-smith but a man who worked in a 'smithies' or had an iron works: 1379 *Johannes Cutyler, Alanus Fox, smethyman*, Askwith (PTWR); 1417 'John *Passelewe, smythyman*, diverted the water course so that it ran to his smithies', Thurstonland (MD225/1/143); 1562 *Robert Humblocke, Ecclesfeild, smethyman* (YRS14/86). See also oliver, smithy.

smithy place See smithies.

smithystead A rare alternative to 'smithy place': 1454 *hafe latyn to ferme* [let to farm] ... *all his watyrr and smethystedys*, Farnley (YRS120/64); 1486 *Smethystedehey*, Mytholmroyd (PNWR3/167). A reference to *Oldesmythystedes* in a Derbyshire deed of 1387 hints at how old the term might be, Barlborough (TWH16/43).

smoke penny Possibly a payment linked with the right to have a fire: 1309 'every house in ... Barkisland and Stainland whence smoke issues shall give by custom for one day's harvesting 1d' (WYAS813). It occurs in land deeds for Lealholm in North Yorkshire from 1686, where *green pennyes and smoake pennyes* were paid to the landlord (MD34/15). A Wolds parish terrier has: 1764 *1d for every house called smoke Penny*, Kirby Underdale (HKU102). See also greenpenny.

smoot A dialect word for a hole at the base of a wall or hedge. It allowed animals to pass from one enclosure to another, from hares to sheep, and differed from a 'gap' which was a much larger opening, either purpose made or the result of neglect, one that people and carts might pass through: 1572 *warning to all them that hath any smoughte or gaps in Long Newton ... that they be made ... before Sunday next*, Doncaster (YAJ35/298); 1642 *soe may the Shepheard have an eye to them all, both to stoppe the smouts and to see that none of them bee ... hanged in bryers*, Elmswell (DW87). The same word was used for small holes that gave bees access to a hive: 1642 *sette downe the hive on the sieve, leaving an open smoute for them to goe in*, Elmswell (DW65). See AW58.

smoothing-iron An iron with a flat face for smoothing linen, etc. It appears to be earlier than the term flat-iron, which has not been noted before 1810 (OED). Examples of 'smoothing-iron' are on record elsewhere from 1627, and Yorkshire references date from roughly the same period: 1613 *one toasting iron, one smoothing iron*, Ripley (YAJ34/193); 1628 *one smothinge yron*, Pudsey (LRS1/76); 1637 *two smoothing irons*, Knaresborough (YRS134/82). A word with much the same meaning was 'smoothing-box' which is on record from before 1700 (OED): it did not displace 'smoothing-iron' which remained in everyday use until more modern irons were invented. It survives as the business name of a Staffordshire ironing service. See also box-iron.

smoothing-iron maker A maker of smoothing-irons. The occupation is not listed in dictionaries but it was not uncommon in Sheffield from the mid-seventeenth century: 1654 *William Tickhill of Sheffeld smoothing ironmaker* (PR3/190); 1656 *William Nunns of Sheffield smoothing ironmaker* (PR3/201). Richard Smith was described as *Smoothing Iron maker* in both his will and his inventory. Other instances occur in the Cutlers' Company records but the lack of references from soon after 1700 can be explained by the development and popularity of the 'smoothing-box' or 'box-iron'. When William Harrison died in 1692 he described himself as a 'boxmaker' whereas the appraisers of his inventory referred to him as a 'smoothing-ironmaker'. The 'boxmakers' produced a great variety of wares but the likelihood is that at least some of them were really making box-irons, n.b. 1767 *William Newton, box iron maker* (HCC302). See also box-iron, boxmaker, smoothing-iron, stithy.

smore A spelling of 'smother' which captures the dialect pronunciation. The one example is the burial entry for a youngster who died in a coal-mine: 1597 *Richard Maukenoole* [sic for Mankenoole] *sonn smored with the dampe*, Leeds (PR).

smowing iron A dialect spelling of 'smoothing iron', that is an early type of flat iron: 1655 *a pare of iron bridges, one iron bestell, 2 smowing irons*, Selby (YRS47/110).

snag See snig.

snart An obsolete word for sharp, strong, severe, used as a nickname in the Wakefield area in the early fourteenth century: 1313 *Richard Snart*, Ossett (YRS57/4); 1333 *Thomas Snart*, Alverthorpe (WCR3/212).

snathe, snathing axe To 'snathe' was to cut off twigs and branches: 1570 *great timber … muche spoiled with snaithinge*, Topcliffe (YAJ17/148); 1642 *yow are to snath of all the small twigges and boughes*, Elmswell (DW127). It gave its name to a type of axe, one used to make husbandry implements such as flail staffs, rake shafts and the like: 1642 *Hee hayth for this purpose a little broad snathinge axe*, Elmswell (DW127).

sneck (1) The evidence for this word is found mostly in the northern counties and parts of Scotland, and references in the OED take its history back to the early fourteenth century. The etymology is said to be obscure but a 'sneck' was most commonly the iron latch of a door and that meaning has changed little over the centuries. Early Yorkshire examples serve to confirm that meaning, with *snekkys* made for a cupboard in Beverley in 1409 (ERAS4/35) and *bandis, crokis and sneckes* purchased from a York blacksmith in 1443 (SS35/58): in 1419 Edmond Loksmyth provided *j snek ad ostium pulpiti [1 snek for the pulpit door]* in Ripon at a cost of one penny (SS81/147). Similar references occur frequently through the sixteenth and seventeenth centuries in accounts concerned with building and property repairs, e.g. 1534 *the keys and sneke of the churche dore* in York (CCW163); 1615 *1 doer with bandes and crookes, lock and key, iron snecke and slott with all belonginge* for Mr Cholmeley of Brandsby (NYRO44/34). In 1673, the churchwardens of Bradford paid *for door bands and sneck mending* (BAS3/484).

In witness statements made before the magistrates the word occurs in quite different contexts. In 1701, a Bewerley bailiff called Thomas Simpson was reported as having come *to the house, the door being shutt, and opened two snecks or latches* (QS1): the clerk evidently recognised 'sneck' as a dialect word and added 'latch' so that there was no room for doubt. In Calverley, in 1738, a witness *heard the sneck of Dobson's shop door lift up* (QS1).

A series of East Riding title deeds provides possibly the most interesting use of 'sneck'. In 1538–9 when property in North Cliff changed hands, the deeds had on the reverse side full details of the 'livery of seisin'; that is the formal recognition of the change in ownership. In one case it is stated that the grantor, by his own hands, had delivered possession *by the snekke of the dore in the name of the hole lands*. In this case it seems that the sneck may have been removed and handed to the purchaser as a symbol of the property that he was entering into (YRS102/47). See also seisin.

sneck (2) The EDD has several late examples of 'sneck' where the reference is to a small piece of land jutting into a neighbouring field; an irregular projection in the boundary line. A Holmfirth document in my possession, written by a solicitor in 1872, reports that a quantity of stone was piled up in the corner of *a sneck of about 5 feet*

... at the division fence between the lands of Anthony Green and Messrs Moorhouse. A small explanatory sketch accompanies the text. This meaning of the word is listed in Carr's *Craven Glossary* (1828).

snickle, snittle A snare or gin, for trapping hares in particular, and used as a synonym of hare-pipe. It was made of wire, a loop with a running knot: 1673 *hath knowne John Warde to make haire pipes or snitles and seen him set them in hedges*, Doncaster (QS1/14/3); 1677 *Richard Wadsworth saith that hee hath lately taken from John Horsfall six snickles, snares or harepipes of yellow wire*, Heptonstall (QS1). The use of 'yellow wire' for snares was usual in the 1600s, possibly wire made from an alloy of copper and zinc. In 1693, a Heckmondwike man was said to have *set severall snares both yallew and blew wyer* (QS1). Snittlegate is a late minor place-name in Scholes near Holmfirth (PNWR2/248).

snig A difficult word. The OED has no early examples but Wright offers 'to chop' or 'to lop off branches' as possible meanings (EDD). Those would fit the contexts in which it appears in coal-mining records from the eighteenth century: 1720 *14 score and 7 poles sniging out of Tong wood*, Farnley (MS11); 1765 *for 100 poles sniging and leading*, Tong (Tong/4c/9). It may be a variant spelling of the verb 'to snag' which had similar meanings but a much longer history: 1608 *Richard Marshall stubbes and snagges wodd in Brandesby oxeclose* (NYRO44/45). A very early by-name takes the connection with wood-cutting back to the fourteenth century: 1339 *William Snaghasel*, Sowerby (WCR12/64).

snip (1) The meaning is explicit in the only example noted: 1738 *out of that snip or passage between Lord Wentworth's room and the room above the parlour* (MS595/51). The various colloquial usages of 'snip' suggest that it was a narrow access which allowed people to slip from one part of the house to another.

snip (2) A white mark down the face of a horse: 1531 *a blake stag stonyd with a white snype of the snote and a sterne in the forehead*, Kirby Underdale (HKU144); 1588 *one blacke meare with a white snippe in the snowte*, Monk Fryston (Th27/227); 1614 *a bay mare with a starre and a snippe*, Coxwold (NRQS2/37); 1631 *sould one blacke maire with a little white snip ... unto Wm Jennings*, Adwalton (BAS7/64). In 1626, Richard Brigham of South Cave bequeathed *one blacke maire named Snippy* to his son (Kaner328). See also snout, starn.

snittle See snickle.

snout Noted in connection with carts and wains but of uncertain meaning. It was probably a projecting attachment at the front end: 1671 *1 pare of wane blads, 1 cupe* [coup] *snout*, Thorpe Willoughby (YRS47/62); 1677 *Thomas sonne of Abraham Lockwood ... buried ... he beeing slain by a waine snowt which was full of coales falling one him*, Kirkburton (PR). See also coup, slidder.

snuffle To show disdain or disagreement by 'snuffing', that is drawing in air through the nostrils (OED). Wright has 'to snub' (EDD): 1651 *to make that good which was Concluded at a Generall Meeting and not to be Snuffled and have our orders contradicted*, Almondbury (YDK45).

soap ashes The ashes of ferns and certain kinds of wood were used to form a lye in soap-making: 1587 *payd for the stubbing ... 20 loods of soope ashe*, Woodsome (KayeCP); 1644 *manure and sope ashes*, Lepton (HM/C/181); 1791 *1000 acres are Rocks where the Poor burn Fearne and raise £120 by the Ashes*, Stannington (HS4/51). In a case at the Quarter Sessions in 1715, two men from Yeadon said they *were partners and did Joyn in Burning Bracken to Ashes for the soape makers* (QS1/54/9). See also ashburner.

sobbed Soaked or saturated, a regional usage: 1562 *in the same Intake there nether* [sic] *was … any moorishe weet sobbed or rotten ground but … ground meet for gyrs and corne*, Rawdon (YRS114/101).

sod Charcoal-burners used sods or turves to cover and seal the cordwood in their pits, thus preventing combustion. The right to get these within the wood was often written into the terms of a lease: 1549 *shall have Such lyke turffe and hyllynge … for colyng of the seyd Woodes*, Bradley (DD/WBD/8/60); 1720 *to dig and get Clods and cover in the said woods for covering the said Barke and coaling the charcoale*, Carlton (SpSt); 1766 *liberty to dig sods in convenient parts of the said woods … for coaling the said wood*, Quarmby (DD/T/33/1). See also dust (1), hilling (1).

sod cup, sod pot See pot.

soe A large tub: 1412 *Et de una Sue de empcione [And for a soe purchased]*, Selby (YRS118/41); 1459 *cum tubbes, soes, alepoittes*, Ripon (SS64/86); 1566 *Item iiij skeiles a soa with other implementes iiis iiijd*, South Cave (Kaner65); 1590 *everye ayle brewer … sell their aile for ijs xd the soe every soo contayninge seaven gallons at the fatt syde*, York (YRS138/126); 1698 *For a ridle, a soe, 5 scutles and 1 hand barrow 3s 2d*, Pickering (YAJ35/217). They were evidently quite large tubs: 1580–1 *Johane Calame beinge about a year and a half oulde by misfortune drowned in a soo of water*, York (SS35/352). See also say (1).

soe-stang The soe or tub had two 'ears' so that it could be carried on a stang or pole (OED): 1611 *1 soe & soestange*, Brandsby (NYRO44/39); 1612 *40 longe yonge ashes thicker then a soestange*, Brandsby (NYRO44/56). Doncaster had a street called *Sostange Lane* in 1572 (YAJ35/294). See also stang (1).

soft coal Inferior coal: 1705 *soft coal good for nothing but Limekilns and is not very good for that either*, Colsterdale (BM82/53). See also cabin, coal-bed, stand (2).

soign To excuse or make a payment for non-attendance at a court: 1661 *Everyone that neither appears nor soynes this Court 4d*, Acomb (YRS131/163) 1685 *Laid down for Thomas Gill for soning 2d;* 1692 *Tho. Gill … For an Assoine 2d*, Conistone (RW13,38). See also soigner.

soigner, soygner A short form of 'essoiner', that is the man who excused the non-attendance of another at the manor court. The evidence suggests that some men, possibly with legal training, did this regularly enough for it to be seen as their 'office' or occupation, as in the case of a Wharfedale man: 1297–8 *Et Alano le Soignour;* 1308–9 *Pro j equo vendito Alano essoniatori [For 1 horse sold to Alan the essoiner]*, Bolton Priory (YRS154); 1323–4 'Adam son of Alan *Soygnour*', Nesfield (YRS69/115). It was not uncommon in the south Pennine parishes where it is likely to be one source of Senior as a surname, conceivably the major source: 1307 *William le Soyngur*, Flockton (YRS102/61); 1379 *Thomas Soignour*, Flockton (YRS102/66); 1391 'Thomas *del Overhall of Flocton, soignour*' (YRS69/60). Possibly belonging here also is: 1421 *Thomas Lyndesay, synyar*, York (SS96/132). See also essoin, soign.

soil, soil tree A dialect spelling of 'sole': 1383–4 *ij dies facientium pyles, soilles & trabes & cum eisdem emendacionem … defectus stagni molendini [2 days making piles, soils and traves & the repair with them of breaches in the mill dam]*, Leeds (Th45/116); 1501 *to bild up right from his soile tre upward*, York (SS85/22); 1612–16 *all the tymber that shalbe needful for ground works … also sufficient soyle trees … and plankes for the whole forebaye*, Golcar (DD/RA/f/4a); 1667 *Paid R. Nayler for 1 Soyle tree for church gates 5s*, Bradford (BAS3/474). See also sole, sole tree.

soken Within the manorial system this was a right attached to a mill which required the tenants of certain lands to have the corn they produced ground there, or the cloths they made fulled there: 1522 'an estate in fee in all his cornmills and *walkemyllnes* and all the suit and *sukken* of the freehold tenants belonging thereto', Brighouse (YRS69/10); 1591 *I geve unto Ellyn my wife … my mylne called Dareley mylne with the soken and suite there to belonginge*, Winsley (SS104/175); 1653 *Tolls, Mulctures suite, Soaken, Commons*, Ingleton (GRD).

sole A horizontal piece of timber, especially one used in the foundations of a timber-framed house: 1335 *et panni tredecim enchiarum et septem enchiarum et solos ejusdem formæ [and thirteen inch and seven inch squared timbers and soles of the same size]*, York (SZ1/431); 1358 *Item pro gistez et soles xxs [Item for gists and soles 20s]*, York (SS129/14); 1417 *that [John] Hesyll may hafe rowme thar to lay hys sole and rayse hys house*, York (SS85/12); 1433 *In diversis peciis meremii … videlicet … vij bandclogs, iij soles, 1 quercu curva [For various pieces of timber … that is … 7 band clogs, 3 soles, 1 rounded oak]*, York (SS35/53); 1661 *laders, rakes, solles and loose wood*, Langfield (YRS134/119); 1739 *three soale balks*, Lofthouse (QS1/80/1). More particularly it could have the same meaning as 'sill': 1419–20 *et ij soles de esch emt. pro ij sperys de novo faciendis in prædicta domo [and 2 ash soles bought for renewing 2 spars in the aforesaid building]*, Ripon (SS81/144); 1464–5 'two great timbers called *solis* for the windows there', Hull (YRS141/101); 1731 *layed a Sleep on a window soal*, West Riding (QS1/70/6). Used occasionally as a verb: 1525 *payd … for a day soling off the stable xijᵈ*, York (CCW103). See also groundsel, soil, sole tree.

sole leather Leather of a thick or strong kind, suitable for the soles of boots and shoes: 1458 *unum daykyr de overledder et unum daykyr de soleledder [one dacre of over leather and one dacre of sole leather]*, Wakefield (SS30/218); 1627 'part of any hide from which the sole leather is cut', Beverley (YRS84/79). See also back, over leather, salt hide, upper leather.

sole-stone A horizontal stone which served as a foundation for a timber-framed building, a term explained under the headword groundsel: 1463 '20 cart loads of stones called *sole stones*', Holmfirth (MD225/1/189). See also soil, sole, sole tree.

sole tree A beam or piece of timber used as a foundation or support: 1527–8 *in evis bordes, severns et j soletre*, York (SS35/101); 1581 *the sole tree thereof to lye even with the sole tree of Mr Edmond Thwenges stall*, Hutton Cranswick (YAJ37/172); 1707 *for a soale tree … 4 spurres … for making the beacon*, North Bierley (QS1/46/9). See also howetree, soil, sole.

sollar An upper room or apartment: 1365 'Grant … of two rooms and two *solers*', York (YRS111/184); 1611 *The wall … that goeth … to the soller end*, Oakwell (Th41/117). See also cellar.

somedeal 'Somewhat', that is in some degree or measure, now archaic: 1546 *of hooll mynde and perfite remembrance … notwithstandinge somedeal vexed by the sekenes*, Halifax (Crossley15).

somewhat A certain amount, the source of dialect 'summat': 1499 *I will also that my son John Malhom reward my servantes with ilkon of them sumwhatt*, Skipton in Craven (SS53/168). See also steeve, sunder.

sop A piece of bread soaked in milk, wine, hot dripping or other liquid: *c.*1588 *put into a manchet cut in sopps*, Almondbury (DD/RA/f/4a). See also sippet.

sore (1), sored The colour 'sorrel', that is reddish-brown or chestnut, used especially of horses: 1420 *I will that … Acris Mersk haue the grey geldyng; Gerard and John my brethir liard botiller and a sorede horse,* York (SS116/31); 1541 *Also I give to John Hadlesay one sored stage to make hyme one horse of,* North Duffield (HAH334); 1587 *I give to my doughter Jane Barowbie a sowerde mare and a fole,* Knaresborough (SS104/158). The spelling 'sore' was less common: 1564 *Item 2 fylles a dappell graye and a sowre baye,* Marske (YRS152/131).

sore (2) A buck in its fourth year: 1523 *where as the prior and convent of Monkebretton clayme of me of olde custome a buck or a soor against Mary Magdaleyn day yerely I am content they have the same* (SS116/116); 1621 *as fast before the hownds as he could … thorow my this yere spring … wher presentlye they brought back by us a fresh sower,* Brandsby (NYRO44/227); 1698 *An Account Sander gave me of the male deer … of full bucks four brace … that were this year sores six brace,* Woodsome (C86).

sorrel, sorrelled Reddish-brown or chestnut coloured, used particularly of horses, sometimes as a name: 1257 *j pullum sorellum [1 sorrel colt],* Harpham (ERAS21/72); 1406 *et equum meum vocatum sorell [and my horse called sorrel],* York (SS4/341); 1515 *iij horses viz Gryme, Brun and Sorell Gosell,* North Frodingham (YAJ36/436); 1541 *my sorolde gelding,* Aughton (SS106/143); 1620 *one graye mare, one sorrel mare and one sorrel fillie,* South Cave (Kaner299); 1637 *one graye meare & her fole & one sorrill coulte,* Brayton (YRS47/148); 1697 *to Francis Thinkell of Gateforth my sorrell'd gelding* (YRS47/130). Occasionally used of a cow: 1551 *a cowe called Sourell,* Great Ouseburn (YAJ14/418). See also sore (1).

souder, souther Regional forms of solder; that is a fusible metal alloy used for uniting metal parts: 1400 *Custus plumbi: … Et in iij dos' tyn emptis pro soudre 8s 8d [Lead costs: … And for 3 dozen of tin bought for souder 8s 8d],* York (SS35/20); 1450 *In mercede eiusdem Willelmi operantis dicti soudour et reparantis gutter' ibidem per ij dies xijd [For the same William's pay for two days making the said souder and repairing the gutter there 12d],* York (SS192/66); 1595 *Item to the Plumer for lieing downe lead … to him for sex pounde souther,* Howden (YAJ19/457). See also sawther, sowthering iron.

sough An artificial water course, drain or sewer; a word commonly found in documents which relate to works associated with bridges, mills, the farming landscape, and coal-pits in particular: 1665 *wee paine Michell Woodhead that hee open his soughholes to vente the water betweene his lands and the lands in Michel Efwick occupation,* Northowram (WCR5/194). In coal-mining, the channel often started underground where it might be walled, and once on the surface it would usually be roofed in with bricks or stone and then turf. There are some references to 'open' soughs but in general the coal-owners were conscious of the danger and inconvenience of their sewers. A lease of 1597 states that it was not lawful to make water courses *under the howses and buildings, orchards, gardens, yeardes, garthes and Bakesides,* Beeston (WYL160/129/4).

The word occurs in many of the earliest leases, both as a noun and a verb: 1582 *the said myne of coals, with free liberty from time to time to make and dig the soughs and new pittes,* Northowram (HAS31/74); 1599 *libertye for sinkeinge and diggeinge of pittes … And for Sougheinge … and dryeing of the said Cole myne,* Shelf (MMA/249); 1720 *walling a peece of the sough,* Farnley (MS14). The lower end of the sough was referred to as the 'tail': 1692 *for the sough tayle feying,* Farnley (MS11); 1814 *railing sow tail,* Ovenden (HAS32/280). The Tong accounts of 1761–2 have payments to John Cowburn *for throwing up an open tail* and entries for *6 days at the open tail* and *78 yards driving open tail.* In the same sequence is a payment of 3d for *a load of Sods to Cover Sow with* and *Michael Crossley 1½ days leading Stone to Cover Sow* (Tong/4c/6). See also sow (1).

sough pit In Mr John Stanhope's *Coal Book* are entries in 1728 *for sinking a Water Pit* and *for sinking a Sough Pit* (SpSt). The precise meaning of these terms is not absolutely certain but they seem likely to refer to sumps where waste water was stored before being disposed of. *The Compleat Collier* (1708) has the following interesting piece: 'if we meet with a great Feeder of Water in Sinking a Pit in a Working Colliery … which Water … is by a drift or Watercourse from the old Pits, set away to the place where your Collery Water is all drawn' (CC5). See also sump.

sough tail See sough.

sourdock The common sorrel, noted as a minor place-name: 1595 'a messuage commonly called *Souerdockhill*', Barkisland (HM/A/96). The dialect equivalent was *Sourdocken*, recorded in 1788 (OED). See also docken.

sour milk See sweet milk.

souter A maker or mender of shoes, derived from a word meaning to sew or stitch: 1202 *et terram Thomæ Sutoris*, Swillington (SS94/31); 1298 *Adam Sutor*, Hunmanby (YRS31/67). It was particularly common in Yorkshire in the poll tax of 1379, with a count of thirty in the wapentakes which include Bradford and Wakefield, mostly as an occupation but occasionally as a by-name, e.g. *Johannes Mylner, sout[er]*, Flockton; *Johannes filius Galfridi sutor [John son of Geoffrey sutor]*, Dewsbury (PTWR). At that time these tradesmen were closely involved in the tanning of leather: *Hugo Souter* of Quarmby, also taxed in 1379, is mentioned in the court rolls in 1386 undertaking both crafts – *offic. sutor et tannator [trade of souter and tanner]* (MD225/1/112). In a city such as York the terms 'shoemaker' and 'souter' continued to overlap in meaning through the fifteenth century. In a case heard in the *Counsail chaumbre* in 1490 the words of Sir Thomas Gribthorp, a priest, were reported by two different witnesses: firstly *ther sholdbe ijc men that was no shomakers to take the part of shomakers* and secondly *ther woldbe iijc or iiijc men not being sowters that wold name thame selfs sowters* (YRS103/57).

southern See sudderon.

sow (1) A common alternative spelling of 'sough': 1539 *shall kep oppyn his watter cowrce cawilyd a sowe*, Ossett (WCR9/122): 1590 *turne one water course … or else sowe it under the grounde into the Calder*, Dewsbury (YAJ21/453); 1598 *liberty for sinkeinge, soweinge and making of pitts*, Thornton (DB1/C1/28); 1655 *opening a sowe upon Baildon Moor* (WPB2/306); 1701 *for repair of the way … damaged per that coal pitt sow*, Horton (MM/E/99); 1718 *John Smith for by worke in the Sow*, Farnley (MS14). See also fore, sough.

sow (2), sow metal Workmen used the word 'sow' for a large oblong piece of solidified metal, from the fifteenth century at least. The cast pig-iron at a furnace flowed into a 'runner', a depression in a bed of sand, and then into branched channels known as 'sows'. The name is said to have arisen because this pattern resembled piglets feeding from a sow. In 1701, Robert Sorsby's shop in Sheffield contained *sow metall Boxes*. The analogy is absolutely clear in the accounts of ironworks in Sussex: in 1542–3, for example, money received for swine pannage drew a distinction between *Sowes, pygges and shottes*: stocks of iron in 1563 were similarly referred to as *Sowes* and *Shott* (C50, C184). The 'shott' was a young pig, one that had been weaned. See also pig, pig-iron, shoat, stithy.

sowned For swooned, that is fainted, pronounced 'sound' in Cleveland: 1606 *making an assault on … his wieff … breaking her head so that she sowned two or three times*, Langthorne (NRQS1/55).

sowre See sore (1).

sowthering iron The tool used by plumbers for soldering: 1685 *2 ieron vieses, 7 sowthering ierons & other working toules* £1 2 6, Selby (YRS47/69). See also sawther, souder.

soygner See soigner.

spandrel The space between the roadway and the arches and piers of a bridge (DHB127). The word is seldom met with in Yorkshire documents: 1713 *the spondrell of ashlar*, Aldham Bridge (QS1/52/3).

spane To wean, especially calves and lambs: 1508 *40 yowes with their lames to they be spaynede*, Morker (YRS140/234); 1578 *Item calves that is spaned* £1 0 0, Stockeld (YRS134/45); 1593 *to every one of them a callf of thos in the laythe when they ar spayned*, Hudswell (YRS152/310). See also spaning.

spanged A regional word used in descriptions of an animal's skin colour, particularly cows. It has been said to mean flecked, speckled, spotted, and even pied (OED): 1552 *to Agnes my doughter one read spanged cowe*, Wakefield (Th19/332); 1558 *to Mathewe Henrye son on spanged oxe calf*, Whitkirk (Th27/195). Several variations in the vowel, and the word's use as a noun have been noted: 1540 *to ... my sone elawe* [sic] *a whit spanke, a cow*, Houghton (Th19/33); 1559 *two bigge bullokes, a brownne and a spvnget*, Treeton (YAJ17/364); 1570 *one spencket qwye*, Grinton (YRS152/198); 1591 *a whye stirke spinked*, Wensley (SS104/176); 1600 *one blake spinkedd que styrke*, Marrick (YRS152/358); 1756 *1 Speng wye calf*, Cawood (MH/DC). See also spangled, spink.

spangled A form of spanged which can be compared with sterneld, taggled: 1600 *Mye will is that one spangled cowe with a broken horne ... shall ... paye the moneye*, Knaresborough (SS104/223). In Kirkheaton there is a public house with a long history named *The Spangled Bull* (NH148). See also starn.

spaning Used of calves, lambs, etc. during the weaning process: 1543 *to little Richard Walker a spanynge calf*, Birstall (Th19/80); 1573 *to Peter Jeffraison a gymer lambe at the spaininge*, Hudswell (YRS152/179); 1672 *8 yonge beast* £9; *6 spaininge calves* £2 10, Thorpe Willoughby (YRS47/9). See also spane.

Spanish iron When we read that the Sheffield cutlers argued in favour of importing Spanish iron in the 1660s that may seem to signal a new departure but it is known that in the Tudor period high-grade Spanish ores were preferred by the Hallamshire cutlers to the local Tankersley ironstone. It was a move encouraged by the Earl of Shrewsbury whose steward was responsible for their importation via the river port of Bawtry, some twenty or so miles to the east (FBH9,55). In 1537, Henry *Rensha'* of Chesterfield had *Speynyshe yron unwroight* worth £9 recorded in his inventory (IH). There is proof of much earlier imports: 1377–8 *In ferro de Spayne empto de Johanne de Gysburn*, Bolton Priory (YRS154/564); 1454 *iij libris Spanysyren, precii petre viijd*, York (SS192/79); 1490 *two hundreth of Spanyssh iren*, York (SS53/60). The term is recorded in the Customs accounts for Hull from the same period: 1453 *5 ton-t' ferri ispanie [5 ton-tight of Spanish iron]* (YRS144/7). Iron from other countries is listed in the same Hull records. 'Osmunds', for example, were imported on a large scale, and the word is dealt with separately. See also Dansk iron, German steel, osmund.

spanker The name of a horse belonging to Sir Hugh Cholmeley, so probably one that could move at a fast pace: 1657 *my bay bald Barbary mare called Spanker*, Whitby (YRS9/164).

spannall A fabric, possibly one imported from Spain or imitating one from Spain: 1475 *Item for v yerdes and dimidium [a half] of spannall to two serkes and making of the sam xxd*, York (SS129/72). The same spelling was formerly a variant of the 'spaniel' dog.

spar It can mean a roof rafter, as in Henry Best's description of a thatcher at work: 1642 *They … fasten the bottles* [bundles] *to the sparres*, Elmswell (DW145). In many early Yorkshire references though it was a pole or piece of timber, typically fir imported from the Baltic, and under six inches in diameter: 1357 *Item, pro v sperris emptis, ijs vjd [Item for buying 5 spars, 2s 6d]*, York (SS129/11); 1409 *pro sparres cum cariagio [for spars and transport]*, Beverley (ERAS4/32); 1463 *2 c fyrsparres*, Hull (YRS144/58). Later, it was used of home-grown timber: 1614 *twenty sparres of oake wood, value 20d* (NRQS2/45). See also deal (2), scaffold.

sparable A small headless wedge-shaped iron nail, said to be a spelling of 'sparrow-bill' (OED). It was used in the soling and heeling of shoes: 1686 *two peniworth of sparribelles*, Conistone (RW24). Sparable Clough is a late Sowerby place-name (PNWR3/154).

sparing Respite or delay: 1528 *they require his said grace to gyf sparyng unto suche tyme that the Kings grace … may be farther knowne*, York (YRS106/111).

sparling (1) Found once only; possibly a diminutive of spar, or a mistake for purlin: 1642 *700 deales 1000 spars 100 balks 100 sparlins*, Bridlington (BCP178).

sparling (2) A small fish, also called a smelt: 1512–13 *iiij lez sperling nettes et ij lez heryng nettes*, Hornsea Beck (SS79/152). 1516–17 *with ix last of heryng wherof was vj full heryng and iij shotyn heryng and iiij last of sparlyng*, Hull (YRS45/40). Found as a by-name: 1259–60 *William Sperling*, Scarborough (YRS44/139).

sparrow-gray A shade of gray inspired by the sparrow: 1656 *for stealing a pair of britches colour sparrow-gray*, Nosterfield (NRQS5/213). It can be compared with crane-coloured, glede-coloured, mirk-gray, etc.

sparrow-hawk The OED has this as the name for a small anvil used in silver-working, with examples from 1869. The following reference in a goldsmith's inventory takes its history back to the Tudor period: 1490 *De ij sparhawke stethez xd* York (SS53/58). See also stithy.

sparrow-net A type of net with a small mesh for catching sparrows, probably to eat: 1390 *quatuor recia vocata Sparwes videlicet ij de melioribus et ij de mediocribus [four sparrow-nets that is to say 2 of the better ones and two of the middling ones]*, Hornsey Beck (SS4/139).

spar-stone Gypsum or plaster, used to give walls a white coat: 1299 *Emendacio domorum: Pro sparstan … de Rither [Building repairs: For spar-stone … at Ryther]*, Bolton Priory (YRS154/91); 1395 *Item pro sperstane*, Whitby (SS72/623); 1481 *quandam querruram de plaster vocatam sperre stone [the quarry for plaster called spar-stone]*, Ripon (SS64/345). The minor place-name *le Sparstoncliff* or *-clyff* was listed by Smith in Scriven in 1439 and 1469, with a note of purchases of *petrarum voc. sparstonez [of stone called spar-stone]* (PNWR5/116).

sparver A canopy for a bed: 1444 *iiij peir of common shetis, a sparver with covering of lynnyn clothe*, Lincolnshire (SS30/112); 1526–7 *my best fether bed … on sperver of Dornyx*, Whitkirk (HAH220); 1547 *with a fether bed, a bolster, a pillowe, a sperver, valaunces of tawney damaske*, Lead Hall (Th19/179); 1568 *an olde sparver of Donex not Serviceable*, Healaugh Park (YRS134/26).

spavin A tumour on a horse's leg, caused by inflammation. As an adjective it was used in the more general sense of lame: 1726 *an old mare and her spavin fole*, Wooldale (IH).

spaw A medicinal or mineral spring, named after Spaw in Belgium: 1574 *Mr Hattoun be reason of his greate syckenes is minded to gowe to the Spawe for the better recoverie of his healthe* (JHS112); 1662 *lent to my nephew Burdett att the spawe att Knaresbrough* (DD/WBL/107); 1665 *I went to Knaresborough spaw and lodged that night at an inne*, Northowram (OH1/256).

speak, speke A wooden spoke of a wheel: 1557 *xx^tie gauge* [sic] *of speakes ... and also xx^tie gauge of fellowes*, Creskeld (Th27/111); 1639 *speakes for wheeles*, Swinsty (YRS134/91). See also gang (1), spokeshave.

spectacle-maker A maker of glass spectacles for those with defective vision: 1423 *Et de xxs receptis pro pare de spectakeles de argento et deaurato [And for 20s for a pair of silver gilt spectacles]*, York (SS45/75); 1468–9 *De Alberto(?) Johnson spectaclemaker*, York (SS192/122). This man was almost certainly not English and his name suggests a German or Low Countries' origin.

speke See speak.

spelded Used of cattle, but of uncertain meaning: 1558 *ij quies, a branded and a speldyd*, Birstall (Th27/277); 1574 *one speldid cowe*, Hipperholme (HTu224); 1636 *Item one spelded oxe*, Eldwick (LRS1/108).

spelk (1) A thatching-rod or small strip of wood: 1563 *iij spelks and iij carres xixd*, Brantfell (SS26/169); 1699 *for Theaking 4 days ... for spelkes and thatch drawing*, Batley (Sheard217); 1798 *five bundles of wood or spelks in Dovecliff*, Worsbrough (IH).

spelk (2) A verb meaning to 'bruise' beans in a mill, a rare term noted in the OED: 1726 *a Horse-Mill ... ready for making Shillin, Spelking Beans and grinding Malt or Shillin*, Swillington (Th22/203).

spell A wooden bar, a rail. See also dagger (2).

spell-bone A spelling of speel-bone, that is the small bone of the arm or leg: 1307 'they assaulted and beat her and broke the *spilebon* of her arm', Wakefield (YRS36/131); 1690 *his left leg was sore hurt and his surgeons informe him that the end of the spell bone is broke*, Idle (QS1/29).

spelter Zinc, or an alloy in which zinc is the main component. In 1720, Luke Winter of Coal Pit lane, Sheffield had *spelter* worth £1 5s 0d in his Work Chamber (IH).

spence Usually a small room where food is kept, a pantry, but in Swaledale it may have been a type of cupboard or container: 1574 *A cupburd and a spence xxs*, Richmond (SS26/248); 1594 *Item a nolmarie and a litell spence 6s 8d*, Marske (YRS152/314); 1599 *Item one old mylk spenc' one arke ... one old ambre*, Marrick (YRS152/359). That meaning may have evolved quite late since this was where Spence as a surname origi-nated: 1327 *De Roberto del Spens*, Thoralby (YRS74/122), and the reference there is likely to be to a pantry or buttery.

spencket, speng See spanged.

spetch As a noun this could refer to a small piece of wood, a strip of undressed leather, a trimming of hide used in making glue or size (OED); 1664 *for spetches, haire and a kettle for lime*; 1666 *Tho: Hebden pro blew powder, white lead and oaken spetches pro sizing*, Ripon (YRS118/113,122). It is in evidence as a noun and a verb and it referred especially to leather patches or clouts used in the repair of shoes and boots: 1582 *the shomakers of this Cyttie … shall not in any wise spetche, clowte or coble any manner of bootes*, York (YRS119/59); 1639 *sufficient mending or spechinge lether*, Austonley (G-A). It was used by all classes of society: in the memorandum book of Miss Mary Worsley of Hovingham, in 1715, is an entry of 2s 10d spent on *a pair of shoes & a pair spetching* (ERAS9/21). Cobblers may have seen it as an alternative spelling of 'patch' and a cobbler's account book for 1770–7 has the following: *heelespecht with strong leather; soald and backspecht; shoo toospecht; Benjamin shoo specht o'th side of too*, South Crosland (GRD). Perhaps it contributed to the development of the surname Spetch, a variant of Petch which is first recorded in 1609 (GRDict). In fact, there is an early example of its use as a minor place-name: 1592 *a close or parcel of land … called the Spetche*, Barkisland (YRS50/34).

spice bread The OED has a reference to 'speysse-bred and wine' in 1550 and the inference is that this was richly flavoured bread or cake which contained raisins, plums, figs or the like. As a delicacy it actually has a much longer history and was being imported into Hull in the fifteenth century, from Danzig: 1453 *1 bar' spycebrede*; 1465 *8 skok spysed brede* (YRS144/6,86). It was almost certainly being made in some of the monasteries from the late thirteenth century, for Selby Abbey allowed small quantities to certain privileged tenants as part of their 'payment': 1320 'and he shall carry half a skep of wheat at Christmas to Seleby and shall have a loaf of *Lespeys bread*' (YRS94/49). Perhaps it was a seasonal delicacy. See also spice cake.

spice cake This may have been a later version of spice bread for very early references are lacking. In 1660, John Gill of York was *allowed to bake spiced Cakes and none other* (GWK64) and the Mirfield attorney John Turner occasionally bought *spice cake* for his sons in the 1740s (MS757). A boy accused of theft in 1721 claimed to the magistrates that he

> *was Incouraged therto by the wife of Joseph Milns of Bradford, alehousekeeper who told him … she would give him anything that was good and accordingly did burne and sweeten his ale for him and gave him spiced Cakes and Gamon Collopps* (QS1/60/6).

It is on record from the sixteenth century: 1589 *nowe the searchers of bakers compleaned of dyvers poore wedowes and others for bakeinge spiced cakes*, York (YRS138/47). Peter Brears lists mace, cloves, nutmeg, currents and sugar among the ingredients (GWK70). The term is still commonly used for a rich mixed-fruit cake which is traditionally eaten with a crumbly cheese.

spice plate A plate on which spices were placed: 1358 *cum uno plate argenti pro speciebus inponendis [with a silver plate for serving spices]*, York (SS4/69); 1399 *unus discus pro speciebus [a dish for spices]*, Ingmanthorpe (SS4/252); 1400 *filio meo predicto melius meum spiceplate [to my said son my better spice plate]*, Castle Bolton (SS4/278). In the will of a York apothecary were: 1398 *ij spiceplates de peudr', spicechargeours depictis & ollis pro viridi ginger [2 pewter spice plates, decorated spice chargers and pots for green ginger]* (SS4/245); 1423 *pro j spysce-plate deaurato [for 1 gilt spice plate]*, York (SS45/78). See also ginger, greenginger.

spiking A spike-nail; that is a large and strong nail: 1299–1300 *Et in spikynges ferris emptis ad eandem bercariam xxvjs ixd [And for spikings bought for that sheepfold 26s 9d]*, Bolton Priory (YRS154/105); a.1360 *Pro clavis ferri, videlicit, spykynges et broddes et aliis 16s [For iron nails, that is spikings, brods and other suchlike 16s]*, York (SS35/3);

1446–7 *c dimidia clavis vocatis spykyngs [150 nails called spikings]*, Beverley (ERAS6/78). References to single, middle and double spikings were also frequent and these words gave rise to by-names: 1379 *John Spikyng*, Bishop Monkton (PTWR), and field names: 1323 *Spikyng*, Snaith; 1516 *Dublespyk(inges)*; 1541 *Singlespyk(inges)*, Tadcaster (PNWR). Such names were common enough for us to suspect that they described a narrow triangular piece of land and that this was the shape of the nail. See also lath-nail.

spile sapling Probably for 'spire': 1555 *one holte of yonge okes called spile sapplyns*, Sowerby (Crossley111).

spilltimber, spillwood The term 'spillwood' has been explained as waste wood of little value (EAH87) but it is found in the court rolls of Wakefield manor as a by-name, along with 'spilltimber'. These take the history of the words back to the early fourteenth century. In 1306, *John Spillewod* of Rastrick had to pay damages in a dispute over rent (YRS36/54) and in 1331 *Richard Spiltimbir* surrendered 3 acres in Warley near Halifax (YRS109/186). In 1390, *Thomas Spilwode* held land in the parish of Snaith (YRS111/98). In fact, these were probably pejorative nicknames, of a type used for individuals deemed to be responsible for waste: *c.*1290 *Willelmus Spillebrede de Daneby* (SS89/134); 1301 *de Johanne Spilhaver* [oats], Guisborough (YRS21/33).

spink A coloured mark or spot on the skin of an animal: 1551 *too blake whies, one with a whyte spynke of the backe*, Gisburn (SS106/306); 1618–19 *a brandid spink cow*, Harrogate (SS110/54). It was a name given to cows and oxen: 1572 *a yorke* [sic] *of oxen called Brighe and Spinke*, Catwick (YAJ36/440); 1697 *Spinke buld June the 28th*, Conistone (RW50). See also spanged.

spinked See spanged.

spire (1) A sapling, used especially of young oak and ash trees. In 1389, Richard Saunderson of Yeadon was fined 2d because he 'cut down *hesshpires*' in the Yeadon woods (SW84); in 1392–3 the fabric rolls for Ripon record the purchase of *xxxij spyres* for 16s 4d. In fact the entry also gives details of costs for felling the trees, transporting them and paying wages, both to labourers and to Thomas *Wright* for working the wood (SS81/116). They were evidently used a great deal in building projects, and feature in the fabric accounts for York Minster: 1421 *in lx spierres de quercu* [oak] *emptis apud Northdyghton; in xxiiij parvis spires de fraxino* [ash] *emptis pro j ustrino in Petergate [for 2 oak spires bought at North Deighton; for 24 ash spires for 1 bakehouse in Petergate]*, York (SS35/44–5). Other examples are found in lists of manorial offences: 1537 *Robert Sergeantson ys a trespasser of fellyng and beryng away hys neghburs spyars and of other wod*, Alverthorpe (WCR9/68); 1620 'for cutting and stealing in *Watlas Springe* two *ash-spires* value 20d' (NRQS2/234). Angus Winchester noted a reference in 1579 to *spier toppes* and *esshe leaves* used as cattle fodder in winter, Buckden (AW57). See also oak, spile sapling.

spire (2) As a verb 'to spire' meant to send out a shoot; to sprout. In an undated seventeenth-century manuscript, gardeners were advised to set walnuts *in some mould … not too dry and then some time in February by which time they may begin to spire for root you are to set them in some good ground*, Farnley near Leeds (MS14).

spit A cooking device with a sharp-pointed metal rod, designed to impale pieces of meat for roasting at a fire: 1380 *ij spites ferreas meliores [2 better iron spits]*, York (SS4/113); 1458 *gallows, rakkis, spittis de ferro in coquina [gallows, racks, iron spits in the kitchen]*, Howden (SS30/212); 1462 *j laver, j spit, ij cobyrens*, Wawne (SS30/261); 1546 *one of my grett spittes and one little spitt and one pare of yron gallos,* Wakefield (Th19/164); 1612 *j racke of iron and 2 spitts,* Brafferton (NYRO44/37).

spital, spittle (1) Aphetic spellings of hospital: 1368 *le spitel-land juxta Hospitale sancti Johannis [the spital-land next to St John's Hospital],* Nottingham (SS4/85). In early records hospitals were charitable institutions, founded by religious bodies, guilds or individuals and they were remembered in wills and land grants: 1500 *to every masyndew and spitil-hous in Beverley xijd* (SS53/177); 1606 *the somme of £3 6s 8d for the use of the Spittle-house in New Malton* (NRQS1/43). A description of York city boundaries in 1443 referred to the *Maudeleyn Spetell;* that is the hospital of St Mary Magdalene (SS186/132), and in 1490, an indulgence of forty days was granted to those who gave money to 'the lepers in the house called *le Spitall* outside the south gate' of Doncaster (CYS231). It was a major element in place-names from the thirteenth century at least, e.g. 1294 *Spitle Hardwicke,* so named because it belonged to the Hospital of St Nicholas in Pontefract (PNWR2/79).

spittle (2) Sometimes a small spade (OED) but in these references an iron baking implement, a sort of peal or shovel used to remove hot loaves from an oven: 1621 *a baking stone, a kneading tubb, an iron spittle,* Slaidburn (YRS63/49); 1698 *one bakeing spittle,* Barnoldswick (YRS118/59); 1727 *had five baking spitles, thre axes and ten iron wedges,* Bowling (QS1/67/2).

spittle-staff A staff with a wedge-shaped piece of iron at the end, used for cutting up weeds, especially thistles: 1592 *spitle staffe viijd,* South Cave (Kaner170); 1605 *to Marmaduke Coghill one spitbell staffe* [sic], Knaresborough (SS104/252); 1614 *two night staves, one daye staffe, one spattell* [sic] *staffe,* Brandsby (NYRO44/75); 1731 *struck him with a spitling staffe,* Leeds (QS1/70/2).

splents Two overlapping pieces of metal armour, designed to protect the elbows in particular: 1453 *7 paribus splentes [7 pairs of splents],* Hull (YRS144/11); 1510 *oon coyt of plate, oon shirte of mayll, a pair splentes, a salett with oon skull,* Sherburn in Elmet (Th33/37); 1559 *3 Jackes 2 paire of splentes and 2 salletts and a sheaf of arrows, £1 6s 8d,* North Stainley (YRS134/5).

splint See splents.

spoil As a noun, 'spoil' referred initially to loot or plunder, that is the 'spoils of war' and it was only much later that it came to be associated with damage. A Ripon document is quoted in the OED as the first use of the word to imply that the landscape had been spoiled or 'rendered unserviceable': 1609 *Commons, Wastes, Spoils, Heaths, Moors* followed almost immediately by *the spoil of the same Woods* (SS81/334). Similarly, a survey of the king's woods in the North Riding, in 1608, lists several woods in the East Ward and then has a marginal note saying *Waste* followed by *it is not above 16 or 17 yeares since that they weare spoyled* (NRR1/12). In fact it is not certain that we should understand 'spoil' in these cases to mean 'damage', since 'the spoils' were assets, like the 'wastes'. The meaning may be that the trees had been illegally lopped and topped – plundered that is. If that is the correct interpretation, it marked a transitional stage in the word's meaning: in a survey of 1568 it was said that *theire hath bene muche spoile and wayst maid in the said Park of Blansbye ... to the value of one thousand lodes* (NRR1/208) and at the Leeds manor court in 1666 Richard Maud presented a tenant *for trespass of swine eating and spoyling his grass* (Th26/133).

Be that as it may, 'spoil' in the sense of refuse material from industrial workings, and the verb to spoil, are first noted in the seventeenth century, explicitly linked to damage done by coal-mining. Leaseholders of the Earl of Cumberland's pits in Craven were required in 1629 to deliver up the work site *unspoiled and tennentable* at the end of their term (YAJ64/160). Compensation was made further south in 1699 *for the spoile and damage done to the … owners of the respective lands and grounds*, Goldthorpe (WN). The modern meaning was by then established: 1702 *no unnecessary spoyle or destruccon*, Thornton (DBB1/2/30); 1732–3 *if the Spoil and damage done to my lands … was to be added to the Expences it would reduce the neat profits*, Horsforth (SpSt).

spokeshave A form of drawing-knife, originally used for shaping and finishing spokes, chair legs, barrel staves, etc.: 1622 *Item, three wimbles, thistle, speak shave*, Cottingley (LRS1/63); 1638 *a handsawe, a hatchett, a speake shawe and a broad chessle*, Tankersley (YRS54/74). 'Speak' was a common regional spelling of spoke: 1698 *new speaks & 6 new boards, 3s*, Salterforth (YRS118/59). See also gang (1), speak.

spool-wheel A wheel for winding thread onto a spool or bobbin: 1615 *a whele, a spoylewhell*, Bingley (LRS1/24); 1639 *Item three spinning wheels & one spoyle wheele 3s 4d*, Swinsty (YRS134/90); 1690 *one spinning wheel, one spole wheel*, Hepworth (IH).

spotted knife The manufacture of so-called spotted knives became widespread in the cutlery trade. Scales of horn were burnt or 'spotted' to resemble tortoiseshell and a directory of 1787 listed 85 manufacturers who specialised in that technique in and around Sheffield. It was recognised as a product aimed at the cheap end of the market (FBH107).

spout A pipe by which water is carried off a roof: 1392–3 *Et in salario Ricardi de Bettes facientis guturas cum spowtis super quondam novam cameram [And for Richard de Bettes' pay for making gutters with spouts on the new chamber]*, Ripon (SS81/113). Similar spouts drained excess water from bridges, and in 1683 the tenancy of Wakefield bridge-house carried with it the obligation to scour *the Water course, on both Sides of the said bridg, And keep open all and every of the Spouts thereunto belonging* (QS1). Evidence for 'spouts' on vessels used to hold water dates from the fifteenth century: 1444 *lego eidem j laver cum ij spowtes deaurat. [I bequeath 1 gilt basin with 2 spouts]*, Beverley (SS30/101).

The earliest evidence for spout meaning a spring of water is in minor place-names, as in an undated thirteenth-century Bradfield document: 'the brook called *le Sputesyke* (TWH14/1). This was possibly the source of the place-name Spout House: 1316 'all that messuage … at *le Spouthous* … in *Bradfeld*' (TWH20/9), although Smith noted three places so called in the township which could not 'be distinguished' (PNWR1/239). 'Spout' was actually a very common element in the Pennines, with numerous Spout Houses and minor names such as Spout Field, Spout Hole, Spout Ing (PNWR8/171). More directly linked to the meaning suggested is the Cumbrian *Sputekelde* of *c*.1200 (PNCu).

The springs from which people formerly fetched water were certainly called spouts, and yet references are scarce: 1775 *neither will fetch the Spoutwater of John Armytage without leave*, Lindley (G-A). More specific is an entry in the court roll of Heptonstall which links the vocabulary item to a particular name: 1577 'a croft called Wellcroft … from the *spowte called the Middle Spowte*' (HAS37/133). See HPN32 for Bradley Spout.

spreckled A dialect spelling of speckled: 1730 *some hens in a basket … one of which was a spreckled one*, Honley (QS1/69/6).

sprent (1) A word for a spring in a lock, so possibly used also of clock springs: 1652 *Item for mending Clocke sprents 6d*, Elland (PR2). It could also be a type of snare: 1620 *taught me with sprents in woods to take feozants*, Brandsby (NYRO44/204).

sprent (2) A young turbot or other flat fish, on record in county Durham from 1324–5 (OED): 1416–17 'And for 7 salmon and 2 *sprentz* at 13d a fish', Selby (SAR162).

spring (1) The source or head of a well, included here because of the possible confusion with spring (2). In many references the meaning is explicit: 1552 *awarde that the heade sprynges of water begynyng to spryng at Lightleroydnoke shall cum and serue as well the howses of … William Yllingworth as the howses of … John Ramsden* (YRS50/24); 1594 *a place there called Uskell heade is a springe and springethe upon Usborne Common or mower … descending … to the river of Ouse*, Great Ouseburn (MD69/2/4/2).

spring (2) As a noun in a woodland context this had several related meanings. It was, for example, the young growth of trees, especially coppice trees: 1425 *The forsaid Abbot sall noght be letted for to close the … wood and hald it in seuerell qwen hym lykes to fell his wode unto the tyme that the springe be reasonably waxen*, Newton (Th4/109). It was also the word for the coppice itself: 1390 'all the wood in *le spryng*', Aislaby (YRS102/1); 1399 *Pro xxj rodis de hegyng circa le spring in Langwath 21d* (SS35/132). When a wood was managed so that a section might be felled in each year of the coppice cycle the sections could also be called 'springs': 1599–1600 *The woodes beyng deuyded into 8 springes every yeare is one spring felled wich at 8 yeares growth is worth 20s the acre*, Settrington (YRS126/29). In some districts the term 'spring wood' became usual for a coppice: 1514 'the hedges between his *Spryngewoddes* and those of John Stone', Shepley (MD225); 1766 *All such Trees & Polls as are set out to be felled in three Spring Woods in Quarmby:* in the same document it was used as a verb and verbal noun in the sense of 'to grow' and 'growing': *the future Springing and Growth of the said woods* (DD/T/33/1).

At some stage the verb also came to mean 'to fell'. It seems to have moved already towards that meaning in a lease of 1684 which referred to *the last fall or spring of the same woodes … brush & underwood taken out … all sprung and cleansed*, Tong (Tong/3/372); 1743–4 *Joseph Dyson for springing Hutchen Wood 15s*, Kirkheaton (DD/WBE/1/18). The *Leeds Mercury* of May 6 1740 has the following notice: *To be Sold, The Spring Wood called Moseley Wood, in Cookridge … a large Quantity of Oak-Poles and Timber Wood proper for Carpenters and Coopers. Likewise a large Quantity of Birch Wood proper for Cloggers, Patten-Makers* (Th26/85). See also blackbark, hagg, waver (1).

spring (3), springer The springer is the supporting stone from which an arch 'springs', and the two words are typically found in the same context: 1682 *two plaine stones at the impost or springing of the arch*, Scriven (YAJ16/111). In 1705, Downham Bridge had *one Arch of hewn stone twelve yards long betwixt springer and springer* (QS1); on a smaller scale was the *bow of five yards within the springers* which described a sluice at the west end of Paythorne Bridge in 1687 (QS1). In 1701, repairs to the east end of a bridge in West Bradford required *one Land Stall* to be *built up to the Springer* (QS1/40/4). The earliest reference is in the Elland Bridge contract of 1579 which referred to *the setting of the … springers* (BAS6/139). See also foot bridge.

springing house In an appeal to the magistrates, in 1724, Zacharia Cooke of Knottingley claimed that he was *much oppressed with extortion* by a bailiff named Jonah Benson *who keeps a Springing house and when he arrests anybody hurryes them thither and exploits large sums of money from them under colour of his office* (QS1/63/4). This sounds as if money had to be paid before a prisoner was released, in which case it approaches the American slang expression 'to spring' someone from gaol. Wright has a dialect use of 'to spring' in the sense of advancing a sum of money (EDD).

spring knife This was the term which became popular for penknives and pocket-knives in the latter half of the seventeenth century. In 1690, George Harrison of Sheffield had in his possession *6 olivante Spring knives 6 plain Springe knives ... 3 dozen horn Spring knives* (IH). The inventory of Lewis Nawl of Sheffield Park (1697) shows that he made spring knives but neither he nor his contemporaries was called a 'spring knife maker' (IH). See also penknife, pocket-knife, trumpmaker.

sprout Used as a verb in an intriguing description of a poke or bag, possibly meaning to fray:

> 1665 *it is his poake ... hee knowes it by severall marks ... the length of it is the breetch of the cloth the selvidge is both at the top and bottom and but one seame at the side dubble sewed for sprouting*, Treeton (QS1).

spruce The spruce fir is not a native English tree but takes its name from Prussia, a state known in the Middle Ages as Pruce or Spruce. The wood was imported (see pruce) and probably used to make chests, coffers and the like, although such items may themselves have been imported: 1429 *lego Johanni de Kyrkby meum sprus kyst [I bequeath to John de Kyrkby my spruce chest]*, Kippax (Th22/246); 1433 *unum spruce coffre*, York (SS30/49); 1485 *una cista de spruse*, Ripon (SS64/368); 1500 'the ... *sprewskyste* in the chamber', Bradford (BAS2/171); 1519 *a spruce ark*, Roundhay (Th9/89). Less frequent usages include: 1528 *a chest with xv sprewes skynnes*, Hull (YAJ2/251); 1549 *one spruce counttar, a langsettill, a side burde*, Elland (Crossley42); 1622 *bo[ug]ht me 30 sprusedeale boards*, Brandsby (NYRO44/232). See also deal (2), pruce.

spur A prop or buttress, a short strut set diagonally to support an upright timber. When Revey beacon in North Bierley was erected, in 1707, *four spurrs* were among the timber supplied (QS1/46/9). The allusion is less clear in 1655 when two North Riding gentlemen were despatched *to view the spurr in Yeddingham Bridge, being in decay and insufficient*: they had to determine what the cost of repairing it would be (NRQS5/188). The editor Canon Atkinson thought it might be the angle of the pier, although this meaning is not recorded in the OED until 1736. See also groyne.

spurging tub A tub in which fermenting liquor was left to cleanse itself, throwing off impure matter: 1559 *The buttry ... iiij spungin tubbes* [sic], Hipswell (SS26/133); 1567 *3 spurging tubbes and ij seayes ijs*, Well (SS26/209); 1568 *tenn spowrging tubbes 3s 4d*, Healaugh (YRS134/35); 1578 *fower sponging* [sic] *tubbes, two tunnels*, Ripley (SS104/133).

spurn A wooden prop or stay, described by Halliwell as a support for a gatepost, and noted in Lincolnshire. Yorkshire examples are: 1500–25 *thair yates sporns*, Healaugh (YRS92/199); 1621 *committed to the House of Correction for cutting downe a windemill spurne*, Helmsley (NRQS3/110); 1739 *spurns and coller beams*, Lofthouse (QS1/80/1).

spurrings Notice given that the banns of marriage are to be published: 1726 *At church. That day there were five spurrings; Thomas Garner and Hannah Booth one*, Dodworth (SS65/260).

spur ryal A gold coin, so named because a Tudor rose on the reverse resembles the rowel on a spur. Although it is chiefly associated with the coinage of James I, examples occur through Elizabeth's reign: 1575 *To Alice and Isabel ... two spurre rialles of gold*, Huddersfield (HTu225); 1595 *I give unto my good neece Katheren ... one spurre ryall as a token of remembrance*, Wiganthorpe (YAJ8/369).

spur-wheel A gear wheel with cogs or teeth on the periphery which could be attached to the axle of the water wheel (OED). The term is on record from 1731 and it was used in an estimate for Sandbed Wheel on the river Don in 1863 (WPS17). In *c.*1760, a Wakefield clothier wrote:

> *How to make wheels in the spur way best and cheapest. Bye a strong bar of iron of 4 or 5 inches brood so piece both ends together and cut pieces out in the edge has thus for iron cogs and those sorts of wheels will work easey and keep them oyld with cow foot oyll* (YRS155/41).

spynget See spanged.

square To make timber square in preparation for its use by the house builders. In 1418, the purchase of seven oaks was followed by a payment for them being squared: *In expensis iiij carpentariorum squarrancium quercus [For the expenses of 4 carpenters who squared oak]*, York (SS35/38); 1486 *xxx squared trees and half c waynescotes to the reparaciones of the stalles*, Beverley (SS53/19); 1544–5 *payd … carpenters for 6 days fellyng and squarryng of tymber*, Bridlington (YRS80/68); 1619 *40 foet of squared tymber is a loade, 6d each wrought square foet or so many inshes as will make a square foet is an ordinary price, be it jeysts, sparres*, Brandsby (NYRO44/174). See also post (1), sware, wainscot.

squib A firework or explosive device: usually a slight explosion: 1678 *to prepare a squybb and to throw the same in att the window*, Huby (SS40/229).

squynchon See scuncheon.

stack A pile or heap, commonly of farm crops: 1658 *a hay stacke in the hay stead & hay at home*, Selby (YRS47/5). References to stacking coal are late, probably because the use of land for that purpose was not readily granted: agriculture took precedence over coal-getting for centuries. The term 'pit-hill', which is dealt with separately, is evidence that coals might be laid or stacked on the ground surface, certainly from the seventeenth century, and leases confirm that: 1659 *with free and sufficient grounde leave for the layeinge of all such coals as shall be … had or wrought*, Wibsey (MMA/255); 1699 *liberty of getting coals, sinking pitts, laying, stacking, stadleing and carrying away coals*, Goldthorpe (WN); 1729–31 *for a man stacking of the coals*, Swillington (CKY37).

In Lepton, the right to stack was clearly linked with commercial interests: 1739 *liberty … to get and Sell and Carry away … and Liberty to stack Coals* (DD/WBD/4/320); 1792 *liberty to open and sink pitshafts … and the coals gotten to draw out, sell and dispose of at their will and the same coals … to place, stack and continue upon the ground*. However, the permission to stack was not indefinite, lasting only until the coals *be conveniently sold* and carried *away with horses* (DD/WBD/3/222). The right to stack pit waste soon followed: 1813 *liberty to … place and stack the Coals and Earth and Rubbish dug out of the pits on the Ground adjoining such Pits making reasonable satisfaction to the occupiers … for all Damages*, Beeston (WYL160/129/1). The following minor place-name may be a reference to charcoal but it points to coal-stack as a much earlier term: 1577 *two acres of land at Colstackehill*, Ripon (YRS27/204). See also bank room, damage, pit-hill.

stack-bar A hurdle used to fence a stack in an open field: 1617 *one stacke of hay and 12 stack barres*, Ripley (YAJ34/183); 1657 *5 cart loads of haye … 5 stackbarrs*, Knaresborough (SS110/223); 1658 *12 stacke barr & the rest of the wood about the house*, Barley (YRS47/17).

stacker A labourer responsible for building stacks, a word used in farming contexts: 1642 *hee that forketh the waine is to stande on the stacke and forke them to the stacker,*

Elmswell (DW62), and also in collieries where both coal and waste were stacked: 1752 *one stacker at 7s 6d a week*, Elsecar (HS9).

stack-garth, staggarth A regional alternative of stack–yard, an enclosure close to a farm where hay, corn, and the like might be stacked: 1402–3 *In alloc. Rectori de Hemmyngburgh pro le Stakgarth 2s [For the allowance to the Rector of Hemingbrough for the stack-garth]* (OED); 1546 *one oxgange land … a kylne house, a stacke garthe*, Hull (SS92/339); 1571 *a peasestacke in the staikgarthe*, Elmswell (DW233); 1597 *In the laith & stackgarth … corne threshed and unthreshed*, South Cave (Kaner200); 1616 *felled … my ellers … and my Stackgarth hedge*, Brandsby (NYRO44/109); 1642 *five score and nine grasse-cockes … of these the little Staggarth had 7*, Elmswell (DW41). In 1338, 'that messuage called *le Stacgarth*' in Easthorpe was leased to William Michel (YRS120/55).

stack-prod A wooden peg or stick, used to fasten the thatch on a stack: 1884 *To 800 Stack prods @ 1/6*, Kirkburton (GWW133). Also referred to in 1914 as *stack-brods* by the author of *A History of Honley* (p.100).

stackstead See stead.

staddle This word of Old English origin had the basic meaning of 'foundation', a place where something might stand: *c*.1530 *he knoweth that Richard Longbothome … paid fyne for a myllstedyll or rode of land nigh where the said mill now standeth*, Halifax (YRS51/114). It was commonly used in connection with stacks of agricultural produce, referring to the foundation materials: 1614 *one stadle of rye*, Stockeld (YAJ34/178); 1642 *that they rake cleane … the staddles of the stookes after-that they have given up the stookes*, Elmswell (DW48). The inference in coal-mining contexts may be that the coal stacks were built up on some kind of framework or platform: 1699 *the liberty of laying, stacking stadleing and carrying away coals*, Goldthorpe (WN). See also stack, stead.

Staddle Bridge This bridge crosses the river Wiske and it is first referred to in a lease to the Prior of Mount Grace which gives the boundaries of property in East Harlsey: 1508 *incipiendo apud Stathelbrige descend per cursum aque usque pasturam vocatam lez pyttes in campo de Estharlesay [beginning at Staddle Bridge going down along the course of the river as far as the pasture called lez pyttes in East Harsley field]* (YAJ7/486). Smith made the point that the river was quite narrow here, with flat land on either side, so this may originally have been a timber bridge standing on four posts.

staddle hay Hay from the base of the stack, probably spoilt as animal fodder: 1642 *Thatchers … usually make theire sowing bandes of staddle-hay and soe fasten the bottles to the sparres*, Elmswell (DW145); 1702 *warned the colliers to keep out … they had staddle hay enough and brimstone which they would put in amongst it*, Bradford (QS1).

staff, staffer See stave hedge, staver.

staff-herd Literally to herd animals with a staff in hand, that is: 1558 *sub baculo pastorali*, a phrase found in an early Malham court roll (DDMa). It was the herdsman's responsibility to prevent animals from crossing an unfenced boundary, and a by-law of 1608 indicates that he might sit at the boundary, staff in hand, from morning to evening during the summer (AW115). The OED has examples of the verb from 1563 but earlier Yorkshire evidence shows that it is likely to have developed from an unrecorded noun: *c*.1530 *the tenantes of Holmfirthe hath taken in theire owne common and putte their bestes of the common of Thirlston and kept them there with staffe herde dayly* (YRS45/79); 1579 *no sheepe should depasture upon or in any common grounds, viz laines or other common pastures but onely as they are driven from there owne houses or grounds to other of their owne pastures … and that without any stay or stafhirdyng of the same*, Beverley (YRS84/30);

1615 *watchers to staffeheard untill the fence was mayd*, Brandsby (NYRO44/101). A much later reference links the practice with the East Riding Wolds: 1734 *that no Sheepherd shall Staff-herd his Sheep in the Cow Pasture or in the Corn Field*, Lund (YRS69/101). See also common herd, herd, townherd, waif.

stag (1) A young horse: 1357 *dunstagg*, Bradford (CR); 1399 *lego Domino Roberto Broune capellano j stagg [I leave to Sir Robert Broune chaplain 1 stag]*, Ingmanthorpe (SS4/252); 1434 *And to Thomas Busham my rede bald stagg*, Ousefleet (SS30/41); 1514 *To William my sone a stagg whiche I promised to hym what tyme he was a yong foolle*, Ingmanthorpe (SS79/60); 1557 *I giue to Sir Thomas Gargrave my stagge that was of the Chrawshaw meare*, Elland (Crossley142); 1606 *unum equum testiculatum, Anglice a stoned stagg [one gelded horse, in English a stoned stagg]*, Middleton Tyas (NRQS1/55). See also stoned.

stag (2) An occasional spelling of 'steg', the regional word for a gander: 1637 *two geese and a stagg 4s*, Hambleton (YRS47/98).

staggarth See stack-garth.

staggett A diminutive of 'stag', a young horse, probably a stallion: 1307–8 *Rem(anent) ibidem de jumentis iij ... Et j stagg(ettus) [There remain there 3 horses ... And 1 staggett]*, Bolton Priory (YRS154/238).

stained Ornamented with coloured images, used especially of wall hangings: 1410 *de j aula stenyd [for 1 stained hanging]*, York (SS45/44); 1426 *le steyned hallyng pertinentem ad aulam de Spaldyngton [the stained halling belonging to Spaldington Hall]* (SS30/11); 1457 *et unum hallyng cum pertinentiis steyned cum ymaginibus [and a halling stained with images with its accoutrements]*, York (SS30/214); 1464 *j stevened cloth cum arboribus et vj imaginibus [1 cloth stained with trees and 6 images]*, York (SS30/262). See also halling, painted cloth, steeve.

stainer In York, the stainers were probably working with cloth rather than with wood. Inventories provide occasional information: in 1565, the Earl of Lennox had property at Temple Newsam which included *two benkers stayned with armes*; that is two coverings for a bench or chair which had his coat of arms 'stained' on them, perhaps to resemble tapestry. Similar items were *imbrodered* or had *crewlez nedle worke* (YAJ25/95). There were stainers in the city from the mid-fourteenth century, for *Willelmus le steignour* was enrolled as a York freeman in 1353 (SS96/49). The *stenours* were a small group, linked with *peyntourz*, and *goldbetours* in the fifteenth century (SS120/164–6) and, in 1421–2, they belonged to the guild of *Payntours, Steynours, Pynners et Latoners*. There were just six members of the *steynourcrafte* on that occasion (SS125/102–3) but the numbers increased in the 1440s and 1450s by which time the by-name was in the process of becoming hereditary: 1443 *Hugo Stenyour, stenyour, fil. Ricardi Stenyour* (SS96/162). Subsequently, the craft declined and it may have been absorbed into the painters' guild: 1491 *Thomas Gynderscale, payntour alias stenour* (SS96/216).

stainwath Stone ford, recorded as the minor place-name *Staynwath* in an undated charter for Isle Beck of *a*.1225 (YRS50/95). It can be compared with place-names such as Stainforth and Stamford. See also wand (2), wath.

staithe (1) In the Old English period the word referred to a river bank or the shore: the OED notes that 'staithe' in the sense of a landing-stage is 'current only in districts where Scandinavian influence is strong'. The earliest Yorkshire references are minor place-names, starting with one in an undated thirteenth-century document: i.e. *Quenstayth*, Drax (PNWR4/11). The distinction in meaning is not always absolutely clear: 1283 *culturam meam in … Overstathecroft [my plough land in … Overstathecroft]*, Acaster (YRS10/325); 1380 *in the northern meadows of Snaythe on the east side del Stathe* (YRS111/159). On the other hand Hull had numerous staithes used by shipping from the fourteenth century: 1347 *the common staith called Aldburgh stathe, Munkegate staith* (YRS141). In York and other inland ports the evidence is a little later: 1404 *Resumptio stathe, pavimenti et inclusi [The taking back of the staithe, the pavement and the enclosure]*, Selby (SAR138); 1434 *pro reparacione stathe fracte super ripam Use [for repair of a damaged staithe on the Ouse bank]*, York (SS192/18).

By the fourteenth century there were landing stages in Newcastle upon Tyne where coal might be loaded onto ships but the staithes which served collieries in Yorkshire were much later:

> 1778 *the Town and Neighbourhood of Leeds have not, of late Years, been sufficiently supplied with Coals from the Coal-Staith* (Th40/60); 1833 *Walker is going to drive a great trade and is … setting up coal staithes at Halifax, Bradford, and other places*, Shibden (HAS31/110).

Such coal-staithes were erected later on sites away from the navigable rivers but accessible by wagon-ways, as at Staygate near Bradford, formerly Staithgate. The detailed accounts in this last case makes it clear that the staithe was built of stone. See also land-staithe, stay (1), wagon-road.

staithe (2) As a verb the meaning 'to strengthen a river wall' was transferred to house-building: 1524 *for two daysse taking downe the tymer off the for sayd howsse and staythyng the walls xij^d*, York (CCW102).

stallage A toll for the right to erect a stall in a market or fair: 1494 *Also on seruante of Thomas Asbrygg off Nafferton … gaue to the said William Haule for stallage off xx^{ti} shepe ijd* (YRS51/37); 1543 *for stallege that he receyved*, Kendal (SS26/39); 1619–21 *Whether is there a market … And whoe hath the toll pickage and Stallage of the same*, Pickering (NRR1/18). It could be used as a verb: 1529 *if any of the said conysellers be disposyd to have a daily market then if they come and be fraunchesyd and stallegyd they shall have a place*, York (YRS56/126).

stamin Possibly an alternative spelling of stammel: 1423 *curtinis de stamyn viridis et rubei coloris*, York (SS45/70); 1520 *ij newe stamyn shyrtes and j olde*, Mount Grace (YAJ18/295); 1553 *my blew stamyng jacket*, Kendal (SS26/77). For a similar interchange of final 'l' and 'n' see sameron.

stammel A coarse woollen cloth, commonly dyed red: 1637 *to Alce Denmer my cosinge … one stammell petticote*, Selby (YRS47/162); 1683 *my gown, stamell petticoat, 2 red petticoats*, Selby (YRS47/105). It gave its name to a red dye: 1617 *Broadcloth stammell dye for a carpet*, Brandsby (NYRO44/145). See also stamin.

stamp A small stack or pile of hay, grain, peas, etc.: 1592 *a stampe or mowsteed of rye unthreshed … a stampe of peas unthreshed*, South Cave (Kaner176); 1647 *one stampe of hay lying in the balkes in the lowe barne*, Hampsthwaite (YRS55/113).

stanchion An upright bar, especially in a window. In early references they were often made of wood but some were of iron by 1472–3 (OED): 1335 *Stanciones vero erunt novem enchiarum [The stanchions moreover were nine inches]*, York (SZ1/431); 1433 *iij balkes, iiij stanzones, vij bandclogs*, York (SS35/53); 1454–5 *et j quart' meremii in burdis, stauns(cions) [and 1 quarter of timber in boards and stanchions]*, York (SS192/97); 1490 *De viij bordes cum j stannshon stantibus inter coquinam et lez bowyltyng-hows [For 8 boards with*

1 stanchion standing between the kitchen and the boulting-house], York (SS53/57); 1637 *tenn windowe stanchions of iron*, Liversedge (YRS54/29); 1726 *the persons which stole the goods did take out a window stanchion in order to get into her house and went out at the back door*, Bretton (QS1); 1779 *For Iron Stanshals for the church*, Kirby Underdale (HKU153).

stand (1) A kind of tub or barrel: 1412 *Et de j standa de empcione [And for buying 1 stand]*, Selby (YRS118/41); 1567 *fowre fattes, fyve standes with theire coveres*, Fixby (YRS134/15); 1644 *tubbes, barelles and standes*, Lepton (HM/C/180); 1671 *found a stand which had within it eleaven peeces of mutton*, Rathmell (QS1). See also knop (3).

stand (2) When a pit, mill or factory was not working it was said to 'stand': 1695 *the pitts stood from the time that John Smith went away*, Farnley (MS11). The Kayes of Woodsome operated a coal-mine in Honley for which a rental survives from 1651, but after 1677 most entries simply say *the coal pitt stands*: a variation in 1685 which confirms the meaning of this phrase is *the coal mine not now wrought* (HAB34). In 1720, a Staveley ironworks journal noted that Robert Thompson had died and that *the cutler wheel stood* (WPS189). In Colsterdale, it was decided in 1721 to *let all Dead workes there stand* (BM82/81) and at Elsecar payment was made in 1769 for *nine pulls of soft coals burnt in the cabin when the pit was standing* (HS9). The term has remained in common use.

stand (3) standall, standard (1), stander 'Standard' was a word used in connection with wood management, especially in the phrase 'coppicing with standards', where the standards were the trees that the woodcutters left standing when the coppice had been felled: they were destined to be timber trees for eventual use in building projects. However, wood leases and other documents have a variety of alternative forms, including 'stand', 'stander' and 'standall': 1574 *one woodd contening xxx acr. ... th'old standes beinge left*, Fountains Abbey (SS42/411); 1594–5 'the sale of all the wood saving a thousand sufficient *standers of okes and ashes'*, Beverley (YRS84/99); 1608 *2 hagges ... in which are noe Standalls nor any other trees*, Pickering (NRR1/10). See also waver (1).

standard (2) A minor place-name noted several times in the West Riding with three examples in the neighbourhood of Skipton: in each case Smith gives the meaning as 'tree stump' although he had found no early forms, and evidence for that interpretation in Yorkshire is lacking. There are one or two thirteenth-century place-names which have 'standard' as an element in other parts of England, and Smith offered the same meaning for these (EPNE2/145). 'Standard' was certainly a word used in connection with wood management but it would be inaccurate to call it a stump.

In boundary descriptions, where examples of 'standard' are not uncommon, the term may originally have referred to a standing stone and then to a more substantial cairn of stones. In 1705–8, for example, witnesses in a Swaledale boundary dispute referred to boundary markers called *Browney gill standard* and *Ridmer Standerd* and these were probably stone cairns. More explicit was mention of *a hurrock or standard called Gibbon Hill Standard*, for 'hurrock' is a more common dialect word for a pile of loose stones (YRS162/12,156,303). At the west end of Swaledale is the prominent cairn called Jack Standards, thought to be a Bronze Age burial site (AF128), and Dent had its *three standerts* (PNWR6/260). The best known of all the 'standards' though is Nine Standards Rigg: these are relatively tall cairns and references to the name date from the first half of the seventeenth century (PNWe2/29). See also hurrock, standing stone.

standard (3) An upright bar, as in the railing of a bridge or in a window frame, of wood or iron: 1502 *To John Conewey, smyth, for foure transoms and xij standardes ... in lede* *for the fastening of the same iron,* York (OED); *a.*1580 *For helping to carry into the wryghte house standerdes, powles and boordes,* Langwith (SS35/118); 1589 *for fleakes and wood laid over the water for passengers … for wood for standerds, railes,* Malton Bridge (NRQS3/24).

stand-bed A high, standing bed as distinguished from a truckle-bed: 1557 *a stand bed in the litle chamber,* Adwick le Street (BIA15/2/185); 1567 *one stand bedde with all thinges perteyninge thereunto,* Fixby (YRS134/14); 1635 *one standbed which is now in making,* Emley (FACccxxi); 1658 *j stand bed which I lye in,* Hampsthwaite (SS110/243). See also standing bed.

stander See stand (3).

stand heck A rack or frame which stood on four legs and held animal fodder. It can be compared with the fixed hecks inside farm-buildings which served the same purpose: 1570 *one stand hecke with all wodd about howse,* Hutton Conyers (SS26/229); 1580 *payd … for maykinge two stand heckes, and other worke,* Stockeld (YRS161/17); 1647 *wood for husbandrie geare 4 stand heckes,* Denton (YRS134/96); 1731 *a crib, a standheck and a ladder,* Austerfield (QS1). See also heck.

standing A regular position for a market stall or booth, subject to tolls: 1538 *we the said sadillers presentts … that all such persones … kepe stalls and standyng to gedder In one place … and to pay thar toills,* Wakefield (WCR9/86); 1579 *a lease … of a rowm or standinge in the old wast in the Weddensday market,* Beverley (YRS84/29–30); 1663 *one standinge and one shoppe in the Shambles in Hallifax in the tenure of Henry Crofte* (MD149).

standing bed An alternative form of stand-bed: 1545 *one stondyng bedde withoute clothes,* Harrogate (SS104/47); 1562 *One standing bed with curtings of dornyxe, viijs,* Richmond (SS26/162).

standing piece An upright ornament, or an item of kitchen or tableware, contrasted with 'flat piece': 1482 *shall have my standing pece gilt called a hande haldyng a cope of the facion of an akorne,* Halsham (SS45/280); 1520 *my white standdyng pece to remayne in the place perpetually,* Hull (SS79/117). See also flat piece.

standing stone A large block of stone standing upright. In an exchange of lands in Gilling, in 1540, a description of the boundaries says: *westward bie the heid of a … quarell … vnto the crose of stone standing at Gilling wood heide.* In the survey of those lands was: *At the Standing Stone and Skelbery di. acre erable* (YRS63/42). In 1619–21, the boundary between Wheeldale and Egton has: *Et inde per eandem viam … usque ad lapidem qui dicitur le standing stone [And from there by that way … as far as the stone called the standing stone]* (NRR1/23). In 1722, on the boundary with Lancashire, was a place in Stanbury called *the Standing Stone* (QS4/24/135). It was a common minor place-name in the Pennine landscape but the evidence is almost always late (PNWR8/173). The exception is in Sowerby where references date from the early fifteenth century: 1403 *Standandstoneroyd* (PNWR3/149).

stang (1) A dialect word for a wooden pole or stake: 1379–80 *Et in viij stanges meremij sarrandis [And for sawing 8 timber stangs],* Ripon (SS81/99); 1472 *in viij sparres of fyre, ijs … for j pottyng stang, jd,* York (SS129/71); 1658 *4 balks, 2 stangs,* Selby (YRS47/94); 1718 *had broken open a door with a stang,* Langfield (QS1/58/2); 1728 *the meat hanged upon a stang in the pitt* (QS1/67/10). Specific uses are implicit in 'potting' above, if this not a misreading, and in *nowte* [cattle] *stanges,* recorded in Richmond in 1574 (SS26/249). Used also for the shaft of a cart or pairs of shafts: 1589 *twoo boarded coupes and two payer coupe stanges,* Downholme (YRS152/285). It gave rise to a rare occupational term: 1488 Robert *Boyth, stangmaker,* Sandal (Clay24). See also soe-stang.

In the east of the county it can be compared with 'rod, pole and perch', as a measure when referring to the divisions in the town fields: 1348–9 'a strip of land … called *Fourstanges*', Adlingfleet (YRS120/18); 1431 'two acres of meadow, a *stang less*', York (SS186/106); 1582 *an acre iij stange of wheate*, South Cave (Kaner122); 1595 *three stanges thereof abuttinge towards the easte on the Twyer*, Ganstead (YRS65/73–4). See also soe, tenter.

stang (2), stank A dam or pool. They were often mill dams and served as fish-ponds: 1497 *and ther riotously brak and kit out a stank … and let the water out and also brake the mylnestone … and distroid grete nombre of pykez, bremez, tenchez and other fyssh*. Tockwith (YRS41/18); 1568 *le grete Stank sive stange cum omnibus pooles and watirs ibidem currentibus [the great Stank or stang with all the pools and waters flowing there]*, Steeton near Tadcaster (YAJ38/227); 1615 *hath promised to fornyshe me … with carpes breams and tenshes when he drawes his pond or great stanke*, Brandsby (NYRO44/95); 1633 *All the stancke or dam of the mill*, Myton on Swale (NRQS3/347); 1736 *all dams, stanks, banks, ponds*, Driffield (MD74–5/33). The earliest references are in Latin: 1148–54 *me concessisse abbati et fratribus ecclesie … stangnum suum super terram meam firmare ad piscacionem et molendinum construendum [that I have granted to the abbot and brothers of the church … their stang on my land to farm for fishing and for building a mill]*, Sawley (YRS87/127); 1227 *licenciam et libertatem attachiandi stangnum suum molendini sui … super terram meam [permission and freedom to embank his mill stang … on my land]*, Hunslet (YRS90/72). In his *Ducatus Leodiensis* (1714), the Leeds historian Thoresby wrote of New Hall in Beeston, which adjoins Hunslet: *The ancient Name of this Place was Stank. Which implies its abounding with standing Waters or Pools, Places so situate being frequently so called in these Northern Parts*. See also attach (2).

staple (1) A piece of 'U' shaped metal which had sharp ends so that it could be driven into wood. It is found frequently from an early date, often linked with 'hasp' which points to its use as a fastener for a gate or door: 1371 *Et in haspis et stapils emptis pro berefrido [And for hasps and staples bought for the belfry]*, York (SS35/12); 1394–5 *Item pro j stapill ad hostium [Item for 1 staple for the door]*, Whitby (SS72/606); 1469 *pro ij staples et j crouke*, York (SS192/130). In colliery accounts it occurs independently but in pairs, so it probably referred there to the handles of a corf: 1754 *2 plates for a corf 2d; two staples 2d*, Beeston (WYL160/129/4). See also corf, hesp (2), holdfast, shackle.

staple (2) A word of Old English origin for a post, pillar or column, usually of wood or stone. It was an element in the Yorkshire place-name Stapleton and the thirteenth-century *Altunstapel* (PNWR7/250) and retained this meaning over the centuries: 1619–21 *a crosse in the grounde where sometime was a stoope called the Staple stoope*, Tollerton (NRR1/56). An OED reference shows that it could be used of a steeple, possibly by association, so it may lie behind the place-name 'dumb steeple': 1771 *a Pyramidal Column or Pillar usually called the dumb Steeple*, Grange Moor (KHPN19–20).

starn, stern Early spellings of 'star': 1454 *to Bossall kirke a vestement of rede cloth of gold and the awter cloth thare … and rede cape with starnes of gold* (SS30/176); 1498 *an old vestment of rede sylke … Floured with starnys*, Wakefield (YAJ15/93). It was used particularly for a white marking on a horse's face: 1531 *I witto my said cosing … a blake stag stonyd with a white snype of the snote and a sterne in the forehead*, Kirby Underdale (HKU144); 1578 *a blacke colte with a white starne*, Loversall (YAJ36/451).

start The handle of a broom or vessel: 1380 *unum possenett cum stert*, Durham (SS4/110); 1421–2 'repairing *le Stert* of one *Amphore* for ale', Selby (SAR196); 1445 *j parvum [small] posnet cum le starte*, York (SS30/195); 1486 *the barne pan with a stert*, Hull

(SS53/17); 1562 *A pan with a start, a lyttill pan*, Allerton Mauleverer (SS26/155); 1562 *iij old panes and one start pane iijs* (SS26/163); 1736 *a beesome start*, Baildon (QS1/76/2). A Calverley field had a shape which earned it the name *Frying-pan start* in 1755–60, no. 80 on the map (Th6/xviij). See also started.

started Having a start or handle: 1529 *a hyngyng panne, a startid panne*, Ingmanthorpe (SS79/277).

startover Recorded as a by-name: 1308 *Henry Stirthover*, Alverthorpe (YRS36/171); 1320 *Robert Styrtover*, Doncaster (TWH14/8). The meaning remains uncertain although Reaney suggested it may have been a nickname for a messenger. He had examples also of startout, startaway and startavant [forward], the last of these also in Yorkshire. See also startup.

startup Originally a boot worn by countrymen but applied later to leggings or gaiters: 1517 *Willelmo Robynson famulo meo j par sotularium quæ dicuntur stertuppes [To my servant William Robynson 1 pair of boots called startups]*, Seamer (SS79/83); 1552 *no person … shall ship … over the seas … any shoes, boots, buskins, stertups or slippers* (SAL5/382). The word is found in by-names but the meaning in such cases is not certain: 1278 *William Styrthupe*, Church Fenton, Tadcaster (YRS12/183).

starve To suffer from the cold, to die of cold: 1716 *not quite drowned but starved so that he died soon after he was drawn out of the water*, Kirkby Wharfe (PR); 1782 *was starv'd almost to death in coming from Manchester … he lay a long time insensible and is very poorly*, Slaithwaite (KC242/1); 1798 *I called at Leonard Manfield's and got myself warmed being almost starved and not very well*, Sessay (WM65).

stationer A book-seller or one working in any of the trades connected with books. Not an itinerant vendor but one with a 'station' or shop: 1335 *Adam de Hustwayt, stationer*, York (SS96/30); 1400 *Roberto Hode, stacionar, pro labore suo ijs [To Robert Hode, stationer, for his work 2s]*, Richmond (SS45/21); 1678 *Mr Fugil, Stationer*, Hull (YAJ14/209).

statutes The Statutes, or Statute-sessions, were fairs or gatherings during which servants were hired, and they are said to have had their origin in two early Elizabethan statutes. The customary arrangements involved the chief constables, the petty constables, the masters and the servants: instructions had to be sent out, warrants issued, and a sequence of 'sittings' arranged. The procedures were complicated, but they are explained in detail in 1642 by Henry Best, an East Riding farmer. Things were set in motion he said at the beginning of November and the hirings would usually be completed by Martinmas (Nov.11). A short extract from his farming book gives us some idea of what took place on the day of the fair:

> When yow are aboute to hyre a servant, yow are to call them aside and to talke privately with them concerninge theire wage. If the servants stande in a church-yard, they usually call them aside and walke to the backe of the Church, and their treate of theire wage. And soe soone as yow have hyred them, yow are to call to them for theire ticketts, and thereby shall yow bee secured from all future dainger. Theire ticketts cost them ijd. a peece, and some Masters will give them that ijd. againe, but that is in the Masters choise, unlesse they condition soe before the servant bee hyred Elmswell (DW140).

The 'tickets' referred to by Henry Best were explained as the papers given by masters to their servants as confirmation that they had completed their contracts and were free to be re-engaged. In many cases the bargain was sealed when the servant was given an earnest or god's penny.

The custom may have differed from one region to another. According to Peter Brears the statutes took place 'in all the market towns' of the East Riding on 23 November, and the diarist Arthur Jessop noted that in 1741 *Huddersfield Statutes* were on 21 October (YRS117/65); in 1760 the Wakefield cloth 'frizzer' John Brearley wrote in his memorandum book: *On the 11th of November there is a fair att Wakefild for fatt cowes and bullocks and horses and on the 12th men and women hires themselves.* In the margin he added the words *called stattues,* a spelling influenced by the colloquial form of 'statutes' (YRS155/56). The Fishlake constable wrote in 1689 that he had spent a shilling *goinge to Hatfield stattis* (GRD), a spelling similar to the 'stattice' or country statute recorded in the OED (1847). Peter Brears must have encountered this version of the word very frequently since he described the fairs as the *stattis* or Martinmas hirings (TFY27). In George Eliot's *Adam Bede* the fairs were called 'stattits' (1859).

stave hedge A fence of staves or wooden posts: 1651 *George Clarke ... did unlawfully breake and enter into six roodes of hedgins called a stafe hedge,* Royston (QS1); 1669 *an encroachment of four or five yards in length of a stafe hedge at the back of his quickset,* Leeds (Th26/143). Wright also has 'staff-and-band hedge', defined as a hedge of stakes interlaced with twigs (EDD). See also staver.

staver A form of 'stave', that is a stake of the kind employed in strengthening and repairing hedges: 1572 'Oliver Harpyn, by his servant, has cut down wood, viz. *staffers and 2 loads of hedgewod',* Farnley Tyas (DT/161/13); 1623 *that no person ... take any stauer or stauers out of anye hedge but their owne,* Lepton (DD/WBM); 1701 *for staffers and bindeings for repair of the fence,* Barkisland (HM/E/99).

stay (1) A regional spelling of 'staithe' which captures the dialect pronunciation: 1567 *le comon stay called lee Burges stay ... abutting on the water of Idyll,* Bawtry (YAJ12/108). Bawtry was an important medieval port.

stay (2) Support or maintenance, used in the phrase 'stay of living' in marriage contracts: 1603 *and for some staie of living for John and Anne during the lieff of the said Robert Kaie,* Woodsome (YDK15); 1704 *for their better support and stay of liveing,* Adwalton (MD292/55).

stay (3) As a verb it could mean to be delayed, as by bad weather and floods: 1488 *I wyll thay take in aged folke ... for a neght logyng, or lange, and* [if] *tha be weder sted or seke,* Ingleby Arncliffe (YAJ16/223–4); 1708 *passengers, horsemen as well as footmen must of necessity either stay the falling of the water or else are forced to goe over to the great hazard of their lives,* Buckden (QS1/47/6). More generally it was to prevent, delay, hold back: 1575 *the people will not be staied from ringing the bells on All Saints daie,* Weaverham (PTD65); 1586 *I stayed the suyte I had already commenced against him,* Woodsome (KayeCP); 1688 *took holde of her Apron and staid her,* Rotherham (QS1/27/9). In some contexts the meaning 'hold back' was more threatening: 1670 *he asked who it was ... I answered one that would stay him ... having an iron forke in my hand said unto him ... that I would stab him,* Thurgoland (QS1).

stead Used extensively in compound terms, especially for the site of a building: 1305 *le Kylnestedes,* Flockton (YRS69/56); 1454 *the seid smethystedys ... and mynes of iryn ure,* Farnley (YRS120/64); 1482 *le husthedelandes,* Rowley (MD335); 1517 *two messuagez steddes ... a cottage sted,* Threshfield (YRS140/62); 1546 *a barne stede,* Doncaster (SS91/181); 1590 *a messuage called a meestead,* Dewsbury (YAJ21/454). It later identified places within or close to a dwelling: 1646 *in the dore stead,* Ecclesfield

(PR); 1654 *liberty to lye in the hallstead of the sayd house*, Abbotside (YRS130/61); 1689 *a range fixed in the chimney stead*, Bewerley (QS1/29/1); 1690 *the viccaridge gate stead*, Huddersfield (DD/R/M/3).

It was used also of places within farm buildings, and enclosures attached to them: 1546 *a garden stede*, Doncaster (SS91/181); 1560 '*le Baystede*, one barn … *le Outshutte* … a small part of *le Foldstede*'. Dungworth (TWH26/111); 1572 *grownde to be used for a dongesteade*, Barnbow in Barwick (PR); 1573 *for one middenstead*, Doncaster (YAJ35/302); 1578 *a jettie and a mowsteade in my overbarne*, Newton in Bowland (CS3/7); 1590 *my wief to have the thirde parte, with one stacke stead*, Abbotside (YRS130/17); 1586 'One *le Fronstead* or curtilage', Aiskew (YAJ20/360); 1621 *one fotheringe stead*, Glaisdale (NRQS4/153); 1642 *the staddlestead wheare the stooke stood*, Elmswell (DW54); 1651 *a sufficient Yate stead being a common way in a place called Hurwood Yate* (NRQS1/201); 1711 *a milking stead*, Kirkby Malzeard (MD16).

Localities associated with water mills or access to water include: 1472 'a parcel of land called *le Damestede*', Wombwell (YRS63/145); 1507 *as myche coste of mendyng of the watteryng-stede as men goys to the Dringhowses*, York (YAJ22/282); 1579 *one wearesteade in the side of the becke*, Dewsbury (YAJ21/408); 1604 *a passable foard or wath-stead for cart and carriage*, Topcliffe (NRQS3/47). See also dial stead, gapstead, lair (2), marketstead, nawtmarket, stack.

steal A wooden handle or shaft: 1520 *a lytell brasyn skelett with a stele*, Mount Grace (YAJ18/296); 1570–80 *For mending the masons towles in ther worke and for style to them, 4s 3d … For mending and styling four chesells*, York (SS35/117); 1639 *Rakes and rake steals*, Swinsty (YRS134/91); 1695 *a fire shovel steyll*, West Riding (QS4/17). In 1712, small amounts of wood at Cawthorne were used for *Punchwood* and … *Besom stales* (OC8). See also start.

steaner A piece of land within an oxbow, formed by a change in the course of a river: 1562 *a close called Steaner or Steyner … on the north side of the river Calder alleged to be abrupted and ryven by violence of the river … from certain grounds the inheritance of Sir George Savile*, Southowram (DD/SR/10/99). The land would at one time have been formed of sand and stones and the origin is likely to be Old English *stæner*: 1494 'a close of land called the *Steynour* lying between the water of *Keldre* and a close called *Wydkynrode*', Mirfield (KM150); 1581 *one parcell of lande and water Contayneinge by estimacion one acre or thereabowtes Commonly callid a steanor adioyninge and lienge alongest the sowth syde of the Callder*, Kirklees (KM431); 1608 'certain parcels of land called *le Stayner* lying between *Thornes* and *Dirtcarr*, the ancient course of water there and to whom *le Stayner* belonged … and who ought to make fences from the water' (WCR11/10); 1649 *a banck or sandbed neare to the said bridge … did hinder the straight Current of the … Calder … to Cutt the said banck sandbed or stayner through*, Horbury (QS10/2/248).

Place-names testify to a much longer history and a related meaning associated with land by mill dams: 1292 *le Steenre, Damheuedsteenre*, Rothwell (PNWR2/145); 1333 'Henry *Presteman* … says Richard [son of John Huddeson] wrongfully seized 8 of his cattle in a certain place called *Stenner* in Horbury' (WCR3/201); 1699 *Mr Fenton Mil Steaner*, Aire (Th9/193). The huge bend in the river Ouse at Stainer near Selby suggests that this twelfth-century place-name may commemorate an ancient steaner.

As the use of the term declined and the meaning became less transparent the spellings were more variable, and the acquisition of a final 'd' helped transform some 'stennards' or 'stannards' into Stone Yards: 1665 '4 closes of arable meadow or pasture commonly called *Stannardwells*', Horbury (WCR5/66); 1731 *she had stacked coal upon the Stenard at Wakefield* (QS10/16/146); 1800 *Stoneyard, Lower Stoneyard,*

Linthwaite (OWR1/1/25–9); 1838 *Stone Yard*, Honley (M). See also cringle, stonery, and NH77–80.

stee A north-country word for a ladder, noted in counties where Scandinavian influence was strong: 1522 *paid for a ste to the kirk, xvij^d*, York (CCW88); 1559 *two longe stiis*, Castleford (Th27/287); 1561 *Item 3 stees or Ladders*, Spaldington (YRS134/10); 1563 *Thre stees alias ledders*, Knayton (SS2/207); 1596 *Item Fyve stees Longer and shorter*, Knaresborough (YRS134/61). See also nawgur, stee-room.

steel The word dates from the Old English period and in many of the earliest references it is linked with iron. Chaucer wrote of arrows that were made of gold: 'sharpe for to kerven weel But iren was ther noon ne steel'. Steel is actually a general term for several alloys of iron and carbon that have been produced artificially so as to have greater hardness and elasticity: this makes them more suitable for industrial purposes and the production of edge tools.

It is difficult to define the word in the early period, for steel was being made in different places using different methods. A Hallamshire account book records the arrival in 1574 of *vj Barrells of Steele … Layd in the stawre howse at Sheffield Castle* (MD192): this cargo had been imported from the Continent via Bawtry. Even in the mid-1600s, Britain still lagged behind several other European countries in its manufacture, and relied heavily on imports. That began to change once the cementation method had been introduced, and Huntsman's invention of crucible or cast steel finally helped Sheffield to become the steel capital of Europe. The product there was more uniform in composition and freer from impurities than any steel previously produced.

steele A regional spelling of stile, that is a passage over or through a fence: 1572 'that they make and maintain *le stele apud tofte gap*', Farnley Tyas (DT/161); 1583 *Arthur Beeston shall set a steele at Rawcroft head under payne of 3s 4d*, Ilkley (CHT126); 1648 *timber for carts and yeates and steeles*, Meltham (G-A). It is an element in minor place-names such as Steel Bank (Ecclesall) and Steel Lane (Barkisland): the latter is likely to be linked to 'the messuage called *Stelerode*', held by the Woodhead family in 1448 (YRS39/12): in 1465 there was 'a meadow called *le steledoyle*' in Rowley near Lepton (YDK52). In 1884, the Rev. Lewthwaite of Newsome near Almondbury wrote in the chuch magazine: *leaving Steel Common, now commonly called Stile Common*. See also kirk steele.

steelmaker An occupational term which occurs infrequently in early Sheffield records: 1700 *Georgius Ball steelmaker* (PR5/65).

steem To bespeak something, a regional word: 1674 *thy father went to John Walker's to steime a pare of shooes, and he would not let him have them without he had money in his hand … Likewise he went to George Coppley's to steime a wastcoate cloth*, Denby (SS40/210). It is likely to be a spelling of 'steven' which could have the same meaning (EDD).

steep-fat A vessel in which brewers steeped malt, possibly made of wood originally: 1377 *2 stepyngfattes*, Hackness (YRS76/129); 1438 *ij plumbaria [2 leaden vessels], j Stepefatt, ij Relyngfattes*, Sherburn in Elmet (Th33/45); 1522 *I wytt that John Derluff, my son, have … a stepefatt with the kylnehayres*, Knaresborough (SS104/16). A leaden vessel with the same function was usually called a steep-lead, but not always: 1376 *do et lego j stepeled Alicie [I give and bequeath 1 steep-lead to Alice]*, Ripon (SS115/34); 1419 *Item j stepeled 24s*, Ripon (SS81/142); 1542 *Item a steyp fat of leed*, Bedale (SS26/30); 1545 *on seystern of leyd for stepyng of maulte*, Brettanby (SS26/56). In a York indenture of 1338 is a reference to '*le Malthous* with a piece of ground on which the *stepeleder* is usually placed'. The editor speculated whether this was for 'stepladder', otherwise first recorded in 1751 (OED), but the lessee was a skinner, so it is possibly where leather was 'steeped' (YRS111/183). See also steep-house.

steep-headed Of uncertain meaning but used of an animal, possibly one with an upright or high forehead: 1617 *one stepeheaded black oxe hide 20s*, Huddersfield (DD/RA/f/4a).

steep-house A building where the steeping of malt could take place: 1444 *j cisternam ad ordium stantem in le stipehouse [1 vat for steeping barley in the steep-house]*, Beverley (SS30/99). See also steep-fat.

steer A young ox, especially one which has been castrated: 1607 *did drive at Steresby 8 oxen 15 kyne one bull & 7 steares* (NYRO44/42); 1623 *6 young beasts, 4 of them steares and 2 whyes*, Elmswell (DW173); 1644 *1 steare, 1 quye*, Lepton (HM/C/180). Modern glossaries say that a steer hide shows 'a tight grain structure' which makes it an ideal choice for leather upholstery. Since it is distinguished from other hides in early accounts it is likely that its distinctive qualities were recognised by tanners in earlier centuries: 1617 *my black steare hide xxvijs vid*, Almondbury (DD/RA/f/4a); 1645 *20 country steer hides and 50 cow hides*, Kirkheaton (YRS18/44). In the cordwainers' ordinances in Beverley its quality was recognised: 1627 'nor into the outer sole any other leather than the best of the ox or steer hide' (YRS84/79). See also segg.

stee-room The owner of a house was often granted the right to place a ladder on ground which adjoined his property, so that he might carry out necessary repairs. This was originally referred to as 'stee room' and then as ladder room as the use of dialect in official documents declined: 1539 *we say that William Mawncell shall challenge no ground bot to sett A steye to messe or Amend his bildyngs at reasonable tymes*, Ossett (WCR9/122); 1589 *shall permit John Parkyn to sett steys or ladders in his fold for the repayringe of his houses*, Meltham (MD63/A6); 1656 *1 slated barne or laithe below Kilnsaye nether yeat together with a stee room … or sufficient roome for setting up a stee or ladder in the garth*, Kilnsey (MD247). Quite often the space allowed would be explicit: 1600 *one ladder or stee roome at the sowthe end of the house being threequarters of a yard onlie for the theaking of the same*, Malham (RMM23). See also ladder room.

steeve To compress, to make tight or solid: 1695 *Old widow Banks … was busy making hen meat, bid a lasse stieve it while she did somewhat else*, Northowram (OH2/180). In the following reference it was probably for 'stained': 1489 *one frontall, one steuened clothe, and ij lynyn clothes*, Hornby (SS53/41).

steg A gander: 1563 *two gese, a stegg, sixe hennes and a cock 4s*, Clint (YRS55/93); 1570 *vij geyse and steygs, price iijs*, Hutton Conyers (SS26/229); 1581 *one stege & iij gesses with x geselines iiijs*, South Cave (Kaner113); 1682 *4 gese, 1 stege 4 henses & 1 coke*, Brayton (YRS47/53); 1727 *one stegg was taken out of the place where his geese sits*, Pontefract (QS1/66/4). On the Leeds-Liverpool canal Lock 35 is named Stegneck, no doubt 'borrowed' from the field in Gargrave so called (PNWR6/54). Nearby in Addingham is Stegg Holes recorded in the tithe award of 1844. See also goose, stag (2).

stell A north Yorkshire word for a dike or open drain: 1651 *the inhabitants of Pottoe, Traineham and East Rownton for not scouring their proportion of Traineham Stell … for not making a sufficient horsebridg over Traineham Stell* (NRQS5/76). It could also be a place on a stream or river where fish were netted: c.1362 'ancient fisheries … called *Byshopstelles* … the fourth is called *Hudstell*', Cawood (WYAS747). See also stelling.

stelling Sometimes a place of shelter for animals, but in this minor place-name possibly a location where salmon could be netted: *c.*1570 *knowithe a plase … callide Marrigge stelling … the saide damme callide Marrige stelling dubbe* (YAJ6/283). See also stell.

stengraft One example noted, either a right to dig for stone or a place where stone might be quarried: 1370 'he may dig in the turbary called *Stengraft* … to maintain his household', Gristhorpe (YRS120/86). See also flawgraft, turf-graft.

–ster Historically this was predominantly a feminine suffix, as in spinster, but it was widely used in Yorkshire in occupational terms for both men and women; 1297 *Thomas le Wollestere*, Sowerby (YRS29/291); 1301 *De Ada Dreyster*, Hunton (YRS21/103); 1379 *Johannes Thekester*, Clint; *Thomas Waddester*, Painley (PTWR). In the place-name Colsterdale, where coal was mined from the fourteenth century at least, the first element may be a form of 'coler' or collier. See also tippler.

sterlings The protective piling round the piers of a bridge, driven into the river bed. The meaning is clear but the origin and early history of the word are obscure. The OED headword is 'starling': 1739 *to contract with such workmen … for the making of sterlings or frames round the main pillars of the said bridge*, Yarm (NRQS8/229).

stern See starn.

sterneld A popular name for cows which had a white patch on the forehead: 1486 *a cowe called Sternelld, with calfe*, Felixkirk (YAJ22/204); 1545 *to John Hogson one quye called Stornylde*, Featherstone (Th19/140); 1546 *ij kie, the one called sterneld and the other Browne*, Great Preston (Th19/184); 1553 *to my said sonne … one gray nague and one cowe called sternelde*, Wakefield (Th19/332); 1677 *an heifer or qui called Starnill*, Batley (YRS74/73). See also flowereld, raggled, spangled, starn, taggle, and NH144–9.

steven It has several related meanings in northern dialects, of which one is 'an assembly, a gathering, an appointment' (EDD) and that may explain the following manorial order: 1593 'that no man be involved on the sabbath in *lez goose eatinges, pigge eating … steavens sive helpales*', Slaithwaite (M/SL).

stew A place where fish can be readily caught, a dam, moat or pond. In 1603, the lease of the manor of Skerne included rights to the *ponds and stews and closes* (MD74–5/309).

stick (1) A measure of quantity used for eels, twenty-five according to some writers, a term noted as early as 1086: 1394–6 *Item pro iiii styk browet eyl iis iiiid … ii styk rostyng eyls*, Whitby (SS72/624). See also stick-eel.

stick (2) This verb occurs three times in the accounts of Farnley colliery: 1692 *for gate stickeinge and dressing*; 1695 *for the end sticking; and for sticking the drif* [sic] *4d* (MS11). The meaning is unclear but the reference may be to placing sticks or props of wood in the galleries. It was said in 1933, by a member of the Yorkshire Dialect Society, to mean 'to channel' (YDS34/20) but more evidence is needed.

stick (3) To stab with a knife, to kill by stabbing: 1669 *Thomas Walker threatened to stick him, meaning to take away his life*, Thornhill (QS1); 1672 *the black lamb … broke its neck and he did stick it with a penknife*, Purston Jaglin (QS1). It occurred much earlier in by-names: 1296 *Walter Stikebuc*, Ripon (YRS31/44); 1355 *Et predict Radus … dicit quod … predict Steph plus est cognit per illud agnomen Stykebich [hind] quam per illud agnomen fil Thom [And the aforesaid Ralf … says that … the aforesaid Stephen is known by the name*

Stykebich which name his son Thomas (is also known)], Aldborough (YAJ31/66). Evidently these names commemorated the killing of deer, possibly unwelcome nicknames.

stick–eel The 'stick' was a quantity of eels, although in later references 'stick-eels' may have been the smaller fish (OED). Numbers of eels were often part of tenancy agreements: 1417 *pro ij mesuagiis cum uno crofto duobus bovatis terre … viij centenis anguillarum vocatis stykell vel xvjs [for 2 dwellings with a croft two bovates of arable land … 7 hundredweight of eels called stick-eels or 16s]*, Stork, Beverley (SS108/321).

stick leathers A term of uncertain meaning which occurs quite frequently in documents relating to tanners: 1541 *ij styk lethers dighted and half a hydd ixs*, Knaresborough (SS104/35); 1589 *to John Wislon* [sic] *one hyde and a litle sticklether* York (YRS138/82); 1622 *Item 3 sticke lethers, 7 calfe skines xjs vjd*, Cottingley (LRS1/62); 1660 *16 hides, 4 sticklethers, 3 veal skins & a foale skinne £16*, Selby (YRS47/170). It is possible that 'stick' was a reference to rolls of leather but in these typical contexts it seems more likely to have been a type of skin. In Selby, the tanner John Titlow had *6 stick lethers in the baite* in 1660; that is immersed in an alkaline solution, a pre-tanning process. See also bate (1).

stiffen To make the soil heavier, a verb used in Stovin's manuscript of husbandry practices in the Levels in the early eighteenth century:

> *c.1745 Industrious farmers began to manure the Levil Land with Lyme … they spread it with Shovels … and they often mix Sand or Ashes or Light Earth with it … this Lyme Destroys the worms or Grubs … and stiffens their Land*, Hatfield (ERAS12/49–50).

stillatory A still, a vessel used for distillation: 1463 *j par de wafryirins, j stellatory et j ollam [1 pair of wafer irons, 1 stillatory and 1 pot]*, Leeds (SS30/259); 1508 *a marbyll stone with a styllytorie for aqua vitæ*, York (SS53/275); 1548 *a stillitorie that is in my parlor*, Bishop Burton (SS106/274); 1567 *A stylletorye and a salt fishe arke, iijs*, Richmond (SS26/197). See also limbeck.

stillingfleet nails Almost certainly nails purchased at Stillingfleet where 'stubs' were on sale in the same period: 1539–40 *Item for di. Mˡ of styllyngflet dubyll spykynges, xviijᵈ*, York (CCW215n). See also thornhill nails.

stilt (1) The handle of a plough: *c.1570 plowbeams, great stiltes, lytil stiltes*, Woodsome (KayeCP); 1648 *certaine plow stilts & harrowtines*, Sharlston (YRS134/99). See also plough.

stilt (2) A crutch or long thin pole, possibly a walking aid in this early by-name: 1291 'by agreement … of *Agnes-with-the-Stilte*, his late sister', York (YRS12/128). The following name may have originated as a pejorative nickname: 1472 *Richard Styltbayne*, Scampston (YRS6/161). See also bain.

stint As a noun this was an allotted number or amount: 1541–2 'no husbandman shall … keep more than two geese and one gander or a *gresseman* more than one goose and one gander … for each goose beyond *le stynt* … 4d', Scruton (YRS39/149); 1584 *to goo and depastour … wytheout stynt or number*, Tong (Tong/8b/1); 1660 *Noe person shall putt more goods into the Meanefield then their stinte*, South Crosland (DD/WBR/2/17). It was also used as a verb with reference to common pastures: 1599–1600 *The stinted pastures be all stinted after the ancient rent*, Settrington (YRS126/13); 1670 *on the west stinting of the Wetlands of Thirske* (NRQS4/143). Used occasionally of the pasture itself:

1668 *such parte of that stent and pasture belonging to Hebden called Hebden Pasture* (MD87).
See also tether.

stirk The meaning could differ regionally and chronologically, but generally it
meant a bullock or heifer up to two years old: 1292 *In equis, bovettis et stircis cxvijs
vjd [For horses, steers and stirks 117s 6d]*, Bolton Priory (YRS154/44); 1346 *lego Elenæ
de Lathum iiijs et unum stirk [I bequeath to Helen de Lathum 4s and a stirk]*, Sutton on
Derwent (SS4/19); 1446–58 *iij twynters j sterke j vacca*, Fountains Abbey (SS130/123);
1524 *certain styrkes delivered to the Cellerar of Fontance … and seyn the burning of the
same*, Kirkby Malzeard (YRS114/5); 1607 *with ten stirkes coming out of the calfe close*,
Airton (DDMa). It was not unusual for the sex and age of the animal to be made
clear: 1548 *to the saide Henrie Waddisworthe an oxe stirke*, Halifax (Crossley28); 1551
6 stirk milk kye prised to £6, Marske (YRS152/81); 1607 *7 yearing stirkes*, Brandsby
(NYRO44/42). It remained active in the farmers' vocabulary: 1816 *Jany 7th Stirk bulled
at John Roberts*, South Crosland (GRD). Stirk is a well-established Yorkshire surname
and the by-name provides an early example of the word: 1275 *Ricardus Styrke*, Sandal
(YRS29/52). See also nawt, quy-stirk, strike (2), and GRDict.

stirket Technically a diminutive of stirk but the evidence suggests that it may have
had the same meaning: 1312–13 *Pro viij stirkettis emptis de executor(ibus) magistri Ade
de Hertford et venditis xvjs [For 8 stirkets bought from master Adam de Hertford's executors
and sold 16s]*, Bolton Priory (YRS154/335); 1456–7 *j stirkett vs iiijd*, Fountains Abbey
(SS130/19); 1485 *x stirkettes precii unius iijs viijd [10 stirkets each priced at 3s 8d]*, Ripon
(SS64/372). See also staggett, sturdy.

stirk house A farm building where stirks were housed: 1675 *One Cow one Heiffer
and Two Stirkes at the new House £12; Foure Kine at the stirke House £16*, Admergill
(YRS118/66). In 1301, Rievaulx Abbey had property *apud Stirkhous* on which taxes
were paid (YRS21/56). A fine seventeenth-century hall in Ribblesdale has the name
Stirk House: 1550–1 *Laurence Lyster of Stirkhowse … gentleman*, Gisburn (SS106/306).

stithy An anvil: a word with an Old Norse origin which is on record from *a*.1295
(OED). Examples are frequent in Yorkshire from the fourteenth century: 1374 *lego
Willielmo consanguineo meo unum magnum stythy [I bequeath to my kinsman William a great
stithy]*, York (SS4/92); 1445 *Johanni Ulron, unum stethy de ferro [to John Ulron, an iron
stithy]*, York (SS30/116); 1510 *2 stythes … all oder smithy gere*, Ecclesfield (PR); 1600
all my geare and toyles in the smythye except my stythye, Cottingley (LRS1/1). The will
of Hugh Sponer of Sheffield in 1539 suggests that some cutlers had much of their
capital tied up in anvils for he made bequests of six *stethies* and they were all in the
separate 'occupation' of local men (TWH13/66–7). The anvils used by different kinds
of smith had a variety of names and some of these are dealt with under bighorn,
bolster, crooked stithy, cutting stithy, and sparrow-hawk: additional names found in
the Hallamshire cutlery trade include: 1692 *7 box Stythies*; 1701 *one sow metle stithy*
(FBH121–7). See also planish, swaging stithy.

stithy stock This was a stand for an anvil, and originally it will have been a solid
block of wood, a section of a large tree. Such a block was noted for a *stythistok* at
Scarborough in 1284 (SZ1/347). Later, some 'stocks' were of metal. In 1689, Francis
Brownell's possessions included a *Stithie and Stock* and in 1734 John Fearnally had a
Stiddy Stock, Sheffield (IH). See also stock (1).

stob A short thick nail, probably a variant or cognate of 'stub': 1578 *Item payed for
a hundredth plow stobbs iiijd*, Stockeld (YRS161/43); 1580 *wayne clowtes & a C stobes*,
Stockeld (YRS161/19).

stock (1) The stump of a tree; the part left standing when a tree has been felled. It occurs commonly as a place-name element, some of them dating from the twelfth century (PNWR7/251). It was used as a prefix, e.g. Stockbridge, Stockwell, and as a suffix, e.g. Hagstock (PNWR7/251). Several such localities were minor settlements, close to or in woodland clearances, whereas others such as Stockbridge and Stockwell more probably point to the use of timber in the construction of bridges, floodgates, wells, and the like. See also goit stock, shuttle, stithy stock, stock bridge.

stock (2) In connection with bees it was usually a swarm but it may occasionally have been a reference to the hive or a wooden block on which the hive was placed: 1500 *to my parish kirke on old stok of bees with a swarm*, Bishopthorpe (SS53/174); 1600 *I geve to Anne … one old winter stocke of bees*, Knaresborough (SS104/223). See also bee-stock.

stock (3) A term found in the inventories of clothiers which referred to card stocks and comb stocks, dealt with separately. The will of John Haigh of Binn in Marsden has: 1697 *Item stocke Cardes and Litel Cards and paire of Lomes* (BIA). See also card stock, comb.

stock bridge A common term or minor place-name in Yorkshire, with examples from the twelfth century: 1166 *Stochebrige*, Arksey (PNWR1/25). A 'stock' could be a post, a log or a tree trunk (OED) but its exact meaning in this compound is not certain. Smith said of some of these names that they were bridges 'made of logs' and of others that they were made 'from a tree trunk', but these could have been quite different types of structure. In any case, the early dates invite a comparison with fleak bridge, rise bridge, stone bridge and trowbridge, providing us with a range of possible generic terms in the Middle Ages.

stockfish Cod or ling, split open and cured without salt, dried in the wind and sun. It came principally from Norway and Iceland and was imported into Hull and Scarborough from a very early date: 1305–6 *c stockfische vii^li ix^s ix^d*, Bolton Priory (YRS154/196); 1446–58 *In expensis Rad. Snayth versus Hull pro … stokfysch [For Ralph Snayth's expenses in going to Hull for … stockfish]*, Fountains Abbey (SS130/111); 1510 *of ylke hundredth stokfysshe jd*, York (YRS106/33).

stockfishmonger A dealer in stockfish, possibly with trading links between London and provincial towns: 1527 *Thomas Ilderton, citezen and Stokfishmonger*, Chigwell and Alnwick (SS116/280). In 1542, a Nottinghamshire man called Leonard Johnson who died in London was also described in his will as *citezen and stockfisshemonger* (SS116/288). Ekwall noted the by-name and occupation in London in 1308 (EE25).

stocks An obsolete instrument of punishment which consisted of two adjustable planks of wood set one over the other, with holes at the junction to confine a seated prisoner's ankles: 1619 *That the inhabitants … shall forthwith … make a paire of Stockes for the punishing of rogues*, Gunnerside (NRQS2/196); 1653–4 *for not making a sufficient pair of stocks*, Theakston (NRQS5/150). In a violent, early sixteenth-century dispute, the stocks at Sutton in Craven were destroyed by one of the parties involved:

> c.1522 *one Hugh Blakey … with an axe dyd cut at peces the stokes made and ordined by the inhabitants of Sutton … for the punishment of vacabondes and beggers … and dyd cast great peces of them in to the fyre* (YRS41/86).

See also timber (1).

stock well Not uncommon as a minor place-name but not a recognised word in the vocabulary. It occurs several times in Yorkshire, for example: *a*.1189 *Stockewell furlangs*, Denby (SS208/82); 1334 *Stokwelleynge*, Ardsley (TWH30/56); 1401 *Stockwell Lane*, Hedon (PNER40); 1637 *the Stockwell Greene*, Sheffield (HSMS116). The precise meaning is not clear but the probability is that the 'stock' was some kind of timber framework for a well, perhaps in the shaft of a draw well: 1751 *John Robinson … was sinking a well at Hunsingore and had occasion for some old wood to make well stocks* (QS1/90/4).

stomacher In the context noted it was probably a waistcoat, of the type worn by men: 1720 *stole a stomacher lapped in a riding hood*, West Riding (QS1/59/8).

stone As a verb it described the actions of poachers who sought to stun or kill fish by hurling stones into a confined stretch of water: 1693 *I see severall persons … stoneing the water for catching and destroying of fish … see William Holden with heapes of stones … to throw into the river to beat the salmon out*, Timble (QS1).

stone-blind Blind as a stone; that is completely blind. The OED has 'stane-blynde' in Scotland *c*.1375 and occasional examples in England from 1591. In Yorkshire, a witness in a Star Chamber case gave evidence of an assault upon her by several men: *c*.1535 *wiche grevoslye and riotoslye dyd stryk and wound your said poer orratrix in here hede, so as she … is now at this day ston blynde*, Sharlston (YRS41/52). I have noted one further example: 1711 *a poor old man stone blind and above 80 years of age*, Rotherham (QS1/50/7).

stone-bow A kind of catapult or cross-bow, used for shooting stones: 1613 *with my lesser stonebowe & mowldes*, Brandsby (NYRO44/73); 1632 *one morter, one stonebow and one gavelocke*, Ripley (YRS55/115); 1656 *a muskett and a stone bowe*, Eshton (YRS134/116); 1667 *one fowling peice … two Carbines, one stone Bowe*, North Bierley (YRS134/125).

stone-brag A type of nail, possibly an alternative of 'stone-brod': 1580 *Item payd for stonebrages and spykyns for mendinge the hay barne*, Stockeld (YRS161/23). See also brag.

stone-breaker In several bridge contracts there are references to workmen 'breaking' stone, a term which seems to have a straightforward meaning. The OED entries for 'break' do not link the word with 'masoncraft' and it is presumably excluded for the reasons given there in the preliminary note. The examples quoted here suggest that 'breaking stone' may have had a more precise meaning than at first appears, defining just one of several distinctive practices, for which three fourteenth-century by-names are the evidence: 1327–8 *Roger le Stonhewer*, Stannington (TWH20/12); 1348 *John le Stonebrekar*, Holmfirth (WCR2/26); 1350 *Adam Staynwright*, Holmfirth (WCR2/214). These seem to represent three different phases in the preparation and use of stone for building purposes; that is 'breaking', 'hewing' and 'working'. These were different tasks and they required different skill levels, which may have been reflected in the rates of pay: 1322 *in stipendio vnius Cementarii & vnius hominis lapidos in quarrera frangentis & eosdem in dicto stagno cubantis [for the pay of one mason and one man breaking stones in the quarry and laying them in the said mill dam]*, Leeds (Th45/88). There were no doubt times when a mason had to cross the boundaries: when Thomas Kidd was contracted *c*.1690 to build a shippon at Conistone he was *to breake all the greet Stone … & to hew one doore* (RW28).

The distinctions appear to be borne out by the terms of the Kirkstall Bridge contract of 1619 which referred to *the breaking, hewing and workinge of the severall sorts of stones thereto belonginge, after theise severall rates* (BAS6/147). A later paragraph records the *confesion of the Stonebreaker that he hath received xij^li*. In 1422, it was agreed that the masons building Catterick Bridge should have free entry to two specified quarries *for to brek the stane that schalle go to the said brigge*. The occupation of stone-breaker would have been even older, and the wage accounts for Bolton Priory in 1296–7 contain the entry *Et cuidam fractori lapidum iijs vjd [And to that stone breaker 3s 6d]* (YRS154/71). Similarly, payments were made to several stone-breakers in York, for example: 1399 *Et in fractura lapidum per Johannem Waryn per xv sept. et iij dies, cap. 18d. per sept [And for stone breaking by John Waryn for 15 weeks and 3 days, he taking 18d per week]* (SS35/14). In the *Kirkstall Abbey Coucher Book* is a reference to a tenant called *Walter Stanhewer* in an undated memorandum of *c*.1200 (Th8/76).

stone bridge The Catterick Bridge contract of 1422 was for *a brigge of stane oure the watir of Swalle*, one with three arches, to replace *the olde stane brigge* (NRQS3/33): Lady's Bridge *over the watyr of Dune* in 1486 was *a Brygge of ston* with five arches (HS1/59). These were not the earliest stone structures in the county, for the Ripon place-name *Staynebriggegate* is on record from the very early thirteenth century (SS74/60). The street led to a stone bridge across *Skyteryk*, a sewer which flowed into the Ure east of the town (SS74/62). In fact, there were stone bridges in York and on monastic sites even earlier. Once stones had been worked by the masons they were valuable and it is noticeable that accounts often include a reference to recovering them from the river after a bridge had been damaged: 1616 *getting stones oute of the water*, Kirkstall (BAS6/147). See also skitterick.

stone-brod A wooden nail or peg for fixing stone slates, a slate-pin: 1351 *Et pro iiijm stonbrod' emptis pro eisdem domibus faciendis et cooperiendis cum petris iiijs vjd [And for buying 4000 stone-brods for building those houses and roofing them with stones 4s 6d]*, Dewsbury (YAJ21/381); 1391–2 *Et in v^ml Dcc. stanebrodd' emp. pro dicto stauro [And for buying 5700 stone-brods for the said store]*, Ripon (SS81/110); 1419–20 *Et in vj mil. stanbrod emt. in festo Philippi et Jacobi, 7s 9d [And for 6000 stone-brods bought on the feast of St. Philip and James, 7s 9d]*, Ripon (SS81/145); 1450 *et iiijMDlx stanebrod, precii M' xvj d [and 4560 stone-brods, cost per 1000 16d]*, York (SS192/66); 1543–4 *xix.m stone broddes, 19s*, York (SS35/111); 1615 *2000 stone brod nayles, 2000 latt nayles*, Brandsby (NYRO44/97); 1705 *thre hundred of stone brods and nales*, Methley (Th11/279). See also brod.

stone coal A term for any hard variety of coal, especially anthracite (OED): 1690 *the stone at 4s 6d a yard and the rest at 3s 4d a yard*; 1710 *began at Moore to sinke at the Stone Coale*, Farnley (MS11); 1819 *a bed of stone coal about 20 yds from the surface which is four feet thick*, Birstall (DD/CA/5). See also cannel.

stoned Of a horse, entire, not castrated: 1520 *to my yonger son ... a fole to be a stoned horse*, Fewston (SS104/12); 1563 *I give ... a graie stoned horse to serve the towneshippe for ever*, Thruscross (SS104/93); 1639 *Item one Stond horse £7 0 0*, Swinsty (YRS134/92); 1664 *as for scabed horses or stonde horses on our Common wee have none*, Wadsworth (WCR5/134). See also stag (1), snip (2).

stone-delf A small stone quarry: 1538 *James Mawde for a stone delfe in the hyeway for to be amendyd*, Ovenden (WCR9/90); 1651 *Thomas Brooke ... doe paine John Beamond ... to fill up the delfe on the Hollinwellgreene ... because that the last Stones that was gotten ... was by the apountment of John Beamond*, Halifax (WCR8/171). See also ironstone, slate-stone, stone-pit. Stone Delves in Huddersfield gave rise to a place-name before 1553 (HPN132).

stone fence In use quite late for a stone wall: 1770 *the House ... walled with a good Stone Fence*, Slaithwaite Chapel terrier (IMF). Probably a dry-stone wall: 1779 *have got*

Stone Lying upon the said parcel of Waste ground wherewith to inclose the same ... give to my said Brother William the said stone and Fences already made, Slaithwaite (IMF).

stone-getter Sometimes a man who mined iron-stone rather than one who worked in a quarry: *c.*1573 *our charges for our smythies came to the some of £40 10s 10d which we have discharged, viz. for smithy geare and to the stone geaters,* Honley (KayeCP); 1568 *For iren stone to the lorde of the so[i]le for everye lode wyche ys 6 kettes 3d, and to the getteres for a lode 12d,* Esholt (BAS10/246). It was also used of a quarryman: 1651 *Richard Hanson, stone getter,* Halifax (WCR8/171); 1654 *given to the stone getters ... to drink ... and give them earnest for millstones, 5s* (HP). See also get, stone-delf.

stone hammer A mason's hammer: 1389 *unum stanhamyr de ferro [a stone hammer made of iron],* York (SS4/130).

stone-hewer See stone-breaker.

stone lath See latt.

stone-pit A small quarry: 1664 *wee lay in paine John Longbottom that hee fill up two stone pitts neare the highway on the wast,* Northowram (WCR5/142); 1786 *Cuddy with 3 Horses leading Wall Stone undrest from Stone pit,* Slaithwaite (KC242/1). It gave rise to a number of minor place-names (PNWR8) and some East Riding examples date from the twelfth century: 1190–1220 *Stainpittes,* North Dalton (ERPN168). See also stone-delf.

stonery A place where stones could be quarried, specifically those regions in lower Airedale and Wharfedale where limestone boulders could be extracted from glacial deposits: 1619 *all manner of mines of coals ... stonearyes or slate,* Austby (YRS65/20); 1629 *all that Stonerye of Lymestone,* Addingham (GRD); 1685 *quarries of stone and stonaries,* Austby (YRS65/21). It was used occasionally instead of 'steaner': 1717 *For making a getty in the water and cutting a cutt through the stonery 4 yds broad to be wear'd on each side,* Hampsthwaite (QS11/57/8). See also steaner and GRYD23–4.

stone-wright See stone-breaker.

stook A regional word for a shock of corn, that is twelve sheaves: 1598 *gleanynge of Corne amongst the stowkes in Harvest tyme,* West Riding (YRS3/87); 1612 *for stealing a stowke of rye value 2s 4d,* Tanton (NRQS1/243). In 1642, Henry Best wrote: *A good shearer will sheare constantly 10 stookes of Winter-corne in a day ... it is usuall for one man to binde and stooke after 6 or 8 shearers ... stookers have (for the most parte) viijd a day,* Elmswell (DW45,50).

stoop A pillar or post, usually of wood or stone: 1463 *for a newe stowpe to the grate yates 10d,* Bubwith (SS35/134); 1553 *againste the stowpe of the stall which was sett harde in the grounde,* Terrington (YAJ37/167); 1626 *for setting stowpes and rales in the arch of a woodden bridge near Sowerby Milne,* Thirsk (NRQS3/259); 1650 *did pull and afterwards broke ... two rayless and six stoopes out of a foote wooden bridge,* Huddersfield (QS4/3). At Kirkstall, in 1686, it was ordered that *stoopes of wood or stone* be set in the sides of a causey *to guide persons when the water is high and to keep waynes, Carts and Carryages from destroying the said Cawsey* (QS1). It was used occasionally as a verb: 1607 *the inhabitants in Acome to stoupe and rayle their several lands* (YRS137/282). See also lead stoop, stulp.

stooth (1) A stud, that is a short piece of timber, particularly such as were used for the uprights in a timber-framed house: 1284 '27 *stodes,* 14 ft in length', Scarborough (SZ1/205); 1434–5 'for *stothes* ... for the house', Selby (SAR246); 1446 *vj quercus ...*

pro les stothes grangiæ et les screnes et ostiis [6 oaks ... for the barn's stooths and the partitions and doors], Beverley (ERAS6/78); 1582 *iiij plough heads iij stothes a molde borde balkes*, South Cave (Kaner122); 1658 *severall deales and stoothes*, Selby (YRS47/94); 1739 *90 yards of stoothing for the petitions* [sic for partitions] *at 1s a yard*, West Riding (QS1).

stooth (2) An obsolete spelling of stud, that is the ornamental studs on a belt or girdle. Used as a verb and noun: 1530 *a gyrdell stothed with sylver*, Clint (SS104/26); 1538 *Unto ... my doughter a ledder belt with syluer stothes*, Thirsk (YAJ22/223); 1543 *my best girdle harnessed with a rede corse and xxxiiij stothes of siluer and gilte*, Adel (Th19/84). See also harness (1).

stope Examples noted in mining records are late and the exact meaning is obscure. The contexts link it with opening up soughs and ventilation gates: 1640 *I did stope the soowe*, Sharlston (GSH2); 1692 *the sough opening at wood which was stoped*, Farnley (MS11); 1765 *one day making stopings to get vent to back ending*, Tong (Tong/4c/9); 1774 *Towards the sow 15s; Borin 7s 6d; Stopin 2s 6d; 3 yards of Ending*, Tong (Tong/4c/11). These seem to refer to the manner in which an excavation was being carried out but Greenwell explains a 'stopping' in Northumberland and Durham as a wall built for the purpose of conducting air further into the workings, and in 1708 'stoppings' were seen as essential to the ventilation of a mine (CC38).

stoprise The wood and timber requirements of lead-miners included huge quantities of stoprise, that is thin pieces of timber, a word noted in Derbyshire and Lancashire from 1630 (JHR149) and soon afterwards in Swaledale: 1671 *stoprice paid to Geo. Spensley (for) 8,800 at 2s 6d per thousd*: this was described by Arthur Raistrick as 'lighter stuff which was put behind the timber framing' (NYRO31/57). See also rise (1).

storer One who keeps in store: 1309 *et Willelmo le Estorur*, Guisborough (SS89/278). As an early by-name it was for an officer with some responsibility for livestock on a monastic estate: 1321–2 *De ix bidentibus de instauro Roberti le Storour' ex legato venditis viijs [For 9 sheep from Robert le Storour's livestock sold out of the legacy]*, Bolton Priory (YRS154/496).

storth A place-name element of Old Norse origin, usually said to mean 'plantation, brushwood'. These may have been accurate when the names were coined but many of the earliest Yorkshire examples are linked to woodland clearance and settlement: 1286 'one and a half acres lay in the assart called *Storthe*', Elland (YRS65/53); 1297 *Thomas de Askebaldstorthes*, Ingleton (YRS16/8); 1316 Henry *del Storthes*, Thurstonland (YRS39/171). An undated reference points to wood management in Oxspring near Penistone: *c*.1300 'a broad path through *Molgerode* and *Coppicstorye [Coppicstorthe]*' (YRS111/133). Also possible is Storwood in the East Riding, with the spelling *Storthwait* in 1219 (YRS62/17).

stot A young castrated ox: 1346 *lego Agneti de Thornton duos stottos cum vj porcis [I bequeath to Agnes de Thornton two stots with 6 pigs]*, Catton (SS4/18); 1395–6 *De xix stottes, j vacca de stauro vijli [For 19 stots, 1 cow from livestock £7]*, Whitby (SS72/575); 1488 *Unus boviculus vocat. stott iiijs [A young ox called a stot 4s]*, Beverley (SS53/37); 1535 *xiiij yong Stottes and quyes*, Stillingfleet (YRS45/126); 1588 *Item two oxen and two Stottes*, Dalton (DD/WBW/19); 1642 *There was att that time a bull, 11 milch kyne, 2 fatte kyne, 2 fatte stotts, 2 leane stotts*, Elmswell (DW150). It gave rise to the common surname Stott and an early by-name: 1166 *Gamel Stot* (R&W). See also steer.

stotterel A diminutive of stot, a word recorded in the unpublished stock book of Fountains Abbey in 1481 (YRS140/215) and later in leases and wills: 1518 *to keipe ... within the seide groundes, woddes ande pastures yerly ... threscore stottes and stotterelles or whyes, of the aige of two yeres ande abown*, Braisty Wood (YRS140/191); 1542 *to every one off my dowtres ... one why strik or one stotrell*, Cundall (SS26/37); 1574 *xxij stotes and stottreles*, Brough near Catterick (SS26/248).

stoup A frequent spelling of stoop, stulp.

stouping-brod Possibly a nail used in setting up stoops or posts, but the one example noted occurs in a context of daubing, walling and roofing, so it may be for 'stouring brod': 1443 '1,555 nails called *stoupyng broddis*', Bedale (HH5). See also stouring-nail.

stour An alternative spelling of 'stower', a wooden pole, stake, or the like, used here in connection with building and repair work: 1316 'for buying ... *stouros de paliacer 40s*', Sowerby (YRS78/145–6); 1371 *amputanti stoures apud boscum de Acom pro parietibus domorum [cutting stours in Acomb wood for walls of the houses]*, York (SS35/355); 1419 *In stoures emptis pro emendacione ustrinae ... 12d [For stours bought to repair the bakehouse ... 12d]*, York (SS35/41). See also daub, estover, stower.

stouring-nail For securing stours or stowers: the Selby examples below were among items used in the re-building of a stable and the repair of a house: 1413–14 'And for 360 *stovres* ... 240 *spikyng* ... 3600 *stovryngnayll*', Thorpe Willoughby (SAR126); 1416–17 'For 60 *daubingstoures* ... and 180 stowering nails', Selby (YAJ48/127)'. The following may be a transcription error: 1504 *Item v^m scowryng nayll iiijs*, York (SS53/191). See also stouping-brod.

stove, stow To cut down or shorten: 1606 *from one gappe in the south side of the said parke unto one oak tree heretofore stoved*, North Bierley (LRS2/132); 1608 *Thomas Boake stowed ashe trees on the 14 lands*, Brandsby (NYRO44/44). I note the verb 'to stowen' in a much earlier Suffolk lease: 1447 *only to stowyn & to schredyn in swych places ... as William Payn stowyd and schredde in*, Dunwich (TWH14/328). It was also used of the identifying cuts made on the ears of farm animals: 1617 *both ther eares being stowed*, Brandsby (NYRO44/134); 1692 *the near ear stov'd*, Spofforth (QS1/30/1). See also brash, nar.

stoven The stump or stool of a tree from which young shoots spring: 1524 *To keep and ... fence all trees, stoven, and undergrowth, so that it be not destroyed or lossed*, Blubberhouses (YRS50/39); 1672 *all the springe woodes, underwoods and stovens now growinge*, Tong (Tong/3/320). Perhaps also the tree's base: 1622 *every Timber tree ... ought to be sex foote long above the stoven and a foote square at the Topp*, Pickering (NRR2/5). See also stove.

stoving, stowing The action of lopping off branches, or the branches and twigs cut off in that process: 1563 *to take for their fuel or firewood all plashings of hedges, and shreddings and stovings of trees growing in the hedgerows*, Scagglethorpe (YRS50/165); 1622 *and stowing of all trees and hedging in the said Grains*, Glaisdale (NRQS4/155). See also stove, stoven.

stow See stove.

stower A piece of wood such as a pole or stake, but with a wide range of applications: 1380 'John Pye is charged ... for cutting greenery and for one wagon-load of *Ellerstowrs*', Yeadon (SW63); 1409 *Et pro stowres et j syff ixd*, Beverley (ERAS4/36); 1463 *12 duss' fyrdelys 4C smalle burdes 4C bowstaffes 4C smalle stowres*, Hull (YRS144/58); 1575 *no person ... shall ... pytch any stowres, powles or staves in any street*, Beverley

(YRS84/2). The upright poles on carts were called 'wain stowers': 1600 *not one Ashe fit for a waynestower*, Settrington (YRS126/88); 1617 *yonge ashes to sell, oxe bowes, wayne stowers*, Brandsby (NYRO44/148); 1642 *see that the … waines be sownde and … putte in stowers wheare any are wantinge*, Elmswell (DW38). It is considered to have an Old Norse origin but may have been influenced by estower as a form of estover: 1619–21 *for estowers and pawnage in the Princes woodes*, Pickering (NRR1/21). See also daub, stour, wiver.

stowing See stoving.

straight head An alternative spelling of 'strait head' that is a narrow head driven into the coal: 1713 *the straight head from the old pitt eye is 10 score and half a yard*, Shibden (HAS30/143). See also strait board.

strait A narrow cloth: 1394 *5 duzen straytes*, Hull (YRS64/58).

strait board, strait work Literally 'narrow passage' and 'narrow work'. These terms appear to have much the same meaning and they feature regularly in colliery accounts from the seventeenth century: 1693 *Ro: Kendall straite worke 1y½; strait board 2y½*, Farnley (MS11); 1760 *pd Jos. Cowburn for 10 yds of strait work 5s 0d*, Tong (Tong/4c/5) Their precise significance is far from self-evident and neither term is well documented but Wright defines 'strait work' as 'narrow roads driven in the coal to facilitate the winning in a mine' (EDD): his information came from a West Riding correspondent. The OED also has 'strait work' and quotes Gresley (1883): 'the system of getting coals by headings or narrow work'. The 'headings', which seem likely to be what were called 'headways' in *The Compleat Collier* (1708), were not 'wrought so wide as the other Works or Boards' but from them the individual work-places branched off to either side (CC34). It is employed as a verb in the Farnley accounts: 1704 *straitebord the Watergate* (MS11), possibly a reference to cutting through for a drainage channel. The excavation of such passages was skilled work which gave the workman the same status as a 'pickman'. See also head (2), pick (5), straight head.

strake (1), stroke (2) A strip of iron along the left-hand side of a plough: 1395 *Item pro ij dosan plewstrakys iiijs*, Whitby (SS72/618); c.1426 *bad hym that he suld make hym osmundes of the drosse and landyren … and na plughstrakes*, York (SS85/5); 1579 *ij yron howpes vj plowghe straikes with wayne clowtes*, South Cave (Kaner103). Also a section of the iron rim or tyre of a cart wheel: 1597 *Item 6 newe tyre strokes with other iron stuffe*, South Cave (Kaner194); 1619 *Iron for bynding a payre of wheeles … 2 dozen wayneclouts and one dozen stroakes*, Brandsby (NYRO44/175).

strake (2) An alternative spelling of stroke (1), and strike (1): 1400 *j siffe, j buschell, j strake*, York (SS4/270); 1558 *to Jenet Scamonden a strake of wheate*, Ackton (Th27/248).

strake-nail The nail used to secure the iron rim on a cart-wheel: 1320–1 *Pro clutis ad caruc(as) et plaustr(a) emptis apud Harewod iijs iiijd. Pro c. strakenayl emptis ibidem xviijd [For clouts bought for ploughs and carts at Harewood 3s 4d. For 100 strake-nails bought there 18d]*, Bolton Priory (YRS154/482).

strand Low-lying land which borders a river or stream: 1637 *not cleansing a water-sewer betwixt the Long Holme and Swainby and the strand leading down to Pickall* (NRQS4/72). Minor place-names with this origin are *the Strande* (1580) by the Wharfe near Hubberholme and *the Strennes* (1543) by the Calder in Shitlington, both listed by Smith (PNWR).

strandling The fur of the squirrel, taken in the autumn: 1300 *cum duabus furruris de strandling [with two strandling linings]*, Harpham (ERAS21/74); 1415 *j togam … furruratam cum strandlyng [1 gown … trimmed with strandling]*, Wollaton (SS4/382); 1429 'to Agnes Crawen a green gown with *stranelyn* fur, a black gown furred with *meniver*', York (SS186/99).

straw-brod A type of nail used to attach the laths, or 'straw-laths', in a thatched roof: 1358 *Item, pro strabroddis j mill', xvjd [Item, for 1000 straw-brods, 16d]*, York (SS129/15); 1415 *In v.c. strabrod, 6d [For 500 strabod, 6d]*, York (SS35/35); 1433 *In m.m.m. strebroddes emptis pro dictis strelattes [For 3000 straw-brods bought for the said straw laths]*, York (SS35/54); 1446–7 *Mille cc clavis vocatis strawbrod 16d [1200 nails called straw-brods 16d]*, Beverley (ERAS6/78).

straw-lain Evidently a tie used in thatching, made of straw or for attaching straw: 1391–2 *Et in viii*ˣˣ *travis straminis ordii emp. pro coopertura cujusdam domus in tenura Joh. Knygth … Et in cc stralanes emp. pro domo in tenure Joh. Knygth [And for 8 score thraves of barley straw bought for roofing the house in John Knygth's tenure. And for 200 straw-lains bought for the house in John Knygth's tenure]*, Ripon (SS81/107). See also lain.

straw lath See latt, straw-brod.

strawthack Straw used as a roofing material: 1534 *to kep upe the said house with straw-thake at al tymes*, Little Preston (Th11/66).

streaker I have noted only one use of this word, in a carpenter's accounts for bridge timbers: 1699 *For long Streakers & cross Binders 174 ft at 12d per ft*, Tadcaster (QS1/38/4). It may have been a reference to wood used in the making of a centre, possibly a regional spelling of 'stretcher', that is a tie-beam. See also bind (2).

stream In many early documents this was not a synonym for brook or beck but a reference to the current or main flow of a river, especially where it provided power by turning a water wheel: 1491 *inter Bulderclogh et Styes cote long egge et le streme de Caldre*, Sowerby (MD225/1/216); 1580 *and the streame or course of water running from the upper end of a little holme … until the Milne damme*, Barkisland (HM/B/140); 1628 *occupieth one Corne millne and two Fulling Mylnes upon … Ayre and paieth for the Streame*, Leeds (Th57/158). In 1683, after serious flooding at Harewood Bridge, reference was made to *the Streame of the said Water which used to rune under the South side of the said bridge, now is turned and doth rune to the North side* (QS1/22/6). In Kettlewell, in 1686, *the landstayes* were *in danger to be carried away by the violence of the stream* (QS1/26/1).

street The element 'street', and forms derived from it, were the specific or first element in certain major place-names, evidence of an ancient paved way, especially a former Roman road, e.g. Strafforth, Sturton (PNWR7/252). That use of the word persisted long enough to feature in minor names such as Tong Street, and *The hye Street* in Lindley, on a Robert Saxton map (1609) in Kirklees archives: both these are on the line of Roman roads.

It was used also of a paved way between buildings in a town or village, with examples from the eleventh century, for example: *c.*1090 *Nordstreta*; 1150–61 *Cuningesstrete*, York (PNER295,285); 1318 *strete in front of the Friars Preachers*, Beverley (PNER195); 1415 *Fynkelstrete*, Hull (PNER211); 1557 *in every of the three stretes in Wakefelde* (Th27/124). Even though 'gate' was the usual word for a way or street in Yorkshire, 'High Street' has a long history there, recorded in Hull as *le Heighe Streete* in 1321 (PNER212) and subsequently over a wide area: 1536 *his movable guddes and howssehold stuffe dyd cast forth of the sayd howsse into the Hygh Strett*, Whiston (YRS70/139); 1563 *one common*

Street commonly called the hieghe streate, Aldborough (YRS74/35); 1585 *They lay in pain that Henry Nayler do remove his maner and donnge which he hathe laid in the hie streete, that others may leade there*, Dewsbury (YAJ21/428); 1609 *le Highestreete in Earlesheaton* (WCR11/39). In some individual cases it is not certain how High Street should be interpreted, whether as a highway or as a major street in a town.

Nor can we ignore the influence of clerks who were not local men, especially from the seventeenth century when 'town street' began to feature in the records, replacing the regional word 'town-gate': 1654 *those of Crathorne and Yarm for not repairing their town streets or gates* (NRQS5/155); 1730 *the Town Street in Hallifax* (QS4/27/27). The history of 'kirk' and 'laithe' is evidence of how certain important regional words were being relegated to the status of dialect terms from the sixteenth century. See also town-gate.

streetway A paved road or highway: 1526 *I gif xij^d to the amending of the street waye*, Burley (Th9/191); 1642 *upp Barney Gill to the Streete Waye*, Helmsley (HRD433). In this latter example the editor noted that it referred to 'the paved causeway from Bloworth to the Face Stone'.

strickle A wooden tool which was used to whet or sharpen a scythe: 1620 *three sithe strickles worth 9d*, Helmsley (NRQS3/108); 1642 *The tooles that Mowers are to have with them are Sythe, shafte, and strickle, hammer to pitte the strickle with to make it keepe sande, sand-bagge, and grease horne*, Elmswell (DW34); 1657 *a scith and shaft and strickle*, East Rounton (NRQS5/257). In the *Craven Glossary* (1828) it was 'a piece of wood besmeared with grease and strewed with sand'. Alternatively it could mean the smooth straight piece of wood used to strike off the surplus grain from the top of a corn-measure: 1423 *pro ij buss' cum j strekill et j peke [for 2 bushels with 1 stickle and 1 peck]*, York (SS45/80); 1642 *When wee goe to take up Corne for the mill, the first thinge wee doe is to looke out poakes, then the bushell and strickle*, Elmswell (DW108).

strike (1) A dry measure for corn, peas, etc. and the vessel holding that amount: 1316 'demands against Adam Kenward for 2 full strikes (*strokas*) of oat meal & 2 separate strikes (*strikatas*), Holmfirth (YRS78/103); 1527 *euery on of them oon strike barlie*, Sherburn (Th9/252); *c*.1534 *4 new mawndys for hoppes … one Stryke*, Bridlington (YRS80/2); 1558 *I gyve to Jenet Smyth one strike of malte*, Monk Fryston (Th27/166). Used also as a verb. The measure was considered to be levelled by the hand or a strickle, not heaped: 1642 *When wee sende our Corne to mill wee allwayes strike all cleane of, yet the use is in most places to hand wave it and not to strike it*, Elmswell (DW109). See also strake (2), stroke (1).

strike (2) A metathesised spelling of stirk, a bullock or heifer up to two years old: 1457 *duas vaccas et ij strikkis de stauro meo [two cows and 2 strikes from my stock]*, Howden (SS30/211); 1495 'to keep … twenty cows and … deliver annually … ten *strykes* worth 4s each', Burton on Ure (YRS140/144); 1589 *unto me two doughters Jene and Margret ether of them one cowe and two partes of two strykes and one stryk to Margret only besyedes*, Abbotside (YRS130/16).

strike (3) The verb could mean 'to paint an image': 1639 *To Mr Horsley for strikeing my Lord Deputyes coate on the organs 4s*, York: Edward Horsley was a painter and stainer of note in the city, in whose will were *books of armory … coulors … grynding stones and oyle belonging to* [his] *trade* (SS35/120).

strike a mark Cutlers had their own marks, and the idea of 'striking a mark' is explicit in a Latin entry in the Sheffield court roll of 1554. William Elles was assigned a mark for his knives (*pro cultellis ferreis signando*), and provision was made lest any other person strike [*percutiet*] that mark (TWH28/57). The use of the expression in English soon followed and in 1590 the Sheffield cutlers were ordered not *to stryke anye marke* on their knives except the one assigned to them, and not to *stryke anye other marke* (HCC3). In 1730, Thomas Warburton was accused of *engraving upon his razors contrary to his Mark* (HCC17). The marks were made on forged items such as knives and scissors by hammering the blades with a mark punch, about 8 cm long and 1–5 cm across. Little is known about their manufacture and it was assumed by Unwin that cutlers made their own. See also mark.

striking A regional word for a kind of coarse linen, a variant of 'straiken' which has been recorded in Scotland and north-east England: 1535 *vij lynyn schetys, ij strykyns*, Mappleton (SS26/12); 1536 *ij payre of sheites of strykynges*, Killingwoldgraves (SS106/53); 1558 *to my sister … two paire of strikings*, Beverley (Crossley168); 1588 *3 peire of harden sheetes one paire of strikinges*, South Cave (Kaner150).

stringer Occupational, sometimes for the craftsman who made bow-strings: 1359–60 *Thomas le bower, Thomas le stringer*, York (SS96/54); 1420 *in arte quadam que vocatur stryngercrafte … et quod lez strynges pro arcubus qui inventi erunt defectivi [in that trade called stringer craft … and that the bow strings which had been found were damaged]*, York (SS125/122–3). Away from towns and cities the stringer was more likely to be an iron-worker, a smith or nailer who worked at the string-hearth: *c.*1270 *Thomas called le Strenger*, Bramley; 1379 *Johannes Strynger, nayler*, Thornhill (GRDict). See also stringfellow.

stringfellow An iron-worker, an alternative of 'stringer': 1308 *John the Strengfelagh*, Thornhill (YRS36/160); 1547 *the stringefelloe wages, for … breakeing of the blowme and heweinge*, Sheffield (HS2).

string-hearth A specialist hearth in iron-making, with the earliest examples found in Durham: 1409 *le stryngherth* (OED) and Derbyshire: 1507 *strynge herth*, Norton (TWH14/124). In the West Riding, the accounts for Esholt ironworks have a more detailed reference: 1567–8 *Harre Wylle blowmer for wages … for evere blome in the blome harthe … and helping the smythe in the strynge-harthe* (BAS10/247). See also bloom, hearth, smithies, string smithy.

string-layer 1641 *Thos Robinson of Scarborough, stringlayer* (NYRO49/7).

string smithy In 1569, Thomas Wille [*sic*] of Shipley reported to Sir Thomas Danby on the state of his iron works:

> *The smithies are not repaired according to covenant for your smyths cannot work at the string hearth neyther the bellowes can lye dry for that space is no charge upon the string smithies nor the coles in the blome smithies can be kept dry* (BM82/15).

Catherine Collinson comments on the use of this 'stringsmithy' in 1579 (YAJ68/195). See also bloomer.

strinkle A holy water sprinkler: 1449 *unum halywatirfatt et unum strynkyll de argento [a holy water vessel and a silver strinkle]*, Everton (SS30/138); 1455 *j litill holy water fatt with j strenkill of silver*, York (SS30/190); 1493 *To a well disposed preste … I will that he … take the holy water strynkill and goe to the grave … and cast holywater on the grave*, York (SS53/86); 1520 *paid for ij strynkylles, jd*, York (CCW78); *c.*1537 *j holywater fatt with a strynkyll of sylver ungilt weyng liiij unces*, Fountains Abbey (SS42/290). As a verb it meant more generally 'to sprinkle': 1707 *Thomas Calvert's shoes were all strinkled with red wares*, Baildon (QS1); 1741 *strinkle it over with bread Crumbs*, Pontefract (GWK30).

strip Found several times in church terriers and tithe disputes, where it referred specifically to cows. In 1743, for example, the Easter dues in Kirkheaton parish included a penny *for every strip* (LTK110): the editor took this to be a reference to a strip of ground in the open field but a South Crosland farmer makes the meaning clear in his day book: 1768 *If a Cow Renew not within the year She is called A strip; the Town of Marsden by specious [sic] Custom pays Nothing for A strip* (GRD); in the Almondbury terrier of 1770 it was *by special custom*.

The OED has no examples of the noun but quotes uses of the verb 'to strip' from 1610 which point to a connection. It is defined there as 'to extract the milk remaining in the udder after the normal milking, especially by a particular movement of the hand'. The EDD has similar examples in counties from the midlands to Scotland, the earliest being for the East Riding in 1788. In fact, a tithe dispute takes this use back to 1553 when the Proctor family were farmers of Gargrave vicarage. In a deposition relating to payments for tithe milk Roger Wigglesworth said: *the custome in the parishe is that for everie cowe which reneweth … they use to paye ijd. and for everie stripte mylke cowe a penny* (YRS114/49). It was in use across the county: 1567 *two strippe milke kye*, Mortham (SS26/203); 1664 *3 stripmilk kine £7 0 0*, Elmswell (DW238); 1672 *3 kine, one new calved & 2 stript milked*, Selby (YRS47/187). See also renew.

striving irons Part of the harness for draught horses, found only in the East Riding. It may have been a local alternative for iron traces since the two terms do not occur together: 1570 *two payer of strivinge Irons*, Spaldington (YRS134/37); 1575 *ij yockes a teame, a payr of strifyng iorons*, South Cave (Kaner93); 1582 *a plough shackle another little shackle striving irons horse geare*, Faxfleet (Kaner122); 1624 *teames & yoakes striving irons & harrowes*, South Cave (Kaner318).

stroke (1) A denomination of dry measure and the vessel holding that amount: 1533 *every pore bodye … to have one stroke of peese*, Fryston (SS106/34); 1577 *one stroke of shilling at harvest*, Kirkburton (FACcciii); 1601 *a strooke of vnwynded barley*, Campsall (YRS3/186); 1676 *1 salt bushel, a stroak with other small mesures*, Selby (YRS47/41); 1728 *saw the stroke that Mr Chamberlain sould by measured before Mr Horton which was found to be just*, West Riding (QS1/67/6). See also multure, strake (2), strike (1).

stroke (2) See strake (1).

stroller An itinerant beggar, a vagrant: 1763 *Edward, son of Thomas Jones, a soldier (whose wife is a stroller)*, Hunslet (Th23/351). The word's pejorative associations were implicit in the verb: 1743 *John Allen … about 10 was apprenticed … served 2 years and ever since has strolled and wandered about the country*, West Riding (QS1/82/4).

strong water Any form of alcoholic spirits used as a beverage: 1674 *hath distreyned the goodes of severall persons for distilling strong waters*, Sandal (QS1/13).

strum, strum maker A strum was a wicker-work basket, used in the brew-house to keep the malt in the vat: 1394–5 *It. pro strom pro le brewhous, iiijd*, Whitby (SS72/606); 1446–58 *pro cirpis … et pro factura le stromes [for rushes … and for making the strums]*, Fountains Abbey (SS130/202); 1616 *2 men … was whitinge [sic for whitlinge?] streight saughe wodd to make trellesses, strums, maundes, baskets or it may be rydles and sives*, Brandsby (NYRO44/115); 1629 *makers of Baskets, Bottells, Seves, Temses, Strumps and Kitts*, Beverley (YRS84/81). In 1617, Richard Cholmeley of Brandsby made the following entry in his memorandum book: *Gray the strumme maker of Haxbie Henry Jackson* *overtooke him on the forest beyond Sutton … with a great burthin of streight Yonge saughes which he confessed he had gotten in Spellow Wood* (NYRO44/135). See also carpenter.

stub (1) A short thick nail: 1394–5 *It. pro i^m stubs iis*, Whitby (SS72/615); 1504 *xv^c stubs xviijd*, York (SS53/191); 1535 *Item a thowsand stubbes ijs*, Stillingfleet (YRS45/130); 1615 *100 of stubbes, iijs vjd*, Brandsby (NYRO44/97); 1715 *for stubs to mend corves*, Farnley near Leeds (MS14); 1776 *latt nails, spar nails, stubs*, Holmfirth (G-A). See also stob, stillingfleet nails.

stub (2) By the sixteenth century to 'stub', or more explicitly to stub up a tree, was to remove the stubs or stumps of those that had been felled, so that the land might be ploughed. In 1520, a Fountains Abbey lease granted Ralph and Robert Scayfe of Bishopside *libertye to stube upe and clense certain growndes … to ther more advantage and profett* (YRS140/170): in 1587 Sir John Kaye of Woodsome and his workmen *dyd stubb a pece of the Carr beyond the Brodyng, calling yt the Great Stubbing* (KayeCP), and in Ilkley *verie woddy and bushey grounds* were *stubbed and made arable* in 1591 (YNQ2/26).

The West Riding Quarter Sessions record a tragic accident in 1675 which paints a vivid picture of the dangers that such work involved: Joseph Hirst of East Ardsley testified that he had been

> *stubbing of a tree … And being fetching of this blow with his axe, Stephen Allen, unknowne to [him], was betwixt his blow and the root of the tree that he was then stubbing and by that meanes was Accidentally sore cut into the head.* The blow was not fatal but the unfortunate man was taken *home to his Masters … who doth maintaine him* (QS1).

'Stubbing' remained a common practice and the diarist Adam Eyre noted in February 1648 that his man was *stubbing the ashes in the croft head* (SS65/95): in 1732, John Hobson wrote of *ploughing in a close where there had lately been some wood stubbed* (SS65/316) and in Beverley in 1774 the rents from the town pasture called Westwood were used in *stubbing up old tree roots … and clearing the said pasture as far as the money will allow* (YRS122/21). The word eventually acquired a number of related meanings and in Kirkheaton in 1604 Mr Stocke was fined 12d for *stubbinge and fellinge whinnes*, that is gorse bushes (DD/WBR/11): in 1837 the Thurstonland churchwardens accounted for *stubbing Docks in the Churchyard* (KC271/67). See also stubber, stubbing, stubbs, thorn.

stubber *The Bolton Priory Compotus* has an interesting sequence of references to 'stubber' as an occupational term from 1311 to 1319. It begins with sums of money paid to *Willelmo le Stubber* which is likely to have been the workman's by-name not a hereditary surname: he was once referred to just as *Stubber*. He might at that time have been cutting down trees or helping to manage the woods but unfortunately the entries are not detailed enough: they include *una magna falce liberata xiiijd [equipped with a large billhook 14d]* and *amputanti boscum xijd [for cutting wood 12d]* (YRS154). In 1379, *Robertus Stubber* was a taxpayer in Crigglestone near Wakefield (PTWR).

stubbing This occurs frequently as a minor place-name element from the thirteenth century, although many early examples are in undated charters: in Worsbrough, for example, *Rokelaystubbing* was an assart (YRS39/183) as was *Hemmingstubbing* in Ilkley (YRS69/103): a grant of lands in Thorp Salvin mentions *le Heyestubing*, 'Willstubbing', and 'Aldanstubbing' (YRS83/169). In 1344, a plot of land called *le Stubbing* in Denby near Penistone contained fifteen acres (YRS65/48). Such 'stubbings' referred to assarts where the 'stubs' had been removed so that crops might be grown there: n.d. *in predicta* *cultura que vocatur Stubyngs post fena et blade asportata [in the aforesaid ploughland called Stubyngs after the hay and corn has been taken away],* Healaugh (YRS92/75).

Although the suffix was widely used in that period, its precise interpretation is not always certain. A dispute in Sowerby near Halifax, in 1275, had to do with 'a bovate of land with a garden and a stubbing', leased to William Brun. William then accused the owner of breaking their agreement by throwing down the stubbing and carrying it away: *et dictum stubbing prostravit et asportavit [and they threw down and carried off the said stubbing]* (YRS29/37,115). This was clearly not a direct reference to a clearance and in view of meanings discussed in woodland glossaries it should perhaps be interpreted as coppice wood or brushwood. It may be that in some early clearances the stubs were left standing for a number of years, serving as pollards or stovens. See also ridding, royd, stubbs.

stubbing boon On some manors, tenants were expected to take part in clearing woods as a condition of their tenure, and the men of North Bierley were given the option in 1548 of paying 2d to the lord annually or performing *five stubbinge boynes*; that is five days work on clearance (EH/68D82). See also boon, sickle boon.

stubbing hack The tool used to stub up tree roots, whins, docks, etc.: 1759 *j Stubbing Hack*, Barnoldswick (YRS118/74).

stubbs Both 'stubbs' and 'stubbing' are common place-names in Yorkshire, although each had a variety of similar spellings. They occur frequently also in compound names, and Smith lists scores of examples across the county. Typical examples under 'stubb' are *Apeltrestubbe, Burtrestubbys* and *Stobtrees* (PNWR7/253). In general, it can be said that they identify places where trees were cut down, often so that the land could be brought under cultivation. However, the stubs or stumps may not always have been removed immediately.

stub cross See stump cross.

stud See stooth (2).

stuff, stuff-maker The word 'stuff' was used of a woollen fabric which was described late in its history as not having a pile (OED): 1653 *some holland for my selfe and stuffe for her*, Stockeld (YRS161/125); 1657 *to John Fawcett my sonne one little trunck & my stufe suite*, Thorpe Willoughy (YRS47/61); 1675 *The persons who tooke the monies had their faces covered, one being mounted on a gray horse being in a close gray coate, th'other on a lusty bay gelding in a brone stuffe coate*, Tadcaster (QS1). The occupational term occurs later: 1709 *John Candler of Selby stuffe maker* (YRS47/38); 1785 *Samuel Clapham of Leeds, stuffmaker* (MD292/13).

stulp An early spelling of stoop: 1454 *Et in mercede Johannis Stede carpentarij ponantis unum stulpum in Walmegate [And for the carpenter John Stede's pay placing a stoop in Walmegate]*, York (SS192/78); 1490 *the wyff of the said Richard Wryght [ought to knell] next to the stulp of the said fourem end*, Kirkburton (Morehouse63); 1579 *Thomas Hirste … shall make a newe gate and new stulpes at the water side*, Dewsbury (YAJ21/410). It apparently gave rise to a by-name, possibly an uncomplimentary nickname: 1333 'William *Stulp* was seised of a moiety of a bovate in Thornes' (WCR3/223); *c*.1344 'Thomas *Stulppe* of Catthal', Hunsingore (YRS76/86).

stump cross A cross with a broken shaft. The index to PNWR includes nine examples of Stump Cross as a place-name, in localities as far apart as Wadworth which lies south of Doncaster, Bolton by Bowland in the western dales, and Aldborough near Boroughbridge. The meaning is not in doubt but the evidence on the whole is late, and my interest in the place-name lies in the evidence that 'stump cross' was a term in everyday use from the sixteenth century. The destruction of crosses is associated with the Reformation and its challenge to the Roman Catholic Church, and monuments continued to be destroyed through the Civil War period. The standing crosses were seen as symbols of Catholicism, and for zealous Protestants the breaking of their shafts was an irresistible challenge.

Of course, many of the crosses were simply waymarkers, standing at major junctions, and they were not in themselves religious symbols although some undoubtedly came to be associated with the church, if only because they were halting-places during the processions at Rogation tide. A witness in a tithe case in 1556 recalled how before the Dissolution they would go in procession *to a crose in Westowe parishe*, or *to the Crose at Whitwell Beacon*, saying *a Gospell* in each place (YRS114/80). That did not save the waymarkers from the hammers of the iconoclasts. In a visitation of 1567, it was noted that in Warburton they had *a Stumpe of a crosse in their churchyeard, the head beinge smitten of*, and in churchyards where that had not been done the parishioners were enjoined *to pull downe and deface the same utterlie* (PTD177).

In many early cases therefore 'stump cross' was a vocabulary item, not a place-name. J.K. Hammond's work on Eccleshill contains details of the township boundaries in 1585 which ran from *a close dyke and a stump cross ... to Bolton out lanes:* in 1607, a section of the highway from Stockton to York was reportedly in great decay; it led *from Moncke Bridge end to a stompcross*: the editor attempted to explain the term 'stump cross', saying that it was not infrequently met with, but he did not understand its meaning (NRQS1/68). It remained in use beyond the Civil Wars and a Worsbrough by-law of 1688 required tenants to *scour their ditches in the lane ... up to the Stumpcross* (JWW).

It is to be expected that some examples of Stump Cross as a place-name will go back to the 1530s when Henry VIII broke with Rome, and the Act of Supremacy recognised him as head of the English church. In fact, it seems to have acquired that status almost immediately for when Thomas Percy of Scarborough bequeathed land to the Black Friars in 1536–7 one acre was described as *lying at Stompe crosse* (SS106/56). In 1578, a Beverley butcher had to pay 4s fine *for his sheep depasturing in a Close at Stumpe Cross* and that is possibly the Stump Cross in Bishop Burton (YRS84/27). William Brooke *of Stumpcross in Batley* was married at Leeds in 1739 (PR).

The frequency of the evidence from the 1530s actually makes a contribution to the history of 'stump' as a word. This is on record from the fourteenth century and for much of its earliest history it referred to the part of a limb which remained after amputation. From *c.*1440 it was used also of a standing tree-trunk and that may have played a part in the popularity of stump cross as a vocabulary item. In 1577, for example, the mayor of Beverley received 5s *for 2 stump trees in Westwood* (YRS84/8). There is also interest in the parallels that exist between 'stump' and 'stub', although 'an etymological connexion is difficult to make' (OED). Of course 'stub' has a much longer history, as a word for the rooted portion of a felled tree, but it is worth noting that 'stub cross' is in use as a place-name earlier than stump cross. Two examples are *Stob crose* in Brampton Bierlow in 1516 (PNWR1/109) and *le Stub crosse in Pontefract* in 1475 (Th26/220). There were evidently broken crosses before the Reformation.

sturdy A brain disease in sheep and cattle which causes them to be giddy, to turn round and round: 1642 *A 3 sheare ewe is allwayes better for the buyer ... for then is all dainger past ... of sturdie*, Elmswell (DW4); 1653 *received of Robert Fish for a whye that had the sturddy 13s*, Stockeld (YRS161/78). The word was also used adjectivally: 1446–58 *Item in j sturd sterkett communitatis xxd [Item for 1 sturdy common stirket 20d]*, Fountains

Abbey (SS130/224); 1642 *If there bee any of the hogges that bee sturdy, lame, weake … putte them into the closes … wheare there is grasse sufficient*, Elmswell (DW77). Early by-names seem likely to have referred to a person's character but whether or not complimentary it is difficult to say: 1301 *De Rogero Sturdy*, Bainbridge (YRS21/89).

sty A footpath or narrow way. It is of Old English origin and occurs quite frequently in minor place-names: *c.*1275 *as far as Rauenestih*, Hipperholme (YRS83/124); 1366 *le Wyndmilnestigh*, Woolley (YRS102/169). There are also early examples as a vocabulary item: 1289 *one acre of meadow at le Sty*, Habton (YRS69/74); 1350 *le stye a capite de Twonges usque ad le watermilne [the sty from the head of Twonges as far as the water mill]*, Holmfirth (G-A). It survived into the modern period: 1699 *Bridlestie to the Lock below fleet mill*, Rothwell (Th9/193). See also styway.

styth Foul air in a mine. It is a rare word in the West Riding but occurs occasionally from the nineteenth century: 1829 *for avoiding or carrying away water or styth*, Leeds (WYL160/129/2). It was used regularly in *The Compleat Collier* (1708) and like 'tentale' it occurs in a part of Leeds where coal-owners had direct links with Northumberland.

styway A late alternative of 'sty' which may have developed when the meaning of that word was no longer transparent: 1432 *a way called a stighway*, Hipperholme (WYAS618); 1509 *a styway goyng frome Crosseland to a house called the helme*, Meltham (DD/WBD/2/30). The OED has no references to 'sty' later than 1430, except in the alliterative phrase 'by sty and street'. The EDD has 'sty-road' in Wakefield in 1865.

such-like Of such a kind, similar: 1600 *hath not payd any rent therfore to her majestye wich after the auncient rent of other such lyke landes … is worth yearly 3s 4d*, Settrington (YRS126/96).

sudderon Southern, that is from the south of England: 1508 *every man … that sells and cuts sudderon cloth … shall pay yerly to the well of the pageant of the sayd draypours xijd each*, York (YRS106/25); 1522 *those that dothe selle brode sotheron clothe*, York (YRS106/83).

sufficient Qualified by talent or ability. See also put forth, turf-gate.

summer (1) A pack-horse: 1350 *jeo devise a Roger mon chambreleyn xx lvyres* [sic] *et le melior robe que j'ay et le melior somer [I bequeath to my chamberlain Roger £20 and the best robe that I have and the best summer]*, Ayton (SS4/62); 1400 *De xvjs rec. pro j equo vocato somer coquinæ [For 16s received for 1 horse called 'summer kitchen']*, Richmond (SS45/15); 1617 *and vnto Mr Brigges my parson a summer nagge*, Hinderwell (YRS63/54).

summer (2), summer-tree A summer was a horizontal bearing beam and its use is implicit in Latin documents: 1335 *Ad hoc lignea summaria interlacia ac omnia alia genera meremiorum [For this wooden summer lying about and all the other types of timber]*, York (SZ1/431). Later we have: 1589 *for 33 sommers and 30 planckes*, How Bridge (NRQS3/24); 1682 *the summers to be eight yeards long, fifteen inches and twelve in gage*, Scriven (YAJ16/112). Summer-tree has the same meaning and is on record from the eighteenth century: 1733 *roofe cast, goists and summer trees*, Wakefield (QS1/73/4); 1788 *sumertrees, beams, reafters, sidtrees, bindings, spars, planks*, Meltham (G-A). *Sommertree Bridge* was the name of a bridge in Pickering in 1633 (NRQS3/343). See also dorman, jobby, sleeper.

summer (3) It is an ancient practice to have cattle, horses or sheep use different pasture grounds at different times of the year: 1349 'from summer agistment in Erringden Park', Sowerby (WCR2/231), and the verbs 'to winter' and 'to summer' were used in this context:

1598 *the horses and beastes of … Fountance Abbey were kepte on the same pasture in sommer tyme from about May Day unto Mychaelmas beinge … an highe moorishe and mossy grounde fit onely for someringe and not for wynteringe of any cattell* (YRS114/168).

1634 *Wee lay in paine that noe man dwellinge within the … Lordshipp shall winter any Cattal in any other Lordshipp and bringe them to be … somered upon the mores*, Meltham (G-A).

The practice was responsible for a number of minor place-names: 1577 *my lease of Somerlodge in Swadaile*, Easby (SS26/267); 1608–9 *Somerboothlee … Wynterboothlee*, Warley (WCR11/157); 1634 'John Dyson holds a close of arable and meadow in Meltham called *Somerhey*' (G-A). See also ought (2), winter.

summer games This referred to a festival held at Midsummer with dancing and dramatic performances, often associated with a light kept burning in the parish church: 1464 *lumini vocato Somer-game light iij buz. brasei ordei [for the light called summer games light 3 bushels of barley malt]*, Kirk Deighton (SS79/103n); 1496 *lez Somergame in Capella [chapel] de Kirkham* (PTD161); 1519 *To the Somer-game light in my parishe chirche ijs*, York (SS79/103); 1569 *admonishe youe to be … cercumspecte what lycences yow geyve to persones to kepe common somer games for we here of some great abuses therein*, York (YRS112/155). It is likely that the celebrations took place in a traditional location: 1605 'abutting towards the east on *le Somergames*', Swine (YRS65/78). The word 'summer' can probably be taken to refer to summer-games in certain contexts: 1469 *ad orreum quo ludus tentus fuit vulgariter dictum Somerhouse [at the barn where the games were held commonly called Somerhouse]*, Wistow (PTD160n); 1571 *the minister and churchewardens shall not suffer any lords of misrule or somer lords or ladyes or any disguised persone … at May games or any minstrels morice dauncers or others at Rishebearinges*, Diocese of York (PTD160-1). Possibly also: 1462 *j almery in the somerhall*, Wawne (SS30/261).

summer-tree See summer (2).

sump In coal-mining, this was a hole or depression set beneath the lowest landing in a shaft, where water gathered before draining away or being pumped to the surface: 1704 *Jo. Harrison paid Ad. for sump*, Farnley (MS11); 1763 *for a boy ladeing water a week in the sump*, Tong (Tong/4c/7). See also dress, sough pit.

sumpter cloth, sumpter saddle Pack-horse accoutrements, but not necessarily workaday in character as references make clear (OED): 1568 *Item 3 Sumpter Clothes … with my lordes Armes upone the same*, Healaugh Park (YRS114/33); 1569 *One sumtar sadle, one trouncke sadle*, Sizergh (SS26/219).

sunder Separate, apart, perhaps 'in pieces' in some cases: 1508 *I witt to Thomas my brother my secondary gowne, beying sondre*, Ripon (SS64/330); 1552 *a reed jackett taken sunder and lyinge in quarters*, Garforth (Th19/300). As a verb it meant to separate or move apart: *c.*1620 *a workeman … did Cast some what Iron firth of the harth … amongst the … persons soe struggling whereupon they sundred one from another*, Bradley, Huddersfield (HOW41). It occurs several times in the place-name Sunderland: 1274 *Matheus de Sundreland*, Halifax (YRS29/1); 1424 'dwelling in *Sondreland*', Tickhill (YRS120/166).

sunderly Separately: 1439 *To whilke witness the forsaid parties … ther seales sonderly has putt*, York (SS186/122); 1496 *in witnessing for trowth … we have to this present testament and will sunderly putto our seales and subscribed our names*, Newark (SS53/118).

sun–end, sun–side Commonly used of locations which benefited most from the sun: 1379 *Adam at Sonnend*, Handsworth (PTWR); 1510 *To be buried in the parishe churche ... upon the son–side*, Sherburn in Elmet (SS53/206n); 1556 *to be buried within the parishe churche yearde of Ledes of the sonnsyd* (Th27/76); *c.*1571 *one Acre and a half ... Lyinge on the Sun side of Huddersfield grene* (OHR12); 1592 *John Eastwod of Crosland of the Sunne end of the towne* (DD/RA/f/4a); 1703 *from the Lower Thunderyate ... to the sunside of the said Senier's Garden*, Shelley (YAS/DD181).

sup To take sips, to drink, now chiefly regional: 1642 *and for the old Ewe to suppe on the river is thought to bee much avaleable for bringinge of them to milke*, Elmswell (DW86); 1725 *when he had supped his milke he sett down the meale pott upon her dresser*, West Riding (QS1/64/1).

surcingle A girth for a horse, especially one which secured a pack on its back: 1615 *sterop irons xd; 2 sursyngles xvjd; saddles mending*, Brandsby (NYRO44/104). See also cingle, packsaddle.

surfle To embroider: 1399–1400 *Et in salario j mulieris surfuland prædictum baner 4d* [*And for the pay of 1 woman for surfling the aforesaid banner 4d*], Ripon (SS81/133).

surrender with straw A tenant was said to surrender an estate when he relinquished his interest in copyhold lands, yielding them directly to the lord of the manor, or via the lord to another person. The piece of straw was a symbol of the crops the land was capable of producing: 1545 *accordinge unto a surrender which I haue given upe with a strawe into the hands of Richard Mawde*, Shelf (Crossley8). Its importance is explicit in the following Chancery case: 1671 *Remembers the surrender with a straw into the hands of Henry Haigh ... all was upon the delivery of that very straw*, Marsden (G-A). See also seisin.

surveyor One who has oversight of something, a word on record from the mid–fifteenth century (OED). It came into prominence nationally via the Act of 1555 which made provision for the election of *twoo honest persons ... to be surveyours ... of the highways* (SAL6/71). Previously, in 1531, Justices of Peace had been given the power to name and appoint two surveyors who would be responsible for the maintenance of bridges. They had to be *substantial and indifferent persons* who would view a bridge and then consult with skilful workmen to determine what sum of money would be needed for its repair. The number of surveyors later appears to have been increased, and their status reviewed, for at the Quarter Sessions in Richmond in 1607, four gentlemen were nominated *to take survey of decayed Bridges in Richmondshire* (NRQS1/97). Later still the post would be salaried and the bridge surveyor himself had the power to order repairs. In 1710, it was noted at the West Riding Quarter Sessions that Mr William Ettie was offering himself *as surveyor of bridges* (QS1/49/4).

suster A regional spelling of 'sister', a vowel change formerly common in dialect speech. The surnames Rushworth and Rushton derive from places named Rishworth and Rishton and illustrate a similar development: 1538 *to Jennet my suster 6s 8d*, Pontefract (Th19/2); 1541 *to be devyded betwixte her breder and her susters*, Hemingbrough (HAH334). See also kid.

swab A regional pronunciation of squab, that is a newly hatched or unfledged bird: 1558–9 *That the Swanherd ... shall make no Sale nor take up no wabes* [sic] *nor mark them*, Hatfield (ERAS12/59).

swage The noun 'swage' is on record from 1374, descriptive of the grooving or moulding on metal objects such as basins, candlesticks and salt cellars, e.g. 1503 *an ewere of silver, the swages gilt*, Stoke Rochford (SS53/216). From the latter part of the seventeenth century it was associated also with anvils and tools which were used for shaping or bending metal, and the term 'swage-anvil' occurred in 1854 (OED). According to Wright, a 'swage-anvil' was used for making agricultural implements (EDD). One early example in the inventory of a Yorkshire goldsmith seems likely to refer to a specialist tool capable of producing decoration on metal, a link in the word's semantic history: 1490 *De ij lez spoyn tayses xd. De ij lez stampis xiiijd. De iij lez swages vjd*, York (SS53/58). A glossary of words used in claims after the Sheffield flood of 1864 defines it as a tool used in bending or shaping cold metal, or a stamp for marking metal (online). See also swaging stithy.

swaging stithy In 1690, a file-cutter called Edward Hellifeild had in his smithy *5 cuting Sithies* [sic] *and two Swageing Stithies* (IH).

swale Substantial pieces of timber, planking: 1508 *De ijs iiijd pro v lez swailles like shamels*, York (SS53/288); 1520 *Fabricæ pontis le Hew xij lez swalles*, New Malton (SS79/118); 1541 *Item for a gret longe swayll that lyes under the gutter*, York (CCW237); 1600 *a swalle of timber lyinge at Beckwithe*, Harrogate (SS104/222); 1634 *bords, swalls, sleighes and all other lose wood*, Eldwick (LRS1/100). See also swawle.

swallow A deep hole or opening in the ground. The word has a very long history and is now associated particularly with landscape features in limestone country. Less obviously it was used when the piers of bridges had their foundation timbers swept away by the scouring action of the water: 1705 *wanting Twenty Four yards of Oake frameing under the Swallow att the south end*, Newton Bridge over the Hodder (QS1/44/1). Such holes or pits were formed by the whirlpool action of the water: 1673 *late greate flood … the stones that fell downe being driving* [sic] *away into deepe turne-pitts not to be recovered*, Bolton Bridge (QS1/11). Usually, the reference is simply to 'holes'. In 1686, John Rhodes of Harden agreed to *fill up and Sett with stone A great hole worne by the River under the East bow* of Kirkstall Bridge: it was 15 yards long, 8 yards wide and 4 yards deep, and had been there so long that it was *called the Fowle hole* (QS1).

swame A variant spelling of 'swalm', that is an attack of faintness or sickness: 1659 *Mary dropped down in a swame but after standing at the door recovered*, Hackness (PR).

swang A low-lying piece of grass land subject to flooding: 1642 *When wee used to mowe rounde aboute the Corne-Sikes, viz the balkes and swanges att the farre ende, that was accounted three dayworkes*, Elmswell (DW42). Although it is generally a rare word it occurs frequently in one set of Bridlington records: 1636 *the Mill Hill and swang*; 1668 *for an incrochment … Adjoyne upon the swange*; 1683 *for plowing further into the swang then the bounder stones 2s 6d* (BCP).

swanherd A keeper responsible for the swans: 1558–9 *ordayned that no Person or Persons being Swanherds … begin a marking without the master of the Kings Game of Swannes … be there present*, Hatfield (ERAS12/58); 1652 *their honors armes graven and quartered for the wearing of there hon'rs Swanherd on the carrs in Holderness* (Whit2/321). The sites where the swans were kept were called pools or carrs: 1508 *the goyng of a payr of swans in the carre of Newsom with ther brewde and brewdez*, Breckenbrough (SS53/272); 1558–9 *their swan Poles … are by now … Converted into Dryland*, Hatfield (ERAS12/59); 1570 *And there are in the Carre … by the confession of the swannerdes xlvij whyte swannes and all the sygnettes are to be marked*, Leconfield (YAJ17/144); 1598 *Low Holling Closes or Swankare Close*, Thorpe near Ripon (SS104/213).

swanimote A forest court, responsible for controlling the pasturage of swine and other livestock, and dealing with woodland offences: 1349 *Willelmus de Kyrkeby nuper ballivus de Pykerynge, colore officii sui qualibet vice quando ipse tenuit swanemota Foreste de Pykerynge* [William de Kyrkeby lately bailiff of Pickering, by reason of his office at whatever time when he held the swanimote of the Forest of Pickering] (NRR4/171); 1547–57 *Cur' leta & swaynnimot forest [Courts leet and swanimote forest]*, Langstrothdale (AW37); 1619–21 *they saye that there are theis severall Courtes yearlie kepte for the Honor and foreste, vizt a view of franck pledge, Turnes, Wapentack Courtes, Swanimotes and attachment Courtes*, Pickering (NRR1/35).

swan-pie A dish enjoyed occasionally by the Saviles of Thornhill, even when they were away from home: 1642 17 Feb *swan pie to London to my master £1 4s 6d* (BN2/29).

swape A wooden implement, a handle or lever, although Wright offers a number of other possibilities (EDD). It occurred several times in one *accompte of … the clerk of the works* for York: 1568–9 *To Edmonde Dakers for making a swape to the Minster gates 16d; For making an iron pynne to the mason well swape, 15d; for a pece of tymber to make the swape on, 14d* (SS35/114–15). Such items could be made of holly wood: 1606 *Edward Mylson got hollinge swaypes in Awmett wodd*, Brandsby (NYRO44/42). It was possibly responsible for an early by-name: 1297 *William Swaype*, Sowerby (YRS29/291).

sware, swared Regional spellings of square, squared: 1423 *uno veru magno swarrd de ferro [a large swared iron spit]*, York (SS45/79); 1433 *unam peciam argenti coopertam, swared, signatam sub pede [a covered silver article, swared, marked beneath the foot]*, York (SS30/47); 1490 *De j lez fowir swared bord jd*, York (SS53/57); 1578 *Item sware trenchers … Item rownd trenchers*, Stockeld (YRS134/50); 1581 *hath not used decent apparell and sware cap lyke a minister of his vocation*, Rufforth (PTD168).

swarf (1) The tiny particles of metal which a grindstone throws off when knives and tools are given a cutting edge. It was apparently used as a black dye: 1565 *no person … shall dye or cause to be dyed black, any cap, with bark or swarf* (SAL6/247); 1568 *In swarffe xxviijs Ireon in the shope*, Kendal (SS26/224). The Sheffield cutlers had a protective shield which caught moisture and the stone and metal particles from the grindstone (CAT19): in 1714, a Wadsley grinder called Henry Shaw had *2 swarfing boards* at his grinding wheel (IH).

swarf (2) An occasional spelling of sward, via swarth, in this instance used as a verb meaning to pare the top sods: 1747–8 *swarfing in Park*, Whitley (DD/WBE/1/21).

swarth An alternative spelling of 'sward', as in green-sward, that is grass land: 1549 *leve the same grounde three yerez swarthe and not pluyd afore the ende of the seid xij^ue yerez*, Manston (YRS50/112); 1562 *the moore parte of the ground taken in was fair and good grene gyrs [grass] and swerth ground … and noo heath growing upon yt* Rawdon (YRS114/100); 1619–21 *about the skirtes of which hill on everie syde there is arable land excepte the south syde which is swarth or ley grounde*, Pickering (NRR1/37); 1634 *noe person … shall grave any bent, swarthe or greenesword ground*, Meltham (G-A). See also pare, swarf (2).

swartmold Literally 'black earth', formerly a frequent minor place-name in east Yorkshire, referring usually to land in the town fields: *c*.1316 *half an acre at Suardmold*, Constable Burton (YRS83/62); 1408 *one acre on Swertmollde*, Skelton in Cleveland (YRS59/71). Undated thirteenth-century references include: *unam rodam in cultura mea de Swartemolde [a rood in my ploughland at Swartemold]*, Guisborough (SS86/153);

dim. acram supra Swardemolde [half an acre above Swartemolde], Normanby (SS89/6). See also mire pits, mould (1).

swash To behave noisily or in an unseemly way, to swagger: 1581 *a lusty dauncinge preist and offensive to many both by his dauncinge and swashing in apparell, not minister lyke*, Rufforth (YAJ15/243).

swath The space covered by a sweep of a mower's scythe: 1642 *A goode Mower will … take a broade lande and more att 4 sweathes and … yow shall scarce perceive his sweath-balke*, Elmswell (DW34). It was used as a measure for a division of a meadow: 1348 'all her meadow in the great meadow of Walton, namely one swath (*swatha*) at *le nuhengthorne*, two swaths in *Lefall* and a share of a swath in *le Drihalges*', Chevet (YRS106/28); 1664 *all those sixteene swaithes of meadowe-ground lyeing within the lordshippe of Cropton* (NRQS4/162).

swath-rake A large drag rake, the width of a swath, used for gathering the scattered hay or corn: 1577 *ij sweathe raikes*, North Frodingham (YAJ36/450); 1648 *3 swathrakes, 2 horse harrowes* Sharlston (YRS134/99); 1727 *no Person … shall make use of any Sweath Rake or any other large Rake to gather Corn in the field*, Reighton (YRS74/102); 1835 *1 Swaith Rake head making 1s 6d; 24 teeth 1s*, Darton (GRD).

swattle To make a splashing or spluttering noise in water:

> 1671 *she did take the ax and knocked him in the harnes* [brains] *her owne selfe … carryed him downe and threw him in the becke and that he swattled after he came in the becke*, Pickering (SS40/186).

swawle A spelling of swale, that is a piece of wood or timber: 1574 *Foure swawles and foure trists vs*, Richmond (SS26/249).

swayed Swaying of the back, a kind of lumbago when used of a horse: 1565 *an olde white gelding sweyde in the backe*, Temple Newsam (YAJ25/99).

sway pole A word noted by Wright which was used of a pole serving as a lever (EDD): c.1620 'Nor had he seen him *Cutt or Cropp in peeces the sway poles of the Bellowes*', Colne Bridge (HOW41).

sweal To singe or burn: 1760 *lett two people have hold of either end of each hank and keep pulling itt bak and forward over the blase … while all the coarse hairs are swealed*, Wakefield (YRS155/39). See also swill (2).

sweet milk Fresh milk having its natural sweet flavour as distinct from sour milk, that is buttermilk, on record from c.1420 (OED). Both are noted as by-names: 1258 *Peter Swetemilk*, Rothwell (YRS12/59); 1325 *Ivo Sourmilk*, Sowerby near Halifax (YRS109/67). Sweet milk occurs as a minor place-name in an undated thirteenth-century deed: 'in the fields of *Farnelay* in the place called *Suet Milke Riddinge*', Otley (YRS111/78).

sweet mouth Possibly a nickname for a flatterer: 1324 *Margaret Swetemuth*, York (YRS158/99); 1357 'the chantry lately founded by Robert *Swetmouth*', York (SS91/49n).

sweet wort A sweet-flavoured wort, before the hops were put in: c.1534 *2 swett wortt fatts*, Bridlington (YRS80/2); 1567 *a swete worte toube*, Mortham (SS26/203); 1568 *a Sweyte worte fat*, Healaugh Park (YRS134/34). See also wort.

swelly Spellings recorded elsewhere include 'swally' and swilly', so they may derive from the dialect pronunciation of 'swallow', in the sense of a hole. In west Yorkshire it refers to a hollow place in the coal stratum, often filled with water. The word is used here in conjunction with 'dike', since both hindered normal productive working: 1714 *your field of coal … is a Crabbed and uncertain works by that reason of so many Dikes and Swellies, and the coal lying partly Rigg and Furr*, Colsterdale (BM82/73). Greenwell described it as a depression in the strata, where the seam of coal might be thicker.

swift Part of the clothiers' equipment, a machine for winding yarn, although Wright has several regionally distinct definitions (EDD): 1753 *4 looms and utensils, a pair of bartrees, 2 pair of swifts*, Burnt Yates (QS1/92/1).

swill (1) A large shallow basket, woven from oak laths and characteristic of Cumbria (CDD): 1395 *pro ij cannis et j squill*, Whitby (SS72/604); 1562 *In the loft, barrells, swills, stolles … with other woodde gere*, Kendal (SS26/153). In Yorkshire contexts it may occasionally have been a shallow tub: 1658 *In the Milkehouse 5 milke bowles, 1 swill, 2 kitts, 3 shelves*, Beckwithshaw (SS110/234).

swill (2) A verb which related to the movement of water and other liquids: 1747 *a violent torent of rain … sweel'd the waters over where the bridges are, one of them entirely drove down*, Kirkby Malzeard (QS1/86/8). Regionally it described the practice of spreading liquid manure over the fields via a system of shallow channels: 1783 *I worked in the fields Shreading, Swilling, &c*, Ovenden (CA114). Some spellings are similar to those of 'sweal'.

swine grease The fat of a swine: 1576 *Swine greace xvjd*, Scriven (SS26/260); 1587 *Item in swine greise xijd*, South Cave (Kaner141). See also grease cake, tallow.

swineherd A herdsman in charge of the swine, working on behalf of a township or group of owners: 1472 *Also xij men has ordan & chosyn ij men of ather gatt for to gedyr the swyn hyrd hyrez with the constabylle*, Selby (SS85/23); 1579 *no inhabitant … shall keep any swine saving within their own several grounds … and the said swine … shall not go in any of the said laynes, common pastures or streets before the Swyneherd blowe his horn*, Beverley (YRS84/30); 1608 *William Splett of Nunnington being the hired servant for keeping there towne-swyne* (NRQS1/99); 1668 *The Swinard is Will Hobson and … hee is to repaire the fould … and if any beast be impounded by his neglect the pouncill is to be paid out of his wadgis*, Bridlington (BCP238); 1747 *George Ruddock appointed swineherd until Michaelmas next and to have 20s salary and 10s towards a cloth coat*, Beverley (YRS122/28). The Latin *porcarius* is on record much earlier, especially in monastic accounts, and only occasional by-names provide evidence of the English word: 1377–8 *Johanni Swynehird operanti in carpentaria [To John Swynehird working in the carpenter's shop]*, Bolton Priory (YRS154/567); 1379 *Willelmus Swynhyrd*, Halton East (PTWR). See also common herd, townherd.

swine root Manorial by-laws obliged tenants to 'ring' their swine at certain times of the year, in order to control their routing for food: 1548 'If any person keep his swine unringed [*si aliquis custod porcos suos non anulat*] … after 3 May he will be fined 4d for each animal', Lepton (DD/WBM); 1609 *that every man doe ringe and yoke his swine before the tenth day of May next and soe kepe them ringed until the 29 day of September*, Upperthong (WCR11/185). In 1629, *for the maintenance of good … neighbourhood* a lease threatened distraint *for anie … ofence or default Except for Swynewroot*, Buckden (GRD). See also ring (2), rout (1).

swingle-stock The swingle was a sword-like implement used in the dressing of flax and hemp and it gave rise to both a verb and an adjective (OED): the 'stock' was a wooden board on which the fibres were beaten: 1579 *iij swingle stockes*, South Cave (Kaner109); 1581 *payd for spynnyng swynglyn towe*, Stockeld (YRS161/45); 1634 *a pair of garnewingle blades and stocke and a swingle stocke*, Elmswell (DW234).

swingletree In a horse-drawn plough or carriage this is a cross-bar, pivoted at the middle, to which the traces are attached: 1618 *the horse mill with the furniture a swingle tree & the linkes 5s 6d*, South Cave (Kaner270); 1639 *three paire of traces & three Swineltres*, Swinsty (YRS134/91); 1681 *4 payre of hames with the traces and swengletrese*, Lund (YRS47/66). It derives from the verb to swing and this influenced some spellings: *c.*1742 *stave body, raiths, swinging tree*, Holmfirth (G-A). In some contexts the meaning is not absolutely clear, for it could also be a board on which flax and hemp were dressed (OED).

swipple The part of a flail that strikes the grain in threshing. Mr Cholmeley complained in 1617 that Seth Lazenby had been in his woods *cuttinge flayle swipples with a knyfe and great whittle*, Brandsby (NYRO44/148). In 1642, the East Riding farmer Henry Best made allowances to his *thrashers … furnishing them with swipples and Flailebands*, Elmswell (DW148).

switch As a noun 'switch' was a slender tree shoot or branch, used by farmers as a whip to control animals: 1642 *a small switch in your hande, and to switch her sowndly*, Elmswell (DW84). The verb could also refer to cutting off the switches from a tree or hedge: 1688 *that everie one shall cutt and swich thiere hedgs where they are annoyance to the hye way*, Kirkburton (WCR14/122); 1763 *occupiers of land adjoining to Mean Lane switch the hedges and scour the ditches*, Meltham (G-A). See also walking rod.

swithen To singe, scorch or burn, a regional word of Old Norse origin although the vocabulary references are quite late: 1681 *the grasse upon the hay-ground went back so that many fell to mowing to take what there was, lest all should be swithend away*, Northowram (OH2/186). Minor place-names provide much earlier evidence: 1246 *Swythengate* (PNWR7/254); 1404 'one piece of land called *Swythenknoll*', Old Lindley (YRS65/90); 1472 'an acre of land in *Swythenhyll*', Barnsley (YRS120/29). See Swithenbank (GRDict).

swoon See sowned.

sword-sliper A sword sharpener (OED) but also the craftsman who made sword sheaths: 1479 *Et solutum … Robson swerdsliper pro j vagina de novo facta magno gladio maioris [And paid to … Robson the sword-sliper for renewing the sheath of the great mayoral sword]*, York (SS192/165); 1596 *arte of smithes, armourers, cutlers, swordslipers and hardeway-remen*, Beverley (YRS84/69); 1638 *Jonathan Worrall, Halifax, swordsliper* (YRS4/63). By-names provide the earliest evidence: 1305 *Peter le Swerdslipere*, Northallerton (YRS127/53); 1316 *William the Swerdslyper*, Wakefield (YRS78/110); 1379 *Johannes Swerdslyper*, Rotherham (PTWR); 1425 'Thomas *Swordsliper* holds seven acres of land', Leeds (Th24/20).

sycamore A tree of the maple family which is said to have been introduced into Britain but is now thoroughly naturalised. The Romans are considered by some to have brought it here but one argument against that is the absence of 'sycamore' in early place-names. Rackham thought that it came from the Continent in the sixteenth century which seems possible since the first reference in the OED is from Shakespeare. On the other hand it has been suggested that if it were known earlier as 'maple' it will have had a much longer history. In Yorkshire, it was grown as a hedgerow tree in the seventeenth century: 1653–5 *Item given to Taskard and Hodgson of earnest for making the sickamore hedg*, Stockeld (YRS161/83) and was later used occasionally for building: 1741 *oke plank, seckamor plank, felks*, Wakefield (QS1/80/9). On some estates it became customary to plant sycamores close to exposed farms, and that practice is recorded in the accounts of the Earl of Dartmouth, held in the Slaithwaite estate office: 1808 *Make the tenants, each of them, plant 8 or 10 sycamore about their Homeflatts*: two years earlier it was said that a few sycamore and ash *at each fold would look picturesque*. See also chatt.

syke A regional term for a stream of no great size. It occurred commonly as the name of hillside becks, especially those which defined boundaries: 1502 *inter un syke vocat Dyksyke ex boreal [between a syke called Dyksyke on the north side]*, Hepworth (MD225/1/228); 1574 *one sicke or brook which parts Derbyshire and Hallamshire* – later referred to as the said *sicke or ditch* (JHS12). 1635 *certain bounderes sett amongest the Peatepittes … one syke or water which runneth by the horwithens*, Northowram (MD225/1/361).

It was also the word for the water channels used as boundaries in the open arable fields, and this may explain the frequent plural which is a feature of the surname. Many early examples are in undated documents: n.d. 'and 1½ roods of land in three selions abutting on *le Sykes*', Hornington (YRS50/81); 1291 'half an acre by *Stokeldsyk* … one acre between *le Sykes*', Hackness (YRS69/45); 1352 'and by *le syk* an acre of land abutting on *le Wellecroft*', Parlington (YRS39/132); *c.*1490 *the whyche syke was wonte in my tyme and in my fadyr days as he sayd me to be drawyn with a plough for a mere on that syde bytwene Sand Hoton and Brakynbargh* (YAJ2/91); 1612 'land … in the West Field … abutting on a certain stream (*gurgitem*) called *le Sewer vel le Kirkesicke*', Methley (Th35/88). Early by-names include: 1275 *Richard del Syk*, Langfield (YRS29/105); 1309 *Richard del Sikes*, Langfield (YRS36//227). See also overwhart, and Sykes (GRDict).

syle An alternative of cruck: 1422 *iiij romes of syelles and two henforkes*, Catterick (NRQS3/36). Probably more characteristic of the north-east of England since other examples quoted by Salzman were from county Durham.

syling, syllyng Variant spellings of ceiling or seiling: 1565 *plew tymbre and sylinge bourds*, Knaresborough (SS26/179).

T

tabby A word applied from the seventeenth century to a type of material, generally silk taffeta (OED). It is said to derive ultimately from the quarter of Bagdad where it was originally made: 1655 *my blacke suite, the cloake of cloath lyned with tabby*, Babthorpe (HAH194).

table (1) As a verb this could mean 'to provide board', a sense recorded in the OED from the fifteenth century. An early example shows how the two words inter-related: 1577 *for the board and tabling of William Gilby … 12d weekly*, Beverley (YRS84/12). A workman might have his board provided as part of a contract or pay for it himself: 1640 *William Tadman the shepherd to have £5 per annum … and he to table himselfe*, Elmswell (DW192); 1672 *went to worke at Almondbury by dayes and out of his hand labor tabled his child at Honley* (QS1/11/7). More usually it meant to take one's meals at a certain place or with a certain person or family: 1633 *we tabled all the time of our aboad in that country* [Devonshire] *in the house of Mr Roger Skinner* (SS65/127). Examples are found in parish registers: 1656–7 *Anthony Smith, sep: the 19 Januarie who was tabled att Philip Scatcherdes, att Arthington*, Adel (PR); 1664 *Thomas Briggs who were tabled with John Cozin*, Horbury (PR). See also board (2), tabler.

table (2) A mason's word for a horizontal piece of stone: 1618 *Window tables 72 yards and 2 foote at 9d a yard: Ground tables 50 yardes at 6d a yard … 29 yardes of hollow table at 3d the foot … towards the capping the wall*, Almondbury (DD/RA/f/4a).

tablemen See tables.

tabler A boarder: 1707 *Agnes Jennings a tabler with Richard Firth of Keighley* (QS1/46/6); 1722 *Mary Baites a tabler or boarder with George Whiteley of Sowerby* (QS1).

tables The game of backgammon (OED) but possibly used more widely for other board games. These were being imported into Hull in the fifteenth century: 1453 *2 duss' par' playng tabilles; 60 scok tabylmen* (YRS144/4,61); 1472 *suffers me(n) to play in his hous at the tables for mony*, Selby (SS85/25); 1490 *De j pari tabellarum [For 1 pair of tables]*, York (SS53/56); 1568 *Item 3 pare of plaing tables with men for the same*, Healaugh Park (YRS134/34); 1607–8 *Richard Fawcett of New Malton for keeping unlawfull games or play at cardes and tables in his house* (NRQS1/101). A Ripon inventory of 1485 has: *tabula lusoria cum hominibus [a game table with men]*, possibly chessmen, and a Bury will of 1459 has *unum par de tablis cum chesemen et tabilmenys* (SS64/366). In 1619, 5s was *Given to my lo[rd] to play at Tables in the Great Chamber* of Skipton Castle (Whit2/321).

tache A clasp or buckle, used to attach two parts of a garment: 1532 *one pare of new siluer crokes and my best tache*, Swillington (Th11/50); 1535 *j tach with j ruby ston*, Ripon (SS64/359); 1542 *my best gowne with the siluer tache*, Leeds (Th19/59); 1558 *vnto Elsabethe Cowper my doughter my best gowne, a paire of Syluer Crokes and a tache of Syluer*, Rothwell (Th27/175).

tack (1) A small, sharp-pointed metal nail: 1504 *Item vj takkes iiijd*, York (SS53/191).

tack (2) A lease or tenancy: 1510 *I will that my sonne have the takke of my water wheles*, Ecclesfield (PR); 1547 *one tacke or terme which I haue of James Grenewood ... as moore playnelie apperithe in a paire of indentures*, Heptonstall (Crossley25).

tack (3), tacked Alternative spellings of tag, tagged: 1515 *an oxe called Takke*, South Otterington (YAJ36/438); 1558 *ij oxen the blacke and the tacked*, Newton Kyme (Th27/146); 1652 *two quies, a brouneish black & a blacke with a tacke taile*, Gateforth (YRS47/158).

tacket A very small metal nail, a diminutive of tack: 1413–14 'And for *takettis* purchased for joining together the boards (*pro tabulis conjungendis*) 2d', Selby (SAR212); 1526–7 *Item for naylles and brages and takyttes, iiij^d· ob*, York (CCW117). Note the by-name: 1276 John *Taket* or *Takel*, Cottingham (YRS12/239). *Taket* was one of the carters employed at Bolton Priory from 1311–12, but he had no surname (YRS154/319).

taffeta A name given to various fabrics, often a bright lustrous material, usually silk: 1378 *Deux courtyns de taffata rouge [Two red taffeta curtains]*, York (YAJ15/480); 1392 *et unum vestimentum integrum de viridi tafata [and a full vestment of green taffeta]*, Ingmanthorpe (SS4/179); 1567 *usethe veine undecent apparell, namelie great britches cut and drawen oute with sarcenet and taffitie*, Ripon (PTD28); 1568 *a quilt of black velvet yellowe and red taffetay*, Healaugh (YRS134/25); 1612 *1 pare of silver color taffetye skirts*, Brafferton (NYRO44/34); 1621 *taffety to face both hands of the ould dublitts ijs*, Brandsby (NYRO44/214). See also tippet.

tag The tip of an animal's tail, especially a white tip: 1543 *a blake stott with a tage of the tale*, Ardsley (Th19/96). It was regularly used as a name for oxen and cows: 1543 *towe stottes the ane called Raven the other Tagge*, Castleford (Th19/87); 1558 *ij oxen called fedder & tagge*, Fairburn (Th27/194). In *Wharfedale*, by Ella Pontefract and Marie Hartley, the authors quote from the will of Anthony Craven, undated but probably 1617, *one oxe called Tagge to bring me forth to my burial* (BIA34/602). In rural areas it may also explain the by-name: 1275 *Bateman Tagge*, Stanley (YRS29/155). See also tack (3), tagged, taggle.

tagged, tagtailed Used regularly to describe a bovine animal with a white-tipped tail: 1458 *j bovem vocatum taggyd ox [1 ox called the tagged ox]*, Ripon (SS64/75); 1540 *a tagged whie*, Spofforth (Th19/14); 1544 *one taged whye*, Timble (SS104/42); 1556 *a tagged cowe*, Halifax (Crossley128); 1588 *a tagged cowe spinked*, Birstwith (SS104/163); 1610 *my other whie being a black tagged*, South Cave (Kaner236); 1616 *one black tagged oxehide*, Huddersfield (DD/RA/f/4a); 1707 *1 tagtailed why for his childs part*, Hambleton (YRS47/20). See also tack (3), tag, taggle.

taggle, taggled Used as a name for a bovine animal with a white tail: 1412 *lego Johanni Rihell vnam vaccam que vocatur Tagill [I bequeath to John Rihell a cow called Taggle]*, Winestead (ERAS10/7); 1588 *twoe kye called Taggelde and Cherie*, Hudswell (YRS152/281); 1670 *to my doughter Mary ... [a] tagel why in ful for a portion*, Brayton (YRS47/165); 1707 *Tagill Buld June the 11th*, Conistone (RW50). This can be compared with flowerill (see flowereld), raggled, spangled, sterneld, and possibly featherill (see feather). See also NH144–9.

tagtailed See tagged.

take care on Regional for take care of: 1690 *a child ... laid upon a bench ... for the towne to take care on*, Skipton (QS1/29/5).

tallow, tallow cake Tallow is the fat of an animal, especially the fat around the kidneys and liver of sheep and oxen from which suet was rendered: 1510 *ylke hundredth groce of talghte*, York (YRS106/33); 1619 *Tarr 3 gallons ijs vjd, tallow one stone iiijs vjd*, Brandsby (NYRO44/181); 1642 *the salve* [for sheep] *beinge made partly of molten tallowe*, Elmswell (DW31); 1654 *paid to Canby for five pound of tallow to grease the waines*, Stockeld (YRS161/93). Its use in the tanning process and the manufacture of candles and soap explains its frequency in inventories and the like, especially attributively: 1567 *iij caiks of talowe*, Mortham (SS26/203); 1725 *sold a tallow cake* [which] *came out of a cow of his own … weighed 2 stone*, Wakefield (QS1/64/2). A North Riding farmer recorded the following: 1798 *Mar. 23 We cut up bull this morning. He very fat. Weighed 86 stones 6lbs … Tallow 13st 3lbs which I sold at 5/6 stone. I went with cake to Thirkleby* (WM67). The word influenced the spelling of surnames such as Talbot or Tarbutt: 1660 *Thomas Tallowpot*, Emley (PR); 1669 *George Tallopot*, Thurgoland (QS1). See also candle, grease cake, tapett, and S&G74.

tally, tally board, tally stick A piece of wood on which notches, numbers or letters might be incised in order to keep an account of debts, payments or work done. In some cases identical tallies were kept by each party to an agreement: 1728 *he took the tally stick along with him*, Wakefield (QS1/67/4). In a dispute at the Quarter Sessions in 1638, Mr Lionel Copley was criticised for not restoring *to the poore men their Tallyes of the coals led to him* (YAJ5/372). On that occasion the coals were actually charcoal but it was a practice used also in coal-mining, and a tally board from Dark Lane Colliery in Mirfield has survived (DHH24). Gresley noted that in some pits tallies were attached to corves to credit men working below.

tammy A fine cloth woven with a worsted weft and cotton warp, dyed fancy colours and having a glazed finish: 1724 *theft of 7½ of greeneyard broad tammy*, Hemingfield (QS1/67/4); 1783 *Edward Holland of Lightcliffe, Halifax, Tammy Maker*, Emley (PR); 1785 *I wove Tamy in Charles Crowther loom in the day*, Ovenden (CA180). The origin of the word is obscure so it is worth noting that Halliwell has a material called 'tamine'. In Yorkshire, 'tammet' occurs from the early seventeenth century: 1619 *Taylor of Malton for making up my wif's tammet gowne xxxvs*, Brandsby (NYRO44/170); 1693 *1 piece of stript searge £2 … 1 piece of tammet £1 5s*, Selby (YRS47/22). Tammy Hall in Wakefield, of which a substantial section has survived, was built in 1766 for the sale of tammies.

tane A spelling of 'taken' which represents the dialect pronunciation: 1533 *we present that every man that hays haue stowpes & rales & stones that tha be tane up be twene thys & halathoresday*, Wakefield (YRS74/17); 1550 *he hathe tane paynes for me right oft*, West Layton (SS26/87).

tang From an Old Norse word which meant 'point' and could be applied to 'points' or spits of land in place-names, for example Tang (Felliscliffe) and Tang Hall (Osbaldwick). In connection with cutlery it referred to the metal extension by which a blade is fitted into its handle, and in this sense it is on record from the fifteenth century: 1483 'A Tange of A knyfe' (OED).

tan-house The building in which tanning is carried on: 1574 *all the tanne howses, barnes … and croft*, Bradford (MMB/57); 1626 *all the tubbes and seasterans in the tanhouse*, Bilton (SS110/102). See also tanyard.

tanner craft This term dates back to the late Middle Ages when tanneries were mostly located in the great towns or cities and tanners operated within the guild system: 1476 *in the counsaile chaumbre of … York, by the instaunce … of all the hole craft of* *the tanners of the said cite* (SS125/166); 1539 *Ordinaunces and constitucions of the tannere crafte in Beverley* (BTD114). The guild system survived in Beverley and the renewed ordinances of 1596 provided for the election of one *Rewler* or warden, *two Stewards and two Searchers … to survey, vewe and searche all the tanners* (YRS84/74).

tanten For Anthony. 'Tant' was the colloquial pet-form of Anthony, certainly in the Sheffield area and in this case it was probably a name for the inmates of an alms-house dedicated to St Anthony: 1515 *To every Tanten man ther dwelling iiijd to pray for my sowll*, Holme in Derbyshire (SS79/65).

tanyard The yard attached to a tannery, where the tan-pits were located. It was sometimes used of the tannery itself: 1673 *In the Tan Yard, 39 uper leather hides*, Selby (YRS47/33); 1709 *also the New Erected building and the Tan Yard to the same belonging*, Mirfield (RD/A/434/687); 1739 *one tanyard on the premises and all the pyts and housing for tanning*, Austonley (G-A); 1754 *the Tanyard with all my stock of leather in the Pitts and out of the Pitts*, Kirkburton (G-A). In 1860, Thomas Walker leased property at Whitley near Mirfield to Hamoth Fell which included a *Tan House, Tan Yard with 54 Pits, 5 Lime Pits, Water Dyke, 3 Bates, Sheds, Cottage, Warehouse* (GRD). No earlier references have yet been noted and in Yorkshire its use in minor place-names is on record only from the nineteenth century.

tapet A piece of figured cloth which could serve as a hanging, a carpet or a table-cover: 1287–8 *et in tapetis et sotularibus et pelliciis emptis ad opus canonicorum xxixs ijd [and for tapets and shoes and cloaks bought for the use of the canons 29s 2d]*, Bolton Priory (YRS154/38); 1342 *lego Roberto Coltebay unum novum tapetum [I bequeath to Robert Coltebay a new tapet]*, York (SS4/5); 1391 *tribus cortinis et tribus tapetis de blodio [for three curtains and three blue cloth tapets]*, Harewood (SS4/150); 1485 *vj cusshyns de tappett xxd*, Clotherholme (SS64/368). There were tapiters in York from the thirteenth century: *c.*1280 *Willelmus Tapiter* (YAJ50/85) but the guild may have been established later, possibly from *c.*1375 when no fewer than ten men were enrolled as freemen, e.g. 1375 *Thomas de Coppegrave, tapetter* (SS96/72): several of those names were included in their undated ordinances (SS120/84). See also arras, happing, ridel, tester.

tapett The contexts suggest that these were candles, possibly tapers: 1527–8 *for iij quartes of wax to iij tapyttes v^d ob … for makyn of them ij^d*; 1545–6 *for making of iij tapertes at Crystynmes j^d ob … iij^li of tallow candylles*, York (CCW123,291).

tar A dark, viscous liquid which consists mainly of hydrocarbons, produced by the destructive distillation of materials such as wood, coal and peat. It was much used by shepherds: 1291–2 *oleo et ter ad oves lxs viijd [oil and tar for sheep 60s 8d]*, Bolton Priory (YRS154/44); 1530 *pro … tar barels ad comburendum calcem, 8d [for … tar barrels for burning lime, 8d]*, York (SS35/105); 1579 *payd for a gallon of tarre for mending shepe*, Stockeld (YRS161/12); 1617 *Stray tuppes … challenged by Anthony Watson of Sutton … by his name marked with tarr*, Brandsby (NYRO44/133); 1642 *The manner is to give lambes a tarre-marke before they goe to the feld*, Elmswell (DW13). It had a wide range of other attributive uses: 1627 *a tarbox*, South Cave (Kaner333); 1642 *a tarre-kettle*, Elmswell (DW25); 1678 *a tarring trough [for a ropemaker]*, Selby (YRS47/102); 1686 *3 tar cartes … 1 new tar pan, 1 tarcan*, West Riding (QS1). See also costrel.

tar band A length of tarred rope or string: 1762 *A Tar Band 3d*, Tong (Tong/4c/6). When this was lit at one end it was difficult to extinguish and would burn uniformly for hours. It may have served to ignite the gunpowder which was in regular use in the Tong coal-pits by that time. See also gunpowder, rammer.

tartarin A rich material, apparently of silk, which was imported from the east, probably from China through Tartary: 1388 *Trois courtyns de tartaryn rouge, pris c.s [Three red tartarin curtains, cost 100s]*, York (YAJ15/480); 1421 *cum capucio lineato cum viridi tarteryn [with a hood lined with green tartarin]*, York (SS4/400); 1444 *myn aucter clothe of reed tarteryn with the corteyns* (SS30/110).

task The phrase 'by task' was a reference to piece-work, and *c.*1570 John Kaye wrote *owt with thy plowghe Lett taskers thresh more strawe* (KayeCP). Employers would take on men at such rates under certain conditions: 1690 *by Taske*; 1694 *paid for getting by Taske*, Farnley (MS11). The word has a much longer history and is the origin of the surname Tasker: 1341 *Thomas Tasker*, Ousthorpe (YAJ17/107); 1379 *Johannes Tasker*, Sprotbrough (PTWR). Found also in a minor place-name: 1544 *un claus' voc' Taskerrod [a close called Taskerrod]*, Whitley (DD/WBE/7).

tavelin A term used in the fur trade, said to refer originally to the boards between which skins were packed. Examples of it in York suggest that by the sixteenth century it was being used of the skins themselves: 1500 *Item for a furre of purde maid owt of tavillions of iiij yerdes wyde and j yerd depe viijd. Item for a fur of brode menevere makynge of tavilions vjd*, York (YRS106/190); 1582 *Item for a dosen tavilions making*, York (YRS119/63). See also timber (2).

tavern As a verb this occurs in Yorkshire from the fourteenth century and it was quite frequent in the Tudor period. It evidently has a longer history, for Latin references have been noted in county Durham from 1365 (OED) and in north Yorkshire in 1453 (AW158). In most contexts the practice clearly had to do with sub-letting property, and the first English usage is in an undated fifteenth-century document: *yhe schall inquiere if any man have tavernede his place … or any parcel of his lande*, Fountains Abbey (AW158). It was seen as an offence in most places, since it led to smaller holdings, especially in regions where partible inheritance was general. In 1511, when the Hardcastle family held the tenancy of Thrope in Nidderdale they were instructed not *to taberne nor lat to ferme thair said tenement ne no parcel thairof unto any oder persone* (SS42/320). In 1551, Christopher Dodsworth left an instruction in his will that if his wife happened to *latt or taverne any parte of the said fermehold*, his son was to have it, Jolby (SS26/72).

There were other considerations, especially where the tenement was barely able to support one person. In 1575, in State Papers the argument was that if such a tenant died and divided the holding between two sons 'the taverninge of the Queynes lande ys hinderance for kepinge of hors and armor' (OED). The latest reference that I have noted is in a survey of the East Riding village of Settrington in 1600. A clause inserted into tenancy agreements there restricted sub-letting, saying that no part of the tenement was *to be tauerned butt so as all may returne & continue together the last five yeares before the end of the lease* (YRS126/82). The use of the verb in this way appears to have been a northern practice but the word shares the same origin as tavern in the sense of 'public house'. The OED explanation is that both referred initially to sheds or small buildings, and that to 'tavern' first meant to build a cottage on a tenement.

taw The word is of Old English origin and the OED has references from that period. The early evidence in Yorkshire actually links the word with cloth: 1394 *2 taude cloths*, Hull (YRS64/52) but mostly it described the process by which skins are converted into leather by steeping them in a solution of alum and salt. In 1500, it was agreed in York *that … no skynner … from hensfurth wyrk no stuffe tawed by any glover … and that no skynner … wirke ne tawe no prest stuff that is brought rawe*, York (YRS103/152). Later examples include: 1713 *skins tanned, tawed or dressed*, West Riding (QS1). See also tew, whittawer.

tawne, tawny Initially a colour which is described as 'brown, with a preponderance of yellow or orange' (OED). It came to be used frequently of cloth which had that colour: 1341 *lego Agneti … tunicam meam de tawne [I bequeath to Agnes … my tawny tunic]*, York (SS4/3); 1395 '10 ells of *Tawne*', York (YRS64/117); 1493–4 *Item sol. pro xij virgis panni coloris de tawne pro vestura choristarum [Item paid for 12 yards of tawny coloured cloth for the choristers' clothing]*, Ripon (SS81/164); 1517 *meam nigram togam duplicatam cum le tawne sarcynet [my black gown lined with tawne sarsenet]*, Rudby (YAJ6/229). The modern form of the word may date from the early sixteenth century: 1504 *oon tawney gowne*, Ripon (SS64/295); 1526 *a tawney jackett*, Halifax (Clay72); *c.*1537 *certen remanents of tawny … a pece of tawny chamlett*, Halifax (YRS45/188).

tawpe A foolish or slatternly woman. As 'tawpie' or 'tawpy' it is found in Scotland from 1728 (OED). The burial register of Leeds has: 1588 *Jenett Lantome alias Tawpe, Ratten rowe, widow* (Th1/152).

team Part of the gear by which oxen or horses were attached to a plough or wain, the harness and chains that is: 1481 *meo duo plaustra … cum aratris et jugis et temez ferreis [my two carts … with ploughs and yokes and iron teams]*, Featherstone (Th22/261); 1485 *j sokke et j culter viijd, iiij^or temes iijs*, Ripon (SS64/373); 1544 *ij oxen iij iron teymes*, Scriven (SS104/39); 1561 *all my plow geare and wayne geare with yokes and teames*, Denton (Th27/355); 1634 *the ploughs and plough gear, harrows and sleds, 2 teames*, Elmswell (DW235).

tear Of the best quality, fine, delicate, used especially of hemp: 1532 *ij pare of harden shettes, ij pare of hempe tere*, Water Fryston (SS106/34); 1558 *a smocke of hemp teare*, Pontefract (Th27/152); 1637 *lynnen yearne & lynnen teare 4s*, Selby (YRS47/93); 1668 *Item foure pund & ½ of teare yearne 6s 9d Item six pound of Courser yearne 4s 6d*, Slaithwaite (YRS134/136).

teasel A plant, the heads of which have hooked prickles. These were used by clothiers to tease cloth, thereby raising the nap. Some were imported in earlier centuries and Somerset later provided large quantities to the trade. However, from the mid-eighteenth century Sherburn in Elmet was at the centre of a teasel-growing area which supplied local demand until *c.*1850: 1461 *10 skyve tasells*, Hull (YRS144/30); 1562 *Taysles iijs iiijd*, Kendal (SS26/153). See also card (1), handles.

ted To spread or scatter new-mown grass so that it might dry more easily: 1537 *Ralph Waiddelay for teddyng his mow and a foild In the feld 2d*, Sandal (WCR9/69); *c.*1570 *to mawe, to rake, to tedd, to stack*, Farnley Tyas (KayeCP).

teem To make empty: 1642 *if two of an equall strength goe with a waine the loader ought then to teame the waine*, Elmswell (DW48). It was used particularly meaning to empty of water, to pour out: 1703 *being in the mault kiln … teeming the cesterne*, West Riding (QS1). In a mining context it referred to primitive methods of baling or draining: 1755 *For teeming water*, Beeston (WYL160/129/4). See also lade.

teg A doe, or female deer in its second year: 1607 'John Thorneberry … for deerstealing (*unum parem damarum, Angl. a doe and a tegg*)', Downholme Park (NRQS6/70).

teind In parts of the north the tithe was commonly known as the 'teind', a collateral form of 'tenth': 1444 *to the vicer … for offeryng and forgetyn tendes xs*, Hull (SS30/105); 1472 *as for the teynd of Trinites … I have takyn itt … for xvj yere be Indenture*, Pontefract

(Th26/327); 1521 *hys seruande there, one Richard Orome ... manurid and maide the teynde hey within the seid towne*, Middlethorpe (YRS41/31); 1648 *payinge all teand moneys*, Meltham (G-A). Used occasionally as a verb: 1511 *corne, haye and grasse teyndyng ... left in the feld*, Moor Monkton (YRS41/167); 1642 *with teendinge of our lambes; as for the wooll it may bee teended and wayed*, Elmswell (DW28). See also manure (1), tendings.

teind-barn, teind-lathe Regional words for tithe-barn, first recorded as by-names: 1327 *De Johanne Teindebarne*, Silpho (YRS74/155); 1379 *Johannes Tendlathe*, Leeds (PTWR); 1426 'between a barn (*orrium*) called *Teyndlath ... and a garden*', Askwith (YRS65/17); 1510 *the tend laith is blawne downe ij yers syne*, Ampleforth (SS35/264); 1527 *the town of Semer with the teyndlathe and tenements* (YRS88/144). Some clerks replaced the regional word with its English equivalent, as in Whitkirk where a tenant's holding close to the church was called the *Tendlathgarth* in 1522 and the *Tythe Laith Garth* the following year (WYAS832). In Almondbury, the barn was referred to as the *tithe laith* in 1584 (MS205) whilst in Kirkburton the terrier of 1693 noted the existence of *an old Barn, commonly called the Teanlathe or Tithelathe* (PR2/4).

teld Linen for a ship's awning: 1453 *2 rolles teldes; 1 C 60 ulnis canvas*, Hull (YRS144/13); 1463 *1 rolle teldes*, Hull (YRS144/50). In the following context it was possibly a protective sheet: 1549 *one horse and paksadle, one paire of hampers, a teylde, withe all other thinges belonging vnto a packhorse*, Wakefield (Th19/230).

tempering house To 'temper' metal is to bring it to a suitable degree of hardness by heating, sudden cooling, and reheating. In 1716, Mr George Turner of Norton, a prominent figure in the scythe trade, had a *Tempering House* with *1 Little pair of Bellows 1 Anvil*, as well as a smithy (IH).

temple (1), templewand 'Temple' was a word for the long wands, probably of hazel, which were used to hold down the thatch on a roof (EDD). Salzman noted that 'templewand for thatching' was used at Scarborough in 1284 (SZ1/227) and examples elsewhere include: 1432 *Pro virgis pro templis et wethis emptis, 16d [for buying rods for temples and withes, 16d]*, York (SS35/48); 1446 *v* dimidia templewande pro sutura ejusdem coopertura 4d [550 templewands for stitching that roof 4d]*, Beverley (ERAS6/78); 1446–58 *et pro successione et carr. temple 8 [and for cutting and transporting temples 8d]*, Fountains Abbey (SS130/182).

temple (2) A contrivance for keeping cloth stretched to its proper width in the loom during weaving: 1611 *First 2 lomes 11 peire of geires ... barr trees ... temples*, South Cave (Kaner235).

templer An ornament of jewellery or needlework, formerly worn by ladies on both sides of the forehead: 1429 'a pair of *templers de perle de Treyfoillez*, in the custody of William Smyth', York (SS186/99); 1459 *j par templeyrs cum peryll ornatum [1 pair of templers decorated with pearls]*, Hull (SS30/235).

templewand See temple (1).

temse A sieve, especially one for bolting meal: 1377 'j sieve (*temps*) for bolting meal', Hackness (YRS76/129); *c.*1535 *a kettle and a tempse*, Bridlington (YRS80/2); 1622 *3 sives, 2 tempses and 2 ruddles iijs iiijd*, Bingley (LRS1/56); 1674 *a Tiffany Tems a haire Tems*, Doncaster (YRS134/142); 1739 *two silk themsis two hair themsis*, East Riddlesden (MD194).

It was used occasionally as a verb: 1626 'No baker to teach any person *to bolte, tems or weigh any kind of meale*', Beverley (YRS84/82); 1642 *to measure the meale therein ... before it bee tempsed*, Elmswell (DW109), and in a variety of compound terms: 1598

One temsinge troughe, Wearmouth (SS38/287); 1674 *in the Meale Chamber ... a Leaven Tubb & Temsing Tubb,* Doncaster (YRS134/142). See also ring sieve.

temse-bread, temse-loaf Bread made from the best bolted flour: 1601 *3 ownces of wheaten bread called temsed breade,* Scarborough (NYRO47–8); 1642 *a mette of Massledine for our owne temps'd breade baking; a tempseloafe* Elmswell (DW109); 1683 *For a ... Loafe of Temsed Bread 3d,* York (GWK59).

temse-maker A maker of temses, that is sieves: 1584 *Robert Gaden, Nunington, temese maker* (YRS19/59); 1657 *Mr Joseph Harris, Temes maiker,* Hull (YAJ14/206). In Beverley, the craft was linked with that of carpenters and joiners: 1596 *Disheturners, Temesmakers, Syvemakers* (YRS84/67).

ten-bones A game for young people, noted by Halliwell in 1655 but occurring regularly in Yorkshire records: 1606 *one Tho. Wildon, a person excommunicate ... for keeping Guile-bones or Ten-bones and other unlawfull games at his house for mens servants and apprentices to play,* Sheriff Hutton (NRQS1/49); 1619 *Thomas Hodgson for bowlinge att tenn bones in time of divine service,* Thorp Arch (YAJ15/238); 1623 *for playing att x bones upon the Saboath day,* Bishopthorpe (YAJ15/230).

tendings Tithes, a rare alternative to 'teinds': 1482 *for my tendynges forgetyn xs,* Halsham (SS45/279).

tenell Evidently iron forceps or tongs, from the Latin word: 1392 *j scomyr de ferro, j par tenellarum de ferro [1 iron scummer, 1 pair of iron tenells],* York (SS4/173); 1399 *j wod ax ... j scomor ... et j par tenell [1 wood axe ... 1 scummer ... and 1 pair of tenells],* York (SS35/18); 1468 *j pari tenellarum, j craticula ... et j scomour ferri [1 pair of tenells, 1 griddle ... and 1 iron scummer],* Sewerby (SS45/161).

tent To watch over, take care of: 1556 *soo that the said William, my sone, haue the tenting of the same mylne,* Wadsworth (Crossley136); *c.*1570 *tent shepe upon dry ground,* Farnley Tyas (KayeCP); 1615 *for looking to my shepe and tentinge corne ... each weke vs,* Brandsby (NYRO44/105); 1654 *to the boy for helping to tent the sheepe one the Faugh,* Stockeld (YRS161/92).

tentale An advertisement for a new colliery in Beeston, the *Leeds Mercury* of 4 Jan. 1780, has a Yorkshire example of this word:

> *To be Lett, the Working of the abovesaid Colliery, by the Great or Tentale as practised in the North. The Undertaker to defray all Expenses as Colliers, and all other Workmen's Wages; to find materials of every kind necessary for the working of the said Colliery, as well as for keeping in Repair the large Engine lately thereon erected: as also the Roads already made, as well as making and repairing new Roads necessary to new Pits; to make and repair all Ginns and other Utensils necessary for the same; to sink such fresh Pits as will be needful during the Remainder of the Lease, having Twelve Years unexpired ... to be Let at so much per Dozen of Twelve Corves ... for a specific Quantity, not less than Ten Thousand such Dozens per Ann. the Dozen of Corves ... are expected to weigh not less than 26 Cwt of well-dressed coals* (Th40/128).

'Tentale' here is used as an alternative to 'by the great', an expression which was commonly employed in the West Riding with reference to piece work as opposed to an hourly rate. The 'tentale', that is a count of ten, was a term used in the north-east and according to Greenwell it originally referred to a system of payment based on the amount of coal mined, which varied under different landlords: in some leases the 'ten' was fixed at 50 tons. Gresley said that it was a rent or royalty paid by a lessee upon every 'ten' of coals worked in excess of the minimum or certain rent. As the Brandling family had moved from Northumberland to Leeds they had almost certainly brought the word with them, hence the reference *as practised in the North*. See also great, styth, wagon-road.

tenter The tenter was a simple wooden structure on which cloth was stretched after the fulling process, and it consisted of posts and two bars, the upper and the lower. The earliest references are in the towns: 1506 *cloth taken of the tentours*, York (YRS106/21); 1648 *the abuse of Clothyers in making tenters of greater Chase than by the statute is limited*, West Riding (QS4/2/196); 1727 *tenters not marked or numbered each yard distinctly, fairly and plainly to be seen upon the top bar*, West Riding (QS1/66/9). The long history of the word is clear from by-names: 1250 *Adam del Tentur*, York (YRS12/22) and from minor place-names, as in Pontefract where 'a messuage called *le Tenturgerde*' is mentioned in 1322 (YAJ12/302). In those towns, areas were set aside where the tenters might be permanently placed, and such sites can be identified on maps, especially from the eighteenth century. However, rural clothiers had to find temporary accommodation for the tenters near to the house, in a close or croft, and these might survive as the minor place-names Tenter Close or Tenter Croft.

Such names do not reveal the problems raised by this change of land use but the spaces where tenters were sited were temporary, certainly at the outset, and they are referred to in early deeds as 'rooms': 1575 *with on tenter rowme where there is one tenter now standing in the crofte upon the south ende of the howsinge*, Sowerby (YRS50/175); 1598 *one garden, one fold, two tenterrowmes where as they now stande*, Thurstonland (G–A). Such rooms had to be accessible and this inevitably gave rise to questions about rights of way. An enclosure was the subject of an agreement in 1653 which allowed John Cowper to *quietly enjoy the said close … excepte one tenter rowme …* and granted to Richard Dison *liberty to fix and sett one tenter there … with sufficient ways and passages … at all times to and from the same tenter*, Dalton (KC6/15). There will have been close supervision of the sites so granted:

> 1651 *license to erecte, sett up and use two paire of tenters for tentering of woollen Cloth within the Crofte before the dore of the messuage … soe as the ground whereon the same Tenters are to be sett doe not extend twenty yeardes in length and twenty yeardes in breadth And soe as the same tenters be sett upp within twenty yeardes of the aforesaid house*, Lepton (DD/WBD/4/194).

The tenter frames could be easily dismantled: 1562 *Stees, stanggs … old tenture tymber*, Kendal (SS26/152). A bequest in the original will of Richard Williamson in 1686 was *one tenter wood as the same is broken and ready for setting up* (BIA/VR/478). An agreement entered in the accounts of the Green-Armytage family is evidence of how late such arrangements could be:

> *Memorandum. This first Day of November 1813 John Kinder of Greave in the Township of Netherthonge has paid me one shilling as One of the Lords of the Manor of Meltham for the priviledge of putting down a Tenter near Gilbirks … & also agrees to pay one shilling yearly for the standing of the said Tenter until he has Notice from any of the Lords of the said Manor to remove the same and no longer* (G–A).

tenter hook One of the hooked or right-angled nails set in rows along the upper and lower bars of the tenter frame: 1490 *Et idem magister petit allocacionem pro le tenterhukes [And that master asks for an allowance for the tenter hooks]*, York (SS129/82); 1526 *iij.m* *lattnaill, iiij.c tenter hukes,* York (SS35/101); 1543–4 *j.m tentre houkes nailes, 16d [1000 tenter hook nails, 16d],* York (SS35/111); 1673 *for turnestyles tenterhooks stubbs & pikes 2s,* Ripon (YRS118/136). Note: 1728 *nineteen iron tenter pinns,* Sowerby (QS1/67/2).

tenting house The verb 'to tent' is a northern form of 'tend' and it could mean 'to attend to' or 'look after'. In 1735, George Roper of Handsworth leased *All that Steel Furnace … with the Smithy and Tentinghouses* to George Steer (FBH188) and the inference is that these were warehouses of some kind.

tester A canopy over a bed, either suspended from the ceiling or supported on the posts: 1377 *unum lectum integrum cum testers, howcez, tapetis [a full bed furnishing with testers, houses, curtains],* Bewick (SS4/101); 1470 *a white hangyng for a bedde, that is to saye a celour and testour with curteyns,* Doncaster (SS116/55); 1490 *De j lez teister cum imagine B. M. vjd [For 1 tester with an image of the Blessed Mary 6d],* York (SS53/57); 1542 *a … teister of white and tawney saten embrothered,* Bretton Hall (YRS134/2); 1695 *the roofe … redy to fall downe upon them when it raines they are forsed to get any thing they have upon the bed teasters to keep the water forth of the beed,* Wetherby (QS1/35/1).

tether To make fast with a tether. The practice of tethering animals on patches of waste or in the open fields was formerly subject to strict control: 1556 *haithe aswell of use and custome as of right eaten the edishe of Hardye Flatt with there cattell … And aswell tethered … there Cattell there at edishe after corne haith bene gonne and … when it haithe beyne faughe,* Bulmer (YRS114/79); 1580 *have forfayte one paine laid at the last Courte for tethering and gayting cattell in the Byerdole feildes,* Dewsbury (YAJ21/413); 1590 *common stynt which was for every oxgan a gate … and they used to kepe ther horses tethered at ther land ends, one horse for two oxgangs,* Kirby Underdale (HKU63). The practice was explained fully by East Riding farmer Henry Best: 1642 *Our townsfolks … just on St Hellen-day … beginne to teather theire draught Cattle … abroad in the field, on the heads, common balkes, bounders of fields and their owne lande ends,* Elmswell (DW124). See also stint.

tew To tan, a variant spelling of 'taw', with examples in the OED from *c.*1440. It occurs earlier in the North Riding: 1395 *It. pro tewyng xiiij pellium luporum js ixd [Item for tewing 14 wolf skins 1s 9d],* Whitby (SS72/623) and it was common as a past participle: 1488 *j bukskyn tewyd,* Ripon (SS64/286); 1567 *fyve tewed foxe skynnes,* Fixby (YRS134/16). The occupational term is listed in York: 1310 *Andreas de Doncaster, tewer;* 1393 *Thomas Tyas, tewer* (SS96).

It could also mean 'to work with the hands, to pummel or to beat' and these may have derived from the manipulation of leather by hand in the softening process. Examples are quite late: 1642 *grave up some earth and water it and tewe it. Morter neaver doeth well unlesse it bee well wrought in,* Elmswell (DW151); 1695 *she told him the rogue Ely had soe tew'd her till she had noe breath,* Rotherham (QS1/34/4). In 1582, it was used along with 'taw' in the Skinners' Ordinances in York (YRS119/61–3). It survives in dialect with the sense of 'to toil'. See also taw, whittawer.

tew-iron This refers to a nozzle through which a blast of air is forced into a forge or furnace. It derives from the French word which gave modern *tuyère,* and early OED spellings include tewer, tuer, twyer and tewyre. The reference in 1350–1 to 'ij tuers ferri' makes it clear that the nozzle could be of iron, and popular etymology was responsible for 'tew-iron' and similar spellings. That was almost predictable, given that 'ire' was a regional alternative to iron, n.b. 1343 *Roger le Irmongere* (OED). The development may have taken place in the sixteenth century and the OED notes it in Durham in 1570 when a smith gave *vnto John Dycheborne a pair of bellowis with a tewe Ireon* (SS2/329).

The earliest West Riding example is in the will of a blacksmith named Robert Saureby: 1558 *a stithy, a cantell of yron and a tewyron*, Sheffield (TWH16/114). In 1592, an Eckington smith called Richard Gill had two *tew irons* in his smithy and in 1692, Anne Harrison, a Sheffield widow, had *1 pair of bellowes tue irons and 1 double bellow*, valued at £1 1s (IH). The inventory of Godfrey Creswick, a Sheffield cutler, listed *A pair of Bellows and a Tuiron* in 1704 (IH). Closer to the original French word is the plural spelling *Turiors* listed in 1608 among implements in a Cawthorne smithy, possibly at Cinderhill (OC22).

teylde See teld.

thack, thack tile 'Thack' was until recently a common word in parts of Yorkshire for 'roof', and despite its obvious links to the word 'thatch' it could refer to roofs made of slatestones, tiles or shingles. Indeed, there are numerous references to 'thack tiles' in early accounts and Salzman noted the spelling *thakteghell* in York in 1364 (SZ1/230). Later references include: 1404 *In m.m.viij.c thaktell emptis cum cariagio [For 2800 thack tiles bought with transportation]*, York (SS35/27); 1447 *iiij^ml c tegulis vocatis thaktiel 33s 8d [4100 tiles called thack tiles 33s 8d]*, Beverley (ERAS7/60); 1519 *paid for cccc thayke teylle and for ledyng vs jd*, York (CCW75). See also thackboard, thackstone, tile house.

thackboard Salzman considered that these were not wooden tiles or shingles, but boards which were laid across the roof in readiness for thatching, or perhaps tiling, but the evidence is not conclusive: 1327 *cum c thakebordes ad fabricam [with 100 thackboards for the workshop]*, York (SS35/207n); 1354–5 *in ccc de thakbord emp. pro stauro ecclesiæ [for 300 thackboards bought for the church store]*, Ripon (SS81/91); 1377 *de nouo cooperient de unica plita de Thakborde [they will newly roof with one inch thick Thackboards]*, York (SZ1/453–4); 1479 *solutum pro cc de le thakburds pro tegulacione eiusdem domus [paid for 200 thackboards for tiling that house]*, York (SS192/162). See also carpenter.

thacker, thackster A roofer: 1467 *Item ordinatum est quod si quis Carpentarius aut Tegulator viz Tilethakkerr, Tilewaller et Plasterer occupare voluerit in arte sua infra villam Beverlaci, non habens apprenticium habilem … [Item it was ordered that if any carpenter or tiler that is tile thacker, tile waller and plasterer wishes to work at his trade within the town of Beverley, not having a suitable apprentice …]* (BTD55); 1570 *William Diconson, Burton Agnes, thacker* (YRS19/47); 1570 *Watson of Steanburne the thaxster owth me xxd*, Fewston (SS104/106). See also –ster, theaker.

thackstone Stone slates for roofing: 1314 '3d for *thakstones* from Thomas del Northend', Hipperholme (WYAS810); 1416 'that the prioress of *Kyrkeles* took ten cart loads of *petri voc' Thakeston' [stones called thackstone]*, Rastrick (MD225/1/142/1); 1442 *shall have … in the saide toune of Pudsay j acre of soile lying togeder where he may get and tak thakstone at his awen liberte* (Th6/253); 1495 'broke the lord's soil and dug for *petras voc' thakston'*, Hepworth (MD225/1/221).

thack tile See thack.

theak To roof a building, no doubt with thatch originally but also from an early date with stone: 1399–1400 *Et in v^xx travis de stramine ordii emp. 5s, pro tectura j tenementi … Et in salario j hominis tegentis, viz thekand predictam domum [And for buying 5 score thraves of barley straw 5s, for roofing 1 tenement … And for 1 man's pay roofing, that is theaking the said house]*, Ripon (SS81/130); 1429 *to the thekyng of the stepill of my parish kyrke xxvjs viijd*, York (SS4/420) 1509 *cause to be bielded a house of vj Crokkys to be … theked with ston*, South Crosland (DD/WBD/2/26); 1573 *taking the stone all of the oxehowsse dyd* *theake yt a newe*, Farnley Tyas (KayeCP); 1787 *began this Morning to cover in and theak, as 'tis said usually, the new Chapel at Slaighthwaite* (KC242/1).

theaker, theakster A roofer: 1335 *De villa de Daneby pro quadam scala de qua Willelmus Theker de Daneby occisus fuit [From the township of Daneby for that ladder by which William Theker of Daneby was killed]* (YAJ15/203); 1379 *Johannes Thekester*, Clint (PTWR); 1412 *Et in servicio Walteri Theker metentis et ligantis iij^{ml} arundines [And for Walter Theker's labour cutting and binding 3000 reeds]*, Eastoft (YRS118/40); 1537 *Item to a theker for thekyng of the seid thre lode strawe iis xjd*, Bridlington (BCP20); 1610 *Thomas Atkinson of Urebie, theaker* (NRQS1/192); 1658 *To a theaker by the day, with meate 6d, without meate 12d*, Thirsk (NRQS6/4). See also –ster, thacker.

theaking-rake A small rake used by thatchers. One example noted, in the East Riding: 1606 *a turfe spade an old hedged helme a drag & a theaking rake*, South Cave (Kaner220). In his description of how stacks were thatched Henry Best wrote: 1642 *there are to bee two folks, viz. one to sitte beside the strawe and feede the bande therewith and another to goe backewards with the rake to drawe forth and twine the same*, Elmswell (DW64).

theakster See theaker.

thew An instrument of punishment, often for women, evidently one on which a person might be carried: *c.*1450 *schall within the Burgage ordan a pelory and a thew lawfull and strang*, New Malton (SS85/60); 1575 *Thomas Haxoppes wife a skold … to be caryed throughe the cyttie of York … in the market tyme upon the thewe heretofore used in this behalf* (YAJ15/229).

thible Usually a smooth wooden stick with which to stir porridge. However, an earlier meaning is 'setting-stick', quoted by Wright (EDD), and that seems more likely in this context: 1618 *a chiste, a thiple, a tugwythye, a peate spade*, Bingley (LRS1/22).

thick The many meanings of 'thick' which are on record from the Old English period include 'dense', used of trees or woods. The word could be a noun in its own right, and in 1579 a Craven document listed *a certain Thycke or Ryse of Thornes and Underwood* in Littondale (Whit2/492). As an adjective it is commonly found in minor place-names, linked with different types of trees: 1277 *Thyckeholyns*; that is hollies (YRS29/167); 1300 *Thykthorndale*; that is thorns (PNWR7/259); 1421 *Thykwethyns*; that is willows (MD225/1/147) and 1472 *Thekehesils*; that is hazels (MD225/1/198). It was rarely used of the ash or oak but one example has been recorded: 1681 *a close or parcel of ground called Thickoakes*, Selby (YRS47/181). Examples of the word occur in letter books for the Dartmouth estate, kept now in the estate office in Slaithwaite, and they include its use as a verb: 1806 *Thicken Campinot Plantation and Meal Hill Wood*; 1807 *found Owlers Wood growing quite thick from the Larch which I had planted three years since*. It can be contrasted with 'light (2)' above.

thimbles and button A game in which the player has several thimbles and the challenger has to identify which one masks the button, played illegally for money on this occasion: 1717–18 'Robert Saunderson illegally persuaded William Kay, junior, to play the game called *Thimbles and button*', Kirkburton (QS1/23/7).

thiple See thible.

thirl An Old English word meaning 'hole' or 'aperture', linked etymologically with 'through': as a verb it meant 'to make a hole'. It has survived in some dialects but is not now in general use, although many people are aware that 'nostrils' means 'nose holes': the spelling 'nose therlis' in Wyclif's translation of the Bible (1382) illustrates the development.

Both the noun and the verb have already been identified as part of the national mining vocabulary but not earlier than 1686 (OED). Wright comments on the word's popularity in some mining communities, and from a Cheshire source of 1878 quotes: *When a man has … made an opening or connection between a new and old working, he is said to have thirled* (EDD). In fact, a south Yorkshire mining lease of 1486 contains three examples of the word's use, referring to a coal pit *now of new thyreled* and with clauses in the agreement which required the lessees to drive a head *with post and thyrle* in order to drain the mine. Finally they were to keep *a ribbe … unthyreled*, Cortworth (YAJ12/236). There are references later in the accounts of the Farnley colliery near Leeds although the precise interpretation in this case is less clear cut: 1711 *the Thurle 2 dayes and earth feying*; 1718 *Gotten in the Thirle by the Levell gate* (MS11). Much more explicit is an entry in the diary of Ann Lister: 1833 *7 yds distance from the great horizontal shaft runs the windgate from which air is conveyed into the great shaft by thirls at about 25 to 30 yds from each other*, Halifax (HAS31/110). In this instance 'thirling' was clearly a way of ventilating the pit. See also vent.

Thirsk measure A local standard for grain: 1617 *Wheat sould at Thrisk … 6 bushells strucken here and 6 half pecks to make up Thrisk measure for vjs ijd each bushell*, Brandsby (NYRO44/141). See also Ripon measure.

thixel An adze, the usual word in Yorkshire, first noted in a cooper's will: 1400 *Lego Thomæ famulo meo unum [I bequeath to my servant Thomas a] burdhax, unum wyrkyn-ghaget, duo parsures, unum spigot, wymbill, unum thixtill, & unum knave*, York (SS4/265), the second in a carpenter's will: 1505 *To Sanct Peter warkes a gaveloke of irne, a twybill, a thixill, a gret womble with a long shanke, a gret ax callid a bloker, and a chipe ax, othyrwise callid a brod ax*, York (SS53/240); 1535 *Item on Iron wedge, iij exes, ij billes, iiij wymbles, iij axell mylles, a twyble, a thikstelle and a hand saw, ij cheseles, and a pare pyncers, price in all xixs*, Stillingfleet (YRS45/129); 1542 *a tixell and a chysell*, Skelsmergh (SS26/35); 1570 *Item ij hammers & a thewsell*, South Cave (Kaner71); 1628 *3 yron wedges, 5 wymbles, 4 chissells, 1 thissell, 5 hammers, hatchett … 1 axe, 1 handsawe, a shave … 1 payre of pynsors*, Pudsey (LRS1/76–7). See also thwart saw.

thorn Usually a reference to the hawthorn: *c*.1490 *the thorn that stondes at Moskarende*, Sand Hutton (YAJ2/91); 1579 *In another Gyll in Nether Hesseldene are certain Yonge Esshe Spires and Thornes and scrubbie Hessels* (Whit2/492). The tree is remembered in over 100 important Yorkshire place-names, and more than twenty Thorntons are listed by Smith (PNWR8/184). The wood could be used as fuel: 1556 *the Parson had whinnes and thornes opon Whitwell More … so many as served his kitchyn* (YRS114/93). It is of course the traditional hedgerow tree, and information about its role in enclosure will be found under quickfall, quickset and quickwood. References to it as the whitethorn or hawthorn are quite rare but a thirteenth-century deed for Chevet makes reference to an acre of land by *Hahethornstube* (YRS83/66). See also boot (1), saugh.

thornback The common ray or skate, so called because it has sharp spines along the back and tail: 1453 *3 C dry skates 2 C4 duss' thornebakes*, Hull (YRS144/11).

thornhill nails Probably nails bought from the nail-makers in Thornhill near Dewsbury: 1539 *Inprimis for a thowsand of thornell dubyll spykyng, 3ˢ*, York (CCW215); 1542–3 *Item iij C thornell dubyll spykynes, xijᵈ*, York (CCW253). It can be compared with *styllyngflet dubyll spykynges* in the same accounts.

thou As a verb, similar in meaning and use to the French 'tutoyer', that is to address a person as 'thou': 1541 *yt is agreyd that Robert Bold, for such sedicious and slaunderous words as he dyd speyk by Maister Holmes Alderman … in thowyng of hym … shalbe committed forthwith to prison*, York (YRS108/70).

thrave, threave A measure of corn or hay, although the number of sheaves varied in different localities: 1298–9 'the suit … about the thraves (*super trabis*)', Bridlington (SS128/225); 1351 *Et in quadraginta thraues straminis empti pro emendacione grangie de Dewesbury, vjs viijd [And for forty thraves of straw bought for repairing the barn at Dewsbury, 6s 8d]* (YAJ21/381); 1446 *Diversis thravis 10s 0d. Et carectata stramini pro co-opertura grangiæ [For various thraves 10s 0d. And for a cart load of straw for roofing the barn]*, Beverley (ERAS6/78); 1552 *every threave of wheat conteynethe xxiiij sheaffes*, Whorlton (YRS114/39n); 1576 *Edward Dyson, baylyf … had the custodye of certain threves of otes … and did cause the same to be threshed*, South Crosland (DD/WBL/116/2); 1588 *Item xx thrave of rye and three thrave of wheate*, Dalton (DD/WBW/19).

thread The material or fibre of which a garment or accessory is made: 1402 *et ij flameola de threde … et maximum flameolum meum de threde [and 2 thread scarves … and my biggest thread scarf]*, York (SS4/289).

threap In this case 'to insist forcefully': 1515 *And the said Cristofer threpyd vpon the said Sir John that he might doo it*, Guisborough (YRS41/68). However, the word's range of meanings included to bicker or argue and this explains minor names such as Threap Green, Threap Hill and Threaphow, places where boundaries were probably in dispute (PNWR8/185). Several similar names were not recorded by Smith, e.g. 1609 *Greate threape ynge in 12 acres 2 roods £v xijd*, Brandsby (NYRO44/26) and, in an undated thirteenth-century deed, *le Threpcroft* between Illingworth and Holdsworth (YRS65/109).

threave See thrave.

threnter, thrinter Contractions of 'three winter', used of animals such as sheep and cattle which were three winters old: 1446–58 *xij twynters, xij trynters, xij stirkettes*, Fountains Abbey (SS130/120); 1466–7 *to ylkon of my sonnes v twynters and two threnter stottes*, Malton (SS30/285); 1564 *Item 9 twynter cattell … Item 14 threntres of the which 10 ys stotes and 4 qwyes*, Marske (YRS152/131). See also twinter.

throng As an adjective, crowded, busy or engaged: 1620 *all throng in work for tearmers* [sic] *going downe*, Brandsby (NYRO44/198); 1677 *being very throng that day below some went into that false-floore*, Northowram (OH3/149); 1705 *the house being very throng with guests*, West Riding (QS1); 1774 *to York on foot, the City was very throng* (DB1/C6). Occasionally it may have implied 'too busy': 1704 *We are very Throng about setting the Engine in the Colliery*, Masham (BM82/52).

throstle The song thrush. It was extremely popular as a minor place-name element, noted by Smith more than thirty times. Most popular by far was Throstle Nest, with a majority of examples dating from the eighteenth and nineteenth centuries (PNWR8). It also occurred as a by-name: 1301 *de Radulpho Throstelle*, Skelton (YRS21/37); 1306 *Thomas Throstel*, Kirkburton (YRS36/55). Less predictably, it was a popular if ironic name for a horse: 1556 *to Elisabeth my wif on amblinge gray mare called throstell*, Sherburn in Elmet (Th27/53); 1632 *one mare called Throsle*, Hemingbrough (HAH362). See also nightingale.

through, through-stone (1) These words are now met with frequently in accounts of dry-stone walling but they are on record in mason work from a very early date. A 'through-stone' extended through the thickness of a wall, and a certain number were considered essential for its stability. The earliest example in the OED is 1805 but both terms are found in the fabric accounts of York Minster, with references to *j through-stane a quarera [from the quarry]* in 1400 and *in caragio vj lapidum vocatorum thurghes [for transporting 6 stones called throughs]* in 1419 (SS35/21,40). In 1648, a mason who was contracted to build a house in Illingworth agreed to *build up the side with competent number of throughes in the same* (YAJ16/109).

There are frequent references also in bridge-building documents: 1602 *as many through achlers into the stone works as the overseers shall think proper*, Apperley Bridge (BAS6/142). When Methley Bridge was rebuilt, in 1793, it was agreed that the walls which formed the abutments should *be not less than 12 inches in Bed, with proper throughs or Bond Stones* (Th35/86). Occasionally, it was used as a verb, as when the wall of Kildwick Bridge was *well through'd* in 1755 (QS1/94/6).

through, through-stone (2) A horizontal grave-stone, sometimes supported on pillars: 1507 *I will have a thrugh lade upon me after my decesse with iiij stulpis the heght of half a yerde*, Kirk Smeaton (SS53/265); 1521 *I gif to order a through stone to lay on my grave withe scripture of laton of the same xls*, Denaby (SS106/5); 1542 *to be buried within the church yerde … of the northside nere myne awncetors and to have a thrughe stone laide ouer me prepared therfor*, Otley (Th19/79); 1557 *a troughe [sic] stone wythe a remembrance of my selfe wyfe and chyldren in pycketures of brasse to be set … and layd vpon the grave*, Wakefield (Th27/123); 1581 *To be buried … in the middest allie under the through stone where my father's and mother's corps were buried*, Burnsall (YRS39/45n).

through joist Probably a joist running the full length of a floor: 1335 *Gesturae … et thurugistes bene ligati cum … ligaturis [Joists and through joists well tied with … bands]*, York (SZ1/431); 1433 *vj duble postis vj thoregistes iiij balkes, iiij stanzons*, York (SS35/53); 1543–4 *Item for a throght yest, a pane and iij stancions ix^d*, York (CCW266).

through stone See through (1) and (2).

throw (1) To turn on a lathe: 1617 *they will thraw and make such at Robert Peckett's in Stillington*, Brandsby (NYRO44/140); 1663 *pro wheelbands for throwing the bannesters*, Ripon (YRS118/99). The adjective was used to describe items of furniture, particularly chairs: 1490 *a thrawen boxe of tre*, York (YRS103/62); 1499 *a trawn chaer*, Wighill (SS53/160); 1547 *a pare of thrawen bedstokkes*, Lead Hall (Th19/179); 1568 *4 square throwne cubbordes*, Healaugh (YRS134/31); 1699 *six thrown chears*, Meltham (G-A). See also dish-thrower.

throw (2) This was a noun used of objects found in cutlers' smithies. In 1699, William Sherman had *a screwthrow and a foot throw* in his *Work Chamber*, and in 1717 George Cartwright possessed *two old throws* in his *tiphouse* (IH). The exact meaning of the term in a cutlery context is uncertain but some 'throws' were hand-operated lathes which turned objects that were being shaped. These throws may therefore have been used to make knife hafts, employing different methods. See also tip.

throw (3), throw down, throw up The OED has 'throw' as a word for a fault, 'a dislocation in a vein or stratum in which the part on one side of the fracture is displaced up or down'. Three examples from 1796 are listed, including one from a Yorkshire glossary. The following earlier items refer to efforts made in a Tong coal-pit when the miners encountered such a fault: 1760 *Pd Jos. Cowburn for going down the throw down*; 1761 *5 days taking up level from the throw up*; 1763 *Jas Barker 1½ day trying the throw down; Jonas Binns three days trying the throw up*, Tong (Tong/4c/7). Confusingly, the verb 'to throw up' was commonly used also to mean to dig or delve, as in the following extract from turnpike accounts: 1779 *To William Mallinson, about throwing up a Ditch near Ingbirchworth Turnpike to prevent people from evading the tolls* (WRT42). Similarly in a coal-pit: 1761 *throwing up an open tail*, Tong (Tong/4c/6). See also cast down, dike (2), gall (1), horse (1), mare.

throw in This described actions designed to stop a coal-pit from operating, probably by blocking the shaft with debris. In 1698, three colliers *maliciously sett on fire a Colliery of Richard Armitage in Honley*, so that he could not get his coals: soon afterwards, in a further attack, *Jo. Armitage hired Joshua Hallas … to throw in a Coalpitt in Shaw Ing belonging to the same Richard Armitage*, Honley (GRLD35). In Colsterdale, in 1721, colliers were hindered by workmen *throwing in each [pit] and filling up their works* (BM82/80). In Southowram, in 1777, men were warned not *to throw in, crush or prejudice the Coal Mine* (HM/C/10). See also play-day.

throw up See throw (3).

thrum The unwoven ends of the warp threads; short pieces or remnants of thread or yarn. In some sources thrums are referred to as 'waste' but they had many uses and a clear market value: 1401 '9 stone of *thrommes*, val. 20s', Hull (YRS64/24); 1576 *Collered Woll, more certeyne thrumes*, Leeds (Th4/164); 1628 *woollen yarne, thrums & cardes*, Pudsey (LRS1/76); 1668 *Woolle yearne throomes & Nisbetts £2*, Salterforth (YRS118/77); 1760 *the low warp is lin the higher woollen so the are cut about one inch assunder for to make the thrums stick up*, Wakefield (YRS155/11); 1823 *paid for some thrums for mops*, Meltham (G-A). They were in early use to make a kind of hat: 1453 *35 duss' thrumhattes £15 0 0*, Hull (YRS144/3); 1540 *my silke thrummede hate*, Rotsea (SS106/113). In 1559, *one qwyssin thrommed* in Hipswell was probably fringed with thrums (SS26/135). Typical of later spellings are: 1690 *15 pounds of thrumbs*, Lingards (IMF) and 1700 *j thrombs basket*, Holmfirth (IH). Thrum Hall occurs twice as a place-name in the Halifax area and is likely to be a humorous name of the Mouldwarp Hall type: the by-name seems likely to have been derogatory: 1338 *John Thrum'*, Wakefield (WCR12/20).

thrushen A dialect spelling of threshed: 1700 *corne thrushen and unthrushen*, Holmfirth (IH). See also unthrussen.

thuribler The thurible was a vessel in which incense was burnt, and it was in the keeping of an acolyte: 1504 *I witte to the vicars, dekenez, thuribulers, and the choresters … vjs viijd*, Ripon (SS64/295); 1535 *the ministers of the Church, viz. 3 Deacons, 3 Subdeacons, 6 Thuriblers and Sub-thuriblers, and 6 Choristers £16 19 3*, Ripon (SS81/2); 1546 *xvij clerkes … of the seconde forme, viij queristers, ij thuribulers, and fower segersans [sacristans]*, Beverley (SS92/530).

thwart saw A saw used for sawing across pieces of timber, a cross-cut saw: 1578 *one picke, one thwarte sawe*, Ripley (SS104/133); 1614 *a thwart sawe with wimbles*, South Cave (Kaner251). The will of Christopher Halliday, a carpenter, has the following:

> 1613–14 *I give to William my sonne my working toles, half my armesaw which my brother Robert hath, my thwartsaw, my handsaw, if he give my wife his one wood axe, two howing axes, one hatchet, two great wombles, one stowering womble, one small womble, two rake p[ar]cers, three playnes and ij playne stockes, half the rabiting toule which is between my brother John and me, the vth parte of the whipsaw, half the iron gavelock which is between Hugh Lappage and me, one thistle, all my chissils except one for my executrix, and all the rest of my tooles if any be forgotten*, Hampsthwaite (SS110/34).

See also quart saw (a spelling which was equally popular), overthwart saw.

thwittle A knife. Chaucer's reference to 'A Sheffeld thwitel' is often quoted and there are earlier examples of the word in other parts of Yorkshire: 1354 'a small knife called a *twitel*', Bradford (CR); 1374 *lego … unum cultellum cum manubrio de murro, anglice thwetyll [I bequeath a knife with a maple handle, in English a thwittle]*, York (SS4/92). See also whittle.

tick A strong linen or cotton material commonly used for linings, pillow cases, covers, mattresses, etc.: 1467 *5 fedirbedd tykes £3 0 0*, Hull (YRS144/102); 1521 *a gowne lynyd with watteryd tuyke*, Thirsk (YAJ22/219); 1542 *Two gret fether bedds and two bolsters with fyne brisel tikes*, Bretton Hall (YRS134/2); 1591 *A Fetherbedd tyckke which coste xls, the hole Lengthe is iij yardes and a quarterne*, Tong (Tong/4d/77); 1655 *two new bed tickes*, Whitley (DD/WBM/69).

ticking The material of which bed-ticks were made: 1621 *ticken for boulsters & pillowes*, South Cave (Kaner305); 1675 *sold to Urseley, wife of Edward Wharton … a piece of rowd ticking, some white ticking*, Richmond (SS40/218); 1693 *25 yds ticking, 16s 8d*, Selby (YRS47/22).

tickle Ticklish, in the sense of awkward or difficult: 1791 *do not threaten him with suit for the affair will be ticle to manage*, Meltham (G-A); 1853 *We finished shearing Oct' 29th this year A very tickle harvest, and housed 31st*, South Crosland (GRD).

tide A special day in the calendar, marking a fair or anniversary: 1584 *there be three little fairs commonly called tyde days*, Almondbury (DD/R/5/29); 1647 *hee promised to get them before St James' tyde*, Thurlstone (SS65/41); 1658 *the suppressinge of wakes, feasts, tides, revellings at country weddings and sundry others such disorderly meetings*, West Riding (YAJ15/463); 1710 *the Monday night after Bingleytyde Sunday, commonly called Crawmass day*, Wilsden (QS1/49/6). Bradford's Bowling Tide was the first week in August.

tidesman, tide-waiter A customs official who awaited the arrival of ships as they came in with the tide and then boarded them to prevent evasion of custom house dues: 1668 *Mr Coxhead, water of ships*; 1701 *Mr Robert Scott, Tydsman*; 1710 *Mr Samuel Winter, Tide water*, Hull (YAJ12/474,476); 1759 *Robert Richison, Tydewaiter*, Sculcoates (PR); 1823 *Jonathan Bailes, Tide waiter*, Hull (BainesTD).

tidy The chief current uses, that is orderly, neat, etc. are on record only from the opening years of the eighteenth century, and earlier meanings are: timely, in good condition, well-favoured, of good character. Any of the latter might explain the by-name: 1379 *Johannes Tydy*, Grindleton (PTWR). The word was also used as a cow's name: 1486 *to Agnes Chapman a cowe called Tydee*, Felixkirk (YAJ22/204) and this might share the same origin. Alternatively, a tidy cow in Scotland at that time was one that gave milk, and oxen could be described as 'fat and tydye' (OED).

tiffany A kind of gauze, a thin transparent material, silk, muslin or lawn: 1557 *one old tefeny doblett*, Thornton Bridge (SS26/100). Used of objects which were made or part made of tiffany: 1637 *12 lether purses, two dozen of tiffeines, nine silk gairdles*, Bradford (YRS54/47); 1674 *In the Meale Chamber … a Tiffany Tems* Doncaster (YRS134/142).

tile house, tile kiln Places where bricks or tiles were made and stored: 1414 'for transport of *1,500 thaktele* from the *telekilne* at Cawood 6d', Selby (SAR227); 1421 *Soluti pro viij sarcinis de telescarthes a telehouse de Clifton [Paid for 8 loads of tile shards from the Clifton tile house]* (SS35/45). Tiles continued to be made locally: 1703 *William Bothwicke of Selby, tylemaker* (YRS47/73). See also rig tile, thack, wall tile.

tile-pin According to Salzman, tiles and stone slates were hung in the same manner, using wooden pegs driven into holes near the top edge and secured behind the laths (SZ1/233): 1358 *Item, in pinnis pro tegulis, vjd [Item, for pins for tiles, 6d]*, York (SS129/15). See also slate pin.

tile shard Recorded as *Tylescherd* in London in 1370 (SZ1/444) and as *telescarthes* above in 1421. See also tile house.

tilter The workman responsible for operating a tilt-hammer or mill. The occupational term occurs from the mid-eighteenth century: 1743 *John Woollas, tilter*, Sheffield (PR7/166).

tilth Arable land under cultivation. The possession of a certain amount was an indication of status and responsibility: 1598 *euerie person occupieng a ploughe tilth of land … shall send their draughtes & sufficient labourers … and repaire the same waie*, Leeds (YRS3/104).

tilt-hammer, tilt mill Ultimately 'tilt' has its origin in a word that meant to overthrow or overturn, made familiar to us by scenes of combat in which mounted knights sought to unhorse their opponents. In iron working it was the name given to a heavy hammer used in forges: this was fixed on a pivot and acted upon by a cam-wheel which alternately tilted the hammer up and then let it drop (OED).

It is uncertain exactly when the word was first used in this sense but numerous references have been noted from the early 1700s. In 1733, for example, a partnership took a 21-year lease in order *to set up a tilt forge* not far from the Ponds in Sheffield (WPS185) and in 1736, Gosling's map of Sheffield marked one *Tilt Hammer* in the Ponds and another further south: the first of these had already been recorded in a 1716–17 rate book. A writer noted in 1750 that *within these few years past no less than fifteen tilting mills* in and around Sheffield *were erected for reducing iron and steel to a smaller dimension* (FBH181–2). Upper Middlewood Forge was a tilt mill: 1761 *three cutlers wheels and a tilt and a mill for tilting steel*, Oughtibridge (WPS2). 'Tilted steel' is a term recorded from the eighteenth century: in 1734 Samuel Littlewood had *Tilted Steel 5 stone and an half* and in 1735 Joseph Morton had *Tilted Steele £1* (IH).

timber (1) Wood suitable for major building projects, that is houses, mills, ships, etc., sometimes called great timber or timber trees: 1557 *xij posted tymber trees xls, vij rughe tymber trees*, Thornton Bridge (SS26/101); *c.*1565 *delivered of the Quenes Woddes … to William Cawdiner xx timbre trees*, Goathland (NRR1/206); 1722 *Eighty Acres of Wood Ground … consisting as well of Timber Trees as Spring Wood*, Headingley (Th22/191). A lease of 1609 required the tenant to repair the house, the buildings *and the fences therof … with all manner of needful … reparacons … greate tymber onlie excepted*, Kirkheaton (DD/WBD/3/88). In 1619–21, William Wood was fined *xs for taking two timber oke trees in Newton dale*, Pickering (NRR1/29). Which trees fell into the category of timber trees was capable of legal definition but might differ from one region to another: in Yorkshire, for example, in 1818, 'birch trees were timber' (OED). It is an element in some minor place-names, as in the grange that Roche Abbey had in Thurstonland: 1275 'the serjeant of *Tymberwode*', Thurstonland (YRS29/146): when Bolton Priory was assarting land in 1313–14 expenses were incurred at *Tymberwath*; that is 'timber ford' (YRS154/365). A document of 1711 provides evidence of the word's versatility: *The Lord appoints competent timber for making and repairing the yeates of the common, littlestead styles, the stocks, common goat stocks, the clowes & bridges, & boues for mending the highways*, Scalm Park (YAJ7/55). See also great timber, offal, scrub oak, shipping timber, water timber.

timber (2) A word used in the fur trade for a bundle of forty skins. It is thought that they were originally packed flat between thin boards: 1453 *12 tymbres roswek*, Hull (YRS144/6); 1466–7 *12 tymberes rede squerell wark*, Hull (YRS144/106); 1582 *Item for a tymmer of feches tewing viij*ᵈ, York (YRS119/62). See also gray (2), tavelin.

timberware Articles made of timber: 1479 *Item lj shaffe birk and hesh, of temer ware price lez shaffe iijd*, York (SS45/253); *c.*1535 *Item in chestes, cofers, gret arkes, coverters, coberdes, almoys and moche other tymberware*, Halifax (YRS45/189).

tine The projecting sharp point of a weapon or implement, such as a fork or harrow: *c.*1504 *A iij tynd fork, a spayd*, York (SS53/191); 1582 *iij dong forkes, iiij ij tyndyd forkes*, South Cave (Kaner119); 1648 *certaine plow stilts & harrowtines*, Sharlston (YRS134/99).

tingle A very small kind of nail; the smallest size of tack (OED): 1415 *In iiij.m.cccc. tyngilnaill, 4s 4d*, York (SS35/35); 1543–4 *Pro ij.m tingle nailes, 16d*, York (SS35/111). Probably the source of the by-name: 1286 *Thomas Tyngel*, Hipperholme (YRS57/164). See also Tingle (GRDict).

tinkler The regional form of tinker, an itinerant metal-worker: 1446 *Et de Ricardo Walter, tynkler, pro licencia concessa ad occupandum infra civitatem [And to Richard Walter, tinkler, for permission granted to work within the city]*, York (SS192/29); 1520 *To Agnes Sherp a brasse pott with a tyncler clowte*, Ripon (SS79/187n); 1542 *2 litil panes 2 tyngler panes 14d*, Marske (YRS152/58); 1579 *Item payd to tinckeler for mending of panes*, Stockeld (YRS161/11); 1681 *brought a panne to a tinklers house … in our town*, Northowram (OH2/228). By-names provide earlier evidence: 1314 *Gilbert Tynkeler*, Wakefield (YRS57/33). See also Tinker, Tinkler (GRDict).

tinman, tinner, tin worker It is evident in early records of the Cutlers Company that tin was used by the Sheffield cutlers in a variety of ways, not all of them within the rules. In 1625, brass, lead, and pewter were linked with tin as metals that should not be 'intermixed' with gold and silver so as to deceive potential purchasers (HCC9) but that did not halt the practice. A few workers later specialised in making tin items and in 1731 John Walker of Sheffield *Tin-man* had *Tinn Ware made up 2 19 0, a Box with Tinn ware in 15 0* in his inventory (IH). George Close was described as a *tinman* in 1738 (PR7/114) and as a *tinworker* in 1742 (PR7/151). 'Tinner' was an occasional alternative: 1771 *Thomas Hessay, tinner*, St Crux, York (PR).

tin nail A rare word, recorded also in county Durham in 1381–2 (OED). Possibly a nail made of tin but more probably a nail for securing pieces of tin: 1396–7 *Et in Tynnayle pro stauro 12d [And for tin nails for the store, 12d]*, Ripon (SS81/120).

tinner, tin worker See tinman.

tinsel (1) A regional word for brushwood, used as a fencing material: Wright found it in parts of north Wales and the midland counties (EDD), and the OED has an example in Nottinghamshire in 1486. In 1436, Wakefield tenants were charged with felling and carrying away 'green wood called *Tynsill* in the Out-wood' (WCR15/192) and a Bradfield court roll for 1440 has the latinised form *tynsellum*, which the editor translated as 'rails' (TWH26/11). The word was in regular employment in Yorkshire, and Jackson quotes a document dated 1473–4 in which *tynsell* was to be used for making and repairing a weir and mill dam (JB123). Occasionally it occurred as a verb: 1518–19 *to tynsell, to hegge Aboute the same mese*, Tong (Tong/3/3). In a later lease it was linked with 'trouse': 1593 *liberty to cut down and carry away [certain wood] leaving … sufficient crops, lops, bushes, trowse and tynsell for the mowndinge, fencing and hedging of the demised premises*, Bingley (LRS2/7). It can be compared with 'tinnet' found in other

English regions, and with 'garsil', another Yorkshire word for brushwood which has a similar suffix. It may be the origin of place-names such as Tinsel in Midgley and even Tinshill in Adel (PNWR). See also trouse.

tinsel (2) Used of satin or other fabrics which were made to sparkle by the inter-weaving of gold or silver thread: 1558 *one sute of rede silk tynselde with borders of Images of soundry saynts*, Middleton in Teesdale (SS2/171); 1568 *A tester of Russet velvet tinsell fringed with Russet Silke and golde*, Healaugh Park (YRS134/25).

tip, tip house A reference to the tips of horn which were used by Sheffield cutlers, chiefly for knife handles and buttons: the tip house was where they were stored. In one such storehouse, in 1681, was *horn tip* valued at £25 19s 2d: in 1702 Samuel Bothamley possessed *boanes and tipps* valued at £2 3s 0d and in 1717 George Cartwright's inventory recorded *In the tiphouse ... some tips* (IH). When the Sheffield factor John Downes was made bankrupt in 1724 he had in his possession 'over 8,000 tips in barrels and boxes in his stable and tiphouse' (FBH124).

tippet A cape or short cloak, or a garment to cover the neck and shoulders. It could also refer to slips of cloth hanging from a hood or head-dress: 1486 *a typpet of blak velvet with sylver aglettes*, Beverley (SS53/19); 1498 *To Costen Bolling my hat and tippet*, Calverley (BAS2/171); c.1537 *a new typet of blak velvett not lyned*, Halifax (YRS45/188); 1559 *one tipet Lyned with taphetaye*, Wakefield (Th27/289).

tippler A tavern keeper: 1521 *all brewsters and tiplers ... shall pay ther Brewster fines*, York (YRS106/77); 1590 *every tipler ... shall sell their aile being olde and sett ale for vjd the aile gallon*, York (YRS138/120); 1610 *John Riplingham, tailor, Richard Fawcett tipler*, New Malton (NRQS1/1186). Found occasionally with –ster as the suffix: 1527 *every typpylster takyng the said ayle shall sell ... withoute doers fore ijd le gallon*, York (YRS106/109). See also –ster.

tippling-house An ale-house or tavern: 1589 *John Banester inholder and tipler shalbe dischardged of keeping any alehowse or tiplinghowse in respect of great disorder ... in his howse ... at night by diverse disorderd fidlers*, York (YRS138/55); 1596 *ale house, typling house Inn or Taverne*, Beverley (YRS84/38). In such contexts 'to tipple' was to sell ale: 1606 *hath brewed to sell and hath kept tipling without Lycense*, Thirsk (NRQS1/29).

tire, tiresmith Tire is probably an abbreviated spelling of 'attire' which had meanings such as 'dress', 'outfit' or 'equipment'. By the fifteenth century it was being used of the metal rim of a wooden wheel: 1448 *unum par de tyres cum duobus paribus de edges [a pair of tires with two pairs of edges]*, Carlton (SS116/49); 1485 *j tyre pro rota plaustri [1 tire for a cart wheel]*, Ripon (SS64/373); 1597 *6 newe tyre strokes with other iron stuffe*, South Cave (Kaner194). It gave rise to a specialist occupational term: 1727 Thomas Hood, *tiresmith*, St Olave's, York (PR). The modern spelling 'tyre' was a revival, used from the nineteenth century when rubber rims were first made. An unusual nickname may take this meaning back much earlier: 1277 *William de Lynley* called *Tyrewyggel* (YRS29/163). See also hurter, strake (1).

tirl A revolving piece of mechanism such as a wheel or turnstile: 1665 *Item for a Turll for the church gaets*, Elland (PR2/272); 1734 *a wheelbarrow, a turl*, Holmfirth (IH). Note the by-name: 1379 *Robertus Tirlwynd*, Lonsdale (PTLa).

tirl-bed A kind of truckle-bed: 1661 *one Turle bed with bedding*, Hipperholme (YRS134/121); 1661 *a turlbed in the Chamber*, Langfield (YRS134/119); 1700 *One Turle Bed and bedding*, Elland (OWR1/2/8).

tissue A fine, rich material, often interwoven with gold or silver: 1430 *j gonam cum cathena de auricalco cum le tysshewe de serico [1 gown with a brass chain and with silken tissue]*, York (SS30/9); 1463 *et deauratam super unum rubio tisshew [and woven with gold on a red tissue]*, Leeds (Th24/55); 1500–10 *Una virga di. quart. panni auri rubii tissue [One and three-quarters of a yard of golden red tissue cloth]*, York (SS35/228); 1542 *A pair of forsleves of clothe of teishowe*, Bretton (YRS134/2); 1565 *a Frenche gowne of clothe of tisshew*, Temple Newsam (YAJ25/94).

tit Originally a small horse but possibly used here pejoratively:

> 1608 *we lay in paine that no man putt no unlawfull good upon our commons, no sould tytt ridline tupes to avoid them of between this and Trinitie even next in paine of everie horse 10s and everie ridline tup 3s 4d*, Normanton (WCR11/106–7).

titling A small size of stockfish, imported into Hull: 1453 *4 C tytlyng;* 1471 *5 M titlyng* (YRS144/11,146).

toast-iron, toasting-iron An alternative word for toasting-fork: 1468 *j tost-iryn et j scomour ferri*, Sewerby (SS45/161); 1588 *1 gallo balke 3 houkes a paire of tonges and a tostinge iron*, South Cave (Kaner149); 1658 *1 broyleinge iron, 1 toastinge iron*, Barley (YRS47/16); 1677 *One range, gallow balke & dogs, one brogleing iron, one toasting iron*, Selby (YRS47/2); 1693 *1 range, tongues, briges, tosting irne*, Holmfirth (G-A); 1721 *a range tongs toasting iron 5s 6d*, Ecclesfield (EDH57).

tobacco-cutter A rare occupation noted in York: 1716 *Henry Sharpass, Tobacco Cutter*, All Saints Pavement, York (PR).

tod Originally a bundle or pack of wool and then used as a measure. The OED has references from 1425 but the term occurs infrequently in Yorkshire: 1714 *As for the prices of Wooll There is John Stocks of Hallifax Give eighteen shillings A todd for Long Wooll within A good mile of Horncastle* (MD43/E17).

to-fall A lean-to, shed or penthouse: 1416–17 'And for timber purchased for repair of the kiln and *le Tofall* by Henry Joynour', Selby (SAR173); 1446 *quendam murum ad finem ejusdem domus vocatum Tuffall annexæ ad tenementum [a wall at the end of the house called To-fall joined to the building]*, Beverley (ERAS6/80); 1450 *solutum Willelmo Portroy carpentario pro factura unius tufall in Hamertonlan [pait to the carpenter William Portroy for building a to-fall in Hamertonlan]*, York (SS192/66); 1538–9 *for ij sperse of xvij^{th} fotte longe for the toffold in the garth, viij^d*, York (CCW201).

tofore As a preposition this could be 'in front of': 1476 *Thomas Welles … cam to fore the Maire the ix^{th} day of November*, York (YRS98/4). With reference to time it meant 'before': 1504 *all suche bills to be brought in tofore mikelmesse next*, York (YRS106/9).

toft, toftstead A very common place-name element, originally a homestead or dwelling-house, a meaning implicit in a sequence of deeds for Stockeld: 1320 'all her lands, tenements, messuages, tofts' (YRS69/157). It remained in use in the compound 'toftstead' as the site of a house: 1524 *An other toftestede which I have in Lownd and the land belonging therto*, Clarborough (SS79/180); 1609 *one little house and a toft stead lying at the east side of the same cottage*, South Cave (Kaner225); 1653 *unto John Lamm my sonne one toftlande … to Peter Lamm, my sonne, one toftsteade*, Brayton (YRS47/100). 'Toft' itself eventually came to mean a small field or enclosure: 1555 *I … giue the said house, kylne, toft and croft … to my son*, Church Fenton (Th27/44); 1578–9 *I give the* *said house, garth & tofte … to Francise Willson my sone*; 1587 *my hempgarth & ij toftes in the feilde*, South Cave (Kaner105,140).

to-morn A regional alternative for 'tomorrow': 1482 *agreid … that all the Aldermen in skarlet and all the xxiiij in cremyson … shalbe to morn … be iij of clok, at the Miklyth barr*, York (YRS98/56); 1522 *his lordship to take … his part of a pyke at the fisshgarthez to morne*, York (YRS106/83).

tongs A word which goes back to Old English with no real change in meaning. These were the tools which made the moving and handling of heated iron possible and in most smithies there would be a range of such implements: they were an essential part of 'smithy gear': 1374 *unum tayng*, York (SS4/92); 1423 *pro ij par de tangys*, York (SS45/81); 1545 *one little stethie, towe pare of tanges*, Normanton (Th19/104). See also fore-hammer, working tools.

tonnell A large cask or barrel for wine or other commodities (OED): 1380 *le tonel ou le pipe de vyn [the tonnell or the pipe of wine]*, York (SS120/40); 1423 *pro j tonnell et pro j tubb*, York (SS45/80); 1578 *xj barrels … two woodd bottels, fower sponging tubbes, two tunnels*, Ripley (SS104/133); 1694 *to a Cooper for making a tubb 2 daies and a tunell*, Tong (Tong/4a/3). See also dolium, tunnel.

ton-tight A measure of capacity, based on the contents of the 'ton', a cask for holding wine or some dry goods: 1415 *in cariagio ccc lxxxvij tuntight dictorum lapidum per carectas a quarera [for transport of 387 ton-tights of the said stone by waggon from the quarry]*, York (SS35/33); 1472 *viijs receptis de Willelmo Tod pro una tontight in nave vocata Anna a Selandia usque Hullam [8s received from William Tod for a ton-tight in a ship called Anna from Zealand to Hull]* (SS129/68); 1489–90 *a ton-t' ferri [a ton-tight of iron]*, Hull (YRS144/212). In the ordinances of the *Merchant Mistery* in York is:

> 1495 *agreed … that what person … freght any ship outher in England or beyond the see to the beofe of the felisship sall answere to the said felisship of a tontight lyk as the ship is freght or els to the valour of a tontight in money* (SS129/87).

Salzman comments on the weight of a *ton tyght c.*1470 (SZ1/122).

tooth-drawer One who draws or extracts teeth, a dentist: 1414 *omnes medici, sirurgici, fisici et extractores dentium [all doctors, surgeons, physics and tooth-drawers]*, Beverley (BTD111); 1422 *Johannes Clerk treacler et tuthdragher*, York (SS96/133); 1498 *omnes forinsici Tothedrawers et blodelatters qui occupant … infra dicta villam [all foreign tooth-drawers and blood letters who work … within the said town]*, Beverley (BTD113). See also treacler.

tooth-pick An instrument for picking the teeth, often of wood but here of silver: 1558 *a silver whissell with a toithe pike in it*, Richmond (SS26/128). See also ear-pick.

top As a verb this was to cut off the top branches of a growing tree. It was often linked with 'to lop' and the severed branches were called lops and tops: 1543 *which sayed springe the abovesaide Leonarde [Beckwith] occupieth … the loppys and toppys whereof he toke to his own use*, Pontefract (YRS13/361); 1558 *Ellis my sonne shall haue all the tymber saving the toppes therof*, South Milford (Th27/169); 1581 *for fyve ocke topes xijs item more reseaved of him for the topes that was feled in the Rosse Ing ixs*, Stockeld (YRS161/28); 1618 *to fell presentlye, cary away shortly, I to have all topps and bowes cutt off*, Brandsby (NYRO44/155). In 1738, *several young trees … lately planted by Mr Richard Tottie in his Grounds … were … topp'd, cut and destroyed*, Leeds (Th26/69). See also lop, offal.

topping The fore-lock of an animal, used as a name, especially for oxen: 1558 *I gyve to … my sonne … the worst of two foure oxen called by name Topping broodhead, Lyon and Brownberd*, Huddleston (Th27/245); 1584 *also one oxe called Toppin with all my yockes … and plowe geare*, Scriven (SS104/145). Found as a by-name: 1379 *Willelmus Toppyng*, Grassington (PTWR).

Toppit(t) This minor place-name occurs several times in south Yorkshire, and Smith lists examples in Denby and Hoyland (PNWR1/321,327): there was also an enclosure named *Toppit* in Mirfield, on a sales plan of 1829. These are usually explained as 'top pit' but 'the orepit' would have a pronunciation in dialect that could offer an alternative explanation.

top shovel See bank shovel, shovel.

topstailing A regional version of 'topple-tail', a somersault, used by Adam Eyre to describe a riding accident: 1647 *I received a very dangerous fall from my meare, shee topstayleing over mee*, Thurlstone (SS65/69). The expression 'tipply-tails' survives for rolling head over heels downhill.

tortoiseshell This was a material popular with cutlers for making the hafts of knives, and since it is mentioned in the earliest surviving inventories its use is likely to have a longer history. In 1692, Thomas Spooner had *16 dozen of tortoiseshell knives and forkes* in his smithy chamber, and in 1718 John Winter had *30 pounds of Shell* in his cellar (IH). See also spotted knife.

touch (1) An official mark or stamp upon gold or silver which indicates that it has been tested, used as a noun or verb: *c.*1420 *si ascun meistre en dite artifice vende ou mettra a vente ascun choise dore ou dargent que appent a lour dite arte avaunt qil soit touche avec le commune touch de la dite cite … qil forfaite vjs viijd [if any master of the said craft sell or offer for sale any item of gold or silver belonging to their said trade before it had been touched with the said city's common touch … he forfeits 6s 8d]*, York (SS120/75); 1443 *A quart pot of silver with the touche of Parys*, Willoughby, Nottinghamshire (SS30/132); 1561 *the said goldsmythes sholde bring their towche so that thar work might be approved and towched with the pounce of this Citie*, York (YRS112/9).

touch (2), touchstone A fine-grained variety of quartz or jasper which can be used to test the quality of gold and silver alloys. The determining factor is the colour of the mark made when they are rubbed on the stone: 1485 *lapis niger vocatus tuche iiijd [black stone called touch 4d]*, Ripon (SS64/367). When the cutler John Shirtcliffe died in 1713 there was a *Touch-stone* listed in his inventory, worth seven shillings (IH).

touch box A box for priming powder: 1564 *One dagg with flask* [sic] *& tutchbockes* (SS2/226); 1592 *a caliver with flax tuchboxe & head peice*, South Cave (Kaner174); 1599 *one musket with a reste a flaxe and a tutche boxe xvj²*, Rawmarsh (TWH16/162); 1610 *a flax and tutch box*, Kirkstall (SpSt); 1611 *1 fowleinge peese with flaxeboxe & toucheboxe & rammer*, Brafferton (NYRO44/39).

touch prick Of uncertain interpretation but found several times as a by-name in different parts of Yorkshire: 1323 *Willelmus Toucheprik*, Thornton Riseborough (NRR2/99); 1379 *de Roberto Touchepryk, flesshewer*, Howden (PTER196). If 'prick' here is for penis the evidence is early. See also prick (1).

touchstone See touch (2).

tow The fibre of flax, hemp or jute prepared for spinning: 1558 *with the towe in the garth*, South Cave (Kaner52); 1562 *halfe my towe of hemp and flaxe that is brayked*, Sutton Bonnington (YAJ36/440); 1570 *Item towe and lyne soated* [sic] *and unbreakede*, Spaldington (YRS134/38); 1629 *16s in full for flax, towe, nails and other things*, Elmswell (DW182); 1668 *Item two stone of Tow*, Slaithwaite (YRS134/136). See also line-tow, pill.

toward Willing, apt to learn, disposed to do what is required: 1529 *the seide Richerde … byndith hymselfe … to be diligent … and to be ever towarde both in worde and deide … as becommyth eny good servaunde*, Brimham (YRS140/184). In the same indenture is an example of the noun: *the seide abbot grauntith to the side Richerde for his towerdnes … the pasture of 30 sheipe*. See also froward.

towing path We associate the tow path with canals and horse-drawn barges, and references in the OED date from that period. Nevertheless, the men who worked the inland waterways in the Middle Ages must also have used tow paths. When Turnbridge in Snaith was under discussion in Parliament, in 1442, it was confirmed *to the shipmen* that they retained *the right of having towing paths … as of old*, so the practice of towing boats was already well established at that time (JHS122). See also hale.

tow-line A rope by which something can be towed, particularly a boat: 1680 *Best and Second Hausers and towling £5 8s 0d*, Whitby (SAH22/16); 1693 *wee present a rope called a towlin taken up at Scarbrough below the low water marke … about 40 fathome in length* (SAH22/25).

town bull A bull for the use of the town's cattle, kept in turn by the main house-holders: 1563 *I give to the township of Thurscros … a bull to serve the township for ever* (SS104/93); 1595 *Ordered … that every husbandman in Ilkley in his due course shall take the towne bull into ther custodie and meate him well in winter time* (CHT132); 1664 *that noe … person of Billingley or Thurnscoe doe make use of Towne Bull belonging to Boulton … for the service of theire kine*, Bolton on Dearne (WN).

town-gate The regional word for the main street of a village or town: 1523 *to the pavyng of the towne gaite of Tokwith iijs iiijd* (YRS41/169n); 1541 *Also I giue to the churche a tre at lies in the Towne gaite*, Houghton (Th19/33); 1616 *the complainant … came forth of the house … into the street or towngate*, Halifax (BAS10/106); 1668 *Dorothy Blakey … heard a great noise in the Street … did observe that Richard Walker did come downe the Towne gate*, Grindleton (QS1); 1684 *all that one shop … in the towne gate of Kirkby Malzeard late erected upon the waste* (MD15). Most 'town-gates' gave way to 'town street' from the seventeenth century, but it survives quite frequently as a place-name. Huddersfield's *town gate* of 1589 was given the name Kirkgate *c.*1797 by the Ramsden family who held the lordship, no doubt anxious to place the town on a par with Bradford, Leeds and Wakefield (HPN82,139).

townherd The townherd had a role similar to that of the common herd but he may not have been responsible for intercommoning: 1638 *Inhabitants of Snaith petition that Thos. White and his daughter are burthensome to them xijd weekely; said inhabitants having moved him to be Towne heard for Swine* (YAJ5/390). See also herd, staff-herd, swineherd.

town mires An area of carr or marsh which was a town asset in earlier centuries, a location prized for its rich pasturage, supply of reeds and 'black earth': 1570 *for iiij^{or} cattell gaits and iiij^{or} daills in Huton towne myers xxs*, Hutton Conyers (SS26/230). See also mire pits.

town-swine See swineherd, townherd.

toyles, toylles Regional spellings of 'tools': 1479 *Item in toyles that belonges to the occupacon iijs,* York (SS45/253); 1552 *to my sonne … cartes, plowes, yockes with all such toylles belonging to husbandry,* Halifax (Crossley73–4); 1600 *all my geare and toyles in the smithye except my stythye,* Cottingley (LRS1/1).

trace To track by following the footprints: 1598 *William Brotherton of Beckwithshaw fyned vjs viijd for tracing & killing a hare in the Snowe* (YRS3/87); 1669 *did see Thomas Canby traycing haires in the snow with two greyhounds and two mungrell dogs,* Thorne (QS1).

trail (1) A type of sledge used for hauling wood, corn, etc.: 1616 *ashe for a trayle sled,* Brandsby (NYRO44/116). The distinction, which may be one of size, is made in an entry in the Wakefield court rolls in 1433 when tenants were presented by the forester for illegally carting wood: William Burgh's offence was a *sledfull* whereas John Poklyngton had 12 *traylfull* (WCR15/20). In 1576, the inventory of Marmaduke Elderkar of Ripon had a section on his debts and one sequence of three entries recorded payments due to *Christofer Scote for helping hym iiijs, for a traile to hym xijd … for leading the tythe corne xiijs* (SS64/379).

trail (2) Short for trail-net, a kind of drag-net used to catch fish: 1647 *Thomas Pearson indicted … for useing trailes,* West Riding (QS10/2).

trailwing This by-name has been recorded several times in different parts of Yorkshire: 1200 *Geoffrey Trailewing,* Yorkshire pipe roll (R&W); 1346 *Johannes Trailweng,* Catton (SS4/19); 1348 *John Trayleweng of Yokefleet* (ECP21). Evidently a nickname, it may have been inspired by the habit that some ground-nesting birds have of distracting attention from their nesting site by 'trailing' one wing as they move away from it.

train (1) A type of oil imported into Hull from the fifteenth century at least: 1466–7 *6 bar' trane,* Hull (YRS144/99); 1528 *one last of trane,* Hull (YAJ2/248). The editor of the Hull accounts for 1466–7 says that the oil was initially from fish and seals, and later from whales. Train-oil is a term recorded from *c.*1553 (OED). See also blubber, sealsmolt.

train (2) A trick, trickery or deceit: *c.*1530 *Robert Hanson … sayeth that … his brother was by a craftie trayne conueyed to the hows of John Palden … and there murdred by the seruantes of Sir Henry Sayvell,* Halifax (YRS51/37).

tram A word found principally in Scotland and the north-east where its recorded history as a mining term goes back to the early sixteenth century (OED). It could refer to a sled or wheeled vehicle which transported corves: 1711 *For corfe trams 6s per dozen made of Eller* [alder] *and Lugs of Ash,* Colsterdale (BM82/66). It was certainly a wheeled vehicle in the 1800s when it is mentioned in West Riding records: 1828 *a Railway or Tram Road … for the passage of Waggons, Carts and other Carriages,* Astley (CKY39). See also barrower, coal-mining tools and implements.

trammel (1) Of uncertain meaning in some inventories: 1560 *one acre of lande sawne with berlie, lyinge oof Tramelles,* Knaresborough (SS104/85); 1759 *4 soals & Iron Tramels j Corn fork,* Barnoldswick (YRS118/74). The OED has 'shackles' as a contrivance to hobble an animal.

trammel (2), trammel-net A fishing or fowling net with three layers of meshes: 1416 *noctant cum j tramell piscand'* [fishing at night with a trammel], Fulstone (MD225/1/142/1); 1417 'one net called a *Tramaill* … for taking fish in the dam', Selby (SAR168); 1572 *an olde nette with iiij tramel nets,* Skipton (Whit2/336); 1741 *fishing with a trammel,* Horbury (QS1/80/2).

trap door An underground door in a coal-mine which helped to control the flow of air in the galleries. In Colsterdale, in 1737, the blacksmith made fittings for a *trap door* and a boy was paid for *attending the Door for carrying air to the Forefield* (BM82/87). In the 1842 report into child labour Sarah Gooder aged 8 said that she was a trapper *in the Gawber pit*, adding *I have to trap without a light, and I'm scared* (ERP164).

trash Anything of little or no worth: 1543 *ij says, iij seckes with other trasche iijs iiijd*, Brettanby (SS26/41). See also hustlement, truntlement.

trave, traves A metal or wooden beam: 1373–4 *inter trabes cuilibet plaustro vjd*, Leeds (Th45/112); 1468 *j trabe ferri [1 iron trave]*, Sewerby (SS45/162). It could refer to a wooden frame: 1574 *ix hogesheads in the buttrie with the gantrees and traves there*, Wensley (SS26/251), and a pair of traves was a frame with bars which could control a horse that was being shod: 1425 'Thomas Marshall [a farrier] holds a pair of *traves* in the common way beside his forge', Leeds (Th24/17); 1465 *The Traves in the markytt stede called the forge in the tenure of Richard Smyth yerly xijd*, Hull (YRS141/114); 1500 *Thos Kendall, smyth, had set up a payre of newe traves on the common ground without Bouthome Barre*, York. The ownership of the ground on which these traves stood was the subject of a dispute and in later evidence they were called *a payre of horse traves* and *the smyth traves* (YRS103/147–50); 1628 *Wee finde that … George Dixonn doth pay to the Kinges Maiestie for a pair of treyes for a smith in the Market Place*, Leeds (Th57/168); 1748 *one pair of traws*, Sowerby (QS1/87/6). See also soil.

tray A flat board used for carrying food, dishes and other items. The word was formerly applied more generally to shallow open vessels: 1561 *woode trayes*, Spaldington (YRS134/10); 1581 *skelbosses with shepe trayes*, South Cave (Kaner113).

treacle This word derives ultimately from Greek but it was brought here by the Normans. Originally, it was the name given to a salve which was used as an antidote to poison and apparently made up of spices and drugs, in which sense it is on record in England from 1340 (OED): 1457–8 *In triaca pro Joh'e Selby ijd [for treacle for John Selby 2d]*, Fountains Abbey (SS130/67). A North Riding by-name is an earlier example, possibly metonymic for an apothecary: *c.*1211 *William Triacle*, Guisborough (SS86/192).

In 1464–5 John Person on the *Jacob* imported into Hull *23 lib' treacle* and *23 lib' grengyngere*, valued together at £1 10s 0d (YRS144/73). A similar entry links the two commodities in 1467 and the inference may be that they were to be used together, for whatever medicinal purpose. They were almost certainly being brought into Yorkshire from the Low Countries, and in one case the home port was named as Veere. The editor was of the opinion that treacle here was a 'compound of spices and drugs on a honey base, possibly … a sugar base', an explanation which might explain how treacle came later to be thought of as something sweet. Treacle contained in a small box was actually a fashion item from the 1400s, attached to the girdles that ladies wore around their waists: *c.*1504 *Item j dussan and a halfe of trehakyll boxys ijd*, York (SS53/193). In 1693, a Selby shopkeeper had *London treacle 3s; Veanas treacle 1s 6d* (YRS47/22).

In Yorkshire the word was later used for the syrup produced when sugar was refined and crystallised. Treacle parkin is one of the most distinctively Yorkshire cakes, made now with oatmeal and sweetened with sugar and treacle – or 'golden syrup'. At its best it is moist and flavoured with ginger, linked traditionally with several local customs and still popular on bonfire night. It is uncertain how old the tradition might be. The Mirfield diarist John Turner noted on 6 November 1750 that he gave one penny to his wife *for treacle for a parkin* (MS757) and one earlier reference occurs in the Quarter Sessions rolls. The year was 1729 and the offence was one of theft: Ann Whittaker's very full statement told how

> her Mistress did persuade her to ask Sarah Priestley ... to steale meal from her master to make a parkin on ... and sent the meal by a Little lade ... and gave Sarah ... some brass to Fetch Treakle with from Elland to make a Parkin.

The clerk referred to the finished product as *parkins alias cakes* which may imply that the magistrates were unfamiliar with the word 'parkin' (QS1/68/4). In fact, it has an obscure origin and these eighteenth-century references predate those quoted in the dictionaries. See also parkin.

treacler An apothecary, one who gave his patients 'treacle'. The occupation featured in the York freemen's rolls in the early fifteenth century: 1411 *Henry Olyver, triacler*; 1418 *Thomas Chapman, treacler*; 1422 John Clerk, *treacler et tuthdragher*, York (SS96). See also potekary.

treat Food and drink given to a guest at no expense to the recipient: 1768 'the Judges of Assize at Hull to be offered a *cold treat* in the Assembly Rooms', Beverley (YRS122/48).

treate See chisel.

tree Used in the sense of 'wood', as a material of which furniture and a variety of utensils and structures could be made: 1416 *the ... tanneres shall raise upe on[e] castle of tree ... in the Rogacion weeke*, Beverley (BTD115); 1422 *schaffoldynges and other tree werk*, Catterick (NRQS3/35); 1566 *Item thre tre chargers 12d, 7 dussen tre disheis 8d*, Grinton (YRS152/142); 1591 *a tree dubler*, South Cave (Kaner165); 1673 *1 trough tree*, Brayton (YRS47/63). Imported into Hull were *30 tree platers* in 1461, *treen spoones* in 1465, *87 tree cannes* in 1483 and *tre beddes* [beads] in 1489–90 (YRS144). Special types of wood recorded are: 1509 *a long chist of cipresse tre*, Dewsbury (SS79/6); 1565 *a chaire ... of wallenuttree*, Temple Newsam (YAJ25/95). It was contrasted with metal objects: 1462 *all the old pewtr vesell with all the tre vessel*, Wawne (SS30/261). See also doubler, throw (1).

tree-bridge In some cases this may have been a wooden bridge, but it could also be a bridge over a narrow stream, made of a single tree trunk: the OED has an example from 1506, entered under foot-bridge. In 1642, at Ayton in the North Riding the inhabitants were presented *for not repairing their bridge called le Tree-bridge lying between ... Ormsby and the market-town of Stokesley* (NRQS4/224), and in the will of Jeoffrey Charder of Reeth, in 1547, the executors were asked to *bye one tree of one foot brode and laye yt over Waveland becke* (YRS152/32). The 'lost' West Riding place-name *Trowebrigge*, that is tree-bridge, occurred in a Castleford charter *c.*1235 (YRS30/670). See also plank, summer (2).

treenail, trenail A cylindrical pin of hard wood used in fastening timbers together. Those which were provided for the repairs to Bridlington pier in 1717 were 18 inches long and cost 40s per thousand (BCP194): 1441–2 'And for *clavis ligneis*, 2d', Selby (SAR110); 1526 *Item for a leyge and trenaylles, j^d ob*, York (CCW117); 1678 *3000 trenalds besides props and wedges*, Selby (YRS47/195); 1699 *To pilling without Each apron ... to timber groveing driveing & trenayles to Boath*, Naburn Lock (YAJ66/186); 1715 *working for us in riving laths and tree nails*, Maltby (SS65/189); 1717 *For Plank and Trenails from London, £101 8s 4d*, Bridlington (BCP195).

trefoil An ornament with three leaves: 1446 *et sex salsaria argenti signata cum lez trayfulles et le couch [and six silver salt-cellars marked with trefoils and the shell]*, Turnham Hall (SS30/121); 1468 *De ij coverlettes … operatis cum le trayfolis [For 2 coverlets … embroidered with trefoils]*, Sewerby (SS45/162).

trellis, trellis-maker A trellis is a structure of light bars of wood which cross each other at intervals, used as a gate, screen, window, etc.: 1422 *the trelys wyndowe at the somer hall, the glasse wyndows*, York (SS85/16); 1532 *pro v.m les hartlattes pro trelysis*, York (SS35/106); 1616 *streight saughe wodd to make trellesses* (NYRO44/115); 1676 *pro trellises of the windows*, Ripon Minster (YRS118/149). The making of trellises was one of many woodland crafts: 1617 *divers others doe lyve on my wodds … many trellesse makers*, Brandsby (NYRO44/140). It could be used as a verb: *c.*1520 *Will'mo Caruer trelyssyng et carvyng per j diem, 6d*, Ripon (SS81/202).

trenail See treenail.

trencher A wooden platter on which meat was served: 1453 *5 scok trenchours*, Hull (YRS144/5); 1554 *an ewer iii dowsen trenchers*, Brantingham (Kaner48); 1578 *sware trenchers … rownd trenchers in 2 boxes*, Stockeld (YRS134/50); 1617 *Trenchers 2 dozen*, Elmswell (DW161); 1675 *Eleven Duzon of Wood Trenchers*, Bretton (YRS134/150); 1720 *tooke a light out of the window and tooke some Trenchers … she heard them rattle as he ran away*, Wakefield (QS1/60/1).

trenel bed A variant spelling of trundle bed: 1557 *One trenel bedsted, one fether bed*, Thornton Bridge (SS26/100). See also trindle.

trental A set of thirty requiem masses, to be said on one day or over a succession of days: 1392 *pro uno trentali missarum celebrandarum in ecclesia' mea' parochiali … xvˢ [for a trental of masses celebrated in my parish church … 15s]*, York (SS4/175); 1454 *I wyll bedon for my sawle iij trentawls of the Fadyr and Son and Holy Gost*, Hull (SS30/171); 1521 *I wytt xiijs iiijd … to cause oon trentale of messys to be sayd for my husband and me*, Harrogate (SS104/12); 1542 *I wyll that thar be one tryntall of messes doyne … for the heylthe of my soulle*, Grinton (YRS152/57).

trest, trist In early references an alternative of trestle, but perhaps a kind of stool or bench later: 1432 *j met bord with j pare trysts*, Scarborough (SS30/22); 1462 *a lang bord, a par trists*, Wawne (SS30/262); 1542 *an arcke and two trysts*, Bedale (SS26/30); 1618 *one cubward … one table, one treist*, Cottingley (LRS1/49); 1668 *one litle table & one trest 2s*, Slaithwaite (YRS134/134); 1691 *1 buffet, 2 trests, 2 stools*, Holmfirth (IH). See also folding board, trust.

trestle A wooden structure used as a support for boards, usually in pairs: 1396 *unum par tristelles [one pair of trestles]*, Hedon (ERAS10/6); 1410 *de ij tabulis mensalibus et j pari tristellorum [for 2 table boards and 1 pair of trestles]*, York (SS45/48); 1503 *tabulas meas mensales cum le trestels [my table boards with the trestles]*, Ripon (SS64/296); 1588 *two litle trestles*, Dalton (DD/WBW/19); 1694 *2 tressells for the brickmakers*, Tong (Tong/4d/3); 1698 *for makeing ladders and thristles*, Pickering (YAJ35/219). The use of trestles in bridge building is first noted in 1796 and their function was defined in detail by Smiles in 1861 (OED). They formed a part of the complicated timber-work which supported the arch. A reference in the accounts for Kirkstall Bridge in 1616 implies that the trestles were a fundamental part of the centres, if not the centres themselves (BAS6/146):

> For tymber for making the trysletes of the arch   £20
>
> For leading of this tymber over the value of the tymber when it hathe served   £5
> for Set the Arch upon
>
> For working of this tymber and settinge in the Ryver   £25

In 1699, *5 Trissels* and *55 Tressel feet* were part of *a Frame for turning the Arch on* Tadcaster Bridge (QS1/38/4). See also board (2).

treswold A spelling of threshold, that is the piece of timber under the door which has to be crossed on entering a house: 1538–9 *to a wryght for halffe a day for settyng a stancion in his dore syd and for a treswold in his gatt dore ij^d ob*, York (CCW203).

trindle A wheel, especially the lantern wheel of a mill: 1316 'Adam son of Jordan Milner carried from Cartworth mill 2 ironed trendles (*trendellos*) price 2s' (YRS78/104); 1391–2 *In tryndallo pro j porta infra cymiterium 3d [For a trindle for one gate in the cemetery 3d]*, Ripon (SS81/106); 1441–2 'working the said iron into bands and hoops for *le axeltree* and *lez trendells* of the said mill', Selby (SAR109); 1468 *pro j stoke pro le tryndiles … pro le byndynge eorumdem tryndiles*, Brotherton Mill (SS35/134); 1549 *ij watter whells ij Cogge whell troghes and trondyll*, Ecclesfield (Miller85–6); 1618 *2 trimdle heads for a mill*, South Cave (Kaner273).

trindle-bed See trundle bed.

trinket A diminutive of 'trink', that is a kind of fixed fishing net used in rivers: 1657 *And further the statute 2 Hen. VI … doth … forbid the puttinge or settinge of any nets called trincketts … for takeing of fish*, Wetherby (YAJ15/465).

trinter See threnter, twinter.

tripherd A 'trip' was a small flock of animals, especially goats and sheep, and Bolton Priory records contain several references to the animals and the related occupation: 1295–6 *In lib(eracione) de tryphirdes vj qr precium ut supra [for payment of the tripherds 6 farthing at the price as above]* (YRS154/63); 1304–5 *In pane pro triphyrdes et tonsione ovium [For bread for the tripherds and shearling sheep]* (YRS154/187); 1377–8 *In sotularibus emptis pro trypgotes ijs [For shoes bought for the trip goats 2s]* (YRS154/564).

trippett The game of tip-cat, so named from the piece of wood with which it was played, pointed at both ends: 1624 *Francis Milnes … with divers others unknown did on Easter day last in the time of afternoon Service play in the churcheyard there at a game called Trippett*, Aislaby (NRQS3/199).

trist See trest.

trod A trodden way, a footpath: 1709 *Thomas Elliss by several times comeing to Mag Weddell at unlawful times made a perfect trod on the ground where none hath beene*, Pollington (QS1/48/10).

tronell bedde A variant spelling of trundle bed: 1567 *two thrawne beddes … a tronell bedde & two bolsters*, Fixby (YRS134/15).

trotter A horse that trotted briskly, as opposed to one that ambled: 1423 *uno equo gray trottar; uno equo bay ambeler [a grey horse, a trotter; a bay horse, an ambler]*, York (SS45/80). More frequent are references to the verb 'to trot': 1445 'a mare of *myrkgray* colour *trottant*', Bolton (YRS63/8); 1472 *a gra horse trotyng whiche gois in the Parke*, Pontefract

(Th26/327); 1539 *A Blake Fyllye and trots*, Sheriff Hutton (YAJ36/182); 1551 *I giue hyme one grae ambelinge stage … I giue vnto hyme one grae stagge that trottith*, Burley (Th19/274); 1631 *sould one sad bay maire trots*, Adwalton (BAS7/58). See also ambler, and Ambler in GRDict.

trough tree A hollowed out trunk of a tree used as a trough: 1673 *2 packsadles, 1 trough tree, 1 dragg*, Brayton (YRS47/63).

trouse A term for brushwood, that is cuttings from hedges or copses, on record from the Old English period (OED). Oliver Rackham noted its use but it was rare in Yorkshire records. See also tinsel.

trow A spelling of 'trough' which reflects the regional pronunciation: 1440 *In j trow viijd*, Northallerton (SS2/90); 1490 *De j lez grynde-ston, cum j lez troegh*, York (SS53/57); 1549 *one trowe, a worte stone, a maske fatt*, Marrick (YRS152/76); 1568 *In the Back Howse … twoe trowes and twoe bordes 4s*, Healaugh (YRS134/35); 1583 *3 trowes of lead ure and two trowes of sande*, Grinton (YRS152/259). In the cutlery trade the trough held the water that kept the grindstone moist: 1701 *Two stones to grinde and two trowes, 4s*, Sheffield (FBH121); 1769 *one half of all my wheel tools … and one trow at Endcliffe Wheel* (WPS130); 1794 *the number of trows at each wheel*, Sheffield (TWH28/239). In 1739, *the goodwill of one original grinding trow at Morton Wheel* was valued at £70 (WPS19). As a verb it meant to form a trough as a drainage channel: 1668 *carry a sufficient sough and water-gate through the demised ground … and to leave the same trowed and scoured*, Seacroft (YRS50/115). See also trown weight.

trown weight Lead ore has been measured by the 'dish' since the late twelfth century at least (JHR60) but in Nidderdale a smelting agreement indicates that a 'trough' or 'trow' may have served a similar purpose:

> 1527 *the seide parties … shall, durynge the plesor of the seide abbot well and trewly burne and make in cleyn and sufficient leede all suche leede ure as is … delyverde unto theme … at the more of Grenehow from tyme to tyme after trown weight* (YRS140/194).

Swaledale inventories contain evidence for the practice there: 1560 *Debtes awinge … William Skott 8 trowes of ure*, Downholme (YRS152/115); 1583 *Detes … Thomas Cherye 9 trowes of lead ure*, Grinton (YRS152/259).

truckle-bed A low bed running on castors, able to be stored beneath a stand-bed: 1565 *a trokle bed corded iijs iiijd*, Temple Newsam (YAJ25/97); 1621 *One standing bed with a testor … A truckle-bed, a featherbed*, Slaidburn (YRS63/47); 1637 *one truckle bedstead one matteris one pillowe*, Knaresborough (YRS134/81); 1676 *part of a truckle bed 6d*, Barley (YRS47/74); 1691 *1 trunkle bed 1 feather bed 1 blankett*, Selby (YRS47/3).

truelove A precious ornament or symbol of true love: 1463 *j croche [sic] auri cum tribus trewloves de pearl in eodem broch [1 gold 'croche' with three trueloves of pearl in the same brooch]*, Leeds (SS30/259); 1464 *unum anulam argenti et deauratum cum uno trew lyfe [a silver gilt ring with a truelove]*, York (SS30/263); 1471 *Jonett Eland j trewlofe of gold*, Beverley (SS45/194).

trumpery Applied to items of no great value: 1531 *A tub, a hogeshed with other trumperie, viijd*, York (SS79/324).

trumpmaker In the dialect of the West Riding, 'trump' appears to have been a general word for a spring knife, that is a penknife or pocket-knife. It was listed by

Wright (EDD) but he offered no examples, so the earliest evidence of its use is the occupational term in the Sheffield registers: 1659 *Nicholas Stevin of Sheffeld trumpmaker* (PR3/211); 1706 *Robert Bullas Trumpmaker*, Sheffield (PR7/12). The term occurred as late as 1740, when Simeon Handley, *trumpmaker*, was recorded in the parish register, after which it seems to have given way to pen and pocket-knife maker (FBH112).

trundle See trindle.

trundle bed A bed on castors or wheels, low enough to go under a stand-bed, much the same as a truckle-bed: 1542 *A bedsted with a tryndle bed geoned within the same*, Bretton (YRS134/2); 1564 *j standing bed j tryndle bed*, Clint (SS104/94); 1622 *one stand bed & 3 trundlebeddes xiijs iiijd*, Pudsey (LRS1/56); 1669 *a standing bedstead with the bedding, a trundle bed*, Elmswell (DW242). See also trenel bed, tronell bedde.

truntlement Trifles, odds and ends. A term which was noted by Halliwell and occurs in inventories, similar to hustlement but much less frequent: 1613 *a payre of old carte wheeles and other trumplement*, Stockeld (YAJ34/181); 1633 *certaine trenchers with two old stooles and other truntlement ijs*, Pudsey (LRS1/89). See also trash.

truss-hare In 1304, an action was brought by the Prior of Watton against William *Trussehare* and others for breaking his warren (YRS23/47n). The by-name suggests that the offender was known to snatch game illegally, and it anticipates the OED reference to this word which has the eagle *trussing up a hare* (1567).

trussing-bed Adapted for being trussed or packed for travelling: 1392 *unum lectum qui vocatur le trussyngbede [a bed called a trussing-bed]*, Ingmanthorpe (SS4/180); *c*.1537 *as well for stondyng bedes as trussing bedes*, Halifax (YRS45/188); 1562 *A trussing bed, a truckle bed, tester and hangings … in the chambre a trusser of a bed*, Allerton Mauleverer (SS26/154); 1565 *I geve to my awntte Dawson my thrusseyng bedstockes the wiche I had lent to her*, Reeth (YRS152/134); 1572 *One trussing bed for the field*, Skipton (Whit2/327).

trussing-coffer A coffer for use when travelling: 1416 *unum par de old trussing cofres*, Wollaton (SS4/382); 1429 'a pair of *trussyng coffers*', York (SS186/99); 1485 *ij trussing coffers iijs, unum casket xd, unum magnum trussing mayle, precij ijs [2 trussing coffers 3s, a casket 10d, a great trussing bag, price 2s]*, Ripon (SS64/368); 1558 *to Anne Scrope my trussing coffer with all therin*, Danby on Ure (SS26/112). See also mail pillion.

trust An alternative spelling of trest, trist, a bench of some kind: 1661 *a litle table with Trustes, cheares, quishinges*, Langfield (YRS134/119); 1748 *one forme or trust*, Sowerby (QS1/87/6).

tub Water was one of the coal-miner's greatest enemies and over the centuries sophisticated methods of keeping pits dry were devised. Nevertheless, the early records reveal that water was commonly baled out using bowls, and removed from pits in tubs or barrels, even if these had to be drawn up the shaft: 1694 *Paid John Wood towards the pit sinking 1s; to Tubes 1d; to Cartes 2d*, Farnley (MS11); 1713 *two tubs for drawing water*, Shibden (HAS30/147); 1754 *for two New Barrels for the use of pulling water, 11s 0d*, Beeston (WYL160/129/5); 1762 *For 2 Hoops on Water Tubs 8d*, Tong (Tong/4c/6).

tucker A piece of lace or the like worn around the neck by women: 1725 *one chequer'd hand kerchief, three quoifes and a tucker*, West Riding (QS1/64/1).

tug Two examples of the noun have been recorded in coal-mining contexts, one in the inventory of Charles Best of Landimer in Shelf: 1700 *three Tuggs and three shovels* (Corr.) and the other in the accounts of Farnley colliery: 1716 *Tuggs 5* (MS11). The reference may be to 'the iron hoop of a corf', possibly a sort of handle (OED). In farming records it was part of the harness of working horses, a short chain attached to the hames: 1570 *foote shackelles ... one payer of tugges and sex payer of cutwithes* (YRS134/37); *c.*1742 *tug for swingletree*, Holmfirth (G-A). See also cutwithy, lugged, tram.

tugwithy Originally a withe or withy, that is a tough, flexible but slender branch of a willow or osier, used as a tie or shackle, presumably attached to the 'tug' on a working horse. It was later applied to an iron chain which had the same function: 1551 *a ploughe foote shakill, a tugwithe and a plewbyeme*, Altofts (Th19/266); 1559 *too iron tugwythes*, Castleford (Th27/287); 1613 *a harrow, freat & a tugwythye of iron*, Cottingley (LRS1/7); 1675 *2 iron sugwidies* [sic], Selby (YRS47/190). See also cutwithy, thible.

tuke A material such as canvas: 1509 *To Richard Fosgrove my feloy on bag of blue tuke*, York (SS79/7).

tum To card wool by hand, in preparation for finer work and spinning: 1734 *a pair of tuming cards*, Holmfirth (IH). Map evidence shows that there was a *Tuming mill* at Whitley Willows in 1793, possibly so called because scribbling machines had been installed.

tumbler A drinking glass which originally had a rounded or pointed base, so that it could not be set down until emptied: 1647 *one Litle Ladle 3 Tumlirs twoe Tanckards*, Denton (YRS134/94).

tumbling bay The OED offers several meanings for this term, and has examples from 1724 and 1795. It could be an outfall from a canal, river or reservoir; a weir, or even the pool into which water falls from a dam. The details in a Honley agreement of 1796 describe such a feature clearly and they are supported by a plan. One of the parties agreed *to clear away a tunnel above the old weir ... and ... make a new Stone weir or tumbling bay south of his mill six yards in length and of the height of the said old weir* (G-A).

tumbrel A dung-cart which could be tipped so as to discharge its load: 1554 *in the garth a wayn a tomberell ii ploughes*, South Cave (Kaner48); 1561 *Item 3 waynes 3 tombrells ... with all the gere that belonges theym*, Spaldington (YRS134/10); 1582 *a wayne an old tumbrel*, South Cave (Kaner122).

tun Usually a large cask, one to hold liquids: 1453 *6 ton' wadde £30 0s 0d*, Hull (YRS144/2); 1471 *1 ton 1 pipa ferri*, Hull (YRS144/146); 1581 *to John Hudson for maikinge ij newe tonnes & ij pare of laynes of my master owne iron*, Stockeld (YRS161/34). The occupational term for a maker of tuns occurred as a by-name: 1379 *Johannes Tunwright*, Beamsley (PTWR). Alternatively, 'tun' was used of small, metal drinking vessels: 1618 *a pewter salt & a tunn*, Bingley (LRS1/21); 1656 *One silver bowle & a silver tunne*, North Bierley (YRS134/103).

tunicle A small tunic, a type of vestment worn by some clergymen: 1381 *lez trois aubes et lez parures deux tunicles et un cape* [three albs and the embroidery two tunicles and a cape], Guisborough (SS4/114); 1435 *duas tunaklis de nigro arras pulverizatas cum auro* [two black arras tunicles powdered with gold], York (SS30/53); 1497 *iij copes, ij tonnakyls of white lynnyncloth with rosez theruppon, price xxxs*, Wakefield (YAJ15/93); 1518–19 *payd for making of ij tonykylles and frenges to the same ixd*, York (CCW69); 1558 *one tunycle vs*, Knaresborough (SS26/126). See also sandal.

tunnel A typical late spelling of tonnell: 1613 *2 ganteries, j tunnell*, Stockeld (YAJ34/180). See also flight-net.

tun–tight See ton–tight.

tup A ram or male sheep: 1494 *viij hundreth yowes and tuppes*, Barmston (SS53/100); 1554 *twoo twynters waders* [wethers] *and two toppes 9/4*, Abbotside (YRS130/5); 1615 *a humble mugge tuppe*, Brandsby (NYRO44/88); 1642 *Tuppes are eyther hunge t(uppes), close tup(pes), Riggon tuppes*, Elmswell (DW3); 1697 *20 ews and a tup £7 7 0*, Holmfirth (IH). By-names are evidence of the word's much longer history: 1258 *Peter Touplamb*, Pontefract (YRS12/50); 1379 *Willelmus Tuphird*, Beamsley (PTWR). For tup as a verb see shearing.

tup–hog A male lamb from its weaning to its first shearing: 1605 *one other sheep called a tup-hogg, value 5s*, Swaledale (NRQS1/14); 1617 *two sheering shepe viz one gimber and one tuppehogge*, Aughton (YRS55/229); 1723 *a tup hog*, Killinghall (QS1/62/8).

turf–cote A small building in which to store the turves used as fuel: 1579 *one turffe cote*, Langfield (MD297/16). See also turf-house.

turfel Of a hat, furnished with a turn or cock: 1558 *In the Shoppe: Inprimis xxxj feltts, ij turfill hatts, ij ruggid hatts xxxvs*, Knaresborough (SS26/126).

turf–gate, turfway Access routes to the turf-pits: 1317–18 'half an acre on *le Turfgates*', Yapham (YRS76/168); 1528 'a road (*viam*) called a *Turffegate*', Keighley (YRS63/61); 1570 'not keeping the water outside the *Turffe gate*', Slaithwaite (M/SL); 1640 *that euery householder do come or send a suffitient labourer to the mending of the ... turfgates*, Holmfirth (WCR1/169). Turfway was a less common word: 1582 *a waye commonlie called Gisburne turffe waye* (YRS63/45). It gave rise to several minor places, including: 1492 *via voc' Turfewey*, Sowerby (PNWR3/155). The modern spelling of this Sowerby name is Turgate Lane.

turf–graft A regional word for turbary, that is the right to dig for turves or peats: 1313 'with *le turf graft* from either moor', Bagby (YRS50/18); 1584 *common of pasture ... and also common of Turburye and Turfgraft*, Tong (Tong/8b/1); 1624 *trespass in a parcel of land called le Turfe-graftes ... and throwing the turves ... into divers pittes*, Ebberston (NRQS3/206). See also flawgraft, stengraft.

turf–house A small building close to a dwelling-house where turf and peat was stored: 1332 'a house called *le Turfhous*', York (YRS102/176); 1570 'a house called *a turfehouse*, a garden, a croft', Honley (YDK122); 1584 'a house called a *turf hous* on the north side of *le fold*', Holmfirth (WCR4/21); 1622 *one lathe one turffhouse*, Honley (G-A); 1706 *inticed this informant three severall times in the night time to goe alonge to William Hills turfe house and from thence took both turffes and peates*, Pannal (QS1/45/1). It may also have been a kind of warehouse where the turf-getting was part of a commercial operation: 1404–5 'transporting ... the turves by water ... to *le Turfhous*', Selby (SAR138). See also turf-cote.

turf–moss See moss (2).

turfpenny A customary payment for the right to cut turf. See also ground penny.

turf–pit A site where tenants of a manor had the right to dig turves or peat for fuel, noted in an undated deed of the early fourteenth century: *apud Tur(f)pittes versus nord [at Tur(f)pittes towards the north]*, Guisborough (SS89/167). A deed of 1615 has important information about turf-getting practices:

> The said Erle and Lord Clifford shall not permit any forener or stranger to make spoyle or waste of the mosse or turbary of Embsey nor lead nor carry away any of the eldinge

called rowghe flawes or upper flawes without they sufficiently bed and fill such pitt or pitts as they shall make with … graving of any elding, turfes or peats (LRS2/91–2).

turf-spade A spade designed to cut turf, described in 1887 as having a triangular blade of steel with one side turned up and sharpened in front and a long curved shaft with a strong cross-handle (NRQS5/252). The spades referred to in early examples may have been simpler: 1485 *iiij^or vange et j turfe spade*, Ripon (SS64/373); 1559 *j turfspade iiijd ij old leys viijd*, Westerdale (YRS74/57); 1587 *a turfe spade … a dungeforke*, South Cave (Kaner145); 1692 *3 olde turfe spades 6d*, Holmfirth (IH). See also flaw.

turfway See turf-gate.

turkey, turkey carpet, turkey work Originally a carpet woven in one piece of richly coloured wools and having a deep pile, imported from Turkey or woven elsewhere in imitation of the style; often a table covering. Later the word was applied more loosely to a variety of imitative fabrics: 1568 *First one Longe turkey Carpet £5 0 0. Item 7 litell turkey Carpetts £2 6 8*, Healaugh (YRS134/24); 1591 *Three square qwisheons of Turkie worke*, Skipton (Whit2/336); 1620 *payd for forder* (blank) *yerds of Turkye grogram to make hoes & dublitt at 7s the yeard*, Brandsby (NYRO44/203); 1643 *Item j Turkey-worke foote carpet, a large one*, Skipton (Whit2/343); 1656 *Item stuffe for a Turkey worke Chaire with armes 16s*, Eshton (YRS134/107). See also cherkey.

turl-bed See tirl-bed.

turn, turn-stake A word with several meanings, but commonly a type of windlass used in coal-mining. It was described by Wright as a drum turned by means of a handle: a rope passed round the drum and a wagon was attached to each end, so that as the full one was drawn up an empty one descended (EDD).

The documentary evidence dates from the seventeenth century: 1655 *the Roule and Turne, geares and other utensils*, Sharlston (GSH3); 1666 *two turns three Roopes*, South Crosland (DD/WBD/2/81); 1710 *paid for turnestakes making and other wright worke*, Farnley (MS11); 1715 *agreed … to sinke a pitt at Wood to sett on Turne Stakes*, Farnley (MS14). Although it was a primitive method it remained in occasional use well into the nineteenth century, as in 1831 when a pit was sunk in Meltham and *Ropes, turn, gins* were among the items listed (G-A). 'Turn' occurs earlier in lead-mining records: 1630 *findeth all wood to timber the groves, and for turns, corves etc.*, Grassington (BM46/13); 1687 *8 turn trees and other grove tools*, Kettlewell (QS1/26/1). In the cutlery industry it was apparently a lathe worked by a treadle, and in 1702 a cutler called Samuel Bothomley possessed *two Foot turnes* and *one old wheele Turne* (IH). See also gin, roll.

turner The occupational term had a number of possible meanings but usually referred to workmen who turned vessels on a lathe, working with wood, metal or bone. The by-name is on record in Yorkshire from the early thirteenth century: 1227 Ralph *le tornur*, Rudston (YRS62/102); 1284 'Robert the *Turnur*, for a cartload of brushwood', Stanley (YRS29/180). In 1329, William *le Turnour* was brought before the manor court in Wakefield for using the lord's timber to make small wooden vessels without warrant (WYAS689) and in Selby in 1416–17 'wooden dishes, plates, and saucers [were] purchased from Thomas *Turnour*' (SAR168). In York, the turners were too small a group to have their own guild but were linked with 'bollers' [makers of bowls] in 1415 (OED) and with ropers in 1554. Their specialised craft was recognised that year when a dispute broke out among the carpenters and associated craftsmen:

if any the sayd carpentars, carvars or joynars doo throwe or turn bolles, dishes, wheles, chayers or such lyke stuffe as perteynith onely to the turnars craft than every suche to paye pageant sylver to the sayd ropars and turnars accordyngly, York (YRS110/109).

In Beverley in 1596, the *Disheturners* were in the guild of joiners and carpenters (YRS84/67). The adjective 'turned' was used for certain articles of furniture: 1566 *j chair of wainscotte and j chair of turned worke,* Richmond (SS26/193); 1629 *thre furmes a turne chayre two little stooles,* South Cave (Kaner338); 1657 *one little turned chaire,* Selby (YRS47/48). See also alder, cratch, dish-thrower.

turn grece A spiral staircase: 1548–9 *we alowyd hyme to the making of hys turne greyse into his hye chamer ijs,* York (CCW335). See also grece.

turn in All the examples noted are in connection with working the 'banks' or coal face in a pit: 1718 *five bencks turning in 5s 0d,* Farnley (MS11); 1730 *6d for the turning in of every Bank,* Swillington (CKY38); 1761 *for turning in 2 Banks 2 days work 2s 8d,* Tong (Tong/4c/6). Although the exact meaning is unclear it may have referred to preparatory work on the face before coal-getting began. See also inset.

turn-over This was the word for an apprentice whose indentures were transferred to another master, for whatever reason. It is used in those records of the Cutlers' Company which have to do with breaches of the rules: 1736 *Three pounds was paid by Thomas Hancock of Attercliffe for takeing Samuel Birds, the apprentice of Samuel Eardley as a Turnover, his said Master being then living* (HCC18). Less commonly it was used as a verb:

> 1640 *the peticon of John Shemelde, an apprentice to Stephen Metcalfe of Sheffield, cutler, alledgeinge that his maister lyes in prison at London … and desireing that he may be turned over to some other of the same trade, so that he may not loose his tyme* (YRS54/222).

turn-pit See swallow.

turn-press An instrument for pressing cloth, presumably using a screw mechanism: 1545 *iiij paire of loomes, too greate turne presses and iiij paire of tentoures,* Halifax (Crossley17).

turn-pump A kind of light shoe: 1773 *Sally new Turn pumps 3s 6d … Anne pumps Turnd & heelespecht … Wife new Turnpumps to go to Berrin* [burying], South Crosland (GRD).

turn-stake See turn.

tush, tuss These are northern variants of 'tusk', used for stones which formed a projecting course on a building, one on which an additional structure might be built: 1412 *sall putte oute tusses for the making of a Reuestory,* Catterick (OED). In 1704 *three wears or tushes* are mentioned in work done on Burholme Bridge in Bowland but the meaning in this case is not clear (QS1/43/5).

tuts A game resembling stoolball in which the tuts were the 'bases': 1519 *ludi inhonesti … viz [disgraceful games … that is] tutts & handball ac penyston,* Salton (SS35/270). In 1595, several Bilton men were said to have *plaid at Tuts on Lowsoonday at evening prayer tyme* (PTD95).

twibill A kind of axe with two cutting edges, formerly used for making the mortise into which a tenon fitted, noted in the will of a York carpenter: 1407–8 *j chipax, j* *framer, j blokker, j twybill, j mortas wymbyll, j bandwymbyll, j hake, ij planes, j swyer [square], et j treangill [triangle]*, York (SS35/207). See also thixel.

twill A woven fabric with parallel diagonal ribs, used especially for towels: 1400 *j mappa mensali de twill continente xiij ulnas [a twill table cloth containing 13 ells]*, Richmond (SS45/14); 1444 *j mappam de twille continentem vij ulnas iij quart. dim. cum j manutergio de twille [1 twill cloth containing 7 ells 3 quarters and a half with 1 twill tablecloth]*, Beverley (SS30/100); 1498 *Item iiij old awterclothes, one of twille and iij of cloth*, Wakefield (YAJ15/93); 1549 *my table napkynges and on twill towell*, Halifax (Crossley40).

twilled Woven with a twill: *c*.1423 *j fethirbed de panno vocato twylled [1 featherbed of the cloth called twilled]*, York (SS45/71); 1536 *a long twilte towel to serve theme at howsell borde*, Killingwoldgraves (SS106/53).

twilling, twindle Words for a twin: 1583 *twa twyndles of Richard Turton*, Barnsley (PR); 1644 *Aprill Richard sone of Mr Richard Horsfall bapt xxvii*[th] *day. Ricard sone of the said Mr Richard Horsfall and the latter borne beinge twindles bapt same day*, Kirkburton (PR). A word found in the Saxton register may be the clerk's invention: 1626 *William Pearson and Margrett Pearson beinge sonne and daughter of Richard Pearson beinge Twillinges was buried the xvi*[th] *of March*; 1644 *Nicolas the son of Robert Tasker and his brother being Twinlingings [sic] the xxvij*[th] *of December* (PR). A Rievaulx Abbey lease of 1528 has an endorsement *Campe and Twillynge alias Twindill* but the deed itself is illegible (SS83/350).

twilt A regional form of 'quilt': 1528 *A blanket, a coverlet and a twilte*, York (SS79/256); 1559 *ij pyllobers, one pylloe, one twylte and ij bed coveryngs*, Middleham (SS26/129); 1562 *One twylt for a bede of yellow and blew iiijs*, Richmond (SS26/161); 1578 *one paire of shetes, one twilte, two coverlittes*, Ripley (SS104/131); 1662 *tow feincloeth, one twilt*, Brayton (YRS47/49). See also twilled, whilt.

twindle See twilling.

twine (1) To turn, twist or wind: 1619–21 *leaving the beck and bridge on the lefte hande, twyninge southeaste by Sutton Hagg* (NRR1/55); 1642 *take out theire forkes and rakes out of the Waines arse least they bee broken with turning and twininge in the barne*, Elmswell (DW49); 1738 *did threaten to twine or ring the neck about of Mr Tancred*, Whixley (QS1/77/4). Dialect speakers used the form 'to twind': 1758–62 *twinding weft into warp*, Wakefield (YRS155/65). See also cockle.

twine (2) Thread with two or more strands: 1390 *ij stane of prus garne & a stane of twine*, York (SS4/130).

twinter A contraction of 'two winter', used of animals such as sheep and cattle which were two winters old: 1362 '*5 bullocks called Tuynters*', Mitton (YRS111/127); 1446–58 *xvj Twynters et sterkes*, Fountains Abbey (SS130/138); 1541 *my twynters, that is to say, ij quyes and ij stottes*, Otley (Th19/43). It was applied adjectivally in compounds: 1442 *septem animalia vocata twynternawt [seven animals called twinter neat]*, Rylstone (SS30/87); 1545 *Item 11 twenter neytte, £4 8s*, Muker (YRS152/62); 1619 *twinter stages, twinter beastes* (DDKE/100/3). See also threnter, twinter, unlibbed.

twinter gate A grazing right for a twinter on a stinted pasture. See also gate (2), twinter.

twitchel A word formerly common over a wide area, said to mean a narrow passage or alley. It survives in minor place-names such as Twitchill Farm in the Derbyshire parish of Hope, on record from 1376 (PNDb120), and in Nottingham where a street was described as *the common twechell* in 1435 (PNNt21). It is considered to be from an Old English word *twicen* which is a derivative of 'two', descriptive of the fork between two roads, perhaps at a junction or cross roads.

That does not exactly fit the meaning in Yorkshire where it referred in the earliest records to pieces of arable land. A Flockton deed of 1311 describes a holding 'in the fields of *Floketon*' lying in the place called *le Thwychel*, between lands held by Baldwin le Tyas on one side and John the Miller on the other: the same two men are referred to again in 1343 when half an acre of arable lay in different parts of 'the place called *Twechill*' (YRS69/58). Similarly, two Byland Abbey charters mention a 'culture' called *Twychel* in the period 1204–9: this was said to lie 'in the region of Denby'. That reference is to the Denby on Grange Moor (SS208/89–90) which would have been very close to Flockton, but there is nothing in the records which directly links the two localities. Other Yorkshire examples are the 'land called *Twytchill*' in Bradfield in 1568 (TWH28/127), and Twitch Hill in Horbury.

two-hand, two handed Wielded with two hands, as of a sword: 1402 *et j gladium ornatum cum argento quondam patris sui et j thwahandswerd [and 1 sword decorated with silver once his father's and 1 two-hand sword]*, Healaugh Park (SS4/297); 1429 *a dagger harnest with sylver … and a twa hand swerde*, York (SS4/420); 1577 *to Umfray Phillipps my twohanded sworde*, Easby (SS26/267).

tydy See tidy.

U

ulnage, ulnager From Latin *ulna* meaning elbow or arm, a measure of length. These are the usual spellings in Yorkshire records of alnage or aulnage; that is the measurement of cloth by the ell. The alnager or ulnager was an official acting on behalf of the monarch whose job it was to affix a leaden seal to a cloth, which confirmed its measurements and value: the statute in 1350 required all cloths to be measured by the King's 'aulneger' and his deputies (SAL2/45). The term has a longer history, for a 'List of Ulnagers' dates from 1327 (YRS64/115). In *The History of the Huddersfield Woollen Industry* (1935) are details from rolls surviving from 1469–70: 'Robert Nevyl of Almondesbury, subsidy and ulnage of 160 cloths sealed there, 60s' (Crump29), and *ulnage of cloth* is referred to in York in 1474–5 (SS129/65). In 1558, Michael Wentworth bequeathed to his sons his *right in thoffice or ferme of the Alnyger in the Countie of Yorke … the profites to be towards their finding during their minorities* (SS116/245). In 1637, a Northallerton aulnager was fined for extortion, having taken money from clothiers using a counterfeit warrant. The editor noted that he was styled *ulnator* in the Latin entry (NRQS4/73n). See also kersey.

umbras Probably 'vmbras', a spelling of vambrace: 1437 *duas integras armaturas … videlicet duos basynettez, vmbras et rerebrace [two full suits of armour … that is two basinets, vambrace and rearbrace]*, York (SS30/70).

umpirage, umpire From the mis-division of *a noumpere*; that is non-equal. An umpire was one who acted as an impartial third party in a dispute, making a decision on behalf of one of the contestants. The act of umpiring and the decision were referred to as umpirage: 1343–4 *sureit jugge come monepier issi que lez ditz parties oster-reint a son accord [it should be judged as umpirage so that the said parties should cease by their agreement]*, Ingleton (Furn2/295); *c.*1490 *the matter betwixt my servant and John Forest is put to iiij men and the owmpreght of you*, Plompton (PL84); 1552 *bothe the sayd parties are content … to abide … the vmperage of Henrye Savill of Bradleye … the sayd arbitrars and vmper*, Stainland (YRS50/24); 1661 *an Umpier chosen by arbitratours*, Holmfirth (G-A). See also qwerfor.

unbound, unbun In early inventories a variety of articles were said to be 'bound with iron', ranging in size from kettles and chests to wains and their wheels. The same items were sometimes said to be unbound: 1542 *Item 2 old pottes, a unbun' kettill 4s*, Marske (YRS152/58); 1647 *one carte and pair of unbound wheles*, Hampsthwaite (YRS55/114). See also bound, bun wain.

under Denoting position at a lower level, perhaps even 'by the side of' or 'close by': 1559 *the said Edward Brodley, his wyff and chyldreyn shall at all tymes keypp one sufficient yait with locke and keye vnder ther house for ther owne usez*, Shelf (YRS50/168). It was commonly used of enclosures near a dwelling-house: 1652 *one ynge under Crosland Parke* (DD/WBD/2/63) and of low-lying sites: 1545 *underbanke Feld*, Huddersfield (DD/WBD/1/71); 1753 *the road going … to an under Bridge at the bottom of Rawlinshaw Brow*, Clapham (WRT50).

underbit, underbitted A north-country term for a cut or 'bite' on the ear of a sheep or other farm animal, which helped to determine its ownership. It was one of several marks which identified a black wether owned by John Grensyd of Sheriff Hutton:

1539 *a headles crose upon the nar fore shoulder a blot of tar on the tayll head & twyse under byt in the Far eayre & ret in the nar eayre & halteth on a hynder legg.*

His black filly was *ret in the nar eayre and under byt in the same* (YAJ36/182). 'Underbitted' was an alternative spelling: in 1555 William Brerey of Pannal left to his daughter Alice *a browne rigged cowe, under bytted of bothe eyres* (SS104/69). A variety of such marks are illustrated in *The Harvest of the Hills* (AW106). See also nar, overbit, ret, undercavelde.

undercavelde An obscure term, noted just once, in connection with the ear-marks on a sheep: 1546 *his marke that is undercavelde the narre eare and sleyt the furre eare to his own proper use*, Halifax (Crossley20). Possibly a cut made with a 'kevel', a hammer with a sharp point, or 'split', from a dialect word associated with division (EDD).

underdraw To underdraw a ceiling or roof is to cover the underside of exposed beams and joists, either with boards or with lath and plaster: 1764 *Ten of the rooms have board floors, one ceiled … plaister'd and underdrawn … 3 of the chambers, 2 of which … are plaister'd and underdrawn*, Kirby Underdale (HKU98). In dialect the 'underdrawing' is the space between the ceiling and the roof; that is the loft.

undermine Most of the meanings given to this word emphasise its military or negative aspects, literally and figuratively. However, when used in some mining leases it could refer simply to a method of 'winning' coals underground: 1666 *of their owne Coste … shall sett downe and Sincke one other pitt for under myneinge and gettinge of Cooles*, South Crosland (DD/WBD/2/81). Nevertheless, as mining increased in intensity it was linked with damage done to the ground surface and buildings, and that is evident from the sixteenth century: 1580 *yf any person do get cooles … to undermine one hieway called the high Skowte … to forfeite xs*, Dewsbury (YAJ21/412); 1683 *have digged and undermined the said closes … and those Closes will not in all probability be worth 40s per annum which are now worth the summe of 12li*, Whitkirk (YAJ36/330); 1756 *We … have view'd the Barn … and are of the opinion that the damages done … are occasioned by getting the Coal and undermining the said Barn*, Beeston (WYL160/129/4). See also brandreth.

underset A verb meaning to support, used of structures held up by posts or pillars: 1573 *he undersett and selyd the upper end of his hall*, Woodsome (KayeCP). The reference here is to the improvements made at Woodsome Hall by the Kaye family, which confirmed that one end of the main hall was panelled and the dining area on the dais protected beneath an overhang.

undersettle A sub-tenant, one who occupied part of a house but had no direct responsibilities to the lord of the manor. The fear was that such persons might become a charge on the community: 1581 *no inhabitant of Acome or Holgate to keep undersettles in their firehouses under one roof with them* (YRS131/72); 1590 *Uxor Bowes shall avoyd [remove] Uxor Ivison whom she haith latelye taken into her house as an undersettle … before she be delivered of childe*, York (YRS138/124); 1604 *agreed that the constables shall monthly maike searche every man in his warde for undersettells*, Scarborough (NYRO47/32); 1629 *That no undersettle do keep any goods upon the Common, 6s 8d*, Driffield (YAJ35/39); 1734 *no Servant or Stranger, Inmate or undersettle shall have any right of Pasture*, Lund (YRS69/99). See also avoid, inmate, tavern.

undersock, understocking A stocking worn with slops or hose: 1566 *one payre of sloppes … and the undersokes belongynge the sayme*, Catterick (SS26/190); 1593 *my best overhose or sloppes … my best under stockinges*, Killinghall (SS104/195). See also nether stocks.

undertake, undertaker Examples of both the verb and the noun are found in seventeenth-century bridge accounts. In 1673, the constables of Sowerby and Warley, that is the two townships which shared responsibility for Sowerby Bridge, petitioned the Justices of Peace, asking for a surveyor to be appointed so that they might *waite upon with such workemen as may undertake the worke* (HAS5/180). Two years later, the two masons who rebuilt Ilkley Bridge were referred to as the *undertakers* of the work (QS1). The contracts in such cases obliged masons to maintain the bridges for a number of years afterwards and that was often to their disadvantage, as the following extract makes clear:

> *Michael Taileforth and the Rest of the Masons who built Coniston Bridge in 1684 and gave bond to uphold the same for the space of seven yeares, which said bridge being very much ruined by an extraordinary violent flood and two of the years are to expire … wee think they ought to have £100 given them … to be bound and uphould the same seven years longer* (QS1/29/1).

Later, the word acquired a more particular meaning, and the 'undertaker' became an official appointment. In 1712, there was an agreement between the Justices of Peace for the West Riding and four named masons *for putting into repair all the Riding Bridges*. Further to that they were to *keep them so for eleaven yeares … and to leave them in good repairs at the ende of the terme*. They were to be paid a sum of £350 p.a. by the Treasurer. Joseph Pape, the mason who had built Esholt Hall in 1706 was one of those named and soon after his appointment, in 1717, he was referred to as *the Undertaker of Bridges* (QS1/56/1). In 1715, the Wapentake Bridges were *sett of to certaine undertakers* (QS1/53/1).

Some families, like the Carrs and the Ettys, were involved in bridge maintenance over a long period, which suggests that the various offices were looked on as attractive appointments. That seems to be confirmed by a letter written to the Justices in 1743:

> *Wee, Jonathan Jennings of Skipton and Peter Chippindale of Eastbye, masons, desire to be further heard touching our proposal for undertaking the repair of the West Riding Bridges. If the worshipfull Bench would please to divide them wee had rather only propose for those within the wapontake of Staincliffe and Yewcross but if they resolve to let the whole Riding in one Bargain wee have six sons all brought up in the mason trade which wee could disperse into separate parts of the Riding to keep the Bridges in better condition* (QS1/82/4).

underwood Defined in the OED as: 'small trees or shrubs, coppice wood or brush-wood growing beneath higher timber trees', a term on record from the fourteenth century: 1373–4 *boscum lentiscorum corulorum & aliarum minutarum arborum vocatarum vndrewodd [wood of holly hazels and other small trees called underwood]*, Leeds (Th45/110). After the Dissolution, a survey of the woods formerly held by Selby Abbey contrasts underwood with timber and provides details of the different species and their cycles of growth, first in Southwood: 1543 *the underwod wherof standyth moch by hassell and sallowe of sondry ages, wherein are many faire oke spyres of thage of xiiij yeres or thereabowt, And no tymbre within the same wodde*, and then in Aughton: *the underwoode … of the age* *of xvj or xviij yeres is solde ... to be felled within thre yeres next.* Other entries name alder, birch and holly, much of which at that time was *made in faggottes for the repaire of the stathes and bankes of the water of Owse* (YRS13/360–3).

The surname Underwood can certainly be geographic in origin and I have found no suggestion that it may sometimes be an occupational by-name. Nevertheless, it is noticeable how often it occurs on wood-managed estates, e.g. 1258 *Alice sub bosco,* Rothwell (YRS12/60); 1341 *Henry Underwodde,* Roundhay Park (Th2/225); 1379 *Ricardus Undyrwode,* Hambleton (PTWR). Some references are more explicit: 1418–19 *In cariagio earumdem arborum a bosco de Hamelton usque Usam apud Selby per Johannem Underwod [For transporting of those trees from Hamelton wood to the Ouse at Selby by John Underwood]* (SS35/38). I suspect that in Yorkshire it was sometimes occupational and not geographic, and if that is so it has implications for the surname.

undight The verb 'to dight' was used frequently in connection with the preparation of wool, linen, leather, etc. and 'undight' was a reference to articles that had not been fully processed: 1527 *my undight lyne,* Whitkirk (Th9/247); 1533 *in lether dight and undight,* Pannal (SS104/30). See also dight.

undone Brought to ruin: 1674 *sweareing a greate oath saying he might well have undon him by naming his name,* Morley (QS1).

undrawn Said of animals that have not been used to draw carts or the plough: 1567 *Item tenne draught oxen 16s 0d. Item Six stottes undrawen of fowre yere £7 0s 0d,* Fixby (YRS134/17). Probably here also: 1580 *one oxe called Gallande and fower stottes under drawen,* Killinghall (SS104/141). See also drawn.

undressed Not properly put in order: 1657 *for a sewer undressed from the Church Style to John Laykes house,* Patrington (ERAS8/23); 1786 *1 mason dressing Stones ... leading wall stone undrest,* Slaithwaite (KC242/1). In 1709, the inventory of a Sheffield cutler listed *undrest ware* which needed attention before it could be sold (IH). See also dress.

ungain The opposite of 'gain (2)' which is dealt with separately. It had meanings such as 'indirect, severe, awkward', and examples in the OED date from *c.*1400. It is interesting to find it much earlier as a place-name and by-name, possibly a reference to an inconvenient location: 1312–13 *Henry de Ungayn,* Bolton Priory. The priory accounts include several entries which relate to crops in 'Ungain' and the rent or 'farm' in 1377–8 was 6s 8d (YRS154).

unlibbed Not castrated: 1508 *to my cosyn Raulf Nevell, my t'wynter gray horse amblyng, unlybbed,* Breckenbrough (SS53/272); 1552 *one girsell stage unlybbede,* Hardwick (Th19/317). See also lib.

unlike Probably unusual or out of the ordinary. Robert Tordoff of Wibsey *or Torder as he calls himself* was indicted at the Quarter Sessions several times in the period 1680–1700. In 1692, he was described as *an unlike man ... who calls himselfe Robert Tordoff* (QS1).

unmilned Used of cloth that was not milled, that is had not been through the processes at the fulling mill: 1618 *Item one brybe of unmilned cloth beinge fyve yeards, ixs,* Cottingley (LRS1/49).

unpilled To pill was to remove the bark from a tree but this was not done to those reserved for further growth: 1672 *The tanners agree to leave ... unpill'd wavers according to the custome,* Tong (Tong/3/321).

unpounced Not embossed or engraved: 1544 *to M' Nicholas Hall my sonne … a siluer pecie unpounsed, a ryall of golde and a siluer spone*, Sherburn in Elmet (Th19/107). See also pounced.

unrated Not soaked in water or exposed to moisture, as in the preparation of hemp and flax: 1637 *serten hemp unrated*, Selby (YRS47/83); 1747 *forty stones of rated line, forty unrated*, Fishlake (QS1/86/3). See also rate (1).

unsitting Unbecoming, improper: 1483 *for as moch as the said Thomas Watson had unsyttyng and inconvenient langwegh of … Maister Wrangwysh*, York (YRS98/69); 1504 *oon Hesilwode said to Maister Perot, oon of myn officers, many unsittyng words*, York (YRS106/4).

unthrussen Not threshed: 1693 *corne unthrussen*, Holmfirth (G-A). See also thrushen.

unwinded, unwindowed Characteristic spellings of unwinnowed: 1601 *a stroke of vnwynded bar(ley)*, Campsall (YRS3/186); 1612 *rye … in the barne unwyndewed*, Brandsby (NYRO44/59). See also window.

unworkmanlike, unworkmanly See workman.

unwrought Said of coals that have not been 'won' or 'got' and of pits that have not been worked: 1787 *doth sell … his moiety of … all the Pillars of Coal that are now standing and have been left unwrought in the Old Coal Works, adjoining the said whole or unwrought Coal*, Beeston (WYL160/129/4). In the cutlery trade it referred to unfinished items, as in 1713 when John Shirtcliffe had *a parcell of Ivory hafts unwrought, £2* (IH). See also stand (2), undressed, wrought.

upholder A dealer in small wares: 1413 *Johanna Calthorn, uphalder*, York (SS96/120); 1417 *that na upphalder wyrk in girdelercrafte*, York (SS120/183). Elspeth Veale said the word was used of those who traded in used skins and furs (EMV13) and this close link is confirmed in early but undated ordinances of the skinners: *Item que tous gentz uphalders qi vendent fururers deiez la dite cite ou les suburbes soient contributours appaier a lour pagyne de Corpore Christi [Item that all the upholders who sell furs in the said city or suburbs should be contributors paying towards their Corpus Christi pageant]*, York (SS120/61). In a later version of this ordinance, probably from the early fifteenth century, is a reference to *every uphaldster that sellis eny furrez* (SS120/64). See also –ster.

upperbody Comparable with 'overbody', a woman's garment which clothed the upper part of the body and was sometimes quilted and strengthened with whale bone: 1587 *2 reiles, a lose upper body, an apperne, 2 neckerchifs*, South Cave (Kaner143); 1610 *a hatt two upperbodies 2 old safegardes*, South Cave (Kaner230). See also bodies, overbody.

upper end A coal-mining term, probably an alternative word for the rise end: 1760 *pd Miners setting puncheons and Cupplings in the down end and Upper end*, Tong (Tong/4c/5). See also dip-side, rise (2).

upper leather The high-quality leather which forms the upper part of a shoe or boot (OED): 1596 *No tanner dwelling without the liberties of the town shall sell any clout lether or upper lether in any place within the liberties, but only in open market in the place appointed by the Mayor and Governors* (YRS84/76); 1673 *In the Tan Yard 39 uper leather hides*, Selby (YRS47/33); 1708 *17 upper leather hydes*, Frizinghall (YAS/DD187). See also bend (1), clout, over leather, sole leather.

upset, upsetting In the guild system a man was entitled to set up in business only after completing his time as an apprentice and journeyman. In 1417, for example, any qualified girdler who moved into York had *to pay at his first setting up of his shoppe xs* and various other sums to the chamber and the craft (SS120/182). In 1475 the millers would not permit *any estraunge man to sett up as maister* unless it could be shown that he was *able and connyng* in the craft. They expected a qualified person to *pay at his firste upsettyng 3s. 4d.* (SS186/182) which was rather less than the sum paid in 1464 by *any foreine walker* who was expected to *sett up as a maister*. Such a man would *paie at his upsett 13s. 4d. the oone haulf to the chaumbre and use of the citie, and the other haulf to the craft of the walkers* (SS125/207). In Beverley, in 1577, William Blenkarne, a coverlet weaver, paid 20d *for an upsett* (YRS84/13). See also set up.

urchin A hedgehog. They were formerly considered to be vermin and a small bounty was paid by churchwardens for a dead animal: 1667 *Alowd to the Churchwardens of Shipley for 6 uerchanes & for a fox head & for a wild cat 2d*, Bradford; 1673 *given to Willm Ellis & his companye for killing 2 urchants 2d*, Bradford (BAS3/486,490). Similarly in Elland: 1721 *For 8 Urchons from Barkisld:* in the same accounts in 1742 is an entry for *Edge-hogs at 2d a ps* (PR2/284). Richard Wigglesworth of Conistone *c.*1688 spoke of his cattle being *bitten with an urchon or a toade* (RW10).

ure, urre, urstone These spellings of 'ore' and 'orestone' are found regularly in the earliest documents. See also dozen (1), oliver, orestone, and the attributive uses of 'ore'.

urgent Noted in connection with rights of way in the town field, where the meaning seems to be 'short cut' or giving quick access: 1649 *the heade of the Levicarres which is an urgint to the kirkgate*, Lepton (DD/WBM).

urre, urstone See ure.

vaccary From medieval Latin *vaccaria*: 1203–4 *facient logias et vaccarias in eadem foresta de Mewith [they make lodges and vaccaries in the forest of Mewith]* (Furn2/293); 1394–5 *Redditus [Rents] Vaccaria de Kesebek*, Whitby (SS72/556). The word was used in early court rolls and in official documents for the cattle-farms which feudal landlords established in the uplands, especially in the Pennines: 1339 'a sixth part of Saltonstall vaccary which is granted to Richard [son of Stephen] likewise' (WCR12/117).

The thinly populated moorland fringes had abundant grazing and were able to support animal husbandry, so vaccaries could be set up within forests, as in Marsden, or be the main activity within a township such as Scammonden, a development which determined the pattern of settlement. Sometimes the place-names in a particular area serve to identify the sites, especially *booth* as a suffix in the de Lacy territories, and *tūn-stall* on Wakefield manor. The term is now part of the landscape historians' vocabulary. See also within.

vambrace Defensive armour for the fore-arm, a spelling of 'vantbrace': 1380 *j bassinet j par de vaunbrace*, Durham (SS4/110); 1392 *unum bonum par cerotecarum de plate cum vambrase et rerebrase [one good pair of plate gloves with vambrace and rearbrace]*, York (SS4/171); 1402 *j par de wambrace*, Healaugh Park (SS4/297); 1414 *unum par de vaumbrace*, Scrayingham (SS4/371); 1423 *Et de iijs iiijd receptis pro uno pare de vambrace et rerebrace [And for 3s 4d received for a pair of vambrace and rearbrace]*, York (SS45/73); 1572 *xl Flanders corsletts compleat … and also lacking viij p'r of canons or vomebraces*, Skipton Castle (Whit2/335). See also umbras.

vamp, vampet The vamp was that part of a boot which covered the front of the foot, from French *avant pied*, and the verb referred to cutting and shaping the leather used in making or repairing it: n.d. *Item pro la vaumpedyng xij parium ocrearum lowsed aretro xiijd ob [Item for vampeting 12 pairs of boots laced at the back 13½]* (SS120/194); 1582 *Agreed that the shomakers of this Cyttie … may sole and vampett all manner of bootes as well ould as newe with blacke leather onelie and not with bend or reade leather … and shall not in any wise … coble any manner of bootes but onelie sole and vampet them … upon paine of vjs viijd*, York (YRS119/59). They were expressly forbidden from using 'clouts' or 'spetches' for that purpose; that is from doing the cobblers' work. Similarly, in Beverley in 1627 no person was 'to work both old and new wares … or mix old and new leather together except in vamping or soling of old boots or shoes' (YRS84/80).

vang Evidently a type of spade or shovel, although the precise meaning remains uncertain: 1421 *Pro ij vangis emptis pro mundacione quarerœ apud Thevedale, 11d [For 2 vangs bought for tidying the quarry at Thevedale]*, Tadcaster (SS35/43); 1485 *iiij^or vange et j turfspade … iij mukeforkes*, Ripon (SS64/373).

varon Formerly a frequent word for a horse that was wall-eyed: 1403 *lego nomine mortuarii mei optimum equum meum quem habeo nomine Varon [I bequeath by way of my mortuary the best horse that I have called Varon]*, Saxton (Th33/29); 1451 *De j equo trottante vocato Varond xs [for a trotting horse called Varond 10s]*, Strensall (SS45/120); 1553 *my varrant curtall nagge*, Pontefract (Th27/1); 1596 *a graye mare and a varon stagg which was of her*; 1618 *an old varon mare*, South Cave (Kaner191,273).

vasser, vauser See voussoir.

vein A stratum or seam of coal. The analogy is with the veins in the human body which are evidently different from the 'material' in which they are set. References to 'vein' in connection with mining occur from the fourteenth century but are almost always to metals such as gold and tin. Typical examples which refer to coal in Yorkshire date from the fifteenth century: 1464 *veynes of cole* in the manor of Skipton (YAJ64/157); 1538 *Ther be some Vaynes of Coles found in the upper Parte of ... Richemontshire* (YAJ10/476); 1683 *the Seem or Veine of Coale where you have caused to be diggid goes directly underneath it [the church]*, Whitkirk (YAJ36/330). See also coal-bed.

Venice The name of the city and the province in Italy's north-east, used to describe articles made there or traded from there: 1558 *one ounce and a half of Venysse silke ijs*, Knaresborough (SS26/126–7); 1612 *2 crewets the bigger of vennesse mettall*, Brandsby (NYRO44/35); 1693 *London treacle 3s; Veanas treacle 1s 6d*, Selby (YRS47/22).

vennel A narrow lane or thoroughfare: 1376–7 *sibien des fumers en les rewes et venelles [as well as smoke in the streets and vennels]*, York (SS120/17); 1649 *being betweene a vennel or common weind or lane in Yarme* (MD302/3).

vent, vent gate, vent pit The profitable working of a coal-pit depended on how well it was drained and ventilated, and various methods of allowing fresh air to circulate in the workings were tried. These usually involved driving special heads, additional shafts, or holing existing walls but the records are seldom very explicit: in 1702, an agreement restricted the lessees to *one shaft att one time save onely what shall be necessary for vent or Levell*, Thornton (DB1/C2/30); 1760 *for forcing vent in upper end*, Tong (Tong/4c/5); 1792 *air and vent pits to remain open for the more commodious future working of the colliery*, Lepton (DD/WBD/3/222); 1804 *to use the old shaft at Hall Houses as a vent shaft for the High Sunderland mines* (HAS31/85). The term *vent gate* was used at Soil Hill in 1815, in this case a horizontal 'gate' or way (HAS32/282).

ventail Part of a helmet, either the visor or the lower movable section, the mouth-piece: 1391 *lego ... filio meo unum melius basenett cum ventayll [I bequeath ... to my son a better basinet with a ventail]*, Harewood (SS4/151); 1393 *uno bacineto et aventale*, York (SS4/168); 1414 *unum basenet cum vental*, Scrayingham (SS4/371); 1423 *Et de vjd receptis pro uno ventayle veteri et valde debili [And for 6d received for an old and much-damaged ventail]*, York (SS45/73). See also basinet, habergeon.

vent gate, vent pit See vent.

verdigris Basic acetate of copper which occurs naturally as a 'rust' on copper, or can be obtained artificially by the action of dilute acetic acid on the metal. It derives from French 'vert de Grece' that is 'green of Greece' and Latinised examples occur from the thirteenth century: 1291–2 *In pinguedine, vertegreco, lacte, oleo et ter ad oves [For grease, verdigris, milk, oil and tar for the sheep]*, Bolton Priory (YRS154/44); 1472 *xij lib. vertgreas*, York (SS35/77).

verjuice The acid juice of sour fruit, particularly grapes and crab-apples, formed into a liquor and used also in cooking and as a medicine: 1452 *ij barelles pro vergust xijd*, Cawood (SS45/139); 1485 *v vasa cum verjusse vjs viijd*, Ripon (SS64/371); 1528 *6 gallons of varges 4s 8d*, Chevet (Whit2/308); 1562 *One letill barrell for verges ijd*, Richmond (SS26/163); 1596 *towe barrelles of vergies*, Knaresborough (YRS134/60); 1731 *crabjuce, verjise*, Spofforth (QS1/70/4). Note: 1585 *in the vergeshouse – one kymleyn* (SS104/151).

vermyon For vermilion or cinnabar, used by painters and in the illumination of manuscripts: 1456–7 *In cera rubea et vermyon, ijd [For red wax and veryon 2d]*, Fountains Abbey (SS130/25); 1472 *ij lb vermeyon, vj lb plumbi rubei [2lb of vermyon, 6lb of red lead]*, York (SS35/77).

vert A word of French origin, used in legal and manorial contexts for green vegetation in a wood or forest. Typically, tenants were fined for helping themselves to such wood without permission: 1339 'for *vert* in *Horbirylighes*: Thomas Iveson 6d, John Baret 6d, Robert Iveson 2d' (WCR12/58). On the other hand, wood of various kinds could be taken legally: 1251 'they had green and dead wood (*viride et mortuum boscum*) for *husbote* and dry wood (*siccum*) without livery', Pickering (YRS12/28). See also greenhew, green wood.

vestment These were the special garments worn by clergymen and their assistants when performing church services: 1346 *lego eisdem monialibus ad vestimenta inde facienda coccineas armat' cum teguminibus equorum [I bequeath to those monks for making vestments from them the scarlet suit of armour together with the coverings of the horses]*, York (SS4/31); 1485 *a vestment of borde alisaunder*, Ripon (SS64/277); 1497 *Item a vestment of red velvet with a crosse of cloth of gold with the albe, stole and all other thyngez apperteyning therto*, Wakefield (YAJ15/92); 1518–19 *payd for rebon and frenges to the hawbes and for mendyng of iiij vestmenttes ijs*, York (CCW69); 1558 *all suche coipes, vestementtes and the other ornamenttes as I have remaininge in the said churche*, Stanley (Th27/257). See also vestry.

vestment-maker The specialist who made garments for the clergy: 1531 *Robert Locksmith, vestmentmaker*, York (SS79/324). No early examples have been noted which suggests that the following may have been occupational by-names: 1472–3 *8s soluti Willelmo Vestmentmaker pro reparacione vestimentorum in ecclesia [8s paid to William Vestmentmaker for mending vestments in the church]*, Ripon (SS81/246); 1485 *De Roberto vestmentmaker iiijs*, York (SS45/303).

vestry The room in a church in which the vestments are stored, usually close to the chancel: 1494 *Dicto collegio ad faciendum unum vestiarium pro vestimentis dicti collegii xx li [To the said collegiate church for building a vestry for the vestments of the said collegiate church £20]*, Pontefract (SS53/93).

vicar, vicarage In early usages the vicar of a parish was the priest who acted as a representative of the rector, and the 'vicarage' was his benefice or living: 1595 *That there vicar John Richardson is not resident vpon his vicaredg*, Ellerburn (YAJ18/315). Even by that time, though, the word was already being applied to the vicar's dwelling-house, distinguishing it from other buildings in the village: *c.*1540 *a mansion called the vicars mansion … withyn the seid mansion or vicarage*, Swine (YRS80/100); 1596 *they have no vicaredge house*, Wilton (YAJ18/320).

vice (1) A general word for a contrivance which consisted of two 'jaws' that could be opened and closed by means of a screw. Vices were essential to many craftsmen, especially smiths, allowing them to hold and exert pressure on a piece of iron on which they were working. They are found in many inventories, sometimes in good numbers: 1584 *in my shopp … one vice, all my naile tooles and all my hammers, tonges, bellowes*, Knaresborough (SS104/145).

vice (2) A winding or spiral staircase, especially in a church: 1532 *ad hostium les vice doore novæ ecclesiæ [for the door, the vice door, of the new church]*, York (SS35/106).

view, viewer To view had the meaning of to inspect or survey, and the viewer was a person qualified to view or take a view in that sense. The word was in widespread use in all the craft guilds and in subsequent industrial and trade practices: 1596 *to survey, vewe and searche all the tanners*, Beverley (YRS84/74). In 1598, the decay of several bridges in Bradford was under discussion at the Quarter Sessions and finally the court ordered two Justices of Peace *to take a Viewe thereof and certifie … what Some of money* might be necessary for their repair (YRS3/38). In 1605, Yarm Bridge had suffered damage and it was ordered that representatives of the Quarter Sessions court *with thadvise of some skillfull workmen viewe the same what sommes wilbe sufficient to repaire it* (NRQS1/19).

It is a term linked with coal-mining from 1447, in the north-east (OED), but the Yorkshire evidence is much later: 1659 *it shall be lawfull … for John Thornhill … or any other person or persons nominated by* [him] *from tyme to tyme to veiwe the Coale myne and manner of working thereof*, North Bierley (MMA/255). This makes it clear that the landlord had the right to view but could pass the responsibility on to a skilled person: in 1666, the work carried out in a South Crosland pit was *att the discrecion of two men to bee chosen to take a vew thereof to give satisfaccion to the occupyers of the said land* (DD/WBD/2/81) and in 1760, Mr Eltoft was paid *for Severall Journeys to view Collery and give directions about his work*, Tong (Tong/4c/4). In 1695, Richard Ascough was appointed as the *Common Viewer* in Colsterdale (BM82/43) and in 1750 *John Scott and Joseph Knight viewers* were paid for inspecting a coal-pit in Shibden (HAS30/151). See also surveyor, workman.

village A rare word in Yorkshire until the early eighteenth century. From the time when the first settlements were established, even small places were 'towns' but in the Tudor period clerks began to treat this as a regionalism: 1562 *John Teale … haith dwellid … at a litle towne or village callid Small Bankes of the parishe of Addington* (YRS114/105). This clerk was clearly unfamiliar with the region: the parish was actually Addingham and Small Banks may then have been no more than a single dwelling-house on the rim of the moor.

vineyard A word not uncommon as a minor place-name in the seventeenth century, even in the hilly west of the county, almost certainly an indication that grapes were being grown there, possibly in sheltered gardens against heated walls: 1615 *all the messuages … vineyards, willow trees*, Almondbury (DD/R/2/27); 1672 *Samuel Bins … more for the vineyard*, Wakefield (HT). At Thornhill a brick wall with flue holes still visible has survived around the former garden.

virginal A keyed musical instrument, similar to a spinet but in a case without legs, commonly in the plural: 1558 *I giue to Mr More a paire of virgynalls*, Pontefract (Th27/198); 1562 *a set of recorders … a pare of virgenals*, Healaugh Park (YRS134/34); 1658 *one pare of virginals £2*, Selby (YRS47/94).

voider Now a wicker-work clothes basket but formerly a wooden or metal basket or tray used for removing or 'voiding' dirty dishes or food from the table after a meal: 1548 *stuff pertening to the buttrye ther … as … a great voyder*, Denton, Lancashire (SS106/192); 1571 *21 pewter dublers, 3 voiders and 3 sawtes £1 0 0*, Elmswell (DW232); 1621 *three voyders 9s*, Slaidburn (YRS63/48); 1655 *3 wooden voyders*, Whitley (DD/WBM/69).

voussoir, vasser, vauser This French word is found from 1359–60 in building accounts, mostly in connection with churches where it was used for the shaped vault stones of an arch. It must also have been used of arches in bridge building but is not recorded in that sense in the OED until 1739. When Elland Bridge was built of stone in 1579, the request was for *the vassers to be sett forthe on ether side of the arches*

(BAS6/138). In the estimate for rebuilding Clapham Bridge in 1747, one of the items was for *vausers getting* (QS1/86/5). The past participle is on record from 1875 in an adjectival sense meaning 'constructed with voussoirs', and this reference can be compared with the following item in a Halifax building contract over 200 years earlier: 1648 *all to be a yard longe and a foote wide, vocered over and captablde* (YAJ16/110).

vowess A woman who has taken a vow of chastity, used especially of a lady who made such a vow after her husband's death: 1527 *Dame Jane Hillarde, voisse, som tyme wif of Peter Hiliarde Esquyer*, Winestead (SS79/230).

voysome Probably a spelling of advowson, influenced by 'avoid': 1527 *I yeve to Sir John Levett my chaplayne … the voysome and next avodance of my personage of Rither* (SS79/228). See also avoid.

wad, wadde See woad.

wader A dealer in woad, the blue dye-stuff obtained from a plant found originally in central and southern Europe. It was in great demand in England in the Middle Ages: 1185 *William le Waisder*, Yorkshire (R&W); 1274 *Robertus de Walcheford, wayder*, 1293 *Johannes le waider, junior*; 1303 *Stephanus de Whiteby, wayder*, York (SS96/2,5,10). A possible alternative was 'wademan': 1375 *Ricardus de Norham, waddeman*, York (SS96/74).

wadfat A vat to hold the dye-stuff: 1442 *duas vasas plumbeas tunc Anglice wodfattes [two leaden vessels, in English wodfattes]*, Rotherham (SS30/169n); 1533 *the said Henry [Farebanke] to have my lead, wadfattes and a macer*, Heptonstall (Clay85). See also wader, woad.

wadset See wedset.

waferer A servant or tradesman responsible for making wafers: 1348 *Item Roberto Waferer iijs*, Emley (SS4/52); 1373 *legavit Theobaldo wayfarer xxˢ [he bequeathed to Theobald wayfarer 20s]*, York (SS4/89). In 1296 Ralph de Gousill held the free service of 20d from the *Waferur Garthe* in Hedon (YRS23/167).

wafer irons An implement for baking wafers which consisted of two hinged iron blades between the ends of which the paste was held: 1463 *unum par de [a pair of] Wafryiryns*, Leeds (Th24/55); 1528 Item *for wafferens five dares 1s 8d*, Chevet (Whit2/308).

wagon A strong four-wheeled vehicle, used for the transport of heavy goods. This word shares the same etymology as 'wain' which it began to replace after the word was introduced from the Continent, probably in the sixteenth century: 1681 *in the workhouse … a waggon with bark chopt & unchopt*, Selby (YRS47/51). It was in regular use in collieries as wagon-ways were introduced: 1764 *Thomas Atkinson Labourer, Slain, by a Coal waggon running over him at Late Sir Wm Lowther's Colliery*, Swillington (PR). See also coal wain, wagon-road.

wagon-road, wagon-way These were names given to artificial colliery roads, designed to allow horses to draw heavy loads more easily. They were made of rails, originally of wood but then of iron, laid on timber sleepers and they were in use in Yorkshire collieries from the eighteenth century. In 1745, the *York Courant* advertised a coal mine *where a Waggon Way is made from the said Pitts, to Bottom Boat Staith situated on the River Chalder*, Outwood near Wakefield (BAS11/173). In several cases the link with the north-east is explicit: *c.*1772 *opening this colliery and laying a Newcastle wagon-way with wood*, Flockton (OFC2); 1784 *will bring in £3,000 a year if there was a Newcastle Waggon Way made to Brigghouse* (YAJ49/127).
  The alternative 'wagon-road' dates from the same period: 1779 *To be Lett, a Colliery at Houghton near Pontefract … being One Mile of the Navigable River Aire, to which a Waggon Road may be made through the estate* (Th40/78). Some of the roads covered long distances: a Leeds owner called Brandling had a wagon-way 2¼ miles long which

allowed him to convey coal into Leeds, and his right to do that was secured by Act of Parliament: the *Leeds Intelligencer* referred to it as *the intended waggon way* in 1758 (Th4/242) and the work was completed in 1759. The 1803 Inclosure Act for Shelley granted *Liberty of making and repairing Waggonways and other ways in, under and along the same* (GRD). See also rail (1), sleeper.

waif A piece of property found ownerless, especially an animal that had strayed. If unclaimed within a fixed period, and after due notice given, it fell to the lord of the manor: 1612 *All my wayf goods in the back garthe*, Brandsby (NYRO44/33); 1687 *a waife swarme of bees*, Heptonstall (WCR13/92). More often linked with 'stray': *c.*1546 *a parcel of commen grounde belonging to the towne of Cropton to wave and strey and not to drive catall thereunto nor to stafe hirde … comen to all neighbours* (YAJ36/442).

wain (1) Profit, advantage or gain: 1499 *I bequeath xxvjs viijd … to ease the poore folke … for to pay ther fermes with so that the said people sett not ther goodes at waynworth; and they to have a day reasonable to pay*, Wighill (SS53/160); 1609 *We thinke fortie oke trees are as few as we can judge to serve for that purpose … Also we thincke that the workmanshipp of the same will not be made wainemeet under the value of £20*, Whitby Bridge (NRQS2/319–20). See also wainage.

wain (2) A narrow, long-bodied vehicle, with either two or four wheels, drawn by horses or oxen and capable of carrying heavy loads: 1609 *one heighwaie … not suffi-ciently repayred so that carriages [loads] with waynes cannot passe*, Helmsley (NRQS1/141); 1616 *20 hundreth weight is a fudder of lead, a tunne weight or a wayne loade*, Brandsby (NYRO44/113); 1642 *When yow sende your barres to fielde yow are to lay them in 4 severall rowes crosse over the shelvings of the waine and none of them in the body of the waine*, Elmswell (DW18); 1653 *with his drawght and six oxen and a wayne loaded with timber*, Bradley (QS1). See also bare wain, bound wain, bun wain, iron-bound wain, woollen wheels.

wain (3) Used as a verb, to transport by wain: *c.*1570 *to mowe, to rake … to stack, to wayn both to and froe*, Woodsome (KayeCP); 1659 *to drive … Watergates as well for the wayneing of coals as for avoydinge of water*, North Bierley (MMA/255).

wainage The connection here is with 'gain' not 'wagon', that is the profits of agriculture: 1299–1300 *De ij bus. siliginis iiij qr vj bus. avene de wannagio de Conedley venditis xs vjd [For 2 bushels of rye 4 quarters 6 bushels of oats wainage of Conedley sold 10s 6d]*, Bolton Priory (YRS154/101); 1324–5 *De wanagio de Malghum viij qr [For the wainage of Malghum 8 quarters]*, Bolton Priory (YRS154/548). See also wain (1).

wain boot A right granted to tenants which allowed them to take wood for making or repairing their carts and wains: 1587 *sufficient plowbote, waynebote*, Whitley (KM479a). See also boot (1).

wain clout A metal plate nailed to those parts of carts and wains that were subject to wear and tear: 1405 'and for 18 clouts (*clutis*) purchased for the axles of the cart, with nails purchased for the same 20d', Selby (SAR134); 1457 *in vj Wayncloytes emptis per Th. Keyng xijd [for 6 wain clouts bought by Thomas Keyng 12d]*, Fountains Abbey (SS130/11); 1504 *Waynclowtes, xxiij of the leyst sort xijd … xviij byger clowtes xvd*, York (SS53/191); 1580 *Inprimis 9 wayne clowtes*, Beverley (YRS84/33).

wain-gate, wain-road, wain-way Rights of way reserved for use by wains: 1312 'from the path called *Kerbysti* to *le wayngate*', Scawton (YRS120/149); 1516 *le Waynegaite ex parte austral' et unu' Brydilsty ex parte boreali [the wain-gate on the south side and a bridle-sty on the north side]*, Holmfirth (MD225/1/242); 1616 *the common wayne* *gate leadinge through the Kirkfeild*, Kirkheaton (DD/WBD/3/96); 1683 *which lyes in the direct waine roade from Kighley*, Bingley (QS1); 1690 *drayne the water out of the wayne way*, Almondbury (DD/R/M/3).

wain gear The equipment commonly associated with wains and other carts: 1538 *all maner of plewghe geir, wayne geir, coupe geir, and all other tymber out of occupacon*, Coxwold (SS106/75); 1556 *all my wayne geare as waynes, cowpes, plowes, yokes, temes & suche like … & all maner of tymber therto belonginge*, Horsforth (Th27/85). The term no doubt covers a wide range of attributive uses: 1535 *iiij pare of wayne rathes*, Stillingfleet (YRS45/129); 1551 *one paire of whelles, yron bounde, stonding in the laithe, one waynbodie to theym, and one waynehedeyoke, one bolt and one shakill*, Knaresborough (SS104/59); 1556 *the waynhead yocke, shakkell and bolte*, Fairburn (Th27/41); 1557 *a pare of wayne fleaks*, Thornton Bridge (SS26/101); 1558 *a payr of wayne raylls*, Fairburn (Th27/194); 1579 *a payre of wayne blaydes iiijs*, South Cave (Kaner103); 1600 *not one ashe fitt for a waynestower*, Settrington (YRS126/88); 1632 *a paire of wayne blaides and a payre of cowpes*, Ainderby Quernhow (MD338/55); 1667 *a parcell of wane speakes and felkes*, Brayton (YRS47/31).

wainhouse A shed or other building where wains were kept when not in use: 1570 *j layth, j waynhouse, j turfhouse*, Honley (YDK130); 1579 *I amendyd my waynehowse*, Woodsome (KayeCP); 1648 *In the wanehouse: two shilved wanes and two coopwanes … a thorow tree for a wane, 2 paire of wane ronges … a paire of wane blades*, Sharlston (YRS134/99).

wainmeet See wain (1), wainage.

wainpain A domestic servant: 1348 *Johannes de Maldon, waynpayn*; 1350 *Walterus de Wencelay, wampayn* [sic], York (SS96/41,44).

wain-road See wain-gate.

wain-rope The rope used for securing the load on a wain: 1377–8 *trayses … thethers et wauneraps*, Bolton Priory (YRS154/567); 1599 *two olde wayne roopes*, Rawmarsh (TWH16/160); 1620 *two iron bound waines … 2 waine roapes*, Bingley (LRS1/57); 1631 *j payre of wayne naves … 2 wayne ropes*, South Cave (Kaner342); 1644 *certaine harrowes furniture belonging the horses and three Waineropes*, Lepton (HM/C/180).

wainscot A superior quality of foreign oak wood, put to a wide range of uses. In many of the earliest references the word is used in the plural, possibly because it was imported into this country in the form of boards; that is extremely thin planks. Although it is uncertain just when the first boat loads arrived, the east coast trade was certainly established by the middle of the fourteenth century: 1358 *Item, Johanni de Gisburgh [mariner] pro wainscot, j marc*, York (SS129/14); 1371 *et in lx waynscot sarrandis pro orologia et aliis necessariis in fabrica [and for sawing 60 wainscots for clocks and for other requirements in the workshop]*, York (SS35/8); 1409 *et serratoribus pro serratura lx waynscott [and to the sawyers for sawing 60 wainscots]*, Beverley (ERAS4/33); 1486 *to the kyrk werk … xxx squared trees and half c. waynscotes to the reparaciones of the stalles*, Beverley (SS53/19).

In fact, large quantities of both oak and pine came into Hull, especially from the Baltic and Norway, and the evidence of fabric rolls shows that much of it was employed in the great churches. In Beverley, for example, it contributed to the repair of the choir stalls and was used for doors and windows. In Ripon and York it was needed for the reredos and canopy of the altar. Oliver Rackham claimed that it is possible for those who visit churches to 'distinguish the giant, straight-grained, slow-grown oaks of

Central Europe ... from the small, crooked, fast-grown local oaks' (OR1/88). These Continental trees were more versatile than native oak, and the boards were made by specialists who had the necessary skills and equipment. Fifteenth-century accounts for the port of Hull contain details of wainscots shipped from the Baltic. In 1453, the ships *Jacob* and *Catyntroghe*, from Danzig, brought in hundreds of them, along with *deles* and *clapholtes*: ships from Zeeland had *fyrsparres*. The wood came also to be used for panelling in private houses, and to make furniture: 1452 *j parvæ cofre de waynescotes [1 small coffer made of wainscots]*, York (SS45/138); 1525 *a copburde of waynescotte ... a bed of waynescotte*, York (SS79/200); 1558 *a carved chist of waynescott in the parlor*, York (YRS55/224); 1607 *it is my mynde that no glasse, waynescott, iron barres, bedstockes, tables and stoles shalbe removed from my house ... but stand as heirelomes*, Almondbury (YDK39). See also ceiling board, easting board, meatboard.

wain-way See wain-gate.

wainworth See wain (1), wainage.

wait The wait was originally a watchman: 1379 *Johannes Wayte vigilo ville [John Wayte the town wait]*, Derby (PTDb). That was probably the office of individuals so named in earlier documents: 1241 *Helena filia Hugonis le Waite [Helen the daughter of Hugh le Waite]*, Healaugh (YRS30/350); 1301 *De Willelmo le Wayte*, Richmond (YRS21/17). Later, the term was applied to small groups of instrumentalists who were maintained by a city or town at public expense: 1364 *Rogerus Wayte, piper*, York (SS96/59); 1391 *Thomas de Melton, wayte*, York (SS96/90). Their community role is often explicit: 1432–4 *lez Waytes civitatis [the waits of the city]*, York (SS192/15); 1529 *the common waytts of this City*, York (YRS106/129); 1556 *the waytes of the towne*, Wakefield (YRS74/21); 1641 *William Borton watte of this towne*, Hull (YAJ12/468); 1785 *Matthew Gibson, William Rhodes ... chosen town waits at a yearly salary of 50s each*, Beverley (YRS122/67).

Those who performed the office were also provided with distinctive clothing: in 1433, for example, the York waits were given a winter livery *Liberata yemalis* (SS192/15) and in Beverley in 1720 the men received badges, chains and a blue cloak (YRS122/8). Long service was rewarded: Robert Sheyne of York, described in 1486 as *being in so grete age and soo decrepid* was granted an annual pension of 13s and free accommodation (YRS98/170). In 1782, John Leavens of Beverley was allowed 2s a week *having served as a wait for upwards of 50 years*. Some twenty years earlier he had been discharged from his office for *insolent behaviour to the gentlemen in the Chamber*, but was reinstated on begging their pardon (YRS122/41,63).

wake A state of wakefulness, a vigil by a corpse or, as a verb, to watch over a corpse: 1542 *the expenses at was made in his howse ... at his wawke*, Beetham (SS26/29); 1558 *I gyve to xij wedowes to wake with my body one nyght ijs*, Richmond (SS26/113); 1740 *for winding and waking ... a poor vagerant woman, her name unknown*, Knaresborough (QS1/80/8). The wake as a vigil came to be associated with practices which included taking food and drink and eventually with the observance of certain festivals or special occasions. More generally it was then used to describe entertainment or holidays and in the Pennine mill towns 'wakes week' was the annual holiday. See also lyke-wake, night-wake, pot.

walk (1) A division of a forest, the area that one keeper might perambulate or oversee on foot: 1542 *my walkes within the forest of Wyndesore* (SS116/190); 1622 *every woodward maie take Blowen wood or Falne wood within his walkes*, Pickering (NRR2/5). In 1609, fees paid by the Cliffords of Skipton Castle to their *Foresters and Park-keepers* included 16s to William Atkinson for *Walking of Craco Fell* (Whit2/319). See also woodwalker.

walk (2) In the period when cock-fighting flourished it was customary for the birds to be placed in the care of tenants. The practice was referred to as 'walking' the cocks and it became part of tenancy agreements: 1576 *put to walkes in June*, Almondbury (DD/RA/f/4b); 1718 *one of the chickens last sent me is killed at his walk*, Barnsley (MD43/H2); 1728 *a Cuckoo Colour'd Cock … in one of the windows … which cock was kept or walked at this informant's house*, Wakefield (QS1/67/9). Similarly, whelps were kept by tenants but I have not seen 'walk' used in such cases.

walk (3) To full cloth, originally by trampling it under the feet: 1484 *noon inhabitaunt … shall make … eny woollen cloth to be weved or walked … without this Citie*, York (YRS98/95); 1504 *all thinges that belonges to weveyng and walking*, Kirkstall (Th4/9). The East Riding farmer Henry Best used the word for wool that was matted, as though trampled: 1642 *the fleece … walked togeather*, Elmswell (DW22). See also walker, walk milne, wap.

walker A fulling-miller, the person who originally 'walked' or trampled the cloth, a regional term: 1301 *De Rogero le Walker*, New Malton (YRS21/52); 1349 *in illo mesuagio in le Walkmylnbanke … ex dono … Johannis Walker [in that dwelling in the Walkmylnbanke … the gift … of John Walker]*, Ripon (SS74/142); 1379 *fullo Thomas Walker [to the fuller, Thomas Walker]*, Bradford (PTWR); 1436 *Willelmus Brunsall, walker*, York (SS96/151); 1484 *every walker shall walk the said cloth and clothez sufficiently … so that thay be as wele walked in oon place as in an othere*, York (YRS98/95); 1506 *to send for suche on walker as shall walk and wyrk that cloth*, York (YRS106/21); 1540 *George Sympson had two Walk or fulling mills … and in them used Walker Craft by himself or his men*, Leeds (YRS114/8). See also walk milne.

walker shears Used by clothiers: 1499 *entred the house of … Rauf Joynner and … toke and bare awaye a payer Sheres, called Walker Sheres*, Pickering (NRQS1/188); 1549 *too paire of walker sheres*, Halifax (Crossley34); 1592 *a pair of walker sheires*, Rastrick (HTu230); 1620 *walker sheares papers & dightinge towles*, Bingley (LRS1/34). See also paper, press paper.

walking rod A staff or walking-stick: 1593 *thrust his walking rodd through the stone worcke*, Shipley (WPB2/240); 1612 *2 walking rodds & 2 switchers*, Brafferton (NYRO44/35); 1623 *had only a walking Rodd with which he then usually walked … others had walking Rods or hand Cudgells*, Colne Bridge (HOW39); 1710 *knocked with his rod at the doere*, Pudsey (QS1/49/6). See also switch.

walk milne The regional word for a fulling-mill. Early evidence occurs in by-names and minor place-names: 1350 'half an acre in the *Walkmylneholme*', Lepton (YDK2); 1379 *Johannes Walkmylne*, Sheffield (PTWR); 1438 'repairing the *walkemylnedam*', Leeds (Th57/5). As a vocabulary item it is on record from the same period: 1359 *juxta aquam quæ currit usque le Walkemilne*, Ripon (SS74/282); 1488 *ij milnes there, that is to sey a corne mylne and a walk milne*, Woodsome (YDK11); 1519 *a walke mylne with decourse of watir*, Longwood (KM177). The regional term was recognised and 'translated' by clerks, at least partially: 1586 *all that fulling or walke mylne*, Netherthong (MD28/1). See also able (1), milne, walker.

wallet A bag for holding provisions, or items taken on a journey: c.1570 *the good howsbandman to have in store … wallet, botell or cann*, Woodsome (KayeCP); 1670 *one wallit or lethern bagg*, Kirkheaton (QS1/11/1); 1734 *took nine hens and kill'd them and put them into a wallet*, Methley (QS1/73/4).

wall-eyed Used generally of a horse with both eyes excessively light-coloured, or with different-coloured eyes. The meaning is not always certain and 'varon' is a more frequent word: 1618 *a mare, wall-eyed with a starr, value 30s*, West Stonesdale (NRQS2/187); 1631 *a dun fillie whald eyed*, Adwalton (BAS7/64). Also at the Adwalton Fair was *one bay bald gelding with the nar eye whald* (BAS7/62). See also varon.

walling hammer A hammer used by dry-stone wallers for dressing stones. It varies in appearance from region to region but in Yorkshire has one square end and one more or less pointed: 1704 *a walling hammer*, Holmfirth (IH).

wallplate A horizontal timber, supported by a wall or by posts, which in turn supported the timbering of the roof:: 1420 *thay awarde and deme that William Selby hafe abouen the same walle space to ryst hys walleplat apon*, York (SS85/17); 1537 *a payr of forks … vii Sparrs … a Wallplatt*, Bridlington (BCP20); 1538 *the inside of the gatehouse wantes in timber for wall playtes, bandes, entre cases, gestes, window selys*, Knaresborough Castle (YAJ30/222); 1615 *a rough wall to the wall plates and thatch and timber accordingly*, Bowland (CS2/33); 1642 *they will sowe downe theire thatch … first close to the very wallplates*, Elmswell (DW154). See also fork.

wall tile The word 'brick' came into use quite late but 'wall tile' had the same meaning: 1358 *pro xx mille de Walteghill, vjli*, York (SS129/15); 1399 *et in … waltiell cum cariagio [and for … wall tiles with transport]*, York (SS35/15); 1441–2 *And for 200 Walteghell for the said maltkiln, 12d*, Selby (SAR106). See also rig tile, thack, tile house.

walltron See quartern, whartern.

walnut The nuts were a delicacy enjoyed by the wealthy and the privileged, occasionally by the abbot of Whitby along with *fygs et rasyngs*: 1395 *Item pro walnots per vices xxd [Item for walnuts by turns 20d]*, Whitby (SS72/602). See also chestnut, spire (2), tree.

walt See welt (1) and (2).

wand (1) This is found in east Yorkshire as a measure of meadow land: it may have developed there from 'yardwand' or as a variant of 'wang', under the influence of 'wandale': 1583 *Item 4 wands in the south ing meddo*, Kirby Underdale (HKU61); 1596 *two wandes of meadow in the Northe Inges*, Thirsk (YRS50/191); 1723 *one Milnbeck-wand adjoining also on the Milnbeck*, Newton (NRQS9/69).

wand (2) A pliant shoot or sapling used in basket-making, wattle work, etc. They were commonly of willow and hazel and would occur naturally, but the evidence suggests that they were also deliberately cultivated, in riverside locations or in reserved woods: 1364 '*Flekewandes* growing on the banks of the water of the *Eyer* are leased to Hugo Childe', Methley (Th35/140); 1558 *selling wands taken unlawfully from the woods*, Acomb (YRS131/21); 1598 'cut down and carried away one load of wood called *wandes*', Farnley Tyas (DT/179); 1609 *We present Richard Hynde for gettinge of Eight heslewandes*, Malham (DDMa). In the following case it may have referred to a wicker-work fish leap or basket: 1623 *osiers, hopps, fishe wandes, sallowes*, Butterwick (NRQS4/159). The wands referred to in fabric accounts were for binding: 1399–1400 *Et in lxvj wandschothis emp. 21s [And for 66 wandshoots bought 21s]*, Ripon (SS81/130); 1446 *v^r dimidia templewande pro sutura ejusdem cooperturae 4d [550 templewands for fixing that roof 4d]*, Beverley (ERAS6/78). In 1750, the Almondbury constable recorded the expense involved in repairing Fenay Bridge, a wooden construction which had only parish status despite being on a major highway. One of the items listed was *Laying the wans on the Bridge* at a cost of 4s (WDP12/176A). These would have been 'wands' or thin sticks, possibly laid at right angles over more substantial pieces of wood. The minor place-name *Wandwath* was recorded in Hazlewood in 1318 (YRS154/460), and is probably identical with *Wandewat* in 1120–47 (PNWR6/65). It implies that wands were also used at fords from a very early date. See also bushel, fleak bridge, osier hope, stainwath, temple (1), wand (3), wand hagg, wath, writhing wand.

wand (3), wanded Made of wicker work or encased in it: 1563 *On Wandyt leape ij*, Knayton (SS2/208); 1565 *a wanded basket*, Temple Newsam (YAJ15/99); 1567 *In the lawe buttrye … wanded bottles*, Richmond (SS26/197); 1574 *one wanded skeppe to put breade in*, Wensley (SS26/251); 1578 *one wanded screne*, Stockeld (YRS134/52); 1597 *a little wanded arke*, Wakefield (SpSt); 1656 *a wanded chaire*, North Bierley (YRS134/102). It referred also to wattled partition walls: 1634 *one watled wanded or rised woghe*, Addingham (GRD) and occasionally had the spelling 'wand', even as an adjective: 1481 *De j wand busshell*, York (SS45/261); 1490 *de j lez wand-bushell ijd*, York (SS53/57). See also creel (1).

wandale A division of land, possibly the breadth of a 'wand' or perch: the OED has evidence in Yorkshire from *c.*1150 to 1642. An extract from an Elizabethan terrier has: 1590 *Item 1 East Wandale*, with measurement, followed by *Item 4 wands in the south ing meddo 18 fout by ancient mesur to evre wand bred linge north and south utmost eastward to Painstrop nex the outside of the meddo same 4 wand*s, with measurement, Kirby Underdale (HKU61).

wand hagg, wand hagger The wand hagg was a wood or part of a wood set aside for the production of wands, which had a wide variety of uses in the past. The word survived only in minor place-names but the indications are that it may formerly have been in general use across Yorkshire, from the thirteenth century at least: 1505 *the Northewest end of the Waude Hagge* [sic], Healaugh (YRS92/197); 1538–9 *boscum vocatum Whandehage [the wood called Whandehage]*, Bilsdale (SS83/316); 1642 *Also Wand hagg 6 yers growth*, Bilsdale (NYRO23/58); 1770 *Wandhagg*, Great Ouseburn (PNWR5/79). An occupational by-name is confirmation of its early history: 1297 *De Ricardo Wandehagger*, Wawne (YRS16/119). See also hagg, pile hagg, wand (2), wood hagg.

wang, wong Usually found as a minor place-name element, mostly in the southern part of the West Riding: n.d. *le Milnewange*, Thorpe Salvin (YRS83/168). Smith has numerous examples from 1200 (PNWR7/265,284).

want To be lacking or missing: 1472 *To the kirke of Acworth a vestyment that wantys an albe*, Pontefract (SS45/203); 1662 *hee wanted four ew sheepe and two lambs, taken from Kellington Common* (QS1); 1677 *so soone as he awaked and found that he wanted his purse he straightway made enquiry but could not heare what was become of it*, Holmfirth (QS1).

wantow, wanty A rope or leather band used to secure the load on a pack horse: 1377–8 *wambtous trayses kypstryngs*, Bolton Priory (YRS154/567); 1395 *pro iiij pese de waimto-webs xxd*, Whitby (SS72/614); 1416–17 'for 3 *Wambtyes* purchased from William Roper', Selby (SAR166); *c.*1504 *ij pak sadlys with waymtoys and pakes viijd*, York (SS53/191); 1585 *two lodesadles with garthes and wantoes 6s 8d*, Rastrick (YRS134/56); 1676 *they had cutt the wanty that tyed his pack fast to his panyers which he found was fallen downe and most of his cheeses throwne abroad*, Brompton on Swale (SS40/226).

wap A regional word for 'to fold', or to make a careless bundle (EDD): 1484 *ordeynd … that no sherman shall wap ne fold no cloth to be sold as a hole cloth but if it be wele and sufficiently woven and walked*, York (YRS98/96). See also walk (3).

wapentake bridge The 'wapentakes' were formerly the subdivisions of the three Yorkshire Ridings, districts which were equivalent to the 'hundreds' in most parts of England. The word is of Old Norse origin and it reflects Danish influence in the county in the centuries before the Norman Conquest. Wapentake bridges were therefore bridges maintained at the expense of the Wapentake and not the Riding. The status of a bridge could change, for various reasons, and local interests could influence that. A case at the General Quarter Sessions at Pontefract, in 1647–8, serves as an illustration fairly typical: Huddersfield Bridge was *through the violence of water decayed and quyte taken away* and a sum of £30 was *estreated* upon the West Riding towards its repair, and paid over to Sir John Ramsden, not only a Justice of Peace but also the local lord of the manor. A dispute took place over the £30 after the repairs had been carried out and the magistrates resolved the matter in the following order:

> *And whereas it do appear that the Bridge is a Wappentake Bridge and ought to bee repaired at the Countryes Charge, yet in respect of the said order and that the said work is finished, it is now ordered that the said order be confirmed and that the £30 be estreated on the whole West Riding and paid to the hands of those that disbursed the moneys to disengage them, provided that these moneys ... shalbe as a benevolence onely and not to bynd the said Ryding to repaire the bridge hereafter* (QS10/2/75).

–ward Used as a suffix with various nouns to indicate a specified direction: 1417 *in to the streteward un to the third post; in to their garthwarde; fra the waterward of Use*; 1420 *to the kyrkward*, York (SS85/12–16).

warday See warkday.

warden This was an office within the Cutlers' Company which was established after the Act of 1624. From the 1760s, some cutlers declined to serve and were fined: 1762 *By Cash of Mr Edward Shepherd for a fine in refusing to stand as a Warden when chose £5* (HCC20). See also assistant, master cutler, searcher.

warden tree The warden was a variety of baking pear: 1565 *six appletrees, two pearetrees, one wardentree*, Hemsworth (YRS63/51).

ware (1) A word with an Old English origin, used as a collective singular term for items of merchandise or manufacture, goods or commodities. It came also to be used in the plural, and cutlers' inventories for the period 1690–1739 reveal that they were making 'common wares' for the mass market (FBH102). In 1711, when the Cutlers' Company was anxious about immigration into Sheffield and the security of its members, they sought to restrict the number of apprentices each freemen might take because *they make such vast quantities of wares of all sorts that they can't sell them* (FBH141).

Attributive uses include 'ware tools', presumably the tools required to produce 'hardware', that is ironmongery or small metal goods. In 1546, Steven Fox of Ecclesall bequeathed 'all things belonging to his *shope as wayre toylles*' to his son Laurence (TWH13/78). The inventory of Samuel Baylie, in 1737, listed large quantities of files in his *Ware chamber*, an upper room used as a store (IH). This is another word that echoes the earlier vocabulary of the York cutlers: their ordinances in 1479–80 warned that *much evill ware ... be sold ... in greit dissate* [deceit] *and hurt of the common people* (SS120/134–5). See also cutlery ware, hardwareman, undressed.

ware (2) Regional for 'worse': 1553 *he harde* [heard] *Willm Barton ... saye to Dorothie Gett the hence and thowe be well for fere it be not ware*, Terrington (PTD90–1).

ware (3) To spend, lay out money: *a*.1417 *Thare shall comme two of tham to gider and ayther of them shall ware xviijd in fyssch*, York (SS120/222); 1472 *and this money to be waryd of the beldyng of the Mowrouse*, Pontefract (SS45/203); 1545 *I bequeath to the hie altare at Giesley xij^d to be wared of some adornment*, Yeadon (Th19/117). It may have intruded into 'wear out', meaning 'pass away': 1679 *he knew he must wear out the rest of his days in misery in that place*, Halifax (OH2/266). See also arvell.

ware corn Corn sown in spring, especially barley and oats. These were considered less hardy than wheat and rye: 1540 *yf that my ware corne be not sowyn, yt then my be eqally devydyd emongs my said executors*, Yafforth (SS26/19); 1548 *boithe my farmholdes … with the corn sawen theron … And the waire crop to be sawen*, Aberford (Th19/216); 1557 *I wyll that he haue the farmeholde sowne both wyth hard corne and ware corne*, East Keswick (Th27/135); 1620 *Item 10 day-worke of ware corne xvjli*, Bingley (LRS1/57). See also hard corn.

wark The regional spelling of 'work': 1543 *iiij^er warke horses … v draffe oxen*, Brettanby (SS26/41); 1568 *one smythe wylle make in the yere everye warke day a blome*, Esholt (BAS10/246). Attributive uses include: 1503 *one warkbord*, York (SS53/217); 1518–19 *paid … to a warkman x^d*, York (CCW71). See also workboard, workman.

warkday For workday, often used of working attire, especially women's: 1523 *to Agnes Lowkes … my warkday gowne, my warkday Kirtill*, Altofts (Th9/178); 1541 *unto Elisabeth Herrison a warkday cott and a pettecott*, Leeds (Th19/50); 1598 *to Anne Atkinson my warday gowne*, Thorpe near Ripon (SS104/214).

warnestore An obsolete word for provisions put in store: 1287–8 *In pisce et allece emptis … In cariagio eiusdem warnesture viijs ixd ob [For buying fish and herring … For transporting that warnestore 8s 9½d]*; 1318–19 *In expensis hominum et equorum cariancium warenstur[am] ijs iiijd [For expenses of men and horses carrying the warnestore 2s 4d]*, Bolton Priory (YRS154/38,463); 1456–7 *In exp. Joh'is Robynson versus mare pro Warnestura xjs viijd [In John Robynson's expenses going to the sea for warnestore 11s 8d]*, Fountains Abbey (SS130/27).

warp Alluvial soil deposited on land flooded by a river: 1698 *In the digging of the well … they found the earth and stone thus, three yard sand, one foot fine warp … two foot deeper a blew clay*, Winterton (SS54/184). It was common practice in places close to Thorne to recover alluvium from old river beds and spread it over the land, and this gave rise to the use of 'warp' as a verb: 1798 *beyond Cowick … Saw the warping which I think is a great curiosity* (WM77). See also mire pits, warp up.

warper A workman who prepared the yarn for weaving: 1602 *Robert Clughe, Laycocke, par. Kighley, warper* (YRS24/24).

warping Of uncertain meaning but a process in the preparation of skins for the fur trade: 1582 *Item for a warping of all manner of furres of rigges and of wombs – every furre ijd*, York (YRS119/63).

warping vat A textile term, the vat in which the warp could be placed, probably for sizing: 1572 *ij lomes his warpinfat, his barttryses*; 1611 *2 lomes 11 peire of geires … warping fatt, barr trees*, South Cave (Kaner79,235).

warping wough A wooden frame on which yarn was wound to form a warp, ready for weaving: 1639 *two paire of Loames with on warping woaghe in the shoppe*, Swinsty (YRS134/90); 1678 *one paire of Lowmes one warping wough with other things belonging to that trade*, Barnoldswick (YRS118/58); 1691 *One warping Wough with furniture,*

Slaithwaite (IMF). The spelling of 'wough' varied: 1680 *Loomes and warping woake and furnture*, Barnoldswick (YRS118/60); 1690 *one warping woak with creels*, Holmfirth (IH); 1757 *a pair of looms, warping oogh*, Holmfirth (IH). It measured three yards by one foot according to Easther.

warp up Flood water is said to 'warp up' property when it deposits earth and stone on the river banks and the buildings located there. In 1686, a great storm destroyed bridges, houses, and farm land in Wharfedale, an event recorded in the Quarter Sessions Order Book for the West Riding:

> On Thursday the eighth day of June ... betweene the hours of one and three in the afternoone ... there happened an Earthquake with dreadful claps of thunder which was attended with great showers of haile and raine which descended so violently from the mountains and flowed out of the caverns of the rocks that in a very short moment it overflowed the bancks of the River and great streams ran through ... Kettlewell and Starbotton driving along with them great quantities of great stones, land and sludge soe that it overturned, carried away, warpt up and made useless, uninhabitable ... dwelling houses ... Outhouses and Barns And carried, swept away and spoiled ... household goods ... and did likewise Tear up and drive away the Earth of one hundred acres and upwards of arable pasture and meadow ground ... And did likewise cover with great stones, gravel and sand above 100 acres more of arable pasture or meadow ground ... (OWR1/13).

The estimates for repairs by masons, carpenters and surveyors have survived in detail, and for these two communities alone the bill amounted to over £3,000. This early use of the verb 'to warp up' goes far beyond the meanings given in the OED and it paints a graphic picture of houses and land choked up with river debris. The effects were felt as far downstream as Addingham. Similarly: 1697–8 *not having A free Passage to the said Mill, the Beck being warped up*, West Riding (QS1); 1712 *in many places the River is Warpt up 2 foot, in some places 3 foot and in some 9 foot, so yt is impossible it should Contain the same quantity of Water as before*, Knottingley (BAS11/162). See also wrack.

warrap A rope attached to a fishing net: 1391 *et j flew cum warrap et flot* [float], Scarborough (SS4/157); 1530 *And to yonge Richerd Johnson vj stone of hemp and a nett and a warrope*, Whitby (SS79/301).

warren The right to 'warren' was the liberty granted to a landowner to hunt birds and animals on part of his estate: 1524 *wilde bores, dere, heronsewies, shoulardes, fesandes, partriches as othre fowles and beistes of waraunt*, Thorpe Underwood (YRS140/108). These 'reserves' came to be known as warrens and they were watched over by warreners: 1519 *that no man hawke nor hunte within my Lorde's warraunte*, Selby (SS85/32); 1602 *hedgeing the warren*, Brandsby (NYRO44/18); 1726 *Francis Gibson of Rigton warrener of Hornbank Warren* (QS1/65/9).

From the Tudor period the word was more usually associated with the keeping of rabbits or coneys and the landlords' privileges were under increasing threat. In 1498, Miles Willesthorp claimed that a body of armed men had come *to the more of Willesthorp ... and ... there riotously hunted the conyes ... and digged up the erthis* (YRS41/18). In 1599–1600, *the cony warren* within the lordship of Settrington was surveyed and a memorandum noted that *in Anncient tyme the conye warren was planted in the low commons*, but so many rabbits were poached that it was moved closer to the manor house (YRS126/31).

The Quarter Sessions records have details of poaching in such warrens into quite recent times and *a warren or common called Coney Moor in Methley* is mentioned in 1732 (QS1/71/6). The houses occupied by the warreners are quite frequently referred to, and Warren House became a common minor place-name: 1654 *paid for drawinge the thack and for theakinge of the Warrand House, 4s 6d*, Stockeld (YRS161/91). References which list improvements to Richard Cholmeley's property illustrate the word's attributive uses: 1612 *a warren howse wall*; 1614 *my warren yeat stowpes*; *finished my warren dyke burnynge*, Brandsby (NYRO44). See also boon, and GRMH169–71.

warrick A girth for a horse: 1452 *Stabulum … ij warrokkes ijd [In the stable … 2 warricks 2d]*, York (SS45/137).

wash (1), wesh This was one of several words for human urine. A York brewer was accused in 1588 of contaminating his beer with urine, although the exact words uttered by the accused were that *he did put washe in his drinke* (YRS138/29). Until quite recently the untreated liquid had a variety of industrial uses, especially in cloth-making. It was sometimes called 'old wash', and in 1716 John Whitehead spoke of going to his father's house in Almondbury *to begg some old wash to wett some pieces of cloath before he carryed them to Mill* (OWR1/2/16). This practice was commented on by the Wakefield cloth frizzer John Brearley: 1762 *weeting out and washing* leaves some cloths *surpriseing thin* (YRS155/15).

An alternative term for urine was 'lee' or 'chamber-lee'. John Kaye of Farnley Tyas wrote that *upon 26 of Maye 1589 Alice Hepworth* [was] *sentt by hir Master Edmonde Kay for a kytt full of wash or chamber lee* and later in the same anecdote it was called *wesshe* (KayeCP). This was the usual dialect spelling and various informants over the years have told me that the lane which leads from just below the Conservative Club in Longwood to Quarmby Fold is called locally *Weshlickerloyn*. An undated entry in a seventeenth-century account book recommends *howe to die blewe out of white* and it begins with the instruction to *Taike 12 gallans of chamberlee* and *sett it on the fire*. When it was close to boiling it was removed and a quarter of a pound of indigo was mixed in before adding the cloth or wool and stirring well (OWR1/2/16). See also chamber-lee, lant, lee, weeting.

wash (2) To cover with a coating of precious metal, a term regularly used by coiners: 1680 *to search houses for clipping, washinge and diminishing the King's Coyne*, Halifax (QS1/19/8); 1696 *last week I took two or three new counterfeit sixpences but exquisitely made and washed with silver being copper within*, Hatfield (SS54/112).

washing towel In early inventories 'towel' was a word with a wide range of meanings, used of a piece of cloth which could serve as a table napkin, a communion cloth or the covering for the altar in church. This compound was rare but the OED has two fifteenth-century examples, the earliest in county Durham in 1404. In these cases it may have been a cloth used to dry a person's body after washing, possibly a ceremonial washing: 1509 *j par de weshyng toweles de diaper [1 pair of washing towels made of diaper]*, Hedon (SS79/1); 1509 *one awtercloth … with on wasshyng towel*, York (SS79/7).

wash-leather A soft leather, usually of split sheepskin, dressed to imitate chamois leather. 'Wash' seems likely to refer to a process in the production and not to the article's function: 1730 *a wash leather purse made of a woman's glove, without strings*, Southowram (QS1/69/2).

wash-pit A place in a brook where sheep might be washed: 1647 June 26 *after diner I went to the wash pitt where Wm Wordsworth and Geo Morton were washing Winleden sheep*, Thurlstone (SS65/47). Washpit is a minor place-name in Holmfirth and the similar names Wash Dike and Wash Dub probably share this origin. There is a very early reference to the practice: 1307 *Shepewesshe ... Schepewassegrene*, Hepworth (YRS36/103).

wassail Originally a salutation, offered when presenting a guest with a cup of ale or wine. It came to be associated with the festivity and then with a particular celebration: In 1697, Dr Kaye of Woodsome wrote in his diary: *to Claton wassel yestern*. The original diary is in the Bodleian Library (MS.Rad) but Kirklees archives hold a copy.

watchet A light blue colour, although sometimes a material of that colour: 1485 *Unum pece levis wachett [A piece of light watchet]*, York (SS45/301); 1556 *iij pece of watchet clothe price v^{li} ij^{s}*, Halifax (Crossley131); 1596 *for halfe one ounce of Watchet silke 15d*, Howden (YAJ19/463); 1633–4 *Two long clothes of gold & watchet silke*, York (SS35/316).

water In Yorkshire this was the usual word for a river, beck or brook. Catterick Bridge was built *oure the watir of Swalle* in 1422 (NRQS3/33) and Sheffield's Lady's Bridge *over the watyr of Dune* in 1485–6 (HS1/59). It remained in general use through the sixteenth century, and persisted into the eighteenth century at least: 1531 *one close of meadow ... as the same ... abutteth upon the river or water that runneth from the town of Bradford unto the Ayre* (BAS10/26–7); 1582 *a litle water or brooke commonlie called Collerden water* (YRS63/45); 1640 *3 parcells of land ... abutting upon the water or brook there*, Almondbury (DD/R/4/21); 1706 *the water of Colne in Honley* (C296/151). Even by the early 1500s this had begun to be seen as a regional term by scribes and it was regularly translated as 'river' in title deeds, etc.: 1649 *to the water or Ryver of Tease*, Yarm (MD302/3); 1675 *the river or water which runneth betwixt Smithyplacebridge and Honley* (C296).

water-bank A reinforcement of the river bank, made with wooden piles, a weir wall: 1546 *the yerly charges for the reparynge of water bankes xxxs iijd*, Riccall (SS91/56); 1664 *repaire his water bankes ... and make the same sufficient to turne the water*, Rishworth (WCR5/134); 1716 *Ripa vel moles (Anglice the water bank or wear) adjung. [adjoining] Thurgoland Beck* (QS4/22/186); 1717–18 *the wear or waterbank near Gargrave is very ruinous ... both above and below the bridge* (QS1/57/1).

water-engine An early device for pumping water onto a fire so as to extinguish it: 1732 *by the industryus assistance and Labour of the Inhabitants ... with water Engines and other materialles the said Malt Kiln was mostly saved*, Wakefield (QS10/16). See also fire engine.

waterfast The OED has examples of this word from the sixteenth century in the sense of 'waterproof', but in coal-mining it was used occasionally of a pit or gallery that could not be worked because it was flooded: 1701 *Nathaniel Booth of Popeley his Coalpitt being watter Fast Coals cannot be gotten in it* (HM/E/99); 1710 *hath sunke 8½ y^{d} left of being fast with watter*, Farnley (MS11).

water-furrowing A husbandry practice which involved flooding meadows early in spring to promote the growth of the grass (CA45). A weir had to be built across the brook so that water could be run off and distributed via channels: 1783 April 4 *began Water furrowing*, Ovenden (CA119).

watergate The suffix 'gate' is important in this case for it could have two meanings. In the sense of 'barrier' or 'door', it was a contrivance that had to be opened if water was to pass through: in the sense of 'road' it referred to a water course or channel. The first of these meanings applies to references from the fifteenth century where the spelling 'yate' confirms that watergate could be a term similar in meaning to floodgate:

1458–9 *pro factura le Wateryattes per Th. Bute in fontans fell, ijs [for making the Watergates by Thomas Bute in Fountains Fell, 2s]* (SS130/84); 1579 *They lay in pain that the farr watter yate at Roger Gauntes shalbe well made and a good locke kept of it*, Dewsbury (YAJ21/410).

On the other hand, in a mining context the watergate was likely to be a drain, saving the pit from flooding and allowing the miners to get coal in relatively dry conditions. The earliest examples noted are from Rainton in Durham where expenses for making a watergate or drain in a pit are recorded in 1368–9, 'pro uno Watergat pro minera' (OED). The first evidence for such features in Yorkshire is in the court rolls of Wakefield manor: in 1340, the steward or 'grave' granted a tenant permission to dig for sea-coal in Alverthorpe and also 'to make a channel under the earth for draining the water' (WCR12/196). The original text is in Latin, but this translation is clear evidence that drains had to be built in some of the earliest pits if coal was to be easily extracted.

The first Yorkshire examples of 'watergate' in this sense occur in seventeenth-century documents, and one note about coal getting in Barwick in Elmet is particularly detailed. Sir Thomas Gascoigne was working shallow pits there in the mid-1600s and water had evidently been a problem. He says that in 1638 he *did … sinke the Ginn pitt deeper and added another pumpe*, which allowed him to draw the water 20 yards in all, evidently the depth of the pit. The passage that is directly relevant to the draining operation is worth quoting at length:

> *From Parlington Hollins there is two rowes of bottom cole, and one rowe of hardband to be gotten when the ginns shall draw 20 y*[ard]*e: which to recover there must be 2 water gates driven, one for the high cole and another for the low cole. The higher water gate must be taken out of the bottom of the Ginn pitt which is about 20 yarde deep …*

He then comments on the necessity of attending to the water courses lest they be *lost or misspent … by mold warpe holes or choked by sedges, etc., for want of scouring*. His major concern was *the Soughe from the wheele race downe to the Cock* [the name of the stream] which if it were obstructed would *utterly undoe us* (Th17/10–11).

Coal leases in the Bradford area contain additional information about the way problems with water were dealt with. In 1659, pits in Wibsey were leased to Samuel Littlewood of Hunsworth *with free liberty … to drive and make Watergates as well for the wayneing of Coales as for avoydinge of water*. The inference is that the 'gates' here would be wide, serving principally as drains but also allowing coal to be moved out of the pit by some form of vehicle. Littlewood agreed *to maintaine and keep the Watergate or Watergates in good and sufficient manner during the said terme* of ten years (MMA/255) and that would involve maintenance work on the drains. Additional examples are quoted under the headwords 'fettle' and 'fey'. See also dry, sough.

water-gin A 'gin' operated by water power, that is by a water wheel. The drawing of water in this way was a practice commented on in *The Compleat Collier* (1708) and it was known in south Yorkshire from about that time: 1713 *water gin, house and ropes*, Sheffield (HS7). See also fire engine.

waterhead A 'head' driven to serve as a watercourse, although it might also provide ventilation: 1633 *Abraham Shaw shall … drive every sough which he shall take in hand … till he come to take the last waterhead … and shall have allowance of the fourth part of the charges*, Northowram (HAS31/78); 1702 *that the waterhead bee carried on and kept upon a true Levell so that there may bee free Passage for winde and water*, Thornton (DB1/C2/30). See also head (2), sough, watergate.

watering stead A place where livestock could take water from a pond, stream or river: 1507 *I will that my executor make as mych coste of mendyng of the watteryng-stede*, York (YAJ22/282); 1650 *the watering steade close*, Tong (MMB/8). Note: 1620 *with way leave thro' the lands and waste grounds to the Brook for watering Cattle*, Beeston (WYL160/129/4).

water-leader A carrier who made his living by transporting water for sale: 1252 *De dono [By gift of] Willelmi filii Ricardi le Waterleder de Scardeburge* (SS83/399); 1346 *William le Waterleder*, York (YRS111/184); 1411 *Ricardus Menwar, watirleder*, York (SS96/116); 1455 *Et de Johanne Henrison smyth pro ferramento equi Ricardi Waterleder [And for John Henrison the smith for shoeing Richard Waterleder's horse]*, York (SS192/86); 1503 *apon the payment of pagiaunt money of the watterleders*, York (YRS103/183). See also lead (1).

waterleaf Possibly a design in the shape of the leaf of an aquatic plant: 1444 *cum dim. dos. whisshons rubiis cum waterlefe [with half a dozen red cushions with waterleaf]*, Beverley (SS30/104).

water loose See loose.

waterman A mariner, or more usually a sailor working on the inland waterways, with examples principally from Beverley when it was a port: 1520 *Robert Garbrey, Beverley, waterman* (YRS11/68); 1561 *Robert Smythe, Beverley, waterman* (YRS14/148); 1586 *Robert Brakine, Beverley, waterman* (YRS22/16).

water milne See milne.

water-pit A rare term, probably an alternative word for a sump in a coal-mine: 1728 *for sinking a Water Pit £1 5s 0d*, Horsforth (SpSt/5/4/1/5).

water slack A water-filled depression or shallow area between two stretches of rising ground: *c.*1270 *a Waterslakgille usque ad fossum [from Waterslakgille to the dyke]*, Langdale (SS72/449); 1329 'the place called *Watirslack*'; 1331 'and one rood lies at *le Watyrslacke* between the land of the said Adam … and the land of Robert Franckelayne', Hemsworth (YRS120/99). An undated thirteenth-century deed also has the term: 'in a place called *Briggeflat* by *le Water slacke*', Stubham (YRS76/155).

water timber In 1497, the lessee of a corn-mill near Whitby was granted timber from the abbey's forester *vocatum [called] watter tymmer*, which seems to recognise that wood from certain trees was more water-resistant, Ruswarp (MC361).

wath, wath stead 'Wath' is a word of Scandinavian origin which means 'ford', and it is especially common as a place-name element in Yorkshire and Cumbria. As a suffix it came under the influence of similar sounding words and there has been confusion with -thwaite, -way, -with and -worth in particular. It occurs for example in Helwith Bridge and Solway Firth: Beggars Wife Bridge in Giggleswick was originally *Beggerwathe* (1580). The bridge of *Brygwath* is mentioned several times in accounts for Bolton Priory from 1310 but the name did not survive and the site is not known (YRS154). The word remained in use in the northern dialects: 1486 'to *le Wath* above the mill pond', Thornton (YRS63/139); 1655 *the wearing* [weiring] *of the wath*, Kirkby Moorside (NRQS5/195); 1697 *From thence I went over a wath which tradition says was formerly a great river running … into Humber* (SS54/153). It alternated with 'wath stead', the site of a wath, and both are used in references to work on the bridge at Skipton on Swale. In 1604, money was advanced for the making of *a passable foard, or wath-stead, for cart and carriage* (NRQS3/47) but heavy traffic continued over the bridge and it had again become ruinous by 1610. As a result it was decided to improve the *foard* *or wath* and deny heavy carriages access to the bridge, for which purpose *A locke and chaine* was provided. Carriers with *offensive burthens* would therefore be obliged to use the ford (NRQS1/204–5).

wattle Stakes or rods interwoven with twigs or branches, used in house building and to make hurdles and fences. Although the word dates from the Anglo-Saxon period and was in common use generally, Yorkshire examples are infrequent: 1457–8 *In ij foder Watlyng per Joh. Lambart et W^m, xijd*, Fountains Abbey (SS130/54). The Latin accounts for repairs to Otterburn tithe barn in 1454 list expenses for *watlyng* and *thakke* (Morkill238) and details of a house built at Wolviston *c.*1663 had 6s 6d *paid for cutinge the watles and layinge them* (HH9). See also rised wough, wand (3).

wave As a verb it may be linked with 'waive' in the sense of setting aside, for it was used when a wood was being felled, identifying those trees which were to remain standing: 1527 *Also the said Richard Beaumont to leve them abilly waived after the use and custom of the contree*, Denby (MD93). See also avoid, waver (1).

waver (1) At the end of the coppice cycle, when the trees were felled, a certain number were allowed to remain, in order to provide a later crop of timber trees. These were called standards, or more commonly in Yorkshire 'wavers': 1390 'the purchasers should leave … *wayuerez*', Aislaby (YRS102/1); 1462 *to cole the woddes … [and leave] sufficient wayvers*, Norton (HS13); 1548–9 *it is agreed … that weyvers shall be last* [sic for left?] *in the saide two sprynges conveniently according to the most huse of suche spryng woode*, Shelf (YRS39/151); 1720 *reserving out of the said Woodes sixty wavers … and eight Black Barks in every acre*, Carlton (SpSt); 1763 *And if any Reserved Wavers be broke down by Carelessness on felling … In that case they shall pay for the same or Allow as many & as Good to be marked Sett out & left in some other place*, Esholt (MD93/19). It occurred occasionally as a verb: 1496 *to be weyvered workmonlyke*, Beauchief (HS13); 1719 *or els to be wavered and sett oute … by the pillers*, Tong (Tong/3/505). See also short end, weaver (1).

waver (2) A pool, pond or trough, especially a common water supply: 1416–17 'And for the service of the same person cleaning out the horse-pond (*le Wayhour*) there 6d', Selby (SAR170); 1436–7 'on *Mikilbryng Lane* opposite the *Wayver*', Braithwell (TWH14/29); 1556 *neyther man nor woman frome hensfurthe washe anye clothes woole puddynges … in the waver*, Wakefield (YRS74/22); 1584 *in the overfeilde near the wayver*, Almondbury (MS205).

waw A measure of weight, equivalent to twelve stone: 1302–3 *In ij waghis plumbi de Galfrido de Lonesdale vs [For 2 waws of lead from Geoffrey de Lonesdale 5s]*, Bolton Priory (YRS154/149); 1401 'From John Rotse for … 40 *wagh* of salt', Hull (YRS64/26); 1458 *Et de precio vij wawes vitri … prec. waw 12d [And for the cost of 7 waws of glass … price per waw 12d]*, York (SS35/70); 1508 *a waw of glasse*, York (SS35/359); 1580 *John Haykin the smelter of Marricke oweth one foother of leade & moreover one wawe of leade* (YRS152/246). See also wey.

wax To grow, to become: 1428 *he perceived wele that iren waxed skant and dere*, York (SS85/3); 1483 *all ther childer that are waxyn and comyn to aghe has made an eschange*, Ovenden (BAS1/261); 1642 *Tuppes … will beginne to linger after* [crave for] *Ewes and decline theyre flesh waxe reade and rancke*, Elmswell (DW12); 1685 *his wife waxed dime of sight … that she could not helpe her selfe*, Flockton (QS1).

way leave The granting of special rights of way is in evidence from an early date, as when Richard le Walais allowed the prior of Healaugh to use a road 20 feet in width from his old park *usque pontem suum de Haganhou … ad cariandum boscum et maher-emium [as far as his bridge at Healaugh … for transporting wood and timber]* (YRS92/52–3). Springwood leases frequently included clauses which had to do with the use of such rights of way, not just controlling access into the woods but also the transporting of material in and through the fields which adjoined the woods.

They also controlled the pasturing of carriage animals: in 1377 Walter de Calverley granted one lessee and his associates 'reasonable ingress and regress … and pasture for his horses that carry his coal', Calverley (Th6/190). There are similar examples through the sixteenth and seventeenth centuries: 1527 *to have free entree and issue with all maner of cariage into the said two greafes … as afore hath been accustomed withoute vexation*, Denby (DD/WBD/3/32); 1548–9 'Thomas Nailler and Richard Willey, *smethemen …* to have sufficient ways for carrying the wood and bark over Rysheworthe's ground', Shelf (YRS39/151); 1596 *wayeleave for the said Ralph Beistone … with horses, Cartes and Carryages*, Beeston (WYL160/129/7); 1620 *way leave through the lands and waste grounds to the Brook for watering Cattle*, Beeston (WYL160/129/4). Coal-mining leases have similar clauses: 1597 *wayeleave for servantes, workemen … to geat Coales, make sueres*, Beeston (WYL160/129/4); 1659 *waye leave in and through all the ground*, North Bierley (MMA/255).

William Storr wrote of customs that prevailed in the late 1600s, saying in his memorandum book *we have no horss way on the Closses but by leave*, Scalm Park (YAJ7/49). Over the centuries, despite such ways being required only at intervals, their use could evidently become customary: 1672 *to take Cleare Cary away the same … in and throughe all usual ways*, Tong (Tong/3/320); 1763 *Also granteth way and Leive for carrying off the said Trees, Wood, Bark, Cordwood … in over & through the usual ways*, Esholt (MD93/19). See also cheminage, gate-law.

wear See weir.

weaver (1) In coppicing this was a young oak tree left standing when the surrounding trees were felled, an alternative spelling of 'waver' (1): 1640 *dicunt qd John Pogson succidit unum querculum (anglice a weaver)* [they say that John Pogson felled an oak (in English a weaver)], Lepton (DD/WBM).

weaver (2) An alternative spelling of waver (2).

web (1) A measure or sheet of lead: 1457 *quoddam plumbum in fornace cum quodam webbe de plumbo [the lead in the furnace together with a web of lead]*, Kirby in Cleveland (SS30/210); 1476 *Et solverunt Johanni Midilton, plommer, pro castyng de ij webbs plumbi … ijs ijd [And they have paid John Midilton, plumber, for casting 2 webs of lead … 2s 2d]*, York (SS129/74); 1538 *three lodgings are reasonable good reparations saving three webbs of lead for a gutter which is there ready to be laid on*, Knaresborough (YAJ30/222); 1568 *Item thirtene webbes of leadd*, Healaugh Park (YRS134/35); 1576 *for xvj yerds of bourds to make the frame to cast the leade in webs*, Sheffield (HS4).

web (2) A whole piece of cloth, woollen or linen: 1433 *unum par linthiaminum de tribus webbes [a pair of sheets of three webs]*, York (SS30/48); 1578 *Item payd for workinge on blankett webe vjs*, Stockeld (YRS161/3); 1580 *all my webbes … made this yeare*, Full Sutton (YAJ36/440); 1598 *Towe Lowmes and a webb on one of them and all his working geare belonginge thereto 10s*, Knaresborough (YRS134/62). By extension it was associated with the loom itself: 1494 *Et lego Katerinæ filiæ meæ illud instrumentum, anglice weblome, in quo Johannes maritus suus operatur [And I bequeath to my daughter Katherine that equipment, in English the web loom, at which her husband John works]*, York (SS4/191). The OED has: 1538 'the web or lome'.

web (3) A band of woven material, especially those used on pack animals: 1395 *pro vj pes de gyrthwebs ijs … pro iiij pese de waimto-webs xxd*, Whitby (SS72/614). See also wantow.

web (4) The blade of a weapon or carpentry tool: 1676 *came to him with an ax threatning to murder him … And this informant got hold of the head or web of the ax*, Ilkley (SS40/223).

webster A regional word for a weaver, found as an occupational by-name in Yorkshire from the thirteenth century and widely distributed in the period when surnames were stabilising: 1279 *Johannes filius [son of] Rogeri Webster*, York (SS96/4); 1379 *Johannes Webster, textor*, Timble (PTWR). 'Weaver' is on record in the late 1400s but webster remained in use into the seventeenth century at least: 1504 *landes in Barnard-castell late in the holdyng of a webster*, Marske (YAJ6/228); 1634 *Simon Haldisworth of Addingham, lynninge webster* (GRD). See also –ster, and GRDict.

wedge A short but solid piece of metal with a thin edge at one end and the other much thicker. They were used by stone-masons: 1371 *Et in 24 weggis ferri de novo fabricandis [And for 24 newly made iron wedges]*, York (SS35/7), and by colliers. When inserted into a fissure and struck with a heavy hammer or mall they would bring down coal from the face, and the word occurs regularly in colliery accounts, e.g. 1708 *two barrs of Iorne for Coale pitt weges they weighed 4 ston 12 pounds*, Farnley (MS11); 1713 *for the working of the pit, five shovels, five malls, five iron wedges*, Shibden (HAS30/147); 1754 *3 wedges, 7p^d at 4d per pound*, Beeston (WYL160/129/4). In 1569, Thomas Gybson of Wibsey bequeathed to William Rokes his *greatest iron malle, foure wedges and two picks* (BAS1/24). The following entry is in the Leeds burial register: 1706 *Tho: Hey of Banke, a Colyer. This mans scull was broke with an Iron Wedge driven by Gunpowder* (Th13/185). See also latt axe, quart saw, thixel.

wedge-horned Used of cattle, presumably having wedge-shaped horns. It was a frequent term in the accounts of Richard Wigglesworth: 1685 *The wegge hornd why was buld July 30*; 1694 *behinde for the wegghornd 17s 6d for her grasse*; 1719 *Waeg hornd … Augt the 19*, Conistone (RW18,33,52).

wedset An alternative spelling of the legal term 'wadset', that is to pledge land: *c*.1440 *a place here … wolde I wedde-sette*, York (OED); 1505 *My wyffe to have my purchest and my wedsett land in Clyffe*, Hull (SS79/39n); 1541 *ij howses … whiche William Woode of Ricall wedset to me*, Osgodby (HAH335).

weeting In the Huddersfield area, this was a word for human urine which had uses formerly in several local industries (OWR2/1/12) and was commented on in Easther's Glossary (1883). The noun was used by James Hirst of Wortshill in Slaithwaite, writing in the late nineteenth century. When dyeing wool black, he said, *a bucketful of weeting* made the colours brighter (OWR1/2/16). It was probably a spelling of 'wetting' which was a process in cloth-making, and in 1762 the Wakefield clothier John Brearley wrote: *when the [Hudersfild light drab] come from dyeing all the earth is gone out and the are surpriseing thin with weeting out and washing* (YRS155/15). In 1751, a Holmfirth inventory listed *a weeting trough* (IH). See also chamber-lee, lant, lee, wash (1).

weigh-balk A beam of wood or iron used with a pair of scales and weights, a regional term: 1410 *cum le weghbalk [with the weigh-balk]*, York (SS45/48); 1485 *j weybalke cum skales et ponderibus de plumbo [1 weigh-balk with scales and lead weights]*, Ripon (SS64/371); 1493 *j weybalk of iren with the skales that langes therto*, York (SS53/89); 1543 *a webayke with schalls and vij leyd weyghts*, Ripley (SS26/44); 1614 *with a weay* *balke with scales*, Pudsey (LRS1/27); 1676 *j paire of weigh scales with a balke 2s*, Brayton (YRS47/74); *c.*1742 *weigh balk*, Holmfirth (G-A).

weind See wynd.

weir, wear, wer A weir is now most commonly thought of as a dam, placed across a river to restrict and control its flow rather than stop it altogether. Formerly, it had several meanings connected with river defences and these can be linked with bridges and the strengthening of river banks. Most commonly, it referred to an embankment reinforced by piles and that was probably what was meant in 1340 by 'one rood of *wer* at the bank of the water of Colyn' (YRS63/20). This referred to the river Colne at Dalton, near Huddersfield. More specifically, the tenants of Bradford manor 'made a *weyre* with *pylles*' in 1422 (CR). Maps of 1598 and 1625 which had to do with disputes over 'steaners', that is places where a river had changed its course, show *weares* that had been built to defend the new line of the stream (OWR1/1/26–7).

Tenants were often held responsible for making and maintaining the defences: 1512 'enjoined on Robert Ward that he shall make a fence called a *wer* ... next the *Haire*' [river Aire], Methley (Th35/194); 1558 *make and upholde the wayres betwixt the water of Calder and the said holme*, Copley (YDK99); 1626 *making and maintayning ... one water weare att the foote of the said dam twentie yeards in length downewardes along after the side of Damhead Close ... from wasting by the violence of the said river*, Armitage Mill (FAClxxiii). A document of 1581 contains an order to the tenants of Hartshead *to make sufficient the weares and workes defendinge the meadow from the Callder* (KM431). Occasionally the word was also used as a synonym for 'wing' or 'wing wall', most explicitly in 1701 when a new bridge was built over the Laver:

> *Alsoe to make a wing or weare of hewen stone upp above the said road on the East side of the water betwixt the road and where the old bridge now standeth with a point to goe into the watercourse beyond the foundation of the Landstall on that side (QS1/40/4).*

weir-gate Of uncertain meaning, but possibly a 'fence' suspended above a stream, which served to link the walls on each bank: 1759 *to the corner of the Intack where a wear gate is made across the said brook*, Shelley (YAS/DD181/15). In the case quoted here it was part of a boundary.

weirstead The site of a weir or waterbank: 1579 *they lay in pain that one wearesteade in the side of the becke going into Crackenedge be well fenced and mended*, Dewsbury (YAJ21/408).

weir wall Weirs were initially reinforcements to an existing river bank, formed of piles, but the need to heighten and strengthen the defences resulted in the building of stone walls, often but not always linked to bridges. The verb 'to weir' was used in such contexts: 1718 *a cutt 4 yds broad to be wear'd on each side*, Hampsthwaite (QS1/57/8); 1776 *for wairing and walling*, Boothhouse Woods, Holmfirth (G-A); 1839 *It is absolutely necessary that the banks should be stayed by a weir wall*, Golcar (DD/SR/1/273). See also call (3), water-bank, wing (2).

weld See wold (2).

well-gate A road or way to a well: 1516 *inter le Kirkegaite ex parte orient' ... et le Wellegaite ex boreal'* [between the Kirkegaite on the east side ... and the Wellegaite on the north], Hepworth (G-A).

Welsh frieze A kind of woollen cloth with a nap, originally made in Wales, a term noted in the OED from the Act of 1551–2: *All Welch frizes … made and wrought within the shires of Cardigan, Caermarthen and Pembroke … or elsewhere of like making* (SAL5/358). In fact, the practice had a much longer history: 1444 *in panno dicto [for cloth called] Coventr' russet walshefresed*, Beverley (SS30/97).

welt (1) In shoemaking, the welt was a strip of leather that joined and was attached to the sole and upper leather, holding them together. The verb meant to repair or renew welts and this was seen as a cobbler's task not a shoemaker's: 1582 *and to capp and welt both old bootes and shoes with new blacke leather*, York (YRS119/60); 1589 *the cordyners ther servants and apprentices may sole shoes and botes … so they do not welt or clowt any shoes bootes or other wayr*, York (YRS138/68); 1773 *George Shoes Soald & heelespecht and Capild and Welted*, Meltham (GRD).
More generally, the verb and noun referred to furnishing a garment with a border or hem of material: 1540 *my blake gowne of cloth weltede with velvet and faced with bogge*, Whitby (SS106/111); 1545 *to my mother one gowne walted with velvett*, Collingham (Th19/120); 1559 *a blacke clothe cloke with welts of velvet*, Hipswell (SS26/132); 1572 *one overbodie of satten of bridges, and welted with cremyson velvett*, Skipton Castle (Whit2/330).

welt (2) To roll or turn something over. Thoresby (1703) had 'welt' meaning to overturn a cart or wain (OED) and an amusing by-name had that exact meaning: 1263 *Robert Weltecarte*, Harewood (YRS12/96). To 'walt ovver' has survived in the dialect, and is used when a person turns his foot over, or loses his balance when seated.

wen A wart or growth, a tumour on an animal: 1559 *one grey nagge with a wen in his side*, Wycliffe (SS26/133).

wench A girl. See also quenshe, rail (3).

wend (1) To go, return or depart for: 1428 *to wend to Cawod for that cause* (SS85/9); 1429 *a gude trewman that weendes to the courte of Rome in pilgramege*, York (SS4/420).

wend (2) See wynd.

weng See wing (1).

wer (1) See weir.

wer (2), were A dialect form of 'was': 1555 *the stalles standethe … as they dyd in the ould Chapell or Churche befor it wer removed*, Glaisdale (YAJ37/167).

wesh See wash (1).

western man A term used in east Yorkshire for a man from the West Riding: 1592 *the Survayer was Christoffer Saxton a westoran man that mesuryd the land*, Kirby Underdale (HKU63).

wether A male sheep, a castrated ram: 1521 *ij of my best wheder shepe*, Halifax (Clay60); 1559 *in Pennycroft 20 wedders at £4 0 0*, North Stainley (YRS134/4); 1642 *Weathers are such as have formerly been tuppes but now are gelded; and they are usually called cleane weathers … one as hayth had both his stones taken away [or] riggon weathers*, Elmswell (DW4); 1654 *Fourescore wethers at eight shillings apeece*, Stockeld (YRS161/139). The wethers were kept in flocks by Fountains Abbey, under specialist herdsmen: 1297 *Johannes le Wetherhirde*, Horton in Ribblesdale (YRS16/6). See also ridgel.

wether hogg A castrated male sheep, from weaning until first shearing: 1500 *I witt to the kirk ij wedder hoges and ij gymer hoges*, Bishopthorpe (SS53/175); 1557 *72* *sheire wethers at 4s a piece … 58 olde wethers at 3s 4d a piece … 75 wether hogges at 4s a peice*, Marske in Swaledale (YRS152/102); 1563 'two sheep called *wether hogges*', Aldborough (YRS74/39).

wet leather Of uncertain meaning but contrasted with 'leather well tanned and curried', so probably leather still wet from the currying process: 1627 'They are not to make wares of *English leather wett curried*', Beverley (YRS84/79).

wey A measure for dry goods, with values determined by the commodity. It was used particularly for salt in Yorkshire: 1395 *Item pro j wey salis albi xxiijs [Item for 1 wey of white salt 23s]*, Whitby (SS72/620); 1453 *12 weygh salis*, Hull (YRS144/3); 1642 *20 wey of Salte for Thomas Rickaby*, Bridlington (BCP178); 1678 *In the Salt Ding 8 weigh of salt, £20*, Selby (YRS47/42). See also waw.

whale To beat, thrash or flog: 1736 *I whaled thee bravely*, Baildon (QS1/76/2).

wharell, wharl, wherelle These are local variations of 'quarrel' in the sense of quarry or stone-pit, and they occur from the fourteenth century: 1379 *Thomas de Wharell*, Sherburn in Elmet (PTWR); 1422 *free entre and issue to … the wherelle of Sedbury, and to the qwerelle of Rysedale berkes*, Catterick (NRQS3/34–5); 1500 *North Hall wharellys*, Leeds (Th57/25). The diarist Abraham Shackleton of Keighley wrote in 1794 9 October that he *helped to delve at the wharls* (ASh) – a spelling almost identical with one in Westmorland in the EDD where a reference to a quarry was qualified with the words 'or wharle as we call it' (1825).

wharrell See harled.

wharter A regional spelling of quarter: 1515 *a wharter of rye*, South Otterington (YAJ36/438); 1530 *20 qwarters of salt yerely … the saide wharters of salt to be delyverede … ever yere*, Great Busby (YRS140/132); 1540 *xx wherters of whet*, Etton (SS106/102); 1658 *thirteen wharters of mallt £16*, Selby (YRS47/124). See also quarter.

whartern An alternative spelling of quartern, that is a quarter of anything, a measure of various commodities: 1724 *nine wharterons of weft*, Gomersal (QS1/63/9). Note: c.1758 *the prise the give for spinning weft … is never above 10d a walltron that is 6 pound*, Wakefield (YRS155/76).

whart saw See quart saw.

whearn An alternative spelling of 'whern', that is quern: 1561 *The Kytching … one pair of whearnes*, Spaldington (YRS134/12).

wheel 'Wheel', more than any other word in the vocabulary of the Hallamshire cutlers, has the power to evoke the great days of the industry. It came into use in the Middle Ages when water wheels on the fast-flowing Don and its tributaries powered the region's corn and fulling mills, but was used from the Tudor period, certainly from 1496 (WPS166), to refer to the water wheels which drove the grinders' wheels: 1542 *My Weyle in letel Sheyfeld Moore* (WPS140). The 'wheel' therefore had double significance and once it was used in the names given to the grinding sites it developed semantically, similar in some respects to the use of 'mill' in the textile area. By the 1500s, for example, 'wheel' was being used of the buildings which housed the cutlers' wheels and finally it emerged in its own right as a local place-name element. The use of 'wheel' for the water-powered grindstones was explicit in the Cutlers' Orders of 1590 which placed restrictions on *personnes usinge … the said mysteryes or scyence of Cuttlers and having or occupyinge any whele or wheles for gryndinge of Knyves* (HCC2).

The term 'cutler wheel' was in use from the early sixteenth century at least, and a fine in Latin records the sale of lands in Ecclesall and Sheffield in 1607–8 *quatuor rotis cultellariis*, surely a scribal rendering of 'four cutler wheels' (YRS53/79). In Harrison's survey of Sheffield, in 1637, the list of *The Rents of the Cutler Wheeles* had more than forty entries (HSMS31–3). The only inventory noted for a specialist grinder is dated 1728 and *All his Concerns at the wheele belonging his trade* were valued at £2 10s 0d (FBH103). Certain title deeds illustrate the different phases of the word's development: 1530–1 'one messuage with one water-wheel built above called *le Southwhele*', Ecclesfield (TWH20/34); 1715 *the other part of the wheel now fallen down*, Hawksley Wheel (WPS6). In 1547, Richard King of Sheffield left his *wheile* to his daughter, and in a footnote the historian T. W. Hall wrote: 'Wheile is an old spelling of wheel and refers to a building used for grinding cutlery' (TWH13/82). Similarly, C. A. Turner noted that 'The term wheel refers to the building housing numerous shafts and belts working from one power source' (CAT17). Several of the word's attributive uses are dealt with below. See also cutler wheel, end (2), quell, wheelhouse, wheelstead.

wheelband Sometimes the band or tire of a wheel on a vehicle: 1557 *In the hag house … vj pare of plow irens … iiij qwelebannes*, Kirkham in Lancashire (SS26/93). The meaning is not always clear: 1647 *I here bought … 2 wheelebands, 4d … 1 pair of sissors and 3 locks*, Sheffield (SS65/4). In the context of cutlery it was the word used for the driving band or belt of the grinding wheel: in 1697 Michael Fox had *a wheelband certain Puleys* at the grinding wheel (IH) and in 1739 George Greaves, scissorsmith, had at Morton Wheel *9 pulleys, 2 horsings … a wheel band, a wheel kitt* (WPS19). See also throw (1).

wheel bed A trundle bed: 1578 *Chappell chamber … one whele bed*, Stockeld (YRS134/48); 1644 *foure Chists one Coffer and a Whelebedd*, Lepton (HM/C/180).

wheel chimney In 1716, John Green of Attercliffe had *2 bandes 1 wheel chimney and some other geers* amongst his *Wheel tools* (IH).

wheel gear A term which covered the tools and implements that a cutler might need for the grinding processes, distinct from 'smithy gear' since the two occur together in the will of Robert Skergell in 1557. He gave to his sons Hugh and George *all his smythe gaire*, which was in his own possession, together with his *whelle* and *whelle gaire* during his 'terms'. Presumably he had an agreement which allowed him use of the wheel, tools and fittings at specified times (TWH16/109).

wheelhouse This word occurs only rarely but it marks a transitional stage in the development of 'wheel' as a term for a building. One document contains the following illustrative information:

> 1587 *here runeth a water called Porterwater whereupon there is a whele sett and a house over yt for grynding knyves and other Iron worke and whether … ther are now standing … uppone Lyttle Sheyffeild Nethermore any house and wheeles in the same torninge with the watter ther runinge and the said whelehowses* (HS4/41).

The by-name and surname Wheelhouse date from the fourteenth century and are associated chiefly with buildings in lead-mining areas, almost certainly locations where water power was being used in the smelting process. See GRDict.

wheel kit See kit (2).

wheelstead The site of a cutler's wheel. A Latin deed of 1549 conveyed land in *Ashyngcar* in Ecclesfield to William Shoter of Wadsley which abutted on *Lokkysley water* and it was endorsed *Whelested* (TWH20/53). Similarly, a deed of 1557 which relates to the same property has on the reverse the words *concerning a Wheel Sted in Ashincar,* but in a later hand (TWH20/58). Finally, an English deed of covenant in 1578–9 described 'one wheel stead and two *grynding stones* in *Asshing Carre*' which were held by John Creswick (TWH20/84). This last example of 'wheel stead' was probably given its modern spelling by the editor but the document seems likely to mark the occasion when the two earlier deeds were endorsed.

wheelwright A maker of wheels and wheeled vehicles, found as a by-name and surname in different parts of Yorkshire: 1308 *Alcok le Quelewrigh*, Hipperholme (YRS36/181); 1346 John *Whelwryght*, Selby (YRS42/188); 1379 *Richard Qwelwryght*, Halton West (PTWR). The inventory of a certain Thomas Dalby was drawn up in 1400 and it lists his debts to a wheelwright for items which relate to a carriage formerly in his possession: *Alano Quelewright, pro lymers, j codd pour le charet, et j sege, et iiij cloutez … et aliis clavis pur le charet [To Alan Quelewright, for limbers, 1 cod for the charet, and 1 seat, and 4 clouts … and other nails for the charet]*, Richmond (SS45/16). In 1504, land in Thornton le Moor was *in the haldyng of Bulmere, a whele wryght* (YAJ6/227) and in Beverley, in 1596, the *Wheale wrightes* were in the guild of carpenters and joiners (YRS84/67). See also quelewright.

where A dialect form of 'quere', that is the quire or choir in the church: 1466 *my body to be beryed … in the where by syde my husband*, Old Malton (SS30/284); 1510 *To be buried in the where of the chirch of Pall*, Paul Holme (SS53/218n); 1533 *to be bered … in the myd ale [aisle] before the where dore*, Halifax (Clay88). See also quere (2).

wherelle See wharell.

whern A frequent regional spelling of quern: 1518 *on par of whernes*, Barkston (Th9/87); 1558 *a paire of corne whernes*, Whitkirk (Th27/195); 1570 *a payer of whernes*, South Cave (Kaner69). Note: 1575 *one pare of whernestones*, South Cave (Kaner90). See also malt quern, mustard quern, whearn.

wherreours Quarriers or quarry workers. In the contract of 1422 for Catterick Bridge, it was stated that *the wherreours brekes the saide stanes and schapels thaim in the saides qwerrels* (NRQS3/35). To 'scapple' stones was to rough hew them and this phrase neatly distinguishes the work of the quarrymen from that of the masons. The by-name or surname occurs from the late thirteenth century, e.g. 1297 *Ralph le Quarreur*, Bolton Priory (YRS154/81) and 1323 *Henry le Quarreour*, Sandal, near Wakefield (YRS109/17). A second *Henry le Queriowre* lived in Embsay in 1379 (PTWR) and his descendants were still in the parish over 160 years later. The spellings of their surname are of interest: 1473 *Quaryor* (YRS132/4), 1522 *Warrear* and 1543 *Wharrear* (YRS145/15,76).

whick, whik These are variants of 'quick', usually in the sense of living as opposed to dead, and they occurred regularly in the north and north midlands, at least as far south as Lincolnshire, Derbyshire and Nottinghamshire: 1455 *I will … all my other gudes whike and dede … to my doghter*, Kirkby Fleetham (SS30/216). In 1505, Thomas Mighley of Leeds wrote *I gyf … my best whik good in the name of my mortuarie* (Th4/10), and in 1699, a Marsden farmer listed his *goods and chatills, booth whick and deaid* (IMF). In this context it is worth noting that cattle and chattels share the same etymology; that is the Latin word 'capitalis'. See also good, incontinent, quick.

whicken, wicken, wickenberry The mountain ash or rowan: 1562 'one *whykkyn* tree in the hedge', Southowram (YRS69/143); 1650 *unto one Wicken Tree standing in the middle of the same hedge*, Cottingley (YAS/DD187). As a place-name element it is quite common, especially linked to 'clough', but few of the examples have early spellings. In Upperthong, for instance, the hamlet of Wickins is first recorded as *Whickins* in 1709: Wickenberry Clough in Todmorden is on the OS map of 1843. See also quicken, wiggen.

whickfall See quickfall.

whicking See quick.

whickset See quickset.

whickwood See quickwood.

whik See whick.

while, whilst Regularly used to mean 'until': 1674 *forced to charge four men to watch him while I could come before one of his Majesties Justices of Peace*, Quarmby (QS1); 1725 *left his apprentice to worke two or three days whilst he came again*, Kildwick (QS1/64/1); 1741 *broil it before the fire while it be enough*, Pontefract (GWK30); 1774 *I suppose he will expect security for the money whilst it be collected*, Holmfirth (G-A); 1797 *leading wheat while noon* when it came rain, Sessay (WM55). See also sweal.

whilt For 'quilt': 1455 *unum whilt et duo coopertoria de melioribus [one quilt and two of the better covers]*, Newark (SS30/179). See also twilt.

whin This was once the usual word for the common furze or gorse. It was a plant with a variety of uses, and many townships had areas set aside where it could be gathered: 1537 'the township of *Hudderfeld* was enjoined that henceforth they will not carry any *fuell called whynnes* from the common of Dalton' (WCR9/79); 1556 *the Parson had whinnes and thornes opon Whitwell More in the Prior ground so many as served his kitchyn*, Kirkham (YRS114/93); 1612 *John Cade* [presented] *for damaging the hedge of whins of a close … called Chester Close*, Middleton Tyas (NRQS2/4); 1620 *John Pease … did burne and sett on fire most part of the firres or whinnes growing on a pasture of Leon. Cleasbie's … to the number of 200 waine-loades … which pasture he hath letten out … and in the same demise reserved the whinnes … for his house use*, Cleasby (NRQS2/227); 1668 *to my sonn … my part of the cart which is betwixt me & and him, leading my wife her turves & whines (during) her life*, Barley (YRS47/87); 1672 *saw Anthony Young take a shirt of the whinnes or furres where it was laid out to dry*, Darley (QS1/11); 1698 *About Hallifax side … they took green whinz chopt them a little, put them in a trough and stampt them … to bruise all their pricles and then gave them to their beasts* (SS54/178); 1703 *by carelessnesse of a woman fetching fyer from a neighbours house and scattering some fyer which got into a whin heap adjoining … the houses which took fyer and burnt down*, West Riding (QS1); 1740 *two capps and one handkerchief … hanging upon some whinns near the house*, Sheffield (QS1/79/4); 1805 *The young shoots of whins or furze are excellent fotherage for fattening horses*, Huntington (YRS142/18).

whip-cord A tough but thin kind of hempen cord, the material used for whip-lashes or the tips of them: 1377–8 *In qwypcorde empt' per eundem ijd [For whip-cord bought for the same 2d]*, Bolton Priory (YRS154/568); 1504 *Two gros off wypcord and a half xxd*, York (SS53/192); 1642 *two peeces of whipcoarde or plough stringe*, Elmswell (DW68). See also qu–.

whipping stock See whip-stock.

whip-saw A frame saw with a narrow blade, used especially for curved work: 1556 *ij old wood chests and a whype sawe, iiijs,* Thornton Bridge (SS26/100); 1653 *did steale one broade axe 5s, one whipp seage 10s; one hatchett 3s 4d, one hand seage 1s 8d,* Almondbury (QS4/4). See also sage.

whip-stock, whipping stock A post set up in a public place to which offenders were tied and whipped: 1664 *All ouer … whipestocke, butts and pinfoulds are … in good repaire,* Ovenden (WCR5/133). In the following year it was referred to as *the whippingestocke.*

whishing An obsolete spelling of quishing, which is the typical early form of cushion: 1432 *to Annas Drynge a rede docer with a banquere and all the whisshyns,* Scarborough (SS30/22); 1549 *to my sones in lawe … a pare of sheites, my whyssynges, my table napkynges,* Halifax (Crossley40).

whisht A word or sound used to request silence: 1689 *she crying out he bid her whisht,* Holmfirth (QS1).

whisk A neckerchief worn by women: 1691 *one black whiske, a scotch cloath apron,* Adwick (QS1/30/3).

whiteclamed For 'quitclaimed' that is released from an action or claim by a legal document called a 'quitclaim': 1455 *and haife also relesede and white clamed all the reghte that I have in the forsaide landes to Jane my moder,* Whenby (SS30/216). See also whittance.

white coal A rare word of uncertain meaning. It may refer to the ashes which resulted from burning the ramell after woods had been felled: 1720 *coaleing the charcoale … and white coale arising from the said woods,* Carlton near Monk Bretton (SpSt).

whitecock An unidentified type of bird, hunted in woodland: 1285 'Robert the Miller … for killing *wytecokes* in the great wood', Ossett (YRS29/195). The OED has 'widecok' as an early spelling of woodcock.

white herring The meaning clearly depends on the context since the two suggested alternatives are contradictory, that is a pickled herring or a fresh herring. The early references here were probably to salted herrings: 1526 *to have vij saltfeych, lx whyet heryn and lx red heryn,* Skiplam (SS83/355); 1729 *they used frequently to give her wheat bread … and white herring made into pastyes,* Stainland (QS1/68/4). Latin references indicate that the term has a very long history: 1377–8 *In v barellis allec(is) alby emptis apud Ebor' [For 5 barrels of white herring bought at York],* Bolton Priory (YRS154/558); 1395–6 *Item eidem de iij barellis allecis albæ sibi venditis xxviijs [Item to the same for 3 barrels of white herring sold to him 28s],* Whitby (SS72/565). White herring were imported via Hull: 1461 *14½ last' allecis albi [14½ lasts of white herring],* Hull (YRS144/41); 1465 *4 bar' white heryng,* Hull (YRS144/78). An early reference to smoked red herring is in French: 1388 *pur j coupill de haranc sor' et vj pisces sals xvjs [for a pair of smoked herrings and 6 salt fish 16s],* Calverley (Th6/204).

white iron A term for tin-plate, that is iron whitened by a thin coating of tin: 1457–8 *In albo ferro pro absconcis, vijd [For white iron for sconces, 7d],* Fountains Abbey (SS130/52). It was possibly an imported item until the seventeenth century (SS130/257).

white leather Leather of a white or light colour and soft pliant consistence, prepared by tawing (OED): 1395 *It. pro factura xj sellarum … de canwas pro eisdem … pro whitlethir* *pro eisdem* [*Item for making 11 saddles ... for canvas for them ... for white leather for them*], Whitby (SS72/614); 1465 *1 bar' de whiteleder tewed* [imported from Leith into Hull] (YRS144/83); 1532 *one halffe dacre of whit ledder*, Fountains Abbey (YRS140/242); 1579 *Mr Maior for a pece of whytt leather 6d*, Beverley (YRS84/24): 1583 *Rec. of the Glovers for 3 haulf hides of whyte leather taken of one dwelling about Skarbrough 10d*, Beverley (YRS84/32). Latin texts indicate that it has a much longer history: 1299–1300 *In albo coreo, cordis ... et canabo* [for white leather, cords ... and hemp], Bolton Priory (YRS154/106). See also taw, whittawer.

white-limer A plasterer. A woman arrested in the West Riding in 1754, as a vagrant, said that aged 19 *she married John Wood of Burnley, plaisterer or whitelimer* (QS1/93/2). Note: 1333 *Willelmus Whitebrow, plasterer*, York (SS96/28).

white metal Used of various alloys which owe their light grey colour to lead, tin or zinc. It was made use of in the cutlery trade by buttonmakers in particular: in 1726 Stainforth Jennings, a Sheffield barber, had *one Gro*[ss] *of White mettle buttons* for sale (IH).

whitening stone A kind of stone used for the final stage of grinding, of a finer texture than those used generally: 1587 *a delf of whiting stone*, Brincliffe Edge (HS4). In 1714, the inventory of Henry Shaw, a Wadsley grinder, noted *part of Whitning stone* and in 1755 Joseph Swallow of Stannington had *in the Wheel ... a Whitning Stone* valued at five shillings (IH).

whitesmith It has two meanings but is generally used of a tinsmith, that is a worker in 'white iron'. Rather more loosely it was applied also to those workmen who 'finished' off metal goods, as opposed to those who forged them (OED). As an occupational term it is on record from 1302, much earlier than 'blacksmith'. Examples in Sheffield are later: 1700 *fil' [son of] Joh'is Kirke white smith* (PR4/180).

whitethorn The traditional hedgerow tree in many parts of Yorkshire: 1755 *the advantages arising from Inclosures have been long experienced in this Parish. The Fence is white Thorn and thrives greatly with us, being often cut and kept in repair*, Mirfield (WDP1/192). See also quickfall, sallow.

white wood Trees with light-coloured wood, a term generally used to describe the lime, the white poplar and the wayfaring tree (OED). However, there may have been regional differences: 1763 *White Wood as Firrs, Ash, Elm ... to be sold & felled*, Esholt (MD93/19).

whittance For acquittance: 1547 *I will that myne executores ... paie vnto Richarde Morton ... xxs whiche my sone Robert Webster owe to the said Richarde ... and then the saide Richard Morton shall giue to my said sone ... a whittance*, Great Preston (Th19/184). See also whiteclamed.

whittawer The worker responsible for producing white leather from hides and skins. Several alternative forms were recorded in York: 1384 *Joh. Prychet, whit-lether-tewer*; 1469 *Johannes Kyrkeby, whitewer*; 1488 *Henricus Laburn, tewer de le whiteledder*, York (SS96/82,189,214). Examples elsewhere include: 1577 *Robert Gamble, Methley, white tawer* (YRS19/59); 1707 *Thomas Butterwick, whittawer*, Yarm (MD302/9). See also taw, tew, white leather.

whittle A knife: 1617 *cuttinge flayle swipples with a knyfe and great whittle*, Brandsby (NYRO44/148); 1686 *did ... come out of his shop with a drawne whitle in his hand*, Sedbergh (QS1/26/1). See also thwittle.

whole coal See unwrought.

whole deal This term occurs in a context where it is contrasted with 'half deals': 1678 *In the Dealhouse, 1000 latts, 60 halfe deales, 7 spars, 45 hole deales, £3 5*, Selby (YRS47/42). See also slit deals.

wholson Bran sifted from flour: *c.*1760 *Wholson (some calls it pollard) is dressed outt of bran. Itt is about the same roundness as oatmal is ground.* The writer had recommended that *one pek of wholson* be mixed with oatmeal and *bean flower* to *make haver bread a cheap way*, Wakefield (YRS155/30).

whone See razor hone.

why, whye A heifer or young cow: 1444 *shall restore … oon hors & oon and twenty shepe and … foure whies*, Birstall (YRS83/45); 1486 *to Jamys my seruant a why of ij yere age*, Felixkirk (YAJ22/203); 1536 *I bequeathe Margarete Grenwod my doughter one whye*, Halifax (Clay108); 1580 *sold to Lanslett of Herwoode vj whyes att 30s a pese*, Stockeld (YRS161/21). See also quy.

why–stirk A heifer up to two years old: 1485 *that William Sparowe have a whye styrke*, Ripon (SS64/277); 1499 *To Alice Martendale a whye-stirke*, Skipton (SS53/168); 1549 *To my kinsman John Cowtus oyn whie styrke*, Westerdale (YRS74/49).

wicken, wickenberry See whicken.

widow See freeman.

widowman An early dialect word for a man whose wife had died: 1550 *Thomas Barrett, Cromwell, widueman* (YRS11/12). The only example noted is from Nottinghamshire where widow-woman also occurred: 1536 *Isabell Demoke, Newark wedowoman* (YRS11/51).

wiggen The mountain ash or rowan, an alternative spelling of quicken, whicken: 1779 *by a large wiggin tree adjoining Mr Radcliffe*, Holmfirth (MD225/7/4/9). It was considered to protect people from evil spirits, and the following reference is from a witchcraft trial: 1674 *they tye soe much whighen about him, I cannot come to my purpose*, Denby (SS40/209). In 1782, an Ecclesfield man's diary recorded an attack of the ague, from which he recovered after six days *Under Bark of Wiggin* (EDH121).

wilf An obsolete regional word for willow: 1613 *tow pieces of wilfe woodd*, South Cave (Kaner250); 1642 *a Wilfe tree that growth in the hedge*, Elmswell (DW43). These are East Riding examples and the Elmswell farmer Henry Best also mentioned *reade-wilfes, white-wilfes and Saughs.* He advised about planting the different varieties of willow:

> *The course that wee take with our white-wilfes and Saughs is to cutte them up by the rootes or as close to the ground as possibly wee can, if wee can but preserve them beinge eaten by Cattle. And by this meanes have wee greate increase of them, for out of the rootes will growe many younge trees, which in 4 or 5 yeares space will come to that perfecktion and bignesse that they will serve for flayle-handstaffes, Cavinge rake-shaftes, heckestowers … as for reade-wilfes, the course … is to take longe branches aboute 4 yards in length and to thrust them into the grownde about halfe a yard … and this should bee aboute the beginning of March. And afore yow sette it, yow are to snath of all the small twigges and boughs, leaving onely the toppe-bough to drawe up the sappe …* (DW127).

See also mosker, Quickstavers.

wimble The OED has definitions for 'wimble' which include small boring tools such as a gimlet, and some of the earliest Yorkshire references are certain to be to similar implements: 1392 *Item lego [Item I bequeath to] Johanni Goldbeter j wymbill et j par de pynsours*, York (SS4/174). In a Ripon inventory of 1485 *ij wymbels* valued at 6d were in a list which clearly included carpentry tools, so these may have been augers (SS64/373). The wimble used regularly in boring for coal was a much heavier piece of equipment and it appears in coal-mining records from the early seventeenth century: 1615 *to the fellow that boared to fynd cooles with Mr Hyll's wemell*, Brandsby (NYRO44/106); 1642 *certain wymbles for cooles*, the property of Mr Stanhope, Horsforth (BAS7/192); 1720 *Pd for Wimbles bitting 2s 4d*, Farnley (MS11); 1739 *some wimbles to boor with*, Whitley (DD/WBE/1/12); 1814 *wimbles and bits*, Honley (G-A). No wimble was included in a list of coal-mining tools in 1840 (BM101/70) which may suggest that sinkers were by then using augers: 1840 *To 34 boring Rods, 2 Chissels, Shell, catch, Dog and double brace head £6 12 0*. See also bore (1), pump (1), womble.

win The expression 'to win coal' is met with in many mining contexts but its history is far from straightforward. The verb 'to win' can be traced back to Old English and is on record from the ninth century when the associations were with 'labouring' or 'exerting oneself', even 'tilling the ground'. Only later did it come to mean 'overcoming' or 'emerging victorious' although these are the allusions with which we are now most familiar.

From the fourteenth century, crops in the fields could be 'won', and in Scotland the expression to win coal, stone or other minerals was usual from the 1400s (OED). It was probably a regional term, since the earliest examples in England occur in the northern counties, notably in co. Durham in 1447 (SZ/15). In 1708, the phrase 'to win a Colliery' was used in the north-east (CC2) and the same writer spoke of 'Estates or Lands wherein Coal Mines are wrought or may be won'.

The first Yorkshire evidence dates from the sixteenth century: 1591 *works there made for the getting and winning of coals*, Northowram (HAS31/76); 1665 *freedom to … dig and win coal*, Crigglestone (WCR5/97); 1719 *three bencks wining 3s 0d*, Farnley (MS11); 1766 *whereby the colliery when won may be drowned, set on fire, choked up or otherwise damnified*, Boothtown (HAS31/88). It had 'get' and 'gain' as apparent synonyms: 1754 *workmen … employed in or about the gaining, winning or getting of … seams of coal*, Beeston (WYL160/129/9) but emerged as the semi-official term in the nineteenth century, used for example in the Inclosure Award for Shelley: 1803 *to have, hold, win, work and enjoy all mines of coal*, and in other legal documents: 1869 'I conceive that coal is won when it is put in a state in which continuous working can go forward in the ordinary way' (OED). See also gain (1), get.

Winchester measure Used of dry and liquid measures based on the standards at Winchester: 1710 *a bowle full of toppings and a bowle of hinderends … about three Winchester half strikes*, West Riding (QS1/49/9); 1801 *the measure shall be the Winchester bushel & 32 bushels = 1 chaldron*, Beverley (YRS122/83). See also Leeds measure, perch, Ripon measure, Thirsk measure.

wind (1) To wind was a verb in frequent use in pits where 'turns' or windlasses were in operation, drawing up coal, water or workers: 1591 *one pitte for the wyndinge and getting of coles*, Northowram (HAS31/75); 1702 *hath known the smoak come up so thick out of the pitt where* [they] *were winding coals that they could scarce discern the scoop*, Bradford (QS1). In earlier centuries, building materials were moved in this way: 1396–7 *Et j auxilianti ad vyndand petras et meremium per iij dies 12d*, Ripon (SS81/126). See also windas.

wind (2) See windle (2).

windas An earlier form of windlass, a contrivance for lifting or drawing, as water from a well, coal from a pit or sacks of grain in a mill: 1379–80 *Et in potu dato diversis auxiliantibus ad le wyndas eadem die 2d [And for pot given to various helpers at the windas that day 2d]*, Ripon (SS81/99); 1582 *j wyndhouse rope with windhouses & pules* [pulleys], South Cave (Kaner118); 1619 *2 cottrells & 6 bragges for the mylne wyndesses xvjd*, Brandsby (NYRO44/170). See also roll, turn.

wind-balk, wind-band Words for a cross beam which tied the roof rafters: it was also called a wind-beam, or collar: 1522 *paid for ij speryse and for a wynbalke, vjd*, York (CCW84); 1527 *Item for iij coppyll spares and the wyndbandes xvijd*, York (CCW119); 1682 *pans or wall plates, balkes, principles, wind bands and wyvers*, Scriven (YAJ16/112).

wind-cloth Probably for window-cloth, that is a winnowing cloth: 1440 *ij wyndclathis iiijd*, Northallerton (SS2/90).

windfall Used of trees or branches brought down by the wind, a valuable commodity. The OED has evidence from 1464 but it is surely a much older term. In 1274, John de Miggeley was arrested in possession of 'four cart loads of boards' in Sowerby forest: they were from 'a dead tree blown down by the wind', but the charge was dropped when it became clear that 'he had them … of the gift of Thomas le Ragged', the chief forester (YRS29/95). In 1300, Roger de Mowbray granted the forestership of Hovingham with the rights of windfall to Ralph Kirketon, *suam forestarium … cum arboribus vento prostratis et ramis et tanno omnium arborum [his forester … with trees blown to the ground and the branches and bark of all the trees]* (NRR2/232). More explicitly, the rights granted to George Buschell in Fyling included uprooted trees: 1518 *omnia et singula lingna vento prostrata ad terram ac eradicata [each and every tree blown down to the ground and uprooted]* (MC362). Windfall had a clear market value: 1307–8 *De ramillis quercuum, alnetis et de alio bosco prostrato per ventum apud Wygdon' et venditis [For branches of oaks, alders and other wood blown down by the wind at Wygdon and sold]* (YRS154/228). Later references in English include: 1502 *divers Fosters* [foresters] *use to carie on hors bak to Scarburgh suche wyndefallen wodde*, Pickering (NRR1/199); 1549 'And to have, in the name of fuel … the wood fallen with wind called *wind-falls*', Scagglethorpe (YRS50/164); 1622 *every woodward maie take Blowen wood or Falne wood within his walkes*, Pickering (NRR2/5). Fallen trees were listed in the inventory of William Middleton's assets: 1614 *birkes fallen in the woode xxs*, Stockeld (YAJ34/179). In Harrison's survey of the manor of Sheffield is the following entry: 1637 *For Windfall Wood & diging up of Old Roots for Charcoales £103 08s 00d* (HSMS37). See also blown wood, deer fall, fallen, hollin fall.

windgate A ventilation passage in a mine: 1753 *to leave two Pitts open with Windgate and Watergate So as the Said Colliery may continue in a going Condition*, Heaton near Bradford (GRD). See also thirl, vent, waterhead.

windhouse See windas.

winding A flexible rod or withy: 1463 *30 bunch wyndyng*, Hull (YRS144/59); 1617 *tooke a short hande byll from one Sampson … cutting wyndyng in my Spellow wodd*, Brandsby (NYRO44/141). Used as a verb meaning to put the 'winding' in place: 1469–70 'To a wright for *wyndyng* of the Trinity House', Hull (YAJ62/166). See also ring (3), writhing wand, yedder.

winding–cloth Possibly for 'winnowing-cloth', or a winding sheet for a corpse: 1317 'for stealing … a *wyndyngcloth* worth 2½ d', Wakefield (YRS78/186). See also window–cloth (1).

windle (1) An appliance for winding yarn or thread: *c.*1504 *j garyn-wyndyll foytt and the blaytters viijd*, York (SS53/193); 1577 *a paire of yearen windle blades*, North Frodingham (YAJ36/450); 1591 *a yarne windle foote*, South Cave (Kaner161); 1657 *j pare of yearne windles*, Selby (YRS47/48). A by-name, similar to spinster in meaning, suggests that the word has a much longer history: 1275 *Thomas Wyndelester … non venit*, Hipperholme (YRS29/35). See also garn.

windle (2) A measure of certain commodities, mostly corn: 1252 *unum windellum farine avene [a windle of oat meal]*, Flasby (Furn2/442); 1315 'to the value of one *wyndel* of winter wheat', Holmfirth (YRS78/19); 1518 *a wyndyll of barly malt*, Barkston (Th9/87); 1540 *to 18 servants yerely 18 quarters and a wyndyll of whete and 39 quarters and a wyndyll of barly*, Hampole (YRS80/125); 1561 *one windle of barley & one wyndle of pease*, Monk Fryston (Th27/330); *c.*1592 *this yeare I had growing of good rye in the Alanroide xlvj thraves which yelded a wyndle a thrave*, Woodsome (KayeCP). Note: 1286 '*j wynd* of malt', Wakefield (YRS57/167); 1309 'one *wynd* of barley', Thornes (YRS36/194). See also pile (1).

window A characteristic spelling of winnow, that is to separate grain from the chaff: 1508 *sherynge, threshynge, wyndoynge, mawynge and hay-makynge*, Morker Grange (YRS140/232); 1538 *whete … clene dight and wyndowede*, Seamer (YRS102/109); 1612 *a peck of wheat not windowed*, Alne (NRQS1/251); 1671 *was windowinge bareley in a broomefeild*, Lightcliffe (QS1/11/1). See also windower, unwinded.

window–cloth (1), windowing–cloth A winnowing cloth or sheet: 1377 *j window clath*, Hackness (YRS76/129); 1402 *unum Wyndncloth* [sic] *et unum malt arke*, Normanton (Th24/323); 1460 *j cart load of hay … j wyndowcloth*, Sharow (SS64/365); 1567 *14 seckes & one windowe clothe*, Fixby (YRS134/15); 1612 *7 sacks and a window-cloth*, Eccleshill (YRS134/68); 1691 *1 fann, 2 windowing clothes 6s 6d*, Selby (YRS47/4). See also window–cloth (2).

window–cloth (2) A cloth or curtain to put in front of a window: 1562 *a wyndow clothe of whit satten and read velvet*, Allerton Mauleverer (SS26/154). Note: 1731 *one winnowing cloth … one winder cloth*, Spofforth (QS1/70/4).

windower Occupational, for one who winnows: 1540 *to 3 tressheres and 2 wyndowers*, Hampole (YRS80/125).

windowing–cloth See window–cloth (1).

window looker The official who counted the windows in a house when the window tax was in operation: 1791 *Mr Wilkinson the window-looker counted our windows this evening*, Slaithwaite (KC242/1).

windrake A custom of Pickering Forest, considered as an agistment, so possibly the right to graze beasts on fallen branches, either on their way through a forest or on certain special occasions: 1619–21 *The inhabitants of Kinthorpe doe paye yearlie vijs to the graves of Pickeringe … for their winderake there* (NRR1/38–9). A survey taken in the Commonwealth years has the following memorandum: *one Mr Hutchinson doth clayme a windrake in the said West side as in right of the Abbey of Wickham which his ancestors purchased of King Henry VIII* (NRR1/80).

wing (1) The wings of large birds were used as brushes: 1371 *Et in wengges emptis, 4d [And for wings bought 4d]*, York (SS35/9). In 1642, Henry Best wrote: *the man is to stande ready with a winge in his hande and ever as hee taketh out a combe hee is to … winge of the bees*, Elmswell (DW70). See also besom.

wing (2), wing wall The embankments that adjoined bridge abutments were often reinforced and fronted with a stone wall. These wings or wing walls are referred to from the seventeenth century: 1684 *Rampiers and wings*, Conistone (QS1/23/8); 1702 *to make a wing or weare of hewen stone*, Skirden (QS1/40/4). In the latter case the dimensions were given: *one wing wall att the East end of the said bridge twelve yards long and two yards high, with a frame under the said wing wall* (QS1/40/4). See also weir.

wink at To turn a blind eye to: 1627 *whilst poor neighbours got a few turfes* [John Kaye] *winked at, it desirous of peace*, Slaithwaite (DT/211).

winter Used in reference to seasonal rights of pasturage: 1641 *½ oxgang of Wynter stint within the open fields of Hanleyth* (MD217/152). See also fest, summer (3).

winterhedge The dialect word for a clothes-horse. It was formerly the practice to place clothes over a hedge or furze bush to dry but that was not always possible in winter: 1791 *Edmond Dysons wife … having wash'd and gone to the Clothes Hedge with her clothes was found dead*, Slaithwaite (KC242/1). The word is recorded as *winter hedge* in a Holmfirth inventory of 1799 (G-A) and a *winter edge 2 foot 6 inches high* was advertised for sale in a Spen Valley newspaper of 1986. See also whin, wool-hedge.

wipe (1) A regional word for the lapwing (EDD): 1395 *Item pro j dosan partryks iijs … pro j dosan wypis ijs … pro ij dosan feldfars js*, Whitby (SS72/624).

wipe (2) A 'wipe' could be an insult but in this case it may have been a more serious assault: 1664 *for frays and blode wipes we doe nott know of aney*, Warley (WCR5/133).

wiredrawer The drawing of wire is a practice that goes back to antiquity, and the occupation of wiredrawer is on record even in England from the thirteenth century. The earliest Yorkshire references are in York: 1300 *Rad. de Notingham, wirdragher*; 1312 *Rogerus le wirdragher* (SS96/8,15). At that time the technique involved reducing the thickness of a metal rod by drawing it through a series of holes in a metal plate, of decreasing diameter; tongs or pliers were used to pull the wire steadily. By the sixteenth century the craft was established in many parts of the county: 1506 *Garrard Yonger, York, wyrdrawer* (YRS6/192); 1563 *Rauf Beckett, Selbie, wyer drawer* (YRS14/13); 1583 *George Bucktroute … Harewood, wyerdrawer* (YRS19/24). Wire production was mechanised towards the end of the sixteenth century, thanks to technology brought from Germany, and the inventory of Robert Salmon of Sheffield in 1718 records *The Lease of the Wheel and wire miln tools thereunto belonging £100* (IH). There were wiredrawers also in the Derbyshire village of Hathersage from the Elizabethan period, and when Thomas Heaton married he set up business in Sheffield: 1713 *Thomas Heaton Wire-drawer* (PR7/54). See also draw box, wiresmith.

wire hat From the contexts in which the word has been noted this must have been a metal helmet of some kind: 1406 *lego [I bequeath to] Roberto Brid j wyrehatt cum j Carlele ax*, York (SS4/343); 1429 *j wyer hatt harnest with sylver, j schaffe of pakok fedird arrows*, York (SS4/419–20); 1434 *lego Henrico Swillyngton j wyre hatte*, Pontefract (Th26/191).

wiresmith An alternative and rarely used word for 'wiredrawer': 1438 *Johannes Buller, wiresmyth*, York (SS96/154).

wirethorn, wiretree Names for the yew in parts of south Yorkshire: 1657 *my close … called by the name of Wiretree feeld*, Selby (YRS47/69); *c.1750 In these moors is found yew in plenty, which the country people call wire thorne*, Hatfield (YAJ7/206–7).

wiseman, wise woman Although both words might be taken at face value, they more frequently referred to individuals with supposed occult skills, and were used especially of people who might heal sick animals or locate missing objects: 1567 *Robt Garmann parochie de Lowdame … is commonly reputed to be a wiseman or sorceror … he hayth healed beastes beinge forspoken* (PTD199); 1598 *he sent to one Haigh widdowe or widdowe Carr of Darfield reputed wise women to knowe a remedy for his sicknes*, Darton (PTD200); 1657 *Francis Metcalffe of Stanningley Greene, wiseman* (QS4/5/69); 1693 *William Beever whoe the common people call a wise man … can tell where to finde things that are lost … by a booke whiche he calls an alminacke*, Silkstone (QS1). In a court case reported in the *Doncaster Gazette* of 1 July, 1834, John Crossley and his wife denied consulting a 'cunning' man or a wise man.

wisket A regional word for a type of basket: 1686 *In wooll & wisketts £3*, Barnoldswick (YRS118/64); 1693 *In the Warehouse … wiskets, 2s 6d … runlets, barells, empty boxes & other huslements 15s*, Selby (YRS47/22); 1701 *2 whels and wiskitis*, Barnoldswick (YRS118/72). Such baskets were possibly made from a kind of wicker-work: 1650 *one wyskett chayre*, Doncaster (YRS9/18).

wisp A bundle or parcel, a measure of glass and other commodities, perhaps originally wrapped in straw: 1465 *40 wyspe glasse*, Hull (YRS144/78); 1470 *Pro j les wysp vitri rubij 16d*, York (SS35/73); 1530 *for two weyspes of glayse*, Burton Pidsea (SS35/135).

wit (1) To know, to be aware of: 1487 *we grete you wele latting you wit that by sundry reports made unto us we undrestande the faithfull diligence and wise weys that ye have used*, York (YRS103/11).

wit (2) To bequeath: 1393 *Also I wyte for my corspresent the best garment that I for my body ordand*, York (SS4/185); 1434 *I wite to the Trinitee gilde xls*, Ousefleet (SS30/41); 1478 *I witt to the kirkwark of Wakefeld x marcs*, Halifax (Crossley198); 1498 *all my goodes nott wytt nor yeven … I yeve and witt unto my executors*, Ripon (SS64/290); 1518–19 *rasavid of Master Geges wyffe that hyr husband whyttyd to owr kyrke warke iij⁵ iiij^d*, York (CCW74); 1558 *I witt to my mother one bushell of rye*, South Cave (Kaner53). See also bewit, witword.

with, withe A tough flexible twig, as of birch, hazel or willow, used for binding or tying: 1422 *pro virgis pro templis et wethis emptis, 16d [for rods bought for templates and withs 16d]*, York (SS35/48); 1449 'cut *wythes* and other wood', Yeadon (SW158). It is found in early place-names, possibly meaning 'willow', so the *witheker* which is recorded in Bolton by Bowland in the late twelfth century may have been a managed site (YRS87/69). See also alder, eller, withy.

withdrawing chamber An upstairs room to withdraw to, furnished with a bed: 1445 *Item lego eidem [Item I bequeath to the same] j banded-bedd in le withdrawynchambre*, Beverley (SS30/102); 1533 *one paire of bedstokes in the with draught chambre*, Copley (SS106/39). See also wright work.

withe See with.

within A willow tree or, in the plural, a willow copse, found commonly as an element in minor place-names: 1315 'the vaccary of the *Wythenes*', Sowerby (YRS57/74); 1360 'a meadow … in *le Wythyns*', Fixby (YRS63/33); 1539 *John Sutclif of Wethyns*,

Heptonstall (Clay124); 1592 'The *Wythin Carr* pasture', Methley (Th35/124–5). It remained in use as a dialect word: 1697 *carried away a piece of wood called a saugh or within*, Wadsworth (QS1).

withy James defined 'withy' as any species of willow, which is how it is explained in the OED. However, in Yorkshire it appears to be an alternative spelling of 'with, withe': 1563 '2 cartloads of withies', Aldborough (YRS74/37). In 1661, a Glaisdale man was said to be a rogue who *deserves a withy* (NRQS6/34), doubtless a flogging, and in an editorial note Canon Atkinson said '*withy, with* both mean not only a willow rod … but one that could be twisted and would thus become a more stinging instrument of chastisement'. It is found in several compounds: 1550 *one schakill, one plewghe, one fottewethie*, Killinghall (SS104/61). In some cases such 'withies' were specifically made of iron but it is likely that these were seen as an improvement on an earlier willow binder. See also kid, cutwithy, tugwithy, writhing wand.

witword Testament or will: 1393 *And in kase þe that this wytword will noght perfurnysche I will it be a bryged*, York (SS4/186); 1471 *my wytword fulfyllyd then I will that my wife have hal the t'one halfe and my selfe the t'odir halfe*, Beverley (SS45/180); 1491 *Margaret Roberts by her wittword … gaff unto the same Sir Thos Brydlyngton the said girdell*, York (YRS103/77); 1519 *rasavid of Wylliam Prestman wyff for ys wytword vjs*, York (CCW67); 1523 *my witwordes fulfilled*, Heptonstall (Clay67). See also bewit, wit (2).

wiver A long beam, one of the roof timbers: 1527 *ij spare and a wyver xijd*, York (CCW125); 1682 *one well wrought roof … with wind-bands and wyvers*, Scriven. The builder's contract in this case required him *to place his balkes and principle spars soe that the wyvers* [should] *not beare above ten foot. The said roof to be doubly wyverd, both ends and sides* (YAJ16/112). It is on record much earlier as a verb: 1471–2 'For a tree and *stowres* bought for *wivering*', Hull (YAJ62/168). It is said to be a form of 'waver' (OED) but that spelling is late. See also fork, side-waver.

woad A blue dye-stuff: 1258 'the toll of woad (*wayde*) half a marc', Pontefract (YRS12/50); 1453 *6 ton' wadde £30*, Hull (YRS144/2); 1510 *of ylke a town of wadde iiijd … ylke a quart of wade jd*, York (YRS106/32); 1553 *to … my sonnes all my hooll lithowse as wadde, hardasche*, Birstall (Th19/340). See also wader, wadfat.

woake See warping wough.

wold (1) Originally forest land, found in Old English place-names such as Easingwold. However, after the trees had been cleared it came to be used of open upland areas and is on record as a by-name from the thirteenth century: 1254 *John de Wald*, Fawdington (YRS12/39); 1322 *Robert del Wald*, York (YRS102/174); 1370 *Adam del Wald*, York (SS96/68). As a vocabulary item it has remained in use: 1590 *the would was sevred into towe equall parts and halfe plughed one yer and halfe a nother yer*, Kirby Underdale (HKU62); 1600 'that parcel of pasture called *the great wold* between *le greate wowld* and the demesne of *Duglebye*' (YRS126/37); 1619–21 *the agistement of a spacious moorish wolde pasture grounde called Wheeledale, a verie colde and barreyne place*, Goathland (NRR1/49); 1642 *most of the grasse that groweth … on the leyes of the wolds is a small, sparrie and dry grasse*, Elmswell (DW29). It survived as a specific description of the upland region in the county which stretches from Humberside into north Yorkshire. This was referred to as *Yorkeswold* in 1472–5 (OED).

wold (2), would The plant *Reseda Luteola* which yields a yellow dye used by clothiers, known popularly as Dyers' Rocket: 1755 *vetches, rapes and Turnips with Wolds for the Dyers are frequently sown in Mirfield* (WDP1/192); 1760 *Wowlds for dyeing of yellow* with are grown about Wakefild … The farmers grows them so sells them att so much per hundred or by the stone to dyears (YRS155/19). A South Crosland farmer recorded the purchase of Wouldwood seed and would seed sowing in 1815 (GRD). One possible earlier example has been noted: 1390 et ij stane wald, York (SS4/130). These spellings were usual locally but 'weld' is the OED headword.

wolf-fall Probably an alternative for wolf-pit. It is quoted in an account of the farm named Woolrow in Shelley, formerly Wulfwro: 1307 'that field which is called Wolf-falls in which these thieves fell', Shelley (Morehouse94).

wolf-pit A pit in which wolves might be trapped. They feature in Latin in early charters, many without date: 1121 versus Silkstonam per luporum foveam [towards Silkston by the wolf-pit] (YRS25/104); n.d. et inde usque [and from there as far as] Wolf pittes, Pickering forest (NRR1/5); 1278–92 unam acram prati in Wlfepit medu [an acre of meadow in Wolf-pit meadow], Sawley Abbey (YRS87/161). The word was still in use in the fourteenth century but had by then given rise to a minor place-name: 1341 'abutting Est [to the east] on le Wolfepitt', Thorpe Salvin (YRS102/137); 1348 'a rood on Wolpit', Chevet (YRS102/28). See also wolf-fall, wolron-pit.

wolron-pit A pit in which to trap the wolron or wild boar. Noted in an undated thirteenth-century deed: 'one acre of which lay at Wlleronpit, between the land of the prior … and that of William Nobelot', Kilnwick (YRS76/104).

womb The belly piece of a fur skin (OED). In the Act of 1558 it was said 'Two pieces called Wombs shall be cut off of every hide to be converted to sole-leather, commonly called Backs. Both the backs and womb shall be brought to fairs and markets to be sold' (SAL6/137). The term is on record much earlier: 1377–8 liberantur iij cor(ei) ad opus sub celerarii cum v paribus wames per conversum vs xxijd ob [3 skins are delivered for the use of the undercellarer with 5 pairs of wombs for a lay brother 5s 22½d], Bolton Priory (YRS154/569); c.1425 Item for a dosan wames, drissyng coloryng and shafyng als it is a bouen sayd he shall haf ijd (SS120/65); 1465 21 dos' et 9 wombis coriorum vitulinorum, Hull (YRS144/90); 1582 for the potinge, pinsing and righting of wambes and rigges [backs] ij', York (YRS119/63); 1627 'part of any hide from which the sole leather is cut called the woombe, necke, shanke, pole or cheeke', Beverley (YRS84/79).

womble An alternative spelling of wimble, that is a boring tool, used in many crafts, and common in farming and coal-mining contexts. First noted in a goldsmith's inventory: 1490 de j veteri terobro, Anglice a womyll, ijd [for 1 old gimlet, in English a womble, 2d], York (SS53/59) and then in a list of farming tools: 1571 a gavelock and 3 womles, Elmswell (DW233). Sometimes, it was specifically a tool used by carpenters: 1581 payd for a paling womble, Stockeld (YRS161/37). Many different types of wimble are mentioned in the records. See also adge, grope, quart saw, spokeshave, thixel, thwart saw, twibill.

won, wone To live or dwell in a place: 1490 To my wiff the place that I wonne in, the yarde that the hyves standith in and a parcel of a meese, Scrooby (SS53/51); 1512 unto Robert Cliffe the reversion of yeres … which I have in my house I wonne in, York (SS79/39); 1530 lego to Johanne Agawbron wonyng some time in Nonnebrynholme vs, Acklam (SS79/291).

wong See wang.

wont The forms of this word all have to do with customary practice, and it was used several times by Henry Best, an East Riding farmer: 1642 When the Horse close was wonte to bee mowne it was allwayes accounted eight dayworkes; Kellithorpe-greets was wonte to bee a pasture that younge beasts would like very well (DW65,125). More imaginatively, he explained how animals were made accustomed to a new feeding ground: 1642 *The Noutheard hath for every beast jd which is called a wontinge penny. Hee taketh them all in himselfe and perhaps keepeth them a weeke till they bee wonted* (DW126).

wood-cast A pile or stack of wood: 1612 *for building his woodcast and laying his tymber in the Kinges street*, Thirsk (NRQS1/259). In 1796, a Yorkshire farmer wrote in his diary *Cast a long stack in the stackyard*, Thirsk (WM36). See also kidcast.

wood collier In early records the word 'collier' often referred to a charcoal burner: 1567–8 *John Wayed and Christopher Wayde colyeres agreed … to falle the underwood and ockes and saplynges*, Esholt (BAS10//245). However, in those parts of the West Riding where collier could mean coal-miner, the term wood collier had come into use by the sixteenth century: 1577 *Edward Hirste of Smithie Place, wood collier*, Honley (DD/WBD/6/11); 1628 *Richard Coward, wood collier*, Thornhill (YRS35/21); 1675 *Robert Moore of Bradley yate, wood-colyer* (QS1). The term 'charcoal-burner' is on record in the North Riding from the seventeenth century but I have not found any early West Riding references. See also collier (1).

wood geld A payment due to the officers of a forest for wood gathered there. The lands held in the forest of Pickering entitled the prior of Malton to exemption from this tax and also to a range of fines and tolls to which others were subject: 1334 *de Misericordia foreste, vasto, regardo, geldis, wodegeldis, fotgeldis, horngeldis … et amerciamantis [For forest dues, for waste, inspection of the forest, gelds, wood gelds, foot gelds horn gelds … and amercements]*, Pickering (NRR3/107).

wood ground This word was used repeatedly in the survey of Settrington woods: 1599 *Touchinge hir majesties woods and wood grounds in hir lordship of Sittrington* (YRS126/87). It probably distinguished those parts of the manor where there was wooded pasture from the woods, the cultivated grounds and the *wast groundes* (YRS126/96), n.b. *Tymber growing … uppon the woodgrowndes … being butt small yt were most profitable … to sell all her Tymber and underwood And to let out the grownds for pasture* (YRS126/95).

wood hagg Evidently a managed wood, presumably one with 'haggs': 1237 *John de Wodehag*, Flaxley (YRS10/271). It is clearly linked with the following occupational by-name: c.1297 *Matilda le Wodhagg'*, Selby (YRS10/175). See also hagg, hagger, pile hagg, wand hagg.

wood-hewer On record as an occupational term and by-name in Yorkshire in the fourteenth century: 1357 *Item, Willelmo Wodehewer xvjd*, York (SS129/11); 1379 *Johannes Wodhewer*, Headingley (PTWR). Possibly a wood-cutter since no early examples of that word have been noted. However, the wood which carpenters and carvers used had to be prepared or 'rough-hewn', and the wood-hewer may also have performed that task. See also hagger.

wood-house A building where wood could be stored: 1658 *In the wood house, in borde and raile to the vallew of xxxvˡⁱ*, Selby (YRS47/139).

wood-keeper An official whose task it was to oversee the woods on an estate: 1519 *Item that noo wodekyeper take no swyn into the woddys for akecornes*, Selby (SS85/32). See also keeper.

wood knife A short sword or dagger, noted in the OED from the early fifteenth century and said to have been used for cutting up game or as a weapon. In some cases though the bearer used it simply for cutting wood. In 1394, for example, Sir

Brian Stapilton of Wighill left to his keeper a *cutell que jeo solay porter pour le boys [knife that I am wont to carry for wood]* (YAJ8/244). In 1403, William Barker of Tadcaster left his *wodeknyf* to Richard Clerk (SS4/328) and in 1523, Thomas Legh bequeathed to his brother the *wodknyf whiche my cousyng … gave to me*, Rothwell (SS79/164). More seriously, in 1472, *Gerard Melton … stroke a straunger with a wodknyfe & drewe blode*, Selby (SS85/24). In 1566, William Tomson of Sheffield left his *wood knyfe with two knives and a hamer* to his son in law: he was evidently well off, not a cutler, and had connections in London and Wolverhampton (TWH20/71).

woodman Not always an occupational term. In the earliest examples quoted in the OED it could be a hunter of game and even a madman or lunatic. In the sense of a workman employed to look after a wood it is noted only from 1426. However, the following by-name or surname occurred in that part of Kirkburton parish where Roche Abbey had its Timberwood Grange: 1307 *Thomas Wodeman*, Thurstonland (YRS36/79); 1324 Adam son of *Thomas Wodmen* [sic], Fulstone (YRS109/55). The role of the woodman is explicit in York: 1390 *Ricardus Wodeman … Willelmus Wodeman … mensuratores de wode [measurers of wood]* (SS120/43).

wood monger A dealer in wood, a timber merchant. It occurs as a by-name in London as early as the thirteenth century (OED), so the Yorkshire examples are quite late: 1599 'John Hood of New Malton, *wood monger*' (YRS126/9); 1795 *William Roberts and John Parkins of Kirkburton, wood mungers* (DD/T/5/3).

wood pattern A figure from which a mould can be made for a casting: 1761 *Att Rotherham the will cast iron of aney shape provided the have a pattern made of wood to go bye* (YRS155/63). See also patron.

wood stack A wood-pile: 1653 *paid … for the <Riddinge> wood stack*, Stockeld (YRS161/79). See also kidcast, wood-cast.

wood vessel Household utensils made of wood. In a will of 1556, the testator contrasted his *pewther* vessel with his *water kyttes, one chirne, one stande … dyshes, boylles, tubes, and all other wood vessel*, Beeston (Th27/79). It was also used in the plural: 1558 *all arckes and chists with all wood vecels*, Birstall (Th27/277); 1629 *and all others who occupy their trade upon wood or woodvessels*, Beverley (YRS84/81). See also alder, collock.

woodwalker Perhaps a regional variant of woodward, that is an employee who regularly walked in the woods as a keeper: 1616 *Henrye Hall I hyered to … walke woddes and grownds*, Brandsby (NYRO44/120); 1623 *Peter my woodwalker lent me £13 and I owe him forder in wages*, Brandsby (NYRO44/233). See also walk (1), woodward.

woodward The person who looked after the wood or forest, a term in use from the Old English period. The role could differ from one locality to another, and in each community the office would have its own customs. In Pickering Forest, for example, *every severall woodward* might *take Blowen wood … within his walkes but ought to fell none of yt greene* (NRR2/5). It was common as a by-name: 1275 *Richard the Woodward*, Wakefield (YRS29/128) and as a vocabulary item. 1333 *Willelmus Page, wodewardus de Aiton* (NRR2/73). See also windfall.

woodwose A satyr or faun, a wild man of the woods. Reaney has *Wudewuse* as a Yorkshire by-name in 1251. The figures of such beings were decorative motifs: 1381 *lectum meum broudatum cum signis de wodewese et arboribus [my bed furnishing embroidered with devices of woodwose and with trees]*, Durham (SS4/121); 1498 *sex cocliaria optima arg. cum wodwoshes [six of the best silver spoons with woodwose]*, Beverley (SS53/133). It may be that this word influenced the spelling of 'woad-ash', used by dyers: 1520–30 *Item ix ston of wodwys* (SS26/10).

wool chapman See woolman.

wool-gathering The figurative use of this term may have obscured the fact that it referred to the collecting of pieces of wool caught on hedgerows and whins or simply lying in the fields. When such collecting was sanctioned it could be a means of earning small amounts of money but collecting without permission was an offence: 1595 *Item a pair of hoose … 2 pounde of gethren' wull*, Grinton (YRS152/317); 1632 *Woole gathering: A paine laid that noe (man) shall goe to gather any woole at any mans Sheepe fould or upon the more … before seaven of the Clocke in the morneing*, Burton Agnes (YRS74/88); 1688 *never received wages but the keeping of a few sheep and the gathering woole of the hedges with some little milk that the calfes left in their sucking*, Kilnsey (QS1/27/4); 1734 *that none gather Wooll before Sun-rise, for every Default 1s 6d*, Lund (YRS69/98).

wool-hedge A word found only in Leeds, where wool, like clothes more generally, was draped over a 'hedge' to dry. The evidence is not conclusive but it seems likely that such a 'hedge' was made of rails. In the reeve's account for Leeds of 1579–80 mention is made of several *woollrayles*, and a *woolhedge* leased to William *Beicrofte* (Th57/61).

Subsequently, 'wool hedge' is on record in clothiers' wills and manorial court records: 1588 *to my son William my great lyttinge lead, pair of tenters and my wollhedge and all my shope geare*, Leeds (Th1/382); 1650 *James Rider surrenders one peice of ground on Woodhouse Moore conteyning in length 32 yardes & in breadth 12 For a wooll hedge*; 1653 *Wm Taylor … surrenders one Barne one Garth, two gardens two wooll hedges*, Leeds (Th9/63,68); 1700 *Linnen Cloathes … laid out on certain Rails in a croft called the Woollhedge Croft … to dry … she told them … a man had stolen some Cloaths off their Wooll hedge*, Rodley (QS1/39/4). See also winterhedge.

wool-house A building for the storage of wool, noted in an early Wakefield by-name: 1275 *Johannes de Wllehuses*, Sandal (YRS29/25); 1316 *Thomas de Wollehouse*, Stanley (YRS57/141). In the poll-tax returns it was in widespread use, with examples in several townships, for example: 1379 *William de Wollehous*, Ecclesfield; *John de Wollehouse*, Wigton (PTWR). It is on record later in Hull, along with 'wool-porter' as an occupational term: 1377 *Johannes Coke, wolporter pro se [for himself] 12d*, Hull (PTER); 1465 *Hulle strete: The Wolporters for the ocupacone of the Wolhous yerly xls*, Hull (YRS141/111); 1527–8 *The porters of the Wolhous wiche paid at a terme xxs now nothing & thus xxs in decay*, Hull (YRS141/121); 1672 *Robert Downes per Woolhouse*, Brightside Bierlow (HT).

woollen wheels This unusual term had the same meaning as 'unbound wheels', that is wheels without a studded metal tyre. The wheels may also have been padded but I have found no evidence for such a practice. The definition is expressed most clearly in the ordinances of the city of York: 1524 *none … shall … cary any of the said dong furth of the said City with their yrinbonwaines … but oonely waines that hath woulne wheylls or els upon sledds*, York (YRS106/91). Later examples confirm that it is not a misreading and that the term was used over a wider area: 1559 *one cowpe with one whele with iron, one wonne [sic] whele*, Hipswell (SS26/136). The following extract from the civic records therefore makes much better sense if we assume that 'on' in line six is a mistake for 'or':

> 1497 *it was ennacted … that a proclamacion shalbe maid in the opyn market that every denysen and foreyn that bryngez waynez or cartes bound with yren and loden with any maner stuff, except the Kyngs carriage and comez within this Citie upon the*

*Payvement whiche of newe is maid … shall fro noufurth pay for every tyme xijd to
the common well of this Citie; and thei that bryngs wollen on* [sic] *unbound waynes
or cartes and without any naylez with any maner stuffe to be welcome and to have fre
entre and passage,* York (YRS103/132).

The contrast with a bound wain is made in a Ripley inventory: 1578 *a bound wayne
with iron xxxs; a woulne wane xs* (SS104/135). The term is not in the OED but there
is an entry for 'to have woollen feet' which meant to walk silently, as if the feet were
padded with wool. Elsewhere are spellings of 'woollen' which support this interpretation: 1542 *a ston and an half of wonegarne,* Bedale (SS26/31); 1572 *iij wowne gears* [for
a loom], South Cave (Kaner79).

woolman A dealer in wool, or a wool merchant: 1377 *Hegyn Wolman,* York (PTY);
1390 *John de Gysburn, wolleman,* York (SS120/43); 1428 *Robert Appylby, York, wolman*
(YRS6/5); 1441 *John Cardell, York, woulman* (YRS6/32); 1561 *Thomas Wreythe, Ripon,
wooleman* (YRS14/184). Note: 1475–6 *De Roberto Gilmyn de Helperthorp super le
Waldam wollchapman,* York (SS192/146).

wool pack A large bag into which wool or fleeces were packed for carriage: 1445
'Robert Atkinson of Killinghall acknowledges a pledge on behalf of Thomas of
Barnardcastell for the payment of toll on two *woulpakkez* (BJHK89). It was the source
of an occupational by-name: 1377 *de Radulpho Wolpaker,* York (PTY); 1427 *John Lund,
York, woll pakker* (YRS6/107). See also pack cloth to pack ware.

wool-pit See wolf-pit.

wool porter Occupational for the labourer who earned a living by transporting
wool. See also wool-house.

wool wheel Almost certainly a spinning wheel: 1556 *one wooll whele,* Church Fenton
(Th27/45); 1657 *one woule whele,* Hambleton (YRS47/109); 1676 *one woule whele,*
Selby (YRS47/2).

work In 1549, a clause in the lease of Bradley Wood granted the lessees *lawfull egresse
and regresse for theym there workemen and theyr carreges for to worke and cary away the sayd
Woodes at theyre pleasures* (DD/WBD/8/60). This was permission to carry out all
the separate stages of 'work' within the three-year period specified, that is barking,
charcoal-burning, felling and sawing. See also sager, saw-pit.

workboard, working board In smithies of various kinds, references have been
found to a wooden board or table, linked with other furniture, which provided a work
surface away from the anvil or forge: 1374 *unum wyrkyngborde, unum armariolum stantem
super le wyrkyngborde [one working board, one cupboard standing on the working board],* York
(SS4/92); 1490 *De j lez wirkyng-bord cum le deske xxd,* York (SS53/58). Similarly, in
1713, John Shirtcliffe of Sheffield had a *workboard* in his *Work Chamber* (IH). Other
craftsmen had the same facility: in 1503, a York glazier bequeathed *one warkbord, the
best except one* to a fellow workman (SS53/217).

work chamber For clothiers this was a room in the upper storey of a cottage where
the loom was kept: 1624 *one other roome called a mistall and the chamber lying above and
over the same called the worke chamber … and liberty for the standing and being of one paire
of narowe loomes within the same,* Honley (G-A). See also loom chamber, workboard.

working board See workboard.

working tools It is in wills and inventories that we find lists of the tools used in a typical smithy. In 1709, for example, a cutler named Joseph Webster had *2 payr of bellowes A stiddy and Stock, Cow trough and glaszer, £4, 5 payr of tonges 6 hammers, 5s 0d, A pair of Rollers Shears and small working tooles, £1, 5 vices £1 10s 0d,* Sheffield (IH). In 1492–3, the York *founderer* John Brown bequeathed his *wirking irenes* to three apprentices so that they might *continue the crafte* (SS53/78) and in 1544, Robert Whit of Normanton left to his son *all and singler my smyth stuf, as well the towlles and implementes to worke with as also such yren as is maide readie to the working* (Th19/104). There is a more detailed agreement in 1574 between two masons and the Earl of Sheffield's servant William Dickenson: *a Coate also to either of them, the said masons fyndeinge them selves all maner of toyles to worke with pertaining to their Scyence … my Lord gyveing them towards their toyles ii stone of yron* (HS2/189). Some of these implements are commented on in more detail elsewhere in the glossary, as are items such as hammers and troughs if they have a defining first element. See also working tree.

working tree I find no examples of this term in the standard reference works but it occurs several times in documents linked to Yorkshire tanners. In 1658, for example, the final items in the inventory of Richard Wadye of Selby were *The working tree, apron, knife, bill, wood with other huslement* (YRS47/176): in 1660 John Titlow, also of Selby, had *his working tree with the rest of his working tooles* valued at 6s (YRS47/170). In 1686, Samuel Cutler had *In the tan house … 1 working tree and working knife, 1 choping bill,* Selby (YRS47/55). The implement's precise function is not apparent in such contexts but it may have been a section of a tree trunk over which a hide could be draped when it was being 'wrought', similar to the beam used when the hide was converted into a butt, or the scudding-beam in more modern tanneries.

workman, workmanlike, workmanly By the mid-fifteenth century the word workman had acquired the meaning of 'skilled craftsman', and 'workmanlike' meant 'characteristic of a skilful workman'. There is early evidence in bridge-building records: 1422 *quilke forsaide brigge … salle be made sufficient and warkmanly in mason crafte,* Catterick (NRQS3/33). In 1486, Lady's Bridge in Sheffield was judged *after the sight of Workmen of the same Crafte* (HS1/59) and in 1579, Elland Bridge had to be *finished in a workmanlike manner in every respect* (BAS6/139). In 1701, Ambrose Pudsay's report on Skirden Bridge began with the following sentence: *And having taken Some Workmen along with me, the better to informe me what work is necessary … Certifie this Court that there must be erected … one new Land Stall, etc.'* (QS1/40/4). The same standards operated in other crafts, in metal work for example: 1475 *dight no swerdes but warkemanlyke,* York (YRS106/179). An Act of 1624 wanted cutlers who were responsible for *unworkmanly wares* to be penalised (HCC7) and entries in the searchers records mention *sizzors unworkmanly wrought* in 1704 and *Searching for unworkmanlike wares* in 1715 (HCC22).

The terms are found in springwood leases from the eighteenth century: 1766 *workmen shall and will in a … workmanlike manner according to the best and most approved method for encouraging the future Springing and growth … cut down and fall the said woods,* Quarmby (DD/T/33/1). This more specialised meaning of the word is implicit in a Lepton by-law: 1623 *that no man take anye Coles … without workmens consent* (DD/WBM). In a South Crosland lease of 1666, the lessees were to leave the pit in good repair and its condition was to be *att the discresion of two workemen* (DD/WBD/2/81). These men were effectively the 'viewers' named by the landlord. An agreement in Tong in 1744 required *the Coale Mines to be left in a Workmanlike manner* (Tong/3/593). See also view, wark, waver (1).

wormstall As a vocabulary item 'wormstall' is defined in the OED as 'an outdoor shelter for cattle in warm weather', and the inference is that 'shelter' refers to a building, such as a shed. The first evidence quoted is in Philemon Holland's translation of Pliny's *Natural History*, dated 1601: 'Drive thy sheepe and cattail out of the Sunne, into some worme-stalle and place of shade'. Wright defined 'wormstall' as 'an outdoor shed or shelter into which cattle retire to avoid flies in warm weather' (EDD), a meaning previously suggested by other writers. The only evidence for 'wormstall' that I have found is as a place-name, and it was not infrequent in Yorkshire. It is likely though to belong to a much earlier period in English history since Old English *wyrmsteall* occurs twice in charter boundaries (PNBk318).

Many people would therefore have been familiar with 'Wormstall' as a place-name long before the word was used by Philemon Holland in 1601. In Methley, for example, a manorial survey of 1592 has an entry for *two closes called Wormestalles* and the same field name is recorded in the court rolls fifty years earlier: 1543 'the *steiles* outside a close called *Wormstall*' (Th35/126,206). A similar reference is found in a Dissolution valuation of lands in Selby which had belonged to the abbey: 1540 *ij closes called the Wormestall Closes cont. ix acres* (YRS13/350). An even earlier reference occurs in an undated charter for Longwood near Huddersfield, probably executed in the first two decades of the thirteenth century: 'fifteen pence which Thomas his brother ought to pay for four acres of land in *Wrmstalhirst*'; that is a 'hirst' or small wood in or close to a 'wormstall' (Font137). *Wormstall Clough* in Barkisland near by occurs in a title deed in 1665 (DD/SR/10/39).

The spellings in the examples just quoted seem to rule out the possibility that the prefix 'worm' developed as a form of 'oumer, umber', as has been suggested, so it would be more logical to take it at face value and link it with Old English *wyrm*. This had a wide variety of meanings and could be applied to animals as diverse as toads and hunting dogs, for example: 1514 *grewhondis and ratches and other smale wormys*, Moor Monckton (YRS41/168). As a common place-name, 'Wormstall' may originally have meant something like 'worm-place' or 'unpleasant creature-place'.

If that is so, it raises a question about how we interpret Holland's 'worme-stalle' (1601) which has been taken to refer to a building. Perhaps it was simply reinforcing 'place of shade', extending its meaning to 'secluded' or 'out-of-the-way'. Markham used the word to mean a 'shelter' or shed in 1613 and this definition is one that many writers seem to have relied on ever since. It may be a scholarly invention.

worry To kill by strangling or biting the throat: 1554 'Penalty on Robt Peas & all others who have any dogs called *sheepworiers*', Methley (Th35/212).

worsted A woollen fabric made from well-twisted yarn spun of long-staple wool, combed to lay the fibres parallel. Examples from 1296 confirm the derivation from the village of Worstead in Norfolk (OED). In Yorkshire, the evidence dates from the early fourteenth century, and John Lister considered that 'worsted beds' was really a reference to blankets: 1310 *sayes of Worstede* (YRS64/x); 1347 *mon vieil lit d rouge worstede [my old red worsted bed blanket]* (SS4/43); 1401 '1 piece of *wersted*', Hull (YRS64/27); 1455 *vj qwisshyns de viridi et albo worsett [6 green and white worsted cushions]*, Wighill (SS30/183); 1561 *ij hodes lined with wyrsett vjs viijd*, Richmond (SS26/149); 1720 *put six pounds of worset to spin to Mary Clough of Horton*, Bradford (QS1/59); 1741 *a pair of worstit hose*, Kirkburton (QS1/80/6); 1755 *dyed worstit yarn*, Pudsey (QS1/94/6). It gave rise to a rare occupational name: 1805 *George Saynor, worsiter*, Thornhill (PR).

wort The infusion of malt or other grain which produced beer once fermentation had taken place. Items of equipment used for that purpose were lead vessels and stone troughs: 1396 *quatuor wortledes*, Hedon (ERAS10/6); 1423 *Et de xlviijs receptis pro xij worteledes parvis et multum usitatis [And for 48s received for 12 wort leads, small and much used]*, York (SS45/80); 1440 *j maskfat & j wortstan*, Northallerton (SS2/90); 1444 *ij wortledes clausa in j fornas [2 wort leads enclosed in 1 furnace]*, Beverley (SS30/100); 1510 *a wort stoon*, Ecclesfield (PR); 1542 *a maskefatt … a wortston*, Bedale (SS26/30); 1544 *towe worte leades … towe stone work* [sic] *troughes*, Wakefield (Th19/116); 1571 *a brewing lead a maskingphat a woort trowyght*, Elmswell (DW232). See also sweet wort.

wortle An implement used in the drawing of wire: 1546 *to John Hutchenson my best wordle and all Instrumentes therto belonging*, Methley (Th19/174).

wough A partition or internal wall. The OED has numerous examples from the Old English period, with a score or more different spellings. The form quoted here was emerging by the fourteenth century and Wycliffe (1382) has 'a boowid woughe'. It was a not uncommon word into the seventeenth century: 1575 'the east side of a *Bordeshutt woghe*' Halifax (HAS37/123); 1594 *the north end of the barn … divided by one woughe from the residue*, Hopton (YRS39/91). Compound terms provide evidence of the construction materials used: 1609 *le Bordshott woughe*, Hipperholme (WCR11/170); 1627 *the West end … of one lathe or barn containing two bayes … which was lately divided from the East end … with a rysed woghe*, Allerton (MD178); 1630 *one stud woughe devydinge the housbody from the upper end*, Honley (YDK130); 1634 *one watled wanded or rised woghe*, Addingham (GRD). See also rised wough, warping wough.

would See wold (2).

wouse See ooze.

wrack, wreck These are alternative spellings of a word which has a long history in Yorkshire, certainly from the early thirteenth century, since the privileges of the church of Ripon in 1228 included *wrek*, in this sense things lost at sea and whatever was cast up on the shore (SS74/52). It included whales, even as late as the seventeenth century: in 1666 eleven North Riding men were charged at the Quarter Sessions with *taking a whale and other wrecke* (NRQS6/101).

In the sense of river debris it is noted in a Barkisland lease of 1580 which granted the tenant *libertie to skower, clense and empyte the … Streame … from all manner of Sande, wreacke and other noisome things* (HM/B/140). Similarly, payments were made at the North Riding Quarter Sessions in 1743 to William Bielby 'for clearing away the wreck from How and Kirby Misperton Bridges', and the editor noted that in the swift-flowing becks of North Yorkshire he had seen timber and branches of trees carried along by floods of even 'ordinary dimensions' (NRQS1/242). In 1782, the minister at Slaithwaite recorded in his diary: *a heavy storm of Lightning Thunder and Rain. The little Brook before our House was very rapid … it broke down Part of Daniel Eagland's Field Wall and left a great Wreck Heap in Horsfall's Pit* (KC242/1).

Entries in the court rolls of Wakefield manor record the word in 1339–40, beginning with an inquiry into 'five acres of *Wreke* in Pokenale' deposited by the River Calder. The matter dragged on for some time and the amount had decreased to three acres by July 1340, presumably after efforts had been made to restore the land to normal use (WCR12/148,240). '*Pokenale*' is the early spelling of Pugneys in Sandal, where an extensive lake is now the focal point of a country park which serves Wakefield. The word occurs as a verb in a report of 1688 about flood damage at Addingham:

> *And soe it was that about a yeare agoe there fell on a sudden such a violent storme and tempest of raine that the said river was soe great that it did most wonderfully overflow the bankes, tooke downe the said bridge, broak the weares in severall places, endangering severall houses and families and spoiled many meadows to the great loss of the inhabitants, being put to great charges in the repairing the weares and making up the bankes againe as also in making the streets and places passable wher the water had soe wrackt and worne* (QS1/27/4).

It is not an isolated example. In 1634, Thomas Sandal was paid for work on the paving of Rotherham Bridge, *where the water had wreckt up* (OED) and *c.*1685 a Conistone farmer wrote in his accounts of *Corrupt ground Which hath been flouded or wrecced* (RW10). In 1860, when Queen Street in Huddersfield, was flooded, the drains were said to be *wrecked up* (KMT18/2/3/2/2). It is likely that damage occurred in some such cases but that meaning is not necessarily implicit in this use of 'to wreck'. The emphasis seems to be on the accumulation of wreck or debris by the flooding water. According to Canon Atkinson, 'wrack' or 'wreck' were words used for sea-weed in all the maritime parts of Cleveland, and he understood them to mean 'that which is cast ashore'. In 1654, a Brotton yeoman was fined 6d 'for unjustly taking ten horse load of sea-wreck' (NRQS5/160).

As a place-name element the word has received little attention, although several examples can be noted. In Methley, a pasture of 'land lying at the water of *Kelder*' was called *Wrekland* in 1465 and subsequent aliases confirm the origin, e.g. 1572 *Sandbeddes, Stanilees or Wracklandes* (Th35/182,217). Much earlier, in the court roll of 1365, 'it was presented that the land at *Stanleighs* gains by reason of wreck' although by how much they could not say (Th35/141). Tenants were set the task of deciding on the extent of the 'new' land and separating it from other holdings, and in 1472 an inquisition looked into 'dividing a parcel of land lying at the water of Kelder … in *Stanleis* from land … called *Wreckland* there' (Th35/184). Other Yorkshire names which almost certainly have a similar origin are: 1236 *Wreckeflatte*, Fylingdales (PNNR326); 1576 *Wreckeholme*, Hampsthwaite (PNWR5/131). See also reck.

wraith See rathe.

wrangland In the open field system the unit of cultivation was the strip or 'land' and these were in groups, often known as furlongs or shutts. It was usual for the strips to be long and straight with just a slight 'S' shaped curve but the terrain meant that was not always the case. One of the words used to describe certain strips was 'wrang', a spelling of wrong which was common in Yorkshire and survives in dialect speech. It survives also in the place-name Wranglands Drain in Appleton Roebuck and Wranglands in Holderness (PNWR8). The use of 'wrang land' as a vocabulary item seems to be implicit in a North Riding conveyance of 1613, in which six acres of arable, meadow and pasture in the common fields of Huntington included *a brode wrangland … lying between six narrow wranglands* (NRQS4/143). In South Cave in 1618, *a wrangland of wheat* was valued at 10s in the inventory of John Marshall (Kaner270).

Other references are to very early place-names and they possibly record pre-Conquest uses of the term. In 1202, for example, Robt *de Thorenton* granted to William *de Barton dim. acram terrae cum pert. in Wrangelandes [half an acre of arable land with appurtenances in Wrangelandes]*, Thornton le Clay (SS94/69). An undated thirteenth-century deed mentions *Wrangelandes* in Tunstall near Catterick (YRS65/155) and fourteenth-century examples include *Wranglandes* in Marston near York (YRS50/117) and *Wranglands* in Preston in the East Riding (PNER). 'Wrang' was also the specific element in the undated thirteenth-century reference to *Wrangeflath* in Normanby

(SS83/72), *le Wrangakere* in Everley in 1290–1 (YRS69/45) and the *selion called Wrangstang* in Drax in 1352 (YRS76/65).

'Wrang' could mean twisted or crooked, but the exact interpretation in such place-names remains uncertain. It can be compared with 'crumb', which is dealt with under the headword Crown Flatt, and further research may establish whether the meaning suggested there is satisfactory and also whether the two terms were regionally distinct.

wrangwise, wrangwisely In an incorrect way, wrongly: 1468 *grounde ... that the tennauntes ... have wrangwisly halden,* York (SS85/19). It gave rise to a surname which apparently became extinct in the sixteenth century: *c.*1300 *Richard Wrangwys,* Tibthorpe (SS89/445): 1433–4 *William Wrangwys,* Gilling (YRS63/41); 1505 *Agreed that William Wrangwysche for this yere occupye the office of Brigmaister,* York (YRS106/14). The OED has 'wrongous' as the headword. See also rightwise.

wray See rathe.

wreath (1) A dialect word noted in the *Craven Glossary* which means a mark and swelling on the skin, caused by a blow: 1725 *her back full of black wreaths or markes occasioned by ... whipping,* West Riding (QS1/64/9).

wreath (2) See rathe.

wreck See wrack.

wright A worker of wood, a carpenter or joiner: 1379 *Andreas Wright, carpenter,* Stockeld (PTWR). It was a frequent suffix in specialist by-names such as plough-wright, sievewright and wheelwright, all dealt with separately. Such by-names could remain unstable long after surnames generally were hereditary: in 1404–5 the granger at Selby Abbey had the services of John Wright for carpentry work (*carpentantis*) and his accounts show how he was employed: 'searching in the woods and choosing timber for the mills, and renewing one inner wheel for the upper mill ... and making mill spindles, cogs and other necessities' (SAR136–7). In 1518, in the churchwardens' accounts of St Michael, Spurriergate, payments were made to *Emond Wryght* who was also named as *Emond the wright,* York (CCW69). The wrights who worked on York Minster had their own lodge, like the masons, a place where materials could be stored and they could relax: 1570–80 *For helping to carry into the wryghte house standerdes, powles and boordes,* York (SS35/118). The word was part of everyday vocabulary: 1642 *the weeke afore wee intende to leade hey, wee sende worde to the Wright to come and see that the axle-trees and felfes of the waines bee sownde,* Elmswell (DW37). See also felf, frame.

wright work Used in building contracts to identify the carpenters' responsibilities: 1484 *four chawmeres, two withdraghtes and oon kechyn to bee made ... and fynyshed in all kynde of wryghte worke,* Kirklington (SZ1/543). In 1689, William West was paid £20 *for all the wright worke about Hilcastle house ... and for the balkes and bowses in the old Leathe* [barn], Conistone (RW41). See also withdrawing chamber.

writhing wand A pliant shoot from trees such as the hazel and willow, with a range of possible uses: 1600 *to cutt small writhing wandes for the tying vp of ther cattell and making harrow wythes,* Settrington (YRS126/80); 1617 *a burthing of wynding, watlyng and writhing wands,* Brandsby (NYRO44/146). See also wand (2), wand hagg.

wrought An earlier form of 'worked', that is worked by hand or worked up. It has survived in terms such as wrought iron: 1486 *C markys to be paid like as the werk is wroght,* Sheffield (HS1/59); 1500 *stuff ... longyng to the same craft unably wroght and maid,* York (YRS103/152). When said of a colliery, it referred to the successful winning or getting of coal: 1584 *a coal mine of small value digged or wrought by John Lockwood*, Almondbury (MS205); 1705–8 *they have wrought mynes and coles within the moores or commons belonging to Harkaside*, Grinton (YRS162/32); 1713 *caused several experienced workmen to be sent down the pitt to measure how far the same had been wrought*, Shibden (HAS30/142). Used also in the tanning industry: 1662 *any leather or raw hides wrought or unwrought* (SAL8/69). See also stand (2).

wurdyng Possibly compost from the folding of animals: 1533 *I will that nother my wif then any other tenante yeve, sell or put awaye any strowe, haye, wurdyng, dunge or asse but alsuche thynges to be put to the most profitt of the said ground*, Halifax (Clay89). See also fold.

wynd An alley or narrow lane in a built-up area, often at right angles to the main street. It is found in the north and east of the county and the earliest references are in undated thirteenth-century charters for Yarm: *in venella que vocatur le Crossewend [in the alley called the Crossewend]* (YRS92/136); *in venella jacentibus quod dicitur le Kyrkewend [situated in the alley which is known as the Kyrkewend]* (YRS92/133). Later examples there suggest that the clerk may have been 'translating' a word he was unfamiliar with: 1649 *a vennell or common weind or lane*; 1660 *a common weinde or loaning*, Yarm (MD302/3–4). It is found as a by-name in the East Riding: 1381 *Robertus at Weynde*, Southburn (PTER227) and in some other east Yorkshire towns: 1442–3 'a toft lying in *le Wend* in *Tadecastre* as the road *se extendit [continued]* towards the church and abutted on the high street' (YRS39/164); 1505 *a burgage in Richmond lying in a street called Franchgate … abutting on lee Kirkeweynde* (YRS39/142).

Y

yaff For gave: 1517 *for his licens there to shew hys seid heryng and sparling yaff to hym iijs iiijd*, Hull (YRS45/41). See also yeve.

yardwand A three-foot rod for measuring: *c*.1450 *j gallon, j potell and j qварte, j yerde wande and weghttes*, New Malton (SS85/61); 1495 *ordand that the serchours of the craft of mercery sall serche … all yerdwands and weghtes and messors*, York (SS129/92); 1609 *John Proude … for selling clothe with a false yarde wande in the Kinges Markett*, Helmsley (NRQS1/14); 1641 *having a false yeard wand in the markett place*, Scarborough (NYRO49/9).

yarls, yerls Variant spellings of 'arles' or 'earls', which occurred in the counties of north-west England.

yate The regional form of gate, in the sense of a moveable barrier: 1489 *comaunding hym for to go to Boutham barre and to shet the greit yats of the same*, York (YRS103/39); 1546 *fre entre, egresse and regresse … in and thoroughe the dores and yattes of the Northside and of the bakeside of the saide messuadge*, Wakefield (Th19/162–3); 1573 *Paid xviijd for a pece of Iron for the yates*, Honley (KayeCP); 1614 *Richard Lingeard … for takeinge and carrying away a barr out of a yeate called badger yeate in Calton* (DDMa); 1675 *they parted at a yeate or gate called Standing Stone yeate*, Grassington (QS1/14/1). It gave rise to several by-names and was the source of the surname Yates: 1322–6 *John atteyate*; *John ad Portam*, Wadworth (GRDict). See also dearn, gate (1), lidgate.

yate boot The right to take wood for yates or gates. It was recorded as *Yateboote* in a Cawthorne lease of 1626 (OC7).

yate-dearn A gatepost: 1555 *from the east end of the yate dearne to the east syde of the mystall dore*, Thurstonland (G-A). See also dearn, yate stoop.

yate stead The site of a yate or gate: 1611 *John Cholmeley … for not repairing of two yeat steades belonging to the same farme … whereon no man can passe but in great danger*, Pickering (NRQS1/222). See also gate stead.

yate stoop A gate post: 1665 *John Ouldroyd … to remove a yayte stoope which stands in a watercourse*, Alverthorpe (WCR5/69). See also dearn, yate-dearn.

ychone For 'each one'. See also ichone.

yealand From Old English *ēa-land*, that is 'land by water', a word which gave rise to a number of place-names. In the instance quoted it may be a field name but that is not how it reads: 1686 *all the Yealand lying upon the further side of the Water of Wharf*, Conistone (RW7).

yearing A yearling, an animal one year old, usually a calf: 1549 *Item thre yearyng cealves price 15s*, Marrick (YRS152/70); 1557 *Fyve yering calves xxvjs viijd*, Westerdale (YRS74/58); 1559 *two meares, one horse and one yeringe calf*, Stanley (Th27/272); 1567 *one blacke mayre with a yearinge foole*, Fixby (YRS134/17); 1642 *When wee take gates for our younge beasts wee hire usually for all our yeerings, all our 2 yeare old beasts and but seldome* *for oure 3 yeare olde beasts*, Elmswell (DW125); 1699 *two Twinter whyes & one Yeareing Stirke £5 10s*, Barnoldswick (YRS118/56).

yearn A dialect spelling of 'earn': 1577 *3s that the said Henry shall yearne or addle*, Beverley (YRS84/8).

years For gears: 1555 *my broode lowme with horne wheles, baretrees and yeares perteyning the same*, Thorpe near Rothwell (Th27/10).

yedder An osier or pliant branch woven between the upright stakes in a laid hedge: 1616 *Clyff common hedge … they went far to get ther stakes and yeathers*, Brandsby (NYRO44/113). It was an alternative word for winding: 1618 *I founde a burthinge of wynding or yeathering brought forth of Awmett and sealed in the whynnes*, Brandsby (NYRO44/154). See also edder.

yeffin A spelling of 'given': 1455 *I will at it be yeffin to my moder*, Kirkby Fleetham (SS30/215). See also yeve.

yeld For geld, that is castrated: 1557 *to Beatrix Bruke ij yeowes, ij lambes, ij yeld sheppe*, Sherburn in Elmet (Th27/161); 1567 *Item hogges & yeld shepe 38*, Fixby (YRS134/17).

yeld hall, yele hall For guild hall: 1482 *opynlie published tofore the commones in the Yeldhall*, York (YRS98/50); 1490 *In the Counsaill Chaumbre within the Yelehall*, York (YRS103/54).

yeoman A word on record from *c.*1300 (OED), recorded later in Yorkshire: 1416 *Willelmus Fulshagh, yoman*, York (SS96/125). During that early period, and even into the sixteenth century, the word could be used of a man servant in the house of a person of higher rank, not an independent holder of a small landed estate: 1419 *Item lego cuilibet servienti meo vocato yoman vjs viijd [Item I bequeath to each of my servants called yeomen 6s 8d]*, Halsham (SS4/396); 1498 *to every yeoman of the seid Sir William Calverley to by them a bowe ijs*, Calverley (SS53/159); 1508 *I woll that … all my houshold yomen have mete and drynke a quarter of a yere next after my decesse and ther hole yeres wages*, Clifton (SS53/276). It developed certain attributive uses: 1532 *Grant … to George Coottes of Rascall, Yeoman, every weike whiett leveray loves, xij … also of yoman aile of the great fatt v gallons*, Rievaulx Abbey (SS83/335). The 'livery loaves' are referred to elsewhere as 'yeoman bread': 1430 *8 panes secundarios vocatos yhomanbreed [8 second best loaves called yeoman loaves]*, Selby (OED). See also youngman.

yest A spelling of joist. See also through joist.

yetling Evidently a bowl or pot, made of brass or iron, possibly with two 'lugs' or ears: 1445 *ac j ollam eneam meam secundariam vocatam a getelyngpotte [and 1 brass pot, my second best, called a yetling pott]*, York (SS30/194); 1452 *j ollam, j yetlyng de ere, j pelvim [1 pott, 1 yetling with ears, 1 bowl]*, Scarborough (SS30/162); 1459 *I witt to the house of Feryby for to pray for my saule my long tabill and j yetteling with the eres*, Hull (SS30/237); 1533 *iij bras potts, ij pans with a gottlyng* [sic] *xiijs*, Mappleton (SS26/12). The OED has an example in Durham dated 1378–9 and it is described there as a utensil with a bow handle and three feet.

yeve, yeven For give, given: 1487 *Yevene undre our signet at Masham the viij day of Juyn*, York (YRS103/21); 1533 *I will that iiij' be takyn of the said land yerely for euer and iij' ix^d be yeven and diuided equaly unto all the prestes*, Halifax (Clay88).

yew The yew is commemorated in a number of Yorkshire place-names, for example Ewden and The Yews, both in Bradfield parish. Documentary references to the tree itself are quite scarce but it had a variety of uses: 1577 *I … bequithe to Mr Mathew*

Nevell ij large bowes of ewe, Birstall (Sheard342); 1599 *Item one payre of ewe naves with certayne wayne timbre ploughe tymber sawn bordes pannell bordes & lattes*, Rawmarsh (TWH16/162); 1636 *one little yew table, vs*, Allerton near Bradford (LRS1/88). The wood was certainly grown for ornament: 1674 *4 view trees* [sic] *set about my house Sept. 1*, Northowram (OH3/213). See also wirethorn.

yholster One example only has been noted: 1396 *et omnes yholsters crescent' super ripam de Ouse [and all the yholsters growing on the Ouse banks]*, Scagglethorpe. The meaning suggested was 'willows', after consultation between the editor William Brown and other scholars. It was considered to have a Scandinavian origin (YRS50/161).

ylkon Each one. See also ichone.

yoale A spelling of 'yawl', that is a ship's boat, smaller than a pinnace: 1721 'Leave to make a *shade* [shed] at Grovell to put his boat or *yoale* in', Beverley (YRS122/8).

yoke The contrivance which coupled oxen together for drawing a plough: 1484 *cum temmes et yhokkez*, Brandsby (SS45/293); 1544 *I will that … my two sons … have my yokes, temes, waynes*, Kirkburton (FACcc); 1554 *my best bounde wayne, foure of the best yockes and teames, a ploughe and four of my best oxen*, Monk Fryston (Th27/5). The coupled oxen were then referred to as a yoke: 1539 *I witt to the forsaide Thomas one yoke of oxen*, Woodkirk (Th19/4); 1558 *to my sonne … one yocke of oxen with all manner of waines, plowes*, Burley (Th27/230).

A similar kind of wooden frame was attached to farm animals that foraged, to prevent them from breaking through hedgerows or fences: 1578 *A payne that every manes swine be rynged and yoked before Trinitie next comynge*, Lepton (DD/WBR/12/4). Even geese had some sort of yoke to hinder their movements: 1667 *that no person … doe keepe their swine unwringed or their Geese unyoaked*, South Crosland (DD/WBR/12/13). Similar attachments allowed a person to carry pairs of baskets or pails: 1599 *Three slynge yolkes and one heade yolke iiijs*, Rawmarsh (TWH16/160). It occurs in an unusual by-name: 1260 *Hugh Yoktdogge* of Skeffling; *William Yocktdoeg* of Burton Pidsea (YRS12/79,80). See also ring (2), sling yoke, swine root.

yolstoch For 'yule-stock', a contribution to the festivities at Christmas: 1282 'The same [Peter son of Adam] pays 12d at Christmas which is called *Yolstoch*', Buttercrambe (YRS12/242). See also clog.

you See yowe.

youngman A young man in the service of, or in attendance upon, a person of high rank or an official: 1540 *Henrie Hewton, Sherborne, yongman* (YRS11/86); 1563 *Davy Dallison, Yongman*, Howden (PR). The possible connection between this word and yeoman has been much discussed, in the OED, for instance, and in *The English Yeoman* by Mildred Campbell (1942). See also yeoman.

yowe A frequent spelling of 'ewe': 1531 *a you and a lame*, Kirby Underdale (HKU144); 1549 *Item 20 yowes & lames*, Grinton (YRS152/68); 1567 *Of Mortham Moore in yowis and tupis* (SS26/205).

yower A sheep's udder: 1642 *If an Ewe bee kittle on her yower or unkinde to her lambe*, Elmswell (DW84). See also admonish.

ypocras An early spelling of hippocras, used by Chaucer. It was a cordial drink made of wine flavoured with spices, and occurs in a petition by the spicers in York: 1433 *whare as we haf had wythouten tyme of mynde the sherch of swet wynes alswhele grewand as confect, ypocras, clarre and all other* (YRS106/176). See also hippocras.

Select Bibliography

In addition to the sources given in the Abbreviated References.

Anon., *A Glossary of Yorkshire Words and Phrases Collected by Whitby and the Neighbourhood*, London (1855)

Atkinson, J. C., *A Glossary of the Cleveland Dialect*, London (1868)

Baines, E., *History, Directory & Gazetteer of the County of York*, 2 vols, Leeds (1822)

Bardsley, C. W., *English Surnames: Their Sources and Significations*, London (1875)

Bond, E. A. (ed.), *Chronica Monasterii de Melsa a fundatione usque ad annum 1396 auctore Thoma de Burton*, London (1868)

Brayshaw, T., and R. M. Robinson, *A History of the Ancient Parish of Giggleswick*, London (1932)

Brunskill, R. W., *Timber Building in Britain*, London (1985)

Burton, E., *The Elizabethans at Home*, London (1973)

Campbell, M., *The English Yeoman in the Tudor and Stuart Age*, London (1960)

Carr, W., *The Dialect of Craven in the West Riding of the County of York*, Leeds (1824, 1828)

Cawley, A. C., *George Meriton's 'A Yorkshire Dialogue' (1683)*, Kendal (1959)

Chapman, C. R., *How Heavy, How Much and How Long? Weights, Money and other Measures Used by our Ancestors*, Dursley (1995)

Clifton-Taylor, A., and A. S. Ireson, *English Stone Building*, London (1983)

Coote, C., *Ordinances of some Secular Guilds of London*, London (1871)

Corèdon, C., and A. Williams, *A Dictionary of Medieval Terms and Phrases*, Cambridge (2004, reprinted 2005)

Cox, J. Charles, *The Royal Forest of England*, London (1905)

Crump, W. B., and G. Ghorbal, *History of the Huddersfield Woollen Industry*, Huddersfield (1935, reprinted 1967)

Ekwall, E. (ed.), *The Place-Names of Lancashire*, Chetham Society, Manchester (1922)

Ellis, W., *The Timber-tree Improved*, London (1744)

Fisher, J. L., *A Medieval Farming Glossary of Latin and English Words*, London (1968; revised by A. Powell and R. Powell, 1997)

Gales and Martin, *A Directory of Sheffield*, London (1787)

Goodwin, Rev. E., 'Natural History of Sheffield', *The Gentleman's Magazine*, April 1764

Greenwell, G. C., *A Glossary of Terms Used in the Coal Trade of Northumberland and Durham*, London (1888; facsimile reprint 1970)

Gresley, W. S., *A Glossary of Terms Used in Coal Mining*, London (1883)

Grigson, G., *A Dictionary of English Plant Names*, London (1974)

Hammond, J. K., *A Typescript of Data on Eccleshill Gifted to Local Studies*, Bradford (1975)

Hartley, D., *Lost Country Life*, New York (1979)

Hooson, W., *The Miners Dictionary*, Wrexham (1747)

Hoyle, R. W. (ed.), *Lord Thanet's Benefaction to the Poor of Craven in 1685*, Settle (1978)

Hughes, J., *The History of Meltham*, Huddersfield (1866)

Hunter, J., *The Hallamshire Glossary*, London (1829; facsimile edn 1983)

Hutton, J., *A Tour to the Caves*, London (1781)

Jobson, A., *Household and Country Crafts*, London (1953)

Laver, J., *A Concise History of Costume*, London (1969)

Lucas, J., *Local Studies in Nidderdale: Upon Notes and Observations other than Geological*, London; Pateley Bridge (1882)

Mackay, J., *Key Definitions in Numismatics*, London (1982)

Marshall, W. H., *The Rural Economy of Yorkshire, 1788*, London (1796)

McDonnel, J., *Inland Fisheries in Medieval Yorkshire, 1066–1300*, Borthwick Papers 60, York (1981)

Morris, C. (ed.), *The Illustrated Journeys of Celia Fiennes, c. 1682–c. 1712*, London (1982)

Newman, C. M., *Late Medieval Northallerton*, Stamford (1999)

Parker, J. H., *A Concise Glossary of Terms Used in Gothic Architecture*, Oxford (1846; 6th edn rev. 1882)

Peel, F., *Spen Valley, Past and Present*, Heckmondwike (1893; facsimile edn 1987)

Pollard, E., M. D. Hooper and W. Moore, *Hedges*, London (1974)

Quennell, M., and C. H. B., *A History of Everyday Things in England, 1500–1799*, London (1919; 2nd imp. 1920)

Seymour, J., *Forgotten Household Crafts*, London (1987)

Smith, A. H., *The Place-Names of the North Riding of Yorkshire*, Cambridge (1928; reissued 1969)

——, *The Place-Names of the East Riding of Yorkshire*, Cambridge (1937)

——, *The Place-Names of the West Riding of Yorkshire*, 8 vols, Cambridge (1961–3). The index in vol. 8 covers all three Ridings.

Straus, R., *Carriages and Coaches: Their History and their Evolution*, London (1912)

Tate, W. E., *The Parish Chest*, Cambridge (1946; 3rd edn Chichester, 1983)

Thoresby, Ralph, *Diary, 1677–1724*, London (1830)

Tusser, T., *Five Hundred Points of Good Husbandry*, Oxford (1984). This edition includes the text of 1580 and a glossary.

Walker, G., *The Costume of Yorkshire*, Leeds (1814)

Watts, V., *A Dictionary of County Durham Place-Names*, Nottingham (2002)

Whaley, D., *A Dictionary of Lake-District Place-Names*, Nottingham (2006)

Williams, W. O., *Calendar of the Caernarvonshire Quarter Sessions Records*, vol. 1: *1541–1558*, Caernarvon (1956)

Winchester, A., *Lake District Field-Names*, Lancaster (2017)

Woodhead, T. W., *History of the Huddersfield Water Supplies*, Huddersfield (1939)

Wrigley, A., *Songs of a Moorland Parish* (1912)

Headword Subject Guide

This subject guide (and it is presented as no more than a guide) groups terms that have similar meanings, or that are related to similar activities or objects, under appropriate headings. It provides a further way into the Dictionary that complements the alphabetical list and cross references that form the body of the text.

In choosing our subject terms we have been mindful of the needs of the modern reader. At the same time, we have tried to choose terms that do not do violence (or not too much of it) to the ways in which the words themselves were used by the people who spoke and wrote them. Given that the people who used these words lived at any time from the 12th to the 20th century, this is, in truth, an impossible task. Readers will discover some of the difficulties for themselves as they use the guide, and might arrive at different solutions to those we suggest here. Moreover, as more people use Yorkshire's records, new meanings and shades of meaning, as well as new words, will come to light. We welcome suggestions for inclusions in the online version of this Dictionary at: <https://yorkshiredictionary.york.ac.uk/>.

The guide only includes headwords; it does not include terms appearing elsewhere in the text. Thus, under the heading Plants the terms referenced do not include rue, fennel, parsley, sorrel, marigold (which appears as a headword only as a colour), groundsel, celandine, thyme or gillyflower, which are all noted in an example under the headword hyssop. Readers who wish to find terms associated with places (or other associations not covered here) can search in detail in the online version of this dictionary.

The Guide was prepared after George Redmonds died, so it does not have the benefit of his considerable learning, and is the poorer for that. The work was a collaborative project by Alexandra Medcalf (YHD's editor), Brian Barber (the incoming Record Series editor) and Chris Webb (the outgoing Record Series editor).

Agriculture *see also* Animals; Buildings; Manors; Topography

Arable
acre, aftercrop, arder, assart, baitful, big (bigg), breirding, ear, essart, farm (farmer, farmhold), faugh, fey, field, foldage, goit stock, hacking, hade, hard land, hay, headland, husband, in-field (in-ground), intake, land, louke, marl, math, mell (2), met-poke, mire pits, moldbrest, mould-hill, mow (2), mowburnt, mowstead, open time, quick, swithen, twitchel, yoke

Arable crops, processing
awn, dust (2), fey, foist, grain (1), grave (2), groats, hard corn, hattock, haulme, haver, hopper, masleion, maslin (1), massledine, mastlyonis, mell (2), mislin (1), misslegen, mooter, moulter (mouter, mowter), multure (multure ark, multure dish), musselgeom, poland oats, queat, thrushen, unwinded (unwindowed)

Buildings
day-house (dey-house), dung stead (*see* dung), feehouse, field house, fold, folding, foldstead, grange, hind-house, hull, lair (1), lathe, lock, malthouse, mistall, nawt-house, pinfold

Agriculture (cont.)

Communal
agist (agistment), average (averidge, averish), average gate, dale (2), dole, dole stone, edish, farthing time, faughgate, flat, gate (2), grass, hade, hay, headland, house (4), in, intercommon, jaist (jeast, jest, jist), land, lease (2), ley ground (ley land), mean, outmoor, outpasture, ox gate

Hedges, fences
dead fence (dead hedge), defence (defend), garsil, edder (ether), fence month (fence time), gap, gapstead, haye, plash, raw, tinsel (1), trouse, yedder

Pastoral, dairy
arles, baitful, brog (2), depasture, drift (2), drive (2), dung (dung stead), eatage, faughgate, find, finding, float (1) (float gap, float-gate), flood gap, flood gate, fog, fold, foldage, gang (2), grass, haveling, hard land, hay, herbage, hive, holding, hurdle, ing, ing ground, intake, justment, lease (1, leyes), leasow, lick, loggin, louke, manure (2), meat, midden, moorburn, mow (2), mowburnt, mowstead, muck, muck-midden, on-shoot, outgang, outmoor, parrock, pike (3), rake (1), renew, tallow (tallow cake), tether, vineyard, wont

Animals *see also* Agriculture; Anatomy, human; Colours; Disease; Food; Fishing; Furs; Leather; Plants; Travel; Trees

Ants
Pismire

Badgers
gray (2), pate

Birds
dotterel (2), dove dung, dub (2), dunlin, follower, glede, goose, goose call, hawk-bag, hen call, heronsew, howlet, kae, lanner, lark net, lintycock, moor-cock, moor game, nuthack (nuthagg), neb, papejoy (papenye, papingay), piannet, plover net, poot, pudding, pullen, puttock, throstle

Body parts
arse, fillet, geld (gelder, geldherd), hair (1), horn (1), inmeat, interills, lesk, lib, mouthed, nare, neb, panch (paunch), pudding, rig, shank(s), stove (stow), topping, unlibbed, yeld

Cattle
drape, ear-mark, eat, fallen, farrow, follower, geld (gelder, geldherd), gelt (1), gester, good (goods), hackled, ky, made (2), mess (2), murrain, nawt (nout, nowt), nawt hair, neat, nolt, note, nought (2), nout (nowt), noutgang, noutmaysterman, nowt, overbit, prop, quy, quy-stirk, tag, town bull, twinter, yearing, yeld,

Cattle, characteristics, colour, names
aneling, brinded, crumb-headed (crumble headed), drawn, feather (feathered, featherill), flecked, flowereld (flowerill), garded, golding, gored, greenhorn, harled, hassled, haveling, hawked, leming, marigold, merridew, merryman, mopsy, night-ingale, nutt (nutty), quinter, raggled, tack (3, tacked), tagged (tagtailed), taggle (taggled), topping, twinter, undrawn

Deer
buckskin, buck-stall, deer fall, doeskin, firth, hartskin, imbost, pricket (1), salter (saltery, sawtry), sore (2), teg

Dogs
dog pits, grewend (grewhound), mastiff (mastiff-dog), rache (2, ratch), setting-dog

Elephant
olivant

Fish
hardfish, keeling, kipper, kipper time, ling (1), lob, mudfish, shotten herring, thornback

Hares
hare-pipe, jack-hare, truss-hare

Hedgehogs
urchin

Horses
amble (ambling) cover, farcy, follower, galloway, glandered, hackney, hair (1), hames, hest, hobby, horse-bread, jackass, jennet, jockey, kevel (2), mirk, mop (mope), morel, musrol, nag, nawmbling, nazzard, pack-horse, prick (2), pullan, rack (1), remove, tit, trotter, varon

Horses, characteristics, colour, names
curtal, dapple-gray, dunn (dunned), flea-bitten, girsell, grizzle (grizzled), iron-gray, lyard, rache (1, racke), mouse-coloured (mouse-dun), pullan

Martins, related animals
foin (1), gell, mart (marten), otter fur

Moles
Mouldwarp

Pigs
galt, gilt, grice, hog (2), hoggaster (hogget), measled, pannage, ring (2), rout (1), runt

Rats
ratton bread, ratsbane

Sheep
drape, dundley, ear-mark, ewe-hog, fallen, geld (gelder, geldherd), gelt (1), gimmer, hap, hog (1), hoggaster (hogget), huck-bone, kemp-hair, kip (1), lamb gate, lamb-hog, made (2), morling, mort, mugg, overbit, poked, raddle (reddle, riddle), ret, ridgel (riggon, riggot), rud, ruddle, shank(s), share, threnter (thrinter), trip (see tripherd), tup, tup-hog, twinter, underbit (underbitted), undercavelde, yowe, yower

Snakes
hagworm

Anatomy, Human *see also* Animals
air-pipe, ee (een), harns, issue, lee, matter, neafe, nieve, privity, reins (1), rig, thirl

Arms, armour
almain rivets, arridge (arris), baselard, Carlisle axe (Carlisle dagger), dag, falchion (fauchion), fencible, flight-shot, float (2), glaive, glaze (glazer), gorget, graver, habergeon, halberd, hanger (1), harness (1), hauberk, hinger, jestron, jornet, morion, pauncer, plate-coat, pressing-nail, rack (3), raper staff, rear, umbras, vambrace, ventail

Bridges *see also* Buildings; Travel

abutment, alure (aluring), arch, draw away (draw off water), drive (4), egeoves, fleak-bridge, foot bridge, ground frame, ground work, groyne, guttertrees, head (1), hebble, hoop (1), horse-bridge, jewel (jowel), land-staithe, land-stall, land-stay, limestone, milnebrigg, packhorse bridge, parish bridge, pave (pavement), pile (2), pillar (2), plank, ramper (rampier, rampire), plat, Riding bridge, tree-bridge, trestle, undertake (under-taker), voussoir (vasser, vauser)

Buildings *see also* Agriculture; Bridges; Church; Household goods; Tools

Beams, boards, timbers
ashlar, aster (astre), deal (2), easting board (eastland board, estriche board), ligger, overlier (overligger), pan, rail (2), rigald, trave (traves)

Chimneys
chimley, chimneth, crock bank, jawm, kymnay, louvre, pipe (3), raddlings

Constructing
big (2), brattice, daub (dauber), edify, filleting, newark, parget, point (1), raddling (*see* raddlings), rear, theak, underdraw, underset,

Corridors, aisles, walkways
alure (aluring), eyling, passage

Cupboards
jointer

Doors
door-band, door-cheek, door stead, durn, gemew, (gemow), gudgeon, harr-tree, hesp (2), hook (1), in door, jawm, jemmer (jimmer), out-door, treswold

Fireplaces
mantel-tree

Floors
flag (flagstone), gist (1), jeest (jyst), jobby, joist, plancher, through joist, yest

Foundations
footing, grepp, ground-wall, ground work, table (2)

Frame
cruck (1), gavel, groundsel (groundsill, ground-sole), jetty, pan, post (1), puncheon

Nails
dog, double spiking, huding-nail, lead-nail, penny nail, pin-nail, prag, prod, rose nail, tack (1), tacket, thornhill nails, tingle, treenail (trenail)

Roofs, roofing
cruck (1), damthak, ease board (easing board), eavesdrop (*see* eavesdropper), eize (eizing), ewse, gavel, hip, moss (1), purlin, ridge-tree (rig-tree), ridging (rigging), temple (1, templewand), thack (thack tile), thackboard, thackstone

Rooms in
eyling, fire-room, hall, hall-house, hallstead, house (1), house-body, house of office, house-room, house-roomth, jakes, kitchen, loom chamber, necessary (necessary house), outshot (outshut), oven house, pantry, pentice (pentis), room (1), roomstead, roomth, to-fall, ware (1)

Site

area, ash heap (ash-hole, ash house, ash-pit), dearn (dern), dial stead, dry-stone wall, durn, garden stead, garr, garth (1), gate stead, housestead, kiln-garth, kilnstead, mese (mese stead), messuage (messuage stead, mesuage), pace (2), place, toft (toftstead), yate, yate-dearn, yate stead, yate stoop

Stairs

grece (greces), turn grece, vice (2)

Types

big (1), deal house, ding (2), firehouse, fish house, flaught house, gyle-house, hall, herring house, house (3), housen, house-row, kidcote, kid helm, kill, kiln-house, kirk, kitchen, lathe, lead-house, lear, limehouse, lodge, manor house (manor place), measondue, melting house, ostery (ostre, ostry), packing house, packing shop, peel (2), pier, pit house, privy, ratton row, tan-house, teind-barn (teind-lathe), tempering house, tenting house, tile house (tile kiln), tile shard, tilt mill (*see* tilt-hammer), tip house (*see* tip), tippling-house, turf-cote, turf-house, yeld hall (yele hall)

Walls

abutment, ashlar, butment, brattice, limestone, muck-wall, pan, parget, parpoint, raddlings, rised wough, table (2), through (through-stone 1), tush (tuss)

Windows

jointer, locket (locket-nail), loop-hole, luthern, mullion, quarrel (2), table (2), trellis

By-names, nicknames

blunder, cruck (2), cumber, dagger maker, dint, drunken, dunlin, fine (finer), fishwasher, flawn pot, gourder (gourdmaker, gourdskin), green gate, hagger, hard, hardchaffer, hest, hind (hine), hopshort, horn (2, horner), ironhard, ironmonger, jagger, kempt, kendalman, kip (2), knacker, kyrsyn, lad (1) lick-dish, lig, make-blithe, makeshift, marler, maugh, merridew, merryman, milner, moody, moor grave, mothersoul, mucker, mullock, multure-ward, nought (1), noutfoot, painter, palfrey-man, paver, pelter, pick (6), platesmith, prick (2), pricker (2), pudding, sickle, tallow (tallow cake), thrum, touch prick, treacle, truss-hare

Charity

allmesse (almose, almosse), dalt (dalte, delte), god's penny, half-penny bread (half-penny dole), lake (2), maisondieu, measondue, penny dole, tanten

Chemicals

pick (1), ratsbane, ratton bread, roseager, rosell, rosin

Church *see also* Buildings; Clothing; Customs; Law

Buildings, fittings, fixtures, grounds

alley, earth, eyling, kirk, kirk garth, kirkgate, kirk steele, kirk sty, kirk wark, quere (2), rood, rood-loft, rowell, strinkle, through (through stone 2), vestry, vicar (vicarage), vice (2)

Clergy, associated offices

kirk grave, kirk maister, questor, thuribler, vicar (vicarage)

Conformity, nonconformity

kyrsyn, maumet, quaking (quakerly), recusant, runagate

Festivals, rites, services

allmesse (almose, almosse), antiphonar (antiphonary), arvell, bring forth, earthed,

Church (cont.)

forthfare, gaud (2, gaudy), grail, grave (2), half-penny bread (half-penny dole), head mass (head mass penny), hearse, houseling, kirk ale, lair (2, lairstall, lairstead), lake (2), lay-bed, lyke-wake, min, minning, mortuary, mothersoul, night-wake, nobit, obit, pace (1), pageant, pasch, pax (paxbred), penny dole, portas, portiforium, prick (4), pyx, rush-bearing, trental

Jurisdiction, administration
advowson, affinity, grith, parishing, reck, teind, tendings, voysome

Vestments
alb, amice, chasuble, cruck (2), crutch (2), gipcian, nawb, orfray, tunicle, vestment

Cloth, clothworking *see also* Clothing; Occupations; Tools

Colours
brereball, drab, grain (1), Kendal, lake (1), marble, medley, melle, melly, milk and water, mixture, motley, murrey, plunket, puke, ray, russet, tawne (tawny)

Raw materials, making, processing
coverlet webster, dight, draper, dress, driver (2, see drive 3), drysalter, dub (1), end (4), face (2), fell (2), felt-maker, float (1, float gap, float-gate), garn, gig, hackle, hairster, half cloth, heckle (1), hemp (hemp garth), hemp dub (hemp pit), hesp (1), jersey comber, kit (1), lant, lea (1), lead (3), lead-house, leck, line, line-beater, linen-draper, list (1), listing, lit, logwood, loom, loss'd, madder, moise, mote, noil, pack cloth, pack sheet, pack ware (packingware), pane, paper, peark (perk), piece (2), pill, poss, pruce, raise (1), rate (1), rating dub (rating pit, rating pool), rembland (remland), ripple comb, sind, temple (2), thrum, tinsel (2), tod, tum, twine (2), ulnage (ulnager), undight, unmilned, unrated, walk (3), wap

Varieties
applebloom, diaper, dimity, dozen (2), drab, drugget, felt (felt hat), femble, flock, harden, hemp, hemp tear (hempter), huggaback, garsey, ginger, gray (1), grogram, (gruff), hair (2, haircloth), indurance, inkle, kelter, kersey, lampas, lawn, line-tow, linsey-woolsey, maidenhair, mantle, mockado, napery, nettle-cloth, oakum, oiled cloth (oilcloth), pladd, plight (2), plunket, powdered, puke, rugg, rugged, russet, tabby, taffeta, tammy, taw, tawne (tawny), tear, teld, tick, ticking, tiffany, tissue, tow, tuke, twill, twilled

Varieties named after places
abills, brisel, damask (1 & 2), dornick (dornix), duffel (duffle), fustian, fustian of Naples, Halifax, holland, jeans, Kendal, levant, Manchester (Manchester ware), mantua, musterdevillers, pampilion, penistone, pruce, reins (2), tartarin, turkey (turkey carpet, turkey work), Venice

Clothing *see also* Church; Cloth; Furs; Leather; Occupations; Tools

Accessories, decoration, jewellery
acorn, aglet, amber, attire, coverchief, dalk (dawk), demiceint, fillet, gagate, galloon, gard, gawgeye, gimp, gipcian, gray (2), handkercher, harness (1), hoop (3), jet, kerchief, kingle, lamber, miniver, mob (1), muffler, napron, necklace, nouch, ouch, parchment lace, patlet, pautener, pelerine, pendant, pendle, penner, pinner (2), pocket, point (2), portmanteau, pricker (1), purfle, purl (2), putts, querell, tache, templer, treacle box (*see* treacle), truelove, tucker, turfel

Garments

apparel, gaberdine, imp coat, jack (1, jake), jornet, jump coat, kirtle, livery, loose suit, mantua, negligee, overbody, overstocks, pair, pilch, plight (2), rail (3) reparel (2), rochet (rocket), tippet, upperbody, warkday

Shoes, stockings

clog, double soles, galages (galosh), hosen, mule, nether stocks, over leather, pantable (pantocle), pump (2), quarterdware, turn-pump, undersock (understocking), upper leather, vamp (vampet)

Colours *see also* Animals; Cloth

dapple-gray, drab, dundley, dunn (dunned), flea-bitten, flecked, garded, ginger, girsell, golding, gored, grain (1), grizzle (grizzled), harled, hassled, hawked, iron-gray, Kendal, lake (1), lyard, marble, marigold, medley, melle (melled), melly, milk and water, mirk, mixture, motley, mouse-coloured (mouse-dun), murrey, nazzard, nutt (nutty), orange (orange-coloured), plunket, puke, pullan, qwyett (qwyth), raddle (reddle, riddle), ray, rud, ruddle, russet, rust, tack (3, tacked), tagged (tagtailed), taggle (taggled), tawne (tawny), vermyon

Crime, punishment, social control *see also* Law

amazed, ban, bat, brast, bray, bunch (2), call (1), cry, cuck, cucking-stool, cuckstool, cuckstoolpit, disable, discover, distemper, do, dobbin, faighting (feighting), flite, foin (2), grease, harking, hedge-breaker, huddle, keek, kidcote, knoll, knop (1), mone, naked bed, never heed, nifle, own, pause, phillip, pick (2), prepresture, punch (1), purpresture, put off, race out, rake (1), rip, run behind, sharking, swattle, thew, train (2), whale, wipe (2), wreath (1)

Customs *see also* Church

ale, clog, fairing, garray, gunpowder treason day, nale, nobit, prick (4), yolstoch

Dialect, language, local usage

Adjective

better, crimple, fire-fanged, foist, jannock, lang, leak, let, marish, mean, meet, mich, mickle, middling, midward, novel, painful, paled, peckled, rightwise, throng, tickle, ychone, ylkom

Adverb, preposition

aboon, aboven, afore, after, afterlang, after that, agone, amang, anent (anenst), at after, ay, hand over head, hard by, leave, mich, nawn (nown), nans, nar (narr), nay, ne, near hand, nens, nether, over, overthwart, overwhart, pell-mell, potteringly, presently, purpose, quare (quere), qwerfor, sith (sithen, sithence), somedeal, somewhat, tickle, tofore, wrangwise (wrangwisely)

Directions/directional

agateward, overquart, overthwart, wend (1)

Insults

beggarly, caddow (2), call (1), eavesdropper, flite, gamester, gape, loggerhead, malison, mow (1), snuffle, wipe (2)

Noun

middest, midward, moor grime, overplus

Pronoun

at, ichone (ychone), nawn (nown), ought (1), other, quome (qwom), qwhos, qwycche (qwylk), sich, silk, such-like, ychone, ylkon

Dialect, language, local usage (cont.)

Verb
admire, admonish, awght, ax, bounden, clap, cleam, colour, come to, cotte, deny, ding (1), discover, doubt, drownd, fending, fettle, flaine, flit, foin (2), foist, gar, gleam, go off, gotten, grutch, hang, hap, hing, holden, hug, jangling, keep, kip (2), kiss, kit (1), knep, knoll, knop (1), lading (1), lain, lait, lap, let, lig, like on, list (2, 3), liver, loaden, long, look sharp, mar, maze, meet with, mell (4), mend (1, 2), mind, mosker, ought (2), over press, oversight, pash, pull to, put to, reparel (1), sam (1), shape to, sharp (2), shored, sind, sprout, stay (3), tane, tent, twine (1), want, wer (2, were), wit (1), won (wone), yeffin, yeve (yeven)

Disease *see also* Animals; Medicine
badly, bleb, caduke, chincough, distemper, distracted, falling sickness, farcy, gargil, jumbled, kittle, mange, melancholy, nangnail, pick (3), pick (4), ripple, sickle, sowned, starve, stone-blind

Family, friends, kinship, neighbours
affinity, alliance (ally), backword, bide, dandling, eme, find, finding, god-bairn (god barn), godslove child, gossip, grandchild, grandsire, house (2), huddle, husband, lad (1), lass, like on, mammal, marrow, maugh, mopsy, nares, naunt (nont), neighbour, neighbourhood, outfolk, outman, quenshe, resiant, rustic, shot (1), steem, tabler, take care on, tanten, thou, twilling (twindle), youngman

Fishing
alger, bow-net, dogdrave, ebbing lock (ebbing weir), eel-ark, eel-band, farcost, fare, fish-driver, fish-garth, flew, flot, hack (1), halver, kiddle, kimp, lade-net, lading (2), leap, leister, lime, mask, netmaker, pilch, pitch (1), plodding pole, pod-net, pole-net, room (1), tow-line, trammel (2, trammel-net), trinket

Food, drink *see also* Animals; Household goods; Occupations; Tools

Drink, preparation, serving
ale-pot, ale rod (ale stake, ale wisp), draw-well, gyle-fat, hair (2, haircloth), hogshead, keeler, lead (3), limbeck, mash-fat (mask-fat), mash-rudder, mazer, ostery (ostre, ostry)

Drink, types
cowslip wine, geneva, hippocras, posset, ypocras

Fish preparation
fish house, fish shamble, fishwasher, herring house, lamprey spit, mease (1), offal, train (1)

Food, preparation, serving
ameall (amel), churn, cleam, earn, flake, flick, flight-net, goblet, hair (2, haircloth), hanger (2), keslep, ket, kiln-hair, kirn, kiver, kneading kit (kneading trough), laughton, lie, lithe, mashonger, meat, melder, mess (1), moulding-board, paste board, posnet, reap, ree, ring sieve, shive, steeve, thible

Food, types
alegar, brawn, brewis (1), canel, cut groats, filbert, flawn pot, galingale, ginger, greenginger, green sauce, jemmeco pepper, liquorice, maine bread, manchet, meat, neat's foot (neat's tongue), offal, orache, orange, parkin, parsneb, pease (peasen), pottage, print, pudding, pudding grass, ramson, temse-bread (temse-loaf), treacle, Venice

Fuel, lighting *see also* Mining

billet, bren (brend, brent, brint), brewis (2), broom, cannel (cannel coal), casing, chopwood, coal, cordwood, elding, fire-pan, firwood, flaght, flaught (flawt), flaw, flay, flower, gale (1), glut, kidcast (kidstack), kidware, kidwood, mend (2), moss (2), pricket (2), seave, tapett, thorn, turf-cote, whin, windfall

Furs, skins *see also* Animals; Clothing; Leather

back, beast hide, bis (bish), black leather, black work, buckskin, cony skin, crop (2), doeskin, dog leather (dog skins), fitch (1), goatfell (goatskin), gray (2), hartskin, kip (1), lettice, miniver, mort, neat's leather, otter fur, ox hide, pell, pilch, popel, putts, raw hide, roswek, shammy, shank(s), timber (2), womb

Heraldry

ragged staves

Household goods *see also* Buildings; Fuel

Calendar
clog almanac

Chests
ambry (aumbry), ark, boarden, evidence chest, flanders ark (flanders chest), foot-chest, gardeviance, kest (kist), nambry (namery), nolmary, powder-box, trussing-coffer

Child-rearing
child going-frame, craddle (cradle), going-frame

Clothes care
box-iron, clothes presser, heater, maiden (maiden-tub), mangle, prass, press (1), presser, smoothing-iron

Cooking, food preparation, storage
apple cradle, awl, broach (1), broil iron (broiling iron), dish-call, dish-cratch, doaf trough, dresser board (dressing board), dripping-pan, gallow-balk, gallow-crook, gallow tree, gallows, gawbiron, gobirons, grater, gridiron, grip (2), isinglass, jack (3), kettle, kid, knop (2), lamprey spit, meatboard, mincing-knife, pantry, posset pot, pot-crook, pote (poyt), pottinger, pottle, prig, rack (2), rackan (reckan), rackan crook, range, toast-iron (toasting-iron), tray, tun, voider, yetling

Decoration, hangings
appery, arras (arraswork), dosser, garnish (2), gnat (gnatt), halling, hangings, hing, Kidderminster, knop (2), libard, nat (natt), painted cloth, panel (2), parclose, quishing (quissyne), ridel (riddel), tapet, tester, turkey (turkey carpet, turkey work)

Eating, drinking
apostle spoons, butter coffin, cruse, dais, dish-benk (dish-bink), dish-board, dobbin, dresser (1), flat piece, garnish (2), gripe egg, Holland plate, laver, mazer, noggin, nut, posset pot, trencher, tumbler, voider

Fires, fireplaces
andiron, end-irons, fire-point (fire-pote), fire-room, gallow-balk, gallow-crook, gallow tree, gallows, gawbiron, gobirons, gridiron, hud, jack (3), landiron (1), mend (2), pote (poyt), rackan (reckan), rackan crook, range

Household goods (cont.)

Lighting
flower, latten, pricket (2)

Non-specific terms
by-place, clunterment, hustlement, nifle, truntlement, wand (3, wanded)

Pottery
earthpot (earthen pot)

Seating
lang settle, throw (1)

Sleeping
boarden, half-headed bed, happing, harl, hilling (2), knat, lier, nat (natt), pillever, pillow-bere, press-bed, ridel (riddel), tester, tirl-bed, trenel bed, tronell bedde, truckle-bed, trussing-bed, twilt

Tables, sideboards
dish-benk (dish-bink), dish-board, dresser board (dressing board), folding board, lapping board, novel, trest (trist), trestle

Hunting
conyhay, firth, hare-pipe, hay, haze, lark net, leace (*see* leash), poot, pricker (2), pricket (1), plover net, purse-net, rache (2, ratch), setting-dog, teg, trace, trammel-net (*see* trammel 2), truss-hare

Ivory
ebor, ever, evere, every, ivory, olivant

Landscape *see* Topography

Law, legal matters *see also* Church; Crime; Manors

Actions
distrain, distress, estreat, mulcture, pain, quest, riddance

Agreements
assent, avoucher, end (1), harmless, hedge-clipping, letten, penny town, tack (1)

Courts
apparitor, arrest, assize, assoil, attach (attachment 1), pairater (partier, paritor)

Ownership, inheritance, wills
amend, appraise, bide, bring forth, dalt (dalte, delte), dead part (death part), escheat, farthing bread, gavelkind, heirloom, jointure, malison, mell (3), mend (1), min, nares, overlive, rembland (remland), skift, trammel (1), ware (1), whick (whik), yeffin, yeve (yeven)

Records
engross, estreat, evidence (evidences), evidence chest, indented, iron-bound chest (iron-bound kist)

Rights
annuity, dale (2), deodand, ease (easement), graft, halfendeal, herbage, ladder room, newitie, nonage, rake (1), teind, tendings

Status
incomer, inhabitant, tavern

Leather, hides, parchment, skins, tanning *see also* Animals; Clothing; Furs; Tools
bray, couching, dacre, (daker, dicker), dight, dove dung, dress, dyker, fellmonger, flay,
leather workers, lime pit, malt, mossing, offal, ooze (ooze pit), parchmenter (parchment
maker), peark (perk), pell, pelter, pilch, pruce, pured grey, quyssheld, raw hide, red
leather, roswek, ruskin, shot (3), tan-house, tanner craft, tanyard, taw, tew, undight

Manors *see also* Agriculture; Law

Obligations, offences
affeer (affeerance), amercement (amerciament), coul, eavesdropper, encroachment,
essoin (essoiner), foldage, foldbreak, gavelgeld, greenhew (greenhue), greenpenny,
green wood, ground penny, hedge-breaker, help-ale, hollin fall, homage, mercyant,
milnebrigg, milnegate, multure, noutgelt, over-measure, over press, pain, penny ing
(penny land, penny place), pind, serve their turn, turfpenny, vert

Officers
affeeror (*see* affeer), ale-taster, dike grave, grave (1), graveship, moor grave

Rights
axboot (axbote), cow-gist, edish, estover, fire-boot (fire-bote), flawgraft, graft,
grassfarm, (grasshouse), harrow boot, hay boot (hay bote, haynbote), hedge boot
(hedge bote), kine gate, moor gate, pale boot, pannage, plough-boot (ploughbote),
rail boot (rail bote), turf-graft, twinter gate, yate boot

Tenure
customer, garsom, gersum (girsom), gressome, heriot, husband, main (mainland),
manor house (manor place), undersettle

Medicine *see also* Disease
beast leech, bone-setter, grace-woman, horse leech, horse marshall, houseleek,
hyssop, issue, jalap, leech, leech craft, liquorice, look to, midwife, mithridate, potekary
(pothecary, poticarie, pottecary), tooth-drawer, treacle, treacler

Metals, ores *see also* Mining; Metalwork
acier, alchemy (alcomy, alkaymyne), assidue, electre, ewer, German steel, Hungarian
iron, ironstone, Kentish iron, landiron (2), latten, London metal, maslin (2, meslin),
messing, milan, mislin (2), mistiltyn, oregrave, oregraver, orepit, orestone, osmund, pig,
pig-iron (pig-metal), pinchbeck, ure (urre, urstone), Venice, verdigris

Metalwork, metalworking *see also* Metals; Mining; Occupations; Tools

Cutlery
apostle spoons, dagger (1)

Decoration
assidue, dagger (1), damask (2), lozengewise, mark (2), pounce, pounced, touch (1),
trefoil, unpounced

Edgetools
edge (edge tool), end (3), gilding of knives, haft (hafter), heft (hefter), knife, lancet-
maker, penknife, pocket-knife, spring knife

Making
anchorsmith, anvil-maker, ashburner, assistant, awlblade (awlblademaker, awlbladesmith), axesmith, cutler, cutler grinder, dint, doubler wright (*see* doubler), draw
out, ferrour, file-cutter, file-grinder (file-hewer), emery mill, end (3), filemaker

Metalwork, metalworking (cont.)

(filesmith), fine (finer), forge-finer, gilding of knives, glaze (glazer), goldbeater, grinder, hafter (*see* haft), hammerman, hardwareman, hefter (see heft), horse marshall, inkstand maker, ironmaster, ironmonger, ironmongercraft, lancet-maker, lead-man, little mester, locksmith, lorimer, mark rent, marshal, master cutler, menged, metal-man, nail chapman, nailer, nail seller, nallbladesmith, patron, penknife grinder, pinmaker (pinner 1), planish, plumber, razormaker (razorsmith), riveter, roller, tilter, tinman (tinner, tin worker), tiresmith (*see* tire), trumpmaker, turner, unwrought

Materials

acier, alchemy (alcomy, alkaymyne), assidue, cantle, ebony wood, electre, German steel, Hungarian iron, ironstone, ivory, Kentish iron, landiron (2), latten, London metal, maslin (2, meslin), messing, milan, mislin (2), mistiltyn, olivant, osmund, pearl shell, pig, pig-iron (pig-metal), pinchbeck, red tin, rod iron, Venice

Products

bound, flat piece, gad, hang-lock, hing-lock, hing-pan, hollow-ware, kever, lead (3), lugged, maslin (2, meslin), rind, rod iron, silver-plate, ware (1)

Mills, milling

attach (attachment 2), dam, dam stead, damstones, drough (droughty), dust (2), falltrough, hopper, horse-mill, millstone (milnestone), milne, milnebrigg, mooter, moulter (mouter, mowter), multure (multure ark, multure dish), oil-mill, penstock, pentrough, picklock, rind, stand (2), trindle

Mining

delf (delve), gain (1), get, gin, gin driver (gin gate, gin house, gin pit, gin rope), loose, metal, royal aid, stand (2), thirl, throw in, undermine, view (viewer)

Mining, coal *see also* Buildings; Occupations; Quarrying; Tools

Buildings

gin house (*see* gin driver), lodge

Coal descriptions

Rale coal, ruck, unwrought

Drainage

avoid, drive (1), drown, dry, fire engine, lade, level, loose, open, ring (1), strait board (strait work), sump, teem, thirl

Machinery, motive power

fire engine, gin, hand gin, roll

Non-specific terms

holdfast

Seams, faults

coal-bed, dib, dike (2), dip-side, down end, gall (1), hitch, horse (1), mare, outbreak, rise (2, rise-end, rise-side), throw (3, throw down, throw up), upper end, vein

Surface features

damage, groundfield, ground leave, pit-hill, pit mouth, pitstead, pot

Types

day-hole, open cast

Underground workings
dead work, draw (1), drift (1), end (5, ending), head (2), hole (2), hurry, inset, latch, level, pillar (1), pit eye, pit-prop, plate (1), post (2), roof, turn in, undermine

Ventilation
air-box, air-gate, air-pipe, air-pit, damp, drive (1), hole (2), hollow, pot, smore, stope, thirl, vent (vent gate, vent pit), waterhead, windgate

Workers
apparel, day-work (1), Monday pot, outwork, over work, prick wage

Mining, ore *see also* Metals; Occupations; Quarrying; Tools
delf (delve), dial, dib, dish (2), dozen (1), dredge, drift (1), dross, grove (1, grove hole), groving, king's rent, mallienstane, mere (3), metal, minery, phodre, pit eye, Toppit(t), trown weight

Money, coinage, precious metals
angel, checkerside, cracked, ducat, electre, fine (finer), galloon, gelt (2), goldbeater, groat, jeniuy, more sum, noble, overplus, plack, put off, rial (ryal), run behind, spur ryal, touch (1), touch (2, touchstone)

Music, musical instruments *see also* Recreation
gittern, organ-maker, prick song, virginal

Occupations, offices *see also* Cloth; Manors; Metalwork; Mining, coal; Leather; Social condition; Wood; Work

Acrobat
posture master, topstailing

Agriculture
cowkeeper, dairyman, day (dey), driver (1, *see* drive 2), farmer (*see* farm), feeman (feemaster), feemanlike (feemanly, feemanship, feemastership), gelder (geldherd, *see* geld), grass-guard, grassman (*see* grassfarm), grasswoman, herd (hird), hind (hine), horse leech, horse marshall, husband, jobber, moor grave, mucker, nawtherd (noutherd), neatherd, netmaker, noughter, noutmaysterman, oil-miller, palfrey-man, pannierman, ploughwright, quyherd, ripper

Arms, armour *see also* Metalworking
armour dresser, arrow-head smith, dagger maker, glazer (*see* glaze), riveter

Building
dauber (*see* daub), glassenwright, joiner, kidbearer, limeburner, limeman, painter, plasterer, thacker (thackster), theaker (theakster), undertaker (*see* undertake)

Clergy, associated offices
kirk grave, kirk maister, questor, thuribler, vicar

Cloth
arraser (arrasman), coverlet webster, draper, driver (2, *see* drive 3), drysalter, felt-maker, hairster, jersey comber, linen-draper, ulnager (*see* ulnage)

Clothing, accessories
clogger, girdler, jetter (jet worker, *see* jet), kendalman, litster, pattener, point-maker (*see* point 2), vestment-maker

Occupations, offices (cont.)

Drainage
dike grave, diker

Fishing
fish-driver, fishwasher, netmaker

Food, drink
ale-draper, ale rod (ale stake, ale wisp), ale-taster, dresser (2), Flappit, galopin, gourder (gourdmaker, gourdskin), grocer, maltster, milner, milnestone-maker, milnewright, mustard-maker, oatmeal maker, oat shiller, oil-drawer, oil-miller, pennyman, ripper, temse-maker, tippler

Leather
fellmonger, leather workers, parchmenter (parchment maker), pelter

Medicine
grace-woman, horse leech, horse marshall, leech, midwife, potekary (pothecary, poticarie, pottecary) tooth-drawer, treacler

Metalworking
anchorsmith, anvil-maker, ashburner, assistant, awlblademaker (awlblademsith, *see* awlblade), axesmith, cutler, cutler grinder, doubler wright (*see* doubler), ferrour, file-cutter, file-grinder (file-hewer), filemaker (filesmith), finer (*see* fine), forge-finer, glazer (*see* glaze), goldbeater, grinder, hafter (*see* haft), hammerman, hardwareman, hefter (*see* heft), horse marshall, inkstand maker, ironmonger, ironmongercraft, lead-man, little mester, locksmith, lorimer, marshal, master cutler, metal-man, nail chapman, nailer, nail seller, nallbladesmith, penknife grinder, pinmaker (pinner 1), plumber, razormaker (razorsmith), riveter, roller, tilter, tinman (tinner, tin worker), tiresmith (*see* tire), trumpmaker, turner

Military
list (2)

Mining, quarrying
delver, gin driver, hurrier, pickman (*see* pick 5), quarrier

Musical instruments
organ-maker

Non-specific terms
apprentice, by times, cast (6, cast over, cast up), day-labourer, day-tale man (day-taler), dryster, farmer (see farm), janitor, jockey, labourer, lad (1), lodger, maister, master, mystery, occupy, overman, overseer, prentice, pricker (2), room (1), turner, yeoman

Officials, borough, court-appointed, crown, gild, manorial
affeeror (*see* affeer), ale-taster, assistant, bellman, dike grave, fenceman, field master, gamekeeper, gardener, grave (1), graveship, keeper, keywarden, kirk grave, kirk maister, market keeper, meter, moor grave, multure grave, multure-ward, murmaster, noffisour, pairater (pariter, paritor), palership (palisership), paliser, parker, pasture master, pinder, pit greave, porter, tidesman (tide-waiter), townherd, ulnager (*see* ulnage), umpire (*see* umpirage), viewer

Painting
strike (3)

Rope
raper

Sea, waterways
cobleman, ferryman, keelman, lighterman, master mariner, navigator, netmaker, occupier, tidesman (tide-waiter)

Stoneworking
entailer, lodge, master mason, milnestone-maker, paver

Trade
ale-draper, fellmonger, hardwareman, higgler, huckster, ironmonger, jobber, lead-man, linen-draper, metal-man, nail chapman, nailer, nail seller, occupier, oil-drawer, packman, pannierman, pedder, pelter, ripper, tinkler, tippler, tobacco cutter, upholder

Transport
driver (1, 2, *see* drive 2, 3), fish-driver, hardwareman, higgler, kidbearer, palfrey-man, pannierman, porter, post (3), ripper

Wood, woodlands, wood working
dishbinder, dish-thrower (dish-turner), doubler wright (*see* doubler), hagger, keeper, kidbearer, kidder, kitmaker (kitwright *see* kit 2), lastmaker, lathcleaver (lathriver), milnewright, paler, paliser, pannier-maker, peeler, piller, ploughwright, quelewright, raff-merchant (*see* raff), trellis-maker, turner

Personal attributes, race *see also* Social condition
able (1), amazed, blunder, bown, brabble (brabbler), brace, brisk, carriage, cunning, dandling, dark, deuce, disable, doting age, easterling, Egyptian, face (1), fain, fond, gipsy, holsom, jealousy, keb, innocent, lad (1), lass, loggerhead, mensk, middling, nonage, nought (1), quenshe, rackabones, rate (2), rustic, sackless, sadness, sharking, tawpe, toward, whick (whik)

Plants *see also* Animals; Trees; Woods
brereball, canel, docken, fitch (2), gale (1), galingale, ginger, heath, houseleek, hyssop, jalap, kedlock, kelp, ling (2), liquorice, moss (1), orache, penny grass, pile (1), pudding grass, ramson, rish

Quarrying *see also* Mining
delf (delve), get, grit (gritstone), quarrel (1, querrell)

Recreation, games, pastimes, sports *see also* Music
gamester, gell and spell, gig, guiser, gunpowder treason day, handicap, lake (3), kirk ale, mumming, nine-holes, penny-prick, penny-stone, pitch the bar, play-day, playing-table, prick in the belt, rush-bearing, tables, ten-bones, thimbles and button, tide, trippett, tuts

Social condition, status *see also* Personal attributes
able (1, 2), gangrel, gentleman, goodman, grassman (*see* grassfarm), grasswoman, husband, inmate, keb, lad (1), lass, maister, master, nonage, outfolk, outman, resiant, tabler, tanten, vicar, vowess, yeoman, youngman

Stone, stone working *see also* Occupations; Quarrying; Tools
ackerspike, ashlar, damplade, dress, fillet, kevel (1), lump stone, manure (1), mason, pullished, rag, rough mason

Time
Day gate, dead time, nightertale, piece (1), sennight, sparing, to-morn, while (whilst)

Taxation, fees, imposts
acre tale, assess (assessment), cast (1), customer, gabulage, gald (gaud, gauld), garnish (1), gate-law, grassfarm (grasshouse, grassman), groundage (grundage), hearth tax, husband, lay (2), metage, murage, pierage, pontage, primage, rack-rent

Tools, equipment, for crafts, trades *see also* Arms; Buildings; Cloth; Household goods; Metalwork; Occupations

Agriculture
bray, crab (2, crab-brake), crackle, dock fork, drawing gear, farcost, folding gates, goose call, gripe, hack, (1, 2), hames, harrow teeth, hedging mittens, hopp, hopper, laine, lea (2), louke crook, mould-board, mould-rake (mould-staff), muck-drag, muck-fork, muck-hack, muck-rake, nib, nought (1), oxbow, pickfork, pike (2), pipe (1), pitch (2), plough, provin tub, push-plough, tar, team, tug, tugwithy, tumbrel, turf-spade, yoke

Arms, armour
float (2), graver

Building
brag, brod, brog (1), bunch (1), gullet-nail, housewright, lath-brod, lathcleaver (lathriver), lath-nail, latt, latt axe, lead-nail, temple (1, templewand), theaking-rake, tile-pin

Cloth
damsel, garnwindle, gig, hackle, handles, heald, horn wheel, litting lead (litting pan), packthread, plating-board, press (2), press paper, pressing boards, quilting-frame, slay, spool-wheel, teasel, temple (2), tenter, tenter hook, turn-press

Clothing
neeld (nild), pressing iron, thread

Fishing
alger, bownet, eel-band, farcost, flew, flot, hack (1), kimp, lade-net, lading (2), leap, leister, pilch, pitch (1), plodding pole, pod-net, pole-net, room (1), tow-line, trail (2), trammel (2), trammel-net

Food, drink
alger, canel, cowler (cowling lead, cowling tub), cutting knife, dressing knife, kilp (2), dripping-pan, flesh-axe, flesh-crook, flesh kit, galingale, galker, gantry, grind-lestone, grundlestone, gyle-fat, kimlin (kimnel), maltgrinder, malt quern, mash-fat (mask-fat), mash-rudder, mustard ball, mustard quern, peel (1), posnet, posset pot, pot-crook, quern, roast iron, rudder

Fuel
flaght spade, flaying spade

Hunting
cast (3), conyhay, dog pits, hawk-bag, hay, haze, lark net, net prick, plover net, purse-net, setting-dog

Leather
flaying knife, musrol, nail tool, tallow (tallow cake), tavelin

Medicine
gallipot

Metal, metalworking

anchor-stock, andiron, cutler wheel, cutlery ware, cutting stithy, dam stead, Dansk iron, draw box (draw engine), finery, gad, gig, gloring nail, grindlestone, grinding stone (grindstone), haft, hack-hammer, hammer, hammer wheel, harness (2), hearth, hearth staff, hob, hoop (2), horse (2), horsing, horse-nail, hudding-nail, hull, iron, iron gear, iron mill, ironstone ways, iron works, ironware, lay (1), lead (2), lead-pan, kelsetnayles, kette, mandril, melting house, middle brod, middle spiking, nail mould, oliver, plate-shears, plating-hammer, pounce, platesmith, pressing iron, ragmop wheel, razor hone, razor scales, rolling mill, tew-iron, throw (2), thwittle, tilt-hammer (tilt mill), tip, tongs, tortoiseshell, touch (2, touchstone), ware (1)

Milling

blue stones, falltrough, hopper, millstone (milnestone), pentrough, picklock, rind, ring sieve, sailyard, shuttle, temse, trindle, windas

Mining, Coal

air-box, air-pipe, barrow, board (1), boring rod, chain, clatch, coal-mining tools and implements, coal-pit rope, corf, dial, glass, gunpowder, plate (1), priest nail, pump (1), punch (2), puncheon, scoop, scoop shoes, tally (tally board, tally stick), tar band, tram, trap door, tub, tug, turn (turn-stake), wimble, womble

Non-specific terms

apparel, drivel, ear-pick, engine, even, fire-box, fire-pan, fleak (fleik), gauge, grease cake, grain (2), hare-pipe, handbarrow, hand board, hand-saw, hatchet, heckle (1), helm (helm timber, helm wood), heven, hoppet, hovel, jenne, jess, kit (2), knop (3), leap, lock, loose suit, mall, match, mattock, maund, mell (1), nipping irons, packthread, parser, parser bitt, penknife, piggin, pipe (3), pitchaxe, prass, prick (1), pump (1), quart saw, quern, rammer, riddle (2), roll, runlet, tallow, tenell, tine, tirl, tooth-pick, touch box, toyles (toylles), trail (1), trough tree, trow, trumpery, truntlement, trust, two-hand (two handed), vang, vice (1), yardwand, years

Shoemaking

awlblade, boot-tree, clout, elsin, illion, last (1), offal, rosin, shoemaker board

Stone working

hack-hammer, wedge

Transport

cowl, fadge, fardel, frail, hamper, hot (hott), hurter, lin-nail, load-saddle, mail pillion (mail saddle), overlay, pack cloth, pack prick, packsaddle, pack sheet, packthread, pack ware (packingware), panel (3), tavelin, teld, timber (2), wool pack

Water management

flood gate, flood-heck, goit stock

Wood, bone

adge, broad-axe, dagger (2), fuster, grope iron (see grope), ink-horn, knave, latt axe, nadge, nawgur, nib, over, snathe (snathing axe), thixel, throw (1), thwart saw, twibill, whip-saw

Topography, landscape, townscape *see also* Agriculture; Water

Boundaries, landmarks

acredike (acregarth, acrewall), cast (4), currock, dead fence (dead hedge), deal (1), dike (1, dyke), ditch-comb, dry-stone wall, dutted forth, haye, headwall, hedgerow, hoar-stone, hurder, hurrock, hutt, lad (1), mere (1), mere (2), merestone, mete (2), moordike, nook, pale (pale-board), palis, pike (1, piked), pole (2), ruck, ruckle, threap

Topography, landscape, townscape (cont.)

Field names, shapes, types
arse, bren (brend, brent, brint), dearbought, dog pits, downafter, gang (2), gore, green gate, hacking, hing, howe, lairpit, laughton, law, letch, light (2, lights), main (mainland), mean, mould (1), ore-blower, oregrave, over, over-measure, park, pickle, pightel, pingle, place, pogmire, pourprise, pudding, quillet, reap, rein, room (2), swithen, tang, threap, toft (toftstead), wang (wong)

Landscape feature, types
assart, dale (1), drough (droughty), fell (1), ghyll, glen, hard land, holme, hoovy, howe, mould (1), park, slobbery, sobbed, ridding, rotten, rodeland (roydland), royd

Non-specific terms
abbeystead, bield, cast (4), eight, lig, midden stead, milking stead, milnegate, moor gate, nook, noutgang, occupation lane (road), out, outgang, outmoor, outpasture, plat, pourprise, rigg (rigg and furrow), rocher, rotten, under, vennel, yate stead, yate stoop

Structures
hamlet, milnebrigg, mistall, moor barn, village

Urban
gale (2), gate (1), ghaut, ginnel, landing, lead-stoop, marketstead, nowtgate, town-gate, town mires

Water, sea
decourse, eight, fleet, flosh, gall (2), ghyll, gill (1), gime, gipsies, gote, grain (2), grip (1), gull, hippings (hipping-stones), holme, lake (4), letch, marish, moss (2), ness, pant, ratton (*see* ratton-bread), sipe, warp up, water slack, yealand

Woods
grove (2), hacking, hagg, hirst, imp yard, laund, plain

Travel, transport *see also* Bridges; Horses

Equipment
gardeviance, hamper, rathe

Footways, highways
green gate, highgate, ironstone ways, kirkgate, kirk sty, knotty, lead (1), loan, loaning, loin, milnegate, oregate, outgang, pave (pavement), pitch (3), plough-tilt (plough-tilth), rake (1), rise bridge, road (roadway), trod, turf-gate (turfway), urgent, vennel

Non-specific terms
gain (2), loaden, wain (3)

Packhorse
galloway, garth (3), girth (1, girth web), hamper, hot (hott), kip-string, mail pillion (mail saddle), load-saddle, orelay, overlay, pack cloth, pack-horse, packhorse bridge, packing house, pack prick, packsaddle, panel (3), pillion (pillion seat), pillion-cloth, sack and seam, summer (1), sumpter cloth (sumpter saddle), surcingle, wantow (wanty), web (3)

Railways
rail (1, railway)

Vehicles
axle-nail, axle-tree, ear braid, iron-bound wheels (*see* iron-bound-wain), muck-coup (muck-sled, muck-tumbrell, muck-wain), rulley

Water
barge, coble, cock (2), cog (1, cog boat), farcost, farming-boat, ferryman, five-man boat, flete, fly-boat, hoy, keel, keg, ketch, lighter, pick (1), pink, punt

Trees, bushes *see also* Plants; Topography; Wood
acorn, alder (aller), ash, asp (aspen), astelwood, crab (1, crab-tree), ellen (ellentree, ellern), eller (ellerwood), esp, ewe, filbert, firwood, hazel (hazel wood), hollin, hollin fall, hovel, kid, leap, light (2, lights), lind, malacatone, maple, oak, ollar, osier hope, owler, quicken (quickenberry), quickfall, quickset, Quickstavers, quickwood, quince, thorn, yew, yholster

Water, rivers, watercourses, *see also* Bridges; Topography; Travel
avoid, decourse, draw-well, dub (1), fey, flash (flask), float (1, float gap, float-gate), flood gate, flood-heck, flosh, flush, gimbal, gull, gutter, hale, hippings (hipping-stones), holdstock, hole (1), holme, hook (2), horse-bridge, howetree, hulk, hush, jetsam, key, kiddle, landing, land-stay, lode, pier, pile (2), pilerow, purl (1), reach, rundle, steaner, swattle, tumbling bay

Weather
drough (droughty), hush, let, middling, mizzling, moor grime, stay (3), warp up

Weights, containers, measures
batt, cast (2), dacre (daker, dicker), damplade, dare, dolium, dozen (1), dyker, eln, fadge, fall (1), fardel, farthingdeal, fat, firkin, flacket, gad, gage, gauge, gallon, hattock, hesp (1), jack (2), gill (2), hogshead, kette, kid, kilderkin, kit (2), last (2), lea (1), Leeds measure, long hundred, meal, mere (3), met, mete (1), meterod, oxgang, peck, perch, phodre, pipe (2), ponder, pottle, pottle-pot, pottler, poundstone, quart, quarter, quartern, reap, Ripon measure, ruck, Thirsk measure, thrave (threave), tod, tonnell, ton-tight, tun, tunnel, ulnage, yardwand

Wood, woods, woodworking *see also* Trees
acorn, axboot (axbote), breirding, chaff (chawf), clog, cumber, dish (1), dishbinder, dish-thrower (dish-turner), dodded (dodderd, dodderell), double waver, doubler wright (*see* doubler), draught, dry wood, dust (1), dutted forth, ebony wood, fall (2), felf (felk), fence month (fence time), fire-boot (fire-bote), firth, gang (1), garth (2), girth (2), great timber, greenhew, (greenhue), hagg, hagger, half-inch board, half tree, heart lath, helm (helm timber, helm wood), hilling (1), hirst, hollin, holt, howetree, hurdle, imp yard, inch board, keeper, kid, kidbearer, kidder, kidware, kidwood, kirffe, kit (2, kitmaker, kitwright), lag, lastmaker, lathcleaver (lathriver), logwood, lop, lording, lumber, made (1), manure (1), mark (1), milnewright, nadge, nave (1), nave (2), Norway oak, osier hope, outwood, pale-board (*see* pale), paler, palis, paliser, panel (1), pannier-maker, peark (perk), peeler, pile-hagg, pill, piller, plain, plantation, plate-lock, ploughwright, plump, polc (1), polling tree, poplar, pruce, prune, quarter cliff, quelewright, rabbet, raddlings, raff, raff-merchant (*see* raff), ramell, rid, ring (3, ring about), rise (1), rive, roof tree, rotten wood, row, runted oak, shive, snathe (snathing axe), stove (stow), thick, timber (1), timberware, tinsel (1), top, tree, trellis (trellis-maker), trouse, turner, underwood, unpilled, yest

Work *see also* Occupations

Descriptive terms
job, liflode, livelihood, moonlighting, task, wark

Status
able (2), agate, apprentice, datleman (*see* day-tale man), day-tale man (day-taler), loose suit, put forth, turn-over, upset (upsetting)

Trade terms, wages
annuity, arles, addle, allowance, boot (2), common day-work, day-work (1, 2), diet, earls, earnest, fest, floor pot, foot pot, god's penny, great, monday pot, over work, pot, prest, prick wage, tentale, yarls (yerls), yearn